PENGUIN

SINGAPORE BURNING

'A meticulous account of the Japanese advance on Singapore . . .
provides an excellent opportunity to revisit hard questions'
*Sydney Morning Herald*

'All the big themes are there: the hubris of the Allies and the Japanese,
as well as their courage; the pathos of the victims. Smith deftly
describes the complacent world of the rubber barons. It is beautifully
told, shrewd and fair in its judgements and character assessments
and on occasions wryly funny'
*Daily Telegraph*

'As Smith's new book demonstrates, the defeat was less due to acts
of sensational stupidity than a more piecemeal ineptitude. The
British lost this corner of their empire much as they had
acquired it – through bluff and bluster'
*Independent on Sunday*

'The full extent of 100,000 British, Australian and Indian troops falling
into Japanese hands is well documented'
*Sunday Tasmanian*

'A comprehensive and engrossing narrative'
*Herald Sun*

'Smith has a sharp eye for the telling anecdote, and sets his scenes
and introduces his characters with care. His prose is engaging. Even
those incidents well known to Australians such as the ambushing
of the tanks at Bakri or the shooting of the nurses on Bangka
Island and the escape of Sister Vivian Bullwinkel are
fresh in the telling'
*Book Talk*, Australian Broadcasting Corporation

# Singapore Burning

*Heroism and Surrender
in World War II*

COLIN SMITH

PENGUIN BOOKS

PENGUIN BOOKS

Published by the Penguin Group
Penguin Books Ltd, 80 Strand, London WC2R ORL, England
Penguin Group (USA) Inc., 375 Hudson Street, New York, New York 10014, USA
Penguin Group (Canada), 90 Eglinton Avenue East, Suite 700, Toronto, Ontario, Canada M4P 2Y3
(a division of Pearson Penguin Canada Inc.)
Penguin Ireland, 25 St Stephen's Green, Dublin 2, Ireland (a division of Penguin Books Ltd)
Penguin Group (Australia), 250 Camberwell Road, Camberwell, Victoria 3124, Australia
(a division of Pearson Australia Group Pty Ltd)
Penguin Books India Pvt Ltd, 11 Community Centre, Panchsheel Park, New Delhi – 110 017, India
Penguin Group (NZ), cnr Airborne and Rosedale Roads, Albany, Auckland 1310, New Zealand
(a division of Pearson New Zealand Ltd)
Penguin Books (South Africa) (Pty) Ltd, 24 Sturdee Avenue, Rosebank, Johannesburg 2196, South Africa

Penguin Books Ltd, Registered Offices: 80 Strand, London WC2R ORL, England

www.penguin.com
www.colin-smith.info

First published by Viking 2005
Published by Penguin Books 2006
I

Copyright © Colin Smith, 2005
All rights reserved

The moral right of the author has been asserted

Set in Monotype Bembo
Typeset by Rowland Phototypesetting Ltd, Bury St Edmunds, Suffolk
Printed in England by Clays Ltd, St Ives plc

ISBN-13: 978-0-141-01036-6
ISBN-10: 0-141-01036-3

And some there be, which have no memorial, who are perished as though they have never been.

Ecclesiasticus 44:9

# Contents

# List of Illustrations

# Maps

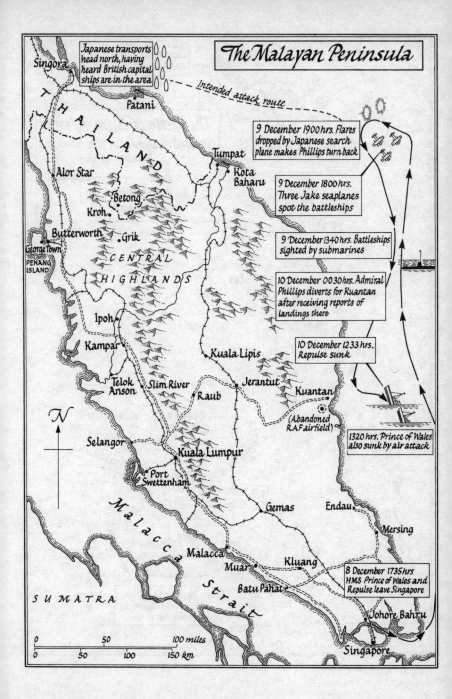

# The Malayan Peninsula

Singora

THAILAND

Japanese transports head north, having heard British capital ships are in the area

Intended attack route

Patani

9 December 1900 hrs. Flares dropped by Japanese search plane makes Phillips turn back

Tumpat

Kota Baharu

9 December 1800 hrs. Three Jake seaplanes spot the battleships

Alor Star

Betong

Kroh

9 December 1340 hrs. Battleships sighted by submarines

Butterworth

Grik

George Town
PENANG ISLAND

CENTRAL HIGHLANDS

10 December 00.30 hrs. Admiral Phillips diverts for Kuantan after receiving reports of landings there

Ipoh

Kampar

Kuala Lipis

10 December 12.33 hrs. Repulse sunk

Telok Anson

Slim River

Jerantut

Kuantan

Raub

Selangor

(Abandoned R.A.F airfield)

1320 hrs. Prince of Wales also sunk by air attack

Kuala Lumpur

Port Swettenham

Gemas

Endau

Mersing

Malacca

Malacca Strait

Muar

Kluang

Batu Pahat

8 December 1735 hrs HMS Prince of Wales and Repulse leave Singapore

SUMATRA

Johore Bahru

Singapore

0        50        100 miles
0    50    100    150 km

N

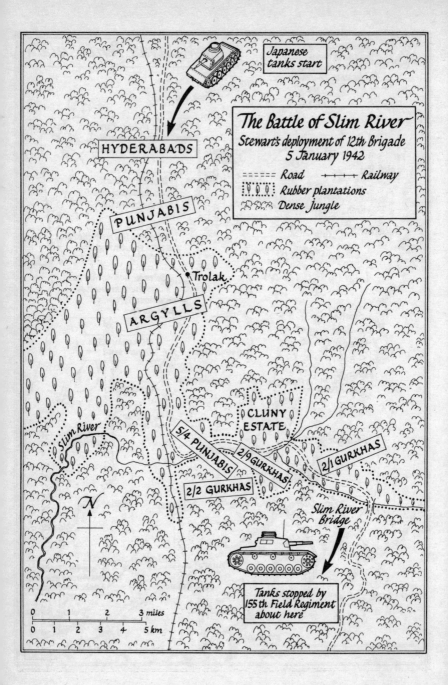

**The Battle of Slim River**
Stewart's deployment of 12th Brigade
5 January 1942

Road ┄┄┄┄┄   Railway ┼┼┼┼┼
Rubber plantations
Dense jungle

Japanese tanks start

HYDERABADS

PUNJABIS

• Trolak

ARGYLLS

Slim River

CLUNY ESTATE

5/4 PUNJABIS

2/9 GURKHAS

2/1 GURKHAS

2/2 GURKHAS

N

Slim River Bridge

Tanks stopped by 155th Field Regiment about here

0   1   2   3 miles
0   1   2   3   4   5 km

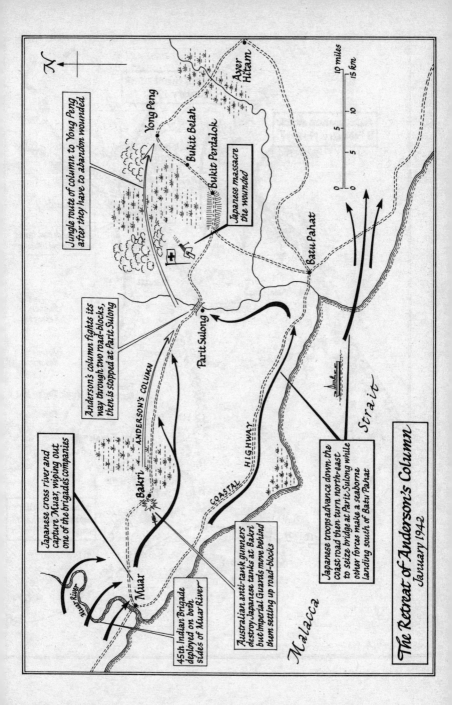

**The Retreat of Anderson's Column**
*January 1942*

N

Muar River

Muar

45th Indian Brigade deployed on both sides of Muar River

Japanese cross river and capture Muar, wiping out one of the brigade's companies

Bakri

ANDERSON'S COLUMN

Australian anti-tank gunners destroy Japanese tanks at Bakri but Imperial Guards move behind them setting up road-blocks

Parit Sulong

Anderson's column fights its way through two road-blocks, then is stopped at Parit Sulong

COASTAL HIGHWAY

Japanese troops advance down the coast road then turn north-east to seize bridge at Parit Sulong while other forces make a seaborne landing south of Batu Pahat

Batu Pahat

Strait

Malacca

Japanese massacre the wounded

Jungle route of column to Yong Peng after they have to abandon wounded

Yong Peng

Bukit Belah

Bukit Perdalok

Ayer Hitam

0    5    10    10 miles
0    5    10    15 km

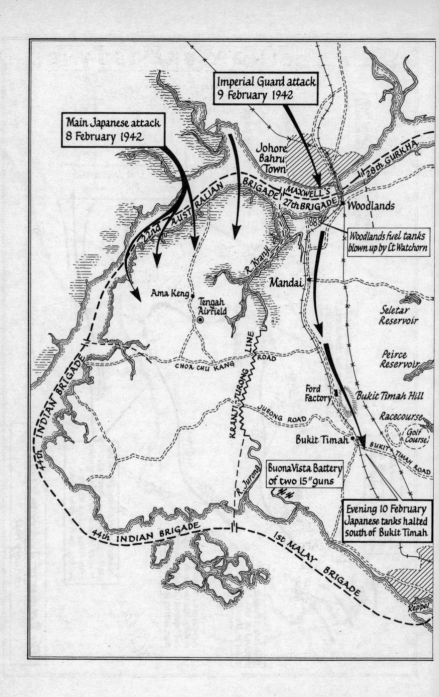

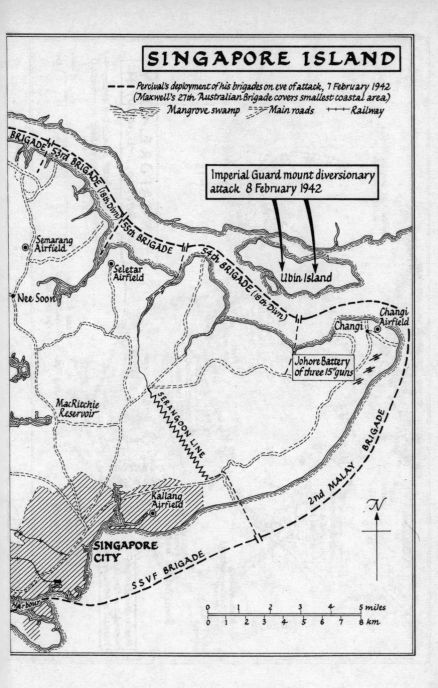

# SINGAPORE ISLAND

- - - Percival's deployment of his brigades on eve of attack, 7 February 1942
(Maxwell's 27th Australian Brigade covers smallest coastal area)
Mangrove swamp === Main roads +++ Railway

Imperial Guard mount diversionary
attack 8 February 1942

Ubin Island

BRIGADE 53rd BRIGADE

55th BRIGADE (18th Divn)

54th BRIGADE (18th Divn)

Semarang Airfield

Seletar Airfield

Nee Soon

Changi

Changi Airfield

Johore Battery
of three 15" guns

MacRitchie Reservoir

SERANGOON LINE

2nd MALAY BRIGADE

Kallang Airfield

SINGAPORE CITY

SSVF BRIGADE

Harbour

N

| 0 | 1 | 2 | 3 | 4 | 5 miles |
| 0 | 1 | 2 | 3 | 4 | 5 | 6 | 7 | 8 km |

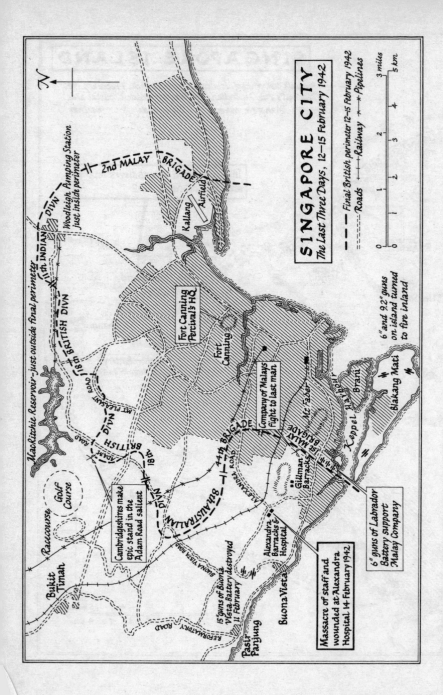

SINGAPORE CITY
The Last Three Days, 12–15 February 1942

– – – Final British perimeter 12–15 February 1942 ····· Pipelines
–·–·– Roads ·+·+·+· Railway

0 1 2 3 miles
0 1 2 3 4 5 km.

N

MacRitchie Reservoir – just outside final perimeter

Woodleigh Pumping Station – just inside perimeter

2nd MALAY BRIGADE

11th INDIAN DIVN

18th BRITISH DIVN

Kallang Airfield

Fort Canning Percival's HQ

Fort Canning

No 4 DIVN

BRITISH

Adam Road

1 BRITISH DIVN

Cambridgeshires make epic stand in the Adam Road salient

18th

44th BRIGADE

8th AUSTRALIAN DIVN

Alexandra Road

Company of Malays fight to last man

1st MALAY BRIGADE

Mt Faber

Gillman Barracks

Keppel Harbour

Brani

Blakang Mati

6" and 9.2" guns on island turned to fire inland

6" guns of Labrador Battery support Malay Company

Massacre of staff and wounded at Alexandra Hospital 14 February 1942

Alexandra Barracks & Hospital

15 guns of Buona Vista Battery destroyed 11 February

Buona Vista

Buona Vista Road

Pasir Panjang

REFORMATORY ROAD

Bukit Timah

Racecourse

Golf Course

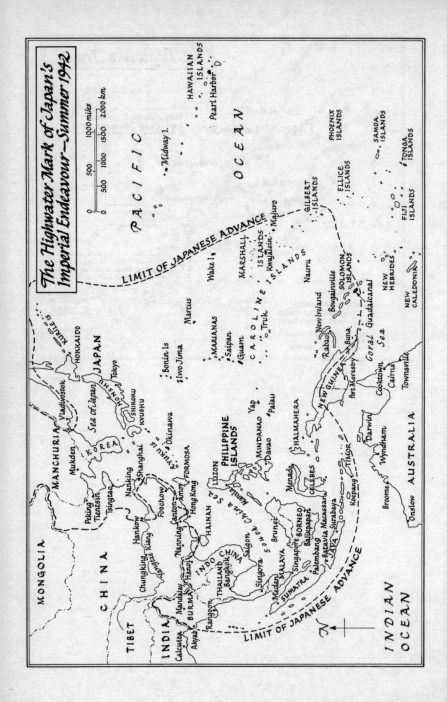

The Highwater Mark of Japan's
Imperial Endeavour—Summer 1942

# The Treasure Island

# The Treasure Island

Singapore, a wet low-lying island some 85 miles north of the equator, lies like the dot to an exclamation mark punctuating an end to the impertinent intrusion of the Malayan Peninsula into the South China Sea. It is separated from this southern extremity of mainland Asia by the narrow straits from which the Sultan of Johore takes his name, and from whose coastal palace the northern shore of the nearby island over which he once held sway can plainly be seen. In Malay its name has a regal sound, for it means 'lion island', though there is no evidence that the long-extinct Asian variety was ever hunted there.

Including some fifty or so islets, Singapore covers about 240 square miles and some of its coastline is fringed by mangrove swamp. British cartographers often noted that it was roughly the same diamond shape and a little smaller than the Isle of Wight due south of the Royal Navy's main channel port at Portsmouth. But the waters which separate its northern coast from Malaya are considerably narrower than the Solent, never being more than a mile wide. The mainland is always in view. Keppel harbour, its main port, lies on the island's southern coast on the eastern end of the Malacca Straits which separate Malaya and Singapore from the elongated island of Sumatra. This is the watergate between the South China Sea and the Indian Ocean, and ideally placed for trade. In the sixteenth century a Portuguese visitor to Singapore noted that vessels from India, China, Cambodia and Siam were calling there. Some of these became victims of the pirates who lurked in the mangrove swamps in their war canoes. From time to time, warlords from Java and Siam made punitive expeditions against these miscreants. Yet, for much of modern history, that is to say 'gunpowder history', despite its strategic position, Singapore was rarely fought over.

In the late afternoon of 29 January 1819 Sir Thomas Stamford Raffles, once a star of the Honourable East India Company but lately regarded as something of a liability by its commercially minded directors, dropped anchor off Singapore. He had recently returned to Southeast Asia from a long leave in England to become Lieutenant-Governor of Bencoolen, a malaria-ridden pepper port on Sumatra's south-west coast. In London he had been knighted, published his *History of Java*, been generally lionized by society, and remarried – his first wife had died in Java. Before he left London George Joseph, a society painter who specialized in the newly elevated, had done his portrait. It shows a shrewd-looking man in his late thirties, with dark good looks; he is modishly unwigged and perhaps a little preoccupied.

No doubt the directors thought he had much to be preoccupied about. During his five years as governor of Java, now returned to the Dutch, Raffles had committed the cardinal sin of putting good administration before profits. Bencoolen was the measure of their displeasure. But now he had been given the chance to redeem himself on a special mission which, providing he obeyed instructions, seemed ideally suited for his considerable talents and background.

Raffles was the son of an improvident merchant navy captain, obliged at the age of fourteen to leave school in order to support his widowed mother and four sisters. He became a clerk with the Honourable Company where, despite long working hours, he found time to continue his studies, paying particular attention to languages and natural history. His energy and ability did not go unnoticed. At twenty-three he was appointed assistant to the Secretary of the Company on the island of Penang, which lay off Malaya's north-west coast just below the border of Siam, where he quickly immersed himself in Malaya's language, history and culture.

Penang had been acquired by the Company from the Sultan of Kedah almost twenty years before, mainly because the sultan thought this was the best way of buying protection from his Siamese neighbours. The British saw the island as a way into the South-east Asian markets, then dominated by the Dutch who controlled most of Sumatra and Java. Before Penang, the only British outpost in the region had been Bencoolen, which was off any significant trade route and did little to earn its keep, though even this toehold was viewed by the Dutch with some foreboding for the English always seemed to have the wind behind them.

Sure enough, in 1795 events in Europe improved the East India Company's standing in the region. The Prince of Orange, seeking asylum in England following Napoleon's invasion of Holland, gave the Company trading rights in Melaka. The old spice trade port was almost 300 miles down Malaya's west coast from Penang on the estuary of the Melaka River. It had been in European hands, first Portuguese and then Dutch, for almost 500 years. But Melaka was in decline, partly because the estuary was beginning to silt up and larger ships had to anchor offshore. What the Company wanted was a place with a good natural harbour at the South China Sea end of the watergate.

When Raffles came ashore at Singapore some four years after Napoleon's defeat at Waterloo the Dutch had reasserted their ascendancy as the major colonial power in the region: the Dutch East Indies were to Holland what India was to the British. Raffles arrived on the Company ship *Indiana* accompanied by seven other sailing vessels, among them the survey ships *Investigator* and *Discovery*. It was not a very formidable force. They were lightly armed with small cannon and swivel guns as a protection against pirates. In addition, the brig *Ganges* was carrying 150 of the Company's Bengali sepoys and a few light artillery pieces manned by European gunners.

Raffles' instructions were to explore the possibility of establishing a trading settlement, 'factory' in the jargon of the Company, around the tip of the Malayan Peninsula. At the same time he was to do nothing to offend the Dutch, who could afford to concentrate their military resources in the region in a way the British, with their much larger empire, could not. It was always a tall order and, in this, Raffles failed.

Singapore was no longer a great trading port. The island Raffles landed on was inhabited by about 500 people, most of them Malay fishermen, some of whom probably dabbled in piracy. The only Chinese were an extended family of about thirty cultivating the *gambir* herb used for leather tanning and making batik.

Occupying the island was relatively easy. Doing so without offending Holland was much harder. Permission for Raffles to set up his factory was readily given by the Temenggong, the resident Malayan aristocrat and, in theory at least, hereditary representative of the Sultan of Johore. 'Our objective is not territory but trade,' declared Raffles, hoping to mollify the Dutch. But local politics were as difficult to navigate as the shoals of the Riau Archipelago, a jigsaw of islands south of Singapore where several of the leading players lived. It turned out that among them were various protégés of The Hague who disputed the Temenggong's authority and took particular exception to his accommodation of the British.

Raffles knew how to soldier. Seven years before, he had apparently reached the pinnacle of his career when he played a leading role in the capture of Java from Franco-Dutch forces. He had hoped for sufficient breathing space in Singapore to erect a Martello tower and other fortifications. Realizing there was no longer time for that, he sailed for Penang where the Company maintained a garrison and he hoped to get reinforcements. Behind him he left Major William Farquhar of the Madras Engineers supervising the manhandling of one of their few cannon to the summit of Bukit Larangan, which means 'Forbidden Hill' in Malay. Larangan was a small hill overlooking the island's southern coast and the locals believed it was haunted, for this ground was said to be the ancient burial place of fierce kings. Not until Farquhar had dragged his gun to the top and fired twelve blank charges from it would the Malays believe that any lingering jinns had departed for quieter graveyards and new rulers could be safely accepted. This assault on the spirit world is the first recorded instance of a cannon being discharged on Singapore Island itself.

Raffles eventually got his reinforcements for Farquhar's meagre garrison, though he was hindered by a jealous Company official in Penang, full of prescient fears that his fief was about to be upstaged. While Farquhar waited for a relief party, a Dutch warship attempted to blockade the island assisted, probably coincidentally, by pirates who had boarded a sampan from Melaka laden with provisions for the garrison and slaughtered its crew. The Dutch, perhaps fearful of starting a general war with the world's biggest and most successful navy, made no attempt to snuff out this British trespass while Singapore was virtually defenceless. Nor was their blockade very effective. In four months the island's population had swelled to 5,000, most of them Chinese labourers.

After a short stay, Raffles went back to Bencoolen and a series of personal tragedies. Three of his four infant children from his second marriage died in a two-year period. The surviving daughter, Ella, was hurriedly shipped out of the pestilential port but it was over a year before her parents learned she had arrived safely in England.

When he returned to Singapore in October 1822, a thriving community now 10,000 strong provided some solace for his recent bereavements and he took pride in 'my almost only child'.

He was less pleased with Farquhar, whose performance he found slothful. The major had not only failed to follow Raffles' detailed plans for the layout of the settlement – there were warehouses where government offices were supposed to be – he had also neglected to build any of the fortifications Raffles had ordered. British merchants with fortunes invested in opium for the China trade were nervous that there was so little security pirates might raid the settlement for their stock. Farquhar was fired.

While Raffles waited for the major to be replaced he concentrated his ferocious energy on various projects. Despite a series of appalling headaches, which made him fear that he would soon be leaving his bones in the new European cemetery, he built an official residence on the hill where Farquhar had fired his cannon to frighten away ghosts, and what had once been 'Forbidden Hill' became 'Government Hill'. Nearby, in a place he had previously earmarked for a fort, he laid out a botanical garden.

Raffles stayed for six months, the longest time he ever spent on Singapore, which he declared to be 'a free port . . . open to ships and vessels of every nation'. In June 1823 he departed for Bencoolen where, by the end of the year, he had buried yet another of his children before she was six weeks old. The following February he and his wife left for England but Bencoolen and its graveyards were reluctant to let the Raffles go. They were back the next day after being obliged to take to the boats when their ship caught fire. All their possessions were lost, including the Indonesian dictionaries Raffles was compiling and his natural history notes. They eventually reached England and their surviving child in August 1824 to learn that, while they had been at sea, the Dutch had agreed that the British could keep Singapore in exchange for awful Bencoolen. Raffles' health was deteriorating, his headaches getting worse, but before he died of a brain tumour in 1826, aged forty-five, he threw himself into a campaign to found a London Zoo of which he became first president. Nor was this remarkable man ever in any doubt about his other legacy, predicting that the faraway island he had acquired would become 'the emporium and pride of the East'.

As it happened, Singapore was slow to bloom. The East India Company lost its monopoly on the China trade and its niggardly bureaucrats in Calcutta mismanaged the island's affairs: it was not to become a Crown Colony until 1867. Singapore not only had to compete with the new port the British were developing at Hong Kong but with the industrious Dutch on the other side of the Malacca Straits and the newly arrived French colonialists in Saigon and Haiphong. The opening of the Suez Canal in 1869, and the new steamships, made it easier for Malaya to sell its tea and tin to Europe. Then, half a century later, as the motor industry took off, these exports were overtaken by rubber, cultivated in Malaya from Brazilian seedlings imported via Kew in 1877 and first grown in Singapore's own Botanical Gardens.

By 1914 Britain controlled all the peninsula up to its northern border with the Kingdom of Siam, the only South-east Asian country never to be colonized by Europeans. For administrative purposes the increasingly prosperous colony was divided into two. The Straits Settlements consisted of the islands of Singapore and Penang, Province Wellesley, which was the coastal strip opposite Penang on the north-east coast, and Melaka port. Most of the mainland peninsula became the Malay States, which were nominally controlled by their individual rulers. In theory, at least, the power behind their thrones was the resident British adviser, normally referred to as the 'Resident' or the 'Political Agent', who gave 'advice' on everything apart from local customs and the Malay interpretation of Islam.

This relationship did not start happily. In 1875, the first British Resident, who was advising, perhaps in rather too loud a voice, the sultan of the northern state of Perak, was murdered. The culprits were hanged, but after this the Residents learned how to deliver their 'advice' in a manner less likely to offend. 'Veiled autocracy' was one description of their technique. But, to a man, the sultans proved difficult puppets to work, sensitive of their honour and requiring careful handling. No visit to London was complete unless they were received at Buckingham Palace.

As the rubber plantations and mines multiplied, thousands of migrants from the south China coast came to help the white man to pick up his burden. In Singapore, the Chinese soon outnumbered the Malays. A small number of Japanese began to settle there as well, mostly as fishermen or running small businesses as artisans and shopkeepers. Soon Tokyo considered there were enough of them to require their own consul-general.

Certain steps were taken to provide Raffles' 'emporium' with the kind of security it deserved. The most visible of these was a permanent garrison of a couple of thousand British and Indian troops on the island, though there were few fixed defences apart from a boom across Keppel harbour. Much more prescient was the accord Britain signed with Asia's burgeoning superpower.

The Anglo-Japanese Alliance of 1902 confirmed the progress Japan had made in modernizing itself in the forty-eight years since it had begun to put an end to two and a half centuries of self-imposed isolation.* It recognized that here was a strong and independent Asian country, as technically advanced as parts of Europe and with an effective military. For the British, competing with Germany to build the most dreadnoughts, the Alliance enabled it to keep most of its fleet in home waters while the Japanese watched Czarist Russia, whose Pacific port at Vladivostok was seen as the biggest threat to Britain's Asian interests. In February 1904, the Japanese went to war with Russia over Manchuria, which both were determined to wrest from the control of a feeble Chinese administration.

Setting the twentieth-century precedent for mega-ambush by dispensing with a formal declaration of war, the Japanese attacked the Russian fleet at Port Arthur, an anchorage west of the Korean Peninsula, which the Russians leased from the Chinese as its ice-free winter quarters. Britain came close to entering the conflict on the Japanese side when the Czar dispatched as reinforcements his Baltic fleet which, at the beginning of its seven months' circumnavigation to eastern waters, mistook some Hull fishing trawlers off the Dogger Bank for Japanese motor torpedo boats and sank one with the loss of two lives. The Royal Navy stalked the Russian ships across the Bay of Biscay until the officers responsible were put ashore at Vigo in Spain and, after international arbitration, St Petersburg agreed to pay compensation. This was only the beginning of the Russian sailors' misfortunes. In May 1905 they suffered a crushing defeat when they were attacked by the Japanese fleet in the straits between Korea and Japan and lost eight capital ships. It was the first time an Asian power, armed with modern weapons, had inflicted a humiliation of this scale on a European one. The Czar agreed to American mediation which, in September 1906, led to a treaty being signed at Portsmouth, New Hampshire.

From the beginning of World War I, the Anglo-Japanese Alliance worked well for Britain, enabling the Royal Navy – as it was always intended it should in wartime – to deploy most of its ships in the cold waters where they would do the most good. At the same time the Japanese fleet rendered valuable assistance in hunting down German

* In 1600 Japan cut itself off from the outside world after its failure to conquer Korea. Japanese were not allowed to go abroad nor could foreigners land there. This ended in 1854 when the US naval officer Commander Matthew Perry turned up with his well-armed ships, some of them steam-driven, and persuaded the Japanese to grant them trading rights. In return they acquired western technology and sometimes improved on it.

raiders and merchantmen in the Pacific, while its soldiers helped the
Australians take over the Bismarck Archipelago and other island
colonies established by the Germans. In China, Japanese troops, sup-
ported by some battalions from the British Indian Army, seized the
German coastal enclave at Tsingtau. But it was in Singapore that the
Japanese rendered the British Empire its most unexpected service.

In February 1915 the Crown Colony's garrison had been reduced
to a skeleton as troops were siphoned off to France or to the Middle
East to fight the Kaiser's Ottoman Turkish allies. The *Singapore Free
Press* reminded its readers that this could only be done because of the
'Sabbath Calm' imposed by the Anglo-Japanese Alliance. Virtually all
that was left on the island were the gunners of the Royal Garrison
Artillery who manned the batteries which covered Keppel harbour,
part-time units of local European volunteers and the 5th Native Light
Infantry, an Indian Army regiment with battle honours won in
Afghanistan and during the Sikh wars. It had one other distinction.
During the Indian Mutiny of 1857 the 5th had remained loyal and not
joined in the uprising against the British.

But in 1915 the 5th, which was recruited entirely from Muslims,
was not a happy battalion. Their colonel was unpopular among his
subordinate British officers, who thought him incompetent and unfit
to command, and their manifest contempt communicated itself to the
entire regiment. The colonel reacted to his officers' hostility by court-
ing the popularity of his sepoys. He set himself up as 'the soldiers'
friend' and often overturned punishments imposed by their company
commanders.

None of this might have counted for much if discipline had not
been further undermined by a malign outside influence. One of the
5th's duties was guarding the 300 or so Germans held in a prisoner-of-
war camp at Tanglin. Some of these were civilians, deracinated adven-
turers long settled in the tropics whose fortunes had been ruined by
the assassin at Sarajevo. But also among them were some sailors from
the German light cruiser *Emden*. Before she was run aground by the
Australian cruiser *Sydney*, the *Emden* had in seven wild weeks accounted
for twenty-three Allied merchant ships and made an audacious raid on
Penang harbour. There she sank the Russian cruiser *Zhemshug* at
its moorings while some of the crew were carousing with Japanese
prostitutes below decks. Then *Emden* capsized a French motor torpedo
boat returning from patrol and escaped to meet its fate with the *Sydney*.

In captivity, some of the *Emden*'s crew made it their business to see that their Indian guards were aware of the Kaiser's alliance with the Ottoman Turks and his friendship with Muslim people everywhere. At the same time, an imam in a Malay mosque attended by some of the sepoys preached that it was forbidden to fight the Turks. Was not the Ottoman sultan also the Caliph, the legitimate successor on earth to the Prophet Muhammad?

On Monday 15 February, a public holiday in Singapore, with the air rent with the explosion of firecrackers for Chinese New Year, the regiment were paraded and told they would shortly be leaving the island for an unknown destination. As it happened, they were not going to war with the Caliph's army. The 5th were bound for Hong Kong and garrison duty in what, in a world at war, was one of the empire's quietest backwaters. Unfortunately, they had not yet been let into the secret. As a result, half the regiment mutinied.

One of the first things the rebels did was liberate the POW camp, killing several of the European militia guards raised from the colonial administration or local houses of commerce. One prisoner was also killed, presumably in crossfire. About twenty others escaped.* The mutineers then started on a random killing spree. In all, about thirty Europeans died. 'Sepoys held up cars in the streets and roads and shot civilians like schoolboys catapulting birds,' according to one account.

There were fears that the mutiny might spark a general uprising against British rule. European women and children left the remoter parts of the island for the town or even ships moored in the harbour. Those with the right connections moved into Government House itself from where Sir Arthur Young was sending frantic wireless messages for help to every Allied ship in the area. Responses came from two Japanese cruisers, the *Otawa* and the *Tsushima*, the French warship *Montcalm* and a Russian vessel which was at Penang salvaging guns from the *Zhemshug*.

While they were waiting for the sailors to arrive, pickets from the garrison artillery and sailors from the sloop HMS *Cadmus* did their best to put up a show of force. In addition, 400 special constables were sworn in. Half of these were European volunteers. The rest were Japanese citizens who had been enrolled by their own consul and,

* Four would eventually reach Germany via Shanghai. Most of the others got as far as the neutral Dutch territories where they were interned for the rest of the war.

though armed by the British, were under their own command. 'Their self-imposed efficiency was in marked contrast to that of the hetero-geneous body of eager Europeans,' observed a British officer cadet in the colony's police.

Soon Nippon's contribution was increased by the 180 rifles in the hands of landing parties from the Japanese warships. Together with French and Russian sailors they joined forces with the British – eventu-ally reinforced from India by a territorial battalion of the Shropshire Light Infantry – in hunting down the mutineers. By now the rebel sepoys had split up into small parties. A few managed to get hold of sampans and cross the straits to Johore, where they were rounded up by French sailors from the cruiser *Montcalm*. The rest were eking out a miserable existence in the island's remaining jungle.

By the end of February, most of the hungry and demoralized mutin-eers had been captured and the courts martial begun. Thirty-seven of the mutineers were sentenced to death. All but one of them, who was hanged, were executed by firing squads supplied by the Malay States Volunteer Reserve, locally recruited British expatriates. A few were shot inside prison grounds but almost fifty Europeans had died and it was felt that a more visible example needed to be made. It was arranged that public executions would be staged against the outer side of the wall around Outram Road jail, near land being cleared for a new general hospital. In an attempt to apply the full majesty of the law these judicial killings often became botched, drawn-out affairs. Death sentences were laboriously translated from English into at least three Indian languages while the condemned sepoys, without blindfolds and tied to stakes only a few yards from their executioners, prayed out loud for an end to it. Some of the weekend soldiers of the Volunteer Reserve, thoroughly unnerved or drunk or both, failed to shoot straight. A lieutenant was aghast to see that, after enduring the trans-lation of their sentences with 'great fortitude', one of the two men his squad were executing was still standing and obviously very much alive. 'The expression on his face was one of such terrible agony that it will for ever remain impressed on my memory.'

In Japan, accounts of the mutiny and the role their troops and civilians had played in putting it down were relished. There were stories of how the fearful British had implored the Japanese navy to rescue them from the rampaging Indians. 'The pitiful state of a colony without effective power was brought home to me,' crowed a Japanese reporter who was present. There was little or no mention of the Russian and French contingents involved.

In Singapore itself, its senior colonial and military officers were inclined to argue that British power had been demonstrated in proxy by the alacrity with which their Japanese, French and Russian allies had cracked heads for them. A few argued that perhaps allowing foreign landing parties ashore was going too far; that the mere presence of warships in Keppel harbour should have been enough. It was feared that Indian nationalists would relish the idea that, for a moment, a part of the empire had been vulnerable. Nor was there any doubt that the tale would grow in the telling. In Sweden, it was widely believed that a mutiny in Singapore had been put down entirely by the Japanese and that the island had since remained in their hands.

By the time World War I had come to an end, it was recognized that Japan, rather than a Russia weakened by revolution, was the most likely threat to Britain's South-east Asian empire. In September 1919, less than two months after the Japanese had marched with the British at the great Allied victory parade in Paris, the Admiralty had decided it was essential to provide 'a secure base well to the southward of Hong Kong, and no more suitable position can be suggested than Singapore. It is sufficiently far from Japan (2,900 miles) to make an overseas attack a very difficult undertaking and it is also an excellent strategical position for a fleet covering the vital Australian and East Indian routes . . .'

So 'Fortress Singapore' replaced the Anglo-Japanese Alliance, which in 1923 was, in the words of the Japanese Foreign Minister, 'discarded like a used pair of sandals'. It was never to be the popular concept of a fortress, no Asian Gibraltar with concreted loopholes covering every likely landing spot. Singapore was far too big for that and, besides, in the aftermath of the bloodiest and costliest war Britain had ever fought, there was little appetite for spending good money on notional threats abroad. By 1925 the major opponent of increasing the navy's budget was none other than the new Chancellor of the Exchequer, Winston Churchill – between 1911 and 1915 the biggest-spending First Sea Lord in the history of that office.

'That extraordinary fellow Winston has gone mad,' declared Admiral Beatty in a letter to his wife. But Churchill, the amateur pilot who had pioneered British naval aviation, switched warships from coal to oil and ensured that they had the 15-inch guns to match the Kaiser's dreadnoughts, was deaf to all entreaties. If the navy got everything it asked for, he said, there would be 'nothing for social reform'. He also wondered if it was not 'provocative' to base twenty-one submarines in Hong Kong instead of six. 'Suppose the Japanese owned the Isle of Man and started putting twenty-one submarines there?' Churchill demanded, in what seems to have been his only known stand against any form of British military expansionism.*

Churchill held to the common and understandable belief that Japan would never risk an Asian war with Britain unless most of the Royal Navy was engaged elsewhere, as it had been when Japan filled the breach in 1914–18. In 1925, with the names of almost a million dead on its memorials, the idea of the British Empire allowing itself to be sucked into another European war was unthinkable. In any case, who was there left to fight? The Germans and the French were equally exhausted. None the less, a mere seven years after the end of that conflict and eight years before Hitler came to power, Stanley Baldwin's Conservative government reluctantly overrode Churchill's objections, and in August 1926 agreed to build the secure Far Eastern base the Admiralty craved. The only dissenting voice was Jan Smuts, the clever South African premier and former Boer guerrilla who had become a firm believer in the benefits of the British Empire and served in the Imperial War Cabinet. Smuts argued that, either way, a Singapore base was pointless. The Japanese would not attack unless there was a war in northern waters, and in the event of such a war the Royal Navy would not be able to send a credible deterrent to Singapore. But it was not Smuts' decision, and to leave a valuable colony defenceless was surely to invite an attack?

At first it was assumed that the navy base would be part of Keppel harbour but this plan was turned down because it was thought incompatible with the harbour's thriving commercial traffic. Eventually it was decided to build the base on the other side of the island, on its northern shore facing the Johore Straits. It had to be on the eastern side of this shore because the causeway being built to the island from Johore Bahru, as both a road as well as a rail link for the Federated Malay States Railway, would make the western side impassable to

---

* Churchill had just left the Liberals to join Stanley Baldwin's Conservative government but, as Admiral Beatty had discovered, he was not as predictable as most fifty-one-year-olds.

shipping. The choice along this mostly mangrove shoreline narrowed down to four sites and eventually Sembawang was chosen, even though this would involve draining swamp land and diverting a river.

The War Office would still have preferred Keppel harbour or some other south coast location. They argued that, in order to defend the base from ground attack, the army would require a perimeter with a radius of some 30 miles. This would take them well into Johore Bahru on the Malayan Peninsula. Sultan Ibrahim, the state's prickly ruler, was consulted. Ibrahim was an Anglophile inasmuch as he felt a certain empathy with the British royal family, whose life-size portraits adorned his palace, though these feelings did not always extend to British subjects in his domain – one of them a Scots lady who was one of his wives. He did his best to allay the War Office's misgivings by promising the utmost cooperation in the defence of the base. He also thought it an opportune moment to point out that he had recently rented 30,000 acres to Japanese interests for the cultivation of rubber.

# PART ONE
# Dancing in the Dark

Rubber was king. Ford and the other car giants were putting the western world on wheels and Malaya was the biggest exporter of natural rubber on the planet. Half of its crop went to the United States. By 1927, its sixtieth anniversary as a Crown Colony, Keppel harbour boasted 3 miles of wharves and warehouses, known locally as 'go-downs'. Its population numbered about 700,000 and was predominantly Chinese, mainly second-generation immigrants from south China, with the Malays and Indians being the next largest communities.

Living with servants from both races, usually in the black and white timber-framed tropical tudor bungalows of its garden suburbs, were the ruling minority: the British colonial civil servants, entrepreneurs and administrators who were almost all, one way or the other, trying to see that the place was run so that the rubber and tin could be extracted at the smallest cost for the greatest profit. As the Jazz Age roared on and rubber prices soared they worked as hard as was considered healthy in tropical climes and many, perhaps, played rather harder than they should have done. A bachelor's evening might start in his club, move on to the ballroom at Raffles Hotel where the number everyone wanted to hear was 'Ain't She Sweet'. Then, if he was unlucky in love – and at any social event available European women were almost always a minority – solace of a kind might be found in one of the better brothels, where Russian émigrés from Shanghai demanded the highest prices, every one a fallen princess.

Up-country, across the Johore Straits in the Malayan Peninsula, miners and planters often did lead hard lives, working from dawn to dusk with their Malay and Tamil labourers in places not long hacked out of the jungle. Some planters, veterans of what was starting to be known as the Great War, had accepted government grants to ex-soldiers of 100-acre rubber plots, sometimes forming consortiums to make sizeable holdings. This was the backcloth Somerset Maugham chose, after a short visit, for his stories of quiet desperation punctuated by drink, adultery, abandoned Eurasian children and vengeful Asian mistresses. Not surprisingly, the European community that served as

Maugham's subject matter was highly indignant at being portrayed in this way. Sport was their substitute for sex and plenty of it: a constant round of tennis, badminton, cricket, rugby football, hockey and what the Malays, an athletic race, called 'kickball'. Furtive visits to the bordellos of Kuala Lumpur – Malaya's capital and always known as 'KL' – rarely made their letters, diaries or memoirs. Nor did the common practice of new assistant rubber estate managers hiring a 'sleeping dictionary' to improve the vocabulary they had acquired from the bestselling *Well's Coolie Tamil*.

The crudeness of South African style apartheid was unknown in Malaya and the Tuans and their Mems, passing through Cape Town on the Blue Funnel line ships that carried them to and from South-ampton, were sometimes surprised to discover the rigid colour bar. In Malaya it was done with more subtlety. Clubs such as the Selangor Club in KL, known as 'the Spotted Dog' for its enormous black and white tropical tudor premises, rarely allowed a non-European membership. Urbane, intelligent, and often deeply Anglicized Malay, Indian and Chinese civil servants were passed over for promotions awarded to less able British colleagues. Only occasionally was the boot on the other foot. In KL some wealthy Chinese started a 'millionaires' club' from which whites were excluded. The young journalist Ian Morrison, son of a famous missionary to China, thought that the Dutch, who had been in the East Indies longer and were far more tolerant of intermarriage, made a better job of things. 'People of mixed blood could, and did, rise to the highest positions in the Indies. They formed a bridge between the Dutch on one hand and the natives on the other.'

Apart from sex, one of the few things that was truly multiracial in British Malaya was sport. A district officer played for a cricket team which included 'Eurasians, Indians, Ceylonese, a Sikh bowler and a Japanese wicket keeper'. But for the young British male seeking the pleasures of the East, nowhere was as glamorous, or sometimes as debauched, as Singapore. The island was rapidly becoming known, even more so than Nairobi, as one of the most hedonistic beacons of the sprawling empire on which the sun never set. ('Because God doesn't trust the British in the dark,' declared nationalists from Peshawar to Penang.) Even when rubber prices slumped in the world-wide eco-nomic depression that began with the New York stock market crash in 1929, and redundant Tuans were being declared 'Distressed British

Persons' and granted government-assisted passages home, Singapore somehow partied on.

On the whitewashed walls of St Andrew's Cathedral there were brass plaques commemorating some of those killed restoring British rule during the sepoy mutiny of February 1915. 'Ready Aye Ready', read the epitaph for a stoker from HMS *Cadmus* assigned to one of the shore parties. But twenty years on it seemed that all most people were ready for was fun. Few of the younger dancers at Raffles, or on the terrace of the Swimming Club with its five bars, or at the Happy World with the professional Chinese dance hostesses known as Taxi Girls, or the spectators at the races at Bukit Timah, knew or cared about the mutiny of the 5th Light Infantry; even fewer about the grisly executions which followed.

The military were no more immune to the spell of Singapore than anybody else. 'Off-duty hours centred round the clubs, to which "Service membership" was open to all officers of the Garrison,' recalled Lieutenant Rex King-Clark whose favourite was the Swimming Club.

Most evenings would find a dozen of us at tables on the edge of the magnificent open-air Olympic style pool, between swims sinking 'John Collins' and *stengahs* served at negligible cost by unobtrusive, efficient Chinese 'boys', and smoking Players No. 3 at a shilling for a round, air-sealed tin of fifty. On Saturday we might dance in the ballrooms of the Club or perhaps, after a delicious meal at a Chinese restaurant in a floating junk, visit the 'Happy World' . . . and though the girls were known as 'taxi girls' there was no way one could get them into a taxi. I know because, like others, I tried!

King-Clark, who thanks to an inheritance had his own private aircraft, had won a Military Cross for gallantry with Orde Wingate's Special Night Squads during the Arab revolt in Palestine. When his battalion of the Manchester Regiment, a heavy machine-gun unit, was sent to Singapore from the Middle East in October 1938 he did not go by troop ship but flew the 6,200 miles from Cairo to Singapore in his single-engined Miles Whitney Straight monoplane. His flight ended at the new grass airport at Kallang – one of the finest in the British Empire. It consisted of a round field about 1,000 yards in diameter and slightly domed for drainage. There was a circular control tower in contemporary art deco style, with long viewing galleries one of which contained an excellent restaurant. Fresh strawberries and cream were flown in from Australia; a spray of orchids could be sent back to Britain on one of the Imperial Airways flying boats which operated from a slip on the edge of the airport, landing and taking off from Keppel harbour. 'The Empire's Greatest Airport,' declared the 1938 edition of *Jane's Aviation Guide*, though the writer could not resist the mischievous, 'otherwise known as Japan's finest target'.

If they dared. After seventeen years of starting and stalling – at one point a Labour government under Ramsay MacDonald had shelved the project altogether – the naval base on the island's northern shore had now been completed. On 15 February 1938, as it happened the twenty-third anniversary of the sepoy mutiny, Governor Sir Shenton Thomas had declared it open for business. It had cost £60 million and provided 22 square miles of deep-sea anchorage, huge fuel tanks and an enormous floating dock, war booty from Germany, which could accommodate the biggest battleship afloat. There were barracks big enough to billet 2,000 sailors, offices, workshops, married quarters, churches, cinemas and seventeen football pitches.

It was about this time that Fleet Street started to refer to the island as 'Fortress Singapore'. But when the amateur pilot Lieutenant King-Clark touched down there some eight months after the naval base was opened, it was not the island's martial profile that impressed him. 'Even so, I was assured by old hands that the tempo was slow compared to the wild days of the rubber boom of the Twenties.'

The look of the city was changing too. The heart of it, including the cathedral with its stained-glass window of Raffles, had been built around the Padang, the large grass square which, despite all the blandishments of Singapore's energetic developers, remained the verdant focal point of the city. It was to Singaporeans of all races a somewhat smaller version of what Hyde Park is to Londoners or Central Park to New Yorkers: a treasured open space and sports ground, home of the Singapore Cricket Club whose veranda overlooked their wicket and venue for all the city's major ceremonials. Many of these started from the steps of the Municipal Building, which was finished in 1929 and bordered the Padang: a large British provincial town hall transplanted to the tropics, a splendid example of Alderman's Neoclassical with a long and elegant Corinthian colonnade.

But by the late 1930s the Singapore skyline was getting bolder and brasher, with a look that obviously owed much more to North America than Britain or Asia. One of the first sights for passengers approaching the island by ship was the ten-storey Fullerton Building with its enormous windows set not in wood but in steel frames. Named after the first governor of the Straits Settlements, it was completed in 1928 on the site of a nineteenth-century seafront fort. It might have been expected that the British, with their ingrained conservatism and feline suspicion of change, would have turned their noses up at this Manhattan import. Not at all. One of the Fullerton's first tenants was the Singapore Club, the bastion of the island's establishment, which took the upper floors including the attic, which they converted into bedrooms for members who wished to stay overnight. Another was the General Post Office, which occupied three floors; one of these boasted a 300-foot curved counter that newcomers were always told was the longest of its kind in the world. Then the Ford Motor Company made its contribution and built an art deco factory with a Pharaonic main entrance on a hill off the main Bukit Timah road leading to the Johore Causeway. This was South-east Asia's first car-assembly plant.

The army, required to provide a garrison that could hold the base for the three months it might take a task force to sail to its rescue, were also building with style. After the festering slums in which British troops were often housed in the Middle East, King-Clark was astonished by the luxurious new barracks the Manchesters were billeted in at Tanglin, especially its spacious officers' mess.

Its main feature was the large, airy anteroom, opening onto a long roofed and beflowered veranda. On the floor above were the single officers' quarters, each with two large rooms and a veranda – all looking across the immaculate nine-hole golf course surrounding the Mess to the massed purple bougainvillea of the Singapore Botanic Gardens. Behind, screened by tall, tropical trees and flowering shrubs, were the excellent barrack blocks and married quarters.

The old military hospital at Tanglin could not meet the needs of the expanding garrison and a new one was built in the suburb of Alexandra. Set in a lush tropical garden with burbling fountains, from the outside the spacious white-painted building resembled an exclusive hotel. Certainly, the Alexandra was yet another indication that, in Singapore at least, the British government had the welfare of its servicemen at heart.

Nor were the basic military priorities neglected. In the 1860s 'Forbidden Hill', where Major Farquhar had fired his cannon to scare away ghosts and Raffles had built his official residence, had become Fort Canning. Now all that remained of the fort whose artillery had once dominated the Malacca Straits was some of the loopholed Victorian brickwork of its elegant gateways. It had been replaced with a more contemporary example of military architecture, apparently inspired by France's formidable Maginot Line along its frontier with Germany. An underground operations centre had been burrowed out of the hill. Almost 30 feet below the surface, the centre consisted of twenty-two rooms, including a communications centre, sleeping quarters and bathrooms. Its reinforced concrete walls were over 3 feet thick in places and it was intended that this bunker complex should be capable of withstanding direct hits from the heaviest aerial bombs and shells.

The most visible manifestation of Singapore's defences were its heavy guns. In May 1935, to mark the Silver Jubilee of His Majesty King George V, the Sultan of Johore had donated an additional half a million pounds towards their cost. Most of this had promptly been spent on providing another brace of 15-inch naval guns to be positioned at Tanah Marah near Changi. 'There are more guns on Singapore Island than plums in a Christmas pudding,' crowed the correspondent for the *Sydney Morning Herald*, who had described Singapore as 'the Gibraltar of the East'. By the eve of the century's second European war, Singapore had twenty-nine garrison artillery pieces in place: five 15-inchers, six of 9.2-inch calibre and eighteen 6-inch guns. All but two 15-inch guns were on full swivel mountings. These enabled them to turn 360 degrees so that, apart from taking on enemy ships, they could traverse in a northerly direction and engage land targets on the Malayan Peninsula.

British thinking about how best to defend Singapore had changed. It was now recognized that, until the Royal Navy arrived in force, it must be prepared to repulse threats to its naval base by both land and sea. The days had gone when the Malayan jungle could be written off as 'impenetrable' with all the aplomb of mediaeval map-makers labelling uncharted waters 'There be dragons'. It was no longer considered that an assault on the island's northern shore by an enemy that had come down the peninsula and crossed the narrow Johore Straits belonged in the same hare-brained category as landings on the moon or tunnels under the English Channel. It was even becoming accepted that the ability of the big guns on the island to pick off enemy ships far out to sea would make it more likely that an aggressor might prefer to establish a bridgehead on the peninsula, then opt for a swift night crossing of the narrow Johore Straits.

From the early 1930s, officer students at London's Imperial Defence College played an annual war game in which they were required to defend Singapore from a Japanese attack. They almost invariably decided that the enemy would choose to land in northern Malaya, or even Siam, then fight their way south. Inter-service rivalry fuelled the debate. The Royal Navy continued to make a convincing case for a defence that was primarily a matter of sea power. They still saw the army's role as hunkering down on Singapore Island and keeping an enemy fleet at bay with its coastal guns until the navy arrived to sink them.

Then, in November 1935, Singapore and Malaya got a new army commander. Major-General Sir William George Shedden Dobbie was fifty-six years old and a member of the Plymouth Brethren, an uncompromising puritanical sect whose devotions were devoid of hymns and ritual, but strong and long on prayer. His nonconformism spilt over into his professional life too. Before long, he was lending his weight to those student war-gamers at the Imperial Defence College who always went for Singapore by the overland route. Had not the British literally paved the way by building a trunk road down the length of the Malayan Peninsula?

In spring 1936, Dobbie acquired a useful and like-minded subordinate. Colonel Arthur Percival joined him as what was effectively his chief of staff. Percival was a tall, gangling man of forty-eight and his appearance belied his considerable ability. Beneath the brim of his Wolseley-pattern sun helmet, the toothbrush moustache, buck teeth and slightly receding chin were a caricature of the haughty rodent features hostile cartoonists loved to bestow on senior British officers. Nor did the pipe-cleaner shanks visible below his long shorts signal his aptitude for long-distance running, tennis and cricket, undiminished by middle age. Only the bits of coloured ribbon sewn above the left breast pocket of his uniform indicated why an immediate superior had once been moved to write of him: 'Exceptionally gifted . . . a very brave and gallant officer.'

Apart from the usual 1914–18 campaign ribbons, and a rarer one earned in 1919 attempting to crush War Minister Churchill's 'typhus-bearing vermin' in revolutionary Russia, Percival's gallantry awards included two Distinguished Service Orders, a Military Cross won on the Somme where he was badly wounded, a Croix de Guerre for leading a tired battalion into a surprisingly effective counter-attack and saving some French artillery during the Ludendorff offensive of 1918 and three Mentions in Dispatches for his coolness under fire. The bar to the DSO had been won in 1919 when he captured a Bolshevik position along the River Dvina from Archangel by making an arduous and unexpected outflanking trek through a thick forest. The following year he received an Order of the British Empire for service as a battalion intelligence officer in Ireland during the Troubles of the early 1920s where, among other things, he doggedly hunted the killers of an off-duty Catholic policeman shot on the steps of a church and survived an ambush in which two other officers were mortally wounded. The IRA would much rather have killed Percival, whom they regarded as obsessive and brutal, alleging that he allowed his soldiers to beat up two of their men so badly that one of them lost his sanity. Their own accolade was a £1,000 price on his head.

Unlike most officers of his rank, there was no military tradition in Percival's family. His father was an estate manager and his mother's family had done well in the Lancashire cotton trade. When he left Rugby School, although he had excelled in its Officer Cadet Training Unit, he found himself a job with some iron ore traders in the City. He was twenty-six when, on the first day of Britain's war with the Kaiser, he enlisted in the Inns of Court Officer Training Corps (OTC). After five weeks' intensive training in infantry tactics, map reading and weapons handling – most of it on Wimbledon Common or in central London parks – he was commissioned as a second lieutenant. Luckily, this was not the end of his training and it would be another ten months before he saw action. Exactly 100 volunteers from the City were commissioned from his day's intake at the Inns of Court OTC. By 1919, twenty-nine were dead and thirty-three had been wounded, often more than once.

Percival was an ambitious man, though his natural reserve tended to conceal it, and he had at first been reluctant to take up the Singapore posting. Four of the last ten years had been spent in England on various staff courses, at which he shone, and the rest abroad. Now he felt that, to start moving up the ladder, he needed the command of UK-based troops. The last thing he wanted was to become a permanent staff officer. He had not won his medals sitting at a desk. The War Office agreed to reduce his tour of duty from three to two years.

He was accompanied by his Irish wife and their small daughter.

Betty Percival was a Protestant from Carrickfergus on the northern shore of Belfast Lough, which was part of Loyalist Ulster. They met there after the IRA leader Michael Collins had signed his treaty in London and British troops had been ordered out of Cork, which had become one of the twenty-six counties of independent Eire.

The Percivals arrived in Singapore expecting it to be something like their last overseas posting in Malta, 'where everybody quickly gets to know everybody else'. Instead, they found that, on the whole, the British civilian community were standoffish. There were obviously some hurt feelings though Percival was loath to admit it, apparently rejoicing in the opportunity to hone his tennis and squash. 'After all,' he reasoned, 'military officers were birds of passage while the majority of civilians were permanent residents . . .'

The truth was that members of the commercial establishment tended to regard the military and their works with, at best, condescension and often with a certain amount of irritation. Singapore was their business and the business of Singapore was business. And while they may well have known that the best way to avoid a war is to show that you are ready for one, they also found it difficult to believe that peace-time military spending – like any expensive insurance – was really all that necessary. In their clubs, over the weak whisky and sodas they called *stengahs*, one did not have to be wearing rose-tinted spectacles to be optimistic about the future. Undoubtedly Japan was in militaristic mood. But it was quite obvious they would never make a move against the Asian colonies of the British, French and Dutch unless another major European war kept most of their fleets in northern waters. And how likely was that? Look how prosperous Germany was under Hitler. Would they risk all that for another war? Trade war more likely! Meanwhile, rearmament kept the price of rubber up. 'Never before had we attempted to build a fortress on top of a rich and prosperous commercial centre,' observed the new chief of staff. 'There were clashes of interests, and important ones too.'

In theory the referee of these clashes was Sir Shenton Thomas, the governor. In practice, Sir Shenton was nowhere near impartial enough to take this role. Quite soon after his arrival in 1934 he had become famous for telling an army staff officer invited to a luncheon party at Government House, 'I wish you bloody soldiers would go away . . . We should be much better off without you.'

Unusually for his generation, and although he had married a colonel's daughter, first cousin of a wiry little Home Counties general called Bernard Montgomery, Thomas had done no soldiering whatsoever. Nor did he appear to think worse of himself for it. In 1914 he was thirty-five years old and serving his country in an African colony when war broke out. He had spent almost a quarter of a century in Africa before coming to Malaya, his last three years as governor of the Gold Coast. Urbane and popular among the British community, even his admirers admitted that he tended to agree with the last person who had his ear. 'I think he wanted to be liked – a weak trait in anyone's character,' observed Arthur Dickinson, the Inspector General of Police, who liked him enough to become a close if not entirely loyal friend.

Certainly, there was a welcome for a governor who sympathized with the right of the hard-working creators of the colony's wealth not to be disturbed by artillery rehearsals and bugles blowing at dawn. One of Singapore's leading English-language dailies congratulated the authorities for having the sense to build a new barracks in Penang, well away from George Town, 'for, without meaning any offence, we all know what soldiers are'. Percival was obviously stunned by this self-centred bunch of expatriates. 'People as a whole were not interested in defence,' he noted with commendable understatement.

Except, of course, for those members of the resident Japanese community, now well over 3,000 strong, whose espionage activities were becoming increasingly blatant. In March 1935 a well-known Japanese contractor called Nishimura killed himself with a hidden phial of poison after he had been arrested by Special Branch detectives in Singapore. He was suspected of being the man who had supplied a Japanese naval officer, who had recently been expelled from the colony, with photographs and plans of the naval base.

In 1937 Japan became engaged in a major war in China. The Chinese had plenty of courage and endurance but they lacked training and equipment, particularly a proper air force. Their other great handicap was a notoriously corrupt government. The Chinese Nationalists under Chiang Kai-shek were first ejected from Peking and then from Shanghai and every other major port.

By the end of 1938 the British colony of Hong Kong was sealed off from the Chinese hinterland following the Japanese capture of Canton. Half a million Chinese refugees swarmed into Hong Kong and over thirty Nationalist government departments set up branches there – many of them to do with procuring arms. Madame Chiang Kai-shek became the first non-European since 1918 to be given permission to have a home in the colony's exclusive 'Peak' district; she divided her time between there and the Nationalists' new capital at Chungking. One Fleet Street journalist declared that the colony had become 'the capital of China'. This was just what the British wanted to avoid. London was sympathetic to the Nationalists but, with the prospect of a European war looming, the British were anxious not to provoke the Japanese, and this, in combination with a long-held conviction that Hong Kong was indefensible however big its garrison, led to the most blatant appeasement. Nationalist radio stations were closed down. Journalists working for the colony's Chinese-language newspapers were forbidden to describe the Japanese as 'shrimp barbarians', 'dwarf barbarians' or 'dwarf pirates'.

In Malaya, wealthy Chinese started support groups among their community to raise funds for the homeland. The struggle also breathed new life into the local Communist Party who would have no truck with Chiang Kai-shek's Nationalists but supported Mao Tse-tung's well-disciplined guerrillas. In Singapore, the Special Branch paid the Chinese Communists as much attention as they did the Japanese because of the influence they had on organized labour in the colony.

Japanese atrocities were widely reported. On 13 December 1937 their army began what western newspapers and magazines would soon refer to as the 'Rape of Nanking', visiting an orgy of massacre and mass rape on the citizens of Chiang Kai-shek's abandoned capital on a scale not seen since the time of Attila the Hun. It went on for seven weeks and exactly how many died has never been agreed. One of the more conservative estimates put the figure at 227,400.

Later the Japanese government tried to cover it up. But its soldiers had taken photographs of bound prisoners being used for live bayonet practice, of naked young women tied to chairs with their legs spread-eagled in preparation for gang rape and then had the gall to take them to Chinese chemists for printing. Extra copies were made and smuggled out to the international community which continued to try and do business in Japanese-occupied Shanghai. A popular Japanese newspaper reported on a competition between two Japanese sub-lieutenants to see how many Chinese prisoners they could decapitate with their samurai swords. Its headline ran: 'Contest to Kill First 100 Chinese Extended When Both Fighters Exceed Mark – Mukai Scores 106 and Noda 105.'

Yet when Japanese forces attacked the Anglo-American gunboats that the Chinese had permitted to patrol the Yangtse River ever since the Boxer Uprising against western influence almost forty years before – sinking the USS *Panay* with the loss of five lives – there were profuse apologies. Killing Chinese, it seemed, was one thing; taking on industrialized western powers quite another. Even so, Percival, who was nearing the end of his tour, had begun to notice how good some Japanese equipment was. He was particularly impressed by the shallow-draft landing-craft and the ships they had developed to carry the landing-craft, enabling them to outflank their enemy and make amphibious landings along the China coast.

The War Office kept its word and the Percivals sailed home in December 1937, slightly ahead of schedule. They left Singapore aboard the liner *Dilwara* with their two small children – baby James had been born in the colony – and memories of a pleasant Asian interlude with plenty of sport for Arthur. Before he left he had written a summary of the tactics the Japanese were likely to use in any attack on Singapore, which assumed that a British task force sailing to the rescue would take more than the expected seventy days to get there. It emphasized the greater need for the defence of 'the back door', as Percival called northern Malaya's border with Thailand. Most of all it demanded more infantry and aircraft to counter Japanese landings along the coast. The senior naval officer in the colony did not share Dobbie's enthusiasm for Percival's conclusions. 'I rather feel that the civilian members of the Defence Committee may regard the whole as too pessimistic, and take the line that we are scaremongers.'

The Percivals looked forward to spending Christmas aboard the *Dilwara*, as the liner cruised steadily northwards and Singapore dropped out of sight, if not entirely out of mind. The ship's radio picked up BBC news bulletins reporting 'profound apologies' from Tokyo for the death of a British sailor when a Royal Navy tug was shelled in the Yangtse River during the Japanese advance on Nanking; a German court had decreed that children of a pacifist couple who refused to bring them up as National Socialists should be made wards of the state; Madrid was under air and artillery bombardment as Franco's German- and Italian-supported forces tightened their siege; in Britain trials were going ahead to determine the best type of air-raid shelter.

Homeward bound through the endless blue of the Indian Ocean, the Percivals could hardly be blamed if they viewed these clouds on the horizon with the kind of equanimity that prevailed among the members of the Singapore Defence Committee. Arthur, who would be celebrating his fiftieth birthday on Boxing Day, was obviously approaching the peak of his career. If he needed any confirmation of this it came in a War Office telegram via the ship's radio room offering him a plum job as Brigadier General Staff at Home Command HQ in Aldershot. Once again Percival would not be commanding troops, but this was too good to refuse.

Behind the Percivals the ripples left by Arthur's presence in Singapore gradually subsided. Copies of his 'scaremongering' summary of how the Japanese might go about things were locked safely away in files marked 'top secret' and the civilian members of the Defence Committee were spared this distraction from their work and play. As 1938, the year of the Munich crisis, slipped by, none of the reinforcements Dobbie and Percival had called for arrived.

It was not until the following year, as Britain began to bow to the inevitable and accelerated its rearmament programme, that the garrison of Singapore and Malaya was strengthened to nine infantry battalions and 100 aircraft. The latter included two squadrons of Vickers Vildebeests, big biplane torpedo bombers that had first come into service about eight years before. The RAF's 36 Squadron was equipped with the latest bigger-engined Mark III version and, though their top speed was still well under 200 mph, they were considered an effective platform for the level runs required for aerial torpedo strikes against shipping. There were as yet no front-line fighters available. The only aircraft that came even close to fighters were ten nippy little yellow-painted Hawker Harts and Audax biplanes, advanced trainers in which the weekend fliers of the Straits Settlements Volunteer Air Force acted out their 1917 Sopwith Camel fantasies.

In August, Dobbie left Singapore to begin what would turn out to be a short-lived retirement. He was replaced as General Officer Commanding Malaya by Major-General Lionel Bond. Like Dobbie, his command was restricted to land forces. The navy was its own boss, as was the air force under Air Vice-Marshal J. T. Babington. Bond and Babington had very different ideas about how Malaya and Singapore should be defended. Bond thought that the only thing that mattered was defending Singapore and the naval base. Babington believed that Singapore was best defended by ensuring that Malaya remained in British hands and that the army should mostly be deployed to defend

the airfields he was busy establishing in the northern part of the peninsula. Soon their relations had reached the point where the smarter
hostesses never invited them to the same dinner party.

Bond's appointment coincided with the arrival of more infantry
reinforcements from India in the shape of the 2nd Battalion of Argyll
and Sutherland Highlanders under Lieutenant-Colonel Ian Stewart, a
Scots laird whose ancestors – the Stewarts of Appin – had fought on
Bonnie Prince Charlie's side in 1745. Really he should have been a
brigadier by now, or at least a full colonel, but he was so devoted to
the Argylls that he had declined the place at Camberley Staff College
that promotion to that rank required in peace-time.

The Argylls were the old 93rd Regiment of Foot, the Crimean War's
famous 'thin red line' at the Battle of Balaclava. To the bewilderment of
outsiders, its men still liked to refer to themselves as 'the 93rd'. For
both officers and men, the regiment was almost a tribal affair, with the
sons of this martial caste following fathers and older brothers into it.
Among Stewart's younger officers was Lieutenant David Wilson who
was just twenty-three and the third generation of his family to serve in
the regiment. Wilson had joined the battalion three years before,
shortly after his father ceased to command it. He had arrived in time
for the 1937 campaign against the Fakir of Ipi in Waziristan where they
had lost twelve killed and sixteen wounded in what the British press
usually referred to as 'skirmishing'.

It had taken the Argylls four days to get to Singapore from Madras. As
they approached the entrance to Keppel harbour, Wilson was impressed
by his first glimpse of the coastal batteries, searchlight emplacements
and concrete pillboxes. He had seen Aden and Karachi and those
imperial ports had nothing like this. Singapore really was a fortress.

But it rained heavily on the King's birthday parade at the Padang
which the Chinese considered inauspicious. Some youths, said to be
Communists, threw stones at the Manchesters' band. Before long the
Argyll rank and file, often small men with even shorter tempers and
reactions honed on the mean streets between the Forth and the Clyde,
would be fighting the Manchesters and any other regiment they could
find. For some, the battalion was their first real home. When they
caroused on pay nights, they were sometimes accompanied by their
buglers, so that the regimental call could be played when reinforcements were needed at a brawl.

Then, at the end of their first month, while the Argylls were still marvelling at the comfort of their new barracks, Hitler invaded Poland and the war the Munich agreement had postponed began in Europe. In Singapore and Malaya Prime Minister Neville Chamberlain's Sunday morning announcement that Britain was at war with Germany for the second time that century arrived via the BBC Overseas Service at 5.45 p.m. local time. Many prominent citizens, the governor and his wife among them, were attending evensong at St Andrew's Cathedral. It was not unexpected news. It was now three days since German troops had crossed the Polish frontier and an ultimatum had been served. The reaction of many of the British in Singapore was guilt: here they were, in safety and ease, while back home everyone was carrying gas masks, including the children being evacuated by train from the big cities.

Rex King-Clark, the Manchesters' flying subaltern, had no such feelings. He was back in England himself, having returned a few months before when a dream had come true and he had been posted to an RAF Army Co-operation Squadron for a four-year attachment. That had since been cancelled and King-Clark was now attached to the 2nd Battalion of his regiment, which was preparing to go to France with the British Expeditionary Force. Most of his brother officers could not believe his luck. Suddenly Singapore had become rather a dull place and unlikely to advance their career prospects.

Many of these men believed in creating their own excitement and the Argylls, who had been given a different pay night from the rest of the garrison, in the hope that they would only find each other to fight, certainly did not hold the monopoly on riot. On the Monday evening following the declaration of war, those Manchesters who were not on guard duty or confined to barracks for various misdemeanours swarmed into town. Bugler Arthur Lane, who was almost nineteen and had already been in the army for four years, having joined as a boy soldier, noticed that, through some unspoken agreement, they had almost all chosen to wear uniform. Normally they did their carousing in civvies. At first the only damage done was to the targets at the rifle ranges in 'The World' funfair, which the Chinese in charge had already turned into German soldiers festooned with swastikas. Then, as the drink began to flow, somebody remembered where they could find a real swastika. The Swedish consulate, which had become the German Interest Section, was flying a small swastika flag from an upper window. Entry was gained and the flag set alight. After that it was the turn of the Black Cat and the Lucky Lady, Chinese-owned girlie bars, for the Manchesters wanted revenge against the Chinese, any Chinese, for stoning their parade. When they had finished, the bars looked like the pictures the newspapers were carrying of bomb damage in Warsaw.

For most people, the transition from peace-time to wartime gave little cause for concern and an editorial in the *Straits Times* advised them that their confidence was well founded. 'At this distance from the scene of battle, with our defences perfected and Japanese participation in the struggle on the side of Germany an extremely remote possibility, Malaya has little to fear.'

Reports, sketchy at first, of a significant Japanese defeat seemed to confirm this. It appeared that a skirmish provoked by the Japanese with Soviet forces on the borders of Manchuria – under Japanese control since they had seized it from the Chinese in 1931 – had flared into full-scale warfare. Almost forty years before, Japan had established itself as a modern military power with its victory over Czarist Russia. But this was a very different story. By skilfully coordinating tanks, artillery and air power, a certain Marshal Zhukov had inflicted a convincing defeat on the Imperial Japanese Army. At least 18,000 were killed before a ceasefire was negotiated.

Unable to endure the shame, two regimental commanders killed themselves, one by ritual disembowelment and the other by hurling himself in a one-man banzai charge at a Russian position. Within days, Zhukov's victory would be eclipsed by the Panzers rolling over the unharvested Polish corn. None the less, it gave comfort to those who viewed Japanese success in China with growing apprehension. Who could doubt that the British and French could match, in quality at least, anything Joseph Stalin might put into the field? Or that Tokyo would draw the right conclusions from such a costly lesson?

On 3 October 1939, when Britain's new war against Germany was exactly a month old, Singapore's first real skyscraper was opened. The art deco Cathay Building had sixteen floors. Radio Malaya had studios there, and its transmitter on the roof. Below them, on the fourth floor, the Cathay restaurant soon acquired a gourmet reputation. There were also thirty-two luxury apartments, several of them tenanted by wealthy Chinese. But its biggest attraction was the ground floor's 1,300-seat cinema, the first in Singapore to be fully air-conditioned, a Hollywood luxury that was almost unheard of in public buildings, and was fitted in very few private ones.

It was here that the majority of the British community first saw Judy Garland's hit Technicolor musical of the year, *The Wizard of Oz*, and heard her yearning to be 'Over the Rainbow'. As far as most of them were concerned, they were already there.

In June 1940, Lakshmi Swaminadhan, fleeing an unhappy marriage, was aboard a vessel of the British India Steam Navigation Company when the ship's radio began to pick up reports of France's collapse and the beginning of the evacuation of the British Expeditionary Force, which appeared to be concentrating around the Channel port of Dunkirk.

Dr Swaminadhan was the daughter of a prominent Hindu lawyer from Kerala who had been born into a poor but literate Brahmin family whose income was almost as low as its caste was hidebound and high. Her father had leapt both these formidable hurdles to finish his education at Edinburgh and Harvard universities. And, although he became a nationalist, famed for procuring the acquittal of a young man accused of murdering an Englishman, he thought a British education the best grounding for beating the '*firangi* rascals'.★

He wanted Lakshmi to follow his footsteps to Edinburgh. Yet, by the time he died in 1930, his hopes had been dashed as both his wife and daughter had embraced the teachings of Mahatma Gandhi. The girl who had once sung 'God Save the King' at her convent school, and learned that the Indian Mutiny of 1857 had been the lowest form of treachery, now called the mutiny the 'The First Great Independence War' and eschewed English frocks for the *pavadai*, southern India's ankle-length skirt. At home she preferred to try and conduct conversations in the Malayalam and Tamil her family used to address the servants, and avoided the English they mostly spoke among themselves. In 1938 she graduated at the Madras Medical College and then started her year's internship for her diploma in gynaecology. Lakshmi's other preoccupation was obtaining a divorce from the pilot with Tata Airlines she had so foolishly married two years before. They had split up in less than six months and, later in life, Lakshmi would say: 'Being self-willed and obstinate I was not prepared to subdue my personality and play the role of a good wife.'

★ '*Firangi*' – foreign.

She was also moving away from the only man who had had almost as much influence over her as her father – Mahatma Gandhi. Lakshmi had come to agree with her Communist friends that what India needed was not civil disobedience and hunger strikes. It was a violent Russian-style revolution which would not only purge India of colonial rule but also of the caste-based feudalism from which her father had made his remarkable escape. The only prominent Indian nationalist who seemed at all likely to achieve this, though he was hardly a Marxist, was Subhas Chandra Bose.

'Give me blood and I promise you freedom,' thundered the Bengali who was Gandhi's chief rival for the leadership of the Indian independence movement and often a much more exciting speaker. As teenagers Lakshmi and her friends had got up at dawn to watch Bose, then the *enfant terrible* of the Congress Party, drilling his admittedly unarmed followers with a precision that 'would have done credit to any crack infantry unit'. Since then there had been developments which the Indian Left could not ignore. Bose's followers were beginning to call him him 'Netaji', which translated into German as 'Führer', and the Bengali himself had expressed approval of some aspects of the mixture of nationalism and socialism preached by Hitler and Mussolini. Even so, no Indian nationalist could fail to admire his spellbinding oratory and courage. Unfortunately, Bose was back in jail again in Calcutta where he had announced that he would go on hunger strike until he was released, daring the British to let him die and allow his funeral pyre to provide the spark that might set the subcontinent ablaze.

Not, she noted, that any of her fellow first-class passengers on the ship were likely to agree with her views. They were mostly professional southern Indians returning from home leave to their well-paid jobs in Malaya and Singapore. Even the BBC news reports of French defeat and British evacuation failed to stir them. Almost their only conversation was about the jobs they were going back to and how quickly they could make enough money to retire comfortably in India.

Occasionally, some misgivings might be expressed about the chances of the war reaching the Far East. After all, the newspapers had been speculating for years that Japan would only strike Malaya if another European war meant Britain's back was turned. Even so, it was easy to brush these fears aside. The power of the empire they had grown up in, which for the educated and enterprising Indian provided such excellent opportunities for financial and social advancement, was self-evident. The British were not the French. They were the greatest power on earth. Anyone who had any doubts only had to look at Singapore's new naval base. Certainly, it was very much business as usual as far as the British India Steam Navigation Company was concerned. The only concession made to the war was the imposition of a strict blackout at night in case there were any German submarines or surface raiders in the area.

There were other Indians on the ship for whom the reasons for this obsession with not showing even a pinprick of light at night, or the very idea that events the far side of the planet could somehow affect lives already a constant struggle for survival, were almost incomprehensible. Lakshmi had watched them come aboard at Nagappattinam, the Tamil port south of Madras and less than 100 miles from Jaffna in northern Ceylon: newly recruited labourers bound for Malaya to answer the almost insatiable demand for rubber of an industrial nation and its allies at war. There was no deep-water harbour at Nagappattinam. The Tamils, who were often accompanied by their wives and children, had to be rowed out to the ship through the breakers and had usually been seasick before they had set foot on board. Their accommodation, with its bucket latrines, was in the hold. Some of them were too weak to leave their fouled bed-spaces for the entire two-week voyage.

Lakshmi's initial reaction to British Singapore was a common one. She was struck by how very Chinese it was, at all levels. Chinese dockers were to be expected, as were the sinewy and often barefoot rickshaw men. More surprisingly, the latter's loads were often also Chinese – fat-faced merchants and middlemen who exuded a cigar-smoking air of prosperous well-being. But it was their lack of servility the young doctor most admired; the way, however humble their occupation, they 'really upheld the dignity of labour'. This pleased her. She had long supported China in its struggle against the Japanese, more than ever regarded by most of the Indian Left as the regional fascists.

By December 1940 the world war had still not spread to South-east Asia. Unlike the mainland Chinese, most of its people continued to live at peace in countries that had long been ruled by Europeans who, for the most part, saw no reason why this should change.

In September Kathleen Stapledon, the wife of a civilian naval architect at the base, had returned to Singapore with her husband Charles, whom she always called 'Steepy', after eight months' home leave.

When they boarded the old liner *Empress of India* in July, the air raids over southern England had begun to hot up. Yet this was not the main reason some friends and relatives wished they could swap places with them, even though the long voyage ahead was not without its U-boat hazards. They envied the Stapledons because, after ten months of hostilities, they were escaping the growing tedium of blacked-out, wartime Britain: a drab and difficult place of endless queues and ration coupons, where all luxuries – and not a few essentials – were in increasingly short supply.

Safely back in Singapore, the Stapledons did notice a few changes but these were all for the better and distinctly uplifting. Kathleen was particularly impressed that the new Supreme Court, with its neat turquoise cupola and Corinthian columns, had at last been completed. And for the first time they visited the Cathay Building, which had been nearing completion as they left. Its air-conditioned cinema, where everybody had gone to see *The Wizard of Oz*, was still the talk of the town.

But the little construction boom that had taken place over the past couple of years had been almost entirely in commercial properties. There had been hardly any private housing built in Singapore since the 1932 slump and a steady trickle of officer reinforcements, mostly staff officers for the newly arrived Indian formations, had further aggravated the shortage. The Stapledons had difficulty finding somewhere to replace the house they had been obliged to give up when they went off for their long leave eight months before. Eventually a Chinese-owned bungalow in the Bukit Timah road was rented and staff engaged. Like many European households the Stapledons' establishment was a good reflection of Singapore's racial mix. The *ayah* (nanny), who had already worked for them for eight years and was also a good cook, was Javanese; the *syce* (chauffeur) Malay; the *kebun* (gardener) Indian; and the 'Boy', as was almost invariably the case, an adult Chinese male, a family man probably in his early thirties. The Boy's role was somewhere between that of a butler and a general factotum, shopping and running errands during the day, serving drinks and waiting on table in the evening. Kathleen found her new Boy 'fat and jovial' and was rather pleased with her choice.

The same could not be said for the house, and her *ayah* lost no time in telling her it was 'terrible'. Her main objection was their Japanese neighbours who played their radio at full volume. But, as far as the

Stapledons were concerned, this was a minor problem and they were soon settled back into the British Singaporeans' round of work and sport and nights at the club, where noisy neighbours and servant problems could be discussed over a couple of drinks.

'Conscience smitten at being so safe from the war,' the Reverend Jack Bennitt, an Anglican Missioner working among the colony's small community of Chinese Christians, noted in his diary. Bennitt and his young wife Nora, a handsome couple, had been out East since 1933 when, newly married, they had first been sent to Hong Kong and then posted to Singapore in April 1938. So far, the nearest they had come to the war had been returning from Britain over their last long leave when, a month after hostilities started, they had been obliged to cross the Channel to Rotterdam at the height of the magnetic mines* scare. But from there it had been safe enough. Holland was neutral and, unlike British and German vessels, the Dutch liner which carried them to Singapore was 'brilliantly lit up'.

Neutrality had not stopped the Wehrmacht invading Holland the following May, part of its right-hook around the Maginot Line. With France, it was one of the two European colonial powers in South-east Asia which had themselves come under occupation. Now, their distant colonies and all the riches they possessed had been cut adrift from their homelands. Naturally, the Germans regarded these orphans as the fruits of victory and meant to plunder all the Dutch and French oil and rubber they could. So did the Japanese who, although they were not a belligerent, had in September signed the Tripartite Pact with Germany and Italy. But this project was not proving as easy as all that.

To bring the Asian spoils of their European victory back home the Germans would have to sail through waters still dominated by Britain's Royal Navy. Furthermore, the Netherlands East Indies was defended by troops loyal to Queen Wilhelmina, who had fled Holland for England in a British destroyer. Seventy million people, of whom some 250,000 were Dutch, inhabited this vast and sprawling territory, which included Java, Sumatra, Dutch Borneo, Dutch New Guinea and Western Timor, as well as dozens of smaller islands. Most of the Dutch army in the region consisted of ill-equipped colonial levies. But the bulk of Holland's small but quite modern fleet, easily the best-equipped

---

* Detonated on the seabed by the magnetic field of a ship's hull, these mines were initially very successful, until one was captured and counter-measures developed.

of its three services, had long been in the East Indies. Apart from three cruisers and five destroyers, it had a dozen or so submarines. Some of them had been fitted with a revolutionary Dutch invention – the *Schnorchel*, which served as both an air intake and an outlet for diesel gases.* Since they did not have to break surface to recharge their batteries, it gave them the longest underwater endurance of any submersibles in the world. If Japan, with its great hunger for raw resources, was tempted to enter the war, the British thought that the Dutch ships might make a useful contribution to the Allied cause.

France also had some warships at its port at Cam Ranh Bay on the South China Sea which was about 700 miles away from the Malayan coast. But French Indo-China – Vietnam, Cambodia and Laos – was controlled by the new collaborationist government the Germans had permitted the French to establish at the spa town of Vichy with Marshal Pétain, the aged hero of Verdun, as its figurehead. The Vichy governor in South-east Asia was Vice-Admiral Jean Découx. In June he had replaced General Georges Catroux, who had promptly defected to Singapore and thence to London to join Brigadier-General Charles de Gaulle and his Free French. So far, Découx had resisted all British blandishments to get him to follow Catroux's splendid example.

In the circumstances, this was hardly surprising. Découx had been appointed governor by Admiral Jean Darlan, who commanded Vichy's military and was a notorious Anglophobe. It was believed that these feelings were rooted in the loss of a great-grandfather during Nelson's victory at the Battle of Trafalgar in 1805. Now the British had provided the French navy with a more recent grudge. When a defeated France had negotiated the best terms it could from the Germans, Darlan had assured the British that the formidable French fleet would never be allowed to fall into German hands and thus tip the naval balance against them. But Churchill did not trust Darlan. The prime minister ordered that French warships which did not rally to de Gaulle be seized or sunk wherever they were found. Almost 1,300 French sailors died when the cruisers *Dunkerque* and *Strasbourg* and the old battleship *Bretagne* were cornered by the Royal Navy in the Algerian harbour of Mers el-Kebir. These were the first naval hostilities between Britain and

---

* Eventually called the 'snorkel' by the Anglo-Americans, the device was turned down by the Admiralty. The Germans immediately saw its potential; fortunately for the Allies they were slow to develop it.

France since 1815. As far as Vichy was concerned, they were also the
death throes of the fading Entente Cordiale and the birth of France's
place in Hitler's Europe.

Yet, if Découx had no reason to love the British, he had no reason
to love the Japanese either. Their troops had long been deployed
around Vietnam's northern border with China, the area the French
called Tongkin, and their war with the Chinese frequently spilt into
Vietnam. Immediately after France's defeat when, so far from hope
and home, French morale had been at its lowest, the Japanese had
begun to increase the pressure. They demanded the closure of a supply
route for Chiang Kai-shek's Nationalist Chinese forces, plus the use of
air bases and a permanent military mission.

On 22 September 1940, Découx reluctantly signed an agreement
granting them all they asked – the main airfields at Hanoi and the port
of Haiphong. It was also agreed that they could station 6,000 troops
on French territory, including air force personnel. On the same day,
the Japanese attacked by land and air the township of Langson on the
Tongkinese frontier. About 150 Vichy troops, 50 of them Europeans,
were killed before a ceasefire was agreed and Tokyo apologized for its
latest 'map-reading error'. Découx was then left to work out whether
the chances of this taking place on the very day he had capitulated and
signed really was coincidence or a warning not to take so long to meet
a Japanese request in future. For instance, it was obvious that it would
suit Tokyo to establish similar bases in southern Indo-China, which
would bring its bombers within striking distance of the Malayan coast
and turn the Gulf of Siam into a Japanese lake.

In November the Siamese themselves, the only uncolonized nation
in the region, started a border war on Indo-China's south-western
flank, having revived ancient claims to parts of Cambodia and Laos.
King Ananata Mahodol was sitting out the war in Switzerland, leaving
Field-Marshal Pibul Songgram, his pro-Japanese commander-in-chief
and prime minister, in charge. One of the first things Songgram had
done was change the name of the kingdom from Siam to Thailand, Thai
meaning 'free'. Among Songgram's demands was the return of Cambodia's 'lost city' of Angkor Wat whose jungle-covered temples had been
rescued from oblivion in the 1860s by the intrepid archaeologists of
the École Française d'Extrême-Orient.

Egged on by the Japanese, who had begun to supply them with
modern aircraft and munitions, the Thais had bombed frontier towns.

At first these raids had been ineffectual, as many of the Thai bombs had not been fused properly and failed to explode. Knowing that the Siamese cabinet was divided over the use of force, Découx hoped they might turn to negotiations, but after a week's bombing and with four civilians dead, the admiral had lost patience and ordered his own small air force into the air with some effect: five Thai aircraft had been shot down. Découx had turned down a Japanese offer of mediation as 'far too dangerous to the independence and integrity of Indo-China', but he had let it be known that he would accept the Americans or even the British in that role – preferably the Americans for Sir Josiah Crosby, for many years the British ambassador in Bangkok, was said to be close to the odious Field-Marshal Songgram and the admiral had lost all trust in the English.

It would have been strange had Découx not felt as bitter over the events at Mers el-Kebir as most senior French naval officers did. And it would have been just as understandable if he did not find the prospect of an equal, or even worse, local humiliation befalling Perfidious Albion a pleasing one. Yet he knew that such an event was not in the interests of the French Empire. Once an Asian power seized a European colony, it would be the beginning of the end. A single crack in the delicate regional acceptance of white supremacy would soon lead to more, and Tokyo was ready to exploit such opportunities. For despite its well-publicized outrages in China, Japan seemed to believe its own propaganda: it was the champion of oppressed Asians everywhere and longed to gather them all under the shield of the Greater East Asia Co-Prosperity Sphere.

With this in view, the admiral was pragmatic enough to maintain diplomatic relations with the British, certainly no longer allies but amicably separated. Both sides still had consulates in the other's territory, though the French preferred that the British consul-general should remain in Saigon, in the south of Vietnam and well away from the Japanese presence in the north, which is what, of course, they were most interested in.

On Boxing Day 1940, as most of British Singapore continued with its Christmas party, Monsieur Pierre Pingaud, the French consul-general on the island, accompanied an important visitor to an audience with Sir Shenton Thomas, the governor-general, and Vice-Admiral Sir Geoffrey Layton. The admiral was the senior Royal Navy officer in the Far East, though his official title, Commander-in-Chief China

Station, had come to sound increasingly operatic as hostilities progressed. The fall of France and Italy's entry into the war had made particular inroads in his command, for ships that might have come his way had been diverted to the Mediterranean, which had previously been regarded as primarily a French responsibility.

The meeting took place at Government House, an imposing white-painted building which easily lived up to the name most of the locals used for it which was '*Istana*', the Malay word for palace. Built on an old nutmeg estate by convict labour in the late 1860s, its famously handsome neoclassical design, high-ceilinged, cool and airy rooms, and wonderful views of sea and lush vegetation had won many plaudits. 'It would be hard to find a more perfect picture of repose in a richer landscape,' one of its Victorian incumbents had reported home.

It is doubtful whether the figure who entered the Istana with Consul-General Pingaud felt very relaxed. Resplendent, like Layton, in naval tropical whites Capitaine de Vaisseau Jouan was Découx's chief of staff. Ostensibly the main reason for his visit was to talk about the renewal, however tenuous, of trade links between Indo-China and the British. Initially, Vichy had wanted to scrap them altogether but Découx had asked them to reconsider, arguing that, in their isolated state, there was no alternative to buying British. High on Indo-China's shopping list were the Calcutta gunny bags made from Bengali jute the British had long sold the French for their colony's rice exports, and flour from Australia.

Having disposed of the vexed question of the gunny bags, Jouan turned to a more delicate matter. His introduction was oblique, a reminder that, as long as Indo-China remained under present management, it would always be a buffer between Japan and Malaya. Why then was Britain disseminating propaganda in Indo-China on behalf of de Gaulle and his so-called Free French? Only a few days before, said the indignant Jouan, they had intercepted Gaullist propaganda leaflets *en route* to the British consul-general and obviously intended for distribution. Was it not understood that, if any 'division' within the French community became apparent, the Germans would encourage the Japanese to intervene and they would undoubtedly 'seize this pretext for occupying the whole of Indo-China'?

It is not difficult to imagine the silence that greeted Jouan's remarks, the soft whirring of the propeller fan over a well-polished table, the slow ticking of a clock somewhere, the feeling, perhaps, of time standing still. Everybody at the meeting knew that the headquarters for all de Gaulle's operations in the Far East was situated in Singapore, though the only territory it controlled were the small Pacific islands of the New Hebrides and New Caledonia, hundreds of miles away. They also knew that at this headquarters off the Orchard Road sat Professor Mayer May, recently a lecturer at Hanoi's College of Medicine and currently employed as the Gaullists' Far Eastern propaganda chief.

None the less, both Sir Shenton Thomas, the governor, and Admiral Layton denied all knowledge of the intercepted leaflets and they were probably telling the truth, for the details of Professor May's activities were not something that needed to concern them. If there were any further cases, suggested Thomas, perhaps the capitaine would kindly arrange with Admiral Découx to send him 'specimen copies of the leaflets, and the wrappers in which they were enclosed'. Meanwhile it was agreed that Britain would 'continue to refrain from active propaganda in Indo-China in favour of the Free French' and Admiral Découx would exercise a similar restraint towards Gaullist New Caledonia. In September, a Vichy frigate from Cam Ranh Bay had attempted to regain control there, but wisely upped anchor when confronted by the heavier guns of an Australian cruiser that had rushed to the scene.

Australia, which had already made a significant commitment to British forces in the Middle East, was also helping to beef up Malaya's defences. Three Royal Australian Air Force Squadrons had arrived, two equipped with twin-engined Hudson bombers and one with Wirraways, the Australian version of the Harvard trainer. The American-built Hudsons were the military version of the sleek Lockheed 14 transcontinental airliner. This plane had a range of almost 2,000 miles, and, although it could carry no more than four 250-pound bombs, was considered a useful anti-submarine and maritime reconnaissance aircraft. It was fast for its size with a maximum speed of just under 250 mph and could carry six machine-guns – two in a rear turret, two either side of the fuselage and two in the nose operated by the pilot. The Wirraway had originally been intended as a fighter bomber and was famous for its engine noise, which sounded uncannily like a motorbike. But by the time this single-engined monoplane was in production, improvements in aircraft design had relegated it to the status of no more than an advanced trainer. None the less, in Malaya the Wirraway was never intended to be anything more than a stopgap, giving their two-man crews an excellent opportunity to acclimatize to local flying conditions while the squadron was waiting to be upgraded to Buffaloes, which would begin to arrive in March 1941.

Sometimes known as the 'flying barrel', the Brewster Buffalo was the first reasonably modern fighter to be earmarked for the Far East. It was a squat, tubby little aircraft, built by the Brewster Aeronautical Company of Long Island, New York, as a carrier-borne fighter for the US Navy. It was not quite 26 feet long, had a wing span of 35 feet, a maximum speed of about 300 mph, and was armed with four 50-calibre Colt-Browning machine-guns, two mounted on the wings and two fired through the arc of the propeller.

Apart from their US Navy contract, Brewster had a lucrative over-seas order from the Belgian air force for 170 of its Buffaloes. Then Belgium came under German occupation and the British acquired them. The Dutch squadrons flying for Queen Wilhelmina in the Netherlands East Indies also acquired Buffaloes, though theirs were a slightly earlier model handed down from the US Navy. The first Buffaloes arrived in England towards the climax of the Battle of Britain. They were never used in combat and trials soon revealed that, in this case, appearances were not deceptive. The 'flying barrels' were simply not in the same league as the Spitfires and Hurricanes, which were just about holding their own against Goering's Messerschmitt 109s. In the circumstances, it was thought that they would be best used in the Far East where there was a desperate shortage of aircraft and they would serve as a stopgap until something better could be spared. It had now been decided that part of the military package designed to deter Japan from entering the war would be 336 front-line aircraft – fighters, bombers and the all-important reconnaissance aircraft required to patrol the South China Sea.

Despite Japan's participation in the four-year-old war with China, reliable intelligence about the capability of Japan's air arm, which functioned as an integral part of either the army or the navy, was remarkably scarce. For some time the views of most western experts on the subject had been at best condescending and often much harsher – 'Japan's Bush League Air Force', snorted the headline in an American aviation magazine. And it was true that in the late 1930s there was something about Japan's latest fighters that looked not entirely finished, as if, having reluctantly given up the biplane, its manufacturers could not quite bring themselves to abandon all the accoutrements of the

Red Baron's glory days. For instance, Mitsubishi produced a carrier fighter which the Americans and the British codenamed 'Claude'. In accordance with the latest thinking on fighters, the Claude was a mostly metal low-winged monoplane, but its pilot sat in an open cockpit and his air speed was slowed by fixed landing gear that could not be retracted beneath the wings.

All this was a cruel addition to the problems he had been born with, for it was generally believed that the average Japanese was just not up to the airman's role. Quite apart from suffering from the same bad eyesight that made so many of the Japanese army poor shots, he tended to suffer from a mysterious congenital inner-ear defect that made high-altitude manoeuvres peculiarly painful. Above all, he simply lacked the coordination to fly high-speed modern aircraft with any finesse. It was pointed out that the Japanese rarely possessed the equestrian skills of aces such as von Richthofen, who started his military career as an Uhlan lancer. The Japanese, it was noted, had no cavalry tradition.

None the less, those western military attachés who had managed to encounter any Japanese aircrews were prepared to concede that, despite these appalling handicaps, they did seem to try very hard. What else could explain the way these same pilots in their funny Claudes had, on occasion, run rings around some of the latest Soviet-built fighters supplied to the Chinese, in one memorable incident shooting down ten of them in a single engagement?

Then, in the summer of 1940, the latest creation from the drawing board of Dr Jiro Horikoshi, Mitsubishi's chief aeronautical designer, made its debut and, by the end of the year, the Chinese air force was in even worse trouble. The Japanese A6M Type O fighter was originally codenamed 'Zeke' by the Anglo-Americans, but it soon became known as the 'Navy O' and eventually this was simplified to 'Zero', even by the Japanese who called it the 'Zero-Sen'. Washington, and through them London, was first alerted to its capabilities by Colonel Claire Chennault, a fifty-year-old retired US Army Air Corps officer who had flown fighters in World War I and taken a job as chief adviser to Chiang Kai-shek's air force.

The Zero was unique in that it was designed for both land and carrier use and was splendid at both. Its undercarriage was retractable and its cockpit covered. It was about as fast as a Spitfire or Messerschmitt 109, probably more manoeuvrable than both, with a very tight turning circle, and reasonably well-armed with two 20 mm cannon and two machine-guns. Most amazing of all, though this was not widely realized at first, was its phenomenal endurance which out-ranged any of its western contemporaries. Fitted with drop tanks on its wings it could fly for 1,000 miles.

Chennault's immediate reaction was that the Chinese had to have both better pilots and better planes. He returned to the United States and recruited, at high wages, about 100 pilots and 200 ground staff on one-year contracts from the US Army and Navy, who obligingly granted them unpaid leave of absence. Officially designated the American Volunteer Group, they soon became known as the Flying Tigers after the fangs, more shark than feline, that they painted on the noses of the American P40 fighters Chennault acquired for them. The RAF, who liked aircraft to have names, called the P40s Tomahawks and were already using them with some effect against the Germans and Italians in North Africa. Chennault's volunteers were keen but green, never having had the opportunity to fire a shot in action. To train them the British gave the American colonel the use of a quiet Burmese airfield at Toungoo, about 250 miles from the border with China's Yunnan province and a half hour's flight north of Rangoon. Here Chennault drummed into them the tactics he had worked out after observing the air war in China. He told them: don't dogfight; instead, make a diving pass, fire close, break off and, if there's a chance, climb and do it again.

There was nothing particularly new in this. These were exactly the methods adopted by RAF pilots during the Battle of Britain once they had learned the hard way that some of their pre-war training in formation flying was tactically unsound. A few of the Few were sent out to stiffen Malaya's four new Buffalo squadrons, which were mostly manned by Australians and New Zealanders straight out of flight school. Among these RAF reinforcements was Flight Lieutenant Tim Vigors who was still six months short of his twenty-first birthday. One clear moonlit night, Vigors had left his spinning bed after a heroically boozy evening, pulled his flying boots over his scarlet pyjama trousers, flushed his hangover with a gulp of pure oxygen through his face mask, staggered into the air and, by a wonderful fluke, shot down a Heinkel which strayed across the moon. In all Vigors, an Old Etonian from a fox-hunting Anglo-Irish background and a Cranwell-trained regular officer, had eight confirmed kills against the Luftwaffe and had been awarded the Distinguished Flying Cross. Bored after Goering had lost the air battle over southern England, he had volunteered to fly Hurricanes catapulted off merchant ships for convoy protection – an almost suicidal undertaking since the only way back to the ship was by parachute or ditching, always a risky proposition in single-engined fighters, which sank nose-first like stones. Perhaps somebody in authority thought Vigors had done enough, for suddenly he was offered the Singapore posting, which was about as far away from the war as it was possible to get. 'I jumped at the chance of a change of scenery.'

Part of this change meant getting used to the Brewster Buffalo which after flying a Spitfire or a Hurricane was like driving a pick-up truck instead of an Aston Martin. Perhaps because there was no way they were going to get a better fighter of their own in the foreseeable future, the RAF refused to get excited about the Zero. 'It is on a par with our Buffalo, certainly not much faster,' a senior officer assured journalists at a press conference in Singapore.

By now some Japanese pilots had acquired, during their long war with China, even more combat experience than people like Vigors, though admittedly Chinese or mercenary airmen rarely matched the calibre of those in the Luftwaffe. Yet there was undoubtedly this underlying assumption that empire pilots, even the green Antipodeans, would be more than a match for Asians, no matter how much technical edge they had. It would have come as quite a shock if Fighter Command had learned how one Japanese expert viewed their recent triumph.

Commander Genda, an attaché of the Imperial Japanese Navy Air Force at Japan's London embassy, reporting to Tokyo on the air battles over southern England, declared that they only confirmed his suspicion that, while the RAF was bad, the Luftwaffe was even worse. Perhaps it was only to be expected that a navy flier like Genda would be much more impressed by the way the Fleet Air Arm had crippled three Italian battleships with torpedoes and bombs during a night attack at Taranto. For the first time, a modern navy had been dealt a devastating blow from the air. The carrier HMS *Illustrious* had come within 200 miles of the port in the toe of Italy before launching twenty of its Swordfish biplanes in two waves. In the space of a six-and-a-half-hour return flight to and from *Illustrious*, the Swordfish inflicted more damage than was visited on the Kaiser's High Seas Fleet at the Battle of Jutland. Air power, even when delivered by middle-aged biplanes, had humbled the battleship.

In London, the Luftwaffe had turned to night bombing. Amidst the Japanese embassy's sandbags and stirrup pumps, Genda wrote a careful appraisal of the Royal Navy's revolutionary tactics against an unsuspecting fleet as it lay in a well-defended harbour, and sent it to Tokyo.

Despite Commander Genda's reservations the British, whose RAF fighters had at last ended Germany's apparently unstoppable roll of blitzkrieg victories, might be forgiven for thinking that they knew a thing or two about air defence and should play to their strengths. In November 1940, Air Chief Marshal Sir Robert Brooke-Popham set up his HQ in the Singapore naval base as the commander-in-chief of all land and air forces in Malaya, Burma, Hong Kong and Borneo. For the first time, an RAF officer had been given overall command of thousands of soldiers as well as his own service.

Brooke-Popham's appointment reflected a growing conviction that, if the Japanese attacked Malaya, it would take at least six months for the Royal Navy to spare enough ships to relieve it. Meanwhile, aircraft would keep an invader at bay by sinking most of his ships with torpedoes and bombs. The idea of creating this post had come to the chiefs of staff after Admiral Layton had informed them that something must be done to stop the bickering and lack of cooperation between the army, the RAF and Shenton Thomas. Somebody thought of Brooke-Popham, who was delighted.

'I hope and believe', he wrote to the chiefs of staff, 'that should an attack on Singapore develop, its defence will not be found wanting of record in the annals of the British Empire, and may even be quoted to future generations as an example to follow.' This would have undoubtedly appealed to Churchill, who, like Brooke-Popham, was of a generation for whom famous Victorian sieges were recent history. Tales of Lucknow, the Residency at Kabul, Rorke's Drift, Gordon's glorious last stand at Khartoum, or indeed Mafeking and Ladysmith in the war both had participated in as young men, were all part of the damp-eyed romance of empire that brought lumps to British throats and raised hair on British forearms.

The only conceivable reason why the air chief marshal should not take a demanding post in an enervating climate was his age. Tall, slim and charming, he was sixty-two, and outwardly he had worn well. In a long career Brooke-Popham had been a soldier, a pioneer airman and a senior colonial civil servant.

Like most senior RAF officers, the air chief marshal started his military career in the army where he first saw action in South Africa fighting the same Boer horsemen who had captured Churchill. But if his military debut was firmly rooted in the nineteenth century his mind was firmly on the possibilities of the one he was going to grow up in. He had been one of the first British officers to learn to fly, taking his first flight shortly after the Wright Brothers. In 1912 his enthusiasm was rewarded by the War Office when Major Brooke-Popham, known to his friends as 'Brookham', took command of the Royal Engineers' newly formed Air Battalion. During World War I, in which he was already considered too old to fly in combat, his unit provided the nucleus of the Royal Flying Corps, which by 1918 had become the Royal Air Force.

Brooke-Popham had been the RAF's inspector general when he retired from the service in 1937 in order to move to Nairobi where the Colonial Office had appointed him governor-general of Kenya. He appears to have got on well with Kenya's white settlers, even those deracinated aristocrats who could be every bit as difficult and mischievous as the rubber barons Shenton Thomas had to deal with. Shortly after the outbreak of war he had returned to the RAF and had been employed to set up flying training schools in the clear, and Luftwaffe-free, skies of Canada and Rhodesia. His recent experience with 'colonials' in a theatre where the Australians were becoming increasingly involved was undoubtedly another reason he got the Singapore job.

In February 1941 the first large contingent of Australian ground troops arrived in Singapore. Almost 6,000 of them sailed into the naval base crammed into the Cunard liner *Queen Mary* whose 81,000 tons, three funnels and top speed of almost 40 knots had made it the star British turn on the transatlantic run. It had been converted into a troop ship at the Singapore naval base's dry dock the year before, well away from prying German and Italian eyes in this remote bastion of empire.

Most of the Australians, the first of two brigades of the 8th Division, were making their first trip abroad. They were thrilled to be aboard 'the *Mary*', as they called her, and in exuberant mood. On the quay to greet them was the band of the Manchester Regiment playing 'Waltzing Matilda', Sir Shenton and Lady Thomas, he in white suit with matching pith helmet, and senior officers of all three services including Brooke-Popham. For some of the Australians lining the rails of the great ship, these Pommy brass hats were too good a target to miss. To show their appreciation for the band they began to shower them with coins. Some of the officers took it in good part but a photograph of Brooke-Popham, arms akimbo, suggests that he was not amused.

One of the offenders was Private Don Wall, a twenty-year-old infantryman from a small country town in New South Wales where his father, an Anzac veteran who had been wounded at Gallipoli in 1915, managed a food wholesaler's. Most of the soldiers on the *Queen Mary* had at least two things in common. They were all volunteers – conscripts were only required to serve in Australia and New Guinea. And, like 90 per cent of Australians in 1941, they were mostly of fairly recent British descent. Wall's paternal grandfather, for instance, had emigrated from England in the 1860s. Some had parents born in Britain who had yet to acquire proper Australian accents. On average they were in their early twenties, but there were fifteen-year-olds pretending to be eighteen and middle-aged veterans of the trenches, including two Victoria Crosses, who had lopped fifteen years off their age and winked at the recruiting officer. Most units, being locally recruited, were closely knit, with a number of brothers and cousins in their ranks. There were also a few cases of fathers and sons serving in Malaya though rarely, if ever, in the same unit. And although they might, as Brooke-Popham had just discovered, like to tease the Poms and beat them at cricket, the Australians were not in the least bit self-conscious about referring to Britain as the 'Motherland' or the 'Old Country', or themselves in certain contexts as British, and even the boys from good Irish Catholic families would not have been there at all had they not found acknowledging George VI as their sovereign King a small price to pay for such a glorious adventure.

This was the 22nd Brigade of the 8th Division, one of the four all-volunteer divisions of the AIF – the Australian Imperial Force. The other three were in the Middle East where the 6th had just distinguished itself by taking the Libyan port of Bardia with 40,000 Italian prisoners. The commander of the 8th Division was Major-General Gordon Bennett, who had served against the Turks in the same battalion as Private Wall's father at the Gallipoli landings, the disastrous attempt to capture Constantinople which, in Australia, had become a symbol of both national fortitude and incompetent British leadership.

Bennett was a small, wiry whippet of a man, with red hair and the short fuse that often goes with it. He was one of Australia's most distinguished soldiers, brave, abrasive, ambitious, arrogant and something of a bully. An accountant in civilian life, during World War I he had served first in Gallipoli, where he was wounded several times, then in Flanders. Afterwards, he returned to his accounting practice in Melbourne with a Distinguished Service Order, eight Mentions in Dispatches and the acting rank of brigadier-general. He also went back to the militia, for he was by no means tired of things military. In many ways he remained a soldier who had become a part-time accountant.

By the time Hitler came to power in 1933, Bennett, now aged forty-six, was the youngest major-general in the Australian army. But this was as high as a militia officer was allowed to go and Bennett was far from satisfied. The militia was run by a cadre of some 2,000 regular officers and NCOs known as the Permanent Staff Corps. Some of the officers, a few like Bennett veterans of the 1914–18 war, had attended staff college courses in Britain. In 1937, with the prospect of another European war looming, Bennett impetuously wrote a series of newspaper articles in which, in so many words, he argued that Australia's defence was jeopardized by a cabal within the Permanent Staff Corps who favoured staff college-trained regulars for senior posts, even if they had seen little or no action. This was the start of a feud that almost resulted in Bennett never leaving Australia in uniform again.

Among those he had offended was Lieutenant-General Sir Thomas Blamey who in 1939 was appointed commander of the AIF. Blamey, who was three years older than Bennett, had spent almost all of 1914–18 on the staff of the Australian Corps and seen little front-line service, though he had been awarded a DSO for his part in planning the fraught withdrawal from the Gallipoli beach-head. Bennett was desperate for a division but the 6th, 7th and 9th were all shipped out to the Middle East with men he believed less qualified than himself at their head. Nor was he originally given the 8th, command being awarded to Major-General Vernon Sturdee, yet another of the Permanent Staff Corps he despised so much. Then Australia's chief of general staff and the army minister, neither of them well disposed towards Bennett, were killed in an air crash at Canberra. Sturdee took over as head of the army and, despite all Bennett's public criticism of the desk-bound Permanent Staff, one of his first acts was to give him the 8th Division.

At that point it was assumed that the 8th would join the other three
AIF divisions in the Middle East, for it was Canberra's policy to keep
all their forces in one theatre, which gave them more say in how they
were used. Then, in December 1940, Churchill was heartened by
Admiral Cunningham's reduction of Italy's Mediterranean Fleet. With
more of this, Britain might soon have warships to spare for the Far
East, and this, he told Sir Robert Menzies, the Australian prime minister, 'will not be lost upon Japan'. Churchill particularly had in mind
the Fleet Air Arm's raid on Taranto, which had so excited Commander
Genda at Japan's London embassy, and in a way he was right. Japanese
torpedo bomber squadrons were now practising their skills more assidu-
ously than ever. Meanwhile, he had 'gratefully accepted' an offer from
Menzies of a 'brigade group' for Malaya as a stopgap until May, when
it would be replaced by Indian troops and sent to Egypt.

'If Australia is seriously threatened by invasion we should not hesitate
to compromise or sacrifice the Mediterranean position for the sake of
our kith and kin,' Churchill assured Menzies. Invasion by land-hungry
Asians had long been an obsession of the white Australians concentrated
in the south-eastern corner of their vast continent. Menzies had a
narrow majority and was under pressure from the Australian Labour
Party to concentrate the AIF where they were best placed to keep the
'Yellow Peril' at bay. Churchill did not for one moment believe that
Australia would ever be seriously threatened with invasion by Japan,
and nor did his chiefs of staff.

In any case what, as far as Australia was concerned, constituted
'seriously threatened'? While war with Japan was a possibility, and
intelligence assessments of its military capabilities were often contra-
dictory or simply ignored, war with Germany and Italy was a pressing
reality. It was obvious that the Axis would like their Asian member to
make threatening noises and draw off men and materials that could be
well-used elsewhere. And, though RAF Fighter Command's autumn
victory had thwarted the Luftwaffe's attempt to gain aerial superiority,
the nearest elements of a vast German army remained some 20 miles
away at Calais. Only Hitler's closest circle knew that Operation Sealion,
the amphibious and airborne assault on southern England, had not
merely been postponed until next spring, but shelved indefinitely in
favour of the forthcoming attack on Russia. As far as Britain was
concerned, the threat of invasion had merely diminished, not disappeared. Most of its army, which since Dunkirk had been frantically

training an enormous intake of conscripts, was still deployed at home. At the beginning of 1941, Britain only had three of its divisions, about 60,000 men, in the Middle East, where the only land warfare against the Axis was taking place. The rest of General Archibald Wavell's desert command, some of them newly arrived and not yet in action, came from Australia, India, New Zealand and South Africa.

It was hard not to agree with Churchill that the Australian infantry, having so quickly proved themselves to be their fathers' sons, would be much better deployed in a war theatre rather than rehearsing for something that might never happen. True, they had a deterrent value; but Bennett and his brigade group seemed to have gone to Singapore to avert the wrath of the Australian Labour Party as much as to deter the Japanese.

'Don't you think they are worthy of some better enemy than the Japanese?' senior Australian officers were fond of asking. Certainly, they looked the part. On average they were bigger men than the city-bred Tommy, proof of what plenty of meat, sport and outdoor living could do for the deracinated Anglo-Celts in the space of a couple of generations. They were also better-paid and better-hatted than their Pommy counterparts, for the famous Digger wide brim was undeniably more rakish than the Tommy's forage cap or the steel battle bowler he was obliged to wear all the time in the field. The Australians were less understated than the UK British too, more like Americans.

The tone was set by Gordon Bennett himself, who declared that one AIF man was worth ten Japanese. His men agreed and told everybody who cared to listen that they could not wait for the little yellow bastards to start something. Senior British officers grumbled, as they had since the Boer War and as they did now in North Africa despite the Australian victory at Bardia, about the Australians' discipline, or lack of it, as demonstrated by the appalling business of the coins tossed at Brooke-Popham from the *Queen Mary*. It was disturbing, too, that officers were not always distinguishable as soon as they opened their mouths, a condition aggravated by the common use of nicknames, even first names, among all ranks. The Australians, of course, found the Poms stuffy, were amused by the way civilian planters referred to each other by their last names, and told each other stories about Aussie buglers being asked not to blow a dawn reveille because it disturbed Pommie officers' wives, or how they had been advised not to get too familiar with the natives.

None the less, Bennett's men were novelties and they received an enthusiastic greeting from the white community who, in this second year of the war, were more enthusiastic about things military than they used to be. Officers were made honorary members of their clubs, and Anzac leave centres were set up for the men, where meals were cooked by lady volunteers who, as one eyewitness observed, 'had never cooked an egg or done a hand's turn for themselves'.

The British propaganda effort was just as welcoming, with information officers laying on visits to Australian units for print and cinema newsreel reporters from London, Sydney and New York, who were beginning to show an increased interest in how seriously the Japanese threat was being taken. In their stories, the Australians were often described as 'the empire's shock troops', especially after Australian infantry had given the newly arrived Rommel and his apparently unstoppable Afrika Korps a bloody nose at Tobruk. Major-General Leslie Morshead, the AIF commander there, was the first to recognize the part played by his UK artillerymen, who had stopped the Panzers at close range by firing over open sights, but the British press loved the Aussies and the gunners' contribution tended to be overlooked. Now, before anybody had fired a shot in anger, the same thing seemed to be happening in Malaya. Yet the UK British, like the Australians, had six battalions of infantry in the colony, three brigaded with Indian troops in the peninsula and three in the Singapore garrison. (The Indians, of course, had more than the two of them put together.)

Kathleen Stapledon, who had delighted her *ayah* by renting another house away from her noisy Japanese neighbours, recalled how irritating this could make a visit to the cinema.

We went mainly in the hope of seeing a British newsreel to see what was going on at home, but almost invariably we would be disappointed, and it would be an Australian one. We saw Australian troops on manoeuvres, in their own country and in Malaya, and work going on in their factories. Judging from these films one would be led to believe that we were being defended entirely by Australians. Many of the British troops got annoyed at this and they could hardly be blamed.

In July, Australian troops in the Middle East were in the news again for the part they had played in defeating the Vichy French in Lebanon and Syria. In a short but surprisingly hard-fought campaign Lieutenant

Roden Cutler,⋆ an artillery unit's forward observation officer, lost a leg winning Australia's first Victoria Cross of the war. On 14 July, Bastille Day, the French surrendered. Thirteen days later, another Vichy colony was invaded.

Japanese troops, without any opposition from Vice-Admiral Découx's forces or any suggestion by the Japanese that they were acting to prevent a British-backed Gaullist plot, began to enter the southern part of Indo-China and establish air bases around its capital, Saigon. The move came shortly after the Japanese had intervened to end Découx's war with Thailand, which had culminated in the French sinking three Siamese ships. 'Japan's peaceful cooperation in the defence of Indo-China', commented the Tokyo daily *Asahi*, 'was brought about by diplomatic negotiations with its legal government and contrasts sharply with Britain's seizure of Syria.'

As it happened, England's recent campaign against the Vichy French had been the only good news for some time. The dispatch of a British Expeditionary Force to Greece, which had been invaded by the Italians, ended in disaster when the Germans came to Mussolini's rescue. First the Greeks had collapsed and those British and Dominion forces that could be rescued had withdrawn to the island of Crete. Here they had at first inflicted heavy casualties on German paratroopers and glider-borne infantry before the Royal Navy once again found themselves coming to the rescue of an army they were beginning to refer to as 'the evacuees'. Around 15,000 who could not get to the boats surrendered, many of them demoralized by the way the Luftwaffe had bombed and strafed them with impunity.

German dive-bombing had proved particularly effective against British warships; among the casualties was the destroyer HMS *Kelly*, commanded by the King's dashing cousin Mountbatten, who had spent several hours in the water with the other survivors. Like the Taranto raid this had been an object lesson in the changing face of naval warfare, demonstrating the vulnerability of the warship to air strikes. On land the 6th Australian Division, the heroes of Bardia, had been badly mauled in both Greece and Crete. In the desert the Afrika Korps had reached the Egyptian frontier, though Morshead's Australians held out at Tobruk, which was supplied by sea. Even more difficult was the

---

⋆ Later Sir Roden Cutler VC, AK, KCMG, KCVO, Australian diplomat and governor of New South Wales.

navy's task of getting convoys through to besieged Malta, which was being heavily bombed, its battered garrison and civilians bracing themselves for the kind of paratroop blitzkrieg with which the Wehrmacht had already captured Crete.

In Singapore, Dr Lakshmi Swaminadhan savoured this litany of British disaster with considerable satisfaction. 'We couldn't help gloating at the beating the British were getting at the hands of the Germans. This, in spite of our being anti-Hitler.' However, being entirely against the Nazis was becoming more difficult. In India, the British had lost their nerve and had transferred the fasting Subhas Bose from jail to what virtually amounted to house arrest only to lose him when, in various disguises, he reached first the sanctuary of Afghanistan and, soon afterwards, Germany. He had since made several broadcasts on Radio Berlin where he had announced the formation of the 'Indian Legion', which was recruiting sepoys captured by Rommel in North Africa. Not all that surprisingly, he had also mentioned his admiration for Germany's New Order. To share her joy at some of these events and analyse their implications Lakshmi had at last found someone she considered worthy of her intellectual mettle. Every Saturday evening, after tennis, she had taken to dining with K. P. Kesava Menon, a veteran of the Indian National Congress usually known to his friends by his first three initials – 'KPK'.

Yet, bad though the news from the Middle East was, all thoughts of sending Bennett's Australians there were apparently shelved, much to the frustration of most of them, who yearned for action with all the longing of young men who have never seen it. Once the Japanese had Indo-Chinese air bases in range of Malaya, the 22nd Brigade not only remained but was reinforced. In August another Australian brigade, the 27th, arrived, so that now General Bennett had a two-brigade division, complete with hospitals, doctors and 130 nurses to look after them. In all, including the signallers, technicians and clerks that went with a mid-twentieth-century army, Bennett now had 15,000 troops under his command.

The *Queen Mary* had sailed to colder waters and this second brigade arrived in Singapore aboard three Dutch merchant ships whose home port was Batavia. This time, their deployment was supposed to be secret and there were no welcoming bands or brass hats to throw pennies at. But their route from the docks took them through Lavender

Street, the city's main brothel area, where a huge banner announced: 'Welcome to the AIF'.

The Japanese Foreign Ministry, as it was hoped they would be, were as aware as the ladies of Lavender Street of these fresh Australian troop movements and took a dim view, for they came at a time when, despite its neutrality, the United States was increasing its aid to the Chinese. Sir Robert Craigie, the British ambassador to Japan, informed the Foreign Office that his host government had complained, and not for the first time, that they were being 'encircled by American, British, Chinese and Dutch forces'.

In London's King Charles Street, sandbagged and window-taped against the further attentions of the Luftwaffe, a Foreign Office mandarin wrote in the margin of Sir Robert's deciphered cable: 'Once again one cannot help thinking that if one is advancing into a wood one is apt to be encircled by the trees.'

At about the same time Ogden Nash, an American writer and poet, was moved to write a few lines on the same subject for the *New Yorker*.

> How courteous is the Japanese;
> He always says, 'Excuse it, please.'
> He climbs into his neighbor's garden,
> And smiles, and says, 'I beg your pardon';
> He bows and grins a friendly grin,
> And calls his hungry family in;
> He grins and bows a friendly bow;
> 'So sorry, this my garden now.'

The effects of America's latest move to evict these courteous Japanese from the gardens of Indo-China were immediately apparent in Tokyo. Washington's total ban on all US petroleum exports had left its citizens choking on the smog created by a growing array of charcoal-powered vehicles. In the Ginza shopping district the Manhattan-style neon lighting had been switched off. Even the opening hours of the city's public bath houses, unisex yet totally asexual institutions, were cut in order to save fuel.

These measures came in addition to the repercussions caused by the gradual imposition of earlier trade embargoes. The lack of Australian scrap metal and Malayan tin meant that new kitchen utensils and children's toys were now only available in wood or bamboo. The stadiums for the cancelled 1940 Tokyo Olympics were being dismembered and their steel girders sent to the Nagasaki shipyards for recycling. Cotton was reserved for military uniforms and much was made of the virtues of rayon and other sweaty new synthetic fabrics.

By the autumn of 1941, as Japan celebrated the first anniversary of its signing of the Tripartite Pact with Germany and Italy, the mood of the nation admirably suited the nationalists around Emperor Hirohito. For some years, Japan had been slipping into a kind of instinctive anti-westernism, and an emphasis on the need to return to traditional values, reminiscent of the mood of much of the Islamic world half a century later. The root of this was discrimination. After Japan had swallowed its considerable pride and allowed foreigners entry, it had emerged from its mediaeval time-warp in a remarkably short time. The 1904 victory over Czarist Russia had demonstrated its success in marrying western technology to the spirit of the samurai. At the same time, various social changes were beginning to take place. Japan had assimilated a good deal of western culture, not only in music and the other performing arts, but through the enormous demand for translations of European literature from Shakespeare and Goethe to Victor Hugo and Charles Dickens.

The Bible was also being read. Some western missionaries were confidently predicting the rapid Christianization of Japan and the decline of the indigenous Shinto, a polytheistic religion with Buddhist influence which reveres the Emperor as a living descendant of the sun goddess and a divine being. The port of Nagasaki was becoming particularly well known for its converts. There was even talk of the Emperor himself being baptized so that he could remain the spiritual head of his people. Yet, despite all this the West, and particularly the Anglo-Americans, had continued to make it obvious that they were not prepared to accept the Japanese as racial equals or as very much different from the poor southern Asians whose lands they had colonized. They were not to be allowed to join the planet's ruling club, not even as junior members. That British arrogance should remain unchecked, even after the events in Singapore during 1915 had, to Japanese eyes at least, revealed the full measure of their decline, was bad enough. But it was their rejection by the Americans, the nation that had played the largest role in bringing them out of seclusion, and the one its diligent pupils had tried hardest to impress, that had been the most hurtful.

From about 1900 the US had encouraged Japanese immigration, making no secret that they preferred them to the Chinese, and before long over 50,000, mostly farmers, had settled in California. By 1920, though they amounted to only 2 per cent of the state's population, the Japanese controlled over 10 per cent of its farmland. At this point alarm bells rang, most of them sounded by the newspaper magnate Randolph Hearst, who for some years had filled the columns of his yellow press with scare stories on the 'Yellow Peril'. California had already enacted an Alien Land Law which made it difficult, not to say impossible, for Japanese-Americans to own the land they farmed. Then, in 1924, the Americans went a step further. To the fury of the Japanese, who had an even higher opinion of themselves than most western nations did of themselves, they were included, along with the Chinese and Koreans, among those Asians who would no longer be allowed to emigrate to the US.

The blatant racism of this legislation released the anger caused by years of heartbreak over Japan's unrequited love affair with America. A mob stormed Tokyo's US embassy, pulled down its flag and, according to one account, 'slashed it to shreds'. Urban Japanese women were urged to put away their cloche hats, high heels and short skirts and return to the kimono. Western hairstyles were also socially unaccept-able and hairdressers would no longer set 'permanent waves'. The distinctly Orwellian concept of *kiken shiso* – 'dangerous thought' – took hold. Nobody in authority could ever bring themselves to articulate a definition of 'dangerous thought', but it certainly covered a wide range of cases. A university professor was sacked for mentioning the promiscuous ways of an empress who had taken her last lover over a thousand years ago. Christian converts found themselves a besieged minority. A Japanese pastor who tried to get around this by suggesting that the Emperor be added to the Trinity was roundly criticized for attempting to lower the Divine One's status. American missionaries were accused of being the hypocritical representatives of a nation that failed to practise what it preached.

Liberals and leftists were invariably branded 'Communists' and har-assed by both the Tojjo, a security service whose full title was Special Higher Police, and the Kempetei military police who would establish a brutal reputation abroad though at home they exercised more restraint and were reported rarely to use torture. In any case, Japan did not have anything like the number of political prisoners of Germany or the Soviet Union and its security apparatus was nothing like the Gestapo or Russian NKVD (Stalin's security service).* Some of the Japanese Left were able to find common cause with their government, and ignore its more disagreeable aspects, because of its pledges to replace European colonialism with a Japanese-led commonwealth to be known as the Greater East Asia Co-Prosperity Sphere. Only the very stubborn insisted that the reality behind this was the Rape of Nanking.

Newspapers, once inclined to celebrate American achievements, now concentrated on stories about speakeasies, gangsters and other symbols of its Jazz Age decadence. Young men were encouraged to devote their energy to the warrior pursuits of the samurai: jujitsu, archery and the double-handed fencing with bamboo staves called kendo. It was decided that baseball, Japan's most popular imported sport, must be purged of its English vocabulary and references to 'strikes' and 'foul balls', particularly by radio commentators, were considered unpatriotic. So was broadcasting 'sensuous' western popular songs. But the love of classical music many Japanese had acquired was

---

* By the end of the war there were still no more than 3,000 political prisoners in Japan.

such that a more lenient view was taken though, as the years went by, with a distinct preference for Wagner, Strauss and other composers identified with the Axis.

Most Japanese had considered themselves to be at war ever since hostilities started with China in 1937 and, on the whole, there was tremendous enthusiasm for it. In Tokyo, on the night Nanking fell, thousands of people staged a lantern-lit victory procession that wound its way around the capital like a luminous snake. One of the places the revellers visited was a statue in Shiba Park which commemorated the three soldier suicide-bombers who, in 1932, had breached a Chinese barbed-wire entanglement during the savage street fighting in Shanghai. That bitter and short-lived campaign, the prelude to the main China war, was famous for another act of self-sacrifice often held up as an example of the true spirit of Bushido, the code of the samurai. A grievously wounded Japanese officer had been rescued by a Chinese lieutenant who had attended university in Japan and recognized his hapless foe as a fellow student. After the ceasefire, the Japanese was released from a Chinese hospital fully recovered from his wounds. As soon as he could, he returned to the place on the Shanghai battlefield where he was captured. There he committed *seppuku*, the agonizing ritual disembowelment by his own hand, vulgarly known as *hari-kari* (literally, 'belly cutting'), and thereby atoned for the dishonour of allowing himself to be taken prisoner.

What better proof could there be of the desire of the younger generation to return to the ancient and honourable ways of the samurai, the warrior caste employed over centuries of clan warfare by Japan's fractious and quarrelsome aristocracy? In 1876 the rank of samurai had been abolished by imperial decree. But the selfless spirit of these knights, legendary protectors of the poor, held too firm a place in the hearts of the Japanese people to be decreed away. In 1906 a bestselling book entitled *Human Bullets* celebrated the courage displayed by the Japanese infantry who suffered enormous casualties in their frontal assault on the Russian lines at Port Arthur. At about the same time, Count Okuma, an English-speaking Japanese aristocrat, responding in a reader's letter to a New York newspaper's latest relapse into Yellow Perilism, warned:

There is nothing more dreadful than crazy persons. The Japanese are a crazy nation in fighting and will display their madness as in the late war. The

Japanese are always ready to throw away their lives for a nation; they regard their lives as lightly as they do the weather. On the other hand, Americans and Europeans attach their chief importance to money. Those who love money love their lives. Suppose the two nations, whose ideas towards death are fundamentally different, should fight? The final result is easily seen . . .

Neither the United States nor any European country, not even Nazi Germany and Fascist Italy, proud as they all were of their martial traditions, saw themselves as warrior nations in quite the same way as the Japanese. In 1934 the Japanese Ministry of War published a pamphlet on its *raison d'être* which contained some lines so breathtaking that even Germany's National Socialists would never have dared to utter them outside their wildest, hate-filled dreams. 'War is the father of creation and mother of culture,' it declared. 'Rivalry for supremacy does for the state what struggle against adversity does for the individual.'

But, seven years later, as the prospects of war with the Anglo-Americans seemed greater by the day, there was in Tokyo far from unanimous approval for this character-building activity. It was fairly well known that Admiral Yamamoto Isoroku, the English-speaking, poker-loving Commander-in-Chief of the Combined Fleet, who had once served as naval attaché in Washington, was against a war with the Americans and the British. One of the reasons he had been sent back to sea was because it had been discovered that some of the more extreme elements of the war faction were planning to assassinate him. Less well known was the fact that Yamamoto, who thought the battleship obsolete and was an ardent believer in air power, had proposed – if war was inevitable – a knock-out pre-emptive strike against the US Pacific Fleet at Pearl Harbor in Hawaii.

The Emperor himself was said to be against a war, or at least ambivalent enough to sit on the fence and, in the way of Gods, let fate take a hand. Perhaps he could do little else. Hirohito reigned but did not rule. His inspiration was said to be Britain's constitutional monarchy, admittedly with the crucial difference that the subjects of the House of Windsor were not encouraged to believe that the incumbent was a living God, merely head of the Church of England. What came out of Hirohito's mouth in the form of imperial decrees were not his own words but words hammered out by his cabinet. And while the navy was generally opposed to a war, the army was generally for it. Undoubtedly the toughest man in the cabinet was General Tojo Hideki,

a chain-smoking workaholic who was the army minister. Round spectacles, and the kind of straggly moustache most senior Japanese officers
tended to avoid, sometimes gave Tojo the harassed and rather furtive
look of an overworked clerk, though few who knew him had the
slightest doubt of the inner steel. It was Tojo who had brought about
the present crisis by persuading the cabinet to advise His Imperial
Majesty that it was propitious to send troops into southern Indo-China.

Hirohito had been on the throne for twenty years, for the first seven
as regent when his father's divine connections failed to prevent his
decline into senility. Now, as the Anglo-American sanctions tightened,
it would be Hirohito who would ultimately announce whether it was
to be war or peace.

If it was to be war, then which war? In June, Hitler had invaded the
Soviet Union and the Führer was pressing Japan, in the spirit of the
Tripartite Pact, to start another front and attack Siberia. On 10 July
1941, General Ott, the German ambassador in Tokyo, had received a
cable from foreign minister Ribbentrop urging him to persuade the
Japanese that 'the natural objective still remains that we and Japan join
hands on the Trans-Siberian railroad before winter starts.'

But, less than five months before, Matsuoka Yosuke, the Japanese
foreign minister, had signed a non-aggression pact with Stalin who,
after several toasts, touched on the realpolitik of the situation with a
vodka-warmed frankness rare in these affairs. 'We are both Asiatics,'
declared the Georgian monster, 'Japan can now move south' – meaning
that Japan, having removed the danger of a two-front war, was now
free to pursue its adventures in China and South-east Asia.

The memory of this convivial occasion did not, of course, stop the
Japanese cabinet from giving the German request serious consideration.
As it happened, most in favour was foreign minister Matsuoka himself,
Stalin's declarations of Asian solidarity being just so much vodka under
the bridge. In the end, the cabinet voted against it. The drubbing
the Japanese army received from Marshal Zhukov at Namonhan in
Manchuria some two years before had taught them there could be no
half-measures with the Red Army, and even Tojo recognized the
dangers of fighting on two fronts. So it was decided that, if there was
going to be a war, it would be in the south, the fragile home of Queen
Wilhelmina's Sumatra oil wells and King George VI's Malayan rubber.

If it was to be peace, then the Americans were asking too high a
price and their demands would have to be whittled down. It was, for

instance, inconceivable that Tokyo would 'guarantee the neutrality of Indo-China and Thailand'. All they were prepared to say was that Japan would withdraw its troops from Indo-China when the China war was finished. And the fighting there would stop when the Americans and the British ceased to arm the Chinese and got them to agree to Japanese demands for trade and territory. If Japan made too many concessions, the oil weapon could be applied any time Roosevelt felt like it. Japan would become like a dog on a leash, jerked to obedience whenever its master wished. As things stood, the Japanese military estimated that they had enough fuel reserves to keep their warships, aircraft, tanks and transport going for another two years. With every day that passed, the situation grew worse and, although all armies make arrangements for various contingencies, Tojo had seen to it that a detailed study of what would be required for the capture and subsequent occupation of Malaya and Singapore was already well under way at the Taiwan Army Research Centre.

The Taiwan Army Research Centre was accommodated in a small house that had formerly been a brigade HQ. Taiwan, or Formosa as the Portuguese explorers called the island, had been a Japanese possession since 1895 when the Chinese, confronted by Asia's Prussians, ceded it to them. The Imperial Japanese Army maintained a large garrison there and the research unit had been set up at the beginning of 1941. Including clerks, radio operators and drivers, its ration strength was about thirty and its commander was Colonel Masanobu Tsuji, a highly regarded staff officer.

At 5 foot 2 inches, Tsuji was small even for his generation of Japanese males though one look at the thin lips and the unblinking gaze behind round, horn-rimmed spectacles suggested that this was not a man to be trifled with. He was born in 1902, the son of a poor farmer, descended from generations of peasants for whom the warrior life had been the privilege of the samurai. He was a bright boy, and when he was fifteen, a local patron paid for him to attend the Nagoya Army Elementary School. He repaid his trust by graduating top of his class and by 1920 he was attending the Officers' Preparatory Course in Tokyo. Most of his fellow cadets regarded him as a dull dog, for Tsuji remained a diligent student and neither drank nor womanized. Nor did he show much interest in sport, with the notable exception of kendo fencing, the samurai's bamboo play-acting for cold steel, that is so much part of the Bushido mystique.

Tsuji was on the staff of the army group in Manchuria that had suffered so badly from Zhukov's Soviet-style blitzkrieg. But if he shared any of the blame for this debacle he avoided taking it. Now married with a young family, he was working at the Imperial Headquarters Staff in Tokyo when he was picked to lead the planning team for the invasion of Malaya and Singapore. Tsuji's cleverness and capacity for hard work was respected by his brother officers, but he was no more popular with them than he had been as a cadet, and he was notorious for his short fuse and violent rages with some subordinates while showing great favouritism towards others. Although later in life he would claim that at this time he was a member of something called the East Asia Organization – a group of officers who believed that Asian should never fight Asian and preached a loose alliance between Japan, China and Manchuria against the whites – he is best remembered for being, even by the standards of the Imperial Japanese Army, an ardent nationalist.

At first Tsuji was told he had a year to complete his project but, at the beginning of 1941, even before the move into Indo-China and the American riposte with the embargo on all petroleum products, this was reduced to six months. The scope of the work to be done was enormous. Apart from isolated actions against the Kaiser's South Pacific colonies and helping to put down the Singapore mutiny, the Japanese had never fought in the tropics. Now the team of ten staff officers was expected to collate 'all conceivable data connected with tropical warfare' for Malaya, the Philippines, Indonesia and Burma. Nothing was deemed too big or too small to merit the attention of the Taiwan Research Department, from the organization of an Army Corps to how to avoid malaria and look after a rifle in humid conditions. Tsuji pulled every string he could to find people who knew something about the potential battleground.

From an old sea captain who had voyaged for many years to the south we received instructions in disembarkation methods and on coastal conditions. From officials in the Ishihara Mining Company we learned useful military facts concerning Malaya's geography. Professors of Taiwan University advised us on tropical hygiene and about counter-measures against malaria . . .

With Malayan beaches in mind, amphibious exercises were staged. The first were on Kyushu, the most southerly of Japan's four main islands. The next were on Hainan, some 600 miles south of Taiwan in Indo-China's Gulf of Tongkin and about as tropical as they could get and still be discreet.

As the troops waded ashore, Tsuji and his team were waiting for them, notebooks in hand, to ask questions about everything from whether they had felt sea-sick to the difficulties of transferring their fully laden selves, plus their weapons and equipment, from the mother-ship to a landing-craft bobbing in a rough sea. Then they had to work out how to disembark men and machines on open beaches, 'with due regard for dangerous coral or hidden and sunken rocks'.

There were some dead ends. Horse transport was widely used by the Japanese in China. Tsuji's team did a lot of work on the sea transport of horses, with great stress put on the need to be attentive and to ensure that they were properly watered and fed and had their heads covered against sunstroke. Then it was decided that the troops earmarked for Malaya would be equipped with motor transport and, above all, bicycles so all this work was wasted.

None the less, their notes on the equine aspect were included in the first visible fruits of their labour, a thick pamphlet boldly entitled *Read This – And The War Can Be Won*, intended for distribution to soldiers crammed into landing ships heading for an enemy coast as the last hours of peace ticked away. As military handbooks go, Tsuji's was a unique contribution. It was partly propaganda, going to some lengths to explain to the fighting man exactly why Japan was at war:

Although our country has sought to purchase them [oil, steel, rubber] by fair methods, the Anglo-Americans have interfered even in this . . . If shortage of oil and steel is Japan's weak point, the greatest weakness in the American economy is the shortage of rubber, tin and tungsten, and these are supplied to America from South Asia and southern China. If Japan can master these areas . . .

Nor did it mince any words about Japan's engagement in a 'struggle between races', revelling in the chance to exploit one of the commonest causes of the national xenophobia:

In the Japan of recent years, where no one who cannot read English can proceed to higher education, and where English is widely used in all first-class hotels, trains and steamships, we have unthinkingly come to accept Europeans as superior . . . this is like spitting into our own eyes . . . classed alongside the Chinese and the Indians as an inferior race . . . we must at the very least here in Asia beat these Westerners to submission, that they may change their arrogant and ill-mannered attitude . . . with no thought of leniency to Europeans unless they be the Germans and the Italians . . .

But, in the main, Tsuji's pamphlet is a soldier's guidebook, full of practical hints, lists of dos and don'ts reminiscent in style of those publications aimed at a gentler breed of backpacker that would come out some forty years later.

In South Asia you must take precautions against mosquitoes and snakes. To fall in a hail of bullets is to meet a hero's death, but there is no glory in dying of disease or accident through inattention to hygiene or carelessness. And a further point you would do well to consider is that native women are almost all infected with venereal disease, and that if you tamper with them you will also make the whole native population your enemy.

Most Japanese live in a mild, temperate climate and there was concern about how the troops would cope with the heat. Some of the advice dispensed by Tsuji's team would have been guaranteed to raise the blood pressure of most British sergeant-majors: 'Clothing should be as loose as possible to allow the air to circulate and it is a good idea *to carry a fan.*'

There were also useful hints about how to get the most out of the local reptile life, advising soldiers to swallow the raw liver of any dangerous snakes they had been obliged to kill before cooking the meat: 'There is no better medicine for strengthening the body.'

And so to battle:

Regard yourself as an avenger come at last face to face with his father's murderer . . . here before you is the man whose death will lighten your heart . . . And the first blow is the vital blow . . . Westerners – being very superior people, very effeminate and very cowardly – have an intense dislike of fighting in the rain or the mist or at night. Night, in particular (though it is excellent for dancing), they cannot conceive as being a proper time for war.

Still the Imperial Japanese Navy was not convinced. Admiral Nagano, its chief of staff, thought that a pre-emptive strike on the

American fleet, however devastating, would not finish the war, and Japan could not afford a long conflict. On the other hand, General Sugiyama, the war minister before Tojo and now army chief of staff, forecast a war of no more than three months. The Emperor reminded him that, when he was war minister, he had predicted that the China Incident would last no more than a month, and that was four years ago.

On 6 September 1941 the Imperial Conference, at Tojo's urging, formally agreed that Japan would set an internal and secret deadline to go to war with the Anglo-Americans if diplomacy had failed to work by early October. Hirohito's only contribution was to recite a poem written by his grandfather, the Emperor Meiji, in praise of peace.

> All the seas in every quarter
> are as brothers to one another.
> Why, then, do the winds and waves of strife
> rage so turbulently throughout the world?

Tojo and the other hawks made their elaborate bows and left. The Emperor was the very soul of Japan and must be protected from those unscrupulous beings who would exploit his divine innocence; and this was no more than His Imperial Majesty would expect of them.

Oh, how I hate this tropic land, its burning sun, its baking sand,
Its heavy humid sticky heat, with odorous decay complete.
I hate the feathery cocoa trees, languidly browsing in the breeze,
The frangipanis' cloying smell and all the other smells as well.

The tropic moonlight leaves me cold and all the myriad stars untold,
The rubber trees, unlovely whores, with obscene scars and running sores,
The black Sumatra's sudden rain, the tom-toms' maddening refrain.
In none of these, for me at least, appeals the glamour of the east.

          (An anonymous member of the Royal Australian Air Force)

By now most of the Australians in Malaya were convinced that they were not going to get into the war they had volunteered for.

'I only wish I could get out of this country and where those damn dirty Huns are,' Private Al Lever of the 2/18th Battalion, whose brother had been killed at Tobruk, wrote to his father. 'That's my only wish now, to get a go at a Hun before this war ends . . . I really don't think the Japs are going to have a go.'

Journalist Gilbert Mant had first arrived in Malaya in the 2/19th Battalion. At thirty-eight he was a bit old for front-line infantry, and before long he was reclaimed by Reuters for essential work as a war correspondent. On a visit to his old battalion he noted 'a hatred of Malaya amounting to a phobia'.

A lot of this was probably to do with homesickness, especially among the younger soldiers, but it seems to have been exacerbated by the feeling that they were away from home on false pretences and merely playing at soldiers. Nor were things helped by an illustrated article on Bennett's command, which had appeared in the *Australian Women's Weekly*, one of the country's most popular magazines. Although there were plenty of warlike pictures of helmeted men clutching weapons against a jungle backcloth, reporter Adele Shelton Smith highlighted what a later generation of English-speaking soldiers in South-east Asia would learn to call 'rest and recuperation'. Soldiers were shown diving

into the swimming pool of a Chinese rubber millionaire who had
befriended them, climbing coconut palms, running along an idyllic-
looking beach, or playfully squeezed into a Shanghai Jar, the large
earthenware pot that was the Malay's cramped domestic bath. Tobruk
it patently was not. Even worse, somebody was quoted as saying that
the Australian nurses 'treat us like film stars'. Soon some of the volunteers began to get letters from the women they had left behind querying
their contribution to the war effort and pointing out that they were
not the only ones who knew how to 'have a gay time'.

The morale of the nurses in question tended to be higher than that
of the men. Kept busy treating tropical diseases and men hurt in
accidents, they were not pining to treat the war wounds available in
the Middle East. Most were fairly recently qualified young women
in their mid- to late twenties who had worked in the hospitals of small
rural towns before they volunteered for the Australian Army Nursing
Service for the same mixture of motives – patriotism and adventure –
as the men they nursed. There was no 'Malaya phobia' here. So
much was new and worth writing home about, from batik prints to
'scrumptious' fruit salads, a culinary concept apparently as novel to
Australia as it was to Britain, which had more excuse as fruit had been
strictly rationed for the past two years. The only frightening thing, as
the monsoon season began, were the tropical storms, especially if, like
Lieutenant Mona Wilton, you had not quite lost your childhood fear
of thunder. 'Hello darlings, I'm just recovering from the very worst of
thunderstorms I have ever had anything to do with,' she wrote to her
parents, dairy farmers near Warrnambool on the Victoria coast. 'I was
alone in my room. Wilma was on duty . . .'

But what the Wiltons' youngest daughter really wanted to tell them
about, before the storm interrupted her flow, was the sultan's ball. The
Australians were based in Johore, the most southerly state on the
peninsula, whose capital, Johore Bahru, was on the northern end of
the Causeway from Singapore. General Bennett had very sensibly
befriended Johore's autocratic sultan, Sir Ibraham, who, heaped with
British honours,\* continued to behave like a mediaeval potentate, and
had a reputation as a great philanderer and very wicked sultan indeed.

---

\* Among them the GCMG (Grand Cross of St Michael and St George). Sir Ibraham
is sometimes thought to have inspired the old jibe that renders GCMG as 'God Calls
Me God'.

Large and dewlapped and almost seventy, he had recently taken as his third wife a young Romanian woman of great beauty who was rumoured to be a few months short of her twentieth birthday.

During an afternoon off, Wilton and another nurse had a face-to-face encounter with the infamous Ibrahim when they went to the Johore Club, of which all Australian officers and nurses had been made honorary members, to call a taxi back to their hospital. Sir Ibrahim, who was present and always eager to help ladies in even the mildest distress, insisted that the nurses joined him for a glass of lemon squash, then, having noted their names, sent them home in his chauffeur-driven Rolls. A couple of days later an invitation arrived for Wilton and her friend to attend the sultan's ball.

What a night we had – we danced from 9 p.m. until 3 a.m. – with nothing below a major in rank . . . The Sultan is supposed to be a bad old thing but we were so surrounded by AIF of high rank we were never safer . . . The Sultan's wife was there – of course – and is the loveliest woman I have ever seen . . . We were 'dressed' for the occasion in our silk uniforms, red cape and cape tails – and caused many comments I think. The General told Matron that he was proud of us and we behaved perfectly – how's that. Some of the other lasses went – but not as the Sultan's guest. They were not called for in the royal car with Indian officer complete . . . When we get home they will think we are making stories up won't they?

Back in Warrnambool, Mrs Wilton jotted some farming news on the back of her youngest daughter's letter and passed it on to a friend, 'I am sending you Mona's last to give you an idea of her goings on. Of course they don't all tell of dancing in sultans' palaces . . .'

But the nurses were in great demand socially and not all the local aristocracy were Malay. Sister Vivian Bullwinkel, a strikingly tall and slim young woman from Broken Hill in New South Wales, where her father had worked as a clerk for the De Bavay Amalgamated Zinc Company, found herself and another nurse being wined and dined by the officers of the *Vyner Brooke*, an island trader owned by Sir Charles Vyner Brooke, the White Rajah of Sarawak.★ The 300-ton vessel,

★ The Brooke dynasty was founded by Sir James who, in 1841, was made Rajah of Sarawak and granted trading rights for putting down piracy and discouraging Dyak head-hunting along Borneo's north-west coast.

which doubled as a private yacht, with luxuriously appointed state-rooms and officers' quarters, was one of a number of local craft recently requisitioned by the Royal Navy, which was desperate for anything that, at a pinch, could sweep or lay mines, hunt submarines and do general patrol duties.

HMS *Vyner Brooke* was now painted battleship grey and fitted out with an old 3-inch gun which the first Rajah Brooke might have found handy for scaring off Chinese pirates. Most of her Australian and UK British officers were members of the Malay Royal Naval Volunteer Reserve and had been asked to remain on board. It was still a rich man's ship. With all its polished mahogany and brass, on formal dining nights, as stewards in white tunics served beneath crystal chandeliers, the *Vyner Brooke*, with its diminutive cannon, could put on a show that was worthy of a battle cruiser. It certainly gave Vivian Bullwinkel something to write about to her younger brother John, who was in Wales learning to fly Spitfires when he was not in London visiting their English relatives and taking nurses to see Flanagan and Allen in *Black Vanities*. He was proud to report that their grandmother 'wouldn't move from her house during the Blitz'.

In Malaya, a new army commander had arrived and for once it seemed that the War Office had put a round peg in a round hole. The return of Arthur Percival on 15 May 1941, after an absence of almost four years, had been generally welcomed by those few officers still around who had known him as General Dobbie's bright chief of staff. And his relationship with Bennett had got off to a good start when he had responded to his badgering for a more designated role by deploying the Australians in Johore, which had previously been the responsibility of the garrison of Singapore Island itself. 'He was very active and energetic,' recalled Bennett, 'playing a good game of tennis which would have been the envy of many younger men.' None the less, Bennett could not resist noting that the Englishman's features were 'intellectual rather than dynamic'.

Percival was now fifty-three. He had left Malaya Command as a colonel and he was returning to it as a lieutenant-general. To date he had had a quiet war. A short stint in France as a senior staff officer with the British Expeditionary Force (BEF) had coincided with the period the French called *Drôle de Guerre*. Well before the German blitzkrieg began, he had been recalled to England to command a newly mobilized Territorial division. After that he did a spell in the War Office as one of three assistants to his mentor Field-Marshal Sir John Dill, the Chief of the Imperial General Staff. But he badly wanted another field command and, after Dunkirk, he was given the task of rebuilding a BEF division which had come back in its socks. Then, in March 1941, he received instructions to get his tropical kit together and report to the War Office.

Percival, though delighted with the promotion – for he had been a rather junior major-general* and had leapfrogged several contemporaries – had found himself wondering whether returning to the Far East was really a good career move, even if it was to command an entire army:

. . . there was the double danger, either of being left in an inactive command for some years if war did not break out in the East or, if it did, of finding myself involved in a pretty sticky business with the inadequate forces which are usually to be found in the more distant parts of our Empire . . .

But the War Office had made its mind up and they wanted him in Singapore quickly. Brooke-Popham was tired of the feud between his army and air force commanders there. He had recently replaced the RAF commander with Air Vice-Marshal Pulford and was anxious to see how his new army commander got on with him. Percival was given three days to put his affairs in order and say goodbye to his family. This time Singapore would not be an accompanied posting. Betty Percival was already reconciled to a long separation, or worse. At the beginning of the war, when he had gone off to France with the BEF, and most people imagined it was all going to be a replay of the trenches with even nastier weaponry, she had tried to explain her feelings in a note, 'as I could not have said it with a dry face'.

Thank you darling for our love, our lovely children and the happy years we have had together. Partings are always sad but we have nothing to look back upon but happiness and good comradeship . . . I pray for your safe return but should it be otherwise I shall try and carry on faithfully until we meet again.

---

* Although a major outranks a lieutenant, a lieutenant-general outranks a major-general because the latter is a shortening of the Cromwellian title of 'Sergeant-Major General'.

As it happened, the flying boat Percival was scheduled to leave on was discovered to have a mechanical problem and, such was the shortage of air transport in this second year of the war, it was five weeks before Percival managed to get away. In the meantime, his mother died. 'The news of my impending departure was too much for that brave woman who, at the age of eighty-three, had stood up unflinchingly to many air raids.'

In broad daylight and without a fighter escort, he flew in a well-armed Sunderland flying boat to Gibraltar, and from there to besieged Malta where his old boss, the pious Dobbie, had been brought out of retirement to be governor. Dobbie showed Percival around Malta's coastal defences and in the evening they watched Axis aircraft being picked up by the searchlights as they dived through the anti-aircraft barrage to bomb Grand Harbour. Next day, the Sunderland slipped out between raids and headed for the Egyptian port of Alexandria, not far from where the only British troops currently engaged in major land warfare were preparing an offensive to relieve the Australians in Tobruk.

A rebellion in Iraq fanned by Axis support meant that the Imperial Airways service between Cairo and Basra had been suspended, but the RAF came to the rescue and got Percival to Karachi in time to catch Imperial's flight to Calcutta and Rangoon. Here Percival again parted company with Imperial, for it was not thought politic to pass through neutral Bangkok. The RAF took him on the last leg to Singapore, stopping briefly at Alor Star, which was just below the Thai border and was the most northerly of Malaya's seven main RAF airfields. It had taken exactly two weeks to get there from England and he had never been out of British-controlled territory or air space for more than twenty-four hours, usually much less.

Percival threw himself into absorbing what reinforcements he could squeeze out of a parsimonious War Office and coordinating the colony's defences. Between work, and sometimes as part of work, there were dinner and cocktail parties. 'A nice shy man who blossoms slowly in conversation,' was the verdict of Megan Spooner, a professional singer and wife of Rear-Admiral Edward Spooner, who was in charge of the naval base.

Yet, for all his shyness, the new mood of cooperation between the army and the RAF was based on the friendship that quickly developed between Percival, who was certainly reserved, and his air force counterpart, Air Vice-Marshal Pulford. Neither man was accompanied by his wife and, since suitable accommodation was at a premium, they agreed to live together in Flagstaff House, the army commander's residence. They hit it off. 'A man of my own way of thinking in most matters military and non-military,' declared Percival. All the major bones of contention between the services were swept away. The RAF consulted the army about the location of emergency landing strips which the army might be required to defend. And since both men understood the air defences that had evolved in Britain over the last year, they were able to plan a coordinated flak and fighter response to any bombing raids on Singapore designed to ensure that, if the island's anti-aircraft batteries ever went into action, what they brought down would be Japanese.

In London the chiefs of staff had promised 336 front-line aircraft for Malaya by the end of the year. But by the autumn of 1941 there were still fewer than half that number in the colony, and these included the lumbering Vickers Vildebeest torpedo bomber biplanes – which had been old when Percival left in 1937 – albeit with new engines. Pulford, who had started his service career in the navy before transferring to the old Royal Flying Corps, was a firm believer in the effectiveness of the torpedo bomber though he was rather hoping the Vildebeests would be replaced by some of the new twin-engined Beauforts that were being made under licence in Australia. As it was, Vildebeest crews liked to tell people that the only way they would ever kill any Japanese was if the latter caught sight of them and died laughing. Despite this, there was considerable affection among them for their aircraft, with their chilly open cockpits, and a firm belief that, granted sufficient fighter cover, the Vildebeest was still a perfect platform from which to launch torpedoes at enemy shipping. The RAF assured Percival that, with their existing strength, they were confident of accounting for 40 per cent of the ships involved in any Japanese attempt to mount seaborne landings on the Malayan or, more likely, the Thai coast.

It had long been obvious that the easiest way for the Japanese to establish a bridgehead in the Malayan Peninsula would be to land troops unopposed on the Kra Isthmus, the narrow neck of land that connects Thailand to Malaya. Their objectives would be the harbour of Songkla, 50 miles from Malaya's northern border, and, to the south of it, Patani, where there was a good airfield. The Thais were only too aware of this, and had already declared their strict neutrality and determination to resist any incursion into their territory, although their army was little more than a gendarmerie.

On his return to Malaya, Percival found he had inherited a plan, Operation Matador, for a pre-emptive strike on southern Thailand, which would see the British crossing the border and dug in around Songkla waiting for the Japanese fleet to appear on the horizon. Matador was a bold plan, a fine example of what the military called 'forward defence', and was favoured by both Brooke-Popham and the commander of the 11th Indian Division, Major-General D. M. Murray-Lyon, whose infantry battalions were already deployed close to the Thai border and would be the ones to carry it out.

If a Japanese landing on the Kra Isthmus appeared imminent, Matador had to be unleashed at least twenty-four hours before they reached it. But Brooke-Popham could not persuade London to allow him, as commander-in-chief, to make the final decision. No matter how inevitable war with Japan was beginning to look, it remained British policy to do everything possible to avoid it. Although Hitler had turned his back on Britain to attack Russia, both Churchill and his chiefs of staff knew they would still be hard put to wage a real world war, with land fighting in both northern and southern hemispheres, and if they tried it, they risked losing both. They felt it was imperative not to be tricked into entering Thailand by a Japanese feint such as a convoy of ships leaving an Indo-China port and then turning back. Over the years, the Thais had been obliged to concede a broad margin of border territory to British Malaya and Burma, just as they had done to French Indo-China. The last thing they wanted was to give the pro-Japanese faction within the Thai hierarchy the chance to invite the Japanese to protect them from western colonialists. And worse, much worse as far as Churchill was concerned, this would give President Roosevelt's isolationist foes in Washington another chance to preach the folly of getting involved in a war to preserve, perhaps even expand, the British Empire.

In this the prime minister had the support of the Foreign Office, which had a powerful voice in Bangkok. Sir Josiah Crosby, a bachelor who had spent thirty-five of his thirty-nine years of service as a diplomat in Thailand, was the British Minister, an exalted ambassadorial rank now extinct. The British had easily as much influence in Thailand as the Japanese, perhaps more. There were British advisers in several government ministries. Tin-mining in the Kra Isthmus was mostly run by Australian, British and New Zealand engineers. Thai princes went to Sandhurst. Sir Josiah's was easily the most important-looking diplomatic mission in Bangkok. His legation worked and lived within an imposing walled compound, with tennis courts, a swimming pool and a statue of Queen Victoria that was sometimes mistaken for a minor deity by country Thais who caught a glimpse of it through the gates. Sir Josiah probably understood the Byzantine ways of Thailand's rulers better than any other westerner, but some considered his empathy had been acquired at a heavy price. 'Crosby is too often influenced by the existing mood of the Thai prime minister and seems inclined to reflect rather than interpret the atmosphere in Bangkok,' pronounced an exasperated staff officer on the War Office's Far East desk. Crosby himself, who regularly complained to the Thais about the number of Japanese sniffing about the border areas with Malaya, thought that, if there was going to be a war, the trick was to let the Japanese make the first move and then get the Thais to invite the British in to protect their neutrality. It was all a matter of timing.

Throughout the summer and autumn of 1941, both the British and the Japanese were quite blatant about their military interest in the Kra Isthmus. Officers in civilian clothes reconnoitred its roads and shore line, took dozens of photographs and even found themselves staying at the same country inns as their counterparts.

On the British side, these trips were organized by a newcomer to South-east Asia. Special Operations Executive (SOE) was the secret sabotage organization set up by Churchill following the German victories of 1940, 'to go and set Europe ablaze'. Since then it had moved further afield. By the end of the war, when it was disbanded, its tactics and increasingly exotic weaponry such as the Welrod, the world's first silenced pistol, effective at 30 feet, would form the basis for generations of spy thrillers. Under Lieutenant-Colonel Valentine Killery, late of the Far East division of Imperial Chemical Industries, SOE arrived in Singapore at about the same time as Percival, intending to lay the foundations for guerrilla and terrorist warfare should any part of Malaya ever be occupied by the Japanese. By July it had established itself on an isolated promontory just outside Singapore city. For a while they went under the alias of School of Demolitions, but this was later changed to 101 Special Training School (STS). The existence of SOE was a secret; it remained so until well after the war, and its initials were never used.

The school was intended to serve the whole of Brooke-Popham's Far East command and, apart from British servicemen and civilians, mostly tea planters and mining engineers, its pupils included Americans, Danes, French and Portuguese from Macau. On its curriculum were a comprehensive small arms course, sabotage with and without explosives, unarmed combat and silent killing, navigation, map reading and a course in fieldcraft, which not only covered tactics but also how to survive in rough country.

This was taught by STS 101's star tutor, Major Freddy Spencer Chapman, a professional explorer, mountaineer, yachtsman, author and expeditions master at Gordonstoun, the Scottish public school that pioneered Outward Bound adventure training for teenagers. He came to Singapore in his prime, thirty-four years old with film-star good looks and a history of rugged adventures in which he had displayed tremendous powers of physical endurance and mental toughness. Shortly after he came down from Cambridge, where he read Natural Sciences, the survey for the British Arctic Air Route had sent him to Greenland where he had shot a rampaging polar bear and ruthlessly kept his husky team alive by killing and feeding them one of the older dogs. (To the outrage of other members of the expedition some of his own appetites were met by an Eskimo mistress.) He had participated in a long trek into Tibet on an intelligence-finding mission for British India and, with the permission of the Foreign Office, published a book on it which was admired as much for its photography as its writing. When war broke out, he was contemplating climbing Everest. He had already scaled the unconquered Himalayan peak of Chomolhari in Bhutan, pressing on after a 30-foot fall when a snowbridge crumbled under him.

Following a spell as an instructor at the commando training school at Lochailort in Scotland, Chapman had been posted to a similar establishment in Australia where his personal magnetism had impressed teachers and pupils alike. 'He talked like a liberal and acted like an anarchist,' recalled fellow instructor Michael Calvert, a regular soldier with a distinguished war ahead of him with Wingate's Chindits. Chapman tended to take a somewhat dim view of regular officers, but in Calvert's case he made an exception. Another exception was Colonel Alan 'Cocky' Warren, his organization's liaison officer with Percival's HQ, a shrewd and innovative colonel in the Royal Marines who was from an Anglo-Irish background and boasted that he had heard his first shots fired in action as a teenager in Dublin during the 1916 Easter Rising. Tall and broad-chested, Warren sported the kind of luxuriant moustache last in vogue among cavalry officers in the Crimea, and had spent a large part of his pre-war career as a Fleet Air Arm pilot when carrier flying was still at its most hazardous, experimental stage. In the summer of 1940 he had pulled off a remarkable feat of endurance and boatmanship. Landed by the Royal Navy with two young army officers on a French beach to investigate whether British troops cut off from Dunkirk might have gathered there, it was soon discovered that their objective was firmly in German hands and the navy was unable to recover them. For several days Warren evaded the enemy until, with French help, he got hold of a blunt-ended, 10-foot fishing coble. Then, with the assistance of only one of his companions, for the other had somehow damaged his wrist, he rowed for fourteen hours across a 35-mile stretch of the Channel until they reached the *Varne* lightship off Dungeness.

After his French adventure, Warren was asked to find a way to land a man on the rocky and fiercely tidal coastline of German-occupied Guernsey from a submarine at night, and bring him back the same way. His answer was a collapsible, rubber-skinned canoe purchased from Harrods' sports department. This was probably the first case of a canoe being used by the British military since Wolfe's conquest of Canada, and turned out to be a great success. Subsequent operations, in which neither Warren nor canoes were employed, all ended in dismal and sometimes farcical failure.

Warren had arrived in Singapore a few weeks before Colonel Killery set up his Special Training School bearing six Thompson sub-machine-guns, the American gangster's Tommy gun, which fired a big .45 bullet and had been used in France by some of the British Expeditionary Force. Most of the troops in Malaya had not yet seen them outside a cinema, but this would change over the next few months as equipment caught up with the reinforcements. Warren thought the Thompsons would be ideal for jungle warfare. But though their close-quarters firepower was appreciated, on exercises men found them awkward to carry, heavier than their Enfield rifles, and with various knobs and projections that caught on clothing. At least one of the instructors at STS 101, a New Zealand tin-miner who had worked in southern Thailand, thought rifles were of more use in the jungle.

For the moment this was all very academic. Warren, like Percival, had to face the awful prospect for a professional soldier that, if he remained in Malaya, he might be in for a very dull war. The massive and lavishly equipped naval base ready to succour a major task force, the untested Buffaloes and their mostly untested pilots who were never out of the newsreels and the newspapers, the unblooded Australians who also photographed so well against a jungle backcloth, might all do the trick. The Japanese might be deterred. There was a lot of steel there, a lot of high morale. If some elements of it were a bluff, and it depended on who you listened to, then much worse ones had helped to make the empire.

Meanwhile, at least SOE did have some operational tasks. The main one was in Thailand, but here they were thwarted by the prickly Crosby whose expertise they had expected to be one of their greatest assets. 'One might as well expect a chief of police to sponsor a guild of housebreakers,' despaired one of Killery's men after the British Minister had tried to dissuade a British expatriate they had hoped to recruit from working for them.

As it happened, SOE fared rather better than another intelligence agency trying to operate on Crosby's turf. John Becker, a forty-ish lieutenant in the Royal Army Service Corps until somebody realized his worth, had been a successful trader in Malaya and Thailand. He spoke excellent Thai and Malay, had good contacts with the royal family and was even rumoured to have fathered a child by a Thai princess. By early 1941 he appears to have been working for the Inter-Services Liaison Department, which was the cover name for the Secret Intelligence Service sometimes known as MI6. They encouraged Becker to return to Bangkok and persuade the Thai royals, or at least a faction of them, to raise the royal standard and rebel against the usurper Field-Marshal Pibul who had declared himself regent. But Crosby got to hear about the plot and made strong objections to Brooke-Popham. Becker was placed under close arrest and, in October 1941, despite an audience with Percival who said he could do nothing about it, was put on a ship bound for the UK where he was transferred to the Army Education Corps.

Apart from their involvement in the Thai briar patch, SOE's main task was to prepare in Malaya 'stay-behind' parties equipped and trained to operate out of jungle hide-outs for several months at a time. If their area was overrun, they would emerge to ambush road and rail traffic and any other soft target they could find. It was envisaged that these parties would be made up mainly of Chinese, who, of all the indigenous communities, hated the Japanese the most, led by Asiatic police inspectors and some of SOE's local European volunteers who spoke the local languages and knew the country. All would be tutored by Spencer Chapman and the other instructors at the Special Training School in Singapore.

Just as he had expected Crosby's help, Killery thought the army would provide him with all he needed. Once again he was in for a shock. SOE and Percival had arrived in Singapore at about the same time, but at first only Brooke-Popham knew of SOE's plans. It was several weeks before Percival discovered what they were up to and when he did he was furious. The general officer commanding's main concern was the effect these cloak-and-dagger merchants might have on morale, both civilian and military. What would people think if they discovered that, before a single shot had been fired, the possibility of parts of Malaya coming under enemy occupation was already being contemplated? His other objection was that it was a waste of his manpower since the Europeans involved, who would probably be the cream of the local volunteer forces, could hardly expect to move about a Japanese-controlled territory undetected as British agents might do in Nazi-occupied Europe.

Killery thought Percival's arguments were totally disingenuous, particularly the last one. His British and Dominion personnel were expected to lead hit-and-run raids from their jungle hide-outs, not mingle with the crowd. Killery told Brooke-Popham that, without the army's cooperation, he would be obliged to tell London to withdraw SOE from Singapore as there was nothing it could do. This did the trick – Churchill had a special fondness for SOE operations – and eventually, after a meeting between Percival, Brooke-Popham and Killery, a compromise was worked out. SOE was to be restricted to the Thai frontier area, to be under Command HQ control and, initially at least, to be restricted to intelligence-gathering.

Percival comes out of this spat in rather a blimpish light and perhaps this had something to do with his experiences in Ireland twenty years before, a professional soldier's disdain for the *franc-tireur*. But if his judgement of SOE's potential was clouded, and they had yet to prove their worth in any theatre of war, his irritation has to be balanced against demands on his scant resources that he had not even sanctioned.

It is in the nature of generals to insist to their superiors that they have so little while the enemy has so much, and that disaster will ensue unless they are given more. The British now had more troops in Malaya and Singapore than at any other time in its history as a colony, and Percival was all too aware that his was not even an active command. And yet he knew that if he did have to fight he did not have enough. He certainly did not have enough to mount Matador, secure the RAF's seven Malayan airfields – there were fears that the Japanese might try paratroop assaults against some of them – and keep enough troops back to defend the coastline of southern Malaya and Singapore itself. Nor could he be entirely confident that what he did have was, for the moment at least, good enough.

The two divisions of Lieutenant-General Sir Lewis Heath's 3rd Indian Corps covered all of northern and central Malaya and, if Operation Matador was given the green light, one was poised to enter Thailand. Yet both were mostly composed of raw, partially trained young soldiers. The rapid expansion of the British Indian Army since the beginning of the war could not keep up with the demands being made on it. Three reasonably well-equipped, and certainly very well-trained, Indian divisions were fighting the Italians and the Germans. Heath had just won the battle of Keren, and his knighthood, commanding one of them in Ethiopia.

In order to maintain these standards in the fighting divisions of the Middle East, the units sent to Malaya had been milked of experienced men. It was true that, like the Australians, all Heath's Indian soldiers were volunteers, as were the old sweats in the three regular army British battalions among them. Almost all the conscripts to be found in his divisions were among the UK British supporting arms – artillery, transport, signals and ordnance units. But a lot of the Indian infantry had only been in the army for a few months. Most were teenaged peasants, Sikhs, Muslims and Hindus from the traditional northern Indian recruiting grounds of Punjab and Frontier province, or Gurkhas only recently descended from their Himalayan foothills. Some were still getting used to wearing boots.

This was cause for concern, though the material was exactly the same as in the divisions that had done well in the Middle East. All that was needed was time to train them. But here Heath was hampered by another deficiency: a grave shortage of properly qualified junior officers, because too many of the professionals – the captains and lieutenants who had passed their Urdu or Gurkhali proficiency exams

– had long been transferred to the battalions in the fighting divisions to keep them up to strength. Their replacements were usually what the War Office termed ECOs – Emergency Commissioned Officers. Occasionally the ECOs had civilian experience of the subcontinent, such as tea planting, and spoke some of its languages. Mostly they were the products not of Sandhurst or Woolwich, but the Officer Cadet Training Units now mushrooming in the United Kingdom and mass-producing 'temporary gentlemen'. Once commissioned, those who responded to the call from the Indian Army for second lieutenants usually did so because they believed it was the quickest way to find themselves fighting Rommel in Libya. Some were right. Others ended up in Malaya. Either way, few were yet capable of communicating with their men, or even with the non-commissioned officers who, at best, had a smattering of English and expected to receive orders in Urdu or Gurkhali.

To a certain extent the problem was alleviated by the existence of Indian officers. These came in three kinds. There had long been a sort of sub-caste known as VCOs which stood for Viceroy Commissioned Officers – veterans made up from the ranks whom Indian soldiers, but not British soldiers, were obliged to salute. But the last twenty years had seen the gradual introduction of Indian Commissioned Officers, inevitably ICOs. There was a third category – a small elite known as KCOs, which stood for King's Commissioned Officers and applied to those few Indians who had gone to England and passed through Sandhurst or Woolwich.

It had long been possible for educated and Anglicized Indians to work their way up to senior positions in the Indian civil service. Nationalists sometimes sneered at these 'Brindians' and, behind their backs, some of the British called them 'Brown Sahibs', but India could not work without them. Towards the end of World War I the Indian Army, after much heated internal debate, decided to follow suit. There was to be a gradual process of Indianization and, by the early 1920s, Sandhurst and Woolwich had opened their doors to Indian cadets. On the whole this was not a success. There were some brilliant and popular Indian cadets, but these had usually attended one of the top British public schools. Otherwise, there tended to be too much culture shock and a high wastage rate. Then, in 1932, the Indian Military Academy was opened at the hill station of Dehra Dun, about 120 miles north-east of Delhi. Inscribed in English on its walls were the words: 'The safety, honour and welfare of your country comes first, always and every time.'

Noble words, but by the late 1930s, when the academy was producing fifty-six Indian Commissioned Officers a year, already a trifle ambiguous. Whose India did they refer to? Was it the India of the King-Emperor, British India? Or some other, future India? By the late summer of 1941, Congress Party nationalists were celebrating a clause in the Atlantic Charter, which Churchill had just signed with Roosevelt off Newfoundland aboard HMS *Prince of Wales*, the new battleship blooded on the *Bismarck* sinking. It referred to 'the right of all people to choose the form of government under which they will live'. Let the British try to wriggle out of that one.

For years the Indian Army had managed to remain aloof from the growing clamour for independence, indeed from India itself, which some of its British officers seemed to regard simply as an exotic backdrop. In its isolated cantonments, loyalty was first and foremost to the regiment. It was a concept the country boys who filled the ranks could, with suitable training, respond to, and a recruiter was considered to have done a bad job if he captured a youth literate enough to read a headline.

Now, educated Indian lieutenants stood alongside British subalterns to toast the King-Emperor in the officers' mess, bright young men who had jumped at the chance denied to the often distinguished lawyers and civil servants who had sired them. True, by the time Heath was setting up his Corps HQ in Malaya, they were still something of a novelty – with about one Indian for every twelve British officers. None the less, it was the most radical innovation the British had ever introduced into their largest colonial army.

Danny Misra, who went from Dehra Dun to the Rajputana Rifles, was the son of a high-caste Brahmin magistrate brought up in a home where English and Hindi were spoken about equally. His father's closest friend was a senior and dedicated British member of the Indian civil service who rarely took home leave. The Indian Army's own 'long leave' allotment was as generous as that of the civil service – four months every three years. There was a vogue for its British as well as its Indian officers to take part of it in Japan, about which there was an obvious curiosity. Misra's first long leave came up in 1938 when he was on garrison duty in Hong Kong, the British colony that was closest to Japan.

I stayed in a Japanese home for some time – the father had been at Oxford, the son at Eton. I could not only sense that war was imminent but also their ambitions ... the military ran the country. They had conquered most of China. It had all gone to their heads – arrogant people ... 'Asia for the Asiatics' ... They welcomed Indians. Their policy was to try and drive a wedge between the Indians and the British.

Misra's generation were dismally aware that the empire had its darker side – exemplified by General Dyer and the Amritsar massacre – and there were some 'who thought the only way to run the country was with the *lathi*★ and the boot'. Once they had emerged from their regimental cocoon, even the most Anglicized Indian officers were not always protected from racial snubs. While serving on the North West Frontier, the polo-playing Captain Prem Sahgal, another Dehra Dun alumnus, had ridden alongside side-saddled English women in pursuit of the jackal with the Peshawar Vale Hunt; but the swimming pool at the local club, where, to the furtive astonishment of its Muslim waiters, mixed bathing between the sexes had recently been introduced, was a different proposition. Some British officers' wives made it perfectly plain that they were not prepared to share its waters with Indians of any rank. Whenever they entered the pool these affronted memsahibs splashed to the edge as if they had seen a shark. Sahgal gathered his brother officers and organized a response. 'When an English girl went in, we went in. And when she got out, we got out. So after a while she got tired of all this going in and coming out and there was no problem.'

Sahgal came to Malaya as a company commander with the 2/10th Battalion of the Baluch Regiment. At first the officers behaved much as they had in India. Birthe Rentse, daughter of a Danish surveyor working on RAF landing strips, was fourteen and has fond memories of Sahgal letting her ride the polo ponies he had acquired. But by November 1941, the 2/10th was busy preparing machine-gun nests, mine fields and barbed-wire entanglements on a stretch of beach south of the coastal border town of Kota Baharu, on Malaya's north-east coast where a huge reclining Buddha in an old Siamese temple was evidence of the Thai influence. If the Japanese were intending to land in northern Malaya as well as the Kra Isthmus, this was thought to be the most obvious place, for its best prize was the RAF airfield there. To his great delight, Sahgal was able to fence in the Kelantan Club's

★ Bamboo cane used by Indian riot police.

beach house, which meant that members wanting to take a dip in the Gulf of Siam had to walk miles before they found the hole in the wire his battalion had left for local fishermen and their own vehicles. The club had offered honorary membership to all the 2/10th's officers except its Indians. 'How can we when we don't take senior Malays?'

Nor was this his only revenge. When the club invited the 2/10th's band, who doubled as stretcher-bearers, to play at one of its functions, Sahgal pointed out to his commanding officer, Lieutenant-Colonel James Frith, that he and the other three barred Indian officers in the battalion contributed to its maintenance costs out of their pay. The band did not go. British battalion commanders such as Frith usually had the common sense to establish a school-masterish accommodation with their young Indian officers, tolerating their 'bolshieness', to use the term of the day. They needed them and, devoted to their men as they often were, acquired insights from these educated young Indians on matters they had never bothered – often never wished – to think about. For instance, Sahgal, a not very observant beef-eating Hindu, persuaded Frith that his Sikh, Muslim and Hindu Viceroy Commissioned Officers would, under certain circumstances, be prepared to sit down and eat their sometimes different rations together. Ever since the 1857 Mutiny, the British had been punctilious about not putting pork or beef into the wrong mouths and, though it was a quartermaster's nightmare, their respect for the dietary laws of Hindu and Muslim knew no bounds. 'I hope you're not trying to rush things, Prem,' Frith told him.

He need not have worried. By 1941 the British Indian Army remained the world's most complex, multicultural, military mosaic, quite unrivalled in its diversity since the collapse in 1918 of the Austro-Hungarian and Ottoman armies. At the top of its Malayan deployment was Lieutenant-General Heath, affectionately known to his contemporaries as 'Piggy' Heath, a nickname he had acquired at Wellington, the army's preferred public school. Heath was a couple of years older than Percival and, more important, technically senior to his new commanding officer, having been promoted to lieutenant-general a couple of months before him. He had never passed through staff college and was very much a fighting soldier, from a family of Indian Army officers – an uncle had been killed in Afghanistan in the 1880s. While campaigning in Iraq in 1916 a Turkish bullet had shattered his left upper arm, rendering the limb almost useless despite a 10-inch graft from one of his shin bones. In the way of childhood nicknames, 'Piggy' bore no relation to the man, who was slim, good-looking and capable of great charm. A widower, he had recently remarried in Malaya a New Zealand nurse whom he had met in India.

At this point very few of the British forces had their wives with them. Most of those who did were regular officers who had been posted to Malaya before the outbreak of hostilities with Germany, or Other Ranks who had married permanent residents, often from the Eurasian community whose women were particularly beautiful. The newly wedded Lady Heath was supposed to remain in the country for only a short while, then return to India or New Zealand. But Percival allowed Heath to persuade him to extend his wife's stay.

Perhaps it would have been impossible to do otherwise and expect to maintain a decent relationship with this rather senior subordinate. And no doubt Percival would have told himself it was a bit dog-in-the-manger to point out that neither he nor Pulford had the comfort of their wives. It did not take long for the Heaths to set themselves up in an airy house with a good garden, tennis court and swimming pool in Kuala Lumpur where Heath's 3rd Indian Corps had its HQ and for Lady Heath, in Percival's words, to 'give a lead to the other British women'. She had already been shrewd enough to start playing a leading role in local civil defence work.

Heath was by no means the only officer to get his wife into Malaya after the European war had broken out and merchant shipping was supposed to have better things to do than carry *bouches inutiles*, however good they were at civil defence. But not everybody was so lucky.

'Why has everyone got their wife here except me?' moaned Kenneth Atkinson in a letter home to his wife Molly dated 25 October 1941. Captain Atkinson RN was 'Captain of the Dockyard and King's Harbourmaster', the senior administrator at the naval base, and was normally referred to by neither his name nor his rank but simply by his job initials, 'CD'. At the end of the last war, Atkinson had been a sixteen-year-old midshipman aboard HMS *Warspite*, escorting the Kaiser's surrendered fleet into Scapa Flow. He had won prizes for his skill at navigation and pilotage and shot up the promotion ladder, though he had not been to sea since 1940, when he was on the battleship *Nelson* when she was disabled by a mine. Now, at almost forty and in one of the senior service's most senior posts on the island, he was beset by periodic bouts of homesickness, yearning for Molly and their three young children. 'I wish I was at Lumley now to see all the aubrietia and other flowers,' he had written in the spring from the ship remorselessly bearing him away from his family.

Six months later super-hawk Tojo had replaced the comparatively moderate Prince Konoye as prime minister, while retaining his post as war minister. Those senior Japanese officers around the Emperor who still wanted peace hoped the Anglo-Americans would treat this as a signal of just how dangerous things were getting. In Singapore, British officers like Atkinson did their best to take these distant events seriously, poring over the Reuters reports in the *Straits Times*. But, however much they tried to prepare for the worst, the colony had them in its spell, and had carried them over the rainbow to a Never Never Land where even the anguish of being away from their families at Christmas was dulled, even vanquished.

The first hint of all the parties in store came one Friday evening towards the end of November when the Base Sailing Club held its annual dance. Red, white and blue fairy lights decorated the club house. It was built on piles hammered into the bed of the Straits of Johore so that the officers in their mess kit or white dinner jackets, and the women in their chiffon dresses, twirled above its waters and the sound of music and laughter rippled across the night. When Atkinson, in one of his almost daily letters home, mentioned sailors building bunkers, it got through the censor because it referred to a new golf course he was laying out, not improved defences. Indeed, Atkinson's letters were full of accounts of the tennis (he had his own court), hockey and squash he played with other officers, the cocktail and dinner parties he attended, and how much he wanted Molly there to share his comfortable home and its seven servants. 'How I wish you were here and we could go out in half an hour's time and have our supper on the lawn and I could tell you all my troubles,' he wrote. 'I suppose you are steeped in the gloom of the English winter with real blackouts . . .'

CD's letters home were probably typical of a garrison doing its best to prepare for a conflict that might never happen while guiltily aware that, compared to the war zone where they had left their families, they were living in a kind of paradise. All Atkinson wanted to complete his happiness was his wife and, in his frustration, he sometimes implied that these feelings were not reciprocated as much as they might be. 'My Darling, I've just met another wife who has come straight out from England without any trouble so it can't be as difficult as the shipping companies led you to believe.'

Several times he mentioned that the safe arrival of her numbered letters are a good indication that the battle against the U-boats is going well; but he knew that it was still a dangerous journey and he really ought to let up. 'I'm terribly sorry I've made you so miserable with my constant reference to you coming here.'

None the less, by the beginning of October things were looking up.

Wednesday 1st October. I've now had your number 40 in which you say the Admiralty has given [you] permission [to travel] and, of course, the Japanese situation has improved again. I'm terribly optimistic at the moment and am almost expecting a telephone message any day to say you're in Singapore. Or at least a cable to say you're on your way.

After Tojo was made prime minister at the end of November, he told Molly, 'I still think the Japanese will hover and bluff until the very last moment and never quite commit themselves unless a German victory is certain.'

A month later Atkinson had not exactly changed his mind but an awful thought had occurred. Could it be that the Japanese had persuaded themselves that it was the British who were doing the bluffing?

December 1st . . . we are in the very middle of one of the periodical Far Eastern crises! They certainly seem to get more critical each time, but I still have faith in my original conviction that Japan will remain on the fence and get just as much as she can by bluffing. She can surely be under no illusion that we are bluffing . . .

The Captain of the Dockyard wrote this in the knowledge that significant British naval reinforcements were due to drop anchor off Singapore the very next day, something he felt he could not possibly mention in a letter that might fall into the wrong hands until their presence was announced. The movements of warships often remained a secret for weeks at a time. Perhaps Atkinson had not yet been told that, in this case, an exception was being made. In an effort to deter the Japanese from going to war, Churchill had decided to give maximum publicity to the arrival of the *Prince of Wales*, the Royal Navy's latest battleship. All the media – print, radio and cinema newsreel – were invited to the naval base to witness the arrival of the *Prince*, one of the slayers of the *Bismarck*, four destroyers, and what the official communiqué described as 'other heavy elements'.

This referred to HMS *Repulse*, classed as a battle cruiser because, although she had the same huge 15-inch guns as most battleships, she was much more lightly armoured and, in 1916, when she was launched, faster than a battleship. By the time the *Prince of Wales* came off the Cammel Laird slipway in 1939, naval architecture had moved on and Britain's latest battleship could sail as fast as the *Repulse*, despite the weight of the armoured plate on her upper decks. The older ship had seen several refits. Its captain's quarters were the envy of the fleet, refurbished to accommodate the newly crowned King George VI and Queen Elizabeth on their state visit to North America in 1939. At the last moment, however, with the prospect looming of more proper employment for battle cruisers, the royal couple went on the liner *Empress of Australia* instead.

Otherwise, everything else about the ship, from her armament, particularly her anti-aircraft guns, to the way her old engines gulped fuel oil at speed, were still a generation behind her glamorous companion which, ever since the Atlantic Charter trip, was known in the service as 'Churchill's yacht'. The 1,600-strong crew of the *Repulse*, which had also been part of the pack around the *Bismarck* until she had to retire to refuel, resented being eclipsed by the bigger ship. When the ship arrived in Singapore and the crew realized that the press was not even allowed to identify them, they began to refer to their ship as 'HMS *Anonymous*'.

There were the usual inter-ship bar-room brawls, though the biggest punch-up, an epic encounter of boots and bottles that put thirty of the combatants into the Alexandra Military Hospital, was an army–navy rumble at the Union Jack Club between sailors off Churchill's yacht, the Gordon Highlanders and some unidentified Australians on leave from Johore. Afterwards, the captain of the *Prince of Wales*, a tall, roman-nosed West Countryman named John Leach and known as 'Trunky' to his friends, mustered his ship's company and lectured them, perhaps a little tongue-in-cheek, on the perils of becoming 'swollen-headed' about their ship.

As it happened, the crew of the *Repulse* were perhaps an even prouder bunch, revelling in the classic lines that made the battle cruiser so much better-looking than the *Prince*, which seemed crammed, inside and out, with every latest naval fad, though not all were visible to the naked eye. The Liquid Sandwich, for instance, was a series of tanks, some filled with fuel oil and others with sea water, installed below the waterline and intended to provide extra protection against mines or torpedoes by dissipating the effect of their explosions. In the thirty years since the *Titanic*, no ship-builder in his right mind was going to use the word 'unsinkable', especially of a warship, but there was definitely a feeling that, should the *Prince of Wales* ever have the misfortune to encounter an iceberg, it would be the penguins who took to the boats.

There was no Liquid Sandwich on the *Repulse*. Instead, girdling the nether regions of her hull was its predecessor: the Torpedo Bulge. Decently out of sight and as unfashionable as a corset, this was exactly what its name suggests: a metallic spare tyre attached to the real hull and intended to absorb the explosions of torpedoes before they did any serious damage. It is unlikely that many of the *Repulse*'s crew lost any sleep over their dated underwear any more than they worried about having old-style 4-inch anti-aircraft guns instead of the eight turrets of double-barrelled 5.25s sported by the bigger ship. Unlike the *Prince of Wales*, which had a high proportion of conscripts – known in the Royal Navy as 'HOs' which stood for 'Hostilities Only' – well over half of them were still pre-war regulars. Morale was high. They had a fine conceit of themselves and, true or false, everybody who had been on the ship since 1939 believed they were part of a hand-picked crew chosen to sail with the monarch. They were, without a shadow of a doubt, the cream of the navy. There was little envy of the *Prince of Wales*, not least because better ventilation made *Repulse* a much more comfortable ship for employment east of Suez, where the Royal Navy had yet to introduce the air-conditioning enjoyed by the patrons of Singapore's latest cinema. They also suspected that theirs was a much more efficient ship, where men and machinery were both well tested. The *Prince of Wales* was regarded as a bit of a Jonah, so new she had never had time to 'work up' properly. Working up was considered vital for a ship and was a process that could last for several months while the hopelessly unsuitable were weeded out, the crew learned to act as a team and the inevitable teething troubles with the ship's working parts were put right. Everybody knew the story of how the *Prince* had made its battle debut against the *Bismarck* with civilian technicians from Vickers still aboard.

Ordinary Seaman Hubert 'Taffy' Bowen, whose unidentical twin Fred was also on *Repulse* as a radio operator, remembers a 'happy ship' and was delighted that his ability to hold top-C had earned him a place in its much-admired male-voice choir. The twins, sons of a South Wales miner turned labourer at the insistence of his English wife, had volunteered for boy service when war broke out. At the time of the *Bismarck* action they were seventeen and among about 120 boy seamen on board. By the time they got to Singapore they had just turned eighteen and passed into man service, although it would still be three years before they were eligible for the daily tot of rum served to all hands on a British warship since Nelson's time. But at least they were no longer eligible for another grand old naval tradition.

Boy seamen were still flogged, admittedly not with a cat-o'-nine-tails but ordered to change into lightweight white ducks and bent over by two of the master at arms' assistants while that beefy figure, the ship's chief policeman, delivered a maximum of twelve cuts across their buttocks with a bamboo cane. Midshipmen, who were rarely much older than eighteen, could receive the same punishment for serious misdemeanours; since they were probationary officers however, in their case it was administered by the sub-lieutenant in charge of the midshipmen's gun room, who was usually a couple of years older. On the *Repulse* the practice had been allowed to fall into disuse, but not on the *Prince of Wales* where the man who preceded Leach made it perfectly plain to Sub-Lieutenant Geoffrey Brooke that he 'wanted a disciplinarian'. Brooke, the lanky regular officer son of a regular naval officer who, not all that long before, had himself been beaten while a midshipman on HMS *Nelson*, rather reluctantly administered two canings during his tenure; much to his embarrassment, he was thanked by one of his victims who informed him it had done him a lot of good.

On the return leg across the Atlantic with Churchill, Brooke had persuaded the prime minister to visit the gun room where he had sat in an armchair with a drink in his hand and allowed the midshipmen to question him at length. Brooke had also had a question. He had asked Churchill about the chances of Japan entering the war. 'No, I don't think so,' said the prime minister. 'If they do, they'll find they've bitten off more than they can chew.'

Among those welcoming the big ships to Singapore, and rejoicing in 'the sense of complete security' they brought with them, was the latest addition to the British hierarchy in the colony. Up until recently Alfred Duff Cooper, known to friend and foe alike as 'Duff', had been minister of information, Churchill's propaganda chief. A famously articulate and literary politician, biographer of Talleyrand and World War I's Field-Marshal Haig, and a competent poet, he was considered ideal for the job. But, more often than not, he not only lacked good news to give, but also the common touch that might have made bad tidings easier to bear. A product of Eton, Oxford and the Foreign Office, his response to the fall of France was to get behind a BBC microphone and read Macaulay's 'The Armada'. The enmity of Beaverbrook's *Express* did not help, and he had welcomed being replaced by Brendan Bracken, his elevation to Chancellor of the Duchy of Lancaster and the job Churchill created for him as his special emissary in the Far East which, though ill-defined, was by no means irrelevant.

In 1918 Duff Cooper, a subaltern in the Grenadier Guards, had almost single-handedly captured two German machine-gun nests for which he had been awarded a Distinguished Service Order, an unusually high award for a junior officer and recognition of how near he had come to winning a Victoria Cross. Twenty years later he had demonstrated considerable moral courage when, while the country celebrated Neville Chamberlain's 'peace in our time', he had resigned as First Lord of the Admiralty in protest at the prime minister's appeasement of Hitler at Munich. 'Disfigured the smiling landscape with a hideous blot,' was Duff Cooper's own description of his actions and it looked like the end of his political career. Now he was just as certain that Tokyo wanted war. Passing through Washington on his way to Singapore, he had warned American journalists that those who thought it would be suicidal for Japan to attack should remember that 'the Japanese were, as a people, addicted to suicide'.

Accompanied by his witty, elegant and sometimes wilful wife Diana, who as a young woman had been an actress and a society beauty of renown, he had arrived in Singapore at the end of September. Since then the Coopers had, like the navy, treated it as their home port and springboard for official visits to Burma, India, Australia and New Zealand in an attempt to assess the state of Britain's Far Eastern defences. The arrival of the *Prince of Wales* and *Repulse* was intended as a strong indication of how seriously these were being taken.

The night after the arrival of the two great battleships, the Duff Coopers attended a reception aboard the *Prince of Wales*. It was hosted by Admiral Sir Tom 'Thumb' Phillips, the commander of the task force, a small, energetic man in his early fifties with ruddy features and piercing blue eyes whom Duff Cooper had grown to like during his own time at the Admiralty. Once again, the purpose of the occasion was to show off the *Prince of Wales*, a cause the admiral could not have believed in more. Phillips was renowned for his faith in battleships, and his impatience with those heretics who prayed to the false gods of air power.

It was a very good party. 'There was a sound of revelry by night,' wrote Duff Cooper, ever the Tory romantic, though Byron's poetic celebration of the Duchess of Richmond's famous eve of Waterloo ball had been written safe in the knowledge that the revellers had won. Under a star-filled sky the ship's Royal Marine band played 'Roll Out the Barrel' and other forces' favourites, often drowning out the bosun's whistle piping homage to sultans and generals as they came aboard. The guests boarded at the front end of the ship, where carpets and upholstered chairs had been placed on the forecastle's wooden deck, which was covered by a striped awning in case of rain. The little admiral, his cap at a rakish angle, greeted all the men with a handshake, sometimes raising himself on his toes so that he could look them in the eye. Smiling sailors in white shorts and t-shirts circulated with trays of drinks including a discreet rum punch for those Muslim dignitaries who were known to like a tipple but had their reputations to consider. One of these turbaned figures was the Sultan of Johore, draped in a luminous cloak of gold thread and attended by his teenaged bride, who was easily one of the best-looking women there.

Many of the Asian males wore western evening dress. One of them, a thin man with horn-rimmed spectacles, was noticed staring intently over the ship's rail at the dark shadow of HMS *Repulse* which, in an attempt to preserve its mystery as 'the other heavy element', was anchored towards the middle of the straits. Nobody was surprised at his interest for this was Mr Suermasa Okomoto, Singapore's Japanese consul-general, who had been invited in the hope that his next telegram to Tokyo might give his country pause for thought. As for the *Repulse*, even if Okomoto knew what to look for when it came to detecting the presence of radar equipment or gauging the calibre of guns, it was well known that the Japanese found it particularly difficult to see in the dark.

In the daylight, more knowing eyes than the consul-general's were not at all impressed. Captain Peter Cazalet, a torpedo specialist who had won a Distinguished Service Cross on land in 1940 for the demolition work he did on Dutch dykes to slow the German advance into Holland, commanded the old light cruiser HMS *Durban* which had been in Singapore for the last four weeks. '*Prince of Wales*, *Repulse*, *Jupiter*, *Electra*, *Express* and *Encounter* arrived from westwards during the afternoon and went to the base,' Cazalet noted in his diary for 2 December 1941.

A great deal made of their arrival. *Repulse* looked smart, *Prince of Wales* looked very war worker and has ugly lines. All the destroyers looked very battered. It seems a very imbalanced squadron to send out but I suppose nothing else can be spared.

Cazalet was not the only one to be unimpressed by Force Z, as Admiral Phillips' squadron was codenamed. Percival, whose many courses had included one at the Royal Naval Staff College, was also perturbed.

I had been told that the essence of naval warfare was a balanced fleet, i.e. a fleet consisting of all types of warships, each with their own part to play, and here we saw these two great ships arriving accompanied only by a few destroyers . . . There were no aircraft carriers . . . no heavy cruisers and no submarines.

Originally, an aircraft carrier had been included in Force Z, but HMS *Indomitable*, a new ship with an armoured flight deck and, among its forty-five aircraft, nine Hurricane fighters, had been slightly damaged when she ran aground while on working up trials in the Caribbean. Her departure for Singapore was delayed for two weeks while repairs were made at the US naval shipyard at Norfolk, Virginia – thanks to Roosevelt, yet another example of neutral America's special relationship with Great Britain. With the demands of the Atlantic and the Mediterranean theatres, there was no question of the Admiralty finding a replacement. As it was, the *Prince of Wales* had been sent despite the fulminations of Admiral Sir John Tovey, the commander of the Home Fleet who, in his worst nightmares, would be left with one modern battleship between the German surface fleet and the Atlantic convoy lifeline from North America. 'Their stoppage would rapidly result in our losing the war. There is no comparable interest in the Far East . . .'

But Churchill was adamant and delighted in sending Roosevelt word of where the great ship on which they had signed the Atlantic Charter was going next. 'This ought to serve as a deterrent on Japan,' he told the president. 'There is nothing like having something that can catch and kill anything. I am very glad we can spare her . . . The firmer your attitude and ours, the less chance of their taking the plunge.'

Quite apart from its deterrent value Churchill had another reason for sending one of Britain's best ships to Singapore: it was a visible demonstration to Australia, whose troops were making such a valuable contribution in the Middle East, that the Old Country cared. And, as *The Times*' journalist Ian Morrison observed, the same could be said for both the garrison and British civilians of Malaya, where 'The sight of the great naval base at last victualling the size of ships it was intended for was a great fillip for morale.'

Since the start of the war, all that Singapore had seen under the white ensign was a scrap-iron flotilla made up of old destroyers and Insect-class gun-boats with names such as HMS *Dragonfly* and *Grasshopper*.

There were even some lightly armed, shallow-bottomed river craft that once did the Yangtse run from Shanghai; these had been requisitioned along with their British merchant navy skippers now newly commissioned into the Royal Naval Reserve.

Not that the navy was the only service that was having to make do. Percival had told the War Office that his minimum teeth arm requirements were forty-eight infantry battalions and two regiments of light tanks capable of crossing some of Malaya's weaker road bridges. And what did he have by the time people were talking about the worst Far East crisis ever? He had thirty-three infantry battalions and absolutely no sign of the armour. What was really annoying was that he had originally asked for tanks during his first tour of Malaya under Dobbie in 1937.

Shortly after Percival had arrived in Singapore it seemed all this might change, when Hitler attacked Russia with the largest army in European history and, no longer constrained by the immediate threat of invasion, Britain would be able to send more men and equipment abroad. But the tanks that might have come to Malaya were all sent to Russia instead. By the end of the year a total of 676 aircraft and 446 tanks had been shipped, despite the protests of General Sir Alan Brooke, then about to become Chief of the Imperial General Staff, who felt there was no way the army could afford this kind of largesse. Nor was it much more than a gesture. The Valentines and Crusaders Britain was sending to Archangel in constantly ambushed Arctic convoys were nowhere near as good as the Red Army's T34s, which had already won the respect of the Panzer regiments. But Churchill thought it was a gesture worth making and so did many of the British people for whom 'Uncle Joe Stalin' had suddenly become as cuddly as their own prime minister.

The RAF, as Percival's friend Pulford never ceased to remind him, was in an even more parlous state. They had been promised 336 modern front-line aircraft by the end of the year. By the beginning of December they had 145 aircraft of which 66 were Buffaloes, 57 twin-engined Blenheim bombers and 22 Hudsons. At first the Buffaloes had been nothing but trouble, requiring twenty-seven different modifications before they were considered battleworthy.

One of the main problems had been their guns. Percival recalled faulty 'interrupter gear', the device that enables the two machine-guns on the nose to fire through the arc of the rotating propeller without shooting it to pieces. But, apart from this, while the Buffalo's total armament of four Colt-Browning .50 calibres – the other two were in the wings – might have packed a punch, they were too heavy for the Flying Barrel, sadly reducing its rate of climb, which was among the most important requirements of an interceptor. In the end, it was decided to replace the Brownings with the kind of .303 machine-guns carried in Hurricanes and Spitfires, limit the ammunition to 350 rounds a gun, and reduce the fuel carried to 84 gallons. When all this was done, the Buffaloes could indeed climb faster, though once they reached the required height, they had neither the fuel nor the ammunition to stay there very long.

Apart from a squadron of Catalina flying boats and half a dozen Wirraways, an Australian version of the American Harvard trainer which in theory could be armed, the only other warplanes available were slow-moving biplanes: twenty-eight Vickers Vildebeests and ten Albacores and Swordfish, the Fleet Air Arm's own vintage torpedo carriers which had worked so well against the Italian fleet at Taranto. All of them could substitute bombs for torpedoes and attack land targets but, whatever they carried, they were not very fast.

There were no long-range bombers, transport or army cooperation aircraft. Percival often travelled about his command in goggles and a leather helmet as he flew low over the jungle canopy seated in one of the two open cockpits of a Tiger Moth. At the controls of the biplane was one of the British civilians of the Malayan Volunteer Air Force who, with little else to fly, sometimes offered their own sports planes as air taxis in the same way that, when war broke out, the officers in English yeomanry regiments had reported for duty with their hunt horses. Percival admired the way these amateur pilots got him about a country where there was often little chance of finding enough open space to make an emergency landing should their flimsy machines suffer one of their not-all-that-infrequent engine failures. His was a generation that had not yet grown accustomed to flying, not even in the services. There was, he confessed, 'a feeling of relief at times when all had arrived safely'.

Percival was quite right to be apprehensive. Even if you survived a crash in a remote jungle area, you could easily end up starving to death or succumbing to one of the several kinds of fatal tropical fevers – blackwater, tick typhus, cerebral malaria, to name but three. Scratches rapidly turned into stinking septic ulcers that rotted the skin to the bone. One of the things that never ceased to amaze was how nasty even the most idyllic setting could swiftly become.

Sergeant Alan Morton, a wireless operator and air gunner with one of the Australian Hudson squadrons, lost his shoes and socks during a crash landing on a particularly inaccessible and delightful-looking east coast beach, fringed by apparently impenetrable jungle. For two nights large sand flies feasted on his bare feet and, by the time the five-man crew was picked up, the bites had turned so ulcerous that parts of his ankle bones were visible. Morton, who was twenty-three, spent ten days in hospital and was told that he had not been far off having one of his feet amputated.

For some time the British had not been the only ones with aircraft over Malaya. From their new base in Saigon, Mitsubishi Ki 46 reconnaissance planes – called 'Dinahs' by the Americans and the British, who gave most twin-engined Japanese aircraft jolly-sounding women's names – had just about enough fuel to make the five-hour round trip across the Gulf of Siam to Thailand's Kra Isthmus and northern Malaya. There had been enough sightings for the RAF to be well aware of these intruders, but the only radar was in Singapore. There was never enough warning for the Buffaloes to attempt an interception, even if they had been fast enough.

Twice, a passenger on an unmarked Dinah over Malaya was the energetic Colonel Tsuji, now transferred from Taiwan to Saigon where, as chief of staff of 25th Army Group, he hoped to see his plans become reality. 'Gambling with human life one must risk one's own,' declared the colonel, an unusual concept for a staff officer, even in the Imperial Japanese Army. The main risk was of drowning in the South China Sea if the aircraft ran out of fuel on the return flight. As it happened, Tsuji had already reduced this risk. Dispensing with the tiresome formalities of acquiring Vichy French permission, he had employed 2,000 coolies to level two runways on Phuquoc Island off the Vietnamese coast. These advance landing strips were 300 miles from the most northerly part of Malaya's east coast and enabled Japanese aircraft to cover all of the Gulf of Siam.

Low monsoon clouds made Tsuji's first flight a failure, but a few days later he took off again and this time overflew Singapore and Patani and two of the RAF airfields in northern Malaya, gashes in the jungle canopy almost impossible to camouflage. Tsuji concluded that aircraft from the Kota Baharu air base particularly threatened their proposed landings. This answered a question he had been asking himself for some time. Should he advise General Tomoyuki Yamashita, the commander of 25th Army Group, to attack Sungei on the Kra Isthmus first and consolidate that before heading south into Malaya? Or would it be better to mount simultaneous attacks on Singora and Kota Baharu, so that the British would have their hands full there, leaving fewer of their aircraft available to harass the landing on the Kra Isthmus in Thailand? Tsuji was in no doubt that the right answer was simultaneous landings, otherwise the British might be able to use their torpedo bombers to sink a lot of Japanese ships off Singora. But would Yamashita listen?

The commander of 25th Army Group was a formidable figure in all meanings of the word. He had recently headed a Japanese military mission in Berlin where the inevitable wining and dining had expanded an already Falstaffian girth that was rare among Japanese generals. 'Of dignified physique' was how the lean and ascetic Tsuji described Yamashita. Tsuji lusted for war and the beauty of a victorious Japan. He had vowed to abstain from alcohol, tobacco and sex until Japan conquered Singapore – not much of a sacrifice for the monkish colonel, who also made a fetish of taking the most frugal of meals. Tsuji's feelings about Yamashita were ambivalent. Instinctively he gravitated towards authority and was anxious to please, but this general was very different from any other general he had worked for and it was not just his Sumo-esque tendencies. Perhaps the most disturbing thing about him for Tsuji was the thought that he was a man tainted by western notions of technological rather than spiritual superiority in military affairs. Yamashita had undoubtedly spent more time in Europe than most Japanese officers. His appointment as head of the military mission to Germany was the natural culmination of over five years of military attaché service, first in Berne and then in Vienna, a city which had a special place in his heart for the affair he had enjoyed with a German woman there. Austria had since become part of the Third Reich and, during his recent mission to Berlin, he had managed to snatch a couple of days off to visit her. It was about this time that his staff noticed that the grey hair around his temples had vanished.

Yamashita was fifty-six and the son of a country doctor who practised in the forested mountains of Shikoku, the smallest of Japan's main islands, famous for the age and size of its cedars. In the 1890s, when he was growing up, metropolitan Japan was modernizing fast but life in villages such as Osugi Mura – the name means 'Great Cedar' – had not changed much for a thousand years. The staple diet was rice from local paddy fields and fish from the rivers and streams that watered them. At night people slept on futons placed on wooden floors. When the winter snows came and there was ice on the fish ponds, they heated their timber houses as best they could with careful charcoal fires standing in a brazier. Inner warmth might be provided by a few cups of sake. In the summer it grew warm enough to slide back the walls, allowing the house to be cooled by mountain breezes. Most of the villagers had never ventured further than Kochi, the island's capital.

One of the first indications of changing times was Yamashita's elder brother's decision to pursue a career in medicine by moving to Tokyo and studying and practising there, rather than doing what was expected of him and working with his father until he was considered ready to take over the practice. Tomoyuki was a bright boy but he had never been as academic as his brother and showed no desire to go into medicine. His mother, who claimed descent from samurai whose seventeenth-century castle still stood on Shikoku, persuaded his father to send him to a military school in Kochi. It was one of those establishments where the curriculum was almost equally divided between the parade ground, the martial arts and lessons but, as his mother suspected he would, her tall and well-built youngest son thrived on it. Before long there was no question about his chosen career.

And yet, through no fault of his own, Yamashita was on the nursery slopes of middle age before he heard his first shots fired in action, as a major-general commanding a division in China. Unlike Percival, he saw no action whatsoever as a junior officer, was never wounded and is highly unlikely ever to have killed anybody. During the Boxer Uprising in China in 1900, when Japanese troops fought alongside the European contingents in Peking, he was a teenaged cadet at an officers' academy in Hiroshima. In 1904, while some of his contemporaries were making names for themselves at Port Arthur and the other battlefields of Japan's war with Czarist Russia, Yamashita had been selected to attend the Central Military Academy in Tokyo where he learned his first German from Prussian instructors. He showed an aptitude for languages and also acquired some French.

He was commissioned into an infantry regiment on garrison duty in Hiroshima. Here he would eventually display enough self-discipline to forgo the pleasures of carousing around the geisha houses with his brother officers and start cramming for the highly competitive Staff College entrance examination to gain a place on the three-year course that was the gateway to high rank. He was thirty-two when he graduated, sixth out of a class of fifty-six officers and awarded an Emperor's sword. Part of his celebration was his marriage to Hisako, the tall, slim daughter of a retired general he had met at a party at his brother's Tokyo home.

Some found his choice puzzling. It was not that the elegant Hisako, with a height to match his own, was anything other than entirely presentable. But since it did not appear to be a love match, rare at any level of Japanese society in those days, his rejection of 'cold-blooded proposals' to marry the equally presentable daughters of serving generals, men more likely to further his career, seemed pointless. Undoubtedly Yamashita had a stubborn streak as well as a growing awareness of his own abilities and, perhaps, an awareness that if he accepted favours from an influential father-in-law he might be expected to reciprocate.

A year after he and Hisako had sealed their vows with the traditional three sips each from three lacquered cups of rice wine blessed by a Shinto priest and proffered by a temple virgin, Yamashita was sent to Europe for the first time as assistant military attaché at the Japanese embassy in Berne. Serving as the attaché was Tojo, who had a year's seniority on him. This was the first time Yamashita had worked under him and they got on well together. It was 1919, World War I had just ended and they spent a lot of their time touring the recently silenced battle grounds of the Western Front.

In 1922 he returned to Tokyo and to Hisako, who had been living with her parents. How much they had seen of each other during his time in Europe is unclear; presumably there would have been some home leave. But even by the standards of that generation of officer-class Japanese, who could usually make the British look thoroughly operatic when it came to a stiff upper lip, their relationship seems extraordinarily constrained. She had been trained from girlhood to be the dutiful wife and he was faithful to the old code of never worrying a woman with anything of importance, even if she was the daughter of a general.

Yamashita, the military bureaucrat who had never been to war, was consumed by his career. All his formidable energy was spent proving to his patrons that he was worthy of their trust. He worked long hours, reviving himself with frequent catnaps which were easily detectable because of his high-decibel snoring. Equally famous was his devotion to the Emperor. Every time he moved into a new office he would work out the compass direction of the imperial palace, rather as a devout Muslim seeks Mecca, then turn his desk to face it.

For the next five years he worked directly under war minister Kai Kazuhige on a plan to streamline the Japanese army by demobilizing four divisions and retiring thousands of officers to the reserve. It was not a task likely to make him many friends, and at the end of it he was rewarded by the posting to Vienna where he was the military attaché for three years. Hisako did not accompany him, though they had no children who might have made the uprooting of a family home difficult.

Their already distant relationship had been further strained by a financial disaster suffered by an entrepreneurial member of her family for whom Yamashita had been persuaded to provide bank guarantees, putting up his Tokyo house as collateral. But the business, which made thermometers for the army and other clients, went bust and Yamashita was told that, unless he could repay the loans, impossible on a major's salary, he would lose his house. For most people this would be a crisis. For an officer of the Imperial Japanese Army it constituted unendurable loss of face and Yamashita was on the brink of resigning his commission when his brother came to the rescue, somehow raised the funds, and saw to it that he took up his posting abroad.

Vienna in the late 1920s was an exciting and volatile place, teetering on the brink of full-scale civil war. By day there was often gunfire in its broad streets as the fascist Heimwehr Freikorps and socialist Schutzbund shot it out. After dark, unless a curfew had been imposed and sometimes even when it had, there were the cabarets and a captivating *demi-monde*. The lady answered to the name of Kitty and, like Hisako, was the daughter of a general. That, apart from Tomoyuki Yamashita, was probably about all they had in common. He met her at the home of the Japanese widow of an Austrian writer who fed him his favourite sweet rice cakes with red bean paste. In a traditional Japanese marriage, only the woman is required to be faithful. It is expected, as elsewhere in Asia, that a married man is unlikely to be unacquainted with brothels, geisha houses and concubines. Kitty seems to have been a decade or so younger than Yamashita, now in his early forties, was German rather than Austrian and was almost certainly one of thousands of war widows living alone in Vienna. A decade after that war had ended, a revisionist examination of its horrors had started with the recent publication of Erich Maria Remarque's *All Quiet on the Western Front*. Together with her friend the Japanese widow, Kitty seems to have introduced her modern samurai to what he must have regarded as a very bohemian crowd. 'Before Vienna I knew little of the world outside the military life,' he would recall. 'There I read many books and met many good and interesting people who became friends of mine.'

Yamashita left Austria in August 1930 after three and a half years there. It is hard to say how much this interlude changed him but perhaps Tsuji was right to suspect undue foreign influence, even the occasional 'incorrect thought'. He did not see Kitty again, for what would turn out to be their final meeting, until the summer of 1941 during his snatched visit to Vienna shortly before Hitler invaded Russia. 'I visited my friend the widow and in the afternoon Kitty came to see me. It was memorable.' This was the only personal entry he made in the rough diary – little more than a list of official functions – he kept during his five months in Germany.

It was a decade since they had last met and though their passion might have been easily rekindled, the camouflaged grey hairs were not the only changes invisible to the naked eye. Yamashita was now a lieutenant-general and one of Japan's most senior and respected soldiers. But getting there had not been easy. In February 1936 he had very nearly left the army again after he had been implicated in a *coup d'état* staged by radical young officers of the Imperial Guard who, naively perhaps, thought the Emperor would welcome them purging him of 'corrupt' government officials who had ruined the economy. One of their chief complaints was that in northern Japan farmers were so impoverished that sales of pre-pubescent girls by their own fathers to big city brothels – traditionally a last resort – had reached epidemic proportions.

Yamashita was not one of the conspirators but he had become involved in a struggle for power with Tojo, with whom he had once got on so well, and there seems little doubt that the plotters regarded him as their spiritual leader. If the Emperor had stepped aside and allowed the army to sort out its own differences, Yamashita might well have emerged at the top of the pile. But the Son of Heaven had no intention of stepping aside. On the contrary, he announced that he was prepared to lead troops against the rebels himself. The *coup* collapsed and the only solace that Yamashita could offer the ringleaders was that he would try and arrange for an imperial representative to honour their ritual suicide by disembowelment. Even this petition was denied and the palace made it plain that it was outraged at Yamashita's involvement, however remote, with the mutineers. As far as Yamashita was concerned, his career was over, but he had enough senior friends in the army to persuade him not to resign. Instead, he took banishment to Korea, a Japanese possession since 1910, as a brigade commander and, for the first time, took Hisako with him on an overseas posting.

They were based in Seoul and later she would remember it as the happiest period of their marriage. Yamashita was resigned to the likelihood that his career would end there and, outwardly, became a much more relaxed man, studying Zen Buddhism and taking up the great Japanese art of calligraphy, signing himself '*Daisen*' which means 'Giant Cedar'. But at heart he remained the Emperor's devoted workaholic and he was full of regret for the intrigue that had cast him out of imperial favour. Then, almost eighteen months after the attempted *coup* by the young Guards officers, the China war began and with it his slow rehabilitation. As a divisional commander, Yamashita demonstrated a sound tactical ability, but he was mostly noted for the enormous physical risks he ran, forever leading from the front in a manner that was rare even for a Japanese general.

In 1939, as the clock ticked towards Hitler's invasion of Poland and the start of World War II, Yamashita became involved in his first confrontation with the British. It occurred in the large northern Chinese city of Tientsin which was occupied by the Japanese apart from a small British trading concession garrisoned by a single battalion of infantry and run by a British municipal council. The Japanese army imposed a blockade and strip-searched British men and women in the street after the British authorities refused to hand over four alleged Chinese terrorists. The idea of Asian soldiers forcing British women to strip to their underclothes in public caused outrage in London and Fleet Street did not have to do much to fan the flames. The Japanese were equally incensed that, in the middle of a war zone, a European power should be maintaining a neutral pocket from which terrorists could apparently operate with impunity. When the British stalled, Yamashita – who was acting as chief of staff to the Anglophone Lieutenant-General Mashuru Homma (a former military attaché in

London) – urged his superior to demand an end to all concessions in Tientsin, something that could have been a blueprint for similar moves against Shanghai and even Hong Kong. Eventually, with Europe on the verge of war over the Danzig Corridor, the British had to climb down and leave the British ambassador in Tokyo, Sir Robert Craigie, to negotiate his way out of it as best he could. This he did with consummate skill, though at the cost of the lives of the four Chinese terrorists, and Tientsin was preserved as a British enclave for almost two more years. It left Yamashita singularly impressed with the power of British diplomacy, if not with their sense of military realities.

In July 1940 Yamashita's supporters in the War Office persuaded the Emperor to let him succeed Tojo, who had just been made war minister, as superintendent of aviation – the man in charge of the army's warplanes. But he had hardly started in the job before he was chosen to lead the mission to Germany and Italy. The mission spent almost six months in Europe and Yamashita had returned, shortly before the Wehrmacht's invasion of Russia, a convinced modernizer. He was certain that Japan would not be ready to wage a major war against the Anglo-Americans for another two years, arguing the necessity for better aircraft, tanks and artillery as well as the industrial capacity to keep them coming. This was exactly what Tojo did not want to hear, any more than he wanted to hear Yamashita's opinion of the Führer, 'more like a bank clerk when I had a talk to him face to face'. Much more to Tojo's liking was Yamashita's conclusion that it was now clearly impossible for the British to defeat Germany and that ultimately British resistance would cease. What better time to strike?

Japanese negotiators were still talking in Washington but, barring a last-minute decision by the Americans to lift the oil embargo, Tokyo intended to launch almost simultaneous attacks over a seven-hour period on Malaya, the US Navy's Pacific Fleet anchorage at Pearl Harbor in Hawaii, the Philippines, Hong Kong and the Pacific islands of Wake and Guam, more or less in that order. Operations in Burma were due to start about a week later.

Because it was considered likely that British Malaya would be the toughest nut of all, two of the four divisions Yamashita had been allotted were probably the best the Imperial Japanese Army had. The 5th and the 18th Divisions had a backbone of battle-hardened veterans who had fought both the Russians and the Chinese. They had now left the Chinese mainland and were on the offshore island of Hainan, where transport ships were being gathered at the port of Timah on the island's southern tip. His third division was the aristocratic Lieutenant-General Nishimura's Imperial Guards. Like Britain's guardsmen, Nishimura's men were selected for their height and general physique, but there the resemblance ended for they had not been given the chance to acquire the consistent reputation for dogged fighting of their British counterparts. The Guards had last seen action against Czarist Russia almost forty years before. They had no recent experience of war and, almost inevitably, they had come to be regarded as chocolate-box soldiers, military confectionery for state occasions. Nishimura and most of his officers were anxious to prove otherwise, but even Tsuji, who warmed to Nishimura because he was a Tojo man, thought the Guards badly trained and wondered if they were up to the job.

Yamashita's fourth division, the 56th, was still in Japan and, for the moment at least, it was staying there. It is an unusual general who does not take all he can get and Yamashita's reasons for leaving it behind were mixed. One was that he thought it would prove a great strain on his logistics to have four divisions on his ration strength, all dependent on a long and vulnerable line of communications. The other was that he had the confidence to do without it. Yamashita was too good a soldier to commit the cardinal sin of underestimating the enemy, but the intelligence reports he had received from Tsuji and his people had convinced him that he had enough to take on Percival's heterogeneous collection of raw Indian colonial troops, swaggering Australians who for the most part had yet to see any action, and a few battalions of UK British infantry. It also helped to know that he had over 200 medium and light tanks, whereas the British had none unless you counted their infantry's Bren gun carriers – small, open-topped, lightly armoured, tracked vehicles equipped with nothing heavier than an anti-tank rifle or their eponymous light machine-gun. To repair the demolished bridges his tanks would have to cross there was a large detachment of engineers. All of them would work under an umbrella of aircraft that were believed to outnumber British aircraft by at least four to one. Between them, the 3rd Army Air Group and the 22nd Naval Air Flotilla could put 600 aircraft into the air. And unless the British had secretly managed to move some Spitfires to Malaya, they did not have a fighter to match the Zero.

Yamashita had been told that he must take Singapore within 100 days so his formations could be used elsewhere, but it was not going to be easy. Even though their best troops and equipment were concentrated in Europe and the Middle East, the British could still be cunning and were quite capable of mounting some nasty surprises. Certainly, nothing could be taken for granted and, this being the case, Yamashita might have wished to be going to war with a more congenial set of fellow officers. He was not on good terms with the ambitious Nishimura and his relations with Field-Marshal Count Terauchi, the commander of all the southern armies, who also had his HQ in Saigon, left a lot to be desired. Even in his own headquarters, Yamashita suspected that Tsuji was a spy for Tojo, storing up anything that could be used against him for the prime minister's office. None the less, he regarded him as an excellent planning officer. Every senior officer he knew found Tsuji difficult and he was determined to get the best out of him.

Percival also had difficulties with subordinates. His relations with Heath remained cordial enough – after all he had allowed his wife to stay – but the older man sometimes found it hard to conceal his awareness that he had more experience of field command. Bennett rarely bothered to disguise his feelings and could be quick to take offence, resenting attempts to reduce the Australian meat ration to the same level as that of the British and Indian troops, or to ensure that War Office strictures were observed and troops required to pay a nominal amount towards transport costs for sports fixtures or trips to the beach. 'It is the policy of the AIF to maintain health and morale at government expense,' snorted Bennett. When the Canberra-based Australian chief of staff General Sturdee visited Malaya, he sensed that things were not as they should be and, pointing out that Bennett was 'very senior', suggested he should be replaced by an 'energetic junior commander'. Nothing came of it.

Nor was the civilian side of affairs as happy as it should have been. The already complex military and civil hierarchy had been complicated by the arrival of the Duff Coopers. Governor Sir Shenton Thomas considered the politician, who had recently been minister of information and was quite close to Churchill, 'a snooper' and possibly after his job. On the surface their relations were friendly enough, but Thomas soon came to detest Duff Cooper, who was all the things, good and bad, he was not: clever, witty, well-connected, a highly decorated hero of the trenches, determinedly bibulous if rarely an incapable drunk, and a compulsive womanizer, even though mere passion never overrode his enduring love for Diana. Thomas, a bit of a dull dog but an honourable civil servant, saw only mendacity and moral turpitude.

Much more to the governor's taste was the amiable Brooke-Popham. Unfortunately, Brooke-Popham's stint as Commander-in-Chief Far East was almost over. He was about to be replaced by a soldier, General Sir Henry Pownall, who had been chief of staff to Lord Gort during the retreat to Dunkirk. At the beginning of November Churchill had given the air chief marshal notice that he was about to be deprived of his chance for a famous siege. Congratulating Brooke-Popham on the 'fine work done' and offering him a baronetcy, the prime minister had sent him a telegram saying that it was now felt his duties 'should be entrusted to an army officer with up-to-date experience'.

There had been mutterings about Brooke-Popham for some time. For irreverent junior officers he was no longer 'Brookham' but had become 'Old Pop Off' for his habit of nodding off during the interminable meetings he was required to chair. Although Duff Cooper knew the chiefs of staff had decided to replace the air chief marshal, this did not stop him from putting the boot in. Shortly after he arrived he had sent a message to London saying that he found Brooke-Popham 'damned near gaga'.

This was not only cruel but untrue. Brooke-Popham's main fault seems to have been that he lacked a politician's ruthlessness. He was too old to play the role of the regional commander selfishly determined to get the very best for his theatre of operations at the expense of others. He was reasonableness personified, unwilling to make a fuss, all too aware that Whitehall must juggle with finite resources and treat each case on its merits. 'We can get on alright with Buffaloes out here,' he had informed the chiefs of staff shortly after he arrived. 'Let England have the super-Spitfires and the hyper-Hurricanes. Buffaloes are quite good enough for Malaya.'

But not even Brooke-Popham could deny that London had miserably failed to meet the promised air-strength. Several of the airfields the army was guarding contained nowhere near the squadrons they were supposed to hold. The largest presence was the army, and it was only common sense that a soldier should be at the top.

Even so, General Pownall was not due to arrive in Singapore until 23 December; meanwhile a demoralized and crestfallen Brooke-Popham was still in charge. It was a humiliating position. It looked as if a shooting war was about to start at any moment, yet no matter how well he did, he would be replaced and required to leave Singapore. Along Pall Mall's clubs the gossip would be that he could not stand the pace, had gone to pieces and had to be relieved of his command. If he was to salvage his reputation the best he could hope for was that Pownall would replace him before the shooting started; even better, that it would not start at all and he would bid farewell to a backwater and return to England and the real war. But the signals from the various intelligence agencies that crossed his desk offered no comfort whatsoever.

Reports continued of the build-up of Japanese troops on Hainan Island, of their aircraft in southern Indo-China, and of their warships in the South China Sea. From Saigon, Edward Meiklereid, the British acting consul-general accredited to the Vichy authorities, sent a message that a local French commercial printing firm had been given a 4-foot square map of Malaya with Japanese characters and asked to make 50,000 copies. They had also received another lucrative order to print copies of a pocket book Japanese–Malay dictionary.

PART TWO

# The Bloody Beaches of Kota Baharu

Big and small, and sometimes highly secret, the portents for imminent war in South-east Asia were increasing. Some were only visible because Washington, recognizing mutual interests in the region, had decided to share with the British its greatest peace-time intelligence triumph. For well over a year, American code-breakers had been able to read the changing codes of Japanese diplomatic traffic by working out how it was encrypted and then building a machine which reverted it. Two of these machines had been given to the British. One was at the decrypting centre at Bletchley Park just outside London, which sent the results to the War Office under the code name Ultra, and the other was at Fort Canning in Singapore. The Americans called the material their wonderful machine produced MAGIC and the Japanese never did discover that they were under its spell.

On 2 December, Brooke-Popham was shown an intercepted tele-gram to Tokyo from Japan's ambassador in Bangkok in which he reported that the pro-Japanese faction within the Thai government had urged that Japan make its initial landing at Kota Baharu. This, it was argued, would provoke the British into invading southern Thailand to prevent landings on the Kra Isthmus and give Thailand the chance to call for Japanese help to eject the western aggressors.

Meanwhile, it had been learned that Giani Pritam Singh, a virulently anti-British Sikh missionary who had lived in Japan for several years, had been allowed to establish an office of his Indian Independence League in Bangkok. He was well funded and was preparing propaganda aimed not only at Indian Army sepoys, but also the Indian population of Malaya as a whole. The Sikh was one of the protégés of Major Fujiwara Iwaichi, an intelligence officer who, like Tsuji, firmly believed that it was Japan's destiny to free Asia from its colonial bonds. His speciality was Indian independence movements and he brought the fervour of the true believer to his work.

On 3 December, thanks to the MAGIC emanating from Bletchley Park, Brooke-Popham was informed that the Japanese embassy in London had been given an order they were only likely to receive if

Tokyo believed Japan was on the verge of hostilities. They had been told to prepare to destroy their (happily useless) cypher machine.

Japanese plans for the invasion of Malaya were now well advanced. As a first step, on 25 November General Yamashita left Saigon and moved away from his objective by going not south but north to the Chinese island of Hainan in the Gulf of Tongkin where Vietnam meets China. Hainan had been under Japanese occupation for two years and was well out of range of British reconnaissance aircraft. Here, in the natural harbour of Samah, a great fleet was being assembled.

Yamashita stayed at the Golden Night Hotel, which was Japanese-run and popular with the officers of the Imperial Navy. Like many Asian hotels of its day it doubled as a brothel, with forty young prostitutes available for male guests. In the Japanese way, the Madam paid him the compliment of sending him her own teenage daughter dressed in her best kimono with the message, 'I have ordered her to do anything you want.' Yamashita asked one of his staff to remove her. 'She's a victim,' he told him. He confided to his diary that he was beginning to feel his age. 'I'm fifty-six years old and I find I cannot write without my glasses,' he wrote in his careful hand.

On 4 December the Japanese transport ships, crammed with the men and equipment of the 5th and 18th Divisions, began to move out of Samah and head south. Ambassador Nomura Kichisaburo's delegation was still talking in Washington, and all it would have taken to send them back was a single code word – that, and the rewriting of a century or so of Japanese history.

Yamashita and Tsuji, along with the rest of 25th Army HQ, were aboard an amphibious landing vessel called the *Ryujo Maru*, which meant 'The Dragon and the Castle'. It looked like an aircraft carrier and was the mother-ship for about thirty landing-craft. By rights they should have been on the *Kashii Maru*, a 10,000-ton former luxury liner which once plied the European and American routes. But the veterans at 5th Division HQ, who had made several amphibious landings along the China coast and were well acquainted with conditions aboard the Imperial Navy's landing-craft carriers, persuaded Tsuji that the *Ryujo Maru* was more suitable because it had better radio communications. They would make do with the converted liner. In any case, it was rarely difficult to make the little colonel wear a hair shirt.

The *Ryujo Maru* was a pig of a ship, where troops lay inches apart in appalling accommodation, and all ranks were served a daily ration of boiled rice, barley and bean-paste soup. For many on board the dreadful food soon became the least of their problems. In even moderate seas, the top-heavy *Ryujo Maru* bobbed like the bucket she was; Tsuji was among the fortunate few who were spared sea-sickness. Yamashita was quite stoical about it all but some of his aides were less forgiving towards the little colonel, who accepted both hardship and wrath with the same relish as he tucked into his rations, not forgetting to add a little pickled radish.

On 5 December 1941, Brooke-Popham was at last given permission by London to launch Operation Matador, the forward defence into Thailand, providing he had 'good information that a Japanese expedition is advancing with the apparent intention of landing on the Kra Isthmus'. But for the commander-in-chief all had changed. He was working out his notice and the free hand he had once yearned for was no longer welcome. What if he got it wrong? The plot sketched out in the intercepted cable from the Japanese ambassador to Thailand was probably typical of the feints he could expect. What if he committed Britain to a conflict they had desperately sought to avoid while the Americans were still sitting it out like good neutrals? It could be one of the worst mistakes of the war. He might never be forgiven.

The weather, too, was making it easier to do nothing as rash as slip the safety catch on Operation Matador. Yamashita and his staff had prayed for bad weather and their prayers had been answered. For two days a storm, almost a typhoon, had made flying impossible. Then, on 6 December, the day after Brooke-Popham had been given permission to go ahead if he thought Matador appropriate, the dawn broke bright and clear with hardly a cloud in the sky.

Shortly after noon, two of three Australian-manned Lockheed Hudsons, which had managed to lumber into the air from a still waterlogged runway at Kota Baharu, made separate sightings of two Japanese convoys headed in a westerly direction towards either the Thai or Malayan coasts. In all, the Hudson crews thought they had seen about seventy vessels, warships and transports. Within a matter of hours John G. Winant, the US ambassador in London, had been informed and sent a 'triple priority most urgent' message to the White House informing President Roosevelt that the Japanese appeared to be on the brink of going to war with the British. Then the Hudsons lost the ships.

This was no fault of their crews. One of the Australian pilots had asked to shadow the largest convoy until relieved by an aircraft with fuller tanks, but was told not to risk running out of fuel and to return to Kota Baharu via his designated search route. It has been alleged that this was the decision of an RAF wing commander of advanced years, at least by the youthful standards of the Australian crews, who was mindful of the steady attrition, through accidents, of the few aircraft Pulford had. Between January and September 1941, Far East Command suffered 67 crashes resulting in 48 deaths, 22 write-offs and 31 aircraft seriously damaged. And it usually took weeks for replacement aircraft to arrive.*

Whatever the reason, this was no time for caution. It was a serious error, compounded by the weather turning nasty again with rain and thick, low cloud, so that even when the Hudsons could get back into the air they could see very little. Brooke-Popham now had no idea where these ships were or any clue as to their intentions. If the Japanese had listened to their Thai friends it was even possible that they were meant to be seen, to lure him into crossing the Thai border. Meanwhile, they might be planning to land behind them on the lower part of the east coast, say in the Endau–Mersing area where the Australians were, and to move directly on towards Johore and Singapore. Or, for all he knew, mischief done, they might be heading back towards their bases in Indo-China.

A brand new Australian-built Beaufort joined in the search, one of six of these twin-engined torpedo bombers and reconnaissance aircraft delivered only a couple of weeks before and intended as the first batch of replacements for the old Vickers Vildebeest biplanes. Then somebody had broken the heart of the torpedo bomber squadron by deciding that, with the prospect of a shooting war imminent, this was no time for aircrews to fast-track into the 1940s and convert to Beauforts, which in any case needed an enormous number of modifications before they could be considered operational. It would take weeks to learn how to handle them properly and, for the moment, it would be best to stick to the old familiar stringbags.

---

* Inexperienced aircrews were blamed. But the worst series of accidents occurred when a decorated squadron leader flying a Blenheim, who was demonstrating to a fighter-pilot passenger that his light bomber was as agile as a Buffalo, collided with two other Blenheims. These aircraft got down safely but the squadron leader's spun into the sea. All three on board were killed – the fighter pilot when his parachute failed to open. An RAF launch, taking a party of ground crew on a day's outing, was rushing to the scene when it hit a British mine. This brought the day's fatalities to twenty-four.

So all but one of the Beauforts, which was retained specifically for photo-reconnaissance, were flown back to Australia out of harm's way. This Beaufort was now ordered to investigate the anchorage at Kas Kong Island, which was just off the coast at the point where the Cambodian part of French Indo-China meets Thailand. It was probably the most advanced aircraft the British had in Malaya, but it could not defeat the weather and RAF Flight Lieutenant Peter Mitchell turned back to Kota Baharu.

Then it became apparent that a Catalina flying boat of the RAF's 205 Squadron based in Singapore, which had been searching an area a little to the east of Mitchell's Beaufort just south of Phuquoc Island where Tsuji had built his advanced landing strip, was long overdue. The aircraft had been out of radio contact for some time. Yet the twin-engined Catalina, the Consolidated PBY-5 to the Americans who built it, had a wonderful reputation for reliability and, with a range of 4,000 miles, also endurance. It seemed unlikely that the weather had brought it down. Of course, the explanation for the Catalina's disappearance was exactly what the RAF suspected it was. The game of hide and seek was over. Flying Officer Edwin Beddell and his seven-man crew had become the first casualties of Japan's war with the Anglo-Americans.

First the Catalina had been bounced by a catapult-launched float plane from a Japanese warship which, coming up behind and below the flying boat, got in a short burst. This appears to have fatally damaged its radio or its operator, perhaps both, for there is no other plausible explanation as to why it did not signal that it was under attack. Then it was finished off by a flight of five Ki 27s, the fighter that had been Japan's mainstay in the China war.

The Ki 27 was a slow though manoeuvrable monoplane with a fixed 'wheels down' undercarriage, which would shortly be superseded by the high-speed acrobatics of the Zero. Its appearance was one of the reasons the British had remained complacent about Japanese air power. The Catalina had three air gunners, but the Ki 27s were more than adequate to shoot it down as their own account makes clear.

Corporal Fujimoto and Corporal Yoshida attacked from the rear while Sergeant Sato attacked from the side bathing it in ferocious fire. The enemy aircraft exploded at 400 metres . . .

For a few seconds its blazing wreckage flickered on the surface of the turquoise waters below, then that too was gone. There were no survivors.

This was about 8.30 a.m. on Sunday 7 December. At Pearl Harbor, on the other side of the international dateline, it was still Saturday 6 December. It would be almost another ten hours before Yamamoto's dive bombers were over the American battleships. At 3.45 p.m. that Malayan Sunday afternoon a Hudson located one of the Japanese ships again, well north of Kota Baharu, with a huddle of khaki-clad men visible on deck. In the same area, another Hudson was fired on by a Japanese cruiser but, despite some slight damage, managed to dodge into cloud and escape.

There was no real doubt which way things were going. All troops were put on full alert and only the administrative headquarters remained in the bunker at Fort Canning. Percival and his operational staff were at the new combined Army and Air Force HQ at Sime Road near the golf club and a good 3 miles out of town. At first Percival was 'a little surprised' that Matador had not been launched, but then he learned that it appeared likely that the two big convoys were following a smaller one north-west towards the island of Kas Kong, the good anchorage 20 miles off Thailand's frontier with French-controlled Cambodia. In view of the official policy of avoiding a war with Japan at all costs, Percival agreed it was probably in their best interest to take no action. By Sunday afternoon he was even beginning to wonder whether he had allowed himself to accept the idea that war was imminent too easily, and whether these convoys were 'only a demonstration against Thailand'.

Sir Robert Brooke-Popham was in no doubt that this was the case. The air chief marshal had already called Jimmie Glover, managing editor of the *Malay Tribune* newspaper group, to remonstrate about the front-page splash in that morning's *Sunday Tribune*, which had led on a Reuters report, cleared by the censor, of Japanese transports and warships off Cambodia Point and speculated that this looked like war. 'It was most improper to print such alarmist news,' Sir Robert had told Glover, adding that things were not half as bad as his newspaper was making out. Most of the *Tribune*'s readers were Asians, its cover price being half that of its main English-language rival, the *Straits Times*. The editor stood by his story and went into the office to read the comment coming over the wires as the news agencies picked up the first Fleet

Street editions. 'Why, if Japan's intentions are honourable and peaceful, does she send twenty-seven transports, heavily laden with troops, even to Siam?' demanded the *Sunday Times*.

Then, as was his habit on Sundays, Glover adjourned to the Tanglin Club where the squash courts emitted their usual thwacking sounds while both the pool and the bar were filling up. Glover noticed, with a bit of a twinge, that few of the civilians sipping their drinks at the bar were talking about the prospects of war. Was it possible Brooke-Popham was right? He was a scaremonger? The editor consoled himself with the thought that the only time he recalled hearing its business members become animated over Japanese intentions was during their heated opposition to Sir Shenton Thomas's proposal to introduce a mild form of local income tax as a contribution towards defence spending.

At 5.50 p.m. a Hudson reported that it had been fired at by what looked like a Japanese cruiser. At 6.48 p.m. another Hudson spotted four small Japanese vessels, possibly destroyers, about 70 miles off Thailand's Kra Isthmus and heading south towards Malaya. As the reports came in, Percival was reminded of the tensions that went with school sports days: 'We were all ready waiting for the flag to fall, and like runners in a race, feeling a bit impatient.'

But not impatient to implement Operation Matador; Percival had decided that the moment had gone. The whole point was to have advanced into Thailand and be dug in on the beach at Singora waiting for the Japanese; but that required a twenty-four-hour start over the enemy and, between Brooke-Popham's cautiousness and losing sight of the convoys for almost thirty hours, the opportunity had been lost. The flag had fallen but not all the runners had left their starting blocks.

Despite its many portents, war came as a shock to Singapore, even to those Cassandras whose predictions had so got under the skin of Brooke-Popham and others. Jimmie Glover, the editor, was dreaming about Barden Ridge, the American-style weatherboard bungalow he and his wife had had built in the Malayan Peninsula's Cameron Highlands, which had only been completed the previous month. Unable to get back home for the long leaves considered necessary for whites working in the tropics, because of the U-boats and the shipping shortage, in the last year many of the British had invested in weekend homes in the almost temperate climes of this hill station with its butterflies

and tea plantations. Barden Ridge was higher than most people wanted
to go but Glover and his French wife Julienne had chosen a plot there
to get away from the herd, fearing that, as the European war dragged
on, a rash of suburban tropical tudor would spread across the foothills.

The Glovers' Singapore home was Dulverton, a late Victorian building in the city's Holland Park district with 2 acres of grounds, including
a tennis court. They had lived in it for ten of the fourteen years they
had been in Malaya and its teak-panelled rooms were packed with the
mahogany furniture and the art they had collected. Jimmie was now
forty-three and, dearly though they loved Dulverton, when he retired
they intended to take their beloved dogs and live at Barden Ridge all
year round.

In his dream, Glover had been putting some finishing touches to
the panelling in the dining room and then decided to spend the night
on the couch in front of the log fire rather than go down to the Green
Cow Tavern in preparation for the morning train to Singapore. It was
raining heavily and the wind was building up. One of the drawbacks
of Barden Ridge were the gales which howled in across the Malacca
Straits, known locally as Sumatras since this is where they started.
Glover hated storms. He had inherited a fear of thunder and lightning
from his mother and she had never been far enough away from their
native Yorkshire to have to put up with anything like the earth-jolting,
sky-splitting tropical spectaculars Malaya could lay on. Gross tentacles
of forked lightning lit up his dream, followed by the most terrifying
thunderclap Glover had ever heard. At which point, and to his considerable relief, he woke up back in his comfortable bed at Dulverton.
The bedroom clock on the chimneypiece, which was always at least
five minutes fast, told him it was 4.17 a.m. and Julienne was trying to
tell him they were being bombed. There were more explosions, the
first crackle of anti-aircraft fire and, through their bedroom window,
they could see searchlights wobbling about a sky that was already well
lit by the moon.

Then, somewhat belatedly, came the sound of the siren. 'Rising and
falling, rising and falling, it cut across the stillness of the tropic night
like some frightful oath uttered in a polite drawing room,' recalled Ian
Morrison, who was about to become *The Times*' South-east Asian
correspondent but at that time was still working for the government
as deputy director of the Far Eastern Bureau of the Ministry of Information. One of the perks of the job was that Morrison and his young

wife Maria lived just above his office in one of the top-floor flats in the Cathay Building, Singapore's only real skyscraper, with its stupendous view of the city. He pulled back the curtains and noticed that, for all their exercises, the civil defence people had not got the street lights switched off and enforced a blackout. They could distinctly hear the drone of aircraft overhead and then came a series of bright flashes as a stick of bombs landed somewhere near the centre of town, then more in the direction of the docks.

Here they woke up engine-room artificer Bill Reeve who had been asleep on a stretcher laid out on the upper deck of His Majesty's Australian Ship *Vendetta*, a small and fairly fast destroyer launched in England in 1917 and one of five of its class transferred to the Australian navy in the early 1930s. *Vendetta*, which had just had its John Brown turbines removed and transported to the workshops at the naval base for a major overhaul, was a veteran of Admiral Cunningham's bloody Mediterranean battles against the Italian fleet and the German air force. Among other things, she had been the star of the 'bombers' alley' run from Alexandria to beleaguered Tobruk, holding the record of thirty-nine round-trips bringing in men and munitions and taking out the wounded. As it happened, the battered Libyan port, where the Australian infantry had played such a big role until their government insisted they were replaced by British troops, had been relieved only a few hours before the bombs started to fall on Singapore after a siege of 242 days – the longest in the history of the British Army. But the news had yet to reach Reeve and the other five men left aboard the destroyers as a 'care and maintenance' party. And when it did it would be so eclipsed by the magnitude of more local events they would hardly register it.

Reeve and his shipmates had been in almost continuous action since hostilities started in the Mediterranean some eighteen months before. They had lost some good friends and were looking forward to a long home leave before they got back into the war. When the familiar whistle and explosion of the bombs began to seep into his consciousness the young artificer thought he was having a bad dream about the Med. 'I said to myself, "You silly bastard, roll over." And then there was this particularly loud bang and I realized that you don't get sounds like that in dreams.'

Nearby the troop ship and former Orient liner *Orion* was having her bow repaired after expensively scraping some paint off the armoured hull of the battle cruiser *Repulse* in the Indian Ocean. Under the glare of floodlights, repairs on the *Orion*'s more substantial wound were going on around the clock. Then, once again, came the crunch of bombs and off went the floodlights but not the street lamps. Reeve had noticed that the electricity company had a sub-station on the quay. He and a couple of others from the crew dashed across the gang-plank, lit up by the flash of the bombs, found the door open and joined some British sailors who were already desperately flicking switches and pulling levers. Eventually somebody chanced on the main switch for all the power in the docks. But this was a mixed blessing because some of the fire-fighting tenders had pumps that were electric powered. Meanwhile, the local street lights shone insubordinately on. It turned out that they were gas lamps and the night watchman who held the key to the gas supply had disappeared.

Glover was utterly amazed at the amount of lights on. Accompanied by his wife, who refused to stay home alone in case she was joined by a Japanese parachutist, he had set out for the *Tribune* office to bring out a special edition. As he drove, the editor was baffled by the absence of a blackout. The new law courts were still proudly illuminated. So were the four faces of the tower clock in the Victoria Memorial Hall, a convenient beacon, he thought, for any Japanese aircrews who might have lost their way.

To attack Singapore the Japanese navy's land-based Mitsubishi twin-engined, twin-tailed Nell bombers had flown through heavy rain some 600 miles across the Gulf of Thailand from Thus Dau Moi airfield north of Saigon. It was a round-trip of almost 1,400 miles and, with full bomb load, as much at the edge of their range as Tsuji's reconnaissance flight in his Dinah. The weather was so filthy that the wing initially ordered to make the attack, the Genzan Ku, which consisted of thirty-four aircraft, had eventually all turned back. Three hours later, while the Genzan Ku endured the loss of face even the most blameless setback could visit on the tender psyche of the Japanese warrior, the task was given to Lieutenant-Commander Yagoro Shibata's Mihoru Ku. Shibata got thirty-one Nells into the air but, by the time they reached Malaya's east coast, fourteen had found the headwinds too much, dropped their bombs into the sea and turned back.

At 3.30 a.m. the approach of the remaining seventeen was plotted at Mersing on the east coast by one of Malaya's few examples of Radio Direction Finding, the detecting system shortly to be known as radar which had helped win the Battle of Britain. The Mersing station, which was housed in a wooden hut surrounded by protective earthworks, was part of a projected network of ten that recently arrived RAF technicians were in the process of installing. From there a warning was radioed back to an RAF communications centre established on the roof of the Cathay Building, below which Ian Morrison and his wife would sleep peacefully on for another half hour or so. The communications centre alerted the RAF at Kallang airfield where the intruders were plotted on a large table map. But the news was not immediately passed on to the Air-Raid Precautions HQ, whose director had been asking for some time for the authority to impose a blackout without first referring to the army.

By this time all the key players in Singapore had been fully aware for the last three hours that Britain was at war with Japan. At about 1 a.m. Brooke-Popham, Percival and Air Vice-Marshal Pulford had all been informed that Japanese ships were off Kota Baharu; shortly afterwards they heard that the beach defences were under shell-fire, and then that landings were taking place. A couple of hours later Duff and Diana Cooper were wakened by an aide who put his head around their bedroom door to announce that the Japs had landed on the northern coast of Malaya. The Coopers, veterans of the recent London Blitz, went back to sleep, 'only to be aroused once more by the familiar sound of falling bombs, followed by explosions, followed by guns and finally by air-raid warnings'.

At Government House, Sir Shenton responded to the news of the Kota Baharu landings by calling the police and ordering the implementation of Operation Collar and Trousers – the rounding up of all Japanese nationals in the colony and the seizure of their assets, particularly the remaining boats of the Japanese fishing fleet. Harvey Ryves, a young policeman at Kuala Kangsar in the northern state of Perak, was appalled to witness one of his senior officers haggling furiously with one of three Japanese shopkeepers they were arresting over a doll he wanted to buy for his daughter. Eventually he got it for one Malayan dollar. Also on the list was Suermasa Okomoto, the Japanese consul-general, who was due to be among the governor's lunch guests in a few hours' time.

Thomas had not ordered a blackout because the military did not advise one. The alarm was about Japanese ships off the east coast of Thailand and Malaya. As far as the governor was concerned, the nearest

Japanese bombers could be no less than 600 miles away in Indo-China. It was up to the RAF to advise him that the enemy possessed aircraft with the range to bomb Singapore from there. They should have been aware of it. In operations over China three years before, Nells flying from bases in Japan and Formosa had made similar long-distance strikes against targets in Nanking and Hankow.

The first inkling the governor had that Singapore was threatened was at 4 a.m. when, some thirty minutes after the Mersing radar had picked them up, Air Vice-Marshal Pulford thought to warn him about the approach of hostile aircraft. 'I asked how far and he said 25 miles,' Thomas noted in his diary. He just managed to get through the ponderous business of placing calls through a manual switchboard to the Harbour Board and the HQ of Air-Raid Precautions when the aircraft were over them. 'Brilliant moon and we had all our lights on,' the governor recalled.

One lot went for the [naval] base area and had lots of wild anti-aircraft fire. The other, about five to six machines, dropped bombs in Raffles Square, near the Chinese Protectorate, in the water, and towards harbour. All over in a few minutes. No fires but about 60 killed and over 100 injured.

Most of the casualties were Chinese. The rest were mainly a few Sikh night watchmen who had been guarding the shops and restaurants around Raffles Square. The naval architect 'Steepy' Stapledon and his wife Kathleen were among those who were awakened by the noise but went back to sleep when, 'seeing the street lights still full on, we thought it could only be a practice'. The night before, Dr Lakshmi Swaminadhan's conviction that war was imminent had been confirmed at the cinema when a message was suddenly flashed on the screen ordering all servicemen to report to their units immediately – a result of the heightened state of alert after the first sighting of the Japanese convoys. But when the first explosions brought her and her partner rushing out on their veranda a passing air-raid warden assured them it was a practice. An English woman, living in a city centre flat above the dress shop she owned, received the same answer when she called the police to ask them if they were aware than an air raid was going on: 'If it's a practice they're overdoing it,' she snapped. 'Guthrie's office opposite is destroyed.' Then the line went dead.

The Reverend Jack Bennitt and his wife Nora, who had felt so guilty at being away from the war and were both Air-Raid Precaution volunteers, went with some stretchers and two Chinese St John's Ambulance men to Fisher Street, where some of the worst damage had occurred. They too had assumed that the absence of a blackout meant it must be another exercise. The sight of coolies from the Public Works Department searching for survivors trapped under the rubble of their homes and three corpses laid out in the street soon disabused them of this idea.

'As I see it, we were all caught on the hop,' admitted Shenton Thomas. He had stood with Daisy at one of the fine picture windows at Government House, sharing with her the sight of the gentle dimming of the city's gas lights, long after the drone of Mitsubishi engines had faded away. Percival agreed it was a surprise and thought it 'a bold enterprise', though he wondered whether the absence of a blackout made much difference, 'for there was no mistaking the water-front at Singapore even at night'.

Even so, among the island's Asians the raid and the reaction to it did pose the question, disturbing for some and intriguing for others, that perhaps the British were not quite as invincible as their newly arrived battleships made them appear. Yet, for all its boldness, the bombing had achieved nothing of military value. None of the island's airfields were badly hit and there was no damage to the naval base from which *Repulse* and a couple of destroyers had disappeared two days before, bound for Darwin on a visit to Australia which the crew were hoping would see them in Sydney for Christmas. When the bombers came over, the *Prince of Wales* was being fussed over in dry dock, having her thoroughbred bottom scraped to remove the various slowing vegetable and mineral accretions of a long voyage. From this rather undignified position she had added her own considerable firepower to what, over-all, had been a splendiferous if almost entirely ineffectual anti-aircraft barrage. Of the fourteen pilots who reached Singapore, only Lieutenant Yoshimi Shirai had the satisfaction of returning an aircraft to Saigon bearing the irrefutable, if slight, shrapnel scars which indicated that running out of fuel had not been the only hazard.

Undoubtedly the most frustrated fighting man on the island that night was RAF Flight Lieutenant Tim Vigors, acting commander of the mostly Australian 453 Buffalo Squadron. The bright moonlight was all too reminiscent of the conditions in which Vigors had won his DFC shooting down the German night bomber. Although few of his

pilots had done any night flying, he had his own and two other
Buffaloes standing by at Sembawang airfield and was raring to go. But
Vigors fell victim to one of the first acts of the *entente* Percival and
Pulford had established between the army and the air force. The
Buffaloes were forbidden to try to intercept because it had been decided
that night attacks would be dealt with by the army's anti-aircraft
batteries and they should not be inhibited by fears of hitting their own.
No doubt another consideration was the presence of the Royal Navy,
whose ships were notorious, in both the Mediterranean and home
waters, for the RAF scalps they had collected. When Vigors threatened
to take off anyway he was told by the station commander at Sembawang
that he would be arrested.

In northern Malaya, some of Pulford's command had been at war
two hours before the Nells appeared over Singapore. These were
the Hudsons of 1 Squadron Royal Australian Air Force under the
wavy-haired Wing Commander 'Curly' Davis. It was one of Davis's
reconnaissance patrols that had relocated the Japanese ships and been
hit by anti-aircraft fire in a wing and its tailplane for doing so. That
was at 5.50 p.m. on 7 December, almost twelve hours before the air
raid on Singapore.

The sightings were exactly what Tsuji and his planning team had
been dreading most. They were willing to submit the troops to any
amount of sea-sickness if heavy seas were the price for low and impenetrable cloud. But Brooke-Popham did not seize on a blatant attempt
to destroy one of his aircraft as enough of a *casus belli* to begin immediate air strikes against the Japanese vessels which were still hours away
from Kota Baharu. Instead, he decided that while negotiations were
still going on in Washington this might be no more than sabre rattling.
A pre-emptive strike, though tactically sound, might be strategically
disastrous. It was against all current British thinking from the arrival of
the *Prince of Wales* and *Repulse*, so ostentatiously there to prevent a war
with Japan rather than start one, to Crosby's desperate messages pleading for no incursion into southern Thailand. Perhaps, too, the war
option was a particularly difficult choice for a man towards the end
of a career which had brought distinction without ever requiring
decision-making of this level.

Wing Commander Davis had worked out that if the ships maintained
the same course they would be off Kota Baharu and inside Malaya's

territorial waters by the early hours of the morning. Then, shortly before midnight, Davis received a telephone call from Brigadier Berthold Wells Key, who commanded the mostly teenaged Indian soldiers spread somewhat thinly behind barbed wire and land mines along 30 miles or so of one of the world's most beautiful palm-fringed shore lines.

A few hours before, the brigadier had been visited at his HQ in Kota Baharu town by Bill Bangs, a British rubber planter in Ulu Kelantan and member of the local volunteer force. He spoke both Malay and Siamese. Bangs had just returned from a spying mission in southern Thailand where, among other things, he had posed as a minister of the Seventh Day Adventists until he met a real one who invited him to take the evening service at his mission hall.

The most important thing Bangs had to tell the brigadier was his discovery that some long-neglected emergency air strips around Singora and Patani had recently been cleared of undergrowth, and drums of aviation fuel had been hidden nearby. Since the small Thai air force had no need of them, it was obvious that they had been prepared for the Japanese, who would presumably secure them with troops before they started bringing aircraft in. Bangs assured the brigadier that it was highly unlikely that the Japanese would try to land that night. On his way down from the frontier, where he had narrowly avoided arrest by Thai border police, some of the biggest waves he had ever seen were crashing down on the beach. 'An enormous number would be drowned,' he told him.

But Bangs had just joined the growing ranks of those who had underestimated the Japanese. Key's call to Wing Commander Davis was to tell him he was about to open fire on three ships that had anchored off Badang Beach, the Australians' nearest bathing spot and the inevitable backcloth of many of the snapshots sent home during the preceding months.

A few minutes after Davis had spoken to Key, the unmistakable sounds of small arms fire and explosions could be heard coming from the beach, which was only a mile away from the airfield. Most of the explosions came from a couple of old 18-pounder field guns which nobody wanted and which for years had been used to fire salutes on ceremonial occasions such as the King's Birthday. In the officers' quarters, Pilot Officer Peter Gibbes,* who had arrived at Kota Baharu less than two hours before following a three-day flight from Australia

---

* Later Squadron Leader Peter Gibbes, RAAF, MVO, DFC, AFC.

and a long train journey from Singapore, was woken by the sound of doors slamming, shouting and people generally behaving in a very inconsiderate fashion. Concluding that it must be some sort of training exercise he got out of bed, stuck his head through the door and told them to pipe down. 'Get up, you silly bastard,' somebody yelled back. 'The Nips have landed on our beach.'

The Wing Commander already had six of his ten serviceable Hudsons bombed up, their machine-guns fully loaded, their fuel tanks filled and ready to go. But even Curly Davis, whose dashing good looks complete with a narrow Clark Gable moustache seemed to promise a man of action, was reluctant to start a war his superiors were obviously anxious to avoid. So was Wing Commander 'Beery' Noble, the RAF officer in overall charge of the station, as opposed to the aircraft that flew from it, who was nominally senior to Davis with whom he got on very well. Radio communications in Malaya were notoriously bad. The wattage of the sets of the day often failed to produce electromagnetic waves capable of piercing soggy jungle vegetation. While the aircrews were standing around their machines smoking cigarette after cigarette and wondering what on earth could be holding them up now, the two wing commanders were trying to place a telephone call to Air Vice-Marshal Pulford in Singapore. But there was only one secure scrambler phone available and all the senior officers, starting with Brooke-Popham, wanted to talk to either the army or the air force at Kota Baharu. A harassed military operator tried and failed to ration these calls, interrupting the speakers every three minutes to ask whether they wanted an 'extension' and getting short shrift for his pains. It had just turned 2 a.m. when Davis emerged from the operations room and dashed down the sodden runway to where Flight Lieutenant Lockwood and his crew, who happened to have been flying the Hudson fired on by the Japanese cruiser some six hours before, were waiting. 'Away you go,' said Davis. 'It's on. It's official.' By this time, some of the Japanese troops had been ashore for almost one and a half hours.

There were three purpose-built military transports anchored off the beach: the *Awagisan Maru*, the *Ayatosan Maru* and the *Sakuru Maru*. They were supported by the cruiser *Sendai* with its ten 5.5-inch guns, four destroyers, two minesweepers and what the Japanese called a submarine chaser, a small vessel with depth charges as its heaviest weapons. The transports carried a brigade group of almost 6,000 men, detached from the 18th Chrysanthemum Division under Major-General Hiroshi Takumi. Most of them were infantry but there was also a battery of four 75 mm howitzers, some heavy mortars, some anti-aircraft guns, heavy machine-guns which could also be used to give ground support, and engineers. The task of the Takumi Detachment was to capture Davis's airfield at Pengkalan Chapa, about 5 miles east of Kota Baharu town. If they failed, it was expected of Takumi that he would fail bloodily enough to divert attention from Yamashita's main landings a few miles up the coast in neutral Thailand. Colonel Tsuji had got his way.

In terms of manpower, Brigadier Key's command may have been thin on the ground; but over the last six months the beach defences that junior officers such as Prem Sahgal of 2/10 Baluch had been preparing had become quite formidable. Land mines started a few yards up the beach from the high-water mark and after them came considerable barbed-wire entanglements.

Behind the mines and the entanglements awaited the men of Key's northernmost battalion, the 3/17th Dogras. They occupied concrete pillboxes about 100 yards apart in between which were L-shaped firing dug-outs and behind them, to give defence in depth, some well dug-in nests for Bren light machine-guns. All the positions were well stocked with ammunition, food, water and medical kits. Each pillbox was garrisoned by about twelve men who had at least two and often three Brens as well as rifles, 15,000 rounds of the .303 ammunition which fitted both weapons, and 100 grenades.

There was one weak link, one gap, and Brigadier Key had done his best to shore it up. At its mouth, the Kelantan River broke up into a delta area of distributaries, lagoons, creeks and low islands that became totally submerged in full monsoon spate. One of these distributaries, the Pengkalan Chapa, had a wide mouth entered between two spits of sand, Badang and Sabak beaches, that curved towards each other rather like the claws of a crab. The river mouth was almost opposite the airfield and Key considered it the most likely landing spot. He had wanted to put a boom across it, which would prevent small craft from entering and worming their way into the labyrinth of waterways behind his lines, but his engineers had been told that the steel cable necessary to construct a boom was not available.

Key had responded to this by making the spits of sand either side of the river mouth as formidable as they could be. As well as pillboxes capable of laying down a withering crossfire, an estimated 300 miles of barbed wire had been strung. First there was what the sappers called a 'Double Apron', in section view an isosceles triangle that presented an attacking force with a 6-foot-high slope of barbed wire as well as an identical slope facing the other way. Next came a Triple Dannert barrier, concertina rolls of barbed wire about ten times nastier than a hawthorn hedge. Just behind this was another 'Double Apron'. And, only a few days before, the last of 4,000 mines had been lightly covered with the beach's fine white sand. The weakest link had been turned into a killing ground.

None the less, Key was right: Takumi was determined to insert a part of his force into the Pengkalan Chapa River. The first to arrive were some scouts in small boats, the sound of their engines muffled by the pounding of the surf that threatened to capsize them. They landed on a half-submerged islet in the river mouth and installed a lamp there which shone out to sea. The defenders did not immediately notice this and, when they did, some thought that fifth columnists must be responsible. The honour of being the first wave of infantry fell to the 11th Company of the 56th Regiment under a Captain Wadar. They approached the shore in two out of the twelve armoured landing-craft from the transports, and the first of Wadar's men hit the beach at around 12.30 a.m. They were very nearly massacred.

Either the moonlight or a mortar-launched parachute flare sufficiently illuminated one of their landing-craft for a shell from the Indians' venerable 18-pounders to score a direct hit and sink it. Many of its fifty or so occupants drowned, but a few struggled ashore to join the men of the other craft on the islet in the river mouth where the scouts had placed the navigation lamp. Here Wadar's company was subjected to the crossfire from the pillboxes on their flanks and eventually reduced to about twenty men, a fifth of its original strength though Wadar seems to have had a charmed life. He and the other survivors pressed themselves into the sand and few dared to rise high enough to return a shot, even if they could make out a target. 'We could not relax for a moment,' one of them recalled. 'Lifting the body even to a slight degree offered a vulnerable target . . . men stuck to the ground as if they were glued there.'

On the *Awagisan Maru*, Takumi and his staff were hearing for the first time in their lives the distinctive sound of British Bren guns and must have guessed by the paucity of the answering fire that all was not going well with the first wave. The general urged the navy to increase their shelling – particularly from the *Sendai*'s 8-inchers – while he tried to take advantage of the inexplicable absence of British aircraft to get himself and as many men as possible on shore as fast as he could.

This proved easier said than done. The wind was building up and the sea was getting heavier. Everybody was soaked to the skin by spray and rain. Alongside the transports the landing-craft bobbed up and down like see-saws; dropping into them from the rope ladders slung over the ships' sides was a matter of exquisite timing. At critical moments clouds scudded across the moon and the boats below were suddenly swallowed up by the darkness.

Everybody had lifejackets but if an infantryman laden with rifle and pack mistimed his jump, the chances of surfacing were not good. As they waited for their lurching craft to fill up, the men already safely aboard clung grimly to the sides and tried to convince themselves they were not feeling the unmistakable first stirrings of sea-sickness. Every time they thought they had arranged themselves into a tolerable position, more comrades clattered aboard and they had to squeeze further up the boat. *Terra firma*, whatever its dangers, was becoming an increasingly inviting prospect. Then, just as it seemed impossible for things to get any worse, Curly Davis's Hudsons at last put in an appearance.

In the space of fifteen minutes six of the bombers had taken off from Kota Baharu's single, waterlogged runway and were in action against the Japanese ships. The second aircraft into the air, commanded by Pilot Officer John Ramshaw, set the tone. Ramshaw, born in 1914 in India where his father was a British officer, made a daring attack on Takumi's command ship, the *Awagisan Maru*, using the 'skip bombing' technique pioneered by RAF light bombers at the beginning of the war in Europe. It took a lot of nerve.

The aircraft had to be flown so low that once the bombs were released they did not have the chance to start falling vertically but struck the sea at an angle, almost horizontally. This caused them to 'skip' across the water rather like flat stones thrown from a beach. Ideally, they would hole a ship's side below its waterline; second best, they would hit some of the higher parts of the vessel. The Hudsons were carrying four 250-pound bombs, two general-purpose and two armour-piercing. They were all set with eleven-second fuses that started to burn the moment they left the bomb bay. Ramshaw did not get a below-the-waterline bull's-eye, but he did score a direct hit with at least one of his bombs on the *Awagisan Maru*'s superstructure, from which a satisfying column of smoke began to rise.

For all the young Australian airmen it was their first time in action. Dressed in their shorts, shirts, knee-high socks and shoes, which made some of them look even more like overgrown schoolboys, they tore into the enemy below: bombing and then strafing, first with the pilot's machine-guns in the nose, then the rear turret, then sometimes banking so that the navigators and wireless operators could have a go with the side guns in the fuselage.

Flight Lieutenant Oscar 'Ossie' Diamond had missed with all his bombs on his first sortie against the Japanese transports and was determined to do better next time. The moon suddenly broke through the cloud and drizzle and picked out the *Ayatosan Maru*, the second-largest of the three transports. Diamond, the son of a Russian Jew whose real name was Dashevsky, made three passes at the ship. First his Hudson machine-gunned the decks and bridge with wing and rear guns; in a second attack, he dropped two of his four bombs. Then Diamond did something that, for cold-blooded nerve, was at least the equal to Ramshaw's skip bombing.

Turning into his third attack to drop his last two bombs, instead of flying as fast as he could, he confused the anti-aircraft gunners on the transport and the escorting warships by doing exactly the opposite. Suddenly the Hudson shuddered almost to a halt as Diamond put up his landing flaps; the aircraft was flying so slowly it was near to stalling and dropping out of the sky. As he passed low over the stern of the *Ayatosan Maru*, the bomb bay opened and the huge ball of flame that followed was accompanied by a blast which lifted the Hudson's tail and seemed bent on tossing it nose-first into the sea. Diamond pulled back on the stick as hard as he could and gradually the front of the aircraft came up, though no sooner had he gained height than he lost his starboard engine, obliging him to make a single-engine landing on Kota Baharu's unlit, if wet and shiny, runway.

Here it was discovered that fuselage, tailplane and wings had all been badly damaged by gunfire, and there was a piece of shrapnel in the starboard oil tank that may have come from one of their own bombs. Casualties among those troops still aboard the *Ayatosan Maru* were heavy, although her crew eventually managed to extinguish the fires the bombs had started. Diamond was awarded a Distinguished Flying Cross.

Few pilots had the nerve to make three passes at the same target. Some released all their bombs at once and beat it back to base. The enemy was so close that most of the aircraft spent no more than three or four minutes over the target, often less. Flying Officer Don Dowie, John Ramshaw's co-pilot, had lit a cigarette as he boarded their aircraft for the sortie that hit the *Awagisan Maru* and stubbed it out when he landed.

The Hudsons were virtually flying circuits and bumps as they took off, bombed, landed and were immediately rearmed in a process that seemed to work with conveyor-belt efficiency. There was no need to refuel for so little fuel was used; ground crews could hear the bombs they had just loaded explode. The armourers and fitters, soaked in oil and sweat, worked methodically, cocking an ear when they had the chance to catch what the aircrews were saying. It seemed the Japs were getting a pasting, though not without cost. The squadron's first casualty was an aircraft piloted by Flight Lieutenant 'Spider' Leighton-Jones, which had simply failed to return. Nobody had seen Jones, a popular officer with the wiry build of a jockey and a perpetual grin, go down. Later there were unconfirmed Japanese reports of a badly smoking Hudson, barely under control, which seemed to seek out a crowded landing-craft and dive into it. Several of his friends watched John Ramshaw crash. He was seen to ditch while making his second skip-bombing attack, this time on the *Sendai* which had much better anti-aircraft defences than the transports. The warship's rudder and perhaps a propeller shaft were damaged and, before long, the cruiser would limp back to Indo-China's Cam Ranh Bay for repairs.

Dowie, the co-pilot and ultimately the only survivor from the four-man crew, was never certain whether they were brought down by anti-aircraft fire or because they were too close to the blast of their own bombs. When they hit the sea, he and Ramshaw had both been thrown through the perspex roof of the cockpit and, for a while, although it was too dark and too rough to see each other, they had been close enough to talk. Then Ramshaw had announced that he didn't think he was going to make it; shortly afterwards Dowie realized he was on his own. He discovered he had little movement in his arms and legs (he had fractured his spine) and was just about being kept afloat by his half-filled Mae-West. His mouth was near the tube used to inflate the lifejacket. Dowie decided to risk removing the plug, which he eventually managed with his teeth. Inhaling was painful but he succeeded in blowing enough air into it to inflate it fully. Then somehow he managed to get the cap back on the tube too. The water was warm and he slipped in and out of consciousness. Sometimes he heard outboard motors nearby and realized he must be in the path of the small craft ferrying ashore the Japanese troops he had been bombing. Dowie half expected a bullet but no doubt their eyes were fixed on the yellow tracer and the flashes that lit up the palm-fringed shore line ahead.

Afterwards, a Japanese journalist called the Kota Baharu landings 'the Hill 203 of the Ocean'. There could be no higher praise. In 1904, Hill 203 was the Russian-held stronghold above China's Port Arthur (now Lüshun) where, in the war against the Czar, Count Nogi Maresuke had sacrificed wave after wave of infantry, among them one of his sons, until the Russians tired of killing and the hill was his.

Nogi* lost more killed than Takumi's entire command, and the only tactical similarity was that Hill 203 and Kota Baharu were both diversionary attacks. What happened to the first Japanese to step ashore in Malaya had much more in common, though again on a smaller scale, with what the American infantry would suffer some thirty months later on Normandy's Omaha beach. It was, by any standards, a sanguinary beginning to Japan's assault on South-east Asia.

For some time, the barbed-wire entanglements continued to prove insurmountable and, as they bunched up behind them, so the Japanese losses mounted. Those who tried to get away from the more obvious fixed lines of the Bren guns began to set off the land mines that had been sown in such profusion. Nearly all the battalion and company commanders were hit, though at least two were trying to continue to lead while being carried about on stretchers. Major-General Takumi managed to leave the stricken *Awagisan Maru* and get ashore with the second wave, sometime around 3 a.m., arriving with a company whose commander had been killed on deck when one of the Hudsons had strafed the ship. Within minutes of getting to the beach the officer who had succeeded him was also killed. Takumi then personally took command of this and another leaderless company and ran and crawled with them towards the wire.

Most contemporary western armies of the day used explosive charges

* Known as 'the Last Samurai', Nogi lost two sons in the 1904–5 war. In 1912 the count and his wife mourned the death of the Emperor by committing ritual suicide. A shrine, still standing, was built next to his house. On the anniversary of his death, Nogi's home is open to the public so that pilgrims can view his bloodied undershirt and contemplate the dedication of the old order.

to get through thick barbed-wire entanglements. The British, for instance, had developed the Bangalore Torpedo: an alloy pipe about 1½ inches in circumference packed with gun cotton and usually 6 feet in length, though sections could be joined together to clear a way through both entanglements and, it was hoped, mines by detonating those either side of it.

For all their intensive preparation, Takumi's men do not appear to have had anything like this at their disposal. Instead, using bayonets, helmets and spoons taken from their knapsacks, his soldiers began to burrow their way like turtles into the soft sand under the wire until they were deep enough to crawl beneath it. According to one Japanese account this was done by lines of men lying abreast, 'digging the ground frantically and gradually crowding forward'. Behind them the next line of crawling men would deepen the trench the vanguard had excavated beneath the wire, gently pulling aside casualties.

Then *Sendai* and the other Japanese warships had begun to lay down accurate fire with their heavy guns. Near misses were blowing sand through the loopholes of the pillboxes which, combined with the sweet-smelling cordite from the Bren guns, made the defenders' eyes water and stung their faces. Soon the air in these concrete boxes became so bad that their defenders started wearing their gas masks. In any case, some of them were already convinced that they were dealing with something more lethal than a cocktail of sand and gunsmoke – 'a kind of tear gas', suspected one of the Dogras' British officers. Japan had acquired a reputation for occasional chemical warfare in China, where neutral observers had accused them of using mustard gas. Whether some of the naval shells that landed on the beaches at Kota Baharu were loaded with gas has never been confirmed. It seems an unlikely tactical risk. The British were not the Chinese. However threadbare their military garrisons east of Suez, the pre-war obsession with gas attacks was such that the one thing they were well prepared for was retaliation. Stockpiled in Singapore were almost 12,000 mustard gas shells for 25-pounder field guns, plus bombs and cylinders for the RAF to drop or spray like crop dusters.

Gas or no gas, here were men trying to defend pillboxes during a night attack who could now see even less through their thick gas goggles. Nor was this their only setback. Brigadier Key's worst fears had come true. Despite the crossfire, armoured landing-craft had managed to get between the two spits of sand where a boom might have stopped them but certainly not the Indians' heaviest weapon, the Boys anti-tank rifle, which fired a huge .55 round, kicked like a mule and had acquired a reputation during the German blitzkrieg across France for rarely meeting its trade description.

By daybreak on 8 December, with the war about six hours old, a good many of the Japanese had penetrated the waterways that jigsawed the land behind the beach defences. Japanese walking wounded on their way back to the beach, some of them helped by comrades, were filing past Takumi's headquarters staff, bloody, muddy, soaked to the skin and utterly exhausted. From where he stood, Takumi was probably within a mile of Wing Commander Davis's airfield, though still on the wrong side of the Pengkalan Chapa River and facing a counter-attack spearheaded by a fresh battalion Key had been loaned from another brigade.

These were Lieutenant-Colonel Arthur Cumming's 2/12th Frontier Force Regiment, although, in the arcane way of the British Indian Army, Cumming would never have dreamt of referring to his battalion as anything other than 'the 2nd Sikhs'. This would have made perfect sense had not the number of Pathans from Frontier province and the Sikhs' Punjabi brethren, who happened to be Muslim, at least equalled and probably outnumbered them. But the mix of races and religions was typical of most Indian infantry battalions. Less typical, especially in the battalions serving in Malaya, was its relatively high number of British officers, and there would have been more had they not lost five to various staff appointments shortly after their arrival in Malaya. There were ten altogether, among them one 'honorary Briton' in the form of Captain Eugene Cowles Pomeroy, an American from Hopetown, New Jersey, who had been working as a journalist in Shanghai.

At 5 a.m., Wing Commander Davis had ordered a brief respite while his Hudsons were refuelled, rearmed, and their airworthiness checked prior to the resumption of bombing at daybreak, about an hour later. For these daylight operations considerable reinforcements were on their way. This was to be Air Vice-Marshal Pulford's big show, his chance to demonstrate that, despite Brooke-Popham's dithering and the government's failure to bring them up to the promised strength, his squadrons might yet destroy the promised 40 per cent of the invaders, leaving the army and the navy to mop up the rest. Davis's six remaining airworthy Hudsons were to be joined by about forty other aircraft, including the twelve Hudsons of the RAAF's 8 Squadron, based 120 miles to the south at Kuantan, a tin-mining port, twenty or so RAF Blenheims, seven from Kuantan and the rest from Alor Star on the west coast, six Vildebeest biplanes in their torpedo-carrying mode and two Buffalo fighters already on detachment at Kota Baharu, although they had not been involved in the night fighting.

At first light, Davis sent up a reconnaissance flight. This established that, apart from the still smoking *Awagisan Maru*, there were no longer any Japanese ships off the Badang and Sabak beaches where anti-aircraft guns were now being dug in. But before the big ships disappeared, they had spawned an armada of at least fifty small craft that were darting about like tadpoles in all directions. Some appeared to be salvaging equipment from the *Awagisan Maru*; others were taking some of the infantry from the beaches to the river mouth and into the labyrinth beyond it. About ten minutes later, the Hudson discovered the missing warships and transports that had supported Takumi's task force, some 40 miles north-north-east of Kota Baharu and close to the rest of the Japanese fleet around the Thai harbours of Singora and Patani. Because Operation Matador had not been implemented, the bulk of Yamashita's forces had been enjoying unimpeded landings there for the last eight hours.

It was decided that a closer look at the southernmost part of the Thai coast was needed, for it was still not clear whether or not the main Japanese landing was at Kota Baharu. Flight Lieutenant Mitchell and the Australian-built Beaufort were the obvious choice, and this time he had more luck with the weather. Mitchell not only photographed the ships but, although he may not have realized it until the photographs he was taking at 20,000 feet were interpreted, he also monitored another chilling development: Japanese fighters parked on the airfields at Singora and Patani that had been prepared for them by Japanese agents and their Thai sympathizers. Very soon, Mitchell had no need of photographs to tell him that enemy fighters were about because his air gunners reported that they had just counted six of them climbing, quite slowly it seemed, towards them.

Mitchell continued to circle, working the switch that controlled the shutter of the wide-angled lens in the belly of the aircraft, confident that he had all the time in the world before any Japanese fighters could get close and, if they did, his twin Pratt and Whitney engines would soon show them a clean pair of heels. 'The next thing I knew they were all around us like hornets. I distinctly remember seeing tracers passing my windscreen and the next second they were hitting the side of the aircraft down by my feet.'

In terms of air combat, this was an historic moment: the RAF's first encounter with the Zero fighter whose phenomenal rate of climb and manoeuvrability, well documented by various Anglo-American intelligence agencies over the last year, had so amazingly eluded the Air Ministry. Both gunners were almost immediately lightly wounded in their legs, though rear gunner Sergeant Bill Barcroft did manage to fire a long burst at the nearest Zero. Some of this hit its engine, obliging Lieutenant Tadatsune Tokaji to break off and nurse his Zero back to Singora for an emergency landing. At about the same time, Mitchell's port engine was hit and the sudden loss of power caused the Beaufort to flip over on its back and develop the kind of slow spin that so often proved fatal. Then, at 10,000 feet, Mitchell managed to regain control and dodge into a cloud where they were able to assess some of the damage. It was discovered that a fuel line, which had been partly severed, could be bridged by using an emergency pump and this restored them to a more or less even keel.

Having lost the Zeros, Mitchell set course for Kota Baharu where the Beaufort was temporarily based, but their troubles were far from over. It was now about 9 a.m., and since he had left the airfield on his reconnaissance mission it had started to come under attack from the squadrons Mitchell had photographed on the ground at Singora. No longer at the edge of their range, both fighters and light bombers made repeated passes, coming in low and fast, strafing and dropping small bombs with impunity. This was despite the best efforts of a recently mobilized anti-aircraft detachment of the Hong Kong and Singapore Royal Artillery, whose old guns failed to down a single intruder. Particularly mesmerized by the performance of the Zeros, Wing Commander Davis did not follow his men into a trench until a Japanese bullet clipped the heel from one of his shoes. Nor was he the only one. Colonel Cumming and some of the newly arrived Frontier Force Rifles were amazed to find curious Asian civilians 'assembled in the pouring rain to watch the bombing of installations as though they were watching a football match'.

Mitchell flew low circuits over the jungle until the last of the enemy had expended his munitions, 'then slipped in for a quick landing and all jumped out'. His air gunners were led away to have their wounds dressed and ground crew worked on the Beaufort so that Mitchell could take it down to Singapore with the pictures. Every time Mitchell started his engines, however, the next sortie of Japanese arrived, spotted the Beaufort's turning propellers and, as Mitchell left the cockpit and scrambled for cover, did their best to see that they turned no more. After several attempts, for like most fighter pilots their marksmanship was not impressive, the Beaufort began to burn, but slowly enough for the camera to be salvaged. Shortly afterwards a Buffalo flew the film to Singapore where the full extent of the Japanese landings on the Thai beaches was at last recognized.

In the meantime, the aircraft Pulford had marshalled for his big show had begun to head towards Takumi's Kota Baharu beach-head. Flying Officer Roy Bulcock woke at dawn at Kuantan airfield. Only eight months before, he had been the director of a commercial printing company in Brisbane. He had answered a newspaper advertisement for men under fifty with executive experience to serve as RAF equipment officers. Kuantan was even less developed than Kota Baharu, an expensive gash in the rubber acquired for £150,000 based on the War Office compensation of one pound for every rubber tree felled. Tigers sometimes left their pug marks in the monsoon mud. Bulcock looked out of his window and thought, they'll never take off in this. The dawn had failed. Thick ground mist obscured the tops of the nearest rubber trees; for a non-flier, the very idea of vaulting them blindfold seemed suicidal. But, even as he was taking this in, he began to hear the sound of twelve pairs of radial engines starting up.

Sergeant Alan Morton, who had almost lost a foot to flesh-eating sand flies when he crash-landed in June, noted the way 'long wisps of smoky cloud' rose from the jungle roof. Then the WAG, as wireless operators/air gunners were known, made his way aft to his position in the rear turret. In the Hudson, this was entered by kneeling on the lavatory and pulling yourself up into the perspex dome they called 'the gunner's office'. Once inside, he released a catch, a seat came down and Morton was at his work station. The gunner sat with his control stick between his legs and in front of him were the cocking handles and working mechanism of his twin Brownings. From the breeches of the guns dangled canvas cartridge belts which folded into the metal ammunition boxes on either side of his feet. Each belt contained 750 rounds of .303, and, if he depressed the button on top of his control stick, the Brownings fired them at a rate of 1,000 rounds a minute: almost fifty in a three-second burst.

Morton and the rest of his squadron were as green as Curly Davis's new veterans at Kota Baharu had been until about six hours before. Now the gunner, a draughtsman from Adelaide of Scots descent who, like everybody else, had joined to fight Hitler but thought the Japs would do, went through all the routine checks and found it relaxing. He moved the control stick to the left and right and rotated the turret in a full circle. When he pushed the stick forwards the guns pointed down; when he pulled it back into his stomach they pointed up. The power came from generators charged by the Hudson's engines. He methodically searched the blue above the pewter-coloured, rain-swollen clouds for the enemy as he had been taught to do and, when he had finished, he started again. Morton, who was three months short of his twenty-fourth birthday, found these checks comforting but he noticed that his hands were sweating. He never did find the answer to that.

'Target coming up,' announced the pilot over the intercom and the Hudson went into shallow dive. Once again the *Awagisan Maru* was bombed and, as they pulled away, Morton told the rest of the crew that he had seen 'a huge fireball'. The gutted transport, which some of the small craft were trying to tow further inshore, remained the most obvious target and several of 8 Squadron's Hudsons decided to cut their teeth on it, though whether it was worth another three or four 1,000-pound bomb loads was questionable.

What was not in doubt was the determination of most of these Australians to wreak as much havoc as they could. When he attacked the *Awagisan Maru* Flight Lieutenant 'Spud' Spurgeon, having already strafed troops and landing-craft on the beach, was trying to ignore his first experience of anti-aircraft fire and concentrate hard on flying low. There was a device in the cockpit for setting the delay fuses on the bombs, but Spurgeon forgot to use it. 'We got the bloody lot back.' His windshield cracked, the barrel of one of the two forward wing machine-guns operated by the pilot was bent back, all the clocks and gauges on the instrument panel broke, and the cockpit was soaked with hydraulic fluid. Unable to lower the landing gear, Spurgeon headed for the handy Kota Baharu strip, where 'I flung the thing down on its belly.' None of the crew was badly hurt, but the Hudson was virtually a write-off.

Most of the Hudson crews soon realized that their prime target was the troops, just offshore and entering the river mouth in their small craft, usually described during debriefing with their intelligence officers as 'armoured barges' or 'armoured power boats'. The latter often mounted a heavy machine-gun slightly forward of amidships and, for a few seconds, Sergeant Morton found himself duelling with one of these.

We attacked in a low pass from behind. As it came into view, I could easily see this big bloke wearing what looked like a brown sun helmet, firing at us with a 50 mm cannon. I got the boat in the sight-ring and gave it a long burst. It did a sharp turn left and was then out of range.

Morton felt it was a hard target to miss and was sure he had inflicted some damage. If he had, it turned out that Brown Hat had very nearly repaid them in kind. The luckiest man on board was their wireless operator. He had stood up to look through the cockpit windscreen just as a round from Morton's adversary had entered the mercifully empty bomb bay, drilled a 2-inch hole through the operator's so recently vacated seat and exited through the top of the fuselage.

On one of the other Hudsons, Pilot Officer Russell Rayson, whose mother was English and who had left his father's advertising business to volunteer for the RAAF within hours of Australia hearing of Britain's declaration of war against Germany, was impressed by the Japanese boat handling. 'They very coolly turned their craft towards us so that it not only reduced our time over them but obliged us to put our nose down, which made the Hudsons a bigger target.' Rayson could see the Japanese, who seemed to him to be about thirty to a boat, as they lay 'herring-bone style' in two rows at the bottom of their vessels, firing at them with rifles.

Others tried to avoid being strafed by steering their boats in constant figure-of-eight patterns. Both of the Australian Hudson squadrons were now above the Kota Baharu beach-head, together with about fifteen Blenheim light bombers from two RAF squadrons. Even some of the old Vildebeests had joined in the strafing, their crews taking out their frustration for a failed torpedo attack on a Japanese cruiser saved by heavy seas. Not all the air gunners were comfortable at first with shooting at defenceless-looking men in boats.

'Right ho, Dusty, there's your chance. Have a go,' crackled Flying Officer Don Stumm's voice over the intercom as he neatly lined up his Hudson for his rear gunner to give one of the boats bobbing below a long burst with the twin Brownings. But back in the gunner's office Sergeant Dusty Hensel, a country boy who had always been a crack shot on a rabbit drive, was not so sure he was ready to 'shoot those blokes down there'. Then a rash of holes appeared on one of the wings and Hensel recalled that he had never met a rabbit with a machine-gun. He held the boat in his sights and pressed the firing button.

In Singapore it was about this time that the atmosphere became markedly optimistic in the large wooden hut, its walls covered with maps, which was the nerve centre of the joint operational HQ Percival had set up with Pulford in Sime Road, next door to the golf club. Up until then, it seemed there was not all that much to be optimistic about, as the magnitude of the surprise attacks unleashed on British, American and Thai territory in South-east Asia and the Pacific had gradually become apparent. In the space of a little over twelve hours, the Japanese had hit seven widely separated places. First they had attacked Kota Baharu; then, about an hour and a half later, about eighty carrier-borne aircraft had caught napping the best part of the US Navy's Pacific Fleet at Pearl Harbor. In Hong Kong, the Japanese were already well into the colony's New Territories and all five of the RAF's aircraft had been caught in the open and destroyed. Hong Kong had always been considered indefensible unless the hard-pressed Chinese could somehow manage to march to its rescue. It was the events at Pearl Harbor that came as the biggest shock. The US Navy was remaining tight-lipped but it appeared that several of the ships that were going to make up for the Royal Navy's present inability to reinforce the *Prince of Wales* and the *Repulse* in eastern waters had, at the very least, been badly damaged.

Then came the wonderful news that at Kota Baharu the Japanese had just got their first bloody nose. The RAF were reporting that they had beaten the Japanese off: that with the exception of one smouldering hulk all their warships had withdrawn leaving some small craft and troops which were being dealt with by themselves and Brigadier Key's Indians. The only person to throw a hint of cold water over the happy, sweating throng watching the yellow pins in the wall map being moved away from the coast was Lieutenant-General Arthur Percival himself. Although he congratulated Key for 'drawing first blood', Percival cautioned, 'the first round does not necessarily decide the contest.'

But beyond doubt it was a taste of victory, and enough to whet the appetite for more. The Japanese had indeed suffered heavy casualties.

It was true they were nowhere near the thousands claimed in some post-war Royal Australian Air Force accounts, from which the reader might imagine clusters of Japanese dead being washed up on the beaches of Kota Baharu like so much seaweed. Colonel Tsuji, the man who planned it all, talked of 320 killed and 538 wounded on the first day; but he admitted that this did not include the losses on the *Awagisan Maru* and the *Ayatosan Maru*, possibly because the navy were less forthcoming with casualty figures. The best indication of how effective the air strikes were on veterans of the China war, unaccustomed to an enemy with even this modest amount of air power, is an account by Tsuji of a rare display of Japanese cowardice.

One section of non-commissioned officers of the Independent Engineers . . . had however become panic-stricken at the enemy's bombing. Without orders from the troop leader, they boarded the large motor boats, crossed to the east of Thailand Bay, and retreated to the open sea off Saigon.

In other words, they bolted and did not stop until they were long out of danger. Even more remarkable for this highly motivated and sometimes brutally disciplined army, Tsuji hints at a cover-up, saying there should have been an immediate court martial, but no court martial was held. How many were involved is unclear. If the 'large motor boats' he refers to were no more than two, and packed with equipment, Tsuji might be talking about less than fifty men. Whatever the numbers, it is a startling, and possibly unique, admission for any Japanese officer to make. Staunchly holding to their code of 'death before dishonour', and believing their immortality guaranteed, Nippon's sons were consistently the bravest in World War II. As the war went on, rear-echelon cooks and clerks frequently demonstrated their willingness to die for their Emperor. And, as in the British Army, engineers were regarded as teeth-arm soldiers expected to clear mine fields and rebuild demolished road bridges while under fire.

Up until now, few British aircraft had been shot down and casualties were low. The Australian squadrons, which because of their anti-shipping role did most of the damage, had lost two out of the twenty-two Hudsons they scrambled and eight aircrew were now 'missing in action'. (It would turn out that seven had been killed and one captured.) Two of the seven RAF Blenheims which joined in the strafing of the Kota Baharu beaches at dawn had also gone down to anti-aircraft fire.

Squadron Leader Estropp-Bennet's aircraft was spotted belching smoke and sinking towards Thailand, where it crashed in a coconut grove killing all on board. Canadian pilot Bill Bowden's Blenheim broke up as he ditched; Bowden surfaced clinging to the tailwheel, the three-man crew's only survivor. He held onto his wheel for twenty-four hours until he was rescued by a Japanese destroyer to become the first Allied airman to be captured by the new enemy.

Some of the Hudsons were directed by radio to go further north in search of Japanese ships. They ran into torrential rain and gave up. On their way back to Kota Baharu for more strafing of the landing-craft, the weather cleared sufficiently for some of them to see a lone figure in a tiny Malayan *prahu*, well offshore without oars, paddles or sail and being blown in a north-westerly direction. This was Flying Officer Don Dowie, the only survivor of Ramshaw's Hudson, whose narrow, 20-foot wooden boat had snapped its moorings in the storm and nudged up to him during the night. Dowie was eventually picked up miles from land by a Japanese patrol boat which took him into Singora, the second of Pulford's fliers to be taken prisoner and, after the best part of thirty-six hours without water, certainly the luckiest.

The loss of four aircraft and fourteen aircrew was a small price to pay for the damage inflicted on the Japanese, and the initial euphoria in the Singapore operations room was entirely understandable. But, for all the blood spilt by both the air force and the army at Kota Baharu, Percival's reminder that a first-round win did not always guarantee the bout was a prescient one.

As Wing Commander Davis had seen at close quarters when admiring the Mitsubishi-sponsored aerobatics over his airfield, Yamashita was already addressing the question of British air power in northern Malaya. So far, all four of the aircraft the Japanese had shot down had been hit by ground flak. But by mid-morning on 8 December, the Hudsons and Blenheims over Kota Baharu were seeing some of the campaign's first air-to-air combat. On the Japanese side, only a few of their superlative Zeros and Oscars, the lesser-known army equivalent, were involved. Most of their fighters were Ki 27s – codenamed the Nate by the Anglo-Americans – the old-fashioned aircraft with the fixed undercarriage that was about to be phased out, one of which had shot down the Catalina the day before.

The Hudsons discovered they were able to hold their own against the Nates. Their sturdy airliner airframes could cope with a lot of ventilation and four machine-gun positions left few blind spots which might be attacked with impunity. A Zero pilot of the 22nd Air Flotilla, who pressed matters too closely with one of them, was obliged to ditch and was rescued by one of Takumi's landing-craft. The smaller Blenheims, which were mainly based on west coast airfields, did not fare so well. Oscars chased some of them all the way back to Butterworth, just across the water from Penang Island, where they were supposed to refuel. Two had to make emergency landings, one bending its propellers as it bumped to a halt wheels-up on its belly. A third was being doggedly pursued a few feet above the jungle canopy when Sergeant Keith Burrill, one of several RAAF gunners seconded to RAF squadrons,* was punched off his seat in the Blenheim's single mid-upper turret by a bullet that shattered his lower jaw and passed through his mouth. Dazed and soaked in blood, the Australian somehow managed to haul himself back behind his guns and, through the turret's splintered perspex, saw that his opponent, obviously convinced he had disposed of the Blenheim's rear defences, was closing in for the kill. At near point-blank range, Burrill gave the Oscar a long burst, then watched as it dropped into the thick, impenetrable jungle that covers much of the hilly spine of Malaya and shrouds its secrets like the sea. Records of the 59th Sentai (squadron) confirm that one of their aircraft engaging British aircraft at about this time and place failed to return. Safely landed at Butterworth, in his holed turret with his feet splayed on a shining carpet of spent cartridge cases and a mouth full of blood and pain, the heroic Burrill must have provided eloquent if mute testimony that the Japanese were not going to be a pushover. (Evacuated to Australia for prolonged medical treatment, he was awarded a Distinguished Flying Medal.)

Having started at Kota Baharu, where the Japanese were hurting most, the battle to reduce British air power rapidly spread to the six other major RAF bases in north and central Malaya. Because of the east coast's poor road and rail communications, only two of the airfields, Kota Baharu and Kuantan, were located on that side of the peninsula. The rest were clustered within 70 miles of each other on the west coast. Alor Star airfield, where Percival had landed as he arrived to take

---

* This is quite apart from the number of Australian, New Zealand, Canadian and South African aircrew who had joined the RAF in the UK and subsequently been posted to RAF squadrons in Malaya.

up his new command, was just below the border with Thailand. Then came Sungei Patani, Butterworth and Penang Island. Within the next forty-eight hours they were all repeatedly bombed and strafed.

By the end of the first day, British air strength in northern Malaya had been reduced by over half – from 110 operational aircraft to 50. Attacks on Sungei Patani started at about the same time as at Kota Baharu. Eight aircraft were destroyed or made unserviceable. Seven of them were Buffaloes belonging to the Australian 21 Squadron, some of them hit by phosphorous incendiary bombs which burnt through their metal skins, exploding their fuel tanks with a whoosh. An RAF Blenheim that was taking off was struck by a bomb within the first seconds of becoming airborne. Other casualties included sixteen of the RAF's Chinese women labourers the airmen called 'Concrete Annies' and two RAF telephone operators.

Two of the Buffaloes did manage to take off in pursuit of the five twin-engined Sallys responsible for this havoc only to find that their guns were not working. After their prompt return it was discovered that, in both cases, they were unloaded, presumably an oversight, although the aircraft had been on standby for at least forty-five minutes before the raid. The disgust these pilots must have felt towards the ground crews responsible – all Australian – can only have been matched by their squadron leader's feelings towards the RAF station commander who, in the few minutes' warning they had before the raid, refused to let him get all his Buffaloes airborne.

About four hours later it happened again. As a formation of twenty-three Japanese bombers was spotted approaching from the west at 12,000 feet, Australian Squadron Leader William Allshorn pleaded with RAF Squadron Leader Frederick Fowle, who also commanded the Blenheim squadron, for permission to get his four remaining Buffaloes airborne. Again Fowle refused, presumably because he feared they would be caught on the runway as one of his Blenheims had been: aircraft were, in theory anyway, replaceable; aircrew were not. This time none of the Buffaloes was damaged, but a fuel dump and buildings were hit. Fowle decided they could no longer operate from Sungei Patani and should make a 'temporary evacuation' to Butterworth, some 50 miles to the south.

On the peninsula's east coast, 120 miles away from Sungei Patani, Wing Commanders Davis and Noble were reluctantly coming to the same conclusion. Some of their ground crew were convinced that, while they were working on aircraft, they were being sniped at by Japanese who must have infiltrated the airfield's outer defences. There had not been any casualties but a few of these Australian fitters and riggers, who like the aircrews had gone without sleep for the best part of twenty-four hours, were getting jumpy and their mood was contagious. An attempt to raise morale by putting rifles in the hands of men not directly involved in keeping the Hudsons in the air was not greeted with much enthusiasm. (Yet some of these technicians would pull every string they knew to be allowed to go on a dangerous operational flight and man the extra machine-guns in the Hudsons' fuselage.)

Noble went off to confer with Brigadier Key at his headquarters. On his return he found to his amazement that the operations room, the nerve centre of the airfield, was deserted, and airmen had set alight several of the station's *attap* palm buildings, claiming they had been ordered to withdraw. It turned out that, while the wing commander was away, somebody gave Air HQ in Singapore the impression that the airfield was about to be overrun and received permission to evacuate. The arrival of an anxious Brigadier Key and a few of his staff coincided with what looked like the departure of some of the Australian ground crews, who were clambering aboard trucks and shouting, 'The Japs are over there.' Key could get very little sense out of them and, accompanied by Noble, the brigadier went to the airfield's perimeter. Here they encountered some concerned-looking soldiers of the 1st Hyderabad Regiment.

The Hyderabads were not exactly part of the Indian Army but on loan to it from the rajah of that ancient and princely state in south-east India as His Excellency's contribution to the war effort. Known as Indian State Forces, there were five such battalions in Malaya, all provided by various despots the Raj had, for one reason or another, seen fit to preserve. A British lieutenant-colonel normally commanded these palace guards, but most of the other officers tended to be Indians. Many were nationalists who disliked their feudal paymasters as much as they disliked British colonialism and were prime targets for Indian Independence League agitators. Nor did it help that the British so obviously regarded these state forces, whose *esprit de corps* could rarely match that of the likes of Cumming's 2nd Sikhs, as anything other than third-rate lines-of-communication troops, fit for guarding bridges and airfields but little else.

When Brigadier Key arrived at their position, the Hyderabads he spoke to confirmed that they had yet to clap eyes on any Japanese; but they had been watching the antics of the Australian ground crew carefully and were beginning to wonder what these sahibs knew that they did not. From the direction of the beaches came a constant crackle of small arms fire and occasionally there would be the unmistakable 'zizz' of a stray rifle bullet passing not all that far overhead. Old soldiers such as Key called these rounds 'overs', but they could unsettle the kind of battlefield novices most of the British forces in Malaya were. This was almost certainly the ground crew's 'sniping'.

Even so, it was undeniable that the position of RAF Kota Baharu had been becoming increasingly untenable ever since the Zeros had stopped Peter Mitchell getting his Beaufort off the ground. The raiders continued to act with impunity. By late afternoon, the airfield's feeble anti-aircraft defences, a couple of old 3-inch guns and some machine-guns, do not appear to have scratched an inch of paint off a single visiting Sally, Zero, Nell or Nate. Nor was there any attempt to provide fighter cover from Singapore to replace the Buffaloes lost in the pre-emptive strike on Allshorn's squadron at Sungei Patani.

In any case, there was less and less point in operating from what was not much more than a jungle air strip. The Hudson squadrons had originally moved north to Kota Baharu and Kuantan from Singapore in order to extend the range of their reconnaissance flights and thus increase their chances of destroying an invasion fleet before it reached the coast. It was too late for that now. For the sake of twenty minutes' or so more flight time, the Australians could operate perfectly well from their old home at Sembawang, on Singapore's northern coast, with its defence umbrella of anti-aircraft guns and fighters and the kind of creature comforts that could keep a man happy in the tropics.

The Australian decision to evacuate the Kota Baharu airfield, which began to take place about dusk, was an ignominious ending to a long day that had started so promisingly for them in the small hours before dawn.

As a first step, all five of Davis's airworthy Hudsons splashed off from their sodden runway for the last time and flew out to Kuantan, carrying as many personnel and stores as they could cram on board. As they lumbered into the air, a rear gunner fired a long burst into a tree where he was convinced he had seen a Japanese sniper. Some aircrew spotted enemy fighters, black specks against a setting sun, but dodged them by wave-hopping along the beach, below the tops of the tall palms that fringed it. One flew all the way with its flaps wired up and its undercarriage down because all the hydraulics had gone. Another, whose pilot had been puzzled by a response to its controls far more sluggish than twenty passengers would warrant, was discovered on landing at Kuantan to be gravid with a full 1,000-pound bomb load somebody had forgotten to remove.

Davis had disregarded orders from Singapore that the last aircraft should bomb the airfield to deny it to the enemy because he wanted to get as much as possible on board his Hudsons, whose ultimate carrying capacity was obviously 1,000 pounds greater than he thought. Besides, he thought the runway was so soggy with rain it was unlikely that the 250-pounders would explode, and that even if they did the holes they made could be filled in within twenty-four hours.

But he did round up some ground crew to try and deal with the five remaining Hudsons on the airfield. Two were airworthy apart from damage to their wheels which needed changing before they could take off. Three were possibly only good for spares and they managed to set two alight. The third, which was the 8 Squadron Hudson Spurgeon had belly-landed, was in a more exposed position and had already been strafed a couple of times.

Davis's demolition party made several attempts to get to Spurgeon's aircraft and the other two Hudsons needing wheel changes. But every time they got close the Australian ground crew became convinced that they were coming under small arms fire and would go no further. By this time they may well have been right, for Hiroshi Takumi's infantry were at last beginning to get close to the airfield's perimeter.

Trucks procured by Wing Commander Noble from the local Public Works Department carried the ground crews the 44 miles to the railway at Kuala Krai where, utterly exhausted, they slumbered uneasily on the platform while a train south was organized. Behind them they left not only the two intact Hudsons but sixty aerial torpedoes, some bombs and a high octane fuel dump, all of which they hoped the army would destroy. 'Thus began the long series of evacuations of aerodromes which had been laboriously prepared and for the protection of which our troops had been specially disposed,' observed Percival who, for all his caution, might have expected the first day of hostilities to end on a more optimistic note.

Davis could at least derive some comfort from the knowledge that, quite apart from suffering eight air attacks, he had not abandoned his airfield until Japanese infantry were within walking distance. No such claim could be made for the next airfield to be evacuated, which did not have a Japanese foot soldier within 100 miles of it.

While most of his squadron went on to Singapore, Davis and sixty of his men left the train at the town of Seletar so that they could drive over to Kuantan and meet their aircraft. They were within about 25 miles of their destination when they met up with a convoy of trucks packed with ground crew. Most of them were from 8 Squadron, the other RAAF Hudson unit. They informed the astonished wing commander that Kuantan had been bombed for the first time that morning and that, as a result, all the aircraft had left for Singapore. They were on their way to join them.

Kuantan, the only sizeable east coast airfield now that Kota Baharu had been abandoned, had not been entirely deserted. Wing Commander Roland Councell, the RAF station commander, and three other officers were still there. One of these was Bulcock, the equipment officer who the day before had heard the Hudsons preparing to take off for their battle debut despite the thick ground mist. Those aircrews had made him very proud of his country, but now he had very different feelings. 'For the first and last time in my life,' admitted Bulcock, 'I felt ashamed of being an Australian.'

And yet the day had started on a very high note. Shortly after 10 a.m.

one of 8 Squadron's pilots, Flight Lieutenant Ron Widmer, had won a Distinguished Flying Cross for accomplishing what must have been a unique feat of shooting down a bomber with a bomber. Widmer was approaching Kuantan after an early morning reconnaissance flight when he saw that his airfield was under attack. After jettisoning his own bombs into the sea, Widmer gained height and dived at the intruders, at least five Nells, which were flying at about 5,000 feet. First he had used his wing guns on them, or rather one wing gun for the other refused to fire, and then turned the Hudson so that his rear gunner could join in. Soon one of the Nells turned away over the jungle canopy with one of its engines on fire and two white parachutes were seen to emerge.

Widmer managed to land safely, though not before an RAAF sergeant drew his revolver on an excited Indian anti-aircraft crew reluctant to accept that this Hudson was not the low, slow target of their wildest dreams. That their desire to shoot something down might overwhelm the constraints of mere aircraft recognition was understandable. Only one airman had been wounded in the attack but, for the price of Widmer's Nell, the Japanese had succeeded in destroying six aircraft: three Hudsons, a Blenheim bomber awaiting repairs and two Vildebeests, one of which was blown apart when flames reached the torpedo slung beneath its canvas belly. In addition, the bomb fusing store had been wrecked and .303 machine-gun ammunition was popping off in the blazing armoury. Despite these depredations, the airfield was still far from out of business. Under the rubber trees dumps of bombs, torpedoes, fuel and oil were still entirely intact, as were most of the aircraft and the men who flew them.

Morale had probably started to deteriorate at Kuantan the night before, with the arrival of the Hudsons from Kota Baharu. Among their passengers were men with nerves already as brittle as melba toast, bearing blitzkrieg tales of bombing, strafing and snipers and gloomy predictions of 'You'll be next.' As far as many of 8 Squadron's personnel were concerned, things were already bad enough.

The unit's deployment up-country to Kuantan in the event of war had long been planned. Yet, despite the pleadings of Bulcock and the rest of the airfield's small staff, RAF Kuantan was still hopelessly ill-equipped to accommodate an operational squadron. Radio and telephone communications were bad and they were short of everything from steel helmets to wheeled transport. It was only after a tiger scare that it was realized there was not a single rifle on the station. Refuelling aircraft was painfully slow because they did not have enough tankers and the ones they had were constantly bogging down on a field turned into a quagmire by the monsoon.

After the evacuation of Kota Baharu there was, for 8 Squadron, a feeling of uncertainty about their own movements, and the news that they had been ordered not to unpack all their equipment was certainly not unwelcome. If there was a certain envy of the other Hudson squadron's return to the old, well-ordered life of Singapore, it is not hard to understand. Bulcock discovered that the first deserters, for that is what they were, had stolen some of his precious commandeered civilian transport and left Kuantan shortly after first light some four hours before the raid. At about the time the all-clear was sounding over the airfield they were already at Jerantut, some three hours' drive away, and drawing attention to themselves by the speed of their passage through a town long untroubled by the press of great events.

But it was not only scared and bewildered ground crew, often left too long to their own devices, who precipitated the panic-stricken flight which followed the air strike. After what had occurred at Kota Baharu, a similar lack of fighter cover and adequate anti-aircraft defences at Kuantan was obviously cause for concern. Shortly after dawn five RAF Blenheims were allowed to return to Singapore on the grounds that Kuantan was becoming too congested. A couple of hours before the Nells arrived, Squadron Leader Peter Henderson, the acting commander of 8 Squadron, 'strongly suggested' to Air HQ Singapore that they be allowed to follow the Blenheims south and get back under a proper defensive umbrella. He was assured, perhaps by somebody who felt Henderson needed cheering up, that bombs on Kuantan were 'not in the scheme of things'.

After this fallacy had been promptly exploded, one of Henderson's officers got on the secure line to Air HQ in Singapore and delivered a damage report with a relish that would have done credit to Radio Tokyo. The alleged response to this would later be the focus of a court of inquiry. The RAAF claimed they were ordered to evacuate Kuantan. Pulford's staff in Singapore insisted that they were merely instructed, as a temporary measure, to bring all airworthy Hudsons back to Sembawang, their old airfield near the naval base. It was not intended to close Kuantan down.

Wing Commander Councell, the RAF station commander who

had been doing his best to accommodate 8 Squadron at his humble aerodrome, had slept through most of the air raid in his quarters, where he was trying to catch up on almost thirty-six hours spent without sleep since the start of hostilities. The operations room was packed, mostly with aircrew, all talking at once. The noise was so bad the Wing Commander couldn't make out what was being said down the telephone from Singapore. He turned to them and yelled, 'If you don't shut up you won't hear the Japs coming back!' In the silence that followed, Bulcock heard Councell splutter into the mouthpiece: 'It's absolutely ridiculous, I tell you. Nothing like that has happened at all. The damage is immaterial.'

But it was too late to stop the Hudsons leaving Kuantan. The order had been given and the Hudsons were preparing to leave, their crews spurred on by an entirely false rumour that was now firmly believed by most of the men on the station. 'We were told that the Japs were landing at Kuantan,' recalled Russell Rayson, the pilot who had so admired the skill with which the Japanese handled their small craft under fire at Kota Baharu. 'There was no time to waste.'

It was never discovered how this rumour started but aircrew are accustomed to reacting quickly. 'The little flame of panic spread like wildfire,' recalled Bulcock.

Saving their aircraft and all the spares and men necessary to keep them in the air was obviously of paramount importance. Anything in the Hudsons surplus to immediate requirements was discarded to make space for men and equipment. Bombs were removed from the bomb bays and left on the airfield, despite the risk that they might provide devastating compound interest for the next Japanese air strike. As soon as they were loaded up they flew away.

Seven aircraft from both Hudson squadrons flew out carrying between them some 140 ground crew. This left at least 600 others, Australian and UK British from the station staff and the Vildebeest squadron, milling about, convinced that they had been abandoned in the face of a Japanese landing and evidently having little faith in the capability of the local Indian Army units to protect them. Although some had rifles and even a few machine-guns, any notion of self-defence seems to have eluded them. Instead there was a stampede to acquire transport, anybody's transport, and put as much distance between themselves and Kuantan as possible. Nor were officers exempt from this panic.

'I saw a bloody Flight Lieutenant soon after the raid started,' an incredulous British captain told his table in the nearby Indian Army officers' mess, where a numbed Bulcock had joined Wing Commander Councell for lunch. 'He ran down the side of the road with two friends, blew the door-lock off a private car with his pistol, drove the car onto the main road so fast that he skidded into a deep drain and couldn't get out. Then he held up the Post Office bus with his gun, made all the passengers and driver get out, and drove off . . .'

RAF Kuantan had taken on the untidy appearance of a recently vacated battlefield or a huge air crash. All that was lacking was bodies. Between the wrecked buildings and the smashed aircraft were littered hundreds of items of kit and personal effects. Bulcock counted 300 steel trunks and suitcases dumped in the mud outside the officers' mess after it was decided there was no room for them on the Hudsons. Some had been left with their contents spilling out where people had delved into them to rescue money and valuables before dashing for their planes. He began to tidy them away.

'How is this possible? They are all sahibs,' a bewildered driver of the Royal Garhwal Rifles asked his officer as they viewed this sad *mélange* of tennis racquets and dress uniforms. 'They are not sahibs, they're Australians,' snapped Lieutenant Richard Clarke. Later it occurred to Clarke that he probably had more relatives in Australia than England.

At RAF Butterworth, 100 miles further north of Kuantan and rather closer to the nearest Japanese infantry, Pulford's Blenheims and Buffaloes were still trying to stay on the offensive and harass the Japanese airfields in southern Thailand. Casualties were heavy. The Japanese had an increasing number of Zeros and Oscars in the air, though some of the Commonwealth pilots were still reluctant to believe that Asians could produce anything as good and insisted on identifying them as 'Messerschmitt-types'. On the morning of 9 December, three out of six Blenheims trying to bomb Singora were shot down by these interceptors. It appears that two of these RAF crews, six men in all, survived their crashes and tried to get back to Malaya only to fall into the hands of the Thai gendarmerie, who handed them over to some of Yamashita's troops. The Japanese vice-consul in Singora later told a Thai judge that three of the airmen were found guilty of 'taking Japanese lives and destroying Japanese property' and beheaded by samurai sword on a beach. The other crew were spared because there was enough forensic evidence around the wreck of their aircraft to verify their claim that a faulty bomb release mechanism had saved Nippon from their evil intent.

Mercifully ignorant of the Alice-in-Wonderland world they were flying into, a few hours later the RAF tried again. Just as they were about to take off and meet up with an escort of four Buffaloes circling above them, however, they were attacked on the ground at Butterworth. Two of the Blenheims were totally destroyed and most of the rest damaged; thick palls of smoke from blazing aircraft and buildings drifted across the airfield. Some aircrew tried to put out fires. A few crouched behind what cover they could find and made ambitious use of Thompson sub-machine-guns fitted with the 'Al Capone' drum magazines. Their targets were usually strafing fighters making repeated low passes at speeds almost as fast as the Thompsons' low-velocity .45 rounds.

Two Blenheims had managed to get into the air, taking off seconds before the first Japanese bomb landed. One was flown by a sergeant pilot from the squadron that had lost three aircraft over Singora that morning. By the time they reached 6,000 feet his Australian gunner was already fighting off a swooping Zero and, seeing no sign of the promised fighter escort which was also under attack, the sergeant got back on the ground as fast as he could.

The other Blenheim was piloted by Squadron Leader Arthur Scarf, who was a Cranwell-trained regular and, at twenty-eight, about to become a father for the first time. His pregnant wife, a nurse at a hospital in Alor Star, had been evacuated to the south the day before. Although it was supposed to be a formation attack Scarf, second-in-command of 62 Squadron, decided the mission was too important to abort. Dodging and weaving, he ran a gauntlet of Japanese fighters until, a little under thirty minutes later, the Blenheim had covered the 110 miles to Singora and was diving towards the Japanese airfield there. His navigator, Sergeant 'Paddy' Calder, worked the bomb release while behind them air gunner Cyril Rich, also a sergeant, hosed down a line of parked aircraft from his turret.

The enemy's response to this impudent lone raider was, by now, entirely predictable. Already damaged by ground fire, the Blenheim was pursued by a wasps' nest of fighters, each focusing its undivided attention on the British plane. That should have been the end of the matter, but Scarf had been honed by over eight years of RAF flying into a brilliant and instinctive pilot: bringing his own wing-mounted front guns to bear whenever he had the opportunity, the squadron leader banked, turned and side-slipped so skilfully that, although the Blenheim was a good 60 mph slower than the Zero, he shook off his tormentors and found cloud cover. But not without cost. By this time Scarf's left arm was shattered, he had a large hole in his back, had lost a lot of blood and was drifting in and out of consciousness. He was also the only one on board with full pilot's wings, although Calder, the bomb-aimer and navigator, had received some basic flying training. Calder called Rich to come down from his turret and help him keep Scarf from slumping onto the controls. Between them they steered the Blenheim towards the abandoned airfield at Alor Star, the nearest landing site. They did not quite get there but Scarf succeeded in making a belly landing on a paddy field about 100 yards from the hospital where his wife had so recently nursed.

Apart from cuts and bruises, Calder and Rich were unhurt and helped carry Scarf inside, where he was immediately given a blood transfusion, but he died the next day. He was buried in a nearby cemetery in a coffin obtained from a local jail by two of the remaining nurses who were friends of his wife. In the fullness of time, when people who had been away for some years were back home and a citation that had been lost was written again, Scarf would receive a posthumous Victoria Cross. His crew were also decorated: Calder, by now Squadron Leader Calder DFC, with a Distinguished Flying Medal, and Sergeant Rich, who had been killed in action some sixteen months later, received a Mention in Dispatches because this, the Victoria Cross and the George Cross were the only awards for gallantry that could be made posthumously.

Scarf's lone hit-and-run raid was a wonderful display of leadership. Unfortunately, the one aircraft that might have followed him, assuming he saw him, chose not to. It had already become apparent that the RAF, under strength at the start, had lost so many aircraft that there was no chance whatsoever of them fulfilling the dominant role the pre-war planners had envisaged. On top of this, two airfields had been abandoned with indecent haste.

Another symptom of panic was the growing belief in the existence among the Asian community of a huge 'fifth column' of Japanese sympathizers. In 1941, the term 'fifth columnists', which had been coined by the Falangist general besieging Madrid during the Spanish

Civil War, was five years old.* But it was still current after nonsensical reports that fifth columnists had paved the way for Hitler's blitzkrieg victories in Western Europe the year before.

Now it was Malaya's turn. Reports that Tokyo's secret army was betraying the British at every turn, particularly by pinpointing airfields, headquarters and other places of interest to overhead visitors, by using banana or palm leaves to make arrows, were rife. Colonial policemen and civil servants tended to be dismissive, insisting that the military's paranoia, not to say xenophobia, was the result of the latter's appalling ignorance of a country most of them had lived in for well over a year.

'It probably led to many innocent men being shot,' thought Harvey Ryves, the inspector in the Perak district who had watched one of his superiors haggling with the Japanese shopkeeper he was about to intern over the price of a doll. Presented by some Indian troops with three terrified and dirt-poor Chinese woodcutters, accused of signalling to the Japanese by burning down their own huts, Ryves let them go with 'a light rebuke that should have been an apology'. They were lucky. As Japanese air strikes increased, summary executions would soon become fairly commonplace. One of the problems was that so few of Percival's army, including the officers, had ever flown and had a very exaggerated idea of what could be seen from an aircraft. People were shot for allegedly calling in dive bombers with the wave of a white topee or by placing newly washed sarongs on a bush to dry. An Argyll, whose younger brother had been killed a couple of days before, was selected by the adjutant to take two civilians suspected of putting down markers 'and do what you want with them'. He got them to walk ahead of him into some long grass, fired a couple of shots above their heads and watched them dive for cover. 'Then I don't know what came over me. They fell down in the big high grass. When they came back up I just took a bead on them and bumped the two of them.'

At least they died quickly. Guy Madoc, a policeman attached to the army as an adviser and general interpreter, heard a pistol shot during an air raid and saw a British NCO walking through some *lallang* grass with a smoking revolver in his hand. 'As the all-clear sounded, there was a commotion and I saw the same NCO running after an elderly Chinese peasant who was staggering away covered with blood. The

---

* He said he had four columns outside the city and a fifth, meaning sympathizers, inside.

NCO went close and shot him dead.' It transpired that the man's only offence was to have been spotted near a forward position. Madoc was convinced that the man was an entirely innocent Chinese vegetable gardener. 'I felt sure there had been a gross miscarriage of justice.'

Undoubtedly a few were guilty as charged, though these were rarely the Chinese, who had been at war with the 'shrimp barbarians' much longer than the British, but mostly Indians and Malays. Indian Independence League propaganda, which was backed by Japanese radio broadcasts, sometimes fell on fertile ground.

There were also occasions when the Japanese dressed as civilians and passed themselves off as Malay or Chinese in order to infiltrate British lines. (Loyal Asians, some of them Indian or Gurkha soldiers, occasionally did similar work for the British.) A member of an artillery battery that had recently had its field telephone wires cut stopped, at a whim, two grinning young cyclists in singlets and shorts who were pedalling past. Wire-cutters were discovered under their saddles.

They were discovered to be Japanese soldiers . . . and were two very frightened men. Since they were not wearing uniform, our troop officer shared the common view that no mercy should be shown to saboteurs. He authorized their execution which was carried out expeditiously.

But by and large, it seems that quite a lot of innocent, bewildered and ultimately terrified people found themselves looking at the wrong end of a row of Lee-Enfields for reasons that were utterly beyond their comprehension. By comparison, it makes the trial and execution of captured RAF crews for damaging Japanese property appear almost sane, although no less cruel. Nor was the hysteria over fifth columnists entirely confined to the usual suspects.

The day after Squadron Leader Scarf and his crew had made their lone attack on Singora, a particularly bumptious and unpopular British Indian Army officer had been arrested at gunpoint. Some eight months before Captain Patrick Heenan had been transferred to an army liaison unit with the RAF, mainly at the insistence of his commanding officer, who disliked him anyway and regarded his unauthorized trips to Thailand as the last straw. Now, Heenan was accused of being the traitor responsible for the series of well-timed raids that had destroyed, among others, so much of Scarf's squadron on the ground.

The prisoner was escorted back to Singapore in handcuffs. There he disappeared. For years there was talk that a British officer had been spying for the Japanese, but it took half a century for his identity to be established and his fate determined: it seems he was sentenced to death by a secret court martial, and eventually disposed of with a shot in the back of the head from a military policeman's pistol. Not surprisingly, none of this has ever received any official confirmation, and there appear to be no official records just as there are none for the Asian civilians who were shot.★

Heenan may have been as innocent as many of them were. It is possible that he got involved with one of the competing British intelligence agencies working around the Malay–Thai border and was a casualty of the SOE, MI5, MI6, Crosby turf wars. This might explain the 'unauthorized trips'. It is possible that he was no more than a role-playing Walter Mitty fantasist. Certainly he liked to mix in the kind of *demi-monde* where policemen and spymasters recruit.

The most damning find against Heenan, who was a Catholic, was that a padre's field communion set in his possession was discovered to contain a small wireless transmitter, or at least something that looked very much like one. Even so, radio communications in Malaya were so bad, especially during the monsoon, that the RAF must have known it was ludicrous to think that the Japanese could have relied on an agent tipping them off that aircraft had been gathered at a certain place and were about to take off.

Otherwise, much of the evidence against him was so circumstantial it might have made a witch-hunter general blush. A search of his quarters had revealed a written assessment of air force strength and a sketch map showing the positions of bomb and fuel dumps, though it might have been assumed that these related to his duties which included deploying men for airfield defence. His Bible was found to be 'full of underlined sentences and an obvious code'.

Like many Indian Army officers, he had been to Japan, spending almost all of a six months' long leave there before returning with an entirely predictable passion for geishas and a newly acquired interest in photography. It had been noted that he often appeared to prefer the company of Indian to British officers, even if they were ardent

★ It would not have come to light at all had it not been for some astute detective work on the part of Peter Elphick, a Master Mariner turned investigative reporter who identified Heenan and filled in a lot of the gaps in his *Odd Man Out* (with Michael Smith).

nationalists. There had also been dangerous liaisons with Asian or Eurasian civilians, particularly women, and unsuitable relations with White Russians, always women.

Tall and athletic and markedly olive skinned, Heenan had a chip on his broad shoulders which won him few friends. His fellow subalterns had regarded him as a hot-tempered bully – he was a good boxer – and definitely 'not quite a gentleman'. His dark skin also raised the possibility that, to use the parlance of the day, he had 'a touch of the tar brush' about him.

Heenan's roots belonged to the kind of by-ways of empire that had inspired Kipling's *Kim*. He was illegitimate. His father was an Irish mining engineer, who was born in India and could have been of Eurasian as well as Hibernian descent. His mother was the good-looking daughter of English immigrants to New Zealand, Heenan's birthplace in 1910. After the death of his father in Burma, where he was working, his mother remained there for a while as a governess. When he was twelve they moved to London where his attractive parent acquired him a reasonably well-off stepfather and with him the fees for Cheltenham College which, like most public schools, had a flourishing Officer Cadet Training Unit. He lacked the academic qualifications to get into Sandhurst but his OTC Certificate 'A', plus a note from his old headmaster, enabled him to obtain a commission in the Supplementary Reserve from which he transferred to the Indian Army.

Heenan had been serving in a battalion of the Punjabi Regiment and, immediately before its arrival in Malaya, was considered to have done well during skirmishing with Pathan tribesmen on the North West Frontier. None the less, his commanding officer was determined to get rid of him and he found himself serving alongside the RAF, in the Air Liaison Unit at Butterworth.

The success of various pre-emptive strikes on the airfields can be put down to Tsuji's reconnaissance flights and reports from local agents who had long ago discovered their whereabouts, plus the gradual build-up of air superiority which enabled the Japanese to keep aircraft over northern Malaya in increasing numbers. There was also an element of that quality Napoleon demanded of all his generals: luck. Heavy rain in Indo-China proved especially propitious for some of the first Japanese raids, delaying scheduled take-offs long enough to bring bombers over RAF airfields with exquisite timing.

By nightfall on 9 December, the first of the RAF's northern airfields was about to fall into enemy hands at Kota Baharu. Every few minutes the darkness would be lit up by lingering sheets of flame as Captain John Close's mountain gun battery, manned by twelve Indian gunners of the Singapore and Hong Kong Royal Artillery, landed another salvo of their small shells on drums of aviation fuel in the abandoned dump. Brigadier Key's day-time counter-attack had failed and since the airfield – the main reason his men were there in the first place – had been abandoned, he received permission to withdraw to a more defensible position.

In the afternoon Cumming's 2nd Sikhs, together with the Dogras and 1st Frontier Force Rifles, had retaken some territory in the wetlands behind the spits of sand either side of the Pengkalan Chapa. But they were too thinly spread and split up by this fissured territory, where gurgling, brown-water streams were now in full monsoon spate. Captain Kysor Medappa, the 2nd Sikhs' only Indian Commissioned Officer, was shot dead from what turned out to be a skilfully camouflaged boat lying alongside a bank. Some men drowned – in one instance after a Japanese fighter had strafed their sampan. Others lost their rifles as they suddenly found themselves under water in places where, earlier in the day, they had waded across with dry belts. Deep mud around mangrove swamps tugged boots off feet which, in some cases, perhaps trod more confidently without them.

Units became hopelessly intertwined. After the Dogras' commanding officer was wounded Cumming, who as a subaltern had won a Military Cross in Britain's successful 1919 campaign in Afghanistan, tried to take overall command, but communications were too bad to do this properly. Radios were not working and Cumming was trying to use runners. Takumi now had most of his men ashore and, despite their casualties, they greatly outnumbered Key's forces as a good part of his brigade was strung out along the coast to the south. As parties of Dogras and 2nd Sikhs straggled back to the airfield in the dark and under relentless rain, the sporadic illumination provided by the exploding aviation fuel revealed nightmare glimpses of their worst fears. The Japanese had beaten them to it: 'bodies of men of both sides were moving across the open space in the same direction in an inextricable muddle,' recorded the regimental history of the 2nd Sikhs.

What the chronicler of the Sikhs' misfortunes is far too polite to say is that the Indian Army component of this race across the airfield was mainly composed of Hyderabads who, unnerved by the panicky departure of the Australian ground crews, had bolted. Behind them lay the stiffening body of their commanding officer, Lieutenant-Colonel Clive Hendricks who, according to one account, may well have died from a British bullet as he pleaded with his men to fight.

'The enemy, realizing the indomitable courage of the Imperial Army, dispersed deep into the coconut groves like little spiders routed by mosquitoes,' wrote a Japanese journalist, probably sometime after the event. The reality was more like murder in the dark, with the lights flicked on every few seconds as another fuel barrel detonated and men were briefly caught in the act of running, shooting, killing and being killed.

The only effective rearguard action for the withdrawal from the airfield seems to have been provided by the mountain guns commanded by Captain Close, 'the hero of Kota Baharu' according to Key, who made sure he was awarded the Military Cross. Only when their ammunition was exhausted did they try to get away. Some escaped but Close, who had delayed his departure to try and wreck the gunsights, left it too late and became the first British Army officer ever to be taken prisoner by the Imperial Japanese Army. It was an inauspicious beginning. Filed as 'Capture Number One' by his interrogators, his hands were tied behind his back with wire and, for at least four days, he was given no food and very little water while he refused to give them any information other than his name, rank and number. He was then shipped to Saigon for more expert interrogation and torture.

Most of Cumming's 2nd Sikhs, with – compared to the Hyderabads – their large number of British officers, fell back through Kota Baharu town in reasonable order. At first the enemy's pursuit was tenacious, although it sometimes displayed a contempt for basic fieldcraft the 2nd Sikhs found puzzling. Relays of Japanese attempting to bring into action a single mortar placed on the road were shot by the same Bren gunner, who was close enough to make them out easily, despite the dark and the rain. After the fourth attempt, they gave up. But if this had been brave to the point of stupidity, the Japanese infantry gave a neat demonstration of what the British would come to learn was their favourite tactic.

While some mortared and held the Indians' attention in front, others infiltrated their flanks and got behind them. Soon they were tightening their noose around battalion headquarters, manhandling along with them a short-barrelled 37 mm anti-tank gun, not much bigger than a wheelbarrow though rather more awkward. Most of the Indians' Bren gun carriers – little open-topped tracked vehicles that looked rather like baby tanks, yet to grow into something lethal – were destroyed. Both sides threw grenades into the darkness. The battalion's second-in-command, Major Lionel Dart, decided they had to break out and led a bayonet charge which found or made a hole in the southern part of the cordon, through which they escaped into swampland carrying some of their wounded with them.

A good 10 miles away from Major Dart's party, in an isolated position still close to the airfield and the beach, Colonel Cumming remained blissfully unaware of Key's decision to withdraw until the next afternoon. He had about 100 men with him. A few were his own 2nd Sikhs but most were from the Dogra battalion, some of them the sepoys who had manned the beach defences so stubbornly and left them with great reluctance. By the time word of Key's order had reached them, they discovered that the Japanese were astride their line of retreat.

Three times Cumming tried and failed to break through, losing two of the Dogras' carriers in the process. In the end, they picked up their wounded and retreated back towards the coast, along one of the gushing distributaries of the Kelantan River, until they found a couple of sampans and were able to cross to its east bank where they rested in a deserted Chinese village. They then turned south again only to discover that the Japanese were across their route in strength. Since it was obvious that they were too weak to break through, Cumming decided that all they could do was disperse. He ordered his troops to disguise themselves as Malays as best they could and slip through the Japanese in ones or twos. This meant discarding rifles as well as boots, though some hid bayonets, grenades and pistols about their persons and a couple accommodated their Lee-Enfields in ingenious bundles.

Not having the option of becoming a Malay, Cumming led a small party of walking wounded slowly south through some paddy fields, hoping to evade the Japanese, although the prospects did not look promising. But help was at hand. The first sepoy to get through guided back a Bren gun carrier containing Captain Pomeroy, the former American journalist. Pomeroy and the sepoy burst through a Japanese road-block, found the colonel and his wounded and led them back.

Cumming was the most senior British straggler to get back to his own lines that day, but what had started as a trickle rapidly became a torrent. On the morning of 10 December, the 2nd Sikhs could only muster 140 men; two days later their numbers were up to almost 700. The same applied to the other battalions in Billy Key's 8th Brigade, and casualties were nowhere near as high as was first suspected. The only battalion that had broken was the Hyderabad State Force, and they did not belong to Key's brigade but, along with most of the rest of these princely Praetorian Guards on loan to the Raj, were part of the 3rd Indian Corps' reserve. In disgrace, they were trucked to the railhead at Kuala Krai and, further down the line, were met by military police who, as a temporary measure, disarmed those who still carried rifles. None of the Hyderabads was ever charged with Colonel Hendricks' murder, but the battalion was never used as a unit again. At least 100 of them found themselves transformed from infantry to uniformed coolies and used as a labour company.

At the urging of the British adviser to the Sultan of Kelantan, most of the European civilians in the area had already taken the same route as the Hyderabads. Since it was perfectly obvious that they would only be away for a few days, 'while the Japs are sorted out', most shut the door on their homes, and often almost a lifetime's acquisitions, carrying not much more than a weekend suitcase. His Highness Sultan Ismail himself, the slim and eternally youthful-looking figure who had ruled Kelantan for just over twenty years, adjourned to a hunting lodge he maintained some 8 miles south of Kota Baharu. In 1909 when Muslim Kelantan discovered, mostly to its satisfaction, that it had exchanged Buddhist Thai for British suzerainty, certain guarantees of protection had been made to Ismail's father. Now the sultan confidently awaited word that the Japanese had been pushed back into the South China Sea.

1. Against the outer wall of Singapore's Outram Road jail in 1915, a British militia begins the botched public executions by firing squad of Indian Army mutineers. Some were captured by the sailors from Japanese warships that had come to rescue the weakly garrisoned colony of their World War I ally

3. Photographers searching for a resolute image were unlikely to be disappointed by the face of a young Gurkha rifleman with 17-inch bayonet fixed, though appearances could be misleading

2. Indian and Gurkha infantry played a major part in the defence of Britain's South-east Asian colonies. Map in hand, an Indian havildar (sergeant) leads his men on a training exercise in the Malayan jungle, 1941

4. Lieutenant-General Arthur Percival arriving at Singapore to take over command in 1941. Too prominent teeth and too little chin might have delighted hostile cartoonists, but he was a brave and clever professional

5. Certainly, Percival had seen more action than his adversary Tomoyuki Yamashita, shown here on the day of his wedding to Hisako, the daughter of a general

6. These Japanese infantrymen gathered around their colours after a formal parade on Hainan Island prior to boarding their ships for the Malayan landings. Their determination is etched on their faces

7. The American-made Thompson sub-machine-gun, the 'Tommy' gun beloved by real and celluloid gangsters alike, was widely used by imperial British forces. But it was heavier than their Lee-Enfield rifles, was prone to jam and was only effective at close quarters

8. With his back to a rubber tree, a well-fed Australian soldier strips and cleans his 'Tommy'

9. Australian signallers (*right*) at a field headquarters. Jungle-covered hills and a humid climate regularly rent by tropical storms combined to make Morse wireless telegraphy unreliable

10. Only in Malaya were the fighter pilots of the British Empire unfortunate enough to have to fly the slow and unlovely American Brewster Buffalo, sometimes known as the 'Flying Barrel', which was no match for the Japanese Zero

11. Even some enemy bombers could get away from it, such as the twin-engined Nell (*right background*) being gingerly 'bombed up' by its own crew

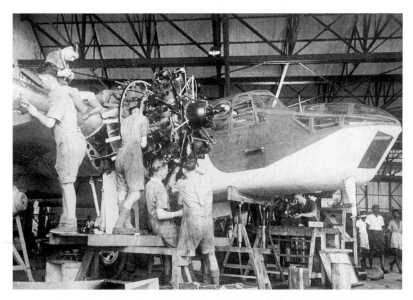

12. A newly arrived RAF Blenheim bomber, about the equivalent of a Nell, being serviced in a Singapore hanger. 'A fresh addition to Malaya's already considerable air strength' bluffed the original caption to this official photograph. Tokyo was unimpressed

13. SOE established a guerrilla training school in Singapore. Handsome, brave and incredibly tough, Colonel Frederick Spencer Chapman, a pre-war Arctic explorer and Himalayan mountaineer, taught fieldcraft and survival and practised what he preached

14. More conventional defences being erected on one of the island's southern beaches, intended to stop enemy landing-craft coming close inshore at high tide. There was little of this on the island's northern shore

15. In Malaya there was probably more fighting in the gloom of the rubber estates than there was in the jungle. Australian troops dig in

16. Lewis 'Piggy' Heath, commander of Percival's Indian forces, winter campaigning at the Khyber Pass about three years before he came to Malaya. He received a knighthood for his victories against the Italians in Ethiopia but found the Japanese a rather different proposition

17. Major-General Murray-Lyon, commander of the 11th Indian Division in northern Malaya, who shot a cheeky Japanese motorcyclist out of the saddle on a bridge but was not quick enough for Percival, who fired him

18. Water obstacles were a problem for both sides in Malaya. Here a Dogra battalion is exercising in cramped rubber boats shortly before the outbreak of hostilities

19. Indian troops demonstrate how two rifles can serve as a makeshift stand to steady a Bren gun against low-flying aircraft. Proper stands did exist but few units had them

20. Two months before the Japanese landing at Kota Baharu, Australian nurses, often from small towns and abroad for the first time, are being escorted around the grounds of a Buddhist temple by an Argylls officer in full dress uniform. Not to be outdone, some of the nurses are wearing gloves as well as stockings

21. Women and children from the substantial Japanese community that existed in pre-war Malaya and Singapore boarding a British ship taking them to continue their internment in India

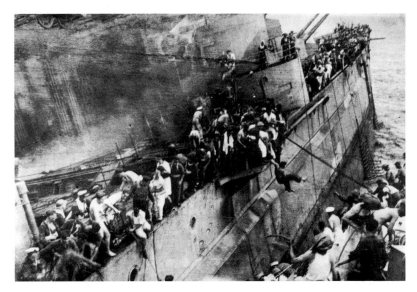

22. Sailors from the listing battleship *Prince of Wales* haul themselves on to the deck of HMS *Express*. Shortly after this photograph was taken from the destroyer's bridge the life lines had to be cut before the sinking giant capsized it

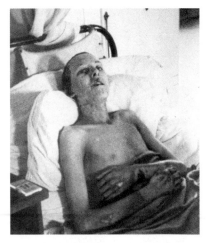

23. One of the teenage seamen off the *Prince of Wales* recovering from leg injuries in the naval base's hospital. Over the next three months many of these survivors would find themselves on other sinking ships

24. The last known photograph of Admiral Tom 'Thumb' Phillips (*right*) taken with Rear-Admiral Palliser, his chief of staff, who remained in Singapore when Phillips took his ships on their ill-fated search for the invasion fleet

# PART THREE

# The 300-year-old Tradition

The sultan's faith was not misplaced. Help was on the way. The Royal Navy, whose well-publicized reinforcements had failed to deter the Japanese from their lunatic folly, were now set to teach them a lesson they would never forget. The *Prince of Wales* and *Repulse* had put to sea along with four destroyers. 'We are off to look for trouble. I expect we shall find it,' Captain William Tennant told his crew on the *Repulse*.

We are going to carry out a sweep to the northward to see what we can pick up and what we can roar up. We must all be on our toes . . . I know the old ship will give a good account of itself. We have trained hard enough for this day. Life saving gear is to be worn or carried . . . not because I think anything is going to happen to the ship – she is much too lucky . . .

Quite apart from being reminded what a lucky ship they were, this was exactly the kind of fighting talk Tennant's mainly regular crew wanted to hear. The trouble with being on the *Repulse* was that she was an old war-horse that had hardly ever been to war. The last and only time her six 15-inch guns had fired a shot in action was in 1917 when she was credited with scoring a direct hit on the cruiser *Königsberg* in the grey waters of the Heligoland Bight. Since the resumption of hostilities with Germany in 1939 she had spent most of her time on convoy protection but had never encountered any surface raiders.

*Repulse*'s big-gun crews, the winners of the Royal Navy's last peacetime main armament competition at Scapa Flow, were still awaiting their chance to show the King's enemies how, without the aid of radar, they could reach them from almost 15 miles away. Ordinary Seaman Bowen, the teenaged chorister whose contribution to his ship's fame had so far been entirely musical, was looking forward to a scrap with the rest of them. 'We thought the Japs would be a bit of a pushover. Little yellow so-and-so's, couldn't see in the dark, probably couldn't see to fly their planes straight. Better than fighting the Germans that was for sure.'

Yet once again the *Repulse* had almost missed out. She had been at the beginning of the third day of her voyage to Australia when, following the first sighting of the Japanese convoys, her wireless room had received the signal recalling her to Singapore. Had this happened twenty-four hours later, *Repulse* would not have had enough fuel left to turn round, and she would have had to press on to Darwin, which, most of the lower deck agreed, was Japan's hard luck not theirs. Even the five Royal Australian Navy midshipmen on board, not one of them over twenty and already a year away from home, were relieved not to be missing out. Originally destined for an Australian cruiser which had left England before they could join her, they had been posted to the *Repulse* in time for the *Bismarck* hunt, and shared in the ignominy of having to break off as their fuel ran low.

Midshipman Guy Griffiths, the son of a New South Wales farmer and grandson of an emigrant from Devon, thought the morale of the Australians on board was high. 'Our minds weren't tuned into going home. We were keen to get into action. You always are when you've never really seen it.'

Unlike his midshipmen, Admiral Sir Tom Phillips, at fifty-three one of the oldest members of Force Z, knew that this was a risky venture. But he also knew where his duty lay and undoubtedly there had been a touch of Nelson, that other small admiral, in his parting words to Tennant and the other captains gathered aboard his flagship, the *Prince of Wales*. 'We can stay in Singapore. We can sail away to the east – Australia. Or we can go out and fight. Gentlemen, we sail at five o'clock.'

It had been the best part of a quarter of a century since Phillips himself was last in action. In 1915 he had been on a cruiser during the ultimately disastrous Gallipoli landings. The following year he had had the great misfortune, for a professional naval officer, of missing the Battle of Jutland. None the less, his intelligence and attention to detail – his hobby was repairing watches – plus a sufficiently well-founded belief in his own convictions, had over the twenty years since earned him one promotion after another, although his was a career that had sailed more desks than ships.

By the time Britain was at last at war with Hitler, Phillips was deputy chief of naval staff. He had taken over the job from Admiral Andrew Cunningham, who had left to command the Mediterranean fleet and to become, with his victorious night action against the Italians at Matapan, in which an enemy cruiser was actually boarded, Britain's most famous sailor since Jellicoe. Cunningham was five years older than

Phillips, and no fan of the younger man whom he considered promoted above his talents. None the less, his successor at Whitehall established a good working relationship with Churchill who always warmed to the warrior breed and probably detected the able administrator's yearning to match Cunningham as a man of action.

This relationship continued to flourish after Churchill moved from the Admiralty to 10 Downing Street. Then came a cooling off. Phillips had not got where he was by being a yes man; he would have regarded it as a dereliction of duty. When the navy was ordered to transport an expeditionary force to Greece, a country that Mussolini's invasion in October 1940 had transformed overnight into the British Empire's only unconquered European ally, the admiral was outspoken in his criticism and rightly predicted a military fiasco.

He could be equally outspoken about things that, on the face of it, were not in his domain. One of them was the retaliatory bombing of German cities. It is not clear how much, if at all, his objections were on moral grounds. In any case, this was early in the war, before the Anglo-Americans began to massacre German civilians in their thousands. But he certainly saw a large investment in offensive air power as a waste of precious resources and argued that bombing civilians had proved counterproductive in both the civil war in Spain and during Goering's attempt to subdue Britain. Yet, despite his well-publicized desire to reduce the RAF's share of the war chest, one of Phillips' friends was Arthur Harris, eventually the air marshal in charge of RAF Bomber Command. Harris, who knew him well enough to make jokes about his height, liked to tease the admiral about his stubborn refusal to believe a battleship could be sunk from the air. 'One day, Tom, you'll be standing on a box on your bridge,' he once told him, 'and your ship will be smashed to pieces by bombers and torpedo aircraft; as she sinks, your last words will be, "That was a fucking great mine!"'

Much of Phillips' attitude appears to have been a reaction against the doom-laden, pre-war certainty that the omnipotent bomber would always get through and render everything else about as relevant as chain mail. Post-1940 Britain, admittedly thanks to heavy last-minute investment in Spitfires, radar and anti-aircraft guns, was living proof that this was far from the case. As for his own service, his faith in the battleship was undiminished.

Seven months before he arrived in Singapore, the final act of the

Greek tragedy had been played out around Crete, where Cunningham persisted in trying to evacuate the army despite the loss to dive bombers of nine of his cruisers and destroyers with at least 1,800 men killed. Far from damaging Cunningham's reputation, these casualties had not only enhanced it but also enabled him to preach the Senior Service's conception of duty and self-sacrifice with some phrase-making worthy of Churchill himself.

'It will take three years to build a new Fleet,' he told General Wavell, who was then the army's Middle East commander-in-chief. 'It will take 300 years to build a new tradition.'

The Royal Navy's belief in its own superiority has always been its most unsinkable asset. As far as Phillips was concerned, it was reinforced by his conviction that a well-handled capital ship, replete with long- and short-range air defences tended by well-trained crews, was a much more difficult proposition than Cunningham's cruisers and destroyers. The Luftwaffe, Phillips would explain, had succeeded against the smaller ships only because, trying to evacuate troops, they had become isolated in coastal waters shielded by no more than their own paltry firepower. Nor would Phillips allow the success of the navy's own air arm against the Italians to change his mind. At Taranto Mussolini's battleships had been ducks in a barrel: torpedoed by the Swordfish when they had been surprised in a badly defended harbour without room to manoeuvre.

Phillips' belief in the ability of big ships to look after themselves, providing they were properly handled, was not a minority one. Cunningham, who as a midshipman had fought with the naval brigade in the Boer War, had himself only very reluctantly come to view the aeroplane as a threat and had actively discouraged young officers from transferring to the Fleet Air Arm. The very air-minded Churchill, who was in his mid-forties before he could be persuaded to give up an often near fatal obsession to qualify for a private pilot's licence, was never in any doubt about the value of air power. Yet he was of a generation brought up to revere the navy, and rightly so, as the source of Britain's greatness. The romantic in him wanted to believe those who insisted that the latest armour-plated battleship, bristling with counter-measures, was far too tough a nut to be cracked by aircraft alone.

If more proof was needed, it had been amply provided by the *Prince of Wales* herself only two months before, while running the gauntlet of Italian and German torpedo bombers into besieged Malta along with the battleships *Nelson* and *Rodney* and the carrier *Ark Royal*. Between them, the battleships had accounted for at least five of their tormentors, of which two had been shot down by the *Prince*. *Nelson*, a battleship that was fourteen years older than the *Prince of Wales*, did stop a torpedo but, thanks to her watertight compartments, the damage had been slight and, despite a slight list, she was able to proceed under her own power. To complete the joy of the *Prince of Wales'* crew, and particularly gratifying for the conscripts on the anti-aircraft guns, once they had returned to Gibraltar the *Nelson*'s air defence officer came aboard to ask the younger ship how they did it. One of the things they told him was that they would have shot down a couple more if it had not been for the large number of stoppages on their eight-barrelled pompom guns, owing to defective ammunition.

Force Z had left the Singapore naval base just after sunset on 8 December, the first clue to their imminent departure being the rattle of anchor chains before they disappeared into the gathering gloom. This was at least sixteen hours after hostilities had started, and the absence of a rapid British naval response had puzzled Vice-Admiral Jizaburo Ozawa, who was almost a decade younger than Phillips and regarded as one of the Imperial Navy's best tacticians. By now he had most of the troops they were landing in Thailand ashore and not a few at Kota Baharu, and was a very relieved man. 'Even if the British attacked there could be no damage done to the military units already landed and any damage would only be to empty ships and to a small quantity of supplies.'

Perhaps a younger, more impetuous commander might have acted faster. Phillips had been in Manila for consultations with the US Navy's Admiral Hart and *Repulse* had been on her way to Darwin when Ramshaw's RAAF Hudson spotted the first convoy in the Gulf of Siam. The admiral, who had been averaging about four hours' sleep a night ever since he left London and not much more there, got back to Singapore the next day, his arrival in the early hours of Sunday 7 December coinciding with the return of the *Repulse*. But before he could go to bed, the representatives of the Australian and New Zealand naval boards were waiting to see him, as were the Dutch and American naval liaison officers based in Singapore. Phillips accepted a Dutch offer to send some of their submarines into the area where the Japanese ships had been seen and, exhausted, retired to his quarters.

On the face of it, if instead of seeing what the morrow would bring

Phillips had decided, there and then, to extract the *Prince of Wales* from dry dock and move Britain's naval deterrent north to meet the Japanese, Ozawa would have had little choice but to back off. The heaviest ships the Japanese had in the area were two old pre-1914 battleships lurking off the Indo-China coast, one of them the British-built *Kongo*, which was the flagship of Vice-Admiral Nobutake Kondo, Ozawa's superior. They had eight 14-inch guns apiece, but no radar, and the Japanese knew that even the *Repulse* had the edge on them. All Ozawa had to protect the landings were four heavy cruisers with 8-inch guns and about eight destroyers which the British battleships could have sunk within minutes before the destroyers got close enough to harm them. For a few hours, Phillips had the opportunity to attempt the most complete destruction of an invasion fleet since Sir Francis Drake was unleashed on the Spanish Armada.

But it was not without risk. Ever since the British had taken such trouble to notify them of the arrival of the *Prince of Wales* and 'other heavy units' the Japanese had taken some well-considered precautions. Had Phillips shrugged off his fatigue when he got back to Singapore and been off before dawn on the most direct route north, there was a very good chance that at least one of his capital ships would have been crippled by one of the 1,000 mines two of Ozawa's minelayers had just finished putting down.

These had been laid across the 100 or so miles of water between Tioman Island, off Malaya's east coast, and the Dutch-owned Anambas group, through which most ships travelling north had to pass. North of the mines were three patrol lines of fourteen submarines, with another two off Singapore's southern shore. Most of them had been there since 2 December – the day the *Prince of Wales* and *Repulse* had arrived at the naval base.

As an added precaution, Admiral Isoroku Yamamoto, the schoolmaster's son who was the architect of the pre-emptive strike at Pearl Harbor, transferred from Formosa to the Indo-China airfields extra Nell and Betty torpedo bombers. Eventually, he had 142 aircraft there, in addition to the army's total regional strength of 682, including all fighters, bombers, flying boats and army cooperation aircraft. It was Yamamoto who had once replied to the 'only a battleship can sink a battleship' argument with an old Chinese proverb Air Marshal Harris would surely have loved to pass on to his friend Tom Phillips: 'The fiercest serpent may be overcome by a swarm of ants.'

Having made his decision to go out and fight, it did make a certain amount of sense for Phillips to delay his departure until dark. With any luck, it would be a good twelve hours before Japanese reconnaissance flights, or the fifth columnists everybody was so sure were everywhere, spotted that the battleships had been let off their leash and the alarm was raised. But this had to be balanced against the risk of getting there too late.

Shortly after midday, both captains came ashore, William Tennant off the *Repulse* and John Leach from the *Prince of Wales*. They had known each other for many years and were good friends. Both were tall men in early middle age who shared the love of country pursuits, particularly fishing and shooting, common to British officers of all three services. Both had been awarded the DSO: Tennant for his work as senior navy liaison officer on the beaches at Dunkirk – he was 'Dunkirk Charlie' to his crew; Leach for the show the *Prince of Wales* had put up against the *Bismarck*, despite its malfunctioning guns – he was very nearly among those killed when a German shell had cleared his bridge. Tennant was the leaner and slightly older of the two, at fifty-three the same age as the admiral. Leach, who was almost bald and looked older than he was, had been a formidable athlete as a young man, a navy racquets, squash and tennis champion.

He was not the only member of his family in Singapore that day. One of the reasons Leach had come ashore was to see his youngest son Henry, who three weeks before had celebrated his eighteenth birthday as a midshipman aboard the new cruiser *Mauritius*, which was undergoing minor repairs in the dockyard. They met up in the late afternoon at the officers' club swimming pool. It was an occasion that was to remain etched in the memory of the teenager.

I've always been a very poor swimmer and was just splashing about to keep cool and chatting to my father until he said he would have to be getting out soon because he had promised to have a drink in the bar with Bill Tennant. 'I'm going to do a couple of lengths now,' he told me. 'You never know when it might not come in handy.'

As far as Leach junior was concerned, this was not a jocular aside but further evidence of the foreboding his father had displayed a couple of nights before when he had invited him to dinner on the *Prince of Wales* while Phillips was away in Manila. It was the first time that they had seen each other for almost a year and they had much to catch up on. Knowing that his father was a stickler for correct dress, despite the sticky night air the midshipman had turned up in long-trousered mess kit complete with short jacket, wing collar and bow tie, only to find that his parent was still clad in white shorts and shirt and obviously preoccupied.

He was a worried man. After dinner in his quarters we sat on the sofa and he offered me his cigarette case. 'I don't know what bad habits you've picked up,' he said. I took one and he asked me what I thought would happen if the Japanese started something. 'Oh let 'em come, let's have a crack at them,' I replied and he gave me a long, thoughtful look. 'I don't think you've any idea of the odds we're up against.'

At least the weather was neutral and it seemed that Phillips, who was maintaining strict radio silence, was going to get the surprise he needed to disrupt the Japanese invasion fleet with one daring raid. Following their departure from Singapore, the same monsoon squalls and low cloud that had shielded the Japanese convoys from the Hudsons now covered Phillips' ships. By another stroke of luck, a Japanese reconnaissance flight over Singapore had reported that the battleships were still in harbour, possibly mistaking the naval base's huge floating dock for one of them.

Phillips was aware of the mines that had been laid to block his passage on the direct route north from the naval base, probably because some of them had broken free of their moorings and been spotted by routine RAF reconnaissance. To avoid them he had taken his battleships and their escorts east around the Anambas Islands and then turned north. They had been at sea for almost twenty hours before they were spotted at a great distance by the most easterly of the Japanese submarines, patrolling at periscope depth north of the mines. Even then their luck held for a little longer.

First the submarine, which had done well to see them in the first place, lost sight of them in a squall. Then bad radio communications delayed by two hours the submarine's sighting report from reaching the cruiser *Chokai*, from where Ozawa was flying his flag. Shortly afterwards any doubts that may have lingered over the identification of the ships, though the submarine had confirmed its first periscope sighting by surfacing and shadowing them for two hours, were dispelled by the latest aerial reconnaissance photographs of the Singapore naval base.

It is not hard to imagine Ozawa's consternation. Orders were immediately given for those transports not already on their way back to Saigon and Cam Ranh Bay to scatter into the northern waters of the Gulf of Siam. Only a few hours of daylight were left but almost sixty aircraft, most of them armed with torpedoes, were sent to find the battleships. If necessary, and if there was enough moonlight, their orders were to continue after dark, and they were not expected to return to their Saigon airfields with more than a sake cup's worth of fuel in their tanks. Ozawa also had his ships increase their radio traffic with each other, in the hope that the enemy would plot their position and be lured away from the transports – a brave move when there was no hope of the 14-inch guns aboard Vice-Admiral Kondo's old battleships getting close enough to cover them before daybreak.

As it happened, the British did not monitor this sudden surge in Japanese radio traffic, or if they did they ignored it. They themselves maintained strict wireless silence, receiving messages but transmitting nothing. Earlier in the day there had been some alarm when an aircraft appeared through the mist, but fire discipline held long enough for it to be identified as the RAF Catalina flying reconnaissance for them. After it was reasonably certain it was not going to be blown out of the sky, the Catalina came in low enough to blink out a morse message with its Aldis lamp confirming that the Japanese were continuing to land troops north of Singora.

On the bridge of the *Prince of Wales*, probably not standing on a box as it was up to Captain Leach to see where they were going, Admiral Phillips was blissfully unaware that Force Z had lost the advantage of surprise. The most troublesome thing that had happened to him all day was that he had developed a bad toothache and Boy Seaman Millard, who was acting as admiral's messenger, had been advised by the coxswain to tread warily. Phillips was not always an easy man to get on with at any level. When Midshipman Leach had asked his father over dinner what the admiral was like, the captain had muttered, 'Difficult man', and changed the subject.

By early evening, Phillips was not letting his toothache stop him sharing his satisfaction at the way things had developed with his sailors, and was explaining what they were going to do next. Clackety-clack-clack, went the Aldis lamps from the bridge of the *Prince of Wales*, as they passed on the admiral's eve-of-battle message to the *Repulse*. On the flagship, it had already been broadcast on the tannoy and pinned to notice boards:

... fat transports lie off the coast ... We have made a wide circuit to avoid air reconnaissance and hope to surprise the enemy shortly after sunrise tomorrow Wednesday. We may have the luck to try our mettle against the old battle cruiser *Kongo* or against some Japanese cruisers and destroyers which are reported in the Gulf of Siam. We are sure to get some useful practice with the h.a. armament [h.a. – high-angle aircraft guns]. Whatever we meet I want to finish quickly and so get well clear to the eastward before the Japanese can mount too formidable a scale of attack against us. So shoot to sink.

Preparations began to be made for a mid-twentieth-century sea battle. In the wardrooms where off-duty officers drank and ate, sports trophies, books and portraits of the royal family were carefully stowed away, for if the sick bay became crowded, wardrooms were sometimes turned into casualty centres. On the *Prince of Wales*, Surgeon Lieutenant-Commander Edward Caldwell discovered there was 'a cold, uninteresting help-yourself supper, the stewards and attendants being already employed on their various jobs in gun turrets, ammunition hoists and shell rooms'.

I thought what a curse a vivid imagination could be and wished we could hurry up and get on with it. Everyone seemed rather quiet. I went down to my cabin ... stuffed some chocolate, a torch, a hypodermic syringe and a packet of tie-on casualty labels into my pockets, adjusted my uninflated lifebelt round my waist and went out ...

On both ships, first-aid bags were filled and distributed. Their contents included padded splints and rubber tubing for tourniquets, 'more practical than the St John's type'. On the *Repulse*, with its slightly smaller medical team, the senior gunnery officer, the senior engineer and the padre were all given morphia ampules and syringes and shown how to use them.

Despite the heat, from action stations at dawn the next day all ranks serving on the upper deck were ordered to cover themselves with long trousers and long-sleeved shirts – boiler suits were considered ideal. This served as a protection against burns inflicted by the searing flash that came when shells failed to pierce a warship's armour-plated hide. For the same reason, gunners covered most of their faces with Chaucerian-looking white cotton cowls, worn under their steel helmets, and put on asbestos gauntlets that went up to the elbow.

But at least one man carried an older remedy for those in peril on the sea. Able Seaman Alexander White, a radar operator on the *Prince of Wales*, had folded into an envelope in his wallet something that looked like a faded piece of ancient, yellowed parchment paper. It was his grandfather's caul, part of the amniotic sac enclosing the foetus sometimes found to be still snugly attached to a baby's head at birth. There is an old sailor's superstition that a man who carries a caul at sea will never drown. This one had been sent to the able seaman handling the most advanced technology on the ship by an aunt who believed in things science could not explain.

Shortly after 6 p.m. the sun would set, the grey, rain-filled sky would give way to a cloud-laden darkness the moon was unlikely to pierce, and they would begin their dash westwards to the coast and death or glory. The off-duty watches swung gently to and fro in their hammocks, or wrote letters home that would not be posted until they were back on land and their contents sweetly dated, though no less heartfelt. The cautious rolled their pound notes into tight cylinders and then waterproofed them by pulling condoms over them. When they had finished, they placed these unlovely packages into pockets which could be buttoned down.

Then, at 4.45 p.m., with no more than an hour to go before dusk started to set in, rents and holes began to appear in the low canopy of pewter-coloured monsoon cloud that had so conveniently covered Force Z ever since Phillips had left Singapore. Gradually, the patches of blue got bigger. Slowly at first, and then with mounting speed, the clouds began to fragment until soon they were reduced to isolated outposts of cumulus besieged by the clear translucent sky of an early tropical evening. This in itself, though nerve-racking, was not disastrous – there was not long to go before the short-lived Asian dusk gave way to night, and the radarless Japanese navy could not see in the dark.

Then, about an hour later, not long before last light, three small blips appeared on the *Prince of Wales'* newly fitted airborne radar screen, an innovation that was still far from infallible and was viewed with suspicion by some. But soon the lookouts confirmed, low on the horizon and hardly bigger than a mosquito on a wall, the existence of three black specks. They were too far away to shoot at. In any case, there was an even chance they were British and the Royal Navy was trying to improve its image in this respect. As they got closer, powerful binoculars showed them to be single-engined monoplanes with big floats. The RAF did not have anything like that. But what about the Americans, the Australians or the Dutch? Even the Vichy French? After all, they were not all that far away from Indo-China.

Identification books were hurriedly consulted, silhouettes matched with what they could see. The reluctant consensus was that they were undoubtedly Jakes, the Allied code word for a Japanese float plane, usually catapulted off warships for reconnaissance. The Jakes circled the horizon with impunity while the gunners manning the most powerful anti-aircraft guns Phillips had at his disposal, the *Prince of Wales*' 5.25-inch dual-purpose, begged them to take a closer look. But they had seen enough.

Admiral Phillips had no knowledge of the brief submarine sighting of his ships that had already caused Ozawa to order the dispersal of his transports, their cargoes mostly discharged and certainly not as fat as they had been. As far as the admiral was concerned, this was the first time he had been spotted and now that he had lost the advantage of surprise he had to decide what to do next.

There was no doubt he was hungry for battle, determined to inflict the maximum damage on the enemy. Being only human, perhaps from time to time over the last twenty-four hours, if only to keep his toothache at bay, the little admiral had mused on the glittering prizes that sinking the transports and their outgunned escorts would bring. Lord Phillips of Singora or would it be Kota Baharu? Yet for all his faith in the ability of battleships to defend themselves against air attack, from the moment he had outlined his plan to his captains aboard the *Prince of Wales* at Singapore, he had made no attempt to hide the risk.

'Like taking the Home Fleet into the Skagerrak without air cover,' he had told them. In 1941, with German air bases on both the Danish and Norwegian coasts, taking the Home Fleet into the Skagerrak would have been, to put it mildly, an unacceptable risk.

Without air support, or even the requisite cruisers and destroyers of a balanced fleet, Phillips had embarked on what was essentially a raid, a daring act of hit-and-run, relying on surprise and his big guns to get them in and out of trouble. Well, he still had his big guns. While the admiral was mulling this over, about 5 miles ahead of them the sea was suddenly bathed in a large white light which just as swiftly dimmed. It was correctly identified as a flare. Phillips immediately ordered a turn to port which put them on a south-westerly course. But if it had alarmed the British, it had given Ozawa much more to worry about.

The flare had been dropped close to *Chokai* by an exultant Lieutenant Takeda, the pilot of a Betty bomber, who had spotted in the moonlight the white froth of the flagship's wake. Takeda had followed it until he could see the dark shadow of the warship and possibly another vessel beneath him, whereupon he announced to the rest of his wing – fifty-three torpedo-carrying or bombed-up aircraft – that he had just located the British battleships, gave his position and urged them to hurry. Ozawa had no direct radio contact with these aircraft and estimated that there were at least three of them above him preparing to attack before he contacted Saigon, who passed on a desperate, 'It is *Chokai* under the flare.' The aircraft returned to base.

At about the same time, a message reached Phillips reporting a large number of Japanese ships around Kota Baharu again, which was a much more attractive target than Singora, being a good 100 miles closer to the safety of Singapore. But fifteen minutes later came another signal explaining that the previous message was based on a reconnaissance flown some seven hours before the Jakes had spotted them, leaving Phillips to ask himself what would a prudent Japanese commander, a fellow professional, do if he knew two fast, big-gunned enemy battle-ships were on the prowl and he lacked adequate means to protect his flock? Easy: he would order them to disperse. Shortly before 9 p.m. Phillips' flagship drew close to the *Repulse* and, on a blue-lensed night-time Aldis lamp less likely to be spotted from a distance, flashed out a message to Captain Tennant.

I have most regretfully cancelled the operation because, having been located by aircraft, surprise was lost and our target would be almost certain to be gone by the morning and the enemy fully prepared for us.

Keyed up for action as they were, Phillips' regrets were probably shared by the majority of officers and men in Force Z. But nowhere was the disappointment more palpable than in the wardroom of the

*Repulse*, where those officers who could get away had just finished their self-service dinner of hot soup, cold cuts and fresh fruit, and the bar had discreetly reopened. A variety of anti-flash ware was being worn, from the blue serge trousers of their cold-water uniforms to cricket flannels and even civilian corduroys.

One of the most disappointed men in the wardroom, and making no secret of it, was O'Dowd Gallagher, who was not a naval officer, nor even in the military, but a war correspondent for the *Daily Express*, one of two journalists aboard. The other was Gallagher's friend Cecil Brown, an American radio reporter for the Columbia Broadcasting System who had come aboard at short notice and was annoyed to find he was still wearing his hand-made, reverse-calf shoes, which were not best suited to salt spray. The newsmen were accompanied by Lieutenant Horace Abrahams of the Royal Navy Volunteer Reserve, an Admiralty press officer who, in civilian life, had worked for a Fleet Street picture agency. Abrahams, whose expanding waistband belied his considerable energy, was to provide the photographs for the press, and he was equipped with the kind of large Speed Graphic plate camera commonly used by most newspaper photographers.

Gallagher, an ambitious young South African of Irish extraction, had reported his first war in 1936, when he was twenty-two – he managed to get to Addis Ababa in time for Mussolini's invasion of Abyssinia. Since then he had covered the end of the Spanish civil war, the blitzkrieg in France and the evacuation from Dunkirk. It would have been a great scoop to be the only Fleet Street reporter to have accompanied a naval raid on the Japanese landings in Malaya, and perhaps his disappointment was greater than that of most of the men on board. 'I may have spoken out of turn in the wardroom by declaring we should have gone on,' he would write, not long afterwards. 'I reasoned that they had found us and, if we were to be bombed, let us achieve something at the same time by attacking the convoy and its escort.'

No doubt there were officers in the wardroom who expected civilian guests to keep their opinions on naval matters to themselves, especially those mature enough to realize that Phillips could not possibly risk badly needed battleships to sink a few cruisers and destroyers for the *Daily Express*. But if Gallagher did raise eyebrows, at least the reporter was not asking his hosts to go anywhere he was not prepared to go himself. And if the worst came to the worst, he was at some disadvantage for, unlike most of the officers present, Gallagher had never learned to swim. He was not alone in this. Non-swimmers were by no means uncommon among the Hostilities Only men.

After dinner, those who were lucky enough not to be at action stations got what sleep they could: Gallagher on a couch in the wardroom; Captain Tennant on the bunk in his sea-cabin where orchids in a glass water jug stood next to the framed photograph of his wife. As they slept, the faintly bubbled wakes of five liquid-oxygen-propelled torpedoes, spread in a roughly parallel formation, silently approached the stern of the *Repulse*, which was well behind the *Prince of Wales*. They missed and went resolutely on their way until their oxygen chambers were emptied and they glided down to the seabed almost as if they had never been.

The torpedoes had been fired by Lieutenant-Commander Sohichi Kitamura, captain of the *I.58*. This somewhat elderly submarine had been on the surface, hoping to catch a glimpse of the British ships on their north-westerly course when, 600 metres away and proceeding in exactly the opposite direction, they had spotted these large shapes bearing down on them at over 20 knots. Coming up to periscope depth after a crash dive, Kitamura had found himself in an ideal position to torpedo the *Prince of Wales*. Then came calamity. The hatches on *I.58*'s torpedo tubes were discovered to be jammed and, by the time they had got them unjammed, the exquisite target was out of danger and *Repulse*'s fast-disappearing stern the only plausible alternative.

None the less Kitamura was still left with the kudos of being the first to report the radical change of direction of the British ships. A later signal, sent not long before his much slower craft inevitably lost contact, took hours to reach Ozawa, after a destroyer with good reception apparently failed to realize that nobody else had picked it up. This reported another change of course, from due south to south-west, and the making of 'much black smoke'.

The *Prince of Wales* had turned to starboard, blue-lamp signals flashing to the *Repulse* and the destroyer escorts, and once again Force Z was heading towards the Malayan coast. Phillips was back into the raiding business.

In his admiral's cuddy aboard the flagship he had probably also slept through the failed torpedo attack, Force Z's combined radar and asdic underwater detection gear having all failed to spot *I.58* either above or below the waves. But at about the time the torpedoes had motored

past the *Repulse*, Phillips had been woken from his slumbers to read a
wireless signal from Rear-Admiral Palliser, his chief of staff who had
been left in Singapore so that he could, among other things, liaise with
RAF reconnaissance. Palliser had informed him that a Japanese landing
had been reported at Kuantan, scene of the hurried departure of the
RAAF's 8 Squadron some hours before. The admiral almost immediately ordered a change of course and increase of speed to 25 knots –
hence Kitamura's 'much black smoke'.

Phillips must have found it hard to believe his luck. Once again he was
unaware that he had been located by a submarine. As far as he was
concerned, the Japanese had no idea where he was and had made a
bad mistake. He thought that the Japanese, convinced that his squadron
was still heading north, had sent some of their transports and escorts to
the Kuantan area – unaware that he was no more than five hours away
and that Force Z could be among their ships shortly after dawn, like a
wolf in the fold. And once the massacre was over, for given his big
guns it could be nothing less, he was well placed for the dash back to
Singapore – 350 nautical miles with the diversion east around the
Anambas Islands again to avoid the Japanese mines.

   HMS *Tenedos*, the oldest of his four escort destroyers and the one
with the least endurance, had already been detached to return to the
naval base while she still had enough fuel to do so. At 8 a.m. on
10 December, by which time Phillips expected to be well into his
rampage off Kuantan, *Tenedos* was instructed to send a radio message
to Palliser asking for the maximum number of destroyers to meet his
two battleships just north of the Anambas Islands the following day.
If possible, this was to include four American destroyers Admiral
Hart had promised him in Manila. He wanted a sizeable escort to take
his two battleships through the approaches to Singapore where the
Japanese were likely to have increased the chances of submarine
ambush.

   *Tenedos*' message would be the first time any ship of Force Z had
broken the radio silence Phillips had imposed. To ensure surprise, he
would continue to maintain it as they went through the night towards
Kuantan. This meant that, after *I.58*'s sighting, the Japanese had a much
better idea of where Force Z were than the British. As far as Palliser
was concerned, Force Z might have stuck to its original plan and be
about to arrive with the dawn off Singora, or chosen the Kota Baharu

option a little further south, or made a major change in course to raid the landing at Kuantan he had reported in his latest message.

On balance, the last was the most likely, because Phillips had a much better chance of catching his 'fat transports' still waiting to put men ashore at a fresh landing. It was also much closer to the Singapore air umbrella. Pulford had made it plain from the beginning that, although he could provide a certain amount of reconnaissance, he could not offer fighter protection as far north as the Thai beaches or even, by the time they had sailed, at Kota Baharu.

Further south was a different question. The Australian 453 Buffalo Squadron, twelve aircraft under the temporary command of Flight Lieutenant Tim Vigors, the Battle of Britain veteran who had so yearned to take on the night bombers over Singapore, had been designated Fleet Defence Squadron. Vigors had been aboard the *Prince of Wales* to arrange a wavelength for an air-to-ship radio link, though there was no time to put it to the test. The squadron was still based at Sembawang airfield near the naval base. It would have made more sense for them to have moved up to RAF Kuantan, forty-five minutes' flying time away, which, thanks to Bulcock and the others who remained, was still serviceable. Then came the reports of the latest Japanese landings.

As Phillips' five ships surged towards them, their 25-knot bow wave leaving great white trails of foam behind, the sounds of a battle royal were coming from Kuantan's beaches. It had started with flares followed by small arms fire, automatic and single shot, from the 2/18th Garhwalis manning defences behind the same kind of barbed-wire entanglements and land mines that had been put down at Kota Baharu. Then came the reassuring sound, for the defenders at least, of the 4.5-inch howitzers of the 5th Regiment, Royal Artillery, systematically flailing the beaches with the batteries they had hidden among the rubber trees a couple of miles behind the infantry. The gunners had plenty of ammunition and were delighted at this first opportunity to fire it in action.

At the airfield, fearing that they were about to be overrun, Flight Lieutenant Bulcock's commanding officer ordered confidential documents to be destroyed. In the process, the can of petrol being used to ensure full cremation caught fire, and the airfield's *attap*-roofed operations room burnt to the ground. Nobody was hurt and, come the dawn, the hut turned out to be the only significant British casualty of the evening. Over 1,000 rounds of 4.5 howitzer ammunition had been expended, but Japanese casualties were even fewer.

Exactly what started the phantom battle of the Kuantan beaches, which would shortly have far-reaching results, has never been decided. It appears to have been a combination of factors, and certainly it seems to have had a little more substance than the rumours which had so spooked the Australian ground crews the day before.

It probably began with the *Larut*, the small British freighter the military used to run people in and out of Kuantan from Singapore, running aground on a sandbank in the Kuantan River estuary at dusk. A Garhwali patrol, seeing a ship where they had never seen one before, opened fire, wounding an airman aboard who was part of a team evacuating equipment used at an RAF bombing range. The *Larut* managed to get itself off the sandbank and escape but, as darkness fell, the howitzer regiment's forward observation post called in fire, though at what and on whose authority was never made clear. 'We all "saw" things from then on and everything looked like an enemy ship,' one of its officers confessed to Bulcock. 'I don't believe there was a Jap within a hundred miles.'

In this the gunner was wrong. There were several sightings of a 'boat-towing barge'. This turned out to be the *Shofu Fu Maru*, a Japanese trawler towing four small craft used for line-fishing. Probably at sea when hostilities started, its crew had yet to be interned and their boat confiscated, though this would shortly be rectified when they were collared by one of the US destroyers Admiral Hart had loaned the British.

Apart from these innocent fisher-folk – and it is hard to imagine so blatant a civilian presence in a war zone was anything else – perhaps the Japanese did do some sort of scouting around Kuantan. Indian troops were adamant that they had seen men getting in and out of small boats, and some reports insist that bullet-riddled lifeboats containing bits of Japanese equipment had come in with the surf; but these could have drifted down from the real fighting up at Kota Baharu.

Late next morning Lieutenant Eric Lomax, a Scots Royal Signals wireless officer attached to the artillery regiment that had spent the night shooting at shadows, walked down to one of the beaches that had come under fire. He stood there, staring out to sea and, despite the barbed wire and recent shell holes, was not unmindful of the beauty of the place.

It was so peaceful standing on a long mile of deserted sand with a long line of palms at my back. I felt I was waiting for the Japanese, at that moment completely alone. Then the loud rumbling started again, a deeper and more distant version of the night's barrage, like thunder but obviously not thunder, drifting in from the sea.

On the *Repulse*, the first shot had almost caused the reporter Gallagher to lose an eye. He had borrowed the Yeoman of Signals' telescope to examine a twin-masted, single-funnelled vessel that was not flying a flag. It would turn out to be the British freighter *Haldis*, recently escaped from Hong Kong. It was undoubtedly the most interesting thing they had seen since 6.30 that morning when all their dashed hopes for action were restored with a brief tannoy announcement: 'The enemy is making a landing 140 miles north of Singapore. We're going in.' Up until then, many of the crew were not even aware that they had changed course during the night.

Breakfast in the wardroom had been quite substantial: coffee, ham and marmalade with freshly baked bread sent up by the bakers who had been on duty since 2 a.m. But Gallagher, Cecil Brown, the American radio reporter, and most of the officers present had rushed it, anxious to be on deck for the first sighting of the Japanese ships they were going to sink. Almost four hours later the voice over the tannoy was telling them what they could plainly see for themselves: 'Well, we have sighted nothing yet but we'll go down the coast looking for them.'

The morning had worn on. Both the *Prince of Wales* and the *Repulse* catapulted off one of their Walruses, the first on reconnaissance, the other circling the ships on anti-submarine patrol. Then, at 10.15 a.m., an unidentified twin-engined aircraft had been spotted overhead, way out of range of the ships' anti-aircraft guns. This was a reconnaissance Nell flown by Midshipman Masame Hoashi, whose radio operator immediately began tapping out the position of the warships below him on his morse key.

About forty-five minutes later, and getting hotter, the radar picked up the freighter and the lookouts soon confirmed it. As the big ships cruised past the variegated greenery of the Malayan coast, the atmosphere on board was becoming increasingly soporific and was about to become more so for petty officers were supervising the unlocking of the barrels for the daily issue of the rum ration. Above them, the silver speck that might or might not be a Japanese reconnaissance plane was still circling.

They began to catch up with the lone ship but it was still too far away to make out its nationality. It was hard to believe that this unescorted vessel had anything to do with a hostile landing, but there was nothing else to look at. Gallagher was focusing the telescope when the shock of the first, unheralded shot made him jab the end of it into his eye. With the eye that wasn't watering Gallagher squinted down at his watch: 11.15 a.m. The shot had come from the *Prince of Wales*, firing with her port side secondary armament at a single, low-flying plane.

On both battleships, the duty marine buglers blew action stations into the same public address system that kept the crew informed of the ship's movements. There were four in all, two on each ship, and they were all aged about sixteen or so. Normally skeleton crews manned the guns. When action stations was sounded, everything was fully manned, 'closed up' in naval parlance; if you were just off watch and looking forward to some hammock time, it was hard luck. Ammunition parties went to what the men on Phillips' ships still called powder rooms, just as they had done in Nelson's navy. Fire-fighting and medical teams formed up; the machine-guns, used as a last resort against low-flying aircraft, were manned. Damage-control parties rushed to close all watertight doors and were not always too fussy about checking whether anyone was left behind them. Marine John Wignall was showering when he realized the cleats were being fastened on the deck hatch that was his only exit. He grabbed his clothes and scrambled up the ladder only to find he was too late. 'I was well and truly locked in. I hammered on the hatch with my shoe in desperation and someone running by heard me and let me out.'

On the *Repulse*, the bugler's call caught Ordinary Seaman Taffy Bowen, one of the stars of the ship's choir, scrubbing a wooden ladder below a pompom gun platform. He stowed away the scrubbing brush and descended to his action station at the aft High-Angle Control Point two decks below, where the occupants could comfort themselves with the knowledge that there was a good deal of armoured plate above their heads.

These Control Points – there was an identical one forward – were a kind of primitive and mostly mechanical computer, which served *Repulse*'s 4-inch guns, in theory dual-purpose but mainly used at high angle in their anti-aircraft role. Under a midshipman wearing head-phones were a team of at least six, sometimes eight, marine bandsmen and seamen. The midshipman was linked by his earphones to the Director Control officer and his men in an enclosed if swaying platform some 60 feet up in the foremast with their calibrated binoculars and other optics.

By way of aligning a cursor with a range plot on a large table, which often involved the simultaneous turning of various wheels, the range, height and bearing of approaching aircraft were calculated and trans-mitted to the gun crews. Then, in the most futuristic part of the operation, the estimated altitude was automatically transmitted into a machine up at the guns, which set the fuses on their air burst shells. The *Prince of Wales*, which had better radar than the *Repulse*, had the same High-Angle Control Positions. This was the core of the complex system that Phillips believed in and it seemed to work surprisingly well – as the Germans and the Italians could testify.

Despite its continued failure to sink a single ship, Phillips' sortie had frightened the Japanese. Once they realized that the British battleships had evaded both their ships and submarines, ninety-four twin-engined Nells and Bettys of the Indo-China-based 22nd Air Flotilla were after them. Nine of these aircraft were given a reconnaissance role, fifty-one were carrying torpedoes and thirty-four had bombs.

First they found the detached destroyer HMS *Tenedos*, which looked so small, and obviously not in its prime, that it was wrongly identified as a freighter. None the less, to the amazement of some of the torpedo carriers, this did not stop the nine bomb-armed Nells from breaking off and assembling into the high-altitude attack formation whereby all the bombs are dropped simultaneously in a murderous volley.

Lieutenant Richard Dyer, in his first command, had already evaded an attack a few minutes before from one of the reconnaissance Nells, which had missed with the two small 50 kg bombs they carried. This was a much more serious affair involving nine 500 kg bombs. The bombers were well out of range of *Tenedos*' paltry anti-aircraft guns as Dyer desperately barked out orders that twisted and turned his small command while the Japanese pilots tried to synchronize their manoeuvres with his.

It took three dummy runs before they felt they had the destroyer straddled and released their combined 4,500 kg of high explosive and steel to see *Tenedos* disappear under great geysers of sea tinged with black smoke. But when the water had subsided, the little ship was still there, zigzagging madly, its drenched white ensign beginning to catch the breeze and flap defiance. The big bombs had missed her port side by a little under 400 feet, felling a sailor hit in the thigh by a splinter but inflicting no other casualties and no serious damage. Having squandered the bomb load they had carried so far, the Nells headed back towards Saigon.

Dyer – now making haste towards Singapore with his one badly wounded seaman – signalled details of the attack, including the number of planes first sighted. These were picked up by Phillips and provided his first indication that a number of hostile aircraft were close by. The news did not reach Singapore, although it was not much further away, so there was no question of alerting Vigors and his pilots on standby at Sembawang. And Phillips was still determined not to break radio silence and risk giving away his position even though Hoashi's reconnaissance Nell had been above them for over an hour.

Hoashi had first spotted the battleships at about the time the *Tenedos* was being attacked. After signalling their position his aircraft became an airborne navigation beacon, circling the ships at high altitude while repeatedly transmitting the same long-wave signal. Like several other Japanese military innovations, this was both simple and effective. A squadron or two at a time, the seventy-six fully armed aircraft that remained after the failed attempt to sink *Tenedos* began to home in on Hoashi with the direction-finders they carried.

The shot which had so startled the *Daily Express* reporter Gallagher had been fired at the first to arrive at the scene: eight Nells of Mihoru Kokutai under the command of Lieutenant Yoshimi Shirai which were flying at 11,500 feet. There were more shots from both ships, while at the same time white ensign battle flags fluttered to fore and main masts, followed on the *Prince of Wales* by a set of signal flags being hauled to her yard arm, instructing *Repulse* and the three destroyers that they should all make a 30-degree turn to starboard. Shortly afterwards, these flags were whipped down and another set went up. Now they were all to turn 50 degrees to port. This kind of maritime dressage, so dependent on timing and having signallers who knew their flags as well as their morse, was something the Royal Navy excelled at. After years of sailing a desk Phillips, his face always a mask with the corners of his mouth turned down, was probably enjoying himself.

Unfortunately, the same could not be said of his gunnery officers, who were horrified to discover that their firepower was reduced by half because, every time they turned, the guns on one side or the other found their field of fire masked by their own superstructure. Despite this disadvantage, those of the *Prince of Wales'* 5.25s and the *Repulse's* 4-inch guns that could fire were doing some damage for, although none of the Nells had yet been shot down, several had been hit.

At first it was thought that the Nells were after the *Prince of Wales*, but then it became apparent they had the *Repulse* in mind, possibly because this was the only squadron carrying two 250 kg bombs instead of one of 500 kg and they had been briefed that the older ship's thinner armoured skin would be more vulnerable to their lighter ordnance. They all waited for the signal from Shirai's aircraft, then dropped their bombs simultaneously from 11,500 feet, just about low enough for the sailors on the upper deck to see them coming and quail at the growing whistle of their fall. Seven straddled *Repulse*, making the usual great water spouts. Only one hit. As it exploded Gallagher felt the battle cruiser rock and noticed large flakes of paint falling off the funnel onto the immaculate flag deck on which the portly Admiralty photographer Lieutenant Abrahams was running from side to side to take his pictures.

The bomb had bored a 15-inch hole through the roof and floor of one of the two Walrus hangars before exploding on an armoured deck above a boiler room, which it failed to penetrate. None the less, the blast or shock fractured steam pipes and their hissing contents scalded several stokers, as the men who tended the diesel-fired boilers that had long replaced coal continued to be known. It appears that the leaking steam prevented them from using the normal exit. In their anguish, some managed to squeeze their raw, half-naked bodies up a ventilation pipe leading to the deck, only to discover that it emerged at a wire grille to which their leader clung, screaming at passing feet to free them. Once they were noticed, the grille was tugged off at the end of a rope and the stokers, who could hardly bear to be touched, removed to a sick bay.

As luck would have it, the hangar contained the Walrus that was not flying. The aircraft had been partially blown off its catapult launch and its petrol tanks were holed and leaking. It was considered a fire hazard and the decision was taken to dump it over the side, though this proved easier said than done. The crane normally employed to lift it out of the water after a landing, was attached to it and, with some difficulty, it was dangled over the side, but then came the problem of releasing it. Sub-Lieutenant Ginger Holden, a red-bearded New

Zealander who was the duty Fleet Air Arm pilot, volunteered to deliver the *coup de grâce* and climbed out along the arm of the crane only to discover that the Walrus was still stubbornly attached to this last link with its mother-ship. In full flying kit, including holstered revolver, Holden straddled the crane, fiddling with the hook, the sea rushing past below him and only too aware that he might well find himself in it should *Repulse* be required to make any more violent evasions.

Captain Tennant, Dunkirk veteran of Stuka dive-bombing attacks, had been impressed by the precision of the Japanese high-altitude bombing, but at first he had been convinced that his ship had got away with no more than near misses. Despite the awful suffering of some of the stokers and at least one fatality, damage to the *Repulse* had been minimal. Its speed was only slightly reduced by the fractured steam pipes and the other boiler rooms were intact; its main anti-aircraft armament was working and the low-level pompoms and Oerlikons had yet to be tested. In all, the combined fire of the battleships and destroyers had hit five of the Nells, damaging two of them badly enough for their pilots to break off, dump their remaining bombs and hope they could keep their machines in the air long enough to make emergency landings at the newly captured Kota Baharu airfield.

There was, of course, no way the gun crews, sweating in their asbestos cowls, could know how accurate their fire had been. The *Repulse*'s gunners were particularly frustrated by the masking brought about by Phillips' Spithead Review manoeuvres, which had left them firing 36 rounds compared to 108 from the *Prince of Wales*. But the admiral had recognized his mistake and ordered the ships to act independently, so there would be a much better chance of getting their eye in next time.

This was not long coming for, thanks to the radio signal being emitted from the reconnaissance Nell, the Japanese aircraft, some of them so low on fuel they had been on the verge of turning back, were beginning, in a piecemeal fashion, to gather over the battleships again. Gradually, as fresh arrivals were recognized as friendly and not the expected British fighters, they began to derive comfort from their numbers: seventy-three, including fifty carrying torpedoes. It had taken just twenty-one old Swordfish biplanes to carry out the devastating torpedo attack on the Italian fleet at Taranto which, twelve months before, had so impressed the Japanese naval attaché in London.

Next in line to try their luck against the British battleships were the two torpedo squadrons that had been grouped in the Genzan Kokutai (a Kokutai was about the equivalent of an RAF wing, rarely less than twenty-seven planes) with the unit that had spent its bombs on the *Tenedos* and gone home. Despite the dipping needles on their fuel gauges they went about it in a measured way, deciding that the smaller squadron of seven aircraft under Lieutenant Sadao Takai would target *Repulse* leaving Lieutenant Kaoru Ishiharu's nine Nells to attack the *Prince of Wales*. For all these torpedo bomber aircrews, this was their debut, often after years of training, and they were a shrewd and dedicated bunch, determined to leave as little as possible to chance. Even as they responded to the radio signal from the reconnaissance Nell, one of the squadron leaders had called their HQ in Saigon to get them to check the sea-depth in the operational area, so they could set their torpedoes accordingly. Air gunners swivelled their turrets, scrunched up their eyes behind tinted goggles as they searched the sky for the fighters they expected to descend on them at any moment. They were already a little puzzled by their absence.

As they lost height for their final approach against the *Prince of Wales*, Ishiharu's nine Nells adopted a loose, crescent-shaped formation. All eight of the port side 5.25-inch guns were firing at them, and then the new Bofors gun which had been fitted on the quarter deck at Cape Town and was manned by some of the ship's contingent of Royal Marines. In a ringside seat was Australian Flight Lieutenant Herb Plenty and his crew, returning to Singapore from a routine reconnaissance patrol in one of the RAAF Hudsons which had so hurriedly vacated Kuantan the day before. As the big 5.25-inch shells exploded around the Nells in grey smoke balls, while beneath them the sea spouted thousands of little geysers where the spent rounds from the pompoms and Oerlikons were falling, they expected at any moment to see the Japanese aircraft turned into balls of flame.

At first the British believed they were about to be subjected to a low-level bombing attack. It appeared that the enemy were flying too high and too fast for torpedo carriers, nothing like the Fleet Air Arm's beloved Swordfish. When at last one of the officers with Phillips and Leach on the flagship's compass platform suggested it might be torpedo bombers after all, the admiral dismissed the idea saying words to the effect that there were 'no torpedo bombers about'.

This left Captain Leach, who was responsible for the handling of the ship, in an appalling dilemma, for the tactics for dealing with low-level bombing and torpedo carriers were diametrically opposed, and the wrong decision could make things much worse. If a ship was being attacked by bombers, it was best that it remained broadside on to them thereby offering the narrowest target, for ships, like bridges, were best bombed lengthways. Against aerial torpedoes exactly the opposite applied. The best defensive manoeuvre was to wait until the torpedoes had been dropped in a broadside attack then turn swiftly towards them, steering the ship, now a much narrower target, through the wakes of the torpedoes which were usually clearly visible. This technique, known as 'combing' – the teeth of the comb being the spread of torpedoes – had been successfully used on the Malta convoys. But the captain who mistakenly turned towards the enemy only to discover that the opposition were carrying bombs and not torpedoes had succeeded in making his ship a much better target.

Now here was Lieutenant-Commander Roger Harland, as it happened the ship's torpedo and electronics specialist, saying to Leach: 'I think they're going to do a torpedo attack.' And there was Phillips, smaller than ever, for he was sitting in his chair, insisting in his calm and deliberate manner that they were not. But if the aircraft off their port side were bombers, why were they not approaching so that her entire length was targeted, unless they intended a last moment change of direction which would make them bigger as they banked and a godsend for the guns? There had been none of this ambiguity about the attack on *Repulse*; they had been flying too high to be anything else but bombers. And, was it his fancy, or were these aircraft a bit lower and slower?

'Hard aport!' Leach had made up his mind. The *Prince of Wales*, which was moving through the water at 25 knots (about 30 mph), probably began its turn just after the first torpedoes were dropped at a distance of about a mile away. Slowly at first and then picking up speed, its 35,000 tons began to swing around, combing through the projected path of the torpedoes so that those dropped by the Nells towards the left of their crescent were already bound to miss.

Shortly before the attack, Geoffrey Brooke, the sub-lieutenant who had been informed by Churchill during the prime minister's visit to the gun room that if the Japanese went to war they would be biting off more than they could chew, had been enjoying the breeze on the Air Defence Platform. The twenty-year-old, who had reluctantly transferred to battleships at his own request from a destroyer because he was unable to get over his sea-sickness, was thinking how lucky he was not to be in one of the boiler rooms where midday temperatures were approaching 136 degrees Fahrenheit. Several stokers were already reported to have collapsed. Then came what he would later describe as 'the most ill-timed call of nature in my life'. To attend to it entailed descending to the heads – lavatories – on the bridge. He was no sooner comfortably seated when most of the ship's anti-aircraft guns started to fire again.

The heavy jarring of the 5.25s, the steady bang-bang of the new Bofors and the rhythmic coughing of the multiple pompoms mocked me as, frantic with annoyance, I sped my departure. I was nearly out when there was a tremendous reverberating explosion that shook my little steel cabinet and had me staggering. It continued as an ominous, muffled rumble that seemed to come from a long way off. My hand was on the door knob when another, peculiar noise percolated through the rest. The gunfire had died down. The noise was rushing water, the sea pouring into our ship, the sound being transmitted up the lavatory waste pipes with chilling clarity. Back up top I was in time to see three or four black dots disappearing towards the horizon.

One of the Nells had been shot down. Trailing black smoke, it fell into the sea near the *Repulse*, killing its pilot, Petty Officer Katsujiro Kawa, and all his crew. But the Japanese were compensated for this loss by a tremendous stroke of luck. Leach had almost finished turning his ship so that only the bows faced the incoming torpedoes when Herb Plenty and his crew in the circling Australian Hudson spotted 'a lurid column of water' rising skywards near the battleship's stern.

From the air this was the only visible evidence of two torpedoes which had caught the *Prince of Wales* before she completed her turn. The one that caused it was not, as it happened, the one that did the most damage. Outrageous fortune decreed that the invisible torpedo, which very nearly missed the battleship altogether, delivered a crippling blow out of all proportion to its 350-pound warhead. It hit the stern near the place, only a few feet away from the rudder, where the outer port propeller shaft, one of four, left the hull. Exploding almost beneath the ship, in the sharp slope going down towards the keel, there was no towering column of water to indicate where a 12-foot-diameter hole had been punched. The sea it boiled was probably lost in the huge wake made by the battleship's propellers.

But far more devastating than the hole it made in a compartment that could easily be sealed off was the destruction of the A-bracket which held the outer port propeller shaft where it emerged from the stern. Although badly buckled, the shaft continued to rotate in an irregular fashion, shrugging off as it did so the watertight seal or cover between the propeller and the hull. Water quickly filled the length of the shaft's 240-foot passage to Engine Room B, which it promptly began to flood. Here Lieutenant Dick Wildish and his artificers were already struggling to turn off the buckled propeller shaft, whose berserk death throes had started a vibration that enabled the wound to be felt in every part of the ship. 'This took some doing at 25 knots,' recalled Wildish. But it soon became apparent that the pumps could not cope with the amount of water now pouring down into this engine room from the uncorked shaft passageway. Before long, with an oily sample of the South China Sea swirling up the steps behind them, Wildish and his men were obliged to scramble out of their workplace, closing a watertight door behind them.

The immediate effect of a water-filled outer port shaft passage, no narrow pipe but wide enough along a third of its length for three men to walk abreast, was an alarming list to port of at least 11 degrees. This, together with the loss of one of the ship's four engines, reduced the ship's speed from 25 to 15 knots. Even worse, the rudder was not answering to the helm because the power supply to its steering motors had been cut, and until this was restored she could do nothing but turn large anti-clockwise circles to port.

The torpedo which caused the 'lurid column of water' spotted by the Australian airmen was probably dropped a couple of seconds after the one that hit the stern and caused the outer port propeller shaft passage to flood. It exploded about 140 feet forward of it, just beyond the aft 14-inch gun turret, and produced the kind of memorable aquatic eruption – one Royal Marine officer aboard estimated 200 feet – more usually associated with bombs or depth charges. The reason for the big splash was that it went off a couple of feet away from the hull without making contact.

Exactly why this premature detonation occurred is unknown. One theory is that it was a sympathetic explosion caused by shock waves from the first torpedo. But although it failed to penetrate the hull, it was by no means a benign event, for its blast loosened enough rivets to flood four watertight compartments beyond the Liquid Sandwich.

Even worse, it thoroughly bewildered the damage-control parties who, totally unaware of the hit by the propellers, could not understand why a single torpedo hitting this part of the ship should cause anything like the degree of flooding and list they were experiencing.

To add to their confusion, most of the electronics started to go haywire. It soon became apparent that several dynamo rooms had been flooded or simply over-heated, and the *Prince of Wales* now had considerable problems making enough electricity to power all its machinery and weapons. The area from the funnel to the stern was particularly affected. Four of its 5.25 turrets were only capable of being turned manually, which made them almost useless as anti-aircraft guns, and both of the steering motors which controlled the rudder had stopped functioning. An attempt was being made to use an emergency system which was steam-powered.

On the bridge, listening to the damage reports as they came in, Admiral Phillips and Captain Leach were reported to be looking some-what stunned. It would have been surprising had they looked anything else unless, in Leach's case, he had been looking reproachfully at the man who had insisted that the aircraft attacking them were not torpedo carriers. By a tremendous fluke, in the space of nine minutes and for the price of four aircrew and their machine, one of the Royal Navy's most powerful battleships had been at least temporarily transformed into a listing hulk by a bunch of Asians flying Asian-designed and Asian-built planes. The time was 11.50 a.m. and there were at least another fifty aircraft around or approaching Force Z with more torpedoes and bombs to deliver.

On the *Repulse*, the reporter Gallagher was crouched behind one of the battle cruiser's two sets of eight-barrelled pompoms known to Fleet Street, if rarely the Royal Navy, as 'Chicago Pianos'. He was watching Lieutenant Takai's squadron begin their torpedo run and taking notes with his fountain pen. For the last few months he had affected green ink, having read that Wavell, the commander of the British forces in India, did the same. But shortly after he came aboard he had run out of it and refilled with naval issue given to him by one of the ship's writers, as RN clerks were called, who had warned him that it was mixed on the ship and 'not up to much'.

Some of Gallagher's journalist colleagues made fun of the young South African's compulsive note-taking, but he was one of those reporters who was always trying to capture the moment, paint a word picture. Now he jotted down the way the pompom's spotter, 'his face tight with excitement', directed the gun onto the nearest aircraft by hammering on the back of the rating in charge of swivelling the gun, 'his forefinger stabbing at the new plane'. The startling sound of the pompom's eight barrels going off at once was followed by a little avalanche of empty brass cartridge cases clattering into the receptacle provided for them. It reminded Gallagher of the time he had won the jackpot playing a fruit-machine in Gibraltar.

The pompom was reckoned to be the Royal Navy's most effective weapon against low-flying aircraft. They had ten-man crews and in theory fired 960 of their 2-inch rounds a minute. But, despite constant attempts to check their belted ammunition for faulty links, which separated cartridges and prevented the next round being fed into the breech, they continued to be plagued by the same stoppages the *Prince of Wales* had suffered on the Malta convoy. Phillips' flagship had five pompoms; the *Repulse* only had two, and by the time they were facing their first torpedo attack neither of them was working properly. The one Gallagher was crouched behind was being turned manually because somehow it had lost its power supply when the bomb hit the seaplane hangar. The other one rapidly developed stoppages in six of its eight barrels.

Some relatively slow-firing Oerlikon, Vickers and Lewis guns offered an additional close-range defence against low-flying aircraft, and then there was its main anti-aircraft armament, its twenty 4-inch guns which, quite apart from their smaller calibre, were not nearly as good as the *Prince of Wales'* 5.25s: some were not much more than secondary surface-to-surface armament, incapable of firing at high-flying aircraft or being sufficiently depressed to hit anything coming at the ship at low level. If he was to get his ship unscathed through the ordeal ahead, it was obvious that Tennant was going to have to be quicker than his friend John Leach when it came to choosing his moment to turn into the torpedoes. In her prime, the battle cruiser could do 32 knots; she could still manage a good 29.

Ideally, the *Repulse* and the *Prince of Wales* should have been attacked simultaneously, so that they were too busy defending themselves to lend fire support to each other. The attack on the *Repulse* had been delayed for a few minutes because Takai and his crew, who were much better briefed on American ships than British, had begun to suspect that the ships below were their own *Kongo* and support units whose whereabouts were uncertain. Mindful of how near they had come to attacking the *Chokai* the night before, they left cloud cover and came down to a level where a better view, and the enthusiasm, if not the effectiveness, of the anti-aircraft fire banished these nagging doubts.

Now Takai led his seven Nells down to about 100 feet above sea level, finding as he did so that he had begun 'to shake from the excitement of the moment'.

The *Repulse* had already started evasive action and was making a hard turn to the right. The target angle was becoming smaller and smaller as the bow of the vessel swung gradually in my direction . . . the airspeed indicator registered more than 200 knots. I do not remember at all how I was flying the aircraft, how I was aiming, and what distance we were from the ship when I dropped the torpedo.

Or not, as the case may be. As it happened, Takai and another pilot both failed to drop their ordnance because the release mechanisms malfunctioned. The other Nell returned to its airfield with the sinister tube still clinging to its belly, which must have encouraged a very concentrated landing. But despite the horribly increased odds against a lone aircraft, a target for every working anti-aircraft gun on the ship, the squadron leader Takai doggedly elected to try again.

Then, suddenly, the torpedo carrier was not alone. Shirai's squadron, which had so far scored the one and only hit on the *Repulse* with the bomb that holed the hangar and scalded the stokers below it, returned to the scene. Their last six 250 kg bombs whistled down in another neat cluster, though this time every one of them was a near miss. But Shirai's parting shots did succeed in distracting some of the guns from Takai's solitary approach.

I pushed the throttles forward to reach maximum speed and flew just above the water. This time I yanked hard on the torpedo release. Over the thudding impact of bullets and shrapnel smashing into the aircraft, I felt the strong shock through the bomber as the torpedo dropped free and plummeted into the water.

Yet for all Takai's boldness it was another wasted effort. As the Nell escaped, its tinfish chugged harmlessly past the weaving ship, as had the other five from Takai's squadron – and as indeed did a further eight dropped a few minutes later by the latest squadron to track to its source the airborne radio direction signal: Mitsubishi Nells from the Mihoru Kokutai which seem to have failed because they delivered their torpedoes from too great a distance, so lookouts could spot the white trails scratching the blue surface of a calm sea from way off.

The *Repulse* seemed to have a charmed life. So far she had survived fourteen torpedoes plus Shirai's bombs. Helmsman John Robson, a leading seaman, could not help reflecting, as he turned the old battle cruiser from port to starboard and back again 'as though we were a destroyer', how he had once been ordered to go easy on wheel movements because her steering mechanism was getting a bit arthritic.

*Repulse* had not got through these latest attacks entirely unscathed. A few men had been killed and wounded when the Nells, finding themselves flying parallel to the ship as it turned into their torpedo tracks, had opened machine-gun fire from their mid-upper turrets. The 4-inch gun crews and pompom gunners were not enclosed in turrets and were particularly vulnerable. 'God, did we move! As one man we all rushed for cover,' recalled one of them.

The utter capriciousness of bullets bouncing off armoured plate at impossible angles was best illustrated by a Royal Marine killed in what should have been one of the safest places on the ship, inside one of the turrets for the big 15-inch guns. By a million-to-one chance, a bullet entered through a narrow slit in the armour plate intended to let out cordite fumes and hit him in the head. Among the return fire were six rounds of .38 revolver ammunition fired by the Kiwi pilot Ginger Holden, who was still straddling the crane like a horse and trying to release his Walrus when a Nell passed close enough for him to see the pilot. He missed his target – though not his place in history.

The *Repulse* was still trying to deal with the effects of the bomb that had hit them when the action started only forty minutes before. Two cooks were trapped in a small galley lift, stuck between decks because its power cable had been severed. Some of the fires that had been started were still being dealt with. Water was being fountained from a split in a high-pressure fire-hose snaking across the deck. Gallagher watched some Vickers gunners, sweating in their anti-flash gear, try to drink it then spit it out when they tasted warm salt water.

But compared to the *Prince of Wales* the *Repulse* was practically untouched, its speed unimpaired, its anti-aircraft guns working if not always as efficiently as they should have been. Tennant could feel pleased with himself and his ship, and even hope that the worst might be over. How many more torpedo carriers and bombers could the Japanese muster at this extremity of their range? In any case, the RAF would surely be getting fighter cover to them before long, and even a few Buffaloes would play havoc with aircraft without a fighter escort forming up for a torpedo run.

He wondered whether Phillips had asked for fighter cover as soon as the Japanese reconnaissance plane had been spotted or waited until the attack began. Tennant asked his Chief Yeoman of Signals for the log of messages monitored from the flagship to Singapore that morning. His reply must have hit him like a bucket of very cold water. There had been no messages. Phillips had stuck firmly to his wireless silence and Admiral Palliser remained a chief of staff with no firm idea of where his boss was or that his ships were under heavy aerial attack. So there were no Buffaloes on their way. Tennant did not bother to contact the flagship to ask why. There could be no justifiable reason for maintaining radio silence when the enemy knew exactly where they were. To try and make up for lost time the first brief morse message his wireless room tapped out was not encoded but sent in plain English:

FROM REPULSE TO ANY BRITISH MAN OF WAR. ENEMY AIRCRAFT BOMBING. MY POSITION 134NTW 22 × 09.

The message was timed at 11.58 a.m. This was exactly forty-five minutes after the *Prince of Wales* had fired the first shot and caused Gallagher to poke his eye with the telescope. This was followed by a coded message which presumably gave what details it could of damage and casualties, and stressed the urgent need for air support which would have been obvious to Palliser as soon as he got the first message. But for some reason this second message failed to arrive.

Then Tennant's lookouts reported that the *Prince of Wales* had hoisted two black balls to its yard arm, the signal for 'not under control'. His own wild 'hard over' turns and the flagship's sad, incessant circling had put them at least 3 miles apart, so now Tennant turned his ship and narrowed the gap, signalling by Aldis lamp as he went: 'Thanks to providence have so far dodged nineteen torpedoes.'

But Leach was too preoccupied to answer his old friend's jaunty message, perhaps understandably envious of his good luck, and as he got closer Tennant could see why. The Royal Navy's newest battleship, in which less than a week before the Royal Marines band had played 'Roll Out the Barrel' for the Japanese consul and Phillips' other cocktail guests, was a pathetic sight. She was moving sluggishly along, still leaning dramatically to port as counter-flooding on the starboard side had reduced her list by no more than 1 degree. Her waterlogged stern was no higher than a coal barge – 2 feet above sea level instead of its normal 24. What Tennant couldn't see was even worse.

So far the efforts of the electrical repair parties, sweating buckets as they crawled into spaces designed for midgets in search of blown fuses and severed cables, had failed to restore power to most of the aft part of the ship. The ramifications of this were enormous and getting worse by the minute. Fan ventilation was off and men were toiling in the two remaining engine rooms in temperatures well over 120 degrees Fahrenheit for a few minutes at a time and then being brought up on deck to recover. Anything like an effective defence against air attack was no longer feasible because, without power, none of the four aft 5.25-inch twin gun turrets could be trained onto their targets. The four forward turrets were in not much better shape because the list to port was now so acute that it was impossible to depress the two starboard turrets against low-level attack. Most of the pompom platforms were working, but they continued to be plagued by defective ammunition. Brave men laboured under emergency battery lighting in the sticky bowels of the ship as they attempted to restore power to the rudder mechanism. Unless they succeeded, Leach would never have a second chance to try his luck at combing torpedoes. For the moment, the only manoeuvre his ship could execute was a slow circle at about the same pace as a metal duck in a fairground shooting booth.

Perhaps now would have been the time for Phillips to detach the only slightly bruised *Repulse* with one of the three destroyers, wish her good luck and godspeed and send her south for Singapore as fast as her old engines would take her, leaving the *Prince of Wales* to take her chances. But who could believe that at any moment Captain Leach would not be told that the rudder was now steering, the ventilation blowing, the huge pumps that could empty flooded engine rooms within minutes pumping with a vengeance, the ship about to be returned to an even keel and the 5.25s able to blow the Mitsubishis out of the sky in any direction? Meanwhile, Phillips needed every anti-aircraft gun he could muster around his flagship and even Tennant's old 4-inchers were better than almost nothing.

If there was ever a chance for *Repulse* to make a lone dash for safety it soon passed. Almost fifty uncommitted aircraft were now gathering over Force Z, most of them torpedo bombers. This was the pack coming in for the kill. Only the capital ships were attacked. No torpedoes or bombs were squandered on the destroyers as they had been on *Tenedos* earlier, though they sometimes drew machine-gun fire from passing aircraft and used their anti-aircraft guns with such enthusiasm that one of them found it had only the star shells used for night illumination left for its main 4.7 dual-purpose gun. A large Australian seaman serving on the British destroyer HMS *Express* became hysterical and had to be held down and given a morphia injection. The Australian destroyer *Vampire* claimed two definite hits on aircraft but, like the British Hudsons, these big two-engined Mitsubishis seemed to take a lot of punishment.

Among the newcomers on the scene were the twenty-six Bettys of the Kanoya Kokutai, slightly bigger and older than the Nells and carrying the heavier Mark Two torpedo with their increased 450-pound warheads. They had given up the search and had been on their way back to Saigon when they picked up the signal, faint at first, from the reconnaissance Nell and homed in like sharks scenting blood.

They peeled off in squadrons. First hit was the hapless *Prince of Wales*, which put up a feeble curtain of anti-aircraft fire as six Bettys approached its higher starboard side and some of them dropped their torpedoes as close as 500 yards away. Even then, two managed to miss this very lame carousel duck, which probably says more about the difficult art of aerial torpedoing than about the competence of these determined Japanese airmen.

The other four hit within seconds of each other, in two cases sending up huge columns of water and fuel oil. One blew a hole straight through the bow from starboard to port. The two that caused the big splashes hit just forward of the bridge and the other further aft beneath the rear 14-inch gun turret. The fourth hit the stern, bending the shaft of the outer starboard propeller inwards and generally doing to it what the first torpedo had done to the outer port some forty minutes before. It did not, as that one had, flood its shaft passageway, but it did reduce the ship's speed to 8 knots. Some men were trapped as the oily sludge swirled into cramped, unlikely action stations, such as the magazine hoists for the big 14-inch guns that had not fired a shot in anger since they helped sink the *Bismarck*.

Otherwise, casualties appear to have been relatively light, though by now enough men had been hurt by machine-gun fire, torpedo blast, or felled by heat exhaustion trying to work below, for an overflow medical station to have been set up in an area known as the Cinema Flat just below the armoured deck. A beneficial side-effect of these latest torpedo hits was that the filling of the starboard side almost righted the list to port and restored the ship to something like an even keel. But it is estimated that the ship had already taken on about 18,000 tons of water and, with only one of its four engines and two of eight dynamos working, there was not enough power left to drive the pumps that would get rid of it. HMS *Prince of Wales* was slowly sinking.

At 12.20 p.m., over an hour after the action started, Phillips at last consented to join *Repulse* in breaking radio silence. The brief message seems to have been transmitted just after the Bettys had attacked, with the latest hits hurriedly inserted.

EMERGENCY. HAVE BEEN STRUCK BY A TORPEDO ON PORT SIDE. NYTW022R06 4 TORPEDOES. SEND DESTROYERS.

But what was needed, though it appears that even at this late stage Phillips could not bring himself to admit it, were fighters not destroyers and these were at last on their way. The signal *Repulse* had sent at 11.58 took twenty-one minutes to travel from the desk of Phillips' chief of staff Admiral Palliser at the naval base to Air HQ alongside Percival's headquarters in Sime Road. Six minutes later the RAF, moving with considerably more urgency than the navy, had scrambled Tim Vigors and his ten Australian pilots waiting in their cockpits at Sembawang, the airfield next door to the naval base.

Reinforcing them were two other Buffaloes from the RAF's 243 Squadron, based at Kallang airfield on the south of the island. Flight Lieutenant Mowbray Garden, who was leading, had been given a course to fly and curiously guarded instructions to look after 'an important ship that was being bombed'. A Buffalo's top speed was 290 mph but this emptied its tanks within minutes and was reserved for dog fighting. At an economical cruising speed of 150 mph, which would give them enough fuel to operate over the area and return or at least get to Kuantan, they could expect to be over the ships in about an hour's time – 1.25 p.m.

By now there were twenty Bettys with undropped torpedoes circling Phillips' command rather like, as one of his officers put it, 'Indians around a wagon train'. From the air, the *Prince of Wales*, some of its guns still flashing and its list almost righted, is unlikely to have looked as hurt as she was. But they had the sense to concentrate on the *Repulse*, Tennant's 'lucky ship' where his crew continued to give a good account of themselves, just as he predicted they would in his message to them when they slipped anchor and left Singapore a thousand years before.

At first aircraft seemed to be coming at the *Repulse* from all points of the compass and once again Leading Seaman Robson found himself frantically turning the old battle cruiser from side to side in an effort to deny the aircraft the beam-on target they needed. Tennant identified the main threat as eight Bettys forming up on his right, which obligingly dropped their torpedoes from well over a mile away. 'It seemed obvious that we should be once more successful in combing their tracks,' observed Tennant in his post-action report.

The *Prince of Wales* was behind them and to the left, her bow about level with *Repulse*'s rear gun turret and perhaps 4 miles away. Three Bettys headed for the flagship, evidently intent on finishing her off. Then suddenly, almost standing on their tails, they executed a 180-degree turn and, at a range of about a mile, dropped their torpedoes. It was a brilliant feint and there was nothing Tennant could do about it. If he turned to avoid them he was going to be hit by the eight he was in the process of combing.

'Stand by for torpedo!' he yelled over the tannoy and then went to the port side of his bridge and stood there staring down, fixated by the remorseless white track propelling 450 pounds of explosives towards his ship. This must have been an agonizing business for it took some ninety seconds to arrive and hit *Repulse* squarely amidships. But the sound of its explosion was something of an anti-climax, much of it lost in the cacophony of their own guns hammering away at the aircraft. Ordinary Seaman Stanley Dimmack, who had braced himself for a very big bang indeed, was surprised when the ship 'hardly shuddered and ploughed steadily on'. Nearer the place of impact, down in the Forward High-Angle Control Point, the Australian Midshipman Guy Griffiths did momentarily feel the hit, 'as if somebody had removed the boat's plug'. Then the ship appeared to steady herself and be back to normal.

It soon became apparent that *Repulse*'s unfashionable 'torpedo bulge' had worked exactly as her designers had intended when she was laid down a quarter of a century before, and proved far more effective than the 'Liquid Sandwich' with which a later generation of naval architects had equipped the *Prince of Wales*. It had touched off the warhead without seriously damaging the main structure of the hull. As the bulge began to fill, the ship took on a list, but this was reduced when damage control started counter-flooding on the starboard side and the battle cruiser could still comfortably work up 25 knots. As if any further proof was needed that she was still a lucky ship, a second torpedo had struck at such an oblique angle that it was observed nuzzling the ship's side, its distinctive yellow head obstinately refusing to detonate.

The 22nd Air Flotilla now had nine torpedoes left and were dangerously low on fuel. For the loss of one aircraft they had already achieved far more than their wildest dreams, crippling the *Prince of Wales*, the ship the British had sent to intimidate them. Even if the enemy managed to get some pumps working and the tugs to tow her the 170 miles back to Singapore, it was going to be a long time before she was a danger to Japan or anybody else.

Whether, even at this stage, they realized this is another matter. No fires had been started, there was no satisfying plume of black oil smoke, she was still shooting back, and the water rushing in through the torpedo holes in her starboard side had, for the moment at least, almost righted her list. As for the *Repulse*, although she had taken hits, she was obviously far from finished and those 15-inch guns and their skilled crews might yet survive to get the targets they yearned for.

Lieutenant Haruki Iki, who commanded the nine Bettys which had yet to drop their torpedoes, was about to follow up the attack on the *Prince of Wales* and deliver what would probably have been a stunning *coup de grâce* when he changed his mind. Later he gave two reasons for his decision. He did not feel his aircraft were in the right position, which presumably meant he would have to take them round again; and he had seen the splashes of water made by the four torpedoes which had just struck the flagship and suspected no more were necessary. So he switched to the *Repulse*.

Iki was a cool customer and it is unlikely that his training had not prepared him for ships making themselves smaller by presenting their narrow bows. Tennant's judicious combing of their torpedoes should not have come as a surprise although in war, as in sport, training drills are often an early casualty. Iki had seen the feint against the *Prince of Wales* which had resulted in the first hit on the *Repulse*. Now he ordered his squadron to divide into two groups of six and three and they attacked the battle cruiser almost simultaneously from both sides. '*Repulse* was confronted by a criss-cross of torpedoes,' recalled Flight Lieutenant Plenty, who was still circling the scene in his Hudson.

Most of the trails were to starboard and it was in this direction that Tennant turned. Meanwhile Iki was approaching the port side with the two pilots he had chosen to accompany him. This honour was reserved for Fukumatsu Yamamoto, a relative of the admiral who had masterminded the attack on Pearl Harbor, and Yuso Nakajima. Iki wanted men who would join him in a point-blank attack and they did not let him down. The three Bettys are estimated to have dropped their torpedoes when they were about 500 yards away from the *Repulse* and every kind of anti-aircraft gun the ship possessed, from 4-inch cannon to Lewis machine-gun, was firing at them. Once his torpedo was running, Iki turned away from the ship, initially a dangerous move because it made him a bigger target, while the other two flew towards their target.

Sub-Lieutenant Dicky Pool, a small, fair-haired young man who irritated Tennant by constantly volunteering to serve on motor torpedo boats, was in charge of one of the ship's two pompom guns. Pool's official title was Fire Distribution Officer, which meant he selected the targets. Common sense dictated that, given a choice, fire should be directed on aircraft about to launch their ordnance rather than those that already had, however close and tempting. But Pool had reached the point where he was determined to spill blood. 'As the ship's position appeared hopeless, I did not shift target after these aircraft had dropped their torpedoes.'

This time the ammunition behaved and an eight-barrel pompom could be deadly at close range – a twenty-second burst delivered 320 rounds. Yamamoto's Betty flopped into the sea on its belly. Some of its crew were seen trying to get out when it exploded in a ball of flame and soon the only trace of it was a ring of fire on the sea. Nakajima's aircraft was slightly higher and for a moment looked as though it might have escaped. Then the first flames were seen flickering forward from the tailplane towards the cockpit and, by the time it hit the water, its whole fuselage was on fire.

From his lofty vantage point on one of the *Prince of Wales'* Air Defence Positions Sub-Lieutenant Brooke, the young officer caught easing his bowels when the first torpedo struck his ship, was among those who saw the Bettys shot down and particularly remembered the descent of Nakajima's aircraft. 'Although it was clear the men inside had only seconds to live I watched with undiluted pleasure . . . We all cheered.'

They were cheering on the *Repulse* too, but not for long. All three of the torpedoes Iki and his wingmen had dropped struck home, followed within minutes by a fourth from the aircraft on the starboard side, making, in all, five torpedo hits in the space of a few minutes. Tennant knew there was no way his stout-hearted old ship, whose luck he and his crew had nurtured for so long, could take this kind of punishment and, heartbreaking though it was, he did not hesitate. 'All hands on deck. Prepare to abandon ship. God be with you,' came the announcement over the tannoy. Even as Tennant spoke, the *Repulse* was already taking on a heavy list to port.

From deep within the innards of the ship men came scrambling up, like miners fleeing from a flood towards daylight, climbing familiar ladders and companionways which were rapidly assuming crazy angles. In the aft High-Angle Control Position Taffy Bowen and his companions, still concentrating on their tasks, had no idea of the seriousness of the situation. The loudspeaker system in that part of the ship had been destroyed by the bomb that hit the Walrus hangar at the beginning of the action. Their midshipman, one of the five Australians on board, eventually heard the news over his headphones and hurried them out.

They made their way up a vertical ladder and then through the captain's lobby flat, part of Tennant's quarters, where about a dozen wounded, among them the scalded stokers, were lying on stretchers. Some were groggy with morphia but others were all too aware of what was going on. As he passed one of the stretchers its occupant tugged at Bowen's leg and asked for a hand up.

Being a kid like, I turned to help him, but one of the Royal Marine bandsmen gave me a shove and said, 'Keep going.' As it was, just after we got out on deck the armoured door slammed shut. There was a warrant officer there shouting 'go forward' because the screws were still turning and they didn't want people cut up.

From the time the last torpedo hit her it took no more than eight minutes for *Repulse* to sink, and it is unlikely that any of the wounded in the Captain's Flat area escaped. Fortunately, most of the casualties were gathered in the two main Medical Distributing Centres, one forward and the other aft and both down three decks, where the cool-headed devotion of some of the medics got most of their patients off the ship, though some succumbed to their wounds either in the water or later.

The last man out of the forward Medical Distributing Centre was Sick Berth Attendant Walter Bridgewater, who had been pushing the wounded up wooden ladders, sometimes into the arms of passing magazine hands on their way up to the top. Bridgewater, who would received a Mention in Dispatches for his actions, got all the wounded on deck except for one man who appeared to be in a coma and incapable of helping himself. 'When the ship gave quite a shudder I just decided I better get out myself and left the last one propped up in a corner . . . I will always remember his helpless, pathetic look.'

Bridgewater was almost on the upper deck when his arm became trapped behind the angle bar of the scuttle covering a porthole he was trying to open and he resigned himself to drowning. 'Then, all of a sudden, I felt my right arm free and I was out in a split second, possibly the last to leave the old ship alive.'

Some of the first to abandon ship had simply swum off the port side as it dipped below water level; but this became increasingly dangerous as the list increased. An avalanche of heavy items including the 4-inch gun mountings began to break free and follow the swimmers overboard. There was obviously a danger that *Repulse* would soon capsize and fall on people not yet far enough away from the ship. Some were already finding swimming difficult as they tried to cough and spit out the fuel oil they had swallowed and get the filthy stuff out of their nostrils and eyes.

It made more sense to climb the sloping deck to the higher starboard side and climb over the guard rail. Then, bending their knees as if they were coming down a steep and treacherously loose hillside, they went down the concave slope to where the torpedo bulge and the red paint above it were now indecently visible. The *Express* reporter Gallagher chose this route. But when he got to the bulge he paused, for beyond it lay an uninviting prospect for a non-swimmer with only his rubber lifebelt to rely on: a 12-foot drop into a darkening sea:

. . . playing for time, I opened my cigarette case. There were two cigarettes in it. I put one in my mouth and offered the other to a sailor standing beside me. He said, 'Ta. Want a match?' We both lit up and puffed once or twice

... He said, 'Well, I'll be seeing you mate.' I replied, 'I certainly hope so. Cheerio.' The sea was black. I jammed my cap on my head and jumped. I remember drawing breath first.

Others got down on their bottoms, almost as if they were on a water slide, gathering speed as they went. This was not always a good idea. Ankles, heel bones and even spines were fractured by hitting the bulge, legs first, too fast; flesh flayed by the rivets and marine encrustations encountered *en route*. One of the luckier ones was Ordinary Seaman Bowen who did part of it this way but arrived intact, climbed the bulge and dived off. Most former boy seamen had been taught to swim properly. Now he swam the fastest crawl he could ever remember doing for, like all young sailors, Bowen had been told how a sinking ship could pull down the men who had abandoned her. Then he heard one of his mates shout, 'You can stop swimming now, Taffy.'

Two sixteen-year-old boy seamen were among those who had the awful luck to leave the starboard bulge immediately over its single torpedo hole and were dragged back into the blackness of what had become stagnant caverns of diluted oil. But a petty officer soon spotted what was happening and warned people off. Otherwise, there was precious little suction from the *Repulse* because, instead of filling slowly from all sides the way an old pot drowns in a pond, she was going down stern first. A midshipman made a 60-foot dive into the water from the gun director's platform on the foremast and survived, though years later friends would wonder if it did not bring on the brain tumour which killed him.

There had been very little time to lower boats, though somebody had got the captain's launch, all polished brass and wood, into the water. Most of the survivors were either clinging to bits of wreckage or one of *Repulse*'s twelve Carley floats, huge rings of canvas-covered cork with slatted wooden floors. Everybody was black with fuel oil, which stung the eyes dreadfully and sometimes made those who had swallowed too much of it retch until it killed them. Gallagher briefly found sanctuary on a round lifebelt already supporting two blackened figures.

I told them they looked like a couple of Al Jolsons. They said, 'We must be an Al Jolson trio, because you're the same' . . . Another man joined us, so we had an Al Jolson quartet on one lifebelt. It was too much. In the struggle to keep it lying flat on the sea we lost our grips and broke up, possibly meeting again later though not being able to recognize each other because of our masks of oil.

The water was warm; fear of sharks, which had beset some people when they first entered it, had largely evaporated, some believing it was the oil as much as the explosions that had kept them away. Sing-songs were started: the inevitable 'Roll Out the Barrel'. As the *Repulse* started to go down, some of her crew gave her a last cheer and officers were seen to salute.

In Bowen's group the cheering stopped when they saw a Marine bandsman they knew hanging in the chains of the paravane mine-sweeping device on the bow. It was well known that the musician could not swim and it seemed that, suspended there at the equivalent height of a four-storey building and getting higher, he was too terrified to let go. Some of his friends began yelling at him by name to drop. Still the bandsman clung on until suddenly, as if he had heard the pleas of the men in the water for the first time, he fell, legs pedalling furiously, to be returned gasping to the surface by his lifebelt. Some sailors paddled over on a Carley float and picked him up.

Another late departure was Captain Tennant. Most of his crew had last seen Dunkirk Charlie leaning over his tottering bridge with a megaphone as he told them, 'You've put up a good show. Now look after yourselves and God bless you.' As if to emphasize Tennant's words of praise, there came from the starboard side the defiant rattle of a lone Oerlikon anti-aircraft gun which could still be depressed far enough to take on low-flying aircraft. Behind it was Midshipman Robert Davies, a cherub-faced Australian always considered a bit on the quiet side by his gunroom messmates. Thanks to Davies, *Repulse* was literally going down fighting, but the eighteen-year-old had harnessed himself to the gun and left it too late to save himself.*

Tennant very nearly went with him. The list was now so steep – his ship was practically on its side – that he chose to walk down to the port gun deck rather than attempt what had become an almost vertical climb the other way. When he met the sea he was still wearing his steel helmet, which he had forgotten he had on. He might have floated

* Davies received a Mention in Dispatches which was the only other posthumous gallantry award that could be granted after the Victoria and George Crosses.

serenely away had not *Repulse*, in her death throes, chosen that moment to turn almost on top of him, taking him down to some black place where he nearly gave up and started swallowing water. Then the rubber lifebelt around his lean frame and his long legs kicking took him back towards the light.

Breaking the surface was marred only by sharing that small piece of it with some hard piece of flotsam. It was then that he realized he still had his helmet on; without it he felt he would have surely been knocked out and might yet have drowned. As it was, he was quite stunned. One of the Carley floats was nearby and somebody was offering him a hand and saying, 'Here you are, sir.'

The *Prince of Wales* was about 4 miles away from the *Repulse* when she sank. Phillips sent the destroyers *Electra* and *Vampire* to pick up survivors and, through binoculars from the bridge, he and Leach watched them begin to close in on an area of bobbing black dots in the place where the battle cruiser had last been seen.

They did not have much time to dwell on this sombre scene, with all its obvious implications, for high above them the last eight Japanese aircraft left with any ordnance to deliver were approaching their port bow at 9,000 feet. They were engaged by those of the twin 5.25 high-angle guns that could still be brought to bear – five were damaged by shrapnel to varying degrees, but this was not enough to deter the Japanese from carrying out their plan. Lieutenant Hachiro Takeda's Nells were each armed with a 500 kg bomb. They adopted the usual tactic of flying in tight formation and dropping all eight simultaneously – the British would soon begin to refer to it as the 'diarrhoea technique'. One bomb failed to release, six missed, though not by far, and the seventh tore through the armoured deck. It exploded, with ghastly results in the Cinema Flat area, where many of the wounded were gathered, along with artificers and others recovering from heat exhaustion after working in the sauna heat below.

It was now about 12.45 p.m., a good ten minutes after *Repulse* had sunk, and it was perfectly obvious that, barring a miracle, the *Prince of Wales* would shortly be joining her on the bed of the South China Sea. That, despite his flagship's many wounds, Phillips had not entirely given up hope, is proved by a signal he sent to Singapore at 12.52 p.m. asking for 'all available tugs'. Even before the final air raid, Lieutenant-Commander Francis Cartwright, the sandy-bearded captain of the

*Express*, had decided that the *Prince of Wales* was doomed. But when he brought his destroyer up to her starboard side in order to take off as many crew as possible, the response rather resembled that of a petulant drunk objecting to being helped to his feet.

'What have you come alongside for?' demanded the Aldis lamp flashing from the flagship's bridge. 'It looks as though you require assistance,' replied Cartwright with admirable restraint.

But though Leach took the ship where his admiral bade him, her management was his. He immediately agreed that the wounded and personnel not immediately required to work or defend the *Prince of Wales* should be allowed to board the destroyer. One of the first across was an officer carrying a briefcase, probably a member of Phillips' staff transferring documents that seemed important at the time. Somebody yelled: 'Come back, you yellow bastard!'

If this was an indication that, compared to the *Repulse*, discipline could be more fragile on Leach's predominantly Hostilities Only ship, it did not show in the orderly way men began to line up after him. At first they crossed easily on gang-planks but as the battleship's list to port increased, so did the distance between the two ships, and the planks fell into the sea. After that, a few leapt down onto the destroyer's deck in running jumps; but the majority used ropes tied between the two ships and crossed hand over hand, their biceps taking their whole body-weight. Among them was Sub-Lieutenant Brooke, who gave the man in front of him a few feet and then seized the half-inch diameter rope which bit into his hands with 'considerable intensity'.

It was surprisingly tiring work, now with the nightmare element that, as the battleship heeled increasingly away, the men at the other end of the rope had to pay it out nullifying most of one's efforts. When the last few yards became a steep uphill haul – the weight of bodies kept the rope well down – I felt for a moment too exhausted to go on but a glance at the oily water in which men were already struggling provided the spur of desperation. A last effort put my wrists within the grasp of eager hands and in one exhilarating heave I was over the destroyer's rail.

Soon, as her list to port increased, all thoughts of tugs and any other hopes that might yet save the *Prince of Wales* had gone. At 1.10 p.m., ten minutes before she finally turned turtle and sank, the order was given to inflate lifebelts and abandon ship, though this process had been under way for some time. For Cartwright, disengaging his destroyer as the battleship began to heel over was a matter of exquisite and brutal timing. If he left it too late, as the nether parts of the battleship's starboard side came towards and under him the *Express* was in danger of being flipped over by the bilge keel of the bigger ship. With this in mind, he had already put a man with a knife at the end of every rope.

Brooke watched the sailor after him come across and then heard Cartwright scream, 'Slip!' – the naval command for undoing a mooring line, though the knives would ensure a faster operation than usual with obvious consequences. 'All the ropes swung down, heavy with men, to crash sickeningly against the battleship's side,' observed the horrified sub-lieutenant. ' "Starboard ten, full astern together" came from the bridge above and, as the engine room telegraph clanged, the grey wall opposite began to roll inexorably away.'

In his desire to collect as many men as possible, it looked as though Cartwright had left it too late. Brooke grabbed for a hand-hold as the *Prince of Wales*' bilge keel suddenly came up beneath the destroyer and levered it to starboard so violently that some of her newly acquired passengers were tipped overboard. For a moment the *Express* teetered on the brink of capsizing until, with a terrible scraping sound that left a 20-foot gash just above her waterline, her propellers and rudder backed her off the battleship's bilge keel.

As she did so her helmsman, Able Seaman John Farrington, glanced up at the battleship and witnessed a 'truly brave sight'. Leaning on his inclining bridge, his chin cupped in his hands, was Phillips, 'looking like some gold-braided "What-Ho", a signalman at his side flashing out hurried messages to our bridge'. The admiral was then seen to give Cartwright a parting wave, an accolade from one professional to another for some bold and effective ship-handling.

Even before she moved away, some men had given up hope of boarding the *Express* and begun to jump overboard. Along with Phillips and Leach, probably about half of the battleship's full complement of 1,612 officers and men was still on the ship. Like the *Repulse*, the battleship was slowly rotating to port, which resulted in the same phenomenon of men walking or sliding down the side of the ship into the sea.

Brooke noticed that some of the men who had smashed against the side of the ship when the ropes were cut, and now found themselves 'lying on a near horizontal surface', managed to get to their feet and join in the move to the water. There was also time for some of the remaining wounded to have their lifebelts inflated and be floated off the port side of the forecastle on makeshift rafts, usually accompanied by at least one able-bodied man. As with the *Repulse*, some of the seriously hurt did not get off, though not all were entirely abandoned. The ship's New Zealand chaplain, the Reverend W. G. Parker, chose to comfort a group of dying men with his prayers to the end, and spurned all entreaties to save himself. There were several instances of swimmers giving up lifebelts to non-swimmers who had somehow become separated from their own; in at least one case it was the swimmer who drowned.

It was perhaps inevitable that a community as big as a decent-sized village, housed in a steel labyrinth of now-darkened passageways and cubby holes in which internal communications had often failed long before it started to go under water, should know mixed fortunes. Some of those closed up at action stations well below decks were simply not aware of the order to abandon ship. A search party looking for trapped men had used ropes to lower themselves like potholers down a hatchway where a wrecked ladder prevented normal access and discovered a startled telephonist still patiently seated at his silent switchboard. He was one of the lucky ones. Several survivors mention the awful wailing sounds that came up the ventilation shafts.

Men lived or died for no discernible reason beyond the general capriciousness of circumstance. Why, for instance, should the magazine party in the working chamber beneath one of the port 5.25 turrets, which was soon under water, survive while the equivalent party on the higher and drier starboard side, who had much more time to save themselves, all perished? Many were inspired by the sight of Royal Marine sergeants calmly falling in and counting off their men. They were then marched to the high side of the ship, where they inflated their lifebelts and were ordered to jump. It was at least 50 feet down. Peter Dunstan, a tall young Londoner who was in a Marine 5.25 gun crew, does not recall anybody hesitating. But discipline could hinder as well as help. 'Guns before men,' chided a warrant officer, blocking the passage of some escaping telegraphists with pompom ammunition for a weapon that was no longer manned. A couple squeezed by; the less insubordinate turned back and searched in vain for another way out.

Able Seaman White, the radar operator who carried his grandfather's caul, reached the safety of a Carley float where he discovered that the membrane, having worked its magic, had disintegrated along with his wallet. White was one of 1,285 saved from the *Prince of Wales*, very nearly 80 per cent of her crew; the *Repulse* sank much faster, with the loss of 513 of the 1,309 aboard. The Japanese aircrews did not molest the three destroyers as they picked up survivors, though some of them circled the scene and got quite close. On the crowded deck of the *Express*, Brooke was crouched with his fingers in his ears under the slowly moving barrel of the ship's dual-purpose 4.7 gun asking himself, 'Why the devil don't we open fire? They'll get us next.'

At the time this was interpreted by some as a wonderful example of 'magnanimity in victory', perhaps stemming from the close training ties that once existed between the two navies. There were even reports that a morse message in English had been flashed instructing the destroyers to hold their fire and pick up survivors. None of this appears to be true and was certainly not borne out by many subsequent actions over the coming weeks. Unknown to the British, all the Japanese aircraft in the vicinity had run out of bombs and torpedoes. They could have machine-gunned the rescue operation but it made sense to husband their ammunition in case vengeful British fighters caught up with them before they were out of range.

The first of these appeared within a few minutes of the Japanese departing the scene in the form of Mowbray Garden's Buffalo. He was just in time to be fired at by guns still being manned on the sinking *Prince of Wales* which stopped when he opened his cockpit and fired the recognition colours of the day with a flare pistol. Next came Vigors and his ten Buffaloes from 453 Squadron – one had turned back with engine trouble. Below them the destroyers were nosing their way into an archipelago of dark blots, each full of wreckage and hundreds of upturned heads. 'Never before have I seen anything comparable with what I saw yesterday,' Vigors, who had patrolled over the Dunkirk beaches, wrote in an emotional tribute he sent to naval headquarters.

It was obvious that the three destroyers were going to take hours to pick up those hundreds of men clinging to bits of wreckage and swimming around in the filthy water . . . Yet as I flew round every man waved and put his thumb up to me . . . as if they were holidaymakers at Brighton . . . I saw the spirit which wins wars.

When they heard about it afterwards, a lot of the sailors said that Vigors was a bloody fool and they'd all been shaking their fists at his Buffaloes and shouting things like 'RAF – Rare As Fucking Fairies'. But it was quite true that morale among the unwounded and those who had not swallowed excessive amounts of oil generally remained high, if only out of a sense of relief that the worst was probably over. None the less, being 'picked up by destroyers' was not, as Midshipman Guy Griffiths found, as easy as it sounds.

Those who reach the destroyer are faced with the problem of getting aboard by clambering up lines, scrambling nets or ladders. The wounded have great difficulty, especially those suffering from burns. With some it was a case of a line under the arms and being hoisted away by the destroyer's crew on the deck above. St John's Ambulance rules are discarded.

One 'very large, unconscious Royal Marine, wounded and clogged with oil' was nearly hanged when Lieutenant John Hayes of the *Repulse*, who had been looking after him, was thrown a rope from the *Electra* which he thought he had tied in a bowline under his arms.

I shouted 'Haul away' a little too eagerly only to find that the noose had slid up round his neck. Just in time. There were ribald comments on my performance by friends in the water and already on deck, and then we were both safe.

The non-swimmer O'Dowd Gallagher was saved by a young petty officer who got him into a boat after he had been in the water for two hours, was exhausted and losing confidence in his lifebelt. His friend Cecil Brown also survived, but not his handmade shoes: the American reporter removed them on the torpedo bulge of the *Repulse* before he dived in, amazing himself by placing them neatly together as if he expected to be reunited with them shortly. In similar vein, Lieutenant Horace Abrahams, the journalists' Admiralty minder, had taken the trouble to place his camera and plates in a lifebelt locker before leaving the flag deck for the last time.

All of *Repulse*'s survivors were rescued by the *Electra* and the *Vampire*, the Australian destroyer. Hubert Bowen found himself on the *Electra* where he was soon in a queue of survivors being given a generous tot of rum. 'How old are you?' asked the suspicious leading seaman in charge when he got up to the barrel. 'Twenty-one,' gasped the oil-soaked eighteen-year-old, determined to get his tot.

His twin Fred was on the *Vampire*, where the Australians had equipped themselves with kerosene-soaked rags for removing oil, the way people clean up polluted seabirds. Vince Cesari, the lanky son of Italian immigrants, grabbed one hand too slippery with oil to grip. He changed tactics, got both his long arms under the survivor's armpits, heaved him unceremoniously over the rail and began gently dabbing eyes and mouth with his rag. To his amazement after a few seconds the man produced a sodden officer's cap he had secreted somewhere about his person, rubbed it until a considerable amount of gold braid had been revealed, placed it carefully on his head and said, 'Thank you. Now could you direct me to the bridge?'

Cesari, an engine-room artificer who had celebrated his twentieth birthday six days before, led the way to his skipper, Captain 'Porky' Moran. 'There's a bloke here called Captain Tennant wants to see you,' he said.

The master of the *Repulse* was the senior survivor. Admiral Phillips was not among the living and nor was Captain Leach. Leach's first lieutenant, Lieutenant-Commander Albert Skipwith, reported that after the *Express* had cast off, they ignored all entreaties to save themselves. It was assumed that Phillips at least had followed the old tradition of going down with his ship.

'They urged them to leave as nothing further could be done but got no reaction,' Skipwith told Henry Leach. Well after midnight, the midshipman had gone searching for his father among the survivors being unloaded from the destroyers at the naval base not far from the officers' club pool where Leach Senior had swum his extra couple of lengths because 'You never know when it might not come in handy.'

Some of the survivors were quite naked except for a blanket wrapped around them. Many were looking for friends. Most still had oil-blackened hair and reeked of that and the rum they had been given which was intended to restore morale. It had sometimes proved more effective as a fast vomitory agent, for it mixed badly with the fuel they had swallowed. One of the older able seamen off the *Prince of Wales*, probably one of her minority of regulars, had put a huge arm around the midshipman's shoulder and said, 'You best get back to your ship, lad, there's nothing more you can do.'

Eventually, Leach had met up with Skipwith among other officer survivors from both ships in the wardroom of the Fleet Shore Accommodation and learned of his father's death. Nearly half a century later the man who, as Admiral of the Fleet, led the Royal Navy to victory in the Falklands War, recalled every word of it.

'Later,' went on Skipwith with infinite sympathy, 'your father was seen in the water looking very blue.'

'Go on, please,' I said. 'Tell me all.'

'He had . . .' he paused, then collecting himself, 'His neck . . . was broken.'

We looked at each other blankly.

'Thank you, sir,' I mumbled.

'I'm very . . . sorry,' he said chokingly. 'He was a fine man . . . and we all loved him.'

I nodded blindly. 'So did I.'

In December 1939 Captain Hans Langsdorff ended the battle of the River Plate against three smaller-gunned British cruisers by scuttling the German pocket battleship *Admiral Graf Spee* and shooting himself in the head. In the North Atlantic some six months later, Britain's Captain Steven 'Go Get 'Em' Smythe was manhandled off the bridge of the sinking armed merchant cruiser *Scotstoun* by his first lieutenant and other officers, having ordered his crew to abandon their torpedoed ship while showing a marked reluctance to follow them.

Usually this kind of ritual suicide, often so appealing to the Japanese psyche, was rare in the European navies. Sometimes a commander could not help dying with his ship – Vice-Admiral Lancelot Holland was blown up with the *Hood* in the *Bismarck* fight – and certainly he was expected to be among the last to leave it. But in the Royal Navy the idea that a captain should die with his ship as an act of contrition for losing it had come to be regarded as wasteful, even defeatist, and made no more sense than encouraging highly trained pilots to stick to their burning aircraft rather than take to their parachutes. It would certainly have led to a dire shortage of destroyer and cruiser captains in the Mediterranean.

No blame could be attached to Captains Tennant and Leach for the loss of their ships and Tennant, who had handled *Repulse* so well, did manage to save himself, though he was undoubtedly one of the last off the old battle cruiser. If Leach's momentary hesitation to turn towards the Nells contributed to the lucky first torpedo hit on the *Prince of*

*Wales*, it was surely caused by Phillips' insistence that they were not confronted by torpedo planes.

Ultimately, the humiliating sinking of the major part of Force Z with the loss of 840 men in a little over two hours must be the fault of the admiral: not because he tried, against considerable odds, to seek out the enemy and destroy them. This was all in keeping with Cunningham's '300 years of tradition' and, had he succeeded, a grateful nation would have had good reason to reward the daring of Lord Phillips of Kota Baharu or wherever. What was indefensible was maintaining radio silence off Kuantan long after it had become apparent that the Japanese had found them. Phillips' failure to call for air cover when he knew, from the destroyer *Tenedos*, that Japanese aircraft were not far away, and the persistent silver speck above them indicated that they too had been located, was simply incomprehensible. Although badly outnumbered, had the Buffaloes arrived some two hours earlier they might well have saved the day. Vigors was certain that as few as six fighters 'could have made one hell of a mess of even fifty or sixty slow and unescorted torpedo bombers'.

Tennant's astonishment that no signal had been sent, and the haste he made to remedy it, is a good indication of how it would probably have been viewed at a court martial of Phillips. By the time he was waving away the *Express* with half the *Prince of Wales*' crew on board some, or even all, of this must been apparent to the brave but stubborn little admiral. Shortly afterwards he dismissed his staff officers – he had brought about twelve of them onto the *Prince of Wales* – with a casual 'Look after yourselves.'

As far as Phillips is concerned, Skipwith's account is backed up by several eyewitnesses on the compass platform, one of whom describes the admiral as being 'in deep despond'. But Henry Leach is quite certain that his father 'would not have subscribed to going down with his ship'.

None the less, the commander of the *Prince of Wales* was in a terrible position for, whatever his personal feelings about Phillips, he was honour-bound not to abandon his ship before him. So was Captain Simon Beardsworth, the admiral's secretary, who had also remained loyally at his side. It appears that at the last moment Leach and Beardsworth may have tried something similar to the frogmarching of Captain Smythe off the *Scotstoun* and taken Phillips into the water between them. There are several reports of the three of them being seen walking down the ship's listing port side, the direction in which she was about to capsize. Telegraphist Bernard Campion, who was also among the last to leave the ship, took the same route and was immediately caught up in a maelstrom of whirling debris 'with a derrick boom wedged firmly over my thighs and all kinds of loose spars belting me about'. Eventually he bobbed up in an oil patch but by now clad in no more than his right sock and his lifebelt, and pummelled black and blue by blunt objects, his worst injury being a broken thigh.

Leach was found by a gunnery officer and some ratings floating face down. When they turned him over it looked as though he may have choked to death, for his face had turned a mottled purple and there were traces of vomit about the mouth. They also thought his neck might be broken and told Skipwith this when they met up with him on the *Express*. Leach was wearing a half-inflated lifebelt and, despite reports that Phillips had declined to get into one on the bridge, an officer who saw his body in the water rather thought the admiral was equipped with one too.

After their astounding victory, a few of the Japanese aircrews diverted to the newly captured British landing strip at Kota Baharu, either because they considered their aircraft too short of fuel or too damaged, or both, to risk the long flight back to Indo-China. But most of them did return, engines spluttering as their fuel feeds began to run dry, to the airfields around Saigon they had left some twelve hours before. One of the Bettys, which had been damaged by anti-aircraft fire, crashed on landing and was written off, though it appears the crew survived. Had all the ninety-five aircraft 22nd Air Flotilla employed on the operation been lost it would have remained an enormous triumph and worth every one of them. As it was, total casualties were the crews in the three aircraft shot down by the ships: 18 Japanese airmen for 840 British sailors.

After a night of riotous *sakai*-fuelled partying, Lieutenant Haruki Iki, who had lost two Bettys from his Chutai during the last devastating attack on the *Repulse*, roused his hungover crew and headed south. It was not hard to find the place, for it was still stained by oil and debris and what might have been bodies. Iki took the Betty down low and circled the spot and then opened the bomb doors. Out of them dropped a small, flat circular object with cork floats, weighted so that it would fall the right way up. The wreath, briefly splendid, settled amidst the flotsam. Iki is sometimes quoted as saying it was for all the dead, and perhaps it was.

# PART FOUR
# Retreat and Reinforcements

Never in its 300-year history had the Royal Navy suffered such a one-sided defeat as the sinking of the *Prince of Wales* and *Repulse*. Never had the loss of just two of its ships been so crucial.

'The worst single piece of news I have ever received,' declared Duff Cooper who for the last twenty-four hours had been revelling in the new title and responsibilities London had just bestowed on him: Resident Cabinet Minister at Singapore for Far Eastern Affairs with authority to form a War Council.

More disastrous things, such as the fall of France, have happened, but the news of them arrived gradually and the mind had time to prepare itself for the catastrophe. Even on this occasion I was buoyed up by the new responsibility that I was carrying. I had so much to do. We agreed that I should broadcast the bad news that evening.

This was done from the Malayan Broadcasting Corporation's studios at the Cathay skyscraper where the man who had become the most senior civilian in the colony – he now outranked the governor – did his eloquent best to conjure up some crumbs of comfort. Duff Cooper reminded his listeners that this would not be the first time the British people had been obliged to overcome disaster, that the Royal Navy had other battleships, that more were being built, and that – surely the most ingenious line of all – meanwhile Malaya was no worse off than it had been a month ago. 'We were not safe then; we are not safe now. But in these great days, safety seems hardly honourable and danger is glorious.'

The monsoon storms had returned with a vengeance that night and disturbances in the ionosphere made for poor radio reception. Kathleen Stapledon and her husband Steepy, the naval architect, found it impossible to hear any of it. Then a friend telephoned. 'His reception was poor but he thought that the two warships had been sunk and he wanted it confirmed. Steepy was furious that such a thing could even be suggested on the phone.'

Those listeners who had been able to pick up the newly appointed

Resident Minister's first broadcast generally failed, as he must have known they would, to share his professed enthusiasm for the prospect of 'glorious danger' now on offer. 'Blown clean away at one fell swoop was one of the main pillars on which our sense of security rested,' noted *The Times'* correspondent Ian Morrison. 'Nor was our despondency in any way mitigated by Mr Duff Cooper's Churchillian heroics and his well-intentioned attempt to reconcile people in Singapore to the news . . . The *Prince of Wales* and the *Repulse* were lost. That was all we knew, all we could think about.'

In London the prime minister's private reaction to the loss of the ships was a sight less Churchillian than the public utterances of his most far-flung cabinet minister. Churchill rarely went to sleep before the early hours of the morning and was a fairly late riser, though this was partly because he began his punishing day by opening his dispatch boxes in bed. His bedside telephone rang and it was Admiral Sir Dudley Pound on the other end. 'Prime Minister, I have to report to you . . .' Churchill thought the First Sea Lord's voice sounded odd. Then he began to absorb what he was saying.

'Are you sure it's true?'

'There is no doubt at all.'

So I put the telephone down. I was thankful to be alone. In all the war I never received a more direct shock . . . As I turned over and twisted in bed the full horror of the news sank in upon me.

Arthur Percival could not afford to be in shock and certainly not in bed past six in the morning; but few generals could have suffered such radical reverses before the bulk of their army had even been committed to battle. After the promising start at Kota Baharu less than seventy-two hours before, when between them Key's Indian infantry and the Australian aircrews had obliged so many of the Japanese with the martyrdom they seemed to crave, the defence plan for Malaya and Singapore had been turned on its head.

The Royal Navy's bluff had been called and, from the Indian Ocean to the South China Sea, Nippon ruled the waves, which meant they could land troops anywhere along Malaya's long coastline. The only effective opposition came from some determined Dutch submariners who severely damaged four transports off Patani, one of Yamashita's two Thai beach-heads, and sank a tanker and a transport off Kota

Baharu. But, within days, the Dutch had lost three of their boats, two depth-charged by destroyers and one sunk on the surface by a British mine while on its way back to its base in Singapore, though its captain, Lieutenant-Commander Arnault Bussemaker, and some of his officers survived because they were on the bridge at the time.

The air force, badly under-strength to start with, had nowhere near fulfilled their promise to destroy at least 40 per cent of an invasion fleet. Instead, the panic-stricken flight of its ground crews had meant abandoning the very airfields that were supposed to be the springboard of a devastating counter-attack. 'In the majority of cases the bombing of aerodromes has been of a far smaller scale than that suffered calmly by women and children in London,' a disgusted Brooke-Popham had complained in a letter to Air Vice-Marshal Pulford. Now its remaining aircraft were being steadily reduced by better machines in the hands of more experienced pilots.

From being cast in a supporting role, protecting airfields and securing the Singapore naval base, the army, grotesquely deployed around places of scant tactical value, found itself promoted to the top of the bill and expected to save the show. But Percival had very little time to rewrite the script. Keen tennis player that he was, all he could hope was that, high on victory, his opponent might start making the kind of unforced errors that would let him back into the match.

One came his way in the north-east. The Japanese were slow, uncharacteristically slow as it turned out, in following up their hard-won victory at Kota Baharu. Despite the lack of decent roads along the east coast, General Takumi failed to cut off Brigadier Key's brigade. Instead, along with most of their vehicles and their stores, it made a remarkable escape south down a single-track railway line that bridged several rivers and ravines. The destruction or capture of any one of these bridges would have finished Key's Indians. It is possible that the Japanese preferred to preserve them for their own use because they never attempted to destroy one by bombing. Instead, they skirmished with the two rearguard battalions, sometimes in a ludicrously over-confident manner as if they were hoping a show of force would make them fall apart as the Hyderabads had done at Kota Baharu.

Once, Prem Sahgal's company of the 2/10th Baluch were attacked in daylight across an open field. 'They came in mass. The light and medium machine-guns made them drop in the paddy. Then the mortars got them.' Later it was discovered from a rare prisoner that these were fresh troops who, like Sahgal's battalion, had not been involved in the fighting at Kota Baharu beach-head.

With the rearguard blowing up some very fine bridges behind it, Key's weary men, collapsed among a great jumble of kit and weapons, rattled into the country station at Kuala Lipis about ten days after the withdrawal started. The town is in the middle of the widest part of the peninsula, some 140 miles south of Kota Baharu. Cumming's 2nd Sikhs went back to the east coast, detached to defend the almost deserted airfield at Kuantan. The rest of the brigade concentrated around Kuala Lipis, a useful reserve poised to go west or east as the situation demanded. But the Japanese made no other unforced errors. In the time it had taken Key's brigade to extricate themselves from Kelantan, Percival had suffered his first defeat and begun a long retreat.

Yamashita had secured Kota Baharu because its airfield threatened his landings just across the border in Thailand. Once ashore, the obvious way to invade Malaya was down the west coast which, unlike the underdeveloped east side of the peninsula, had good north–south roads all the way to Singapore. Major-General David Murray-Lyon, a bagpipe-playing Scot whose 11th Indian Division defended north-western Malaya, had never doubted that war would mean Operation Matador and a pre-emptive dash into Thailand to deny the Japanese a beach-head. Instead, thanks to Brooke-Popham's dithering, they had been stood down and, soaked to the skin by the monsoon rain, begun the demoralizing business of draining and repairing waterlogged trench systems, stringing barbed wire and siting machine-gun nests.

To try and buy time until these defences were ready, Percival had sanctioned a kind of mini-Matador: three short-range raids into Thailand intended to delay the advancing Japanese by destroying bridges and stretches of highland road, and, when they could, ambushing them. One of these raiding parties consisted of an armoured train manned by thirty Punjabis and a demolition team of engineers. A Victorian locomotive coupled to a flat-bedded wagon fitted with sand-bagged machine-guns clattered across the frontier from Perlis, the smallest of the Malayan states in the most north-westerly part of the country, stopped about 10 miles inside Thailand at a bridge with a 200-foot span near Klong Ram, collapsed it and returned safely.

Further to the east, some 200 truck-borne Punjabis crossed the border directly north of the defensive position at Jitra on the trunk road which led directly to the Japanese beach-head at Singora. They had with them four Breda anti-tank guns with UK British crews – booty from the conquest of Italian East Africa in which Indian troops had played a large part – and six Bren gun carriers because the little open-topped, tracked vehicles were useful for off-road reconnaissance. There was also a detachment of engineers with plenty of explosives for blowing up bridges.

They had just set up a defensive position astride the road at the village of Ban Sadao, about 10 miles into Thailand, when, headlights blazing and obviously preferring speed to caution, along came a Japanese convoy of about twenty trucks and ten light tanks. The latter, a mixture of Type 95s, which had a 37 mm cannon as well as two machine-guns, and two-man tankettes armed only with machine-guns, were part of the newly landed 5th Division's reconnaissance unit under Colonel Saeki, who was in overall command. Saeki blundered straight into the Punjabis' road-block and immediately lost his leading Type 95 to one of the Bredas firing at almost point-blank range: screams, shouts, a hailstorm of small arms fire from both sides and the rapid extinguishing of headlights.

The T95 blocked the road. Two other tanks or tankettes which tried to edge round it were knocked out, or at least disabled, by Punjabi riflemen using long-barrelled Boys anti-tank rifles, which sent huge steel-cored .55 bullets ricocheting wickedly about their interiors impartially penetrating men and machinery alike. At 36 pounds the Boys weighed exactly four times as much as the Punjabis' Lee-Enfield rifles, had a recoil that could turn a shoulder black with one shot and were best fired prone. The weapon had acquired a dismal reputation against the Panzers, but the thinner Japanese armour was more vulnerable, providing a man had the nerve to hold his fire until they were no more than 250 yards away.

Saeki's men responded with commendable speed, the infantry dismounting from their trucks and disappearing into the vegetation on either side of the road to work around the flanks of the Punjabis. Badly outnumbered, the Indians began a staged withdrawal, taking it in turns to play rearguard as they started back towards the border, leaving a trail of wrecked bridges and cratered roads as the engineers made enthusiastic use of their explosives. 'It caused great hindrance,' admitted Major-General Saburo Kawamura, who was Colonel's Saeki's immediate superior. But not for long as Japanese sappers gave the first indication of how quickly they could repair bridges and fill in holes.

The third of these raids into Thailand, and by far the most important, was a column which started out from the border town of Kroh. Known to the men who planned it as KrohCol, its objective was to seize and destroy 6 miles of road and thus make it impossible for the enemy to bring up his heavy equipment from Patani, their second and more southerly landing place in the Kra Isthmus.

A glance at the map shows how important it was to hold the Japanese at Kroh. A lateral road ran from there to Sungei Patani on the west coast. If the Japanese possessed this road they would have succeeded in cutting all the north–south communications to Alor Star, the capital of Kedah, the northern state with the longest border with Thailand. The road from the fishing harbour of Patani to the frontier township of Kroh, about 100 miles away, often ran alongside the muddy waters of the Patani River and covered some difficult terrain. The 6-mile stretch that had been targeted – known as The Ledge – had been dynamited out of a steep hillside with a precipitous drop down to the river.

Blowing up a large chunk of The Ledge was a good idea. But, although Heath's 3rd Indian Corps had been placed at first-degree readiness a good two days before hostilities began, it was not until some fourteen hours after the Japanese landings at Kota Baharu that KrohCol moved cautiously across the border. Even then it was at less than half its designated strength, the delay being caused by the failure of a second battalion of Punjabi infantry and a light artillery battery manned by European civilians of the Federal Malay States Volunteers, both based on Penang Island, to get to Kroh. It transpired that it had been difficult to shoehorn the part-time gunners out of their civilian lives quickly enough, and in any case the ferries were not running because their Asian crews had deserted after an air raid. Survivors from the *Prince of Wales* and *Repulse* were sent to take over.

Eventually the commander of the column, Lieutenant-Colonel Henry Moorhead, decided to go ahead with the forces at his disposal. These were the 3/16th Punjabis, his own battalion, some engineers and a collection of leathery Diggers, most of them 1914–18 veterans, from an Australian Reserve Motor Transport Company who were not under Bennett's command but had been permanently attached to the 3rd Indian Corps for the last eight months.

Once inside Thailand, Moorhead's column was further delayed by unexpectedly fierce resistance from the Thai gendarmerie, who shot dead his lead scout and continued to snipe and ambush them. 'A few score men but they fought skilfully,' noted Percival.

Thailand's hopelessly outgunned defence forces appear to have shot at both invaders with equal enthusiasm. Nor were civilians loath to lend a hand. A major of the Imperial Guard, who was part of the Japanese forces that had crossed into the northern part of Thailand from Cambodia, went into Bangkok on a reconnaissance and was dragged out of his car by an enraged mob who beat him to death, along with his orderly. Not long after this Field-Marshal Pibul Song-gram, whose sympathies with Japan had always been obvious, ordered all resistance to cease. As a result the Japanese, though they had the greater distance to cover along a road turned into a quagmire by the rain, won the race to The Ledge by a few minutes. KrohCol's forward company, advancing on foot, was within 5 miles of their objective when, to their amazement, they encountered the first Japanese trucks and tanks. Once again anti-tank rifles were used to good effect and Moorhead handled his column with great skill, making a fighting retreat back towards Kroh where the missing Punjabi battalion had now arrived and was digging in.

Moorhead, forty-three years old and, like some of the Australian drivers, a veteran of the Great War, was one of perhaps a dozen or so military unicorns commanding Indian battalions in Malaya: a dying breed of fluent Urdu-speakers, betrothed to their regiments, who led by example and, though undoubtedly paternalistic, held the respect of their senior Indian non-commissioned officers. Having failed, through no fault of their own, to destroy The Ledge, Moorhead's Punjabis were holding the Japanese at Kroh, though not without cost. Unfortu-nately for the British, it would take more than a few Moorheads to save the day. Elsewhere things were unravelling fast.

Having disposed of the best part of the Royal Navy and clipped the wings of the RAF, the Japanese were beginning to show their superior-ity on the ground. This was hardly surprising. Yamashita had both air superiority and tanks – there was not a single British tank in the whole of Malaya. Above all he had brave and intelligent infantry, many of them China veterans. Against these, while Bennett's Australians languished in the south in case of new landings on the beaches of Johore, Percival continued to deploy thousands of his young Indians. Properly led by people like Moorhead or Cumming of the 2nd Sikhs at Kota Baharu they fought well; but the Japanese responded in the obvious way and picked off white officers whenever they spotted them. With an exceptionally well-placed grenade, Cumming had personally killed three Japanese infiltrators who tried to assassinate him and the commander of 2/10th Baluch at a roadside conference, but this sort of luck was rare.

Mixed in with the brigades of the 11th Indian Division were the three regular UK British battalions from the Argylls, the East Surreys and the Leicesters, all of whom had originally been shipped somewhere east of Suez in colonial gendarmerie roles some years before. They totalled just over 2,000 men, about a fifth of the division's infantry, and were probably the best material Murray-Lyon had.

Even so, they were no longer all the hardened regulars celebrated in Kipling's verse. After Dunkirk, some had been sent back as cadres for fresh battalions being raised at home. Their replacements were often conscripts. Junior officers, though almost invariably volunteers, also tended to be borrowed civilians holding emergency commissions. Many of the professionals had been siphoned off into management and were, often to their great disgust, manning a desk at brigade, division, corps or army headquarters. There was a great shortage of people who – even if they had never been anywhere near a staff college – knew what was needed at the sharp end and might show some aptitude for sorting things out.

The Japanese did not believe in long logistical tails and large staffs. The only European army they had any admiration for was Germany's and that was because they had introduced the world to blitzkrieg – lightning war. It was a Japanese version of this that Major-General Kawamura, who commanded the leading 9th Brigade of the Imperial Army's 5th Division, was about to inflict on Murray-Lyon.

On the British side, frantic preparations were continuing to improve the defences around Jitra, 12 miles north of the now-abandoned Alor Star airfield. At Jitra, the west coast railway and trunk road came together and for the next 50 miles ran south alongside each other until they came to the twin road and rail bridges at Sungei Patani. Here they separated for a few miles, the road curving west to take traffic to Butterworth and the ferry point for Penang Island.

Ever since Heath had taken command of the 3rd Indian Corps, the Jitra defences had been one of the sorest points between the military and the colonial administration. When Heath wanted labour to improve them, he was told that the needs of rubber production and tin-mining came first. When he asked for permission to secure his left flank to the sea by flooding some rice paddy, he was informed that food supplies were sacrosanct. Nor did it make any difference when the army produced statistics supporting their claim that these farmlands contributed no more than three days' worth of Malaya's annual rice consumption.

The lure of Matador and offensive operations into Thailand had made this kind of obstructionism easier to live with, almost irrelevant. But Matador had never happened and now here was Murray-Lyon, three days into a campaign the British had seen coming for over a year, still trying to finish anti-tank traps across a front which stretched some 35 miles from the foothills to the coast. To gain time, substantial road-blocks, deployments of at least 300 men, were set up astride the straight north–south highway running from the border.

Their orders were to give the enemy a bloody nose and only to withdraw if they thought they were about to be overwhelmed. The first one, just north of the village of Changlun, worked well. Some four hours after dusk the 1/14th Punjabis, and the British gunners of a Royal Artillery anti-tank regiment distributed throughout the Indian division, waited until the first two Japanese tanks filled their sights and then ended their joyride into Malaya with a crack some of their crews never heard. The Punjabis inflicted more casualties on the infantry that followed them, then pulled out, whenever possible blowing up small bridges and culverts behind them.

In daylight it was harder. When the Japanese caught up with them at Changlun they captured a damaged but still usable bridge that would have been better demolished. Then, as they retreated from a Japanese flanking party that was about to cut them off, two of the Breda anti-tank guns were lost. But most of the battalion was intact and its morale reasonably unimpaired for there was still the memory of the anti-tank gunners' success the night before.

Lieutenant-Colonel James Fitzpatrick, their commanding officer, intended to get his men back to the next major village of Asun and, more particularly, behind the stream there which would make a handy tank trap. But Murray-Lyon turned up and, still desperately seeking to place extra hurdles in front of the Japanese before they reached the neglected defences at Jitra, told Fitzpatrick to take up a position he had spotted a couple of miles before Asun, where they could fight another delaying action. It was late afternoon. Fitzpatrick and his four company commanders followed Murray-Lyon back towards Asun to see, before it got dark, exactly where he wanted them, and left the battalion to pack up.

It was raining again and most people were trying to keep dry, ground sheets and rubberized gas capes spread over filling fox holes. The sepoys, probably with some relief, started to load themselves and their kit back onto their transport where at least they would be reasonably dry for half an hour or so; the UK British anti-tank gunners, simultaneously sodden and sweating, pulled their guns out of the mud and coupled them to their trucks, which was somehow never as easy as it was supposed to be. Then the rain took on a life of its own, falling in great wind-blown sheets that reduced visibility to a few yards so that Colonel Saeki's T95s clattered among them like ghosts before most of the Punjabis realized what they were.

Half in and half out of trucks, its anti-tank guns limbered up and ready to roll, Fitzpatrick's battalion was at its most vulnerable and Saeki exploited his luck to the full. Lieutenant Peter Greer, the commander of the anti-tank battery attached to the Punjabis, had a ringside seat under a stand of rubber trees beside the road where he was waiting with some of his Bren gun carriers to join the tail of his battery as it pulled out.

Suddenly I saw some of my trucks and a carrier screaming down the flooded road and heard the hell of a battle ... The din was terrific ... almost immediately a medium tank roared past me. I dived for cover ... within the next two minutes a dozen medium tanks and a couple of two-man tanks passed me. They had crashed right through our forward companies ... In the middle of the tanks I saw one of my carriers; its tail was on fire and the Number Two was facing back firing his light machine-gun at a tank twenty yards behind him. Poor beggar.

The 1/14th Punjabis would never be put back together again. No more than 200 found their way back to British lines. Several anti-tank guns were captured. Those who had not been killed or taken prisoner were in hiding. Months later the Japanese would still be flushing out sepoys who had shed uniforms and weapons and were trying to pass themselves off as Tamil rubber estate workers.

The sheer bad luck of having so many of their senior officers absent undoubtedly accelerated the battalion's disintegration. And when they did find out what was happening, few of the officers were in a position to do much about it. The first to understand was Captain Mohan Singh, who commanded the HQ company. Driving back up the trunk road in his truck after inspecting the new position before Asun, Singh met Saeki's tanks coming the other way. He swerved into the rubber, leapt from his cab, heard a long burst of automatic fire and watched from around a tree as the machine-gunner passed by, standing in his open turret 'laughing heartily'.

Further down the road, trying to work out where to deploy his companies so that they had the best fields of fire, Fitzpatrick was at first unaware that his battalion was, according to one contemporary account, being 'scattered like chaff'. When he realized that something was badly amiss he went forward and was trying to organize a road-block of abandoned vehicles when he was badly wounded and evacuated.

The rout of this single Indian battalion was the boulder prised loose that started an avalanche. The remnants of Fitzpatrick's men fell back in confusion upon Asun, where a battalion of Gurkhas was trying to dig in behind a narrow but fast-flowing stream, almost a river. Soon the tanks were approaching its bridge, beneath which, the day before, the Madras Sappers and Miners had placed charges, wired the deton-ators and were ready to blow them to kingdom come. But when the moment came nothing happened, possibly because the charges had become soaked with rain. A British officer seconded to the Indian unit from the Royal Engineers dashed to the bridge to investigate but he was mortally wounded by a burst of machine-gun fire from the oncoming armour.

The Gurkhas had no anti-tank guns; they had been waiting for Greer's battery to fall back on their position. But they did have some Boys rifles. One of them was in the hands of Manbahadur Gurung, a *havildar* (sergeant) with seven years' service behind him who waited until Saeki's tanks were almost on the bridge and then, lying prone, stopped the lead two with his elephant gun, which effectively blocked the progress of the rest. Unfortunately for the British, experienced non-commissioned officers were as yet a rarity in this particular battalion, the 2/1st, of King George V's Own Gurkha Rifles, founded in 1937 and the newest Gurkha regiment. Most of the 2/1st's rank and file were untrained teenagers, many of them rather younger than they pretended to be. If they had to be in a war zone they needed a lot more Havildar Gurungs among them. And they had already had the disconcerting experience of watching trucks full of Punjabis driving through their lines yelling, 'Back to Jitra!'

The Japanese infantry responded to the havildar's good shooting with what was coming to be recognized as their customary speed. They put down mortar and machine-gun fire, then splashed through the water on either side of the bridge with bayonets fixed. Snipers looked for white faces and picked off officers as they tried to rally their men. Soon the young Gurkhas broke, though some paused long enough to remove their boots and other impediments to flight. Out of just under 600 in the battalion, no more than 30 were killed. About 200 escaped booted and armed, most of them in a party held together by the battalion's commanding officer, Lieutenant-Colonel Jack Fulton. The majority were captured, though over the coming weeks a few did straggle back to British lines, usually feverish and in poor health after arduous treks through thick jungle. The wrecked tanks were towed clear of the bridge and, having broken to pieces the best part of two battalions, Colonel Saeki continued his pell-mell progress to Jitra.

There is, of course, nothing on the battlefield more exhilarating than to rout the enemy with little loss to yourself. The British themselves had recently experienced this against the Italians in both East and North Africa. It had been a source of great satisfaction for the British that, for all Benito Mussolini's braggadocio, theirs had undoubtedly been the better troops: better led, often better equipped and, though often greatly outnumbered, able to run rings around the Italians. With victory came confidence and the contempt for the enemy that leads to bold and extravagant bluffs. As long as they kept up the pressure, they expected the Italians to be wrong-footed, then run away or surrender, and they frequently did. Now it looked as though the Japanese were about to inflict a similar series of humiliations on Heath's troops.

Among the defenders along the Jitra line, mixed in with Murray-Lyon's Gurkhas, Punjabis, Dogras and Jats, were two of his three British infantry battalions – the 1st Leicesters and 2nd East Surreys. Despite the borrowed civilians among them, they remained very much regular army units. Both battalions maintained sergeants' messes which waged fierce campaigns against declining standards, delighting in every petty absurdity they imposed to remind the strangers among them of their illustrious pedigrees.

'Did you not observe, sir, that Private Watkins was improperly dressed?'

'I'm afraid I didn't, sergeant-major,' confessed Lieutenant Stephen Abbott, who was twenty-two and had recently reported to the East Surreys with a small draft of reinforcements, mostly conscripts and emergency commissioned officers like himself.

'Sir, the bottom strand of the bootlace on his left boot is twisted.'

Ten months later, after three twelve-hour days working in the tropical slush of the Jitra line, few of Abbott's platoon had seen their bootlaces for some time. Yet, despite the mud and the almost permanently wet feet, morale remained high. The prospect of battle was exciting, probably because few had ever experienced it. Even so, Abbott knew that both he and his men were already exhausted. After dark, despite the long labours of the day, about a third of the battalion at a time took turns to 'stand to' against surprise attack. No one was averaging any more than four hours' sleep a night in leaky tents or under a groundsheet.

After several false night alarms, one of them causing a great waste of 25-pounder artillery shells, the battle started with a series of pre-dawn probes for weak spots. Although the Surreys and Leicesters were in different brigades, the 6th and the 15th, they were deployed next to each other: the Leicesters on the left of their brigade astride the trunk road and the Surreys in the paddy fields and the marshes to the left of them.

The Jitra line was not, and never could be, entirely contiguous in the way that the 1914–18 trenches in Flanders were. Even if Murray-Lyon had had enough men to do this, the terrain, particularly where it became a patchwork quilt of paddy bunds, did not lend itself to it. None the less, it had some good interlocking fields of fire from wired-in strong points. Although he was obviously anxious to galvanize his division with the notion that an attack was imminent, it would not have been unreasonable for Murray-Lyon to nurture secret hopes that Yamashita might wait until he had brought all his forces up.

Which might well have been the case had it not been for Second Lieutenant Oto, a slender young man of epicene good looks according to Tsuji. The colonel had rushed forward from the Singora beachhead to join Saeki, who was an old friend. Oto had commanded one of the probing patrols and when he reported back to Saeki and Tsuji he was covered in blood.

It turned out that the blood was not his own but came from a sentry he had stabbed on a bridge while infiltrating British lines which, he had concluded, were thinly manned. Oto was strongly of the opinion that a night attack at their weakest point might well be successful. This was just what Tsuji and Saeki, who both saw no reason why youth should always hold the monopoly on impetuous behaviour, wanted to hear. The British artillery was expending a lavish amount of ammunition. It was possible they were trying to hold them up with this while rushing up infantry to plug the gaps. It was decided that there was not a moment to lose. They would not wait for the rest of General Kawamura's 9th Brigade to catch up with them but immediately resume the offensive.

As it happened, Oto was wrong. The Jitra line was being held by the best part of a division and Saeki's 500-strong reconnaissance unit was about to attack an enemy that outnumbered it by at least ten to one. A small diversionary party, perhaps 100-strong, was deployed to the east against Murray-Lyon's right flank and began to raid and snipe and generally make as much noise as possible. Before long British troops would be referring to Japanese employed on these tactics as 'jitter parties', and sometimes they would make the British very jittery indeed. A favourite ploy was to use chains of firecrackers lobbed behind the enemy by small mortars to give the enemy the impression that they were being attacked from the rear.

In order to make maximum use of their small number of tanks, the main thrust of Saeki's attack was on the trunk road and a narrow margin either side of it. This was the area held by the Leicesters, who had some anti-tank guns attached, as well as artillery support, and were determined to give a good account of themselves.

By noon the following day the Leicesters were still firmly in place, the Japanese having been ejected from the small gains they had made during the night with vigorous counter-attacks. At one point, when the enemy were reported to have broken through the Jats on the Leicesters' right and to be heading towards an entirely empty prisoner-of-war cage that the British had somewhat optimistically erected, they were repelled by the signallers and clerks of the headquarters company under a lieutenant named Maurice Oldridge.

Among Oldridge's men was signaller Jack 'Becky' Sharpe, a regular from the slums of Leicester's West End, where his father ran a small newsagent's shop. He had just discharged himself from hospital where he was being treated for a skin complaint and hitch-hiked back to the battalion, unable to tolerate the idea that it would go to war without him. Sharpe had last come under fire in Waziristan, where the Faqir of Ipi's men delighted in long-range sniping duels. At Jitra, the combatants got much closer. Oldridge's party was confronted by Japanese infantry led by an officer waving a sword and screaming some terrible war cry. The signaller was amazed. 'It was mediaeval.'

He dropped to one knee and brought his rifle to his shoulder; but he seemed to be doing everything in slow motion, trapped in a nightmare where limbs have turned to water and neither fight nor flight is possible. As this samurai got closer, Sharpe at last began to take first pressure on the trigger. Then suddenly the Japanese began a jerky, puppet-like dance. Sharpe turned to see the corporal who was acting as Oldridge's bodyguard firing from the hip with one of the battalion's new Thompson sub-machine-guns. The swordsman was lying on his back and his men were pulling out. Sharpe and some of the other Leicesters threw grenades at them.

Tsuji watched the walking wounded, with their mud-smeared bandages, helping each other along a deep drainage ditch as British artillery shells exploded along the road. Among them was Lieutenant Oto. This time the blood he was wearing was his own and before long he would die of gangrene in a Saigon hospital. At first the colonel hardly recognized him.

Unconsciously breaking into a run as he drew near he came up and grasped my hand. 'Staff Officer, sir, it is inexcusable. Oto has made a mistake in his estimate of the enemy's strength.' His tears were falling like rain. Was the wound on his right shoulder from a grenade? The flesh, deep red like pomegranate, was swollen. His face was pale as if all the blood had been drained out of it. 'Don't worry,' I said. 'We can win this battle.'

According to Tsuji he now, almost single-handedly it seems, turned the tide by taking Saeki's car and running the gauntlet of artillery fire to contact General Kawamura, who was 4 km to the rear and 'uneasy about the artillery fire so close at hand'. Not surprisingly, this does not correspond to Kawamura's version of events, which nowhere mentions his debt to Yamashita's ubiquitous chief of staff.

But what Kawamura, a shrewd veteran of the China fighting, does acknowledge is the sheer luck his reconnaissance regiment had with the night attack on which they were dispatched against such almighty odds by the misinformed Saeki and Tsuji. 'A blind man is not afraid of snakes,' he would write later. For although it appeared to be a total failure, it had been executed with such *élan* that it had unsettled the British. Slowly at first, cracks began to appear in the Jitra line, then as rapidly as in a sand castle lapped by the incoming tide.

Yet at first Murray-Lyon thought his division had done rather well. An attempt was made to deliver a brigade-size counter-attack, but some of the tired and demoralized Indian troops from Asun were used. A delay caused by a friendly fire incident resulted in their artillery support being fired before they had even reached the start line. When their British officers tried to rally them, several, including a battalion commander, were killed and the counter-attack fell apart.

On the right flank of the line, Saeki's jitter parties started to have some effect. Reports coming in from some of the young and inexperienced Indian units there caused first brigade and then divisional headquarters to believe they were about to be enveloped. A company at a time, reinforcements trickled in from the brigade on the other flank, which had hardly been engaged at all, but they never seemed enough. Soon the East Surreys were the only battalion remaining on the west of the trunk road.

As if this was not bad enough, Murray-Lyon began to receive signals that KrohCol was in serious trouble and there was a real danger that the Japanese were about to reach the coastal road behind him and cut off his communications to the south. As it happened, these fears were as unfounded as the alarums being raised on the right flank. Under Moorhead's leadership, the Punjabis of KrohCol were still putting up a good fight; the Japanese were advancing slowly and were nowhere near the coast.

Bad radio communications, a shortage of liaison officers and the sheer time it took to get around northern Malaya in wet weather often made it impossible to check out dismal tidings at the sharp end. In any case, for Murray-Lyon they were made only too believable by a growing realization that much of his young Indian infantry was no match for the Japanese, who were obviously about to bring up fresh troops. He decided that, if he was to save his division, he had to get it behind another natural anti-tank obstacle, and fast. The obvious choice was the River Kedah some 30 miles to the south, just below Alor Star in the rice-growing lands near the town of Gurun. Percival, rather reluctantly, assented. It was a large piece of territory to lose.

But extricating the 11th Division from the Jitra line was not that easy. As Percival would observe, far from saving the division, it only increased its confusion and exhaustion. Even the Surreys and the Leicesters, with their higher proportion of trained soldiers than most of the Indian battalions, found it difficult enough.

The Leicesters had beaten off Saeki's men and taken less than thirty killed and wounded themselves. When told that, as a first step, they were required to withdraw to a narrow ridge about 2 miles long, where deep paddy either side offered poor fields of fire, their indignant protests were swiftly conveyed to brigade headquarters. They were told to get on with it. After their Bren gun carriers had managed to pull out their bogged-down anti-tank guns, the Leicesters found themselves moving south down the trunk road towards their new location, 'amidst scenes of indescribable confusion':

. . . with small, leaderless parties of Indian and Gurkha troops firing in every direction . . . no one appeared to know what was happening. To add to the confusion, fire from their own artillery was falling short among the British troops.

This panic had mostly been started by leaderless rear echelon troops, sometimes after coming under shelling or air attack for the first time. It was contagious and badly driven trucks careered off the road into drainage ditches with astonishing frequency. When they reached their new position, the Leicesters discovered it was even worse than they had imagined. They had their backs to the brown waters of the River Bata, which were swirling along in full spate. Beyond it was brigade headquarters, where much of their transport was now gathered. In order to reach it, they had to cross a road bridge that was coming under frequent light artillery and mortar fire. Kawamura, having brought the rest of his troops up to Saeki's unit, had been amazed to discover that the British were in the process of abandoning the Jitra line and that he was pushing at an open door. He urged his men on, harassing the enemy at every opportunity, trying to capture bridges before they had the chance to blow them up.

Shortly before midnight, a Leicesters officer, Major Kennedy, swam the Bata rather than risk being shelled on the bridge, and reached brigade HQ just as Murray-Lyon's orders arrived to withdraw immediately to the Gurun position. After his second swim of the evening, Kennedy got back to his battalion HQ at about 1.30 a.m. and told them the news. Runners were immediately dispatched to the four rifle companies. From this moment, the battalion began to disintegrate, not so much through enemy action but because of the sheer nightmare of communications.

Despite repeated attempts, two of the companies, B and D, could not be reached, and it was hours before they and the Japanese discovered how lonely they were. It was no more than half the battalion which, shortly before dawn, found itself trying to cross the Bata in a small boat pulled by a cable of twisted wire set up by the enterprising Kennedy. This proved an agonizingly slow process. During one crossing, the boat capsized and several non-swimmers were drowned. (The Leicesters were very much a county regiment; many of its Midlanders had never seen the sea until they boarded a troopship.) Eventually it was decided that Kennedy and 45 others who had succeeded in reaching the far bank would move off, leaving Lieutenant-Colonel Esmond Morrison, the commanding officer, and about 110 others to find another way.

After an exhausting trek through swamp and paddy, Morrison's party made an almost triumphant entry into the empty streets of Alor Star, marching in a loose formation, rifles slung and singing. Some accounts have it that when the first shots were fired the song really was 'Roll Out the Barrel'. The Japanese had owned the evacuated town for several hours. Morrison managed to keep some forty men around him and escape. The remaining seventy were either cornered or killed in vicious street fighting, or scattered into the jungle where they experienced mixed fortunes.

Apart from loaning the Leicesters their platoon of ten Bren gun carriers to assist in a counter-attack, the Surreys had hardly seen any action before they were ordered to withdraw from their sweated diggings. They were to go back to a new line south of Alor Star. This was the start of an exhausting and demoralizing trek that immediately entailed abandoning all their anti-tank guns and heavy baggage because the first part of it was along a narrow footpath that zig-zagged along the paddy bunds.

Almost the first thing to break down was communications: first with battalion headquarters, then with other companies, then even with individual platoons. Well after midnight, after a particularly gruelling stretch along a broken canal bank where they had to wade and even swim in places, they reached the railway track and the beginning of a 10-mile hike to where it met the trunk road heading south. They had now been walking fast for over ten hours with very little food. 'The fellows are done in by now, and we stumble along the rough stone track like drunken old men,' Abbott would later note in a journal he was trying to keep.

Some of the Surreys had dumped almost everything except their Lee-Enfields. The enormously heavy Boys anti-tank rifles were already a distant memory, and there was an increasing reluctance to share the carrying of Bren light machine-guns, which were lightweight examples of their breed but still weighed slightly more than twice as much as a rifle. Determined to set an example, Abbott had retained a haversack as well as a rifle and his two pistols, one of them privately acquired. He had yet to fire a shot at the enemy with any of them.

Throughout their journey they had heard the artillery and the machine-guns of the rearguard which included one company of their own battalion. Towards dawn it seemed to die down. 'Whenever we stop to listen,' wrote Abbott, 'the men just fall down where they are and have to be lifted bodily to their feet again.'

Watching his weary division cross the River Kedah just south of Alor Star was Murray-Lyon who, attempting to keep the same hours as men half his age, had alarmed his staff by fainting with exhaustion himself earlier that morning. Since then he had responded well to libations of hot sweet tea, the British panacea. The general was standing at the southern end of the road and railway bridges with his senior sapper officer and Lieutenant-Colonel Ray Selby, who was considered the best of the three battalion commanders in the all-Gurkha 28th Brigade.

The road bridge was a bottleneck, with heavily laden trucks and carriers lining up to cross, impatiently hooting at the bone-weary infantry to get out of the way and often getting no reaction whatsoever from men who were virtually asleep on their feet. Demolition charges had already been laid and, though a good part of 11th Division were still the wrong side of the Kedah River, Murray-Lyon and his officers were trying to decide how long they should wait until they destroyed the bridges.

A motorcyclist weaved in and out of the traffic the way motorcyclists do, helmeted and goggled, though the incessant rain was keeping the dust down. Behind him came two more. 'My God! That's a Jap!', shouted Murray-Lyon as the first rider roared by and both he and Selby, recovering from their shock with commendable speed, shot the next two out of their saddles with the big .455 Webley revolvers most Indian Army officers preferred to the smaller .38s the British Army had adopted a couple of years before.

As the bikes went down, machines and riders were riddled by a bunch of Indian and British soldiers who had just crossed the bridge and were resting. The crew of an anti-tank gun also entered into the spirit of things by demolishing a car that appeared in the motorcyclists' wake. The car turned out to be British. It is unclear whether any of its occupants survived.

The motorcyclists made Murray-Lyon's mind up for him. Suspecting that they were the scouts for a tank unit, he ordered the bridges to be blown at once. The road bridge went down easily enough but the neighbouring 500-yard span for the railway was made of sterner stuff. A second attempt, which used up all the engineers' available explosive, also failed, though now there were visible cracks. Then somebody remembered that the steam locomotive of the armoured train which had made the sortie into Thailand was still north of the river. Here was the obvious solution. The boiler was fired, the whistle jammed to a constant scream, the driver leapt from the footplate and the engine trundled innocently onto the cracked bridge, which shivered visibly. Everybody held their breath – still the creaking girders held, a triumph of British engineering and total humiliation for the sappers, unable to deliver the *coup de grâce*. While the audience gasped in disbelief, the driverless machine jumped a broken rail and chugged safely across, its plaintive whistle still sounding as it headed south towards Singapore.

Running alongside it was the officer who had commanded the reprieved engine during its recent adventures in Thailand. Once he had managed to haul himself aboard it became apparent that whatever knowledge he had acquired of the controls did not include braking. At a speed that made it an inviting target for air attack, the locomotive slowly disappeared from view. At what point the amateur in its cab managed to hand over to a professional is not recorded. Eventually the locomotive came to rest in a siding at Kuala Lumpur some 250 miles down the track. It was here, two weeks later, that the luck of the runaway train finally expired and it was destroyed in an air raid.

At Alor Star itself, comedy quickly turned to tragedy as one of Selby's officers, supervising Gurkhas laying mines on the stubbornly intact bridge, was killed when a mine went off while he was handling it.

The name of the first motorcyclist to arrive at the southern side of the Alor Star road bridge – the man whom Murray-Lyon, despite his own chronic fatigue, had immediately identified as a Japanese – was First Lieutenant Hajime Asai. Unlike the British, who generally confined the use of motorcycles to dispatch riders and liaison officers, the Japanese had followed the German example and employed them in the old light cavalry role as scouts and raiders. Asai, who like most of Major-General Kawamura's 9th Brigade came from Hiroshima, had ten men with him when he made his daring attempt to disrupt the demolition of the bridges over the Kedah River so that they could be captured intact.

As far as that was concerned, it was a glorious failure. Although he escaped the blazing .455s of the senior officers, Asai appears to have been killed shortly afterwards. 'Almost all of them died a heroic death,' wrote Kawamura who was under the impression that most of them perished when the British successfully blew up the road bridge. Tsuji, on the other hand, claims that at least one of Asai's men, a corporal, was cut off and fought to the death with his bayonet, and that a man with him was wounded but somehow escaped. He also believed that the railway bridge survived because the motorcyclists managed to cut the wires to the charges, which was not the case: then few if any Japanese eyewitnesses survived to put the record straight.

But their sacrifice was by no means entirely in vain and at least part of the posthumous citation for Lieutenant Asai's unit, signed by Commander-in-Chief Tomoyuki Yamashita himself, got it exactly right: 'The rapid, intrepid charge by those under the section commander caused panic and confusion in the enemy ranks . . .'

At least 300 Indian troops trying to catch up with their sleep beneath some rubber trees reacted to the sound of the road bridge being demolished like a flock of pigeons. Convinced that some fresh hell was upon them, they stampeded down the road and were only halted by Murray-Lyon himself, who pursued them in his staff car and drew his pistol on the leaders. After this, the continued crumbling of his division could not have come as much of a surprise, though some units did considerably better than others.

For several hours Selby's Gurkhas fought a successful rearguard action at the creaking railway bridge. Then, according to plan, they withdrew. Within a very short time, the Japanese had removed the mines that had cost the Gurkhas an officer and crossed the bridge. First it was men on foot, then men pushing the bicycles to which were tied their kit and sometimes, when they felt safe enough, their weapons. Each of Yamashita's three divisions was bringing with them into Malaya about 6,000 bicycles. By comparison the 25th Army had about 1,500 motor vehicles although, as the number of abandoned British transport vehicles increased and not all the occupants cared to linger long enough to destroy them, these began to be augmented by what the Japanese had started to call 'Churchill supplies'.

In the vanguard of the cyclists at the Alor Star railway bridge was Lieutenant-Colonel Yosuke Yokoyama, commander of the 15th Regiment of Independent Engineers who were mainly reservists from Osaka, the port city and heavy industry centre south of Tokyo that is Japan's second city. Yokoyama, a short, rotund man of almost fifty, would rapidly establish a reputation for the astonishing speed with which his unit repaired the trail of broken bridges. Sometimes this owed much to the foresight of the various Public Works Departments to be found in the Malayan states. Envisaging an entirely different campaign, these colonial civil servants had thoughtfully placed piles of cut timber next to their bridges in case they were damaged by Japanese air strikes, and supplies and reinforcements were held up. Unaware of this redundant forward planning, some retreating British troops, Lieutenant Abbott of the Surreys among them, mistook these preparations as yet more evidence of the insolent and widespread activity of fifth columnists.

Abbott was among those fortunate Surreys who crossed the road bridge at Alor Star before Murray-Lyon's hasty response to Asai's motorcyclists left at least 200 of his battalion stranded on the north bank. As the Japanese closed in on them, a Surrey officer was killed leading a fighting patrol, trying to buy time for sampans to be collected while the vehicles they had to abandon were rendered as useless as possible. Most of the Surreys did eventually get across, though some were obliged to swim for it which usually meant discarding rifles.

After a day spent exchanging fire with the Japanese gathering on the north bank, Colonel Yokoyama's fast work on the railway bridge to the east of them and the withdrawal of Selby's Gurkhas resulted in the Surreys being ordered to retire to Gurun before they were outflanked. The Gurun position was 25 miles to the south and no motor transport was available. They set off in the dark, sometimes sliding into waist-deep water as the narrow paddy bunds crumbled beneath them. Soon they began to lose all cohesion: platoons separated and stumbled away in different directions; five Surreys were killed when Indian troops at a small bridge mistook them for Japanese. Lack of sleep, sticky humidity, constant rain, the sheer effort of putting one mud-soaked boot in front of another, brought some men to the point where they could not be persuaded to move another inch. 'There's nothing we can do but leave them – you can't carry a person when you are finding the greatest difficulty in keeping your balance by yourself,' recorded Abbott, who wrote his journal in the present tense.

Before they went into action his company had numbered about 120. Only twenty-six of them reached Gurun as a formed unit, though few of the missing had been in contact with the enemy. Here they were fed 'a hot stew of indiscernible content', and permitted a few seamless hours of sleep before being set to work digging trenches and stringing barbed wire. Percival would later describe the Gurun line as 'one of the strongest natural positions in North Malaya'. It was the kind of bottleneck beloved by defending armies: a pass, 4 miles wide at the most, between the isolated and wooded 4,000-foot Kedah Peak near the coast and the central range's jungled nursery slopes to the east. Both the railway and the trunk road ran through it, close enough together for there to be a level crossing at the village of Gurun itself with its high street of little teak-shuttered shops where, in happier times, the proprietors had sat cross-legged alongside their tills and scales.

But there had been no time to prepare defences, hence the frantic digging by the Surreys, Leicesters and others who had collected there. Colonel Selby, who had been asked to look the position over, had recommended a line north of the village facing some open rice paddy country with reasonable fields of fire. Its most important feature was a crossroads at the hamlet of Yen from where a lateral road ran westwards to the coast and east to a railway station at Champadek.

The Japanese launched a determined assault on Yen, which was held by a single anti-tank gun and a small detachment of Surreys. Abbott, whose company was in reserve just south of the crossroads, was delighted by the sight of 'twelve lorry-loads of fresh Indian troops' going towards the crossroads. Quite why Abbott thought these Punjabis were 'fresh' is not clear. Perhaps he meant that they were more rested than the Surreys, which would not have been difficult. Fifteen minutes later Abbott was horrified to see the same troops running back towards them. He and another officer from the Surreys tried to turn them back but the Indians were not open to persuasion. The Japanese had captured the Yen crossroads and punched a great hole in their line. Abbott and his men, laying extra magazines beside their Bren guns and checking that their grenades were primed, prepared for the worst.

Then, from behind them, coming from Gurun village, where both brigade and battalion headquarters were located, a bunch of about fifty men appeared spread out across the road. They were walking purposefully towards them and at their head was a man waving a walking stick and wearing, Abbott noticed, a battered flat service cap with the red band around its brim which denotes high rank. Brigadier Billy Lay, commander of the much depleted 6th Brigade of which the Surreys were a remnant, had decided to counter-attack with all the forces at his disposal.

Marching behind the brigadier were his mixed Indian and UK British headquarters staff of defence platoon, signallers, clerks and runners, plus some of the UK anti-tank gunners attached to the Indian division under their commander, Lieutenant-Colonel Charles Napier. As he drew level with the Surreys, Lay, who was almost fifty, removed his pipe and shouted: 'Come along, you fellows, we've got to push 'em back. They say there's hundreds of the blighters – all the more to kill!' Abbott did not hesitate.

Well, he may be mad but there's no resisting leadership like that! We join on – all twenty-seven of us – and two carriers, one staff car and two fifteen hundredweight trucks come up to swell the throng.

As they moved closer towards the crossroads they were watched by the crews of a battery of 25-pounder field guns. 'Lob over a few in ten minutes' time just north of the crossroads, will you?' instructed the brigadier, waving his stick in the general direction of the enemy. And on they went. Abbott was close to the brigadier and watched him broaden his line of advance, directing men into the rubber trees and jungle either side of the road: 'Get round the bastards and push 'em out.'

Before long Abbott, who had joined one of these flanking parties, found himself prostrate behind a shrinking anthill whose peak was being relentlessly reduced by a Japanese machine-gunner. This was followed by the crack of mortar bombs landing nearby and then the much heavier drum roll sound of the 25-pounders lobbing their projectiles just ahead, more or less where Lay asked for them.

We arrive back on the road and start to crawl up the ditch. Complete shambles lies around us. Rounding a bend I see our two carriers on the crossroads and blazing away into the undergrowth in front. Our troops start to push on further but the enemy has withdrawn.

Lay's counter-attack, spearheaded by the two Punjabi-crewed carriers that played the largest part in restoring the damage done by their fleeing compatriots, was a splendid if short-lived and costly success. Abbott's company alone had lost fifteen of their twenty-seven in killed and wounded. But even this could not repair the morale of some of the Indian troops (and no doubt some of the British too) against an enemy with tanks and increasingly obvious aerial superiority. There were simply not enough reliable troops to hold the reconquered territory.

Before dawn the next day fresh troops of the Okabe Detachment, who had relieved Colonel Saeki's storm troopers as the Japanese spearhead, were in Gurun itself. Colonel Tsuji, who had attached himself to them, was among their lighter casualties when he suffered the loss of both face and trousers after being hit in the bottom by a shell splinter.

I suddenly felt as if I had been stabbed in the buttocks with burning chopsticks. Blood poured down my thigh and began to seep through my trousers . . . The wound was slight, but it was not in a good area. I felt small while being bandaged in the presence of others. No one spoke . . .

Despite the British artillery, whose surprising accuracy the Japanese would be slow to take into account, the Okabe regiment pressed on with considerable *élan*. First they overran the Surrey's battalion HQ, killing almost every officer and man in it. Then, at about 7 a.m., they went on to storm the nearby headquarters of 6th Brigade, stitching the thin *attap* walls of the stilt-house they occupied with machine-gun bullets before closing in with grenades and bayonets. Most of Brigadier Lay's staff were killed. Also among the dead was the acting commander of the Surreys (their CO had been evacuated with a broken leg following a traffic accident), who had just escaped the holocaust at his own headquarters, and the leader of a company of Leicesters loaned to Lay from another brigade. But the brigadier himself survived. Somehow he managed to hide himself below the first floor of the house, in the space where Malay villagers usually kept their livestock and stored firewood. One account has him arriving there by accidentally falling through a hole in the floor.

Lay waited until the Japanese had moved on, then emerged from his hiding place. The first British soldiers he encountered were the Leicesters who had been put at his disposal, about seventy men under Lieutenants George Chippington and Edgar Newland, Eddie to his friends. Lay had been in the process of telling their company commander, a captain called Bradfield who had gone ahead of them, exactly how he wanted his men deployed, when the Okabe regiment crashed the morning conference and killed him. Now all he could ask the lieutenants to do was to try and secure his brigade HQ area.

Lay's behaviour the day before as he led his ragtag command into a counter-attack had impressed the Surreys' Lieutenant Abbott. He would get a DSO for it. But courage can be a finite thing and this was a different Lay, trying to steady himself with sips from his hip flask after the breakfast massacre of his staff and his own narrow escape. Chippington, the senior of the two Leicester subalterns, described how he approached the place where he had been told he should find the brigade headquarters when 'an elderly officer, a stranger, completely alone, appeared, gesticulating wildly with his arms and shouting'.

I ran forward and realized this must be the brigadier which seemed odd. He was screaming at Eddie, 'Get in there. Get in there,' pointing to the thick undergrowth on the left of the junction just beyond the track to the little bridge, but Eddie, calm and unemotional as always, remained static until I arrived . . . neither of us cared much for histrionics. I told the brigadier my orders were to report to Captain Bradfield at Brigade HQ. When he turned to me I could smell the whisky on his breath. 'Bradfield's dead,' he shouted. 'They are all dead. All my staff are dead.' I could not see how Bradfield could be dead. I had been speaking to him only a few minutes before. I gazed at him in silence, wishing he would calm down. 'The Japs came through the door,' he shouted . . . 'I went through the window.'

Chippington watched as, much against his better judgement, Lay dispatched most of his Leicesters into the nearest jungle, retaining him and about twenty men to guard the road junction before it. 'The Japs are not to get past here,' he told him. 'You are my last infantry reserve.'

The brigadier walked off down the road which led to the railway and, eventually, divisional headquarters, leaving Chippington and his men to listen to the sound of heavy machine-gun fire coming from the direction where his friend Eddie and most of the Leicesters had gone. Soon wounded men began to stagger back through the under-growth, one literally soaked with blood from a throat wound. A man who had been shot in the shoulder told Chippington that the machine-gun fire came from stationary tanks, which the only Bren gunner among them had got close to, firing his weapon from the hip, before he was shot down. A corporal had then been killed trying to rescue the Bren gun. He feared that Lieutenant Newland was also dead.

It turned out that this was not the case. Newland and a sergeant lay next to the two dead men, playing possum until the tanks moved away. They then collected as many men as they could find and, after an arduous twenty-four-hour trek in heavy rain around the eastern slope of the Kedah Peak, including a climb up a steep cliff face using jungle vines, returned to British lines.

Murray-Lyon's division had hardly been able to draw breath after the debacle at Jitra and, once again, it was on the run. Perhaps fresher, better-trained troops might have turned the Okabe's rapier thrust at Gurun to their advantage and punished them for attacking on such a narrow front with no attempt to guard their flanks. Elements from two Indian battalions had not been properly engaged at all. Yet, instead of turning on the enemy and making them pay dearly for their boldness, the commander of the 1/8th Punjabis led his battalion away from the engagement to the coast, where they acquired boats and eventually got back to Singapore via the Dutch administration on Sumatra. He did this on his own initiative, unable to inform a brigade HQ that was no longer answering its radio or field telephone. Lay, dodging mortar bombs which sometimes mercifully refused to explode in the soggy ground, hurried back to give Murray-Lyon the bad news. 'If the 11th Division was defeated at Jitra,' said General Heath, commander of the 3rd Indian Corps and Murray-Lyon's immediate superior, 'it was routed at Gurun.'

Some had tried to make a stand. In Gurun village itself, Abbott and some of the Surreys were part of a mixed bag of troops, including the crew of a solitary anti-tank gun, who had barricaded themselves into its main street shops and other buildings. Among them, calmly directing men to their positions, was the Surrey's regimental sergeant-major, scourge of the twisted bootlace, a parade-ground gloss still amazingly preserved on his toecaps and carrying the venerable silver-topped swagger stick that was his main badge of office. Abbott found him a reassuring sight and thought that 'no one seems particularly frightened'.

The lieutenant had with him about ten men, including a couple of stretcher-bearers. The shop they were in had also been somebody's living quarters because they found mattresses, tables and chairs to barricade the entrance but leave room for a firing position. They had also discovered the tools to make loopholes in the walls so that they could fire in any direction.

'Tanks coming!' somebody yelled, perhaps the sergeant-major. The anti-tank gunners damaged the first two but the third got them and the rest, five according to Abbott, roared through with their cannon and machine-guns blazing. He threw a grenade at one of them, an empty gesture against armoured plate, but fortunately the tank crew did not seem to notice. Then, almost simultaneously, Japanese fighter bombers put in an appearance, one of them landing a bomb close enough to cause the collapse of the best part of the shop Abbott was in.

This coordination of armour and aircraft, such perfect blitzkrieg timing, was too much for the last defenders of Gurun. Those who could left the wreckage of their positions and fled across the railway towards the nearest rubber and jungle, occasionally turning to fire back at the figures they could see milling about in the smouldering village. Abbott hoped they were Japanese.

Once they were in cover the lieutenant and the sergeant-major began to count heads. They discovered that there were about eighty of them, British and Indian. It also became apparent that Abbott was the only officer, albeit at twenty-two a very junior one, and expected to take charge, though the formidable figure of the sergeant-major was never far away. To their delight they found that all but five of the men, and three of these were wounded, had retained their weapons, including two of the heavier Brens. 'Real heroes these!' noted Abbott.

Ammunition and what food they had was shared out and they set off. It took them thirty-six hours to find their way back to what was left of Murray-Lyon's division. Under heavy rain, Abbott led them through the monsoon slime of some of the roughest country in the world until he estimated they had worked far enough around the flank of the Japanese advance and could return to the coast road. Once, the subaltern had to enter the chest-high waters of a river in full spate to attach a rope to a tree on the opposite bank so that his men, who included the usual quota of non-swimmers, could pull themselves across.

Each man was near breaking point – mentally and physically – and as the hours wore on, our exhaustion became complete. Yet, in adversity, we merged into a single community – solid, united, determined. Those who faltered were urged on by strangers who had become comrades.

Not every survivor got away. In Gurun, Colonel Tsuji watched forty or so captive sepoys spring to attention and salute when a young British officer, also a prisoner, was led past. He thought it made the Indians 'seem like slaves'.

The bombing and strafing of those British troops travelling south along the coast road became more relentless. It did not cause heavy casualties. On at least one occasion an aircraft was downed by ground fire, probably from Bren guns, though even that caused delay because it crashed onto a truck, killing three of its occupants, and blocked the road. More important was the effect the almost total absence of the RAF was having on morale.

'RAF – Rare as Fairies.' Once again, the old jibe was on the lips of the sprinkling of Dunkirk veterans attached to 11th Indian Division. Only eighteen months before, men like Corporal Ernest Agass, an East Ender of Huguenot extraction serving in a field workshop of the Royal Electrical and Mechanical Engineers, had been pursued to the French coast by the Luftwaffe. Now, once again, he sat in the back of a 3-tonner with its bolted-down grinding wheels and lathes, a rifle between his knees, looking anxiously skywards, knowing that anything up there was unlikely to be friendly.

Pulford's squadrons were even less blameworthy for this state of affairs than the RAF had been in France, where at least the aircraft had been more or less evenly matched in quality if not in numbers. In Malaya the Buffaloes continued to be shot down with monotonous regularity, or wrecked in bad-weather accidents like the three that got so lost they crash-landed in Sumatra killing two of the pilots.

On 13 December it was the turn of Tim Vigors, the Battle of Britain pilot still three months short of his twenty-first birthday who had got to Phillips' ships minutes after their sinking. The acting squadron leader had been rushed north from Singapore with four other Buffaloes, all with Australian pilots, to protect Penang Island, where Japanese bombing had inflicted the highest civilian losses the campaign had yet seen. In George Town, the island's capital, entire blocks of Chinese shophouses had gone up in flames. The first air raid by about fifty Nells and Bettys had killed over 1,000 people and injured at least 2,000, for when they had dropped their bombs they came back and the turret gunners strafed the panic-stricken survivors below. The fire station had received a direct hit and was not functioning, the police had mostly vanished and looting had started. If the object was to instil terror it worked. Thousands fled to the hills.

The Buffaloes were going to be based at RAF Butterworth, three minutes' flight from the island. As Vigors and his Australians landed, he saw an airman frantically waving the red flag, warning that hostile aircraft were overhead, and ordered his Buffaloes into the air again immediately. He and Sergeant O'Mara, who was acting as his wingman, got into cloud cover high above Penang and then dived on a formation of about twenty-five Army 97s, the surprisingly agile monoplane fighter with the dated-looking fixed undercarriage. It seems that for once the Buffaloes' radios were working, for Vigors was able to tell O'Mara that they were going to get into the middle of the enemy, break them up and watch each other's tails, 'until such time as we got the hell out of it, which wouldn't be long'.

The usual *mêlée* ensued during which time I was pretty certain that I got several Japs but things were far too hot to bother about the score. The Army 97 could turn right inside the Buffalo and I was a little too long in realizing the extent of their manoeuvrability! As a result, I received a direct hit in the petrol tank, which was situated under my feet and which, somewhat naturally, proceeded to blow up in my face.

Badly burned on his hands, arms, legs and parts of his face, Vigors managed to leave his blazing cockpit and release his parachute, but his troubles were far from over. The sheer impertinence of this attack against overwhelming odds seems to have vanquished all notions of Bushido chivalry and sparing a gallant adversary. 'I had what seemed like the whole bloody Japanese air force shooting at me from 10,000 feet down to where I eventually hit the deck, on top of the Penang mountains.'

Fortunately for Vigors, hitting a swaying man on the end of a parachute from a fast-moving aircraft was evidently harder than it looked. He was hit only once. The bullet passed clean through his left thigh without touching bone or vital artery and, though bleeding profusely, on landing he was able to stagger away into jungle cover before he collapsed.

Of the four other Buffaloes under Vigors' command two were shot down shortly after they became airborne and only one of the Australian pilots survived. The other two fighters were both slightly damaged but the pilots, who were unhurt, managed to land them at different airfields. Both Vigors and one of the more experienced Australian pilots who had also served in Europe claimed kills. No Japanese ground wreckage was discovered to confirm them but this could have easily been swallowed up by jungle or sea.

These latest losses left Pulford with about fifty serviceable Buffaloes and, shortly afterwards, the British decided to abandon Penang because they did not have the wherewithal to defend it. This was a momentous decision and almost as big a blow to morale as the sinking of the *Prince of Wales* and *Repulse*. The island was, after all, Britain's oldest colonial possession in South-east Asia, the place where Raffles had started his overseas career with the East India Company.

It was also heartbreakingly beautiful. Few places merited the title Pearl of the Orient as much as Penang, with its fringe of perfect beaches, its variegated interior of spice gardens and jungle-covered granite hills, where waterfalls cascaded into cool swimming holes – 'the like of which we had only ever seen in Dorothy Lamour films,' recalled one of the Leicesters whose battalion was based there for four unforgettable months just before the Japanese war started. From George Town, easily the most cosmopolitan municipality in Malaya with its strong Arab influence, a funicular railway ran to the top of Penang Hill, the town's magnificent backdrop. At sunset the summit offered a stunning view across the straits to Kedah Peak. But by mid-December 1941 sightseers were more likely to be interested in the battle smoke around Gurun where the Leicesters, some of whom once swam in Penang's Dorothy Lamour pools during an exercise against an imaginary enemy called The Slits, were now fighting and dying.

In 1936, during Percival's first posting to Malaya, Penang had officially been declared a fortress, but in the years that followed the wish had never quite been fulfilled in fact. True, two batteries of 6-inch guns and searchlights now commanded the entrance to George Town's harbour, easily Malaya's best port. Yet these were its only fixed defences. There were virtually no anti-aircraft guns. Before the war, the military had been congratulated by the English-language press for building their barracks a discreet distance from George Town, 'for we know what soldiers are'. Now the barracks were half empty, their occupants sent to reinforce Murray-Lyon. Percival had decided that 'every single man we could lay hands on was required on the mainland to avert the disaster which threatened'. All that was left was the gunners manning the harbour batteries and searchlights, and the civilian volunteers of the Province Wellesley Battalion of the Straits Settlements Volunteer Force. And even they were under-strength by one company which had followed the regulars to the mainland.

The evacuation of Penang at last gave Special Operations Executive a chance to show what it could do – albeit against passive British targets. Colonel Cocky Warren, the Royal Marine, and Major Jim Gavin, their demolitions virtuoso, arrived with a twelve-man team and enough explosive to destroy the things the Japanese might have preferred to find intact. They blew up the virgin harbour batteries which had never fired a shot in action, the power station and, because of fears of a typhus outbreak, cremated the uncollected dead that littered the streets.

But they missed important stocks of tin and oil. And, though they made sure they scuttled or took away all the ferries, the harbour's flotilla of privately owned small craft, which the Japanese would shortly put to good use, was overlooked. Most unfortunate of all, for some reason they left intact the studios of Penang Radio which would shortly be asking its listeners, in English and on its usual waveband: 'Hello, Singapore, this is Penang calling; how do you like our bombing?' This would often be followed by members of the Asian communities explaining how much better life was now that the whites had fled, leaving them to enjoy the benefits of the Greater East Asia Co-Prosperity Sphere. Some of Major Fujiwara Iwaichi's team of Indian nationalists also set up shop, urging Indian soldiers to desert and put their martial skills at the disposal of those who wished to liberate Asia from European bondage. They spoke in Urdu, the *lingua franca* of the British Indian Army.

It was easy for the Japanese to exploit the bitterness felt by many Asians in Penang over the way they had been left to their fate by the British, who apparently lacked the guts to stay and fight for their Lotus existence. When Warren arrived he was accompanied by Lieutenant-Commander 'Alex' Alexander, a naval officer and 1914–18 submarine commander. Alexander had been sent to Penang for one specific reason: to organize the evacuation of all Europeans starting with women and children and men in the military hospital.

One of the first to go was Flight Lieutenant Vigors. The fighter pilot had been picked up more dead than alive by two Malays, a father and his twelve-year-old son. Soaked by constant thunderstorms, they had carried him for hours down a treacherous mountain track on a stretcher constructed from tree branches and their shirts until they got to a decent road and could persuade a vehicle to stop. 'They accompanied me to the hospital but the sad thing was that, due to my being nearly unconscious by that time, I never got their names and address.'

Warren and Alexander had been ordered by General Heath, the commander of the 3rd Indian Corps, to get the Europeans out. Those middle-class Asians without enough prescience to have already left soon wished they had. In a three-minute call he had waited six hours to put through, William Paterson, editor of the Penang edition of the *Tribune*, told his boss Maurice Glover in Singapore that Europeans were boarding ferries with luggage and even cars while his Asian friends were being refused permission to board.

Undoubtedly there was a consensus among the military that 'the native population' were in no danger, since Japanese propaganda made much of fighting a war of Asian liberation. One of the first things these liberators did on entering Penang was murder the local head of the United China Relief Fund in front of his entire family. Perhaps it was lack of local knowledge that made Warren and Alexander blind to the peril facing Chinese well known for their anti-Japanese activity. Or did they feel they could not take a few compromised Asians for fear of opening the floodgates and swamping the entire operation? 'Penang was a very discreditable affair, and had a shocking effect on morale throughout Malaya,' declared the governor, Sir Shenton Thomas, who had not been consulted.

Until it sank under the tidal wave of greater events the controversy over the evacuation of the island would do much to fuel the smouldering feud between the governor and Duff Cooper, who apart from being Resident Cabinet Minister was now head of the War Council. Above all, it exposed the dichotomy between the colonial administration and the military who, as part of their fighting retreat, were doing their level best to wreck half a century of hard graft and destroy Malaya's infrastructure in a scorched earth policy. A by-product of this was the growing number of European planters, miners, policemen and administrators blocking the roads south with as much of their property as they could cram into their cars.

Sir Shenton very properly believed that his duty was to all the people of Malaya. If he subscribed to any discrimination, it was his belief that the whites must set an example and not disappear with all the alacrity of Conrad's Lord Jim abandoning his sinking shipload of Asian pilgrims. Otherwise the whole fragile and complex edifice of British Malaya, where so few were able to rule so many in a jumble of crown colonies and states federated and unfederated, would fall apart. He also, like many of the long-serving Malayan hands beneath him, found this scorched earth business simply heartbreaking. Was the army really so weak that it had to destroy Malaya in order to save it?

Duff Cooper, who was by no means without a sense of duty himself, suspected that the older man (there was eleven years between them) simply could not grasp the exigencies of war or how quickly things had changed. He pointed out that, if left to the governor, the British Empire would, for the first time in its history, 'evacuate the troops first and leave the women and children to the tender mercies of a cruel Asiatic foe'.

The last sailing was at night and the harbour was lit up by blazing junks and buildings. Warren and Alexander allowed the evacuees, who by this time were all males, one suitcase each. Among those British citizens who had insisted on staying was the journalist Paterson and his family, a doctor at the local hospital and an elderly man who was looking after two bedridden sisters.

Warren was among the last to leave. As he boarded the truck taking him to the jetty, flames from a burning building briefly lit up a government poster on a wall across the street. The Royal Marine recognized it immediately. There were thousands of these posters all over Malaya, sometimes in Malay and Chinese as well as English. It was an extract in large type from Sir Robert Brooke-Popham's Order of the Day made shortly after hostilities had begun. 'We are ready,' it declared. 'Our preparations have been made and tested: our defences are strong and our weapons efficient.'

Warren boarded and the boat cast off. On the way out Lieutenant-Commander Alexander noticed a small ferry he had failed to scuttle and paused to shell it with a little 12-pounder gun mounted on their bows until the craft slowly began to sink at its moorings, its decks awash. Then they picked their way through the burning junks to the open water and set course for Singapore which, the evacuees could console themselves, was a real fortress and nothing like their lost and lovely Penang.

'Personally I do not feel there is much hope of saving Singapore, but feel that we ought to try and make certain of Burma.'

These were the words of Field-Marshal Sir Alan Brooke, the most senior soldier in British uniform, who was Churchill's newly appointed Chief of the Imperial General Staff. They were written in the Ulsterman's confidential diary on 17 December 1941, the day after Penang had been evacuated, exactly a week after the sinking of the *Prince of Wales* and the *Repulse*, and only nine days after the Japanese infantry had eventually got off the beach at Kota Baharu by tunnelling under the apron wire.

In Whitehall Brooke, who was originally an artilleryman and who was credited with inventing 'the creeping barrage', was known for his incisiveness and clarity of thinking though not, at this point, the iconoclastic diary which remained firmly under lock and key. As far as Percival was concerned, the situation was serious but far from hopeless. He had not even committed the Australians yet, though Bennett was telling everybody who would listen that they were straining at the leash 'to get at our new enemy, the yellow Huns of the East'. For the moment, Percival was reluctant to move Bennett north from Johore in case the Japanese, with their naval and air superiority, made fresh landings further down the east coast or even on Singapore Island itself and they were required to reinforce the garrison there. All he knew for certain was that he must do everything in his power to slow the enemy's advance until help arrived.

Already two new divisions, almost 40,000 men, had been earmarked for deployment against the Japanese in either Malaya or Burma, depending on where they were most needed. One of these divisions was the 17th Indian, a recently raised formation which had been due to go to Iraq to mechanize and train for desert warfare. The other was the 15,000 or so men of the 18th British Division whose infantry core was seven battalions of East Anglian Territorials from the Cambridge-shire, Norfolk and Suffolk regiments. All of them had been brought up to strength with conscripts and a few regular officers and NCOs.

Only three of its infantry battalions were not from the Fen counties: the 5th Bedfordshire and Hertfordshires and the 5th Sherwood Foresters plus a medium machine-gun battalion, the 9th Northumberland Fusiliers. Some of these Fusiliers were so keen that, before the war, they obtained permission to take their Vickers guns home with them so they could speed up their times for stripping them down and putting them back together.

The 18th's commander was Major-General Mark Beckwith-Smith, Becky to old friends in the Welsh Guards, who had commanded a Guards brigade in France then, briefly, a division at Dunkirk, for which he was awarded a DSO to go with the Military Cross he had won in 1917. Guards officers and Territorials were not always a good mix, particularly when the same regional accent could sometimes be heard in both officers' and sergeants' messes. But the sandy-haired and moustached Beckwith-Smith, broad shouldered and quite small for a Guards officer, was both popular and efficient. In war games held during the summer of 1941, his Lancashire-based 18th won Exercise 'War of the Roses' against the experienced 2nd Division, which had been the British Expeditionary Force's rearguard at Dunkirk. To the victors went the spoils of the next overseas posting.

By the time Brooke was writing his gloomy prognosis for Singapore, the 18th had been on the high seas for over six weeks and travelled half the world, but neither they nor the War Office was entirely certain where they were bound. They had left Liverpool on 29 October after unseemly scenes with local dockers, a 'reserved occupation' exempted military service, whose behaviour had thoroughly enraged the Northumberland Fusiliers. First they had been spotted pilfering boxes of U-boat-run Florida oranges. Then the spillage of some of the machine-gunners' ammunition from a dropped box had immediately prompted demands for 'danger money' and a strike until they got it. 'I got so angry,' recalled Captain Henry McCreath as he tried to unload their kits into the SS *Warwick Castle*, a comfortable old ship which had first served as a troop transport in 1914.

In mid-Atlantic an enormous surprise awaited them. On the deck of the transport SS *Orchades* to witness it was Gunner Fergus Anckorn, a driver in a 25-pounder artillery regiment who was better known as Wizardus, the magician in the divisional concert party, a troupe of uniformed strolling players who toured the 18th's units with their show, using whatever props and costumes they could devise. The endless chain of handkerchiefs that appeared from Wizardus' sleeves had started life as the little silk parachutes that drifted Luftwaffe magnesium flares to earth during air raids. Now Anckorn found himself transfixed by something he very much wished he could magic away. 'They were coming towards us over the horizon: destroyers, cruisers, the lot. I thought, it's the German Grand Fleet. We're dead.'

What Anckorn was looking at was a Roosevelt goodwill gesture conceived the previous August at his Atlantic Charter meeting with Churchill aboard the *Prince of Wales*. Although the United States was still neutral, and Roosevelt's clout curtailed by the Isolationists, he had agreed to provide the ships to transport British troops to the Middle East. Anckorn had been among the first to see the battleship, aircraft carrier, four cruisers and eight destroyers which comprised their US naval escort.

Waiting for Beckwith-Smith's division in the Canadian port of Halifax in Nova Scotia were three luxury liners recently converted into troop ships and given new names that suited their grey war paint and anti-aircraft guns. The *Washington* was now the USS *Mount Vernon*; the *America* had become USS *West Point* and the *Manhattan* the USS *Wakefield*. Each of the liners would carry one of the 18th's three infantry brigades and whatever else could be squeezed on. There were smaller vessels for all the auxiliary units – engineers, signals, transport – that went to make up a division.

Gunner Anckorn found himself on the USS *West Point*, which had only been launched two years before, and discovered that at heart she was still a floating palace called SS *America*.

We didn't have companionways, we had marble staircases. We had gymnasiums with gold fittings. We had a swimming pool below decks. I worked in one as a lifeguard and people used to come in batches of ten or twelve for their swim. We had state cabins for royalty with gold and silver in mosaic floors . . . And here we were on this wonderful thing. We had laundries, butchers, bakers and candlestick makers, you name it. The food was terrific. I remember our first meal was a ham omelette. You have to remember we'd been at war for two years and eaten powdered eggs for so long we'd almost forgotten what a real one looked like. And we went out to war in that.

For the moment there was little doubt that their war was going to be against Rommel in the Middle East. Their vehicles and artillery pieces had all received their first coat of yellow desert camouflage paint long before they left England. Most likely they were bound for Basra in the Persian Gulf. Once in Iraq they would acclimatize, train for desert warfare and generally prepare themselves for Libya and their tryst with the Afrika Korps. Meanwhile, they would be on hand to provide internal security on the Mosul and Kirkuk oil fields. Earlier in the year the British had been obliged to put down a pro-Axis *coup* in Iraq, nominally an independent state, and reinstate an administration with a more realistic view of mutual interests.

To minimize their chances of encountering U-boats, the 18th Division, which had started off by going west rather than east, had continued to take the most circuitous route imaginable. From Halifax they steamed down the east coast of the United States to the Caribbean, refuelled at Trinidad, and then sailed on a south-easterly course through the South Atlantic towards Cape Town.

Shortly after the British troops had eaten their first Thanksgiving turkey dinner 'with all the fixings', the alarm went up when a reconnaissance aircraft from the escort carrier attached to the convoy spotted a large man o'war some 45 miles ahead. She turned out to be the Italian-built cruiser the Argentinian navy had named *General Belgrano*, after their national hero. (The next *General Belgrano*, formerly the USS *Phoenix* which had survived Pearl Harbor, was torpedoed by a British submarine during the 1982 Falklands War with the loss of 368 lives.)

The US Navy had been dry since 1914 but, as a rule, only the older officers and men found the absence of drink irksome; the younger ones, once they had got over withdrawal symptoms brought on by the absence of stews with dumplings and treacle puddings, conceded that the food could be very good indeed: 'all Yanky stuff, too light for our British stomachs but it is good', noted Fusilier Taylor, who was on one of the smaller ships keeping a diary of this amazing trip they were having. 'Lots of milk, bread, chocolate, beans, sweet corn, diced spuds in white sauce, also corned beef in white sauce, and all this vitamin stuff which these Yanks go in for.'

Despite the overcrowding on some of the ships – 'the men's quarters stink to high heaven . . . sweat and old socks,' sniffed one of the yeomanry subalterns – the American sailors did their best to provide at least some of the same entertainment their paying passengers had once enjoyed. Their crossing of the equator was marked in a manner appreciated by young men who, in the main, had rarely left their home towns let alone their native hemisphere before. Jolly Rogers fluttered from foremasts as King Neptune and his Court were welcomed aboard. Then the 'lowly, slimy and verminous pollwags' were paraded before them to be introduced, with the aid of hosepipes and buckets, to the Order of the Deep before His Majesty graciously presented them with the certificates dating their birth as 'Shellbacks'. On some ships this was followed by a general *mêlée* and rugby-level injuries.

'When it looked like getting out of hand,' recalled Captain Reginald Burton of the Norfolks, 'the captain sounded the alarm "General Quarters" . . . we went to our action stations but it appeared it had been the only quick and effective way of restoring law and order.'

There were several U-boat 'sightings', but all eventually turned out to be false alarms, mostly sperm whales. Burton, who was sharing a cabin with four others on the *Wakefield* (*née Manhattan*) that had once been occupied by Hollywood's Paulette Goddard, was already a Shellback for this was his third crossing of the equator. As a young regular officer, when war broke out he had been serving in Bangalore with his regiment's 1st Battalion, which returned to the UK just after Dunkirk when the invasion scare was at its height. When that waned he was among a group of regulars sent to stiffen the Territorial Army's 4th Norfolks and now he was going back East again.

'Strange little white bodies are dressing themselves in unfamiliar tropical kit,' wrote Second Lieutenant Stephen Alexander in a letter to his mother, pointing out that the 'scrawny and pallid physique of the Tommies' compared badly to the 'magnificent bodies of the crew'.

Alexander had volunteered for the army from Cambridge having decided not to follow his father into medicine. Now he was a subaltern in what was probably the division's smartest artillery regiment, the Hertfordshire Yeomanry under the command of Lieutenant-Colonel Philip Toosey, a flamboyant merchant banker from Liverpool.

As the American ships approached Cape Town they heard of the landings on the Malayan coast and the attack on Pearl Harbor. Almost immediately the rumours started that it might, after all, be the Japanese and not Rommel they would fight. 'Frankly, at that stage I think some of us were disappointed,' observed Lieutenant Donald Wise of the 4th Suffolks, a tall and debonair young man whose application to transfer to the newly formed Parachute Regiment had been suspended when the Suffolks were told they were going overseas. 'Even after Pearl Harbor we thought the Japs might be a bit Gilbert and Sullivan, sort of oriental Italians and definitely not up to our standards. We wanted to biff the Hun.'

By the end of December one British unit had indeed proved that, given a fair chance, biffing Yamashita's infantry, brave and resourceful as they so often were, was by no means impossible. The undoubted stars of the rearguard fighting down the narrow roads south from Kroh on the Thai border were Stewart's Argyll and Sutherland Highlanders.

It was the Argylls who had relieved KrohCol after they had lost 200 killed and wounded during a hard-fought retreat through the Thai border country from The Ledge, during which Moorhead had personally rescued one of his lance-*naiks* under fire. At Kroh the Argylls had then taken over and, with one carefully laid ambush after another, delayed the Japanese long enough to prevent a pincer movement cutting the west coast road and trapping Murray-Lyon's crippled division.

The man most responsible for this was Lieutenant-Colonel Ian MacAlister Stewart, 13th Laird of Achnacone whose ancestors had fought the English at both Flodden (1513) and Culloden (1746), where two had been lost to the Butcher Cumberland. He was forty-seven, a lean man well over 6 feet tall. Behind his narrow back his men called him 'Busty', one of those inverted nicknames for this was exactly what he was not.

Sometimes people were surprised to discover that Stewart had a wife and daughter in quarters in Singapore, for he appeared to be married to the regiment. He had emerged from the 1914–18 war with three gallantry awards. When wounds left him medically unfit for the infantry he transferred to the newly raised Tank Corps, in which he won the bar to his MC, before negotiating a return to the regiment. Between the wars he had served in India and China and was guarding the International Settlement in Shanghai when he first saw the Japanese in action. This left him convinced that Tokyo would not wait long to take advantage of a European war.

For the past two years Stewart had been training his men to fight in Malaya with an obsessiveness unheard of in the rest of the colony. Other battalion commanders had become rather wary of this wiry beanpole with the piercing blue eyes whose eccentricities knew no bounds, for he was also that rare thing among British officers, a teetotaller. But it was his lunatic energy that really irritated: a caricature of all Noël Coward had ever observed about a man who 'detests a siesta'. After a while other units were calling the Argylls, behind their backs if they had any sense, 'the Jungle Beasts' and finding excuses not to go on exercises with them.

At first Stewart's emphasis had not been so much on jungle training as on building up stamina and endurance, and a psychology among the men of not giving way to the heat. In this respect, the Argylls were not the only regiment that should have been almost half-way there because, like them, several other regiments had come to Malaya from counter-insurgency duties in India or, in the case of the Manchesters, the Palestine Mandate. But most battalions took Coward's little ditty very much to heart. If they could avoid it, they would not join these particular mad dogs and Scotsmen who went out in the midday sun when the enervating humidity reached heights unknown in the sub-continent or the Middle East. One unit even insisted that there were sound medical grounds for stopping work at 10 a.m. and not resuming it again until late afternoon. Shortly before the war in the Far East started, Stewart led his Argylls on an eight-day 116-mile route march from the coastal town of Mersing to Singapore. With two kilted pipers, a drummer and a little dog accompanying the colonel at the head of the column, it was obviously a photogenic occasion. But Stewart was quite shocked, though no doubt secretly pleased, by the attention paid to it by both the local press and even blitzed Fleet Street, declaring that it was 'an ominous reminder of British standards, for it was really of no outstanding merit'.

Less visible was the Argylls' training for what was then normally referred to as 'bush' rather than 'jungle warfare'. Stewart described it as being designed to develop 'resourcefulness, and above all, aggres-siveness and intense speed, for only by these means can the initiative be kept and to lose the initiative in the jungle is death'. To achieve this he pioneered the concept of battle drills whereby, once contact was made with the enemy, every individual soldier knew what was required and did so with the minimum of orders being given. They were something like the game plans adopted for every contingency by rugby or football teams and, by the end of the war, they had become, in theory at least, standard practice throughout the British Army.

This constant training and full-scale battalion exercises led to useful if minor tactical discoveries. When they lay in wait in the gloom of a rubber plantation, the Argylls tied their Brens to trees, which gave them a much better field of fire than lying on their fronts in the standard Bisley match shooting pose the army encouraged. They also developed four-man hit-and-run teams – Stewart called them 'Tiger Patrols' – to get behind the enemy and harass his communications. 'The theme in attack tactics at all levels from battalion down to Tiger Patrols was "Fix Frontally – Encircle",' wrote Stewart. These were the same tactics the Japanese employed, as was an alternative he called 'filleting', which involved an assault on a narrow front straight down the road, 'scattering the enemy into the jungle on either side, where all means of control are lost'. This is what had been done to the East Surreys and the rest of Lay's brigade at Gurun.

The road was the all-important tactical feature, almost the only one. Occupying areas of jungle or rubber any distance from a road was meaningless. Because he recognized this, Stewart had bolstered the mobile firepower provided by the battalion's Bren gun carriers by acquiring four 1927 model Lanchester armoured cars originally destined for the States Volunteer Forces. These constantly needed new parts Coventry could no longer supply, but when the Lanchesters worked they were faster than the tracked carriers, and their twin Vickers machine-guns and Boys anti-tank rifles were in pristine condition.

Above all, Stewart had spent a lot of time getting his battalion to practise the manoeuvres that would equip it with a sting in its tail. Even when Operation Matador's advance into Thailand was regarded as the most likely riposte to a Japanese threat, he had been prescient enough to make sure that the Argylls were trained in rearguard tactics which, he insisted, were all a matter of 'time and space calculation'.

Once a force has been launched into the jungle on a deep encircling attack, and without wireless, effective control of it is lost. The object therefore is to induce the enemy to launch his reserve on such a manoeuvre. The defender then steps back so that the blow strikes his shoulder instead of the undefended road behind . . . if the step back is too late it [the enemy] will have reached and blocked the road behind, and that in all probability is the end . . . it is a fascinating game, embodying as it does appreciations of ground, enemy dispositions, and above all the mind and speed of action of the opposing commander.

Time and again the skills acquired by the Argylls over months of hard training had paid off. In one action along 10 miles of muddy mountain road from Kroh to the hamlet of Grik, a mere thirty-five Argylls under Company Sergeant-Major Archie McDine, the battalion's boxing coach, had held up Colonel Tadeo Ando's detachment of perhaps ten times that number. In a neat demonstration of his battalion's tactical virtuosity, McDine divided his little command into five sections of seven men, one behind the other about 100 yards apart. Each section sought the best ambush position it could find: sharp corners or a hillside with enough gaps in the vegetation to give them a decent field of fire were favourites. The first section ambushed and then fell back through the other six and found a new position. Ando was never given the chance to get behind them.

At Grik, Sergeant-Major McDine's men, who had not suffered a single casualty but were utterly exhausted, met up with Stewart and the rest of the battalion and discovered they were intoxicated by the much larger-scale bushwhacking they had committed west of the Grik Road. 'The force of the bullets was blowing them up,' exulted Corporal Alex McDougall, the third generation of his family to serve in the regiment. 'Knocking them up high from behind the hedges they were hiding behind! They were being flung up and down.'

Hardly less restrained is Stewart's own description of their debut ambush on some 300 Japanese who were noisily sorting themselves out for a move off the road in preparation for a flanking attack while the Argylls, hardly daring to breathe, watched and took first pressure.

They were in close order and the perfect answer to a machine-gunner's prayer. Our fire completely surprised them and at 75 yards' range was devastating. They ran around in all directions in a bewildered way, making no response . . . The Jap losses must have been at least 200 quickly and typically exaggerated to 500 by the time the news reached Singapore.

It is hardly surprising that the exploits of this single British battalion, a candle in the dark for Percival and his staff, grew in the retelling; or that Stewart relates his triumphs with the relish of all those whose ideas and hard work, once the object of scorn and derision, have come to glorious fruition.

At dawn an excellent ambush was sprung on some twelve Japs, evidently an orders group, for it stopped 250 yards from two of our Brens on an open road, carefully put its bicycles in the ditch, and then went into a huddle with maps and field glasses. Its elimination may have been the cause of the rather slow development of Jap frontal pressure.

And again on their withdrawal from a village called Lenggong:

There is rarely a drawn battle in the jungle; it is either a complete success or a complete defeat, and a knife edge divides the two. The follow-up of the forward elements as soon as the withdrawal began was immediate and they had obviously been waiting for the rabbits to be bolted by the encircling move. But the Argyll rabbits could bite, for first the Japs ran into A Company and then, in the gathering dusk, into the ambushes one after the other. Shouts and screams answered the Argyll fire and that was the end of the pursuit . . .

Such close-quarters fighting was not always so one-sided, as Captain Bobby Kennard, a Territorial officer and the son of a naval captain, discovered when he was wounded by a sniper after visiting a forward Punjabi platoon attached to them. Shot in the groin, he had rolled about 5 yards from the track he was on and lay on his back in soft, swampy ground.

Hearing Jap voices I cut some lotus leaves with my parang to hide my body and lay still. Shortly there was the sound of British voices and a Bren opened up. The Japs were about 40 yards to my right and the Argylls about the same to my left, and the bullets from both sides passed over me. There was a lot of talking and shouting from the Japs, and I heard them clapping their hands. The firing died away and shortly afterwards the Japs came along the track in force. I was told later they had tricked our men into thinking they were the Indian platoon by clapping and shouting 'Punjabis'.

Cut off by the enemy's advance Kennard, who was shot during the late afternoon, waited until it got dark before he managed to get to his feet and hobble away, collapsing every time his right foot caught uneven ground. Hearing voices, but uncertain what language they were speaking, he got to within 20 yards of them before he understood it was a Japanese first-aid post. 'There was a lot of moaning and groaning.' After spending the night in the bush he eventually met up with eleven other Argylls isolated when they had advanced too far in a counter-attack. Among them was a Bren gunner who claimed to have killed at least a score of the enemy he discovered clustered in a hollow. Kennard, despite his wound, was among six who managed to get across the 200-yard-wide Perak River while it was in full spate. Some of the others were non-swimmers, reinforcements recently arrived from the UK who had not gone through Stewart's mandatory swimming programme. They were all captured or killed.

There was the usual problem about wireless, and in such a fluid fight field telephones were out of the question. Luckily, another advantage of being a battalion still predominantly made up of regular soldiers was that the Argylls knew their bugle calls, which were lightly coded just in case the clever Japanese had got to know them too. So when Drummer Hardy, who as well as being Stewart's batman was a bugler too, wetted his lips and sounded the regimental call followed by 'The Stand Fast', it meant just the opposite. Usually their Lanchester armoured cars covered their withdrawals and were often in no hurry to leave. The crew of one of these, parked under a few twigs of camouflage at the roadside, permitted a fifteen-strong Japanese reconnaissance patrol to get within 50 yards of their twin Vickers then 'killed the lot'.

Another skirmish became perhaps the Argylls' most famous exploit in Malaya and certainly the one that seemed best to sum up the kind of measured ferocity Stewart had inculcated into his men. It was an impromptu Tiger Patrol led by the very solidly built Captain Bal Hendry, an accomplished rugby forward in his early thirties who played for Edinburgh and might have been capped for Scotland had the war not got in the way.

Hendry, who was commanding A Company, went out with one of the Lanchesters delivering rations to his most remote seven-man section, who were occupying an observation post overlooking a small country railway station. He was accompanied by Company Sergeant-Major Arthur Bing, a deceptively mild-mannered individual, and his batman cum bodyguard, Private James Anderson. Known as 'Big Jimmy' in the battalion, Anderson came from that part of Glasgow where a man's razor was not always kept for his own face.

When they arrived, the corporal in charge was excited. He told Hendry that they had just counted a patrol of about fifteen Japanese, who appeared to have a Tamil guide with them, walking down the track and entering the deserted station. In the distance a larger party, some of them with bicycles, could be made out coming down the line from the same direction. Hendry immediately decided that he, Sergeant-Major Bing and Anderson would attack from a flank while the twin Vickers of the armoured car, plus the seven men they were revictualling, provided covering fire. Bing and Anderson both carried Thompsons and, as well as his revolver, Hendry had acquired a rifle.

Having shot two Japanese who were guarding the approach Hendry had chosen, it was discovered that further progress was blocked by a swamp. They went back a little way and entered from the other side. It soon became apparent that the enemy had taken cover behind the teak walls of the waiting room and ticket office from the gusts of fire the Vickers were putting down on them. Some were firing back through the windows.

The Japanese outnumbered the three Argylls approaching their backs by five to one but the latter had the considerable advantage of surprise. Possessed by some berserker fury, the mild-mannered Bing kicked open the door of the waiting room, emptied the fifty-round drum magazine of his Thompson into five of the men inside, then clubbed a sixth man to the ground by wielding the weapon by its hot barrel. Anderson shot at least two more as they tried to escape down the track while Hendry, the rugby forward, was engaged in the deadliest ruck of his life with four Japanese he had cornered in the narrow confines of the ticket office. Two of these he eventually managed to shoot, but then they all seem to have got too close to use a weapon because a wrestling match ensued with the survivors, who began to use their teeth as well as their boots. Hendry finished it by getting a hand to his steel helmet and then employing it to belabour both his opponents into unconsciousness – probably a unique use of the British battle bowler. By now the larger group of Japanese on the railway track were nearing the station. 'Captain Hendry thereupon picked up the least dead-looking Jap, whom he subsequently sent to battalion head-quarters, and withdrew,' wrote Colonel Stewart in his own account of the action.

For this bold sortie, pressed home against superior numbers in hand-to-hand fighting and culminating in the rare capture of a Japanese prisoner, Hendry only received a Mention in Dispatches, the lowest British award for gallantry in the field, rather than the expected Military Cross. The other two received no recognition whatsoever, possibly because Stewart wanted to make it plain that their conduct, rather like the route march from Mersing, was no more than he expected; to make too much fuss would be yet another indication of declining British standards. Certainly Hendry's success was ample vindication of

Stewart's training mantras, particularly 'Fix Frontally – Encircle'. Twelve of the enemy had been killed without loss and the only member of the encircling trio who emerged with wounds that would need treatment for several days was Sergeant-Major Bing.

As he closed in on his sixth victim, Bing had ignored what the hot barrel of his upturned Thompson was doing to his hands. The next day the sergeant-major was displaying the painful blisters across his palms to Ian Morrison, *The Times'* reporter. He was one of a group of war correspondents who had been taken up-country to visit the Argylls by an escort officer from the Singapore-based Services Public Relations Office, delighted to be able to top up the Argylls' success story with a recent victory, however small. Hendry was away somewhere but Morrison met several of the other young officers and was suitably impressed, even a little moved.

Tired and worn after several days of pretty continuous action, but still amaz-ingly cheerful, they were drawn from the oldest families in Scotland . . . When I hear people inveighing against the degeneracy of my contemporaries, especially those contemporaries who come from the old families of England and have been to the old schools, I like to think (although I know there is something in what the critics say) of those young officers of the Argylls . . . And the men, too. Dour, stocky little men, speaking a tongue so remote from ordinary English that an Englishman had to listen hard to understand everything they said.

Inevitably, UK British troops were going to get more press attention than British-officered Indians. But the Argyll cult must have become galling for the rest of Brigadier Archie Paris's 12th Brigade. Paris had been in Malaya for two years and was reckoned to handle a brigade as well as Stewart commanded his battalion. His two Indian battalions, the 5/2nd Punjabis and the 4/19th Hyderabads (no relation to the sultan's state forces who had mutinied at Kota Baharu), had also in-flicted some cruel ambushes as they leapfrogged down the road with the Argylls. The hair-trigger reactions of Lieutenant-Colonel Cecil Deakin, who commanded the Punjabi battalion, had become particu-larly well known.

During one leapfrog, Deakin was responsible for holding the Merbau Pulas bridge while the Argylls, who had just passed through, prepared a new position some 10 miles to the south. Shortly before dawn

Deakin, his Indian subadar-major (sergeant-major) and three signallers were standing at the bridge's southern end waiting in case any stragglers turned up before the bridge was blown at first light. Suddenly, the crossing was rushed by Japanese infantry covered by mortar and machine-gun fire. Deakin made no attempt to step back but charged straight at these impertinent trespassers like an enraged bull. Hard on his heels came his subadar-major and the three signallers whose duties were normally of a more non-combatant nature. Three of the enemy were killed and the rest fled. The bridge was then blown up. Brigadier Paris made sure that Deakin received the immediate award of a Distinguished Service Order.

By now Paris was an acting major-general. He had just replaced Murray-Lyon, the fast gun at the Alor Star bridge but not a graduate of Camberley Staff College and a late transfer to the Indian Army. On Christmas Eve, Murray-Lyon had been sacked as commander of 11th Indian Division, a casualty of preparing for Operation Matador, the cancelled pre-emptive strike into Thailand, at the expense of making proper defences at Jitra and Gurun. He returned to India and oblivion for shortly afterwards he was 'retired from the service' by General Alan Hartly, the acting commander-in-chief in Delhi. Thus, at the age of fifty-one, this experienced soldier, a DSO and MC, became a civilian in the middle of his country's most desperate war.

Quite why this should have been allowed to happen is unclear. Among senior officers there was some sympathy for Murray-Lyon, who had been fighting a first-class enemy with mostly half-trained troops and without anything to match the armour and air support possessed by his opponents. General Sir John Smyth VC would later call Hartly's decision 'iniquitous', though he admits Percival 'was probably right to make a change'. Percival himself would describe Murray-Lyon as 'a brave and tireless leader' and must have been surprised to learn his fate. For all that, his explanation that he wanted somebody with 'the widest possible experience of bush warfare' is not very convincing. These people hardly existed. As one of Murray-Lyon's brigade commanders, Paris, who was the same age, had no more experience of bush warfare than his old boss although, at his own level, and with the Argylls in his brigade, he had done rather better. Having found Murray-Lyon wanting, Percival was doing no more than reshuffle the pack.

As a reward for the Argylls' performance, Stewart had succeeded

Paris as commander of 12th Brigade. 'Not bad,' as Stewart liked to say, 'for a man who has not been to staff college.' Even so, to date Stewart had met the Japanese in an area where they had been unable to bring tanks and where the vegetation up to the roads was thick and their air superiority of limited advantage. 'It was impossible to make even the remotest guess at the location of our own and the British lines,' reported Tsuji after searching for the Ando Detachment on their calvary from Grik. 'We dropped the plane to an altitude of 100 metres and glared at the ground with eyes like those of an eagle watching a rabbit but we could not see anything.'

Then the terrain began to change. Stewart inherited the brigade which, having done its job and prevented the 11th Division from being cut off, had retreated to the relatively open tin-mining country around the Kampar River. South of the river, at the mainly Chinese market town of the same name, Paris was preparing to make a stand with infantry battalions that in some cases had been stitched together by amalgamating the rested survivors of Jitra and Gurun. Among these were the British Battalion, a mixture of the Leicesters and the East Surreys, and the Jat/Punjab Battalion, which seemed to be a cocktail of almost all of India's northern 'martial races', including Sikhs.

Stewart's task was to deploy 12th Brigade as a screen while trenches were hastily dug, wire strung and, where possible, fields of fire cleared around the ridges of Kampar. There was an increase in Japanese artillery fire and air strikes, the latter killing two Chinese 'mess boys' who had insisted on accompanying the battalion into action. And now for the first time the Argylls, who were the brigade's lead battalion, came under tank attack from Japanese armour which had come down the west coast road and then turned left inland. The action took place along a 3-mile stretch of country road south of the tin-mining town of Gopeng, near one of those specks on the map that suddenly take on a military significance its inhabitants could well do without. This one was a hamlet called Dipang whose little river bridge would mark the northern edge of the Kampar perimeter, about 4 miles from the town itself.

In places the road and river were often no more than 100 yards apart. The Argylls' B Company had a platoon of about thirty men, each under a second lieutenant, either side of the road with its right flank secure against the west bank of the river. Deployed in the rubber alongside the alarmingly pea-green waters of the Kampar, poisoned with mining effluent, was Lieutenant James McLean, an emergency commissioned officer late of the Prudential Insurance Company offices in Berwick-on-Tweed where he had met his fiancée Jean at a tennis party. McLean had arrived in Malaya shortly before hostilities began. He had not yet seen much action being one of seventy or so eve-of-battle reinforcements formed into a reserve company around battalion HQ. The idea was to give them a chance to acclimatize and perhaps imbibe the basics of Colonel Stewart's battle philosophy before they were gradually dispersed to replace casualties.

The arrival of the tanks was heralded by a sudden squall of small arms and heavy machine-gun fire as the Japanese sprayed both sides of the road. McLean's platoon was not engaged. Most of the action seemed to be coming from the one to his left under Lieutenant Sandy Stewart, his closest army friend, a tall, serious young man, the son of an Argyllshire farmer. Both twenty-seven, they were a bit older than most of Stewart's subalterns.

Soon McLean could hear the distinct clatter of tank tracks followed by the sound of trucks. It was obvious that, for the moment at least, the Argylls no longer controlled the road. Then suddenly it went quiet enough for the merged sounds of a single rifle shot and Sandy Stewart crying out in shock to be quite distinct. McLean told his men to stay put and cautiously worked his way between the avenues of rubber trees towards the road, hoping that somehow he might be able to help. Soon he caught his first glimpse of enemy trucks and tanks heading slowly south, all heavily garlanded with recently cut foliage, even though nobody had seen a British plane for days. As he watched, McLean became aware of movement and unfamiliar voices behind him. Then he realized that the Japanese vehicles were dropping off infantry, which had fanned out from the road and were now between him and his platoon. He was cut off.

The Argylls, to use Stewart's word for it, had been 'filleted'. By seizing the road the tanks had deftly removed the Argylls' backbone, bisected the battalion's two forward companies – for behind B there was D. These had been scattered, left and right, into the rubber and jungle where, panting and sweating, they dressed wounds, counted heads, and cursed the lack of decent anti-tank guns, let alone tanks, which had led to this humiliation.

Heavy machine-gun fire and occasional shells from the tanks' little 37 mm cannons snapped the rubber trees with ear-splitting cracks. For a while their resistance was ineffectual: some sniping and occasional pot-shots at the tanks with Boys anti-tank rifles. Then the shock of the tank attack gradually wore off, their old confidence began to return. They started to make it difficult for the Japanese infantry who had been given the task of keeping the road open.

Meanwhile the tanks, advancing alone on Dipang and its bridge, met their first determined opposition. The Argylls' Lanchesters and the little Bren gun carriers, all of which carried anti-tank rifles, went up the road to do battle. 'Destroyers against battleships,' noted Stewart grimly. 'The anti-tank rifles made no impression against Jap mediums, while their 37 mm guns . . . went through our armour like paper.'

Not surprisingly, the Japanese assumed that anything willing to take them on had the wherewithal to do it and this made them cautious enough for the remaining Argylls to withdraw in reasonable order. Once the turret hatches were closed for action, in Malaya's humidity both sides must have felt as if they were locked in a Turkish bath. Air-conditioned fighting vehicles were a daydream and the British wore overalls on top of their shorts and shirts (probably, like naval gunners, to guard against flash burns). To buy more time, Sergeant Albert Darroch deliberately drew fire on his Lanchester, manoeuvring it about the road as its twin Vickers optimistically sought the tanks' vision slits while the Boys pinged screeching ricochets from the unyielding armour.

There could only be one ending. After about ten minutes, a cannon shell demolished the armoured car's tall conning tower, occupied by the sergeant, and, as driver Private Archie Hoggan tried to reverse, he suddenly had Darroch slumped against him and steering was difficult. He pushed him away, not realizing how grievously he had been hurt until he looked down and saw an eye lying near a boot. To attempt to turn the six-wheeled armoured car, which was still running despite the damage to its superstructure, required a suicidal three-point turn offering the enemy its side. The easiest option for Hoggan would have been to abandon the extensively damaged vehicle and Darroch, who appeared to be dying from his head wound. Instead, with great skill and considerable nerve, Hoggan put the Lanchester's power steering to good use and, doubtless expecting another shell any second, managed to reverse it away without dropping it into the drainage ditch that borders all Malayan roads. Before he died Sergeant Darroch was awarded a Distinguished Conduct Medal (which is only bettered by a VC) and Hoggan a Military Medal.

Regimental Sergeant-Major Munnoch managed to hold battalion HQ together which, in Stewart's words, 'refused to let itself be stampeded off the road'. By the time the lead Japanese tank reached the Dipang bridge, having shot up Stewart's brigade headquarters and mortally wounded the Argylls' intelligence officer who had the awful luck to drive into them, a well-positioned 2-pounder anti-tank gun was able to knock it out. This more or less ended the tank sortie, for the Japanese armour withdrew a little way and waited for their infantry to catch them up, possibly because they were running out of fuel. Although the 200 or so Argylls dispersed by the initial attack were still on the wrong side of it, the sappers were told to destroy the bridge. Fortunately the Kampar, although in full spate, was often quite shallow and most were able to wade across about a mile downstream. They were led by Bal Hendry, victor of the ticket office fracas, who knew something must be done to give the non-swimmers confidence to cross. Intending to stretch a lifeline from bank to bank, he had dived in with a rope tied around his waist only to emerge in muddy disarray when he found himself in water no more than waist deep.

Some Argyll stragglers returned to the battalion in twos or threes or even individually. James McLean, the subaltern who had been cut off from his platoon when the tanks first broke through, came back on a stretcher. At first he had done rather well. Distinctly unimpressed by the way the Japs were 'yapping away to each other', which would never have been tolerated under Colonel Stewart's training, he had easily evaded them, reached the river, swam to its east bank and worked his way south along it towards the Dipang bridge. Stray rounds zizzed overhead and in the water he encountered a badly wounded Argyll corporal from Newcastle whom he tried to help. But, in a sudden burst of energy, the Geordie had splashed on ahead of him, desperate to get his injuries treated (in vain, for he died at a casualty clearing station).

Shortly afterwards McLean himself was hit when the Japanese on the opposite bank heard him pulling himself out of the water into the long elephant grass above. The bullet had passed through his right shoulder and travelled across his chest but he was conscious and still able to move on, crouching in the long grass. Some Gurkhas covering the demolition of the Dipang bridge picked him up. The next day McLean found himself crossing the Causeway into Singapore, one of scores of wounded collected from casualty clearing stations in the north and sent south in an ambulance train which, he was slightly surprised to find, was staffed by European nurses. For some reason the pre-war air-conditioned first-class carriages were not among its rolling stock and the heat was almost as bad as inside an armoured car. Stinking, unwashed men, Indians and British, groaned and constantly demanded water while the young nurses scurried around them, doing what they could. It was New Year's Eve.

Back in the perimeter that was building up around Kampar, the Argylls, most of whom had just had their first decent night's sleep in three weeks, were sufficiently rested for the kind of Hogmanay that only forty-eight hours before many would have thought out of the question. Stewart made no bones that denying comforts to the enemy had been, for the Argylls, one of the abiding consolations of rearguard duty. 'All seemed to have a Scottish dislike of seeing things go to waste,' he recalled.

Supply dumps, some containing NAAFI stores, and almost certainly the pantries and wine cellars of abandoned European houses and clubs (though Stewart does not say this) had sometimes been visited. Whisky, champagne, chocolates, canned Australian ham and all the best cigarettes you could smoke were a welcome change from bully beef and the hot sweet tea that Stewart always insisted on having served to his men five times a day as a restorative. In one of their billets, a Chinese school in the village of Bidor, Regimental Sergeant-Major Munnoch distributed the cornets and trumpets of the school band. One of the revellers was the battalion's Irish Presbyterian padre Hartley Beattie, who was from Donegal and held the usual chaplain's rank of captain. Beattie was about the same age as the other young officers and, for most of the time, wore the same uniform. All that distinguished him were the large black crosses sewn on the upper part of his shirt sleeves where sergeants and corporals carry their stripes.

The whisky fell on the fruitful ground of regimental camaraderie. In the last three weeks the Argylls, the old 93rd, the thin red line, had done damned well and they knew it. Notions of rank, class, homesickness and fear for tomorrow were all temporarily banished as bottles and mugs were raised to those old acquaintance who would not be forgot. The sergeant-major sat cross-legged before a small drum and gave his famous impression of the kind of Cairo street percussionists encountered around Kasr el-Nil barracks. 'It was well into the night', remembered Padre Beattie, 'before we stretched out on the floor.' It was a full moon.

In Singapore the full moon brought the bombers back. After the surprise attack at the start of hostilities there had been no more for two weeks. Then a series of nuisance raids had started, all of them at night, inflicting nothing like the number of casualties of the first one. Over the Christmas period, when the worst news had been the fall of Hong Kong on Christmas Day itself, even these had stopped. Some people had persuaded themselves that this was a chivalrous gesture from a non-Christian opponent.

It was hoped, even expected, that this lull would extend to New Year's Eve. However much they thought they had prepared themselves for it, many of the island's British residents still found the suddenness with which their lives had changed utterly unbelievable. 'Even a month ago we were preparing for the usual New Year land and sea sports,' the *Straits Times* reminded its readers, as it looked back on 1941. 'All accommodation at the hill stations was booked, prospects for the Penang race meeting were being discussed and hotels were announcing that very few tables were still available . . .'

In the now rigidly enforced blackout, most of the British community did their best to demonstrate, at parties in restaurants, clubs and private homes, that there would Always Be an England and they were expecting a Very Happy New Year indeed when all the rumours of massive reinforcements for Singapore would come true. Then some Nells of the Mihoru Kokutai ushered in 1942 by killing seventeen Chinese and Indian civilians living around the Sembawang airfield. It was the worst raid since the first one just over three weeks before. Kenneth Atkinson, the Captain of the dockyard, was a couple of miles away attending a party at another senior officer's married quarters in the nearby naval base. They watched the explosions and anti-aircraft fire for a while then left the terrace and went back to their dancing and, as the drink flowed, the inevitable games of sardines: 'all in the dark as there was an alert most of the time but being a full moon we just had most of the windows open and had enough light.'

Playing a more solitary moonlit game in the confines of his cockpit

22,000 feet above them was Flight Lieutenant Mowbray Garden who, along with Vigors, had reached Phillips' stricken battleships too late to save them. His Buffalo was a dedicated night fighter inasmuch as it had been painted black to reduce the chance of enemy air gunners spotting it as it closed in for the kill. Only in the UK were night fighters beginning to be equipped with airborne radar and this was so highly secret that the press were told that Wing Commander 'Cat's Eyes' Cunningham owed his remarkable night vision to his excessive fondness for raw carrots.

The land-based radar at Mersing had given Garden enough warning of the Nells' approach for him to climb above and he briefly caught sight of one darting below him, a fish in a rock pool. Then he lost it and, though he knew they were close, could not find them again. The clock on his instrument panel showed it was midnight. 'What a funny place to be spending New Year,' Garden thought. He was an account-ant who had come to Singapore in 1936. A year before he had been a rather disgruntled pilot in the Straits Settlements Volunteer Air Force, fully mobilized since the outbreak of war but told in no uncertain terms that there was no chance of a transfer to England and Spitfires until all the regulars had gone.

On New Year's Day the War Council met with Duff Cooper pre-siding. Everybody expected fireworks between Duff and Sir Shenton Thomas, who had just returned by car from a visit to Kuala Lumpur intended to raise the capital's shaky morale. As the front line came closer, Kuala Lumpur was coming under increasing air attack. While he was away, another scathing editorial had appeared in the *Straits Times*, written by its editor George Seabridge, which did nothing at all for morale, being a stinging attack on the failure of Thomas's administration to prepare adequate civil defence. It was a well-informed piece and, though he did not reveal his source, it was suspected that a lot of Seabridge's information had come from a certain Frank Bisseker, Deputy Director of Civil Defence. 'It seems to me to be nothing more than the desires of Seabridge . . . and Bisseker . . . to ingratiate themselves with Mr Duff Cooper, by indicating that it would be acceptable to the public if he were to be vested with authority in place of the civil government,' an indignant Thomas would report to the Colonial Office. It was all true. Churchill's bright emissary was seen as a breath of fresh air: they wanted to exchange him for Thomas.

The governor knew that Duff was seeing a lot of Seabridge, who had long been a thorn in his side. He expected Cooper to defend the article. But when Thomas made it plain he considered the piece alarmist and likely to do far more harm than good, he was delighted to find Cooper 'meek and acquiescent'. Perhaps this should have aroused his suspicions, for it was hardly characteristic, though it may have had something to do with his desire not to have a public spat.

Just before Christmas Duff Cooper had sent a letter to Churchill, headed 'Secret and Personal', which was carried to London by Captain Tennant, late of the *Repulse*. In it the Resident Minister reported on Thomas's failure to meet basic civil defence needs in terms very similar to those in the *Straits Times* editorial, and that probably derived from the same source:

. . . there are no air-raid shelters, no trenches even, no tin hats or gas masks for the civilian population. No preparations have been made for a system of food rationing, no registration of the inhabitants nor identity cards. The only sign that the authorities are aware of any danger is a large number of huts that have been set up for the reception of those who may be bombed out of their houses, but these are situated so close together and built of such flimsy material that a couple of incendiary bombs on a windy night would sweep them all away in one magnificent bonfire.

In the same letter Thomas is described as 'the mouthpiece of the last person he speaks to' – an assessment even those who held him in some affection were inclined to agree with. Sketches of some of the other leading players were also included. He made a mistake about Percival's background, having got the impression that he had been a school teacher before entering the army ('I am sometimes tempted to wish he had remained one'). But the rest is a balanced enough profile of the General Officer Commanding, possibly thanks to insights provided by Duff Cooper's military secretary, Major Lindsay Robertson of the Argylls, who had a reputation as a plain-speaking man:

. . . a nice, good man. He is a good soldier – calm, clear-headed and even clever. But he is not a leader. He cannot take a large view; it is all a field day at Aldershot to him. He knows the rules so well and follows them so closely and is always waiting for the umpire's whistle to signal cease fire and hopes that when the moment comes his military dispositions will be such as to receive approval.

He was more impressed by Air Vice-Marshal Pulford, the Air Officer Commanding:

. . . a fine dashing attractive fellow who unfortunately lost half his force on the ground before the battle started. [Some exaggeration here.] He is worried to death and rightly determined to preserve his small resources as long as possible. I like him very much.

Duff Cooper had visited Australia for the first time shortly before the Japanese went to war and been surprised by how much he enjoyed it. 'I found the country far more beautiful than I had expected, and the people warm-hearted, truly hospitable and tremendously alive.'

Apparently, this admiration did not extend to the tall and upright figure of the silver-haired Mr Vivian Bowden CBE, a senior member of Australia's fledgling diplomatic corps who had arrived in Singapore at the end of September. 'The Australian, who is to serve on the War Council in future, is of no account,' Churchill was informed, 'and therefore better than a better man who might give trouble.'

At first glance this seems to show Duff Cooper at his arrogant worst, but he knew that Churchill was becoming increasingly irritated by Canberra's demands for the repatriation of all Australian troops from the Middle East and would not relish the idea of the council being dominated by strident Australians 'who might give trouble'. And Bowden would be Canberra's second voice on the council, for he had invited General Bennett, whom he and his wife saw quite a lot of socially, to attend War Council meetings. In London General Sir Alan Brooke, the Chief of the Imperial General Staff, had already decided that the prime minister's Resident Minister was a bad influence. 'Duff Cooper . . . is inspiring the Australians to ask for more and more for the Far East.'

Bowden was far from being 'of no account' and had the kind of background that might have appealed to Duff Cooper's curiosity. Although born in Australia and already thirty in 1914 he had travelled to England at his own expense and enlisted in the British Army, serving in France in the Royal Engineers. After the war he published two novels based on his wartime experiences, then became involved in the lucrative China silk trade. In 1935 he was made Australia's first Trade Commissioner to China, with an official residence in Shanghai from where he had first observed the Imperial Japanese Army in action.

Bowden, like Brooke, thought there was a good chance Singapore would fall. On New Year's Eve he sent Canberra a message describing British air strength as 'pathetic'. Duff Cooper, a model of positive thinking, was much more optimistic, assuring Churchill: 'Unless the unforeseen happens – such as a successful landing on the island itself – I have no doubt of our ability to hold out for three or four months or even indefinitely provided we can get reinforcements and, later, food supplies.'

The Resident Minister was heartened by the arrival of Lieutenant-General Sir Henry Pownall to replace Brooke-Popham whom he thought 'on the verge of nervous collapse'. Pownall had been chief of staff of the ill-fated British Expeditionary Force to France and then, with post-Dunkirk invasion fears at their height, put in charge of the newly raised Home Guard. He was not much younger than Brooke-Popham but it was expected that his recent experience of the original blitzkrieg would make him better qualified to deal with an Asian imitation. Gordon Bennett, who was still waiting to show what his Australians could do, thought Pownall 'full of fire' and was also impressed. 'He has a heavy task but has, I think, the capacity to handle it.' As it turned out, this was never properly put to the test.

At the beginning of January 1942 General Sir Archibald Wavell, only recently appointed commander of land forces in India and doing his best to deal with the Japanese invasion of Burma, was elevated to supreme commander of all Allied forces in the Far East, such as they were. Pownall became his chief of staff. ABDA – the American-British-Dutch-Australia Command – was the first attempt at a combined Allied headquarters encompassing land, sea and air forces. It was a product of the war strategy currently being hammered out by Roosevelt and Churchill and their staffs at their conference in Washington over the Christmas and New Year period, along with other matters such as the signing – together with Litvinov of the Soviet Union and T. V. Soong of China – of something they called the 'United Nations Pact'.

It was from Washington that Churchill had sent Wavell the long, coded telegram outlining the job. 'The President and his military and naval advisers have impressed on me the urgent need for a unified command in South West Pacific . . .' The territory was enormous. Stretching west as far as the Indian–Burmese border and east to New Guinea, north as far as the southern Japanese islands and Formosa and south to Australia's Northern Territory, it included places that had already been lost to the Japanese such as Indo-China and Hong Kong as well as the current battlefields: the Philippines, where American troops under General MacArthur were putting up some stiff resistance, Burma, Malaya and Singapore. Brooke, who had not gone with the prime minister's party to Washington, thought it was quite ludicrous. 'The whole scheme wild and half-baked and only catering for one area of action namely Western Pacific.'

Wavell's HQ was to be in the Grand Hotel at Lembang in the relative cool of Java's hill country east of Batavia. His second-in-command was an American air force general and his naval commander was US Admiral Hart, commander of what, post-Pearl Harbor, was left of the US Asiatic Fleet. Hart would shortly be replaced by the Dutch Vice-Admiral Helfrich. The second most important Dutchman in the headquarters was a formidable sergeant-major who had been selected as Wavell's bodyguard and insisted on sleeping across the door of his bedroom.

Wavell was fifty-eight, had been commissioned into the Black Watch and saw his first action during the Boer War. In 1915 he had lost his left eye at Ypres, after which he served as General Allenby's chief of staff throughout his victorious campaign against the Ottoman Turks in Palestine. To date Wavell had been Britain's only successful army commander of the war. He had inflicted crushing defeats against numerically superior Italian armies in North and East Africa before the need to fight a simultaneous campaign in Greece and the arrival in the desert of Erwin Rommel and his Afrika Korps had redressed the balance for the Axis.

Temporarily out of favour with Churchill, he swapped jobs with General Sir Claude Auchinleck and became commander-in-chief in India while Auchinleck went off to try his luck against Rommel (not, in the end, a good career move; in August 1942 Auchinleck was replaced by Montgomery). If Japan had not entered the war Wavell might never have held another field command. Now he was getting rather more than his fair share. 'A pretty tall order ... I had been handed not just the baby but quadruplets,' he said in a message to a friend. Nor was Churchill under the illusion that he was doing Wavell any favours: 'It was almost certain that he would have to bear a load of defeat in a scene of confusion.'

Wavell was a clever and cultivated soldier. He was the author of a very readable biography of Allenby and an account of the Palestine campaign, and was shortly to surprise his contemporaries with the publication of *Other Men's Flowers*, an anthology of popular verse that, despite his heavy work load, he found time to select and annotate. Almost half a century after his death it was still in print.

But cleverness and an interest in the arts, even poetry, are not as rare in the British Army as some people imagine. Pownall, a tough character himself who would become one of Wavell's greatest admirers, decided that his greatest strength was 'his immense capacity for taking hard knocks'. This was not accidental. Wavell had consciously developed his mental stamina with all the dedication of a bodybuilder. 'All materials of war, including the general, must have a certain solidity,' he once wrote, 'a high margin over the normal breaking strain.'

Yamashita, also in a more formal way a poetry lover, and even a poet, for a samurai was expected to cultivate the arts, would have no doubt agreed with him, though by New Year's Day he was already beginning to believe that the worst might be over. 'I breathe the air of the South,' he wrote in his diary. 'I was up at 5 a.m. and it was already hot . . . My duty is half done though success is still a problem. The future of my country is now as safe as if we were based on a great mountain.'

Then – and could this have been Kitty's influence? – 'However, I would like to achieve my plan without killing too many of the enemy.'

Arthur Percival was not all that enthusiastic about the appointment of
a new supremo, even one as famous and sometimes successful as Wavell.
He felt that 'continuity was required' and that too many changes could
be bad for morale. However, there had been some good news which,
though he was by no means lacking in the grit Wavell thought so
essential to good generalship, had done wonders for his own spirits.

It had been decided that Malaya would be reinforced by the whole
of Beckwith-Smith's 18th Division, now somewhere in the Indian
Ocean and towards the end of their long and, to date, mostly well-
cushioned odyssey in the borrowed floating palaces of the idle rich.
While the rest of the division went first to Bombay, one brigade, at
the urging of Duff Cooper, was coming directly to Singapore from
Mombassa. At sea it would rendezvous with another Singapore-bound
convoy which was carrying more good news: in the holds of its ships
were fifty crated Hurricane fighters and among its passengers the pilots
who were expected to use them to give the Japanese Zeros a very nasty
shock. Originally it had been intended to ship the aircraft to Sumatra
and assemble them there, but then it had been decided to get them to
Singapore as soon as possible whatever the risk. To increase their
chances of arriving safely, Percival wanted to deny the Japanese the
central Malayan airfields at Kuala Lumpur and Kuantan, which would
enable them to intensify their attacks on the convoy and its valuable
cargo.

Once they were safely ashore Percival was reconciled to the notion
that he would probably have to continue his withdrawal against an
enemy with total naval and air superiority. His fears of the chances of
another landing further down the east coast, or at Singapore itself,
were keener than ever. The latest RAF reconnaissance photographs
of Thailand's Singora harbour showed thirty-four ships at anchor. The
trick was to pick good defensive positions and make Yamashita pay
heavily for every mile he advanced along the Malayan Peninsula without risking heavy losses of men and equipment Percival would need
when he returned to the offensive. Certainly, he could afford no

more Jitras and Guruns. Ultimately, what was needed was to hold the southernmost state of Johore long enough for the 18th Division to deploy there. Then, together with Bennett's unblooded Australians, and under the Hurricanes' umbrella, he could launch a counter-attack against Yamashita's exhausted troops when they were at the end of a long and vulnerable supply line and send them reeling.

There was another famous retreat of a British army along a peninsula which is studied by all of its generals. In Portugal in 1810 the Duke of Wellington made a fighting retreat to the cleverly fortified defensive line he had secretly prepared before Lisbon either side of the market town of Torres Vedras just north of the capital. The Lines of Torres Vedras, almost at the foot of the Iberian peninsula and about 20 miles across, proved to be impregnable and for three years Napoleon's troops wasted away trying to breach them. When they gave up, a reinforced Wellington began to advance, defeated them at Vitoria, liberated all of Portugal and Spain, then scaled the Pyrenees into France itself and saw Napoleon off to his first exile.

There are, of course, important differences between these two peninsular campaigns. Unlike Percival, the Iron Duke had a strong naval presence to patrol both coasts and ensure that his flanks were not turned. Wellington was also holding a much narrower peninsular toe, 20 miles across, while for Percival the narrowest defensive line in Johore was 80 miles or so. Portugal's terraced slopes rather than thick jungle also offered the defender proper fields of fire. Nor did Wellington have air superiority to contend with. Instead he had *los guerrilleros* – about 30,000 of them in all – the civilian insurgents who gave the English language a new noun. Their raiding, ambushing, sabotaging and sniping turned the tortuous French main supply route into a trail of tears.

Percival might have had something like this at his disposal if he had not, in the last months of peace, been against the idea of the SOE preparing 'stay-behind parties' with suitable dumps and wireless links for resupply. Once the fighting started there had been a couple of attempts to interfere with Yamashita's lengthening lines of communications. For a while a unit known as the 'Gurkha Gang', recruited from Selby's all-Gurkha 28th Brigade, roamed the Central Highlands from where, a couple of weeks before the Japanese arrived, most of the Europeans had already fled, mainly because of the growing hostility of the local Sikh community: some had thrown acid in the face of an elderly Englishman who refused to leave his bungalow. But the Gurkha Gang did not achieve very much apart from picking up the Japanese mistress of a planter who had avoided internment and was discovered to have a radio transmitter. She was sent to Singapore under escort.

Major Angus Rose, an Argylls officer of Buchanesque romanticism marooned on Percival's staff since long before Pearl Harbor, had a little more luck. Desperate to catch up with brothers who had, between them, already collected a DSO and an MC in Somaliland and France,★ Rose had originally come up with an ambitious plan. He wanted to insert a battalion-sized clot into Yamashita's supply arteries then hold off all comers until they were relieved by a British counter-attack. Percival said he liked the idea but had no battalions to spare.

In the end, fifty Australian volunteers drawn from Bennett's six infantry battalions congregated at Port Swettenham from where they were to be put behind Japanese lines by boat. They were divided into two platoons and given enough automatics, four Brens and twenty-six Thompson sub-machine-guns, to afford them considerable firepower. The remainder carried rifles, but everybody was issued with two of the new bakelite-cased blast grenades, which fitted snugly into large Australian fists, being smaller and about half the weight of the standard issue 1915 pattern British pineapple grenade. (The downside for the thrower was that they were also about half as effective.) In another effort to travel light, the entire party was shod in black canvas Bata hockey boots. These were similar to the canvas footwear some of Yamashita's infantry wore, except that the Japanese boots had a separate compartment for the big toe, which left an almost cloven-hoofed spoor.

Rose had picked a spot along the main coast road near the village of Trong, which is north-west of Ipoh and no more than 10 miles from the coast. He was responsible for getting the Australians to the ambush site, which he knew well from pre-war drives between Penang and Ipoh. After that, his role was no more than that of observer, or adviser, because the Australians were touchy about their troops coming under local UK British command. Apart from Rose, the only other supernumeraries were six Malay-speaking Europeans, mostly rubber planters, from the Volunteer Forces who would be able to question locals about Japanese movements.

★ A third brother had, for some reason, joined the French Foreign Legion and was missing in action.

On Boxing Day, the navy delivered them in an old coastal steamer to the mouth of the Sungei Tong. There, they were intended to transfer to two shallow-draught motor launches, in which they were to proceed by various creeks to the target area. One of these launches stubbornly refused to start, however, and there was nothing for it but to leave a platoon behind. Rose's raiders were now reduced to twenty-eight including the Argyll and two of the planter guides. They went as far as they could in the remaining boat. Then came an arduous wade through a glutinous mangrove swamp and a mosquito-filled night in the Tamil coolie line huts of a rubber plantation. By 9 a.m. next day – 27 December – they were in position to fire the Australian infantry's first shots against the Japanese.

In command was Lieutenant Robert Sanderson, rather shockingly to Rose's regimental ears known as 'Sandy' to his men. He was twenty-two and had recently been a clerk in Forbes, New South Wales. According to his own account, the honour of the very first shot went to Rose, who makes no bones about how much he was enjoying himself. 'A bird came and perched on a bough near my stand. He preened himself a bit and then started tuning in. This was thrilling work and incomparable to any other kind of sport, such as sitting up for a tiger. Furthermore, it was all being paid for by King George.'

They allowed a couple of large ambulances, heading north from the front, to go by. Rose was hoping for 'a nice cycling party', having observed one the night before while out on a lone reconnaissance. For a while the road was deserted. As they waited, Rose's initial excitement was overshadowed by nagging doubts. He was particularly concerned by the way the Australians were deployed, spaced along a straight length of road in which he was third from the left. 'The field craft was not so hot either. The sun was low down and slap in our eyes . . .' He decided he must have a word with Sandy.

I had gone about 30 yards or so when I heard vehicles approaching from our end of the ambush, so I flattened myself against a tree. As the leading car flashed into sight I saw a blue pennant flying on the radiator cap. I thought instinctively – 'Brigadier! We must have him,' and, in the split second which I had for making a decision, I put up my rifle, swung through on the driver and pressed the trigger. 'Correct!' The driver crumpled up, the car flashed out of sight, the tyres screamed on the tarmac and the vehicle crashed into a ditch further down the road. I was quite pleased with my marksmanship and got a kick out of my shot akin to pulling down a high pheasant at a covert shoot. The fact that I was standing up made it considerably easier and I have an idea that in a cramped sitting position I would probably have registered a wash-out. Behind this first car a whole fleet of vehicles pulled up. They must have been driving at a very close density.

Three trucks and a pick-up screeched to a halt, possibly crashing into each other and certainly stopping within point-blank range of the hidden Australians, who riddled them. Blasts from the bakelite grenades capsized the pick-up. Some of the Japanese were seen to be hiding behind a culvert and more grenades went in their direction. Sanderson personally emptied an entire drum of fifty .45 Thompson rounds into the staff car and later there were claims that at least a brigadier and perhaps a major-general were killed, though this has never been confirmed from Japanese sources.

'Jesus, we didn't half crack the bastards,' the lieutenant told Rose. Undoubtedly the Australians had enjoyed themselves. ('Ambush is murder and murder is fun,' the US Marine Corps would soon be teaching its recruits.) They retired without casualties though, according to Rose, in some disorder. 'There was a good deal of shouting going on . . . Some of the troops were still shooting and others now started to withdraw. One thing that was quite clear was that control had broken down and no one had any idea of their duties.'

Rose tried to talk the Australians into venturing further down the road and 'giving the bastards another crack' but their mood was to get out while the going was good and everybody returned to Port Swettenham. 'The others seemed pleased enough with our achievement but I sat brooding in the motorboat feeling sullen and despondent,' recalled the Argyll, who felt that they should at least have organized a snatch party to remove from the dead the papers, wallets and maps that so often provide intelligence scoops.

None the less, it had not been a bad beginning and should have been the start of greater things. On the way back there was a small bonus for Rose: some Malays brought to them six British stragglers, bearded and more or less clad in the local fustian apart from a pair of dancing pumps on one of them. To Rose's astonishment, two of these apparitions greeted him like a long-lost brother. They turned out to be Argyll NCOs, Platoon Sergeant-Major James Love and Sergeant Albert Skinner, who had been cut off in the fighting along the Grik

Road two weeks before and had spotted a number of juicy Japanese targets as they had trekked around 100 miles south. The Australians were particularly excited about a large airfield and vehicle park the NCOs had seen, though Rose did not think the Australians had received enough training with explosives to destroy aircraft and wondered whether the vehicles would still be there.

In any case, it was no longer his concern. In future the Australians would be operating independently while Rose, to his great delight, had been given his own raiding party in the form of a detachment of Royal Marines, survivors from the *Prince of Wales* and *Repulse*. He had also just acquired the assistance of an officer, like himself an able yachtsman, whose knowledge of the local waters and their islands had secured him a post away from his infantry battalion as a field security officer.

Captain Ivan Lyon of the Gordon Highlanders, who was twenty-six and a distant kinsman of King George VI's consort Queen Elizabeth *née* Bowes-Lyon, had been in Malaya for five years. Now the war had started in earnest he had tired of stalking fifth columnists and trying to locate clandestine radios, sometimes with spectacular lack of success. Once police, acting on one of his plots of an unauthorized transmitter, found themselves standing in the kitchen of one of the British judges of the Malayan High Court.

The son of Brigadier-General Sir Francis Lyon, who was badly wounded at the siege of Ladysmith in the Boer War, Lyon was just under 6 foot, with a wiry, runner's frame and the kind of alert good looks you might expect to find above the ruff of an Elizabethan pirate. There was undoubtedly a wild streak in him, although as he got older his risk-taking became more calculated. As a schoolboy at Harrow he had single-handedly sailed a small boat across the North Sea. In Singapore he had woken after a night's carousing with the 2nd Gordon's other subalterns to discover a large portrait of a snarling tiger tattooed on his chest, not the kind of decoration most officers and gentlemen normally had in mind for that part of their anatomy. Far from regretting it, Lyon rarely resisted an opportunity to show it off.

Then there was the question of his marriage. In peace time, young army officers were not encouraged to marry early. At twenty-four Lyon was not only married but to a foreigner. Gabrielle Bouvier was the daughter of the governor of a French prison island off the Indo-China coast. Something of a free spirit herself, she had already married, divorced and given birth to a daughter before she was nineteen. It is not difficult to understand how the colonel of a garrison duty battalion, well in the public eye, might think he would be doing himself and everybody else a favour if he found alternative employment for this kind of young officer.

Lyon had met and courted his bride when he called at Governor Bouvier's penal colony in his yacht. By the time they married in July 1939, just before the start of the European war, he appears to have been working closely with the Singapore head of MI5, the security service, and using his sailing trips as cover to visit places where Japanese agents were suspected of operating. After the fall of France, Gabrielle Lyon was employed as an interpreter for the Free French mission in Singapore. Her father's sympathies were also with de Gaulle and, at some risk to himself, he began to smuggle out to his daughter titbits of gossip on Découx's Vichy hierarchy in Indo-China. When the SOE's Colonel Warren arrived in Singapore and, perhaps because of the initial clamp-down on SOE activities, became involved in field security, he met and took a liking to Lyon. It was Warren who had introduced him to Rose.

The Argyll had great hopes for his west coast raiders because the Royal Navy had just taken delivery of five American-built Eureka patrol boats, which were ideal for the kind of work he had in mind. They never arrived. Despite abundant evidence of the growing Japanese air superiority, somebody allowed them to complete the last leg of their journey from Singapore to Swettenham in daylight. Three were sunk and two beached and possibly salvageable, though repairs would take some time. At about the same time, the coastal steamer that had taken Rose and the Australian volunteers on the first stage of their raid was sunk in the harbour with all Rose's personal kit on board. A demoralized Lyon, desperate to get into action, wanted to return to his battalion, which was rumoured to be leaving Singapore to take part in the fighting on the peninsula. Warren stopped this. He had other plans for Lyon.

All was by no means lost as far as guerrilla operations were concerned. Since the High Command no longer considered it defeatist to concede that things might get worse before they got better, SOE was at last being allowed to establish 'stay-behind' parties in areas likely to be overrun. In charge was an ecstatic Major Freddy Spencer Chapman, the chief instructor at 101 Special Training School, who seems to have regarded a life already packed with adventure as merely a dress rehearsal for this moment. With Warren at his side, he drove north to the Kuala Lumpur HQ of General Heath's 3rd Indian Corps in a scarlet Ford V8 coupé crammed with Thompson sub-machine-guns, ammunition, grenades, boxes of plastic explosive and detonators. 'I felt so like a Crusader that when we passed a Chinese temple I almost suggested that we should go in and have our Tommy guns blessed.'

Heath was supportive, keen on anything that might take the pressure off his tired and demoralized Indians and demonstrate that the Japanese were not invincible. As a first step, Spencer Chapman suggested a chain of small parties across the 50 miles of territory through which all the main north–south rail and road links pass. Eventually there would be eight of these parties totalling forty-five men, including two Chinese and an Indian. The rest were mostly planters, miners, engineers and colonial civil servants, usually in their late twenties to early thirties. As well as speaking some Malay and Chinese, most had enjoyed a nodding acquaintance with firearms since their early teens: first in the Officer Cadet Training Units of their public schools and then for game shooting or during their weekend soldiering with the Volunteers.

This was just as well for there was no time to give some of the later recruits anything but the most basic training; dropped from the curriculum were practice fighting with blades and bare hands, or alternative uses for bootlaces. If they were lucky they got a week at Special Training School 101. John Wilson, who was twenty-nine and had been working in Malaya for four years as an engineer with the Irrigation and Drainage Department, had just one day there.

During the morning the party did a short course in Tommy gun, hand grenade and revolver training, and in the afternoon, a course on explosives, their uses and the various types. The evening was spent in filling in forms, drawing clothes and arranging for food supplies and the necessary arms, ammunition and explosives.

Rations, which were intended to last for three months, included a dozen bottles of whisky and two dozen of rum, with cans of bully beef, condensed milk, packets of biscuits and porridge, sugar and tea. The cans were dipped into hot candle wax to help preserve their contents when cached in humid jungle hides. They also had fishing lines and, in some cases, shotguns and hunting rifles with which they could supplement their rations.

Wilson had been given the rank of second lieutenant. All members of the 'stay-behind' parties were commissioned. Although leadership and discipline were essential it made no sense to maintain an 'officers and other ranks' divide among men expected to live on top of each other in jungle hide-outs. 'For God's sake stop calling me sir,' Spencer Chapman ordered John Sartin, who had been a Royal Engineers sergeant instructor on explosives at the training school when they first met. 'Call me Freddy and I'll call you John.' In Lieutenant Sartin's case his sudden elevation, though doubtless pleasing, must have been particularly difficult, because he was a regular soldier who had enlisted as a fourteen-year-old boy bugler. None the less, John and Freddy worked well together and would go on to have great success in the bushwhacking business.

Spencer Chapman thought that six was the best size for a party and that at night they should operate in ambushing teams of three, 'as it can move very fast and with practice can almost think and operate as one man'. So that they could move along open roads in daylight posing as Tamil labourers (most were too tall to be convincing Chinese or Malays) they carried dhotis or sarongs to be worn with white shirts and had a paste made up of soot, coffee, iodine and potassium permanganate for blacking up face, hands and feet.

But no amount of make-up could be a substitute for the real thing. Although no Tamils seem to have been available, there were plenty of Asian volunteers in the form of the almost entirely Chinese membership of the Malayan Communist Party. The British had made the MCP a proscribed organization. Until the German invasion of Russia in July 1941 it had done everything it could to disrupt the war effort by fomenting strikes among the grossly underpaid labour force in the rubber industry. Their initial offers of a truce, and even help, following Hitler's assault on the Workers' Paradise were treated with some caution by the Colonial Office. But by 19 December 1941 – eleven days after the first Japanese came ashore at Kota Baharu – the British had swallowed their pride. They agreed first to train and then infiltrate Chinese Communist volunteers into rural areas where the Party enjoyed the kind of local support that would enable them to become, as they would learn to put it, the guerrilla fish in the people's sea. Within a very short time they had almost four times as many trained men in the field as the British. One of their leaders, sitting in a Port Swettenham office beneath portraits of Stalin and Churchill, told Angus

Rose he should not be surprised. 'We have already organized for many years to fight against you British but now we prefer to fight with you against the Japs.'

Before the stay-behind parties started their operations Spencer Chapman had gone on a reconnaissance behind Japanese lines. He went with Sartin and a Malay-speaking inspector in the Malayan Mines Department borrowed from a Volunteer artillery battery where he was serving as a sergeant-major. They paddled themselves across the Perak River in a waterlogged ferry boat with a glass cabin and an engine they could not start. Shortly afterwards they were treated to their first close-up view of the enemy. They lay 100 yards from a road and watched as the Japanese infantry rode towards the sound of guns in cycling packs of forty or fifty, 'three or four abreast and talking and laughing just as if they were going to a football match'. Spencer Chapman was struck by two things: how easy they looked to ambush and the variety of their dress.

Some wore green, others grey, khaki or even dirty white. The majority had trousers hanging loose or enclosed in high boots or puttees. Some had tight breeches and others shorts or rubber boots or gym shoes. Their hats showed the greatest variety: a few tin hats, topees of all shapes, wide-brimmed planters' hats or ordinary felt hats, high-peaked jockey hats, little caps with eye shades . . . Their equipment and armament were equally varied and were slung over themselves and their bicycles. We noticed with delight that their weapons were usually tied onto the frames of the bicycles so that they would have taken some time to go into action had they been suddenly attacked.

By now the metamorphosis of the Japanese from comic, visually impaired Asians with few discernible military virtues likely to concern a Great Western Power, to fanatical, highly trained and superlatively equipped jungle fighters was well under way. Aspects of the later image were no more true than the first. But even *The Times*' Ian Morrison, an excellent reporter who had lived in Japan and covered the war in China from both sides, would be guilty of contributing to it, though almost certainly his information came from army sources. 'Nearly all the Japanese infantry were armed with Tommy guns or other light automatic weapons,' he informed his readers in *Malayan Postscript*, his account of the campaign published by Faber & Faber in London towards the end of 1942. 'They were ideal for this close-range jungle fighting.'

The only people with Tommy guns or any other kind of sub-machine-gun in Malaya were the British, with their heavy American Thompsons. They had bought them as a stopgap while they were developing the Sten, which would not reach the Far East in any quantity until 1944. Yamashita had landed in Malaya before the first Nambu sub-machine-gun, which the Japanese had been working on since the 1920s, emerged from the Naval Arsenal's factory in Nagoya, and only about 20,000 of them were ever produced (compared to an estimated 4 million Stens of various models).

Far from being lavishly equipped with automatic weapons, in Malaya the Japanese not only had fewer of these than their opponents, but also what they did have was invariably slightly inferior to its British equivalent. Their answer to the Bren was the Nambu Type 96 which, with its banana-shaped, 30-round magazine, carrying handle and steadying fold-up bipod near its business end, even looked like the British light machine-gun. But it was nowhere near as good because a design fault made it prone to jamming.

There were usually four of them per platoon of forty or so men, about the same ratio of light machine-guns to rifles that the British had adopted and, as with the Bren, ammunition was rarely a problem because it was the same calibre as the rifle ammunition in almost every infantryman's pouch.

This rifle was the Model 38 bolt-action Arisaka, a Mauser design used by the Japanese army since 1905 and undoubtedly an accurate and robust weapon. But it had one obvious drawback: with its bayonet fixed, the Arisaka measured only 6 inches under 6 feet. It was manifestly unsuited for the average Asian physique and some of the Imperial Japanese Army were so dwarfed by their rifles they tended to look like wicked children. Only a lucky few were issued with the shorter carbine version. Both rifles and carbines fired the same small-calibre 6.5 mm bullet, which was not as effective as the Lee-Enfield's heavier .303 round; there were numerous instances of British soldiers surviving bullet wounds that would have killed them had they come from their own rifles which, as it happened, were both shorter and slightly lighter than the Arisaka.

Nor were the Japanese anywhere near as 'jungle trained' as some of Percival's troops, particularly the Argylls and the first brigade of Australians who arrived in Malaya well before hostilities started. Hardly any of them had ever seen any jungle. But the China war had ensured that far more of them were blooded, and often on victory. Above all, what the Japanese had in abundance was courage, endurance and a discipline that, in their eagerness to see that orders were carried out, did not stifle initiative but encouraged it.

Yet, while there are plenty of eyewitness accounts of close-quarters fighting, there is no record of suicidal banzai charges. Instead there are frequent reports of terrier-like persistence and the tactic of outflanking, of threatening the British rear, that continued to work no matter how predictable it became. Once outflanked, Percival's commanders, who had almost invariably been ordered to do their best but keep their formations intact at all costs, withdrew rather than risk having to fight their way out. Unfortunately, these retreats were sometimes triggered by the kind of bluffs and trickery – the chains of mortar-lobbed firecrackers which could convince a platoon that they had an entire regiment behind them – that should have been ignored or brushed aside.

'I have seen a total absence of the offensive spirit,' reported General Bennett to Australian Army HQ in Melbourne. Bennett did not believe in retreats, however good the Iron Duke might have been at them, and his conviction that, when the time came, his men would put up a much better performance than the Indians or the UK British was unshakeable. 'Frequently one or two men armed with a tommy-gun [sic] have been the only threat to the rear of our positions,' he said in a letter to be read to all the men in his division. 'This is not a new system; it is as old as war itself.'

But then, quite suddenly, it looked as though Percival had found his Torres Vedras.

The lines at Kampar might not be as well remembered as Wellington's lines on the Iberian Peninsula, but they were good enough to stop Yamashita's 5th Division in its tracks. Kampar's eastern backcloth is Gunong Brijang Malaka, an imposing little mountain covered in scrub and secondary jungle which the British knew as 'Kampar Hill'. It is 4,000 feet high, a green barnacle on the edge of the scarred coastal plain, for this was open-cast mining country, fissured with dredged-out, water-filled tin lodes. Stewart's 12th Brigade had bought the time for Chinese labour to help its defenders dig in properly. Percival thought it was the strongest position in Malaya. In particular, he considered the observation posts available on Kampar Hill's forward slopes an artillery spotter's dream.

Artillery was the one arm where the British, virtually without air or naval support, were better off than the Japanese who were not as well trained or equipped in this department – their Krupps-pattern guns, like their rifles, mostly dating from the turn of the century. But up until now there had been precious few opportunities to exploit this advantage. It was difficult to spot targets in jungle terrain and, at the front line, the Japanese infantry tended to hold onto their enemy the way a knife-fighter clings to his opponent's shirt. On several occasions Ian Stewart of the Argylls had attempted, by a surprise withdrawal, to make space for an artillery killing zone, only to find that the target closed to the rhythm of his retreat with all the alacrity of a tango dancer. The scheduled barrage would then have to be called off as it would be liable to kill as many British as Japanese.

Kampar, with its sweeping fields of fire for the defenders, was different. As they neared the high ground the British were holding, picking their way around the stagnant mosquito-breeding farms of used-up tin country, the Japanese came under increasingly accurate harassing fire. Eventually it got to the point where they preferred not to show themselves again in daylight. 'My soldiers began to get tired,' admitted Major-General Kawamura whose 9th Brigade was once again the 5th Division's vanguard.

There was not, as such, a British line at Kampar but something rather better. It appeared on Percival's maps as a goose egg, an all-round defence perimeter. Most of it straddled the hill where the artillery was hidden in the greenery with 200 rounds neatly piled beside each gun and more in dumps nearby. On the western side, the main Kampar position was held by the merged 15th/6th Brigade which also controlled the low ground where the road and railway ran alongside the hill and through the town itself. Alongside them, looking after the right flank and a loop road which went around the hill before joining up with the trunk road just north of Tapah, were the three battalions of Gurkhas who made up Selby's 28th Brigade. They were supported by the old 4.5-inch howitzers of the Lanarkshire Yeomanry, Scots Territorials reinforced with drafts from all over the UK and officially designated 155 Field Regiment, Royal Artillery. The other brigade under the recently promoted Brigadier Moorhead, admired by Percival for the leadership and tactical skills he had demonstrated as the commander of KrohCol during the first days of the conflict, also had an artillery regiment at their disposal, in their case the newer 25-pounders of 88th Field Regiment, RA.

First Kawamura probed the front of Selby's brigade, but his young Gurkhas were well dug in among the kind of hill scrub that might have reminded them of Nepal, and often in the pleasing position of seeing without being seen. When they finally worked out where some of the Gurkhas were and began to form up and close in, the Lanarkshire Yeomanry's forward observation officers picked up their field telephones. Even the China veterans, let alone the boys who had never left Japan before, were unsettled by the fire they called in. A mile or so away, one of the sweating gunners manning the howitzers was Trooper John McEwan, a twenty-year-old from a Catholic mining family in Motherwell, who recalled his delight that they were holding their ground and hitting back.

I remembered a thought from what seemed long ago. 'Wha daur meddle wi' me?' . . . The words of patriotic songs flowed through my mind. 'Britons, never, never, never shall be slaves.' These words accompanied the incessant roar of our howitzers . . .

The Lanarkshire Yeomanry's monocled commander was Lieutenant-Colonel Augustus Murdoch who, like many dismounted yeomanry officers, clung to a cavalry code and, even when astride the thorough-bred BSA motorcycle he had acquired, was rarely seen without his leather riding crop. At midnight on New Year's Eve Murdoch, who was held in great affection by young men like McEwan though they might have come from different planets, ordered a twelve-round salute to be fired at the enemy. About seven hours later, not long after the first Malayan dawn of 1942, Kawamura responded by launching his main attack straight down the trunk road against the other flank of the Kampar position.

The brunt of this was borne by the newly formed British Battalion, the Leicesters and East Surreys who had straggled back after the disasters at Jitra and Gurun and been amalgamated into a single unit. The ex-hausting, mosquito-plagued nights in jungle swamps and paddy fields that followed those battles had further thinned their ranks through malarial fevers. (Among those who had been evacuated with a high temperature was the keen young Lieutenant Abbott of the Surreys.) These losses had been partly made up by the attachment of some sixty European militia from the Perak Volunteers, whose local knowledge and languages were a useful bonus. The battalion was now about 600-strong and commanded by Morrison of the Leicesters, the CO of the Surreys being in hospital. Morrison, who was forty-eight with a 1914–18 Military Cross among his medal ribbons, chose as his adjutant the senior unwounded officer from the Surreys. His sergeant-major was a Leicester.

Morrison's last job had been Director of Military Training to the Johore State Forces. It was said that his main qualifications for the post were that he shared the sultan's enthusiasm for polo and possibly other pursuits. But once war came Esmond Morrison showed himself to be a very serious soldier indeed. Although he was told about his new job three weeks before the Japanese invasion, when his predecessor at the Leicesters had been posted to the staff in Singapore, Morrison had to wait until a replacement had been found for him in Johore. Eventually, he had arrived at his new command just after the Jitra battle had begun. As a result, Morrison had had an awful start to the campaign, losing the best part of his battalion through no fault of his own; and he was lucky to save himself in the ambush at Alor Star.

But the resilience and leadership displayed by this 'polo-playing playboy', as some of the more envious were apt to describe him, must have been remarkable. The Leicesters and Surreys had the same

powerful and exclusive regimental bonds as Stewart's Argylls. Yet by
the time the battle of Kampar, which lasted for three days, was over,
the British Battalion, the hasty improvisation of harassed staff officers,
had acquired an *esprit de corps* that, as word spread, overshadowed its
old loyalties. Undoubtedly this had a lot to do with Morrison's energy
and his habit of sharing the dangers at the sharp end, on one occasion
picking up a rifle and bayonet and helping to clear a road-block.

For two days running the British Battalion was subjected to attacks
at dawn when the shadowy figures of the Japanese infantry would
loom suddenly out of the mist, while behind them their big 4-inch
mortars sought out Morrison's positions among the hill's secondary
jungle. Mortar bombs do not whistle in flight like artillery shells.
Sometimes the distinctive plop they made as they were fired sent men
diving for cover. Otherwise, if their luck held, the nerve-shattering
crack of the first bomb exploding, and perhaps the cries of the less
fortunate, was the first indication that they were being mortared. One
of the early casualties was a company commander who had to be
evacuated when a splinter shattered his jaw.

Thanks to the forward observation officers of 88th Field, one of
whom found himself dictating coordinates down his telephone within
50 yards of the enemy, the British were able to return the high explosive
with interest. None of the Japanese mortars was firing a projectile
anything like as big as the 25-pound shells that were rarely less than
worrying and sometimes scored bull's-eyes that would have broken
lesser troops. Tsuji watched 'a continuous stream' of casualties coming
back down the hill to safety, 'either carried on stretchers or supported
on the shoulders of comrades who were themselves wounded'.

The Japanese tried to locate the guns that were doing the damage from
the air and bring up some artillery of their own. But the 25-pounders and
their limbers and towing vehicles were well concealed in the hill's
secondary jungle. A single lucky shot did mortally wound a gunner
officer at a battery HQ, but although the Japanese had a good idea of the
guns' general whereabouts, they could not be pinpointed for effective
counter-battery fire.

It was possibly out of sheer frustration that the crew of one of the
low-flying open-cockpit aircraft trying to find the artillery dropped a
hand-held anti-personnel bomb on a small group of dug-in Leicesters
they had spotted. Everybody was killed except for a badly shocked
officer, who was unscathed. Seconds later the machine was shot down

and both crew killed when Bren guns further up the hill fired down on it.

In places the ebb and flow of battle, attack and counter-attack, left the British and the Japanese inextricably mixed. One of Morrison's lieutenants, waking alone in a trench shortly before the main action of the day started, heard movement in some neighbouring diggings which were supposed to be empty and found himself face to face with several baleful-looking representatives of the Emperor. He emptied his revolver at them and fled into the arms of his alarmed platoon, who killed some and scattered the rest. A driver from one of the gunner regiments, out delivering rations, saw that a nearby Bren gun position which was below him but overlooking the observation post he was visiting, had just been overrun. Instead of tiptoeing away with the bad news, Driver Walker emerged from his cab with a Thompson, got close to the Japanese unobserved and then delivered a one-man surprise attack which drove away those who could still move. According to his unit's history of the campaign, he was 'immediately awarded' a Military Medal.

This business of immediately awarding medals, which took place within twenty-four hours, was done at the discretion of the man's commanding officer and circumvented the normal practice of post-action recommendations going up a long chain of command. It was done to keep up morale, an indication in a tight spot that displays of courage above and beyond the call of duty were valued. Such recognition of an individual's contribution, common to all western armies, was generally the opposite to the Japanese approach. Their way was to celebrate the nobility of subjugating self to team effort with unit citations which, even in the British Army with its regimental ethos, would have been unlikely to meet most westerners' craving for personal recognition.

Two other of these immediate awards give a good indication of how mixed up the fighting became at Kampar, mostly because of the Japanese infantry's relentless attempts to infiltrate and get around the British flanks. A troop sergeant-major in an outlying observation post connected by field telephone to the main one was awarded a Distinguished Conduct Medal for the way he coolly continued to call in fire to create a wall of fire around him after he was cut off. After the attack had subsided, Troop Sergeant-Major Hugill was making his way back to the main observation post when, in the words of an unpublished regimental history, he 'stumbled across' some Japanese who were as isolated as he had so recently been, and almost as dangerous, having just captured a Vickers-Berthier machine-gun. Hugill responded by 'collecting five or six infantry' and leading a bayonet charge which recaptured the position.

The troop sergeant-major was a regular soldier. Lieutenant Newland of the Leicesters was an emergency commissioned officer who had never been to England, having been born and brought up in Shanghai and Tientsin in China, where his parents were missionaries. Trained under the British instructors of the Shanghai Volunteer Corps, he was one of sixteen considered suitable officer material who came to Singapore to attend the Officer Cadet Training Unit set up to try and make up for the War Office's reluctance to send subaltern reinforcements to a non-war zone.

It is not hard to imagine the initial suspicion with which the products of such pressure-cooker establishments were greeted when they arrived at their regular battalions. Perhaps it made them try even harder. Newland won a Military Cross and his regular platoon sergeant, Euan McDonald, a Distinguished Conduct Medal, for the stubborn way in which they clung onto the British Battalion's most forward position, while attacks and counter-attacks swirled back and forth around them and they were often cut off. Percival singled out Newland and his thirty or so men for special praise for the crucial role they played in holding Kampar. Perhaps he saw something of himself in a young officer who had not chosen a military career (Newland had been working on the production side of the *Peking and Tientsin Times* when he joined up) but so obviously had all the makings of a fighting soldier. Under mortar and machine-gun fire they had stood fast as the Japanese eddied around them, slowly tightening the perimeter of their prickly little bastion as casualties mounted and McDonald had crawled out under fire to give water to a dying man.

Eventually, the Japanese had succeeded in seizing part of some high ground known as Thompson's Ridge. Morrison felt the British Battalion needed a rest before it mounted any more counter-attacks. A company made up of two platoons of Sikhs and one of Gujars, who are mainly Hindus, was given the job, part of another makeshift battalion built from the detritus of Gurun and Jitra. Its commander was a twenty-one-year-old named Charles Lamb, who held the lowest commissioned rank of second lieutenant; this was another indication of casualties, for a company was usually commanded by at least a captain and very often a major. Because of this, Captain John Graham, the battalion's second-in-command, decided to lead the attack himself. Towards dusk, a double dram of rum was issued and, as they sipped, Graham reminded them that, though few would witness what they were about to do, their own honour and that of the regiment were at stake.

Shortly afterwards, having approached their objective using every scrap of available cover, Graham's sixty or so men got to their feet and, screaming their old war cries, followed his charge towards the Japanese with 17-inch bayonets fixed. Young Lamb and several others went down in the first rush, but Graham rallied the rest and pushed on until a small mortar bomb mangled his legs below the knee. Even then he levered himself up off the ground, yelling his men on and, at least one account insists, was seen throwing grenades after he was hit. The only Japanese left on the position were those incapable of leaving it, but they had exacted a high price.

Thirty-four of the Indians died, including a viceroy commissioned officer. Lamb was killed outright. Graham, who would probably have been a double amputee had he survived, bled to death, though he lived long enough to learn they had won the day. Judging from the pep-talk he gave his men it seems obvious that he expected heavy casualties. Nobody was decorated for this epic charge though after the war there was talk in old Indian Army circles of getting Graham a posthumous Victoria Cross. But by that time most of the living witnesses were middle-aged farmers, lost among the mud-brick villages of the Punjab, their youthful valour as dusty as their land.

As it turned out courage, artillery and excellent fields of fire were not enough to hold Kampar. Yamashita had decided to outflank Percival's wonderful defensive position by hooking around it with a series of seaborne landings on the west coast. To do this he was utilizing some forty small craft that had been used in the Singora and Patani landings, then brought by rail to Alor Star. He also had the unexpected bonus of about twenty motor launches, junks and yachts Warren had overlooked in Penang. It was a bold gamble. Tsuji, despite his first-hand experience of the stubborn British defence at Kampar, was vehemently opposed, insisting that they were risking the very boats they would need for the assault on Singapore. So were several other senior staff officers at 25th Army HQ, who all thought that they should stick to land-based operations and not risk their first major setback at the hands of enemy naval and air forces whose remaining powers they grossly overestimated.

For the British, the destruction of the 'Perak Flotilla', the five Eureka patrol boats that Angus Rose and Warren had hoped to use for more raids on the enemy's ever-lengthening lines of communication, had been a major setback. The raids were to have been a subsidiary activity; the Eurekas were intended primarily for patrolling the coast to prevent exactly the kind of thing Yamashita was planning. Their fate had been another sharp reminder of the consequences of mounting almost any kind of naval operation without adequate air cover. The slow and bigger Insect-class gun-boats and tooled-up Yangtse River ferries based in Singapore, all ideal for inshore work against infiltrating small craft, would be even more vulnerable than the Eurekas.

Even so, the fears of Tsuji and the others were not entirely unfounded. One lucky destroyer that had somehow dodged the Nells and the Bettys would wolf down landing-craft like whitebait. But the Admiralty had lost their taste for risk. The cruisers *Durban* and *Exeter*, and the destroyers that had rescued the survivors from Phillips' battleships, were needed to shepherd convoys of reinforcements on the last leg of their voyage through the Indian Ocean and safely into Keppel harbour. And that was risk enough.

The Japanese objective was the Indian Ocean tin port of Telok Anson, which lies about 20 miles upstream from the broad, mangrove-fringed mouth of the Perak River, a good 30 miles south-east of embattled Kampar, and no more than 25 miles west of the main north–south road. If the Japanese could get astride that road, the bulk of Acting Major-General Paris's revived 11th Indian Division, which was doing so well in the defence of Kampar, would be cut off.

Yamashita had decided on a three-pronged attack. From the north, some of the fresh and newly committed Imperial Guards Division, who had just come down from Thailand, would get onto the River Perak and, in sampans and rafts, paddle downstream to the town. From the west his landing-craft, having come south along the coast, would enter the river from the other direction and go upstream to Telok Anson. The third prong would go up the River Bernam. This is the next major estuary to the south, some 15 miles from the Perak. When they reached the little fishing village of Ulan Melintang, they would disembark and head north towards Telok Anson along the 15 miles of good road that connected them.

Since they were considered part and parcel of the same operation, these landings, like the assault on Kampar itself, were handled by General Matsui's 5th Division. Matsui, influenced perhaps by the doubts cast on the operation by Tsuji and other 25th Army senior staff, was not all that enthusiastic, though the China war had given them far more experience of amphibious operations than the untested Imperial Guard. While the British continued to hold the line at Kampar, 1,500 of Matsui's men, crammed into landing-craft and barges towed by rustbucket coastal steamers acquired from the Thais, sailed up and down the coast, looking at their maps and trying to work out whether various gaps in its mangrove hedge were the estuaries they were supposed to sail down.

One party, a steamer with ten landing-craft in tow, went too far south and tried to enter the mouth of the Selangor River which was well defended by a Jat battalion supported by artillery, among them a Volunteer Force battery with European and Chinese gunners. Despite air support, the Japanese were beaten off and at least one landing-craft, possibly three, were sunk before they departed in a northerly direction. British casualties were one killed and one wounded. The Volunteer gunners, with their local knowledge, were certain that this convoy would now head for the Bernam River and begged to be allowed to go there immediately and have their 18-pounders set up and waiting for them. Permission was refused and the Japanese entered unopposed.

But in the Perak, a few miles to the north, Matsui's worst nightmare had come to pass when the Japanese came to grief on a natural obstacle. A tug and four landing-craft had run aground on a sand bar in the river mouth and it would be some time before the tide rescued them. A British boat patrol, probably three or four men in a sampan, soon reported their plight. The fate they anticipated for these sitting ducks is not hard to imagine. Nothing happened. Later Percival, with admirable restraint, could only say: 'Unfortunately neither the navy nor the air force were able to take advantage of this unique opportunity.'

The RAF did attempt to attack the stranded vessels. Three Blenheims could be spared for the job: one turned back to Singapore because of engine trouble and the other two were intercepted by a swarm of Zeros which shot down one and chased the other away. It must have been a grim moment for the army commander, a harsh reminder of just how ineffectual the other two services had become, and of how much of the burden he was expected to bear.

Despite the controversy the idea of seaborne hooks had engendered at Yamashita's HQ, they had hardly surprised the British who were dismally aware of how effective they were likely to be. Several days before the Kampar battle began, Paris had identified Telok Anson and Ulan Melintang as likely landing places to threaten his rear. His response was to have Stewart's 12th Brigade, who were recovering from their exertions of the last three weeks, about 12 miles south of Kampar, on standby to intervene. Meanwhile, he deployed as a trip wire some armoured cars from 3rd (Indian) Cavalry and part of 1st Independent Company which was about 70 per cent Indian and the rest UK British, among them some very hard cases from the Argylls, Leicesters and East Surreys. About 250-strong, they had been equipped with extra Thompsons and Brens and trained for commando-type raids; but they were much too busy plugging gaps and fighting rearguard actions ever to carry them out.*

Supported by armoured cars, including two of the Argylls' Lanchesters, for a while the Independent Company held the Japanese at bay in Telok Anson's narrow streets. At one point they inflicted heavy casualties by pretending to withdraw then rushing back with the armoured cars to surprise the Japanese while they were sorting themselves out in one of the main streets, almost as if they were about to set off on a peace-time route march. Then, as the enemy's numbers began to build up, and, no doubt, their thirst for revenge, they began to fall back onto 12th Brigade.

Stewart's orders were to delay rather than defend. After four days' hard fighting Paris was still holding the Kampar position and Kawamura was showing no sign of breaking through. But, haunted by the usual British fears that his main supply route would be cut off and his division wither away, Paris had received permission from Percival to withdraw to the next defensive line behind the Slim River. As far as the army commander was concerned, his priority remained preserving troops not territory, so that when the reinforcements arrived he would have enough men to counter-attack. 'With no reserves in hand we were still in a position of being unable to accept major losses.'

It was 12th Brigade's job to keep the back door tightly closed while Paris got the rest of the division away. The first of its troops the

---

* Raised about eight months before the invasion, in theory they were all volunteers, though some units probably ensured that persistent troublemakers were made aware of this challenging opportunity.

25. Japanese infantry dump their bicycles by some burned-out Chinese shops and, led by a sword-carrying officer, charge across a stretch of open ground in the northern Malayan state of Penang. In less than two months their bicycles will have carried them to the shores of Singapore

26. European women and children who have been evacuated from Penang Island arriving in Singapore. Governor Sir Shenton Thomas was horrified that the island's Asian community had been left to their fate

27. Almost bent double, some unfortunate Japanese infantry advance along a railway track to draw fire while their officer looks beyond them with his binoculars. If the British disclose their positions they will be fired on by the light machine-gun partially hidden in the long grass to the right of the track, slightly above the soldier

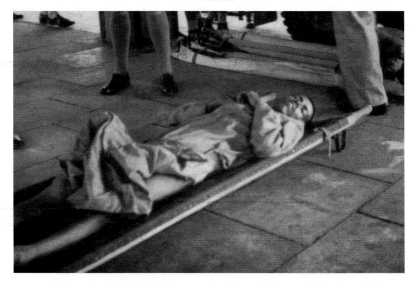

28. That rare thing – a Japanese prisoner. They were almost always wounded

29. Lieutenant-Colonel Ian Stewart (*centre*), the commander of the Argylls, advances purposefully through a mangrove swamp accompanied by (*right*) Sergeant-Major Munnoch and (*left*) Major Angus MacDonald who set up the tank block at Bukit Timah and was lost at sea when his ship was torpedoed

30. Sikh mountain gunners hidden in a rubber plantation about to clean the barrel of their gun

31. Argylls officers and NCOs at an 'Orders Group' in a rubber plantation. They were easily the best-trained British jungle fighters in Malaya

32. Argylls cooling their feet. Apart from jungle training, Lieutenant-Colonel Stewart was keen on route marches

33. Japanese troops storm the Kuala Lumpur railway goods yard that the British had just torched. However, among the undamaged booty were boxes full of detailed maps of Singapore printed by the government

34. Japanese infantry skirmishing with the British rearguard in Kuala Lumpur. The crouched figure in the foreground is carrying a light mortar

35. This was how close the Australian anti-tank gunners allowed the Japanese tanks to get to them on the Muar Bakri road. The 2-pounder gun in the picture was the rear one and it accounted for five tanks

36. A closer view of the jungle defile where the slaughter of the tanks took place. The persistence of the tank crews was typical of the courage displayed by most Japanese troops. The fallen rubber tree was brought down by a stray shell

37. No mercy was shown by the Australian infantry to the surviving crew members. None was expected

38. Helmeted Japanese infantry begin to spread out and advance through young rubber

39. A smoke break for some Australian Bren gunners waiting for the Japanese to turn up in a rubber estate. A spare barrel lies alongside their weapon

40. Lieutenant-Colonel Charles Anderson, the South African-born battalion commander and former big-game hunter, who won his Victoria Cross for the leadership he displayed fighting his Australians through the Japanese road-blocks from Bakri

41. Thick black smoke covers Singapore Island. This time from rubber ignited in an air attack on the godowns at Keppel harbour

Japanese met were the Argylls' A Company under Captain Bal Hendry, the rugby star who had beaten two of their number insensible with his helmet during the scrimmage at the railway station. They tried their familiar outflanking moves and Hendry pulled his company back in stages, blowing up small bridges and culverts and ambushing where they could.

Among their victims, part of a small patrol spotted cycling along a track in the dappled sunlight of a rubber estate, was a European who, according to Brigadier Stewart, was wearing 'khaki shorts and a grey uniform shirt and forage cap'. Early in the campaign a Punjabi sentry on a front-line river bridge already half demolished had shot dead a man whose clothes and manner suggested he might be a British planter until he got close enough to try to snatch the Indian's Thompson. By the beginning of 1942 there had been several such incidents. Hendry's Argylls had no doubt that their dead cyclist in his grey shirt and forage cap was a German. Nor did Percival's headquarters. Shortly before hostilities started they had been warned by the British Legation in Bangkok that deserters from the French Foreign Legion's 5th Regiment in Vichy Indo-China were in town and in touch with the Nazi embassy. Presumably this windfall was offered to their Japanese allies who instantly grasped the awful surprises a friendly northern European face might help them spring.

It is mostly their failures, and their considerable displays of nerve, that seem to be remembered. Certainly Percival was impressed by the 'pluck' demonstrated by the anonymous German who single-handedly tried to disarm a sentry and seize a bridge. There was some indication of more long-term planning. During the opening rounds of the conflict the Argylls shot and recovered the body of another European accompanying Japanese troops. Local police identified the corpse as that of a German political refugee, presumed to be Jewish, who had been working as a mining engineer in the district but had disappeared two weeks before the Asian war began.

Company by company, one covering while the other pulled back, the Argylls gradually withdrew towards the main trunk road to the east of them. It was open tin-mining country and ideal for artillery ambushes on troops who, the British observed, 'often failed to take the most elementary precautions'. Dog-tired as they were after three weeks of almost continuous fighting with the minimum of sleep, Stewart's brigade once again demonstrated the cruel sting in its tail. Its Indian troops fought just as well as his beloved Argylls. A fighting patrol of Deakin's 5/2 Punjabis under a jemadar, a viceroy commissioned rank equivalent to lieutenant and usually an old soldier, made a particularly devastating ambush. Hidden in roadside rubber they allowed the Japanese to get so close they could smell on their breath the tinned fish they had just consumed. Then the jemadar squeezed off the first shot and the slaughter began.

The enemy wreaked a certain amount of revenge by trying to clear the way ahead with air attacks, making it hazardous for vehicles to use the roads in daylight. Stewart estimates that they caused half the casualties among his brigade's ninety killed and wounded. Among the latter was the Argylls' Bal Hendry, who was evacuated to Singapore's Alexandra Hospital with bad head and shoulder injuries after being machine-gunned by a low-flying aircraft.

Ninety casualties out of the brigade's ration strength of at least 4,000, including support arms, was extremely light and Stewart was pleased by the way things had gone: 'It had been an eminently successful battle.' Yet the brigadier's satisfaction is revealing. It had not really been a battle at all but a series of sharp skirmishes leading to an end the British had decided on before the fighting began: delay and inflict casualties where possible but finally withdraw intact. Ultimately, good as it was, there had been no thought of preserving the excellent Kampar position by reinforcing Telok Anson with, say, one of the Australian brigades in Johore or perhaps a couple of the idle garrison battalions in Singapore whose colonels were itching to get into the field. As far as Percival was concerned it was too risky. If he concentrated his forces at Kampar, Yamashita might strike elsewhere and he could end up losing a division or more. Nothing was more important than preserving his army until reinforcements arrived and then he would counter-attack.

And so, shielded by Stewart's brigade, what many of the successful defenders of Kampar saw as yet another inexplicable withdrawal began. This time they were pulling back a good 30 miles to what was known as the Slim River position, though a large part of the 11th Division was north of that stream. It was not as good as Kampar in that it did not have the high ground with open plain below on which an artillery spotter could pour death and destruction. But it was a place where the road and rail exits south were through exceptionally thick jungle, so thick that there were few north–south tracks through it.

Arrogant and vain though he was, Colonel Tsuji was not usually loath to admit that he had acted in error. Indeed, if he suspected that some misjudgement had resulted in his having Japanese blood on his hands these confessions often seem to have been delivered in an ecstasy of self-flagellation. Yet somehow he could not bring himself to acknowledge that the breakthrough at Kampar had been brought about by Yamashita sticking to his guns and delivering the outflanking hook by sea. Instead, he preferred to believe it had been achieved mainly by the Ando Detachment who, after a twenty-four-hour jungle trek requiring god-like powers of endurance, emerged from the last chest-deep swamp studded with blood-sucking leeches to shower the enemy's amazed artillery crews with grenades.

When in doubt, the Japanese always tried to outflank, but whoever they were throwing their grenades at it was not the British gunners. 'The "getaway" was uneventful, except for the usual succession of traffic jams, once the forward area had been left behind,' notes the anonymous narrator in the unpublished account of the adventures of 88th Field Regiment in Malaya. On the right flank of the Kampar position, the Lanarkshire Yeomanry also disengaged successfully, disappointed to find themselves heading south again when they thought everybody was doing so well.

On the east coast, the British were not being allowed to escape so easily. Percival had clung on to the airfield at Kuantan from which, almost three weeks before, a disgusted Flight Lieutenant Bulcock had watched the panic-stricken departure of his fellow Australians. It was all part of the general's plan to deny the Japanese the abandoned RAF airfields of the peninsula for as long as possible, not so the British could use them again – they did not have the aircraft – but in order to reduce the air strikes the enemy could make against ships coming into Singapore with reinforcements.

Now, the first of these convoys was about twenty-four hours' sailing time from Keppel harbour. It had come from Bombay and most of its passengers were a brigade of newly raised Indian infantry who had expected to go to Iraq to finish their training. But Percival would only be a brigade stronger if he could extricate Brigadier George Painter's 22nd Indian Brigade, which held Kuantan and its airfield 9 miles to the east of the port. Painter's brigade was now badly needed on the west coast, where it was obvious that the main Japanese thrust was coming. It was also, to use the phrase of the day, 'battle inoculated'. The half-trained, unblooded new arrivals (the 45th under Brigadier Horatio Duncan) would hardly be a fair exchange if they were lost.

Commanding Painter's rearguard at Kuantan airfield was Lieutenant-Colonel Arthur Cumming who had last been in action during the Kota Baharu landings when his battalion, the 2nd Sikhs, had been loaned to Billy Key and done well for him there. At Kuantan, which is roughly half-way between Kota Baharu and Singapore, they were facing the same enemy: the 18th Division's Takumi Detachment, under the major-general of that name, who was anxious to prove that it was worthy of the unit citation it had earned there.

Since that award, there had been a lot of backbiting and the gossip had gone all the way back to Saigon and Tokyo. Takumi would never have got it, alleged his critics, had he not covered up the shameful business of the engineers running away in their boats because they could not take the British bombing. But this time, by coming down the coast in small craft, they had covered the 160 miles between Kota Baharu and the outskirts of Kuantan and hardly glimpsed the RAF. The only aircraft they ever seemed to see were their own; the only white faces the few British officers among these Indian infantry they were using to defend their colony, who sometimes fought surprisingly well but more often did not.

Cumming had already lost the best part of his A Company, which had been detached from him and sent to reinforce the Royal Garhwal Rifles, alpine herdsmen from India's Himalayan borderlands with Tibet and Nepal, who carried the same curved kukri fighting knife as the Gurkhas. The company had been among about 500 men left stranded on the north bank of the Kuantan River after Painter had been obliged to burn the old wooden winch ferry there once his transport and artillery were safely over: not much of a reward for the men who had bought the time for this to happen. It was hoped that some might get away along the coast. (A few did.)

The destruction of the ferry had not made that much difference to Takumi's infantry, who had soon discovered that the river was easily fordable upstream and were now setting up ambush parties along the start of the brigade's only escape route. This was the highway that went from coast to coast starting at Kuantan on the South China Sea and then, via the foothills town of Jerantut, switchbacking over the peninsula's mountain spine before dropping down to Kuala Lumpur and Port Swettenham on the Indian Ocean. It was central Malaya's only lateral road. Otherwise, in the absence of an east coast highway until Endau, 90 miles north of Singapore, the only solution would have been to persuade the navy to pick them up, which was no solution at all. Even if the Japanese air force failed to sink them (unlikely) they would have had to abandon most of their heavy equipment.

Kuantan airfield almost bordered the highway and had been an obvious place for Brigadier Painter to establish his headquarters. When Painter had ordered his brigade HQ to pack up and headed the withdrawal west, Cumming had moved in, settling his own HQ company around the slit trenches that had once been the property of the Brigade Signals Exchange. Two of his three remaining rifle companies were also deployed on the airfield. The third, D Company under the American 'Pom' Pomeroy, was stationed at the most obvious choke point along the escape route. This was some 6 miles west of the airfield, where the highway narrowed into a gorge, a 'defile' in Indian

Army speak,★ and it would obviously be disastrous if the enemy took control of it. Cumming was confident that Pomeroy would not move until the rest of the battalion had joined them.

Most of Painter's brigade had already passed through Pomeroy's position, often having run the gauntlet of ambushes and hastily set up road-blocks. First came the 4.5 howitzers of 5th Field Regiment, which had made the appropriate calculations and inflicted a wicked artillery ambush as the Japanese entered Kuantan port itself; then brigade head-quarters with their wounded and all the glass broken in their shot-up shooting brakes. They were followed by what was left of the Garhwalis and John Parkin's almost intact 5/11 Sikhs. Parkin, diminutive and full of grit, often wore a Sikh turban, though whether this was to add a few inches to his height or as camouflage against snipers seeking out British officers, nobody dared to ask.

Having covered their escape, Cumming's task was to get his men heading in the same direction before they were overwhelmed. His 2nd Sikhs were spread all over the airfield and involved in several separate moonlit fights with the Japanese, who in places had used blankets to scale the barbed-wire apron fence that ran around the airfield's per-imeter. Now they were running amok, firing their rifles in the air, lobbing chains of firecrackers with their mortars, torching the aban-doned RAF quarters and generally behaving as if the Indians could be persuaded to scatter like startled pigeons. It had, after all, worked with the battalion of Hyderabad State Forces at Kota Baharu who shot their colonel and fled.

But Cumming's battalion were an entirely different proposition. They quickly set up all-round defensive positions and let the enemy surge around them, their gratitude for the target opportunities appar-ently overriding any immediate concerns about being cut off. Tsuji refers to the airfield as being 'obstinately defended'. One reason for this was that someone had made the sensible decision that the best way of transporting the brigade's grenade supply was to issue every man with six instead of the normal two. Grenades are a very practical way of fighting in the dark and can be delivered unobtrusively. A jemadar was observed to roll two of them like bowls into the close confines of an abandoned slit trench into which several of the enemy had dropped.

★ As in Kipling's 'Arithmetic on the Frontier': 'A scrimmage in a border station, a canter down some dark defile'.

One of the main pockets of resistance came from the forty or so clerks, signallers and runners from battalion HQ who had occupied the old Signals Exchange trenches. During one lull they counted all the dead Japanese who had fallen around them and got up to forty-two.

Cumming with his orderly and signals havildar went off to investigate his southern flank where, beyond the barbed wire, a grove of coconut trees lay between him and the main road. A few minutes later they were joined by Captain Ian Grimwood, the adjutant who was an emergency commissioned officer lately of Peterhouse College, Cambridge. It was a scene of incongruous beauty: feathery coconut palms caught in tropical moonlight with only the barbed wire in the foreground, festooned with coconut windfalls, to remind them of the wicked ways of the world. Then they realized that the windfalls were the heads of Japanese soldiers climbing the wire. Soon their bodies were clearly silhouetted by the rising moon. The two officers stepped a few paces forward, their hands going to their holsters.

Both were armed with the world's largest calibre service revolver, the 1894 pattern .455 Webley originally adopted because it fired the same cartridge as the empire-winning Martini-Henry carbine. Since the mid-1930s, the British Army had been phasing it out and most officers and other ranks issued with pistols were delighted to carry the smaller and lighter .38 revolvers. But the Indian Army was always a Cinderella when it came to new kit and weapons. Besides, there was a lingering affection for the .455 among Cumming's generation (he was born in Karachi in 1896 and followed his father into the Indian Army) who swore by the stopping power of its big bullets.

It is not clear how many, if any, of the Japanese were shot on the wire. It seems to have taken Cumming and his companions a few seconds to comprehend what was happening for in that time, according to Grimwood, they were rushed by seven Japanese with bayonets fixed who managed to knock them to the ground. Only after they had gone down did they start shooting, the colonel faster and perhaps more accurately than the younger man. When they had finished six of the Japanese were dead or dying and Cumming was momentarily stunned by his fourth and last victim who had dropped on top of him and knocked him cold with his steel helmet. He was also bleeding badly from two bayonet wounds in the stomach but, though he lacked the protective flab of many forty-five-year-olds, these would turn out to be less serious than they looked.

Grimwood staggered to his feet, reloaded his revolver and was shooting at some more intruders when reinforcements arrived at the scene from battalion HQ. Badly outnumbered on this sector, the surviving Japanese melted into the night. At first it was feared that they might have taken Cumming with them. Then the signals havildar spotted the wiry frame of his colonel trying to crawl out from beneath a small pile of Japanese corpses and dragged him clear.

This was only the beginning of an extraordinary night for Cumming. Taken back to battalion HQ, where a field dressing was put on his bayonet wounds, he began to inspire his men like a man possessed, though at times he was obviously in some pain. When the Japanese renewed their attack on the HQ position and its defenders started to run low on ammunition, Cumming remembered there were five boxes of .303 in his Bren gun carrier and, accompanied by his driver, Sepoy Albel Singh, went and collected them. As they backed the carrier up to a trench and started to unload they were spotted and charged by a few brave men who obviously realized how important the boxes were. But they were bunched together in the way infantry are taught never to bunch, probably because in the heat of battle it is the most natural thing in the world. Singh passed Cumming a Thompson, a weapon he had not used before but sub-machine-guns, like grenades, were ideal at night at close quarters. None of the Japanese got anywhere near the pair. Shortly afterwards he again used the Thompson to good effect when he and Singh got their carrier behind an *attap* house with a raised first floor from which some of Takumi's men were providing covering fire on the HQ slit trenches.

By now Cumming knew that he had to get his battalion out before their escape route was blocked, but there was a problem with communicating with all the isolated outposts around the airfield: in a couple of cases field telephone lines had been cut. So he and Albel Singh set off in the carrier again, touring the airfield perimeter, picking up wounded and telling people it was time to get out and head west while Pomeroy's company was still holding the pass. Here the details start to get a little blurred, but in the course of these perambulations Cumming was wounded at least twice more, probably by a grenade or light mortar bomb while he was standing outside the carrier which had a rabbit-wire screen strung across its open top to prevent grenades falling inside. Whatever it was, it was enough to make the colonel briefly pass out.

When he came round, Cumming was back in the carrier sitting beside Albel Singh and they were parked at the entrance of a cutting leading from the airfield to the main road. Singh told him that they now had four wounded men in the back of the carrier and were facing a Japanese road-block. Cumming looked and saw that immediately ahead of them their way was blocked by a felled tree leaning at an angle from the bank. He also saw that there was just about enough room for the carrier to squeeze under it and ordered Singh to charge.

As they neared the tree the rabbit wire did its job and the grenades that came their way bounced back towards their unseen throwers. Then a mine it had detonated put the carrier briefly into the air and they came down with a bone-shaking thump. Most likely it was a small anti-personnel mine, for the tracks were still taking them forward though now they were subject to increasingly accurate machine-gun and rifle fire. Cumming was hit again and this time an arm was shattered; at least one of the men in the back also received another wound. Then Albel Singh, who until now had led a charmed life, was hit by a .256 armour-piercing bullet designed to be fired from the normal Arisaka rifle. Made of hardened steel with a brass coating, it easily penetrated the thinly armoured Bren gun carriers or armoured cars. Seated behind the wheel, Singh was neatly drilled through both thighs. Somehow, he not only kept control but continued to coax a top speed of 30 mph out of his battered machine as they were swallowed up by the welcoming darkness and the fire behind them gradually receded. Shortly afterwards, the sight of another Bren gun carrier and an armoured car persuaded Singh that his charge was over.

Pomeroy had left one platoon at the pass he was watching and, supported by the armoured car, brought two forward to see if they could be of any assistance. The other carrier had carried the adjutant Grimwood, Cumming's younger partner in the revolver play at the barbed-wire fence, away from the chaos at the airfield. Even by moonlight the appearance of Albel Singh's vehicle, holed and dented and sticky with the blood of all six occupants, must have been a chilling sight.

Yet perhaps for Pomeroy it was also oddly comforting. For this appeared to be all that was left of the rearguard, the last ones through before the door slammed shut. If this was true, it certainly made more palatable the orders he had just received by dispatch rider from Brigadier Painter. He was to withdraw immediately: not just return to the defile but well beyond it to the town of Gamang. Once the Japanese had seized the pass, and they were rarely slow in seizing their opportunities, any 2nd Sikhs still bobbing to the surface from Kuantan airfield would only get through if they left the road for an exhausting jungle detour. This would almost certainly mean abandoning any wounded among them.

Albel Singh was extracted, as gently as could be managed, from the driving seat and Grimwood drove them all up to brigade HQ, where a casualty clearing station and morphia awaited these long-suffering wounded. By this time Cumming, who would receive the Victoria Cross for the heroism he displayed at Kuantan, was lapsing in and out of consciousness again and was in no condition to argue with Painter over whether Pomeroy should be pulled back or not. Even if he had, it is unlikely that it would have made any difference. The brigadier had made his decision under strong pressure from both Heath and Percival that, while he was to deny the Japanese the airfield, he was to do so 'subject to the brigade commander's responsibility for not jeopardizing his force'.

Having held the airfield long enough to allow the convoy in, Painter was doing his best to comply with the second part of his orders, but it was no more possible to make this particular omelette without breaking eggs than any other. Holding Kuantan airfield until the convoy was offshore cost most of one of the best Indian battalions in Malaya. 'It was a tragic error,' declared the regimental history of the Frontier Force Regiment, long after the event. But Painter, like all British commanders in the field, was obsessed with the idea that the Japanese would outflank him: better to lose half a battalion than an entire brigade.

At least 200 of the 2nd Sikhs were missing. Having inflicted heavy casualties on Takumi's reckless infantry, whose officers were determined to make them live up to their Kota Baharu citation, what remained of the British rearguard appeared to withdraw in good order. The first to reach the defile with some 120 men under him was Subadar-Major Rai Singh, who had organized the defence of the brigade signals trenches after Cumming had gone to tell the other positions to pull out. A voice hailed his scouts in English and, no doubt with some relief, they stepped out of the shadows to be mown down by the men behind this linguist. Rai Singh managed to get the survivors away, divided them into three groups under himself and two subadars and they set out to find a jungle route to British lines. The Japanese seem to have learned their lesson from this, for the next party to approach the ambush site were permitted to get well into the gorge and few survived what awaited them there.

Regimental loyalties were as strong, perhaps stronger, in good Indian units as they were among their UK British equivalents: it was the regiment and not King and Country that they fought for. One of the 2nd Sikhs' British officers managed to persuade brigade HQ to allow him to take a small party, including one of their buglers, as far east along the main highway as they dared in the hope that they could rally some of their stragglers. Eventually they reached a demolished bridge about 6 miles from their forward positions and, every few minutes, the bugler sounded the high-pitched notes of the regimental call. The only response, however, was indignant birdsong and the drone of distant aircraft.

Next day they repeated the exercise and Subadar Mehr Khan, a Pathan officer, and about forty men turned up. They were one of the three groups Subadar-Major Rai Singh had divided his party into after they had fallen for the English-speaking Japanese. Utterly exhausted, some of them had wanted to give up, but when they heard the bugle call, faint at first and hardly recognizable, it had given them fresh heart. It was expected that Rai Singh himself, who would be awarded the Military Cross for the part he had played in defending the airfield, would shortly turn up, but he was captured along with the rest of his party.

The 2nd Sikhs had been almost 700-strong when hostilities started. Now their ration strength was down to 220 and their commanding officer, along with several of his men, was in a hospital train bound for Singapore. Under the major who had taken over from Cumming they were given forty-eight hours to rest and sort themselves out at The Gap, a hill resort where clipped yew hedges and beds of zinnias defended the weekend cottages of the increasingly uneasy British civilians in Kuala Lumpur some 7,000 feet below. Their unease was entirely understandable. Yamashita had just smashed through the British defences on the Slim River and was heading their way.

As he stared into his alfresco shaving mirror, artfully arranged to avoid providing their aerial tormentors with a giveaway flash, Captain James Wilson-Stephens became aware of something in the glass that was rather more pressing than his freshly lathered cheek. First one, then two, then three. He turned, razor in hand, and counted no less than six Japanese tanks advancing resolutely towards the headquarters of Ray Selby's all-Gurkha 28th Brigade as if it was the most natural thing in the world to be almost 10 miles behind the British front line at eight o'clock in the morning. Then the shooting started.

The Japanese victory at Slim River was pure blitzkrieg and had precious little to do with jungle fighting. The jungle was where the losers went, usually to waste away of starvation and fever until, if they were lucky, they were captured. At Kampar it had been at best difficult and mostly impossible to use tanks. At Slim, Yamashita's armour, with a full supporting cast of engineers, infantry, aircraft and artillery, won him the day, although for one chaotic hour it had been a close run thing.

The river lies about 50 miles north of Kuala Lumpur. Its source is somewhere beyond the mountain resort of Fraser's Hill, from where it meanders westwards to the coast and its estuary at the little port of Melintang. It is a good anti-tank obstacle, for its brown waters are rarely less than 200 yards across, often more, but the British did not have enough troops to picket its length. This being the case, they decided that the next delaying action would have to be fought at a bottleneck almost 9 miles north of the Slim.

Even in daylight it was a gloomy place. It started with the north–south metalled trunk road and the railway running about 400 yards apart through a 4-mile tunnel of exceptionally thick jungle that really was impenetrable unless you had the machinery and labour to clear it and keep it cleared. Over the last 5 miles to the river, starting at the village of Trolak, this forbidding green wall gave way to rubber estates which had been accommodated by hacking back the extravagantly knitted forest for a mile or more. These places were marginally lighter, though not much. At the river there was a rail bridge, but the road followed the Slim's easterly upstream course for another 6 miles along its northern bank before it came to its own crossing. Ten miles south of this bridge lay the market town of Tanjong Malim where, after his success at Kampar, Acting Major-General Archie Paris had established the latest headquarters of 11th Indian Division.

Originally Paris had expected to hold the bottleneck north of Slim with all three of his brigades. But Heath had felt it necessary to deprive him of Moorhead's 6/15th, 'the heroes of Kampar', and moved them to a coastal position 50 miles to the south in case Japanese landings threatened Kuala Lumpur. This left Paris with Stewart's 12th and Selby's 28th brigades: he put Stewart's battalions up front in the green tunnel that was the narrowest part of the bottleneck and Selby's Gurkhas straddling the road and railway on the northern bank of the river just before the railway bridge, which was prepared for demolition.

Stewart had deployed his three battalions 'in depth', that is, on a narrow front with one battalion behind the other. First came the 4/19 Hyderabads, under the temporary command of a major because their commanding officer, Lieutenant-Colonel Wilson Haffenden, had been wounded in an air attack within hours of them taking up their position. Haffenden was one of a steady trickle of casualties from almost incessant daytime harassment by fighters and light bombers who knew that the British were concentrated on this short stretch of road and could attack them almost with impunity. Apart from shoulder-held Brens, there was little in the way of anti-aircraft guns. Only the Slim road bridge, whose destruction would strand all the division's transport the wrong side of the river, was protected by a battery of four quick-firing Bofors served by volunteers, including some Chinese, of the Hong Kong and Singapore Royal Artillery.

The Hyderabads' role as the lead battalion was to act as a trip wire, alerting the rest of the brigade to any full-scale attack and delaying it for as long as possible. Attached to them was a gunner forward observation team who could call up eight 25-pound shells at a time from a battery set up some way behind the infantry. Stewart had another sixteen guns available from the same 137th Field Regiment, but he did not consider that the terrain offered much scope for artillery and, as he would later admit, it never occurred to him, given his paucity of anti-tank weapons, to use them in that role. Instead, the other two batteries were left under rubber in Selby's area where they could soon be safely south of the river once the scheduled withdrawal started on the night of 7–8 January. This was not very surprising. The 25-pounder was primarily intended to cover large areas with high explosive and shrapnel from a distance. It was hard to aim directly against a specific target over open sights, though it had on occasion been used with some effect against German tanks, particularly in the desert.

Once they judged the time was right the Hyderabads, accompanied by their artillery spotters, would fall back on the next battalion, Deakin's 5/2 Punjabis. Stewart described the Hyderabads' purpose as 'the usual one of gaining time by making the initial enemy blow strike either the air, or at least a situation which had radically changed'.

The Argylls were in the rear behind the Punjabis. Stewart had put them where the rubber started and the vegetation thinned enough for the Japanese to slide in one of their outflanking attacks. They were under their new commanding officer, Lieutenant-Colonel Lindsay Robertson, who had recently been based in Singapore on Duff Cooper's staff. Churchill had just recalled his Cabinet representative to the Far East on the grounds that Wavell's appointment as supreme commander-in-chief brought his mission to an end. This removed the last obstacle to Robertson rejoining his regiment in Malaya, the reason he had had himself attached to the Chancellor of the Duchy of Lancaster's overseas mission in the first place.

Robertson was back with the battalion he loved and, joy of joys, commanding it. When it had arrived in Malaya, before he was posted back to the UK and a tedious staff job, he had been second-in-command. Since then the Argylls had made a name for themselves, but Robertson did not seem to be burdened by any fears that the eccentric Laird of Achnacone, now his brigade commander, might be a hard act to follow. On the contrary, he let it be known that he felt standards of turnout had slipped and the Argylls had become a scruffy bunch during his unfortunate absence. The reaction of men who had just spent the last four weeks learning the hard way that it was more important to pack extra ammunition and food than 'neatly folded shirts' was entirely predictable. Perhaps this curious lack of empathy was no more than a touch of new brooming that would soon have been forgotten as Robertson settled into the job. His battalion nickname had always been 'Uncle' and he was by no means an unpopular officer.

Deakin's Punjabis, the battalion in the middle and immediately ahead of the Argylls, were what Stewart called 'the firm base' of his brigade's in-depth defence. Before the war, part of the road had been straightened and its bends made redundant by cutting through a series of small hills. Two of these cuttings, which were about a mile apart, were in the Punjabis' sector. Since the curves they had replaced, though overgrown, were still passable and could be used by wheeled transport and Bren gun carriers, it was decided to seal off the cuttings with concertina barbed wire and anti-tank mines.

They were also covered by two of the three anti-tank guns under Brigadier Stewart's command, the usual captured Italian Bredas in the hands of UK British gunners from the 80th Anti-Tank Regiment. The third one was further forward with the Hyderabads. Back at the river, Selby's brigade had another two. By this stage of the campaign there was a shortage of Boys anti-tank rifles which would stop the lighter Japanese tanks and at least immobilize the heavier ones by knocking the tracks off. Too heavy for even a strong man to carry for any length of time, they were almost invariably dumped when retreating troops were without transport.

One other anti-tank weapon was generally available to the 11th Indian Division's infantry. It was the Molotov cocktail, the petrol-bottle incendiary invented during the Spanish Civil War and named after Stalin's commissar for foreign affairs. Usually ignited by means of an oily rag stuffed down the neck, these seem to have been a copy of a War Office design for the Home Guard and were of safer manufacture. They were primed by a flat strip of phosphorus-impregnated wood, something like a lollipop stick, which was attached to the side of the bottle and lit by rubbing it with the emery side of a match box. When the bottle smashed against its target the petrol, with any luck, burst into flames. But though they made dramatic if brief blazes, it was difficult to set the interior of a closed-up tank alight with one unless the crew were unlucky enough to get some of the burning petrol into the engine vents.

A little less than twenty-four hours before it started Stewart received his first indication that they might be facing what sounded like the biggest armoured attack of the campaign to date. A Tamil labourer who had wandered through the front lines and been fortunate enough not to be shot out of hand by the British, increasingly the fate of all 'suspicious natives', was brought into brigade headquarters with a somewhat garbled story that he had seen no less than eighty tanks in a village close to the Hyderabads. Then his story began to fall apart when he indicated, probably through a Tamil-speaking rubber planter attached to Stewart's staff, that whatever it was he had seen had wheels.

Of course, tanks do have wheels: a very visible row of sprocket or bogie wheels between the tracks which make them go round. The Japanese Type 95 had six on either side. Judging by subsequent events it seems unlikely that their informant was shown a picture or a sketch of a Japanese tank. Instead, it was decided that trucks and tanks were probably all alike to this simple fellow and eighty did take a lot of believing.

No doubt everybody breathed a sigh of relief. Utterly exhausted by a constant round of moving, digging in, fighting and moving on, the morale in Stewart's two Indian battalions, which had both performed well up to now, was low enough already without any loose talk of mass tank attacks. They were bewildered by the unexplained withdrawals and the unopposed air attacks which meant they only dare work on their defences at night. Were they not serving the largest empire the world had ever seen? Then there were all the minor miseries: being constantly soaked in either sweat or rain; the mosquitoes which plagued them after dusk and were only displaced by the teeth-chattering chill that crept over the jungle before dawn; the absence of organized latrines in crowded overnight bivouac areas where it paid to tread carefully. Unslept, underfed, unwashed and unlaundered, many had had enough.

That morning the Hyderabads, with the help of a few well-aimed salvos laid on by their artillery observers, had repulsed an enemy probe down the railway line without loss to themselves. Sixty dead Japanese had been counted around the track. But, far from restoring their confidence, it had made them even more jittery. Deakin, the commander of the Punjabis who had won the DSO charging the intruders at the northern bridge with his Indian signallers, had warned Stewart that his men were now so tired that the only thing to do with them was to withdraw them from the front line altogether and give them the sleep, decent food and clean clothes they needed to restore their fighting spirit. Stewart thought he exaggerated and the men were in better heart than he imagined. Besides, there was no better position to make the kind of forty-eight-hour stand he had promised Paris. None the less, perhaps he did convey Deakin's misgivings to the divisional commander because Paris told Stewart he was sending reinforcements. Another battalion of infantry, the 5/14th Punjabis from divisional reserve, were coming to give added depth. Stewart decided he would put them behind the Argylls, just south of Trolak village.

The Argylls were just as tired and to date their casualties, about 250 killed, wounded and missing, about the same as the Indian battalions. But their morale was much better. This is not so surprising. They were, after all, the darlings of the brigade, their exploits celebrated by both the local press and Fleet Street. Beneath their cynicism and banter, most Argylls were proud to be Argylls. 'Like all regiments the Argylls had their rubbish for whom the ruthless pressure of the campaign had been too much,' observed Stewart. 'They were few, yet they set a still further strain on the morale of the good, but in spite of this morale held to the very end.'

There was no better proof of this than the reinforcements who, in the early hours of yet another rain-lashed night, turned up at the battalion's rear headquarters at Trolak village. There were about 100 in all of whom perhaps 30 had no choice, being a draft not long arrived from the UK, some of them conscripts and possibly from as far south as Manchester. The rest were almost all volunteers, including some who had discharged themselves from hospital after treatment for wounds or sickness. Among the latter was Platoon Sergeant-Major★ Jimmy Love, one of the NCOs cut off in the Grik Road fighting who, racked by fevers, had trekked 100 miles south in native costume before their unexpected encounter with Rose and his Australian raiders. But the majority were the men who had been steadily milked away from the Argylls over the last two years because of the demand for experienced regular soldiers who could act as instructors, military policemen, drivers or clerks at various headquarters. In Stewart's words they were 'the battalion's best men, those who had been snatched away from it'. Now, determined not to miss out on the excitement any longer, they had seized the opportunity to rejoin the battalion.

Some had been allowed to leave their cushy billets in various base headquarters by understanding superiors; others had not. Captain Drummond Hay, the officer who had delivered them from Singapore, confessed to Stewart that he had been 'expressly forbidden' to take some men with him only to find them parading with the others at

★ Platoon Sergeant-Major was a new rank introduced in the late 1930s when there was a shortage of junior officers to act as platoon commanders. Later in the war, when battlefield commissions were granted to men who had displayed leadership and courage regardless of class, the rank was phased out.

Tyersall barracks, refusing to take no for an answer. Deserting to the face of the enemy was a hard charge to press.

Drummond Hay himself was as determined to get back to the battalion as any of them. Small for an officer, and with the reputation of being a hard drinker, he was popular with the Jocks and long service in India had earned him the nickname 'Pudley', which was thought to be derived from the Urdu word for 'mad'. In Singapore he had been in charge of the officers' mess, paying particular attention to the bar. Stewart, the Episcopalian teetotaller, seemed inclined to leave him there, for 'Pudley' Hay had never been subjected to the rigours of jungle training, yet here he was demanding his place at the front. The Japanese attacked ninety minutes after he and his party had arrived.

Night tank attacks rarely happened in World War II – not in Russia where the biggest armoured battles took place, nor in the North African desert where even Rommel's innovative Panzer regiments generally drew the line at blundering about in the dark. The kind of night-vision equipment that would become standard by the latter part of the twentieth century did not exist. Once the hatches were down, it was often difficult enough to see clearly in daylight.

The Japanese tank commander was a Major Hajime Shimada. He did not have the eighty tanks the Tamil said he had counted. There were about thirty, mostly T95 mediums with perhaps ten of the two-man light tanks which carried nothing heavier than machine-guns, though they were much more tank-like than the British Bren gun carriers, being fully enclosed and better armoured. (Bren gun carriers only had armour plating at the front.) Accompanying them were truck-borne infantry, some of them in captured 'Churchill supplies' manufactured at Cowley in England.

Shimada had persuaded Colonel Ando, whose battle group was once again the Japanese vanguard, to allow his tanks to spearhead the infantry in the first wave of a night attack. Perhaps, after their exertions at Kampar, Ando felt it was time to try something different, and the British positions at Slim looked like another tough nut to crack. They had just taken over from the distinctly chastened Okabe regiment, the unit which had walked into the artillery ambush during their reconnaissance in force down the railway line.

Shimada must have known he was taking a big risk advancing on a front as narrow as a single road even if in places, with its well-maintained shoulders, it was broad enough for four of his T95 mediums to line up abreast. Some reports have it that the overgrown loops where the curves had been straightened were marked on Japanese maps, in some eyes more proof of fifth columnists and the detail of Japanese pre-war preparations. But they could easily have been discovered by a reconnaissance patrol that had inserted itself at night into the quarter-of-a-mile gap of thinner bush between the road and railway and then laid up to observe the British traffic.

By 3 a.m. on Wednesday 7 January it was raining heavily. Huddled in their fox holes either side of the jungle road cutting north of the village, the Hyderabads knew this sort of misery well. Most were trying, with varying success, to get some sleep under their gas capes while the sentries peered into the gloom. They saw little except for the darting glow of the fireflies and, though they always looked like the lamps of determined men who had lost their way, it had been some time since they had last shot at those. At dusk there had been an exchange of fire, but the subadars got them to stop because the Japanese were obviously trying to locate their positions. The first mortar bomb dropped through the rain at 3.30 a.m. and the first artillery shell shortly afterwards.

Fifteen minutes later Japanese infantry were about 300 yards away, down a slight incline from the Hyderabads' leading platoon and trying to dismantle an anti-tank barrier made up of a roll of concertina barbed wire and 40-gallon oil drums filled with concrete. It took the Japanese about fifteen minutes to deal with the barrier. During that time not a single artillery shell or mortar bomb was fired at them, possibly because field telephone lines had been cut.

At 4 a.m. the tanks, heard long before they were seen, came down the road, their machine-guns spitting yellow tracer in all directions, followed by truck loads of infantry. The Hyderabads' only attached anti-tank gun did not fire a single shot. Whether its crew, who were UK British, were dead or had fled is unclear. What is beyond dispute is that the Hyderabads made little attempt to delay the Japanese, and it is not hard to imagine the four-man crew of the anti-tank gun getting swept up in their flight. The pyrotechnics of the tracer ammunition fired at close range from the tanks' heavy machine-guns, probing the darkness with the stabbing yellow lines produced by the chemical at the base of each bullet, were particularly frightening for troops who, in Stewart's words, were not 'emotionally acclimatized'. It was all too easy for a man to imagine that every round was aimed at him, and retreat soon turned into rout.

Most of the Hyderabads fell back on the Punjabis and infected some of them with their panic. But it was here, at about 4.30 a.m., that the Japanese met their first serious resistance. Shimada's leading T95 went over one of the anti-tank mines in the first cutting, which at least blew a track off and possibly did worse. The tank behind it tried to edge round it, was hit by a Boys anti-tank rifle and also stopped. The Punjabis were also in possession of the high ground and banks on either side of the cutting so, until the Japanese infantry began to get to grips with them, they were in the wonderful position of looking down on the tanks. They began to drop Molotov cocktails on them and, before long, at least one appeared to be burning from inside.

Shimada's worst nightmare had just come true and now it was the turn of the Japanese to panic. His armoured column was strung out behind the cutting in a very vulnerable tailback. Any moment now the British were bound to bring their hellish artillery to bear and blow them all to pieces.

As was so often the case with the Japanese, their immediate reaction was to see if they could not frighten the enemy away by making a lot of noise. A kind of primeval bellowing sound ensued from engines being revved as if the drivers were afraid they might stall. Behind their armoured plate the air was a foul mixture of diesel fumes, sweat, urine and the cloying sweetness of cordite as a constant clatter of spent machine-gun cartridges fell around the crew's feet. Use was also made of a small mortar attached to the turret which fired grenade-sized bomblets. The mortars helped to keep the enemy at a distance but for the tanks stuck in the cutting itself their machine-guns were useless. The sides were too steep and in order to clear the edge they found themselves firing almost vertically into the night sky.

More Molotovs exploded around them in great searing flashes, dramatic enough though generally as redundant as the machine-gun fire. Some of the Indians also threw grenades. These were entirely ineffectual against closed armour, though by now some of the tank commanders had opened their hatches and were trying to yell orders above the din. Their tanks were not fitted with radios.

Slowly, with ears cocked for the whistle of incoming British artillery, order was restored. The tanks that could still move backed out of the cutting. Then they found their way into the overgrown loop road, their route helpfully illuminated by stray Molotovs which revealed the broken vegetation and other tracks left by British vehicles since the land mines were laid in the cutting.

Incredibly, Shimada had got away with it. He had cleared his traffic jam without a single shell being fired at it. A golden opportunity to turn his tanks into a charred scrap-heap had been missed because of a breakdown in communications between Deakin and the battery which was meant to be giving him support. The forward observation officers attached to the Hyderabads, who were supposed to have followed their field telephone cable back to Deakin's position winding it up as they went, had disappeared. Then the chance to get the gunners onto the trapped tanks through brigade HQ went when all wireless and field telephone communications were cut. Stewart's last instructions to Deakin were to 'hang on at all costs'.

They did their best. They held the second cutting until shortly after first light at about 6 a.m., though by then most of the tanks had moved on, leaving the mopping up to the infantry. Strangely, the fight there had been a repetition of the first one, as if the Japanese had learned nothing at all. Again the leading tank came to a halt when it detonated one of the mines. Again the Molotovs cracked open against Osaka Arsenal's best armour plate, burst into splendiferous flame and may have left one with more than its paintwork singed. The only difference was that the remaining two anti-tank guns allotted to 12th Brigade were also in the vicinity. They each fired two rounds and one of the tanks was certainly destroyed or at least badly damaged. Then for some reason the guns ceased firing and at least one of them, possibly both, pulled back.

It seems their crews were understandably unnerved by the sight of the growing number of sepoys who, as Ando's infantry closed in, had begun to head for the bush. At least one report suggests that the rot was started by some Hyderabads who had collected around the Punjabis. Long after most of the tanks had discovered the second of the overgrown bends, and pushed on towards the Argylls, a determined band of men led by Deakin himself held out against the Japanese infantry. But shortly after 7 a.m. all organized resistance had ended. Deakin, who was in a filthy temper over the conduct of the early departures, collected together a party of about thirty, mostly from his HQ company, and made for the Argylls' positions around the village of Trolak. They took a circuitous route through the rubber but,

by the time they got close, it was obvious that the Scots were no
longer there.

The Argylls had, to use Stewart's word for it, been 'filleted'. Shimada's
tanks had sliced them away from the road, their tactical backbone, and
left these juicy pickings in some disarray. It would get much worse.
Not since Butcher Cumberland drove Bonnie Prince Charlie's Highlanders into the heather at Culloden had Scots soldiers been driven so
far beyond the edge of their endurance as they were hunted down.

   The Argylls' sector, like those of the battalions in front of them,
straddled the road and railway. But theirs was larger, about 6 square
miles, and entirely in rubber where there were unpaved estate roads
and it was easier to move about. Their first indication of how badly
things had gone ahead of them was the arrival of panic-stricken and
mainly teenaged sepoys, some no longer bearing arms, who demonstrated scant desire to linger. Beattie, the battalion's padre, watched
Captain Kenneth McLeod trying to stop them. 'Turbaned soldiers
ducked around him and under his arms and he stood there like a traffic
officer to whom no one pays any attention.'

   It soon became plain that they were running away from a tank
attack. Road-blocks were hastily improvised, though an attempt to
incorporate one of the anti-tank guns that had been supporting the
Punjabis failed. The gun was under tow but this time McLeod –
'waving my arms like a dervish' – succeeded in flagging it down. He
told the British driver to set the gun up around the corner behind him.
'I heard his engine revving up and continuing to rev up, and he
disappeared without stopping!'

   It was hoped that the road-blocks would hold up the tanks long
enough to blow up the Trolak bridge, which had been prepared for
demolition, though the wires to the charges had been severed by
retreating traffic such as the disappearing anti-tank gun. A hunt was on
to find some sappers to repair them. The first four tanks, which had
left the Japanese infantry still trying to cope with Deakin and his
diehards, appeared at 5.30 a.m. when both sides could still use the
remaining half hour or so of darkness to their advantage.

   At the first road-block some big rubber trees, nearest the road and
therefore the estate's first plantings, had already been partially sawn
through ready to be dropped after the brigade's rearguard had passed
through. These were supposed to be the Hyderabads' Bren gun carriers.

Too late the Argylls realized that these carriers were rather bigger than they should be and Shimada's 15-ton T95s trundled on unimpeded.

Forewarned, the second block, some 300 yards down the road, did a bit better. There were two armoured cars here and besides machine-guns their armament included Boys anti-tank rifles. One of the tanks was set on fire externally by a Molotov, possibly after it had been immobilized by a hit on one of its tracks from the Boys. But it was a very unequal contest. Neither of the armoured cars could conceal their exact location long enough to dodge the shells from the cannon that was the tanks' main armament. Both were wrecked and abandoned with one crew member killed and most of the others wounded and badly shaken up. They must have known it could not have ended otherwise. Certainly, their behaviour was in stark contrast to the shameful conduct of the anti-tank gunners, whose presence might have made all the difference.

The Argylls were not quite finished. Before they were put out of action the armoured cars had fallen back to the southern end of the bridge. Captain Tim Turner, who was in charge of the battalion's armoured vehicles, placed himself and as many men who would join him behind one of the stricken cars and began to push. Although they were under heavy fire they succeeded in getting the heavy Lanchester back to the other end of the bridge and scampered back without casualties. It was a valiant effort but it delayed the T95s only for the few minutes it took for one of them to nudge this obstruction into the brown waters of the Trolak, a tributary of the Slim, and head south. As the sun rose to greet them, Ando's attack was hardly two hours old and no fishmonger could have better 'filleted' Stewart's brigade.

Yet compared to the Indian battalions, the Argylls were, for the moment, relatively unharmed, if neatly divided and quite unable to function as a battalion because of their loss of the trunk road, down which were coming more tanks, 'the Japs sitting on the top as if they were going away on their holidays'. To the east of this were battalion headquarters and two rifle companies, C and B, who soon became embroiled in repelling the expected outflanking infantry attack from the jungle. The reinforcements, none of whom had had a chance to be sent to their companies, joined in and for a while the attack was held, though Drummond Hay himself, who was shot in the back of the knee, was one of the first casualties. Then inevitably they were pressed by infantry coming from the road behind them and if they stayed to fight it out the result was a foregone conclusion. Since it was now impossible to move along the main road they burned all the transport they had hidden among the rubber and decided to get back to Selby's Gurkha brigade on the Slim River by walking east out of the rubber and making a jungle detour.

As the crow flies, the distance between them and the river was just over 5 miles. By the circuitous route Colonel Robertson was planning it was, at the very least, 25 miles. Robertson, radiating confidence as a good leader should, was fondly remembered by Sergeant 'Hoot' Gibson (a long-serving NCO who was about to experience some of the most bizarre and awful adventures of any of that battalion) examining a map while seated on a shooting stick planted in the middle of a jungle stream. It was raining and beside him stood his signals sergeant who, Jeeves-like, was trying to keep both the battalion commander and his map dry by holding a tin hat over his head.

The map was a rough guide to some of the most difficult, unsurveyed terrain in the world, where a hacked mile a day can feel like respectable progress, and Robertson, who held very strong views about surrender, was taking his wounded with them. As Brigadier Stewart reported:

The experiences of this party were similar to those of many others, slow and exhausting progress through the close and hilly country hampered by their wounded, too slow to get ahead of the Jap advance and onto the road again. Then breaking up into small parties to assist foraging as food supplies ran out.

Six weeks later, some of these Argylls, ragged, starving, legs ulcerated to the bone and full of fevers, would still be in the jungle.

West of the road, some of the other half of the battalion fared better. A Company, under Lieutenant Donald Napier, a descendant of the famous Victorian general Charles Napier, was astride the railway line and slightly further back than any of the other companies. Napier sprang a cruel ambush on a party of the enemy who left the cover of the rubber to take the fastest and most direct route to the Slim River rail bridge. Then, falling back in good order, they got to the bridge themselves at 6.30 p.m., shortly before it was blown. They numbered about ninety including two officers and were the only members of Percival's best infantry battalion to reach the Slim's south bank as a formed body.

For a while it seemed as if similar fortune would favour David Boyle's D Company, which came under the command of the Hyderabads' acting CO Major Brown when he fell back onto their position with his HQ company. This mixed force blew up a small bridge on one of the estate roads and an Argylls' armoured car killed the crew of one of the little Japanese two-man 'tankettes' by getting three Boys rounds inside it. Then some of the enemy got behind them and blocked their retreat to the river.

At first they refused to believe they had been cut off like this. Only fifteen minutes before Stewart and brigade HQ had been in the same area. Second Lieutenant Ian Primrose, a tall and powerful young man who had been a useful member of the battalion boxing team, volunteered to scout ahead and see whether it was a case of mistaken identity. It was agreed that if he did discover there were Japanese ahead he would signal their presence with two shots from his Thompson. Primrose, who liked to wear a battered Australian hat and was known in the Argylls for both his courage and a scruffiness unusual for an officer, set off with his Thompson set to 'single shot' in case he had to give the signal.

Well-positioned for an ambush, the Japanese were determined not to give their position away. When Primrose was close enough several of them jumped him but, before they clubbed him senseless, he managed to squeeze off his two warning shots into the belly of the officer who appeared to be his principal assailant.

A confused skirmish now ensued among the rubber during which the Hyderabads' Major Brown was killed. The Argyll armoured car which had knocked out the light tank broke through and got to the river but Boyle, who had now taken command, could not find a way through and eventually gathered together what was left of his company and headed for the river by making a wide westwards detour to where the rubber met the jungle. Like Robertson's party, they found the country too rough for them to overtake Ando's advance and eventually, exhausted by all the usual privations of jungle-bashing, most of them, if not glad to be captured, were indifferent to it.

Not that surrender was any guarantee of survival. Primrose regained consciousness to discover that the Japanese were dividing the Argyll and Hyderabadi wounded they had found around the rubber trees into those who could walk and those who said they could not. Primrose decided he could walk, which turned out to be an excellent choice for the Japanese disposed of the rest with, if they were lucky, a bullet to the head. The British walking wounded heard the shots and realized what was happening with mounting horror. Everybody had heard the stories about Japanese atrocities in China, but that was Asians dealing with Asians. They never expected this sort of thing to happen to them.

Afterwards, the surviving prisoners were made to dig graves for the newly murdered and then used to help carry the enemy's own wounded. To add to their misery they were, at first at least, walking south towards the British lines using the edge of the road the Japanese now owned. Primrose's burden was the Japanese officer he had twice shot and thereby saved his comrades from walking into an ambush. Before long he realized the man was dead but decided it would not be prudent to mention this and staggered on with the corpse in a fireman's lift across his broad back for the best part of a mile. Another Argyll, a private, was carrying a more lightly wounded officer who tipped him for his trouble with twenty cigarettes. It was the first of many examples over the years ahead of just how capricious their captors could be.

As they walked towards the Slim, the prisoners and their escorts were overtaken by tanks and trucks heading in the same direction. Shimada's T95s, having broken through the British crust, were now set to wreak havoc. They shot up everything they could see, often before their prey, who generally imagined they were well behind the front line, realized they were in any danger.

On the menu were targets that must surely have been beyond Major Shimada's wildest expectations. Oblivious to all that had occurred between their early breakfast and a dawn start, the extra battalion Stewart had been given, Lieutenant-Colonel Cyril Stokes' 5/14th Punjabis, was on its way to the positions it had been allotted just south of Trolak. Most of them were on foot, marching by companies with their lorries fore and aft. Some of these vehicles were carrying nothing but ammunition and heavy weapons, including their Boys anti-tank rifles and Molotovs. At the head of the column Stokes, who like most British battalion commanders was in early middle age, was travelling in the back of a car. Bringing up the rear of the convoy and under tow were all three of the anti-tank guns originally attached to Selby's 28th Brigade.

Approaching them was Shimada's lead troop of three tanks, paint-work blackened in places by flaming petrol. Commanding it was Second Lieutenant Sadanobu Watanabe, who was twenty-two years old, had just graduated from the Military Academy in Tokyo and was determined, dead or alive, to make a name for himself. Already that morning he had put to good use the sabre he insisted on wearing even in the cramped interior of his Type 95. Four times he had left the safety of his machine and, while his crew held their breath at his 'god-like acts', used it to sever the wires leading to the obvious demolition packages on the pillars of the small concrete bridges they were about to cross. On each occasion Watanabe had been covered by a platoon of truck-borne infantry under Second Lieutenant Morokuma, also newly commissioned and a classmate at the academy. This had not prevented Watanabe being wounded in the wrist, possibly by a grenade splinter, just as he was clambering down from his tank at bridge number four. Undaunted, he went ahead and cut the fuse wire anyway. As it happened, there was little danger of the British blowing up these crossings beneath their feet; they were scheduled to be destroyed the following day once Stewart's 12th Brigade had withdrawn over them. Nobody, including Stewart, realized that they had lost the road, least of all Stokes' Punjabis, grateful for the cool of early morning and anxious to get to their new position before the Japanese air force spotted them.

It was a massacre. Colonel Stokes was mortally wounded after Watanabe used his 37 mm cannon to destroy his car and then fell, both machine-guns blazing, onto the marching infantry and their transport. The first two companies, about 250 men, were virtually wiped out. (Later it was discovered that one had just twenty unwounded survivors.) The other two had time to scatter into the edge of the rubber and were in the process of re-forming there when a second troop of tanks came along and began scything them down.

Meanwhile, beyond the dead and the dying and the burning trucks where crates of Molotovs exploded with dull whoomphs and thousands of rounds of .303 were beginning to crackle off, Lieutenant Watanabe was dealing with the anti-tank artillery. Two were finished before their crews had time even to start to set them up. But at the end of the column, the four men on the third Breda gun came close to winning their frantic race to unlimber and manhandle it around to face the enemy. As in most duels, there were no second prizes.

Unaware that he had just disposed of the last remaining anti-tank guns between themselves and the Slim River, and expecting resistance to stiffen at any moment, Watanabe pressed on, falling on the enemy's nether parts with all the relish that is the traditional culmination of the successful cavalry charge. By 8.30 a.m. they were well within the area of the Gurkha brigade, magically appearing in the shaving mirror of Wilson-Stephens, who was acting as Selby's brigade major, before shooting up every tent and vehicle they could see in the headquarters area. A signals truck was set on fire and a Sikh officer mortally wounded. The survivors scattered into the rubber.

The Gurkhas had very few anti-tank rifles left. The T95s turned up just as Captain Tom Mooney, a regular officer, was crossing the road. Instead of running for cover, Mooney drew his .455 revolver, stood his ground and fired at them until he was killed. This brave and pointless sacrifice has never been explained.

Certainly, Mooney's revolver about summed up the plight of the defences at Selby's HQ. This was on a slight rise in a rubber plantation, which the signallers hoped might improve wireless reception. The only weapons they possessed that were remotely effective against tanks were a few mortars and then only if the targets obligingly remained stationary. Luckily for them, it was impossible for the T95s to penetrate the trees and overrun them. Nor had Watanabe much time for diversions, however satisfying they might be. His main objective was the Slim road bridge. Capture that and the best part of a British division would be bottled up and those parts that had not fled into the jungle could be dealt with at leisure.

The tanks moved on, following the bend in the river east along the river's north bank towards the road bridge. To their left was the Cluny rubber estate; to their right a thin screen of rubber trees, then the river and swamp and jungle. Watanabe, a bloody bandage on his right wrist, had his hatch up as did the other tank commanders. They could hear the river rushing by below them in full monsoon spate and, through the odd gap in the trees, sometimes caught a glimpse of its swirling brown waters. Then, for the second time that morning, Watanabe had a marching infantry battalion at his mercy. This time the surprise was even more complete for they attacked from behind.

Jack Fulton's 2/1st Gurkhas had been reconstructed since Asun, where many of his teenaged soldiers had removed their boots and bolted. Over the last three weeks, reinforcements from India, the transfer of a few much-needed junior leaders from other Gurkha units, and the return of the more enterprising stragglers after long jungle treks, had brought its ration strength back to about 500. This was enough to enable the 2/1st to function as a battalion again and they had been given a quiet sector. They were going to take up a position in the Cluny estate as Selby's most easterly battalion, to prevent a flanking attack from that direction. Like all the Gurkha battalions they were short of anti-tank rifles, many having been lost with the boots in the north. Even so, as far as Fulton was concerned, there were an awful lot of trees between his battalion and the nearest Japanese tanks and he was quietly confident they would do much better this time. Fulton himself had put in a lot of hard work, sending his wife back to married quarters at the regimental depot in India so there would be no distractions as the war came closer to Singapore. A few days before, he had received his first letter from her, safely arrived in Colombo despite the submarine scares.

When Watanabe's tanks tore into them, Fulton's battalion was marching in two long columns in single file on either side of the road, keeping to the edge so they would be less visible from the air. But it was the rather puzzling sounds of battle coming from the direction of brigade HQ behind them that were beginning to unnerve some of the young Gurkhas. 'I couldn't understand it,' recalled Major Winkfield, Fulton's second-in-command.

True, the battle sounded a bit close but we were miles behind the front and there was no air about. The men behind were looking back and hurrying. They kept pressing forward . . . The next thing I knew a machine-gun blazed in my ear; a bullet grazed my leg and I dived into the ditch as a tank bore down on me. It had passed through half my battalion without my realizing that anything was amiss.

It was soon over, and the death toll was even greater than that of Stokes' Punjabis. Next day a battalion roll call was answered by Winkfield and twenty-seven other ranks. Nobody knew how many of the missing were still alive, for the survivors had fled into the rubber and would soon find themselves cut off. Colonel Fulton had a stomach wound and a fractured thigh and was unable to move. Close by him lay the body of his orderly, whose own injuries had left him in such agony he had shot himself with his officer's pistol. Fulton died two months later in Japanese captivity.

After pausing to machine-gun various patches of rubber estate, where figures could be seen weaving among the trees, the Watanabe whirlwind moved on. His next catch were the two batteries of 25-pounders

Stewart had held in reserve because he could not see a role for them. This time surprise was not quite complete.

To avoid air attack the gunners had hidden their sixteen howitzers and limbers, along with the ammunition trucks and new Morris four-wheel drive artillery tractors known as Quads, about 200 yards off the road in one of the rubber estate's lanes. They were finishing their breakfast when someone rushed up to them and announced that tanks were coming their way. The identity of this messenger is unclear. He was possibly a Gurkha but he could have been from any one of a number of small technical support units – Ordnance Corps or the new Royal Electrical and Mechanical Engineers – which had set up shop in the rubber just north of the river and 15 miles behind the front. There was also 36th Field Ambulance, whose red crosses did not save them from being strafed by three separate groups of Shimada's tanks which passed them that morning.

Major Drought, one of the battery commanders, instantly started to get two of the 25-pounders in action on the road. In North Africa they were beginning to issue armour-piercing ammunition for this contingency but it is a near certainty that none had reached Malaya. Not that it would have made much difference. Like the crew of the last Breda anti-tank gun behind Stokes' Punjabis they were not quite quick enough and the T95s arrived in time to shell and machine-gun them before they were set up. Those that still could fled into the trees and pressed themselves into the earth until they were about 6 inches tall. There was nothing else they could do. Mercifully, Watanabe did not linger. When the tanks had shot up everything they could see, they moved on.

The artillerymen, in twos and threes, gingerly returned to survey the damage and decide what to do next. In this respect, the main problem was their isolation. Dispatch riders and field telephones had not been operating for several hours, and the wireless links that rarely existed below brigade headquarters had, according to Stewart, 'faded' shortly after dawn. There was nobody to tell them what was happening. Had this been a raid or had the division suffered a major defeat? Reluctantly, Drought and the other battery commander concluded that it had been the latter. Since by now the Japanese almost certainly possessed the road bridge and they were cut off, they began to complete what Watanabe had started. Breech blocks were removed from their undamaged guns and buried, sights smashed; transport, including the ammunition trucks and their contents, set on fire. Then, picking up their packs and their rifles, some 120 gunners joined hundreds of other 11th Division troops searching for a way across the deep and fast-flowing Slim River before the Japanese took all the obvious crossing points.

Ten miles south of the road bridge, at his divisional headquarters at Tanjong Malim, Archie Paris was almost as isolated as Major Drought's gunners. He had no idea how fast his two brigades were crumbling away, or even that they were crumbling at all. All he knew was that two hours after the Japanese had launched their surprising night tank attack, information from the innovative and ever-reliable Stewart had begun to dry up. Now people were beginning to turn up at his HQ with garbled reports of some sort of breakthrough. Paris decided to send Lieutenant-Colonel Arthur Harrison, the division's chief of staff, to investigate.

Accompanied by his Indian orderly, Mustapha Ghulam, Harrison drove north in a brand new Ford V8 which was the envy of lesser beings around headquarters. It was a fine morning – too early, Harrison felt, for the Japanese air force, which kept regular hours – and he was in good spirits. The V8 purred along. Approaching them was a British armoured car – except it had tracks and a big gun.

The next thing I knew was a deafening volley as machine-gun bullets shattered my windscreen. I wrenched the wheel hard to starboard, crashed into the ditch, opened the door, leapt out and ran like hell over 50 yards of open ground to the flimsy security of some scattered rubber.

Shortly afterwards he was joined by Ghulam who was clutching a bad shoulder wound and looking puzzled. 'Are those our armoured cars, Sahib?'

Watanabe kept his eyes fixed on the road ahead, moving not much faster than walking pace. T95s had a top speed of 28 mph and a bad reputation for mechanical failure. This was no time to throw a track or come to a halt with an overheated engine. In the distance a motor-cyclist was coming towards them, growing larger by the second. This was Lieutenant-Colonel Charles Holme, the commander of 137th Field Regiment, on his way to visit Drought and the batteries hidden in the Cluny estate. He did not have Harrison's luck.

And then, suddenly, Watanabe was at the bridge and the only people left to defend it were the Bofors gunners of the Singapore and Hong Kong Artillery under a Captain Newington. Two of Newington's crews stuck to their guns, brought their barrels down and opened fire at a range that was closer than most anti-tank gunners would care to get to a hostile tank. It was a brave attempt, but these were anti-aircraft guns firing air-burst ammunition. The rounds exploded harmlessly against the T95s' armour, no more lethal than most of the Molotovs had been.

The gunners fled while Watanabe busied himself cutting the wires to the demolition charges on this, the largest and most important of all the bridges he had captured in the 16 or so miles he had travelled in the last six hours. But this time the wrist wound prevented him from using his sabre and instead he eventually severed the fuse wire with one of the machine-guns, squandering ammunition as a Grand Prix winner squanders champagne.

Perhaps because his wound was bothering him, Watanabe stayed at the bridge and allowed Ensign Toichero Sato to lead a troop of three tanks on a reconnaissance south of the river towards Tanjong Malim and Paris's divisional HQ. Coming up the road towards Sato was another colonel of artillery on a motorcycle, the Lanarkshire Yeomanry's Augustus Murdoch of the monocle and the riding crop. Some way behind him, at quarter-of-a-mile intervals in case of air attack, were his regiment's venerable 4.5 howitzers which had done so well at Kampar and, in their old-fashioned way, fired a shell that was 5 pounds heavier than 25-pounder ammunition.

Murdoch spotted the tanks for what they were in time to turn his heavy BSA around and go haring back towards the guns. Perhaps if he had tried to ride off the straight stretch of road they were on, dumped his bike and sprinted for cover, he might have got away with it. As it was, Sato's second-in-command and hull machine-gunner, Sergeant Matsutaro Higashitsutsumi from Osaka, was given too long to take careful aim at his receding back and killed the Yeomanry colonel with one burst.

But Murdoch's death did give the lead battery some warning of what lay ahead. The first gun crew were wiped out when their Quad took a direct hit as they were trying to turn round and bring their weapon into action. The second gun was commanded by a Sergeant Keen, who opened fire at Sato's tank from about 100 yards and missed twice. (The 4.5 was even less suited for anti-tank work than the

25-pounder.) Sato got to within 30 yards of the gun before the third round hit the machine and stopped it, though enough of its armament was still working for Keen to be killed in his moment of triumph. Bombardier Skone now took command in a contest that was at such close range that it was beginning to resemble one of Nelson's naval battles. He fired two more of the 30-pound shells into it and Sato's tank became silent, though it stubbornly declined to burst into flames. From behind Skone's gun, the rest of the battery began to harass the other tanks with indirect fire. There were more casualties among the gunners, among them the adjutant who lost a leg, but eventually the tanks turned back. After 19 miles it was over.

'Sato died in an officer-like manner, with his hand on the hilt of his service sword,' vouched one Japanese account. Tsuji, who must have visited the wreck at about the same time, was equally admiring, though perhaps a little more honest about what he saw, reporting that one of the crew had 'collapsed beside his gun like a dish of *ame*'. *Ame* is a glutinous jelly.

For the British, the heroes were obviously the gunners who finally stopped them, but Harrison, who wrote an unpublished history of the 11th Division, could not conceal his admiration for the men who almost killed him and Mustapha Ghulam. 'Heedless of danger and of their isolation they had shattered the division: they had captured the Slim bridge by their reckless and gallant determination.'

At about the same time as Watanabe's tanks reached the Slim road bridge, Wavell turned up in Singapore on a Catalina flying boat from Ceylon. This was his first visit to the island since he had been made Supreme Commander of the Allied South West Pacific Command. It had been a mixed Christmas for him: he had been in a Burmese slit trench and almost killed on the day itself during a heavy air raid on Rangoon's Mingaladon airfield and then, a few days later, had gone back to India for some hard sport in Meerut's pigsticking country. Now he was passing through for a chat with Percival before proceeding to Java and Lembang's Grand Hotel where the American and Dutch components of his new headquarters awaited.

The next day, having heard the first sketchy reports of 11th Division's misfortunes, an Australian Hudson with the strongest fighter escort available carried him north to Heath's 3rd Indian Corps HQ at Kuala Lumpur, where motor transport was waiting. At Rasa, a hamlet some 30 or so miles north of there, he discovered brigadiers Stewart and Selby counting heads. 'I have never seen two men look so tired,' thought Wavell's aide-de-camp, Captain Alexander Reid Scott, a desert veteran of the 11th Hussars who, like his boss, was blind in his left eye from a shell splinter.

At the end of the day Stewart's 12th Brigade could muster no more than 430 officers and men, about a sixth of its strength, of whom fewer than 200 were armed. Most of these were Argylls. Selby's 28th were slightly better off at 750. Almost everybody was in a state of utter exhaustion. Wavell was shocked and made it plain that he thought serious errors had been made, his first indication of a loss of confidence in Percival. A report to the chiefs of staff in London described the situation in Malaya as 'somewhat critical'. Those who knew this master of understatement well must have been deeply alarmed.

It was the loss of men and equipment that hurt most, especially sixteen 25-pounders, artillery being the one area where the British enjoyed anything like Yamashita's overwhelming superiority in armour and aircraft. Losing the territory was not so important because it would have been given up anyway, albeit more slowly and at a higher tariff. Forty-eight hours before the Japanese had arrived at the Slim River road bridge, Percival had already decided to abandon central Malaya where the extensive road networks in the heavily populated west coast states of Selangor, Negri Sembilan and Malacca would make it even easier than usual for Yamashita to outflank him. It was by far his most radical decision of the campaign to date, and one that must have delighted Heath, who had always advocated getting back to Johore, making a stand there and forgetting all about this business of denying totally indefensible airfields to the Japanese.

Percival had decided that, in one bound, pausing to burn and blow up but not to fight at any more Kampar or Slim-style bottlenecks, they would fall back some 140 miles. Kuala Lumpur, Port Swettenham and Malacca, all jewels in the Crown of British Malaya, were to be abandoned. The new line was to be in northern Johore where, by the middle of the month, they would be joined by the next batch of reinforcements: a brigade of 18th Division's East Anglian Territorials, who were not much more than a week's sailing time away. This new coast-to-coast defence line, the new Torres Vedras, would be about 100 miles in length and 120 miles from Singapore's northern shore. From the west coast it would begin where the Muar River emptied itself into the Indian Ocean and proceeded eastwards through Segamat to the Australians' territory around Mersing on the South China Sea.

To put it mildly, General Bennett had been disappointed by this plan. Once again his mustard-keen Australians were to be left gazing out onto the South China Sea for a landing that might never come while Heath's tired divisions continued to bear the brunt of the attack on the west coast. Why not simply swap them around? But Percival was adamant. Organizing the transfer of thousands of men from one coast to another would not only be a strain on his transport system but might also make them vulnerable to some lucky Japanese *coup de main* while they were in progress. 'We could not afford to leave the east coast weakly defended even for a day.'

The losses at Slim River changed all this. Wavell agreed with Percival's decision to pull back to Johore but insisted, as Bennett put it, that the Australians were 'going into bat'. 'We must take certain risks on the east coast temporarily in order to organize a good defence on the western side which is immediately threatened,' Wavell cabled London.

The Supreme Commander admired Australian troops. They had

served him well against the Axis in North Africa and also against the Vichy French in Syria and Lebanon. Bennett seemed typical of this pugnacious breed and Wavell decided it was time to give him his head. As a rule senior officers did not interfere with the tactical decisions of their subordinates. 'Sack them or back them,' was the general rule. But on this issue Wavell had decided to overrule Percival, with his nervousness about turning a large part of his army into one huge gridlocked target on the narrow roads.

Bennett was going to move towards the west coast of Johore with one of his two brigades and his divisional HQ. This would be known as Westforce. His other brigade would join him as soon as it could be relieved by troops from the Singapore garrison. Meanwhile, the Australian would also have under his command the fresh, though admittedly half-trained, 45th Indian Brigade under Brigadier Horatio Duncan, and the two brigades of General Barstow's 9th Indian Division. Despite the losses at Kuantan, where Arthur Cumming's 2nd Sikhs had paid such a heavy price at the airfield, the morale of Barstow's men was thought to be much better than that of the 11th Division, which was going to pull back to southern Johore for rest and recuperation.

Even so, most of Barstow's infantry battalions had suffered a steady trickle of casualties and were in need of reinforcements. In the 2/10th Baluch, Captain Prem Sahgal was now commanding a mixed company of Pathans (Muslims) and Dogras (Hindus), in theory a very volatile mix who needed careful feeding. One night a teenaged Pathan reinforcement came to him with a confused story about bayoneting a man who had fallen uninvited into the fox hole he had just dug for himself. 'My God, I thought, he's gone and murdered a Dogra.' Sahgal had visions of his company being on the edge of self-destruction, but the Pathan's victim turned out to be a lone Japanese, possibly a disoriented scout.

While Bennett's Westforce were digging in on the south bank of the Muar River, which was a good water obstacle with a 40-mile stretch without a single bridge, 11th Division would delay the Japanese north of Kuala Lumpur for as long as possible. Since they were now effectively reduced to one brigade, Wavell did not think this would be very long. This would be the start of their long retreat to Johore, with a rearguard to screen sappers who were already scorching the earth with an enthusiasm that bewildered and revolted many of the Asians who were abandoned in the wreckage. It was as if their paternalistic rulers, who, above all else, had imposed a comforting sense of security, were suddenly behaving like spoilt children and smashing everything they could not take with them: policemen breaking windows. Middle-aged tin-mining engineers flooded the mines they had worked on since they were young men and drowned the livelihoods of entire communities. The sensitive Percival was aghast to see the result of his own orders. 'Pillars of smoke and flame rose into the sky as rubber factories, mine machinery, petrol and oil stocks were denied,' he wrote. 'Small wonder that British prestige sank to a very low ebb among the population.'

And here and there, when time and talent and available explosives coincided, booby traps were created. Water tanks in European lavatories, rigged to explode when a sharp tug on the chain plucked the pin from a grenade, were a particular favourite. Others were more ambitious. At Kuala Lumpur's two airfields mines, and perhaps some RAF bombs, were laid to be set off by fine trip wires almost invisible to the naked eye. They would cause several casualties among the ground crews of the Endo Air Group. Sometimes there were inspired moments of improvisation.

Captain David Wilson, who had been so impressed by Singapore's fortifications when the Argylls first arrived, had rejoined what was left of his battalion from a staff job. On rearguard he discovered that gun-cotton charges tied to the girder of a bridge he was supposed to destroy lacked a detonator. Wilson's solution was to tie down the spring-loaded safety lever on a pineapple grenade with string, then lash the grenade to the explosive, gently remove its pin and, praying that the string would hold, tiptoe away to his armoured car. The gun-cotton charges were set off by machine-gunning the girder until the vibrations snapped the string, the safety lever flew off and the grenade exploded.

Wavell predicted that Kuala Lumpur was unlikely to be held beyond 11 January and he was right by a matter of hours. Heath's troops and various attachments blew up the last bridge into the city at 4.30 a.m. and had completed their withdrawal by the time the sun was up. As usual, Yamashita's engineers worked fast and the first of his vehicles were on the streets of the capital of the Malay States by 8.30 p.m., some infantry patrols a little earlier. In the vacuum between British withdrawal and Japanese arrival there was a certain amount of murder, rape and looting, but this anarchy had started some forty-eight hours before, when it became obvious that the city was about to change hands. Utterly astonished by this turn of events, some of the city's British residents, based in Kuala Lumpur for reasons of government or commerce, many with nerves already as brittle as melba toast from a marked increase in the bombing, bolted. To the horror of Asian nurses and air-raid precaution personnel who, inspired by all the newsreels they had watched and newsprint they had devoured on the London Blitz, stuck resolutely to their posts, the British residents began to abandon the town in what one officer described as 'shameful displays of panic'. Some of the soldiers who tried to create some order out of the chaos that ensued around the railway station described it as 'a disgrace which the native peoples are not likely to forget in a hurry'.

To Gunner Bobby Ross of the Malay States Volunteers' Light Battery – twenty-four and a rare wartime recruit to the Malayan civil service, who were delighted to have him with his first class honours from Cambridge in natural science and anthropology – even more shocking were reports of looting by the military. 'One persistent story is told about Kuala Lumpur where British troops were reputed to have driven lorries to the large European-owned shops and mounted guard with Tommy guns while other parties removed the contents of show cases and store rooms . . . There is every reason to believe that it was widespread . . .'

An eyewitness to the anarchy that gripped the Malayan capital the day before the Japanese arrived was Dr Gordon Ryrie. For seventeen years Ryrie had been in charge of the Sungei Buloh Leper Settlement about 12 miles north of Kuala Lumpur where, armed with new drugs, he had carried out pioneering work against the disease. The Scot was dedicated to his patients, who came from all of Malaya's Asian communities, and he had no intention of abandoning them to join the European exodus. He had driven to the city to buy fresh vegetables for the settlement and later jotted some notes in the journal he had begun to keep of the scenes he saw.

An Indian emerges from the crowd holding up a dark green packet of sanitary towels in one hand, and a half empty whisky bottle in the other. Someone shoots him through the chest with a small revolver. The last guard of the British, a little knot of them, naked to the waist, try to keep the crowd out of a licensed shop until the liquor has been smashed. A Sikh manages to get his foot into the door. An officer shoots him through the foot and he sits on the sidewalk moaning and clutching the wound. The blood runs between his toes . . .

As gunfire and breaking glass sounded the end of British rule in Kuala Lumpur, Wavell was preparing to leave Singapore for Batavia, taking General Henry Pownall, who had originally come out as Brooke-Popham's replacement, with him as his chief of staff. Pownall, aware of Wavell's growing and somewhat unfair dissatisfaction with Percival, was rather pleased he had not been asked to take over.

Duff Cooper was also about to leave the island. Wavell had tried to persuade him to stay on, mainly because of the contribution he had made towards improving Singapore's civil defence and his ability, as Pownall saw it, to 'keep Shenton Thomas up to the mark'. Matters had reached the point where Wavell showed Duff Cooper the draft of a telegram he was proposing to send to Churchill asking him to stay. 'I replied immediately that I hoped the telegram would not be sent. I could not remain in my present position, because I had no position at all. Having no position, I had no authority. I was no longer Resident Cabinet Minister.'

This seems somewhat disingenuous. Wavell wanted him and if Duff Cooper had been willing Churchill would have surely created a position for him, perhaps persuaded the Colonial Office to sack Shenton Thomas and make him governor. The truth was probably that, for all the gallantry of 1918 and more recent displays of coolness under fire during the London Blitz, in middle age Duff Cooper was far too much of a hedonist to undergo the privations of a famous siege. Several weeks before the Japanese war started, Lady Diana wrote to a friend of her husband's yearning to get home: 'He is such a one for pleasure. Old English ones, girls, champagne, bridge, clubs, weekends, libraries and a spot of sport. None of them here.' They followed Wavell out to Batavia three days later on the first leg of a long journey to England, their flight delayed by an air raid on the airfield and Diana fortified by a large gin.

Shenton Thomas made public thanks to Duff Cooper for his service but his true feelings were entirely predictable. 'I shall see him out with a sigh of relief,' he confided to his journal. 'A rotten judge of men, arrogant, obstinate, vain; how he could have crept into office is beyond me, indeed beyond us all. Lady Diana has not appeared since the war began and we gather has complete jitters! Their God is publicity.'

The spotlight on Singapore would soon be enough to gratify all lusts in that direction, even those of General Bennett, whom Wavell had just elevated to Corps commander, before he had fought his first battle in Malaya. Perhaps if time had not been so pressing Wavell, with his good nerve ends, might have picked up a hint of Bennett's own staff officers' assessment of their boss after more than a year under his command. Colonel James Thyer, a regular soldier, was his chief of staff.

Between the wars he was a civilian and did not study military tactics but rested on his World War I laurels. He was moved by hunches and believed in the stars. He was tremendously ambitious and had his head in the clouds, which is the last place a good battle commander's head should be.

However fanciful some of Bennett's notions were, and these included a belief in the innate superiority of Australian troops that by far transcended the faith all good commanders must have in the quality of their men, nobody can deny that he eventually got off to a good start. In the five weeks since hostilities began the only Australian soldiers who had seen any action at all were the raiding party the Argylls' Major Rose had accompanied behind enemy lines and the 1914–18 veterans of the independent transport company attached to 11th Indian Division who, on at least one occasion, had joined in a fire-fight with some effect. (Among the Argylls and the British Battalion these older Diggers were also appreciated for their reliability and the generous way they had with their whisky.)

Then, at about 4.20 p.m. on Wednesday 14 January 1942, Captain Jack Duffy whispered the word into his field telephone – whispered because the Japanese cyclists he had already allowed over the bridge were now riding four or five abreast only a few feet from his hiding place and he was convinced they would hear him. Not having done this sort of thing before, Duffy was astonished by what happened next. 'Japanese bodies, bicycles, timber, rocks and earth flew far and wide in a huge red flash leaving a gaping space where the bridge had been.'

The ambush at the Gemencheh River bridge, a structure of willow-pattern innocence some 7 miles north-west of the railway junction town of Gemas, signalled the entry of Bennett's 8th Australian Division into the Malayan campaign. The cyclists blown up on the bridge were only the beginning. Company commander Duffy had allowed at least 250 to go through to be dealt with by the rest of the battalion further down the road while he estimated that he had at least 400 in the ambush area itself. Their best killing ground was a high-banked cutting just beyond the bridge, where the Australians were waiting with Brens, Thompsons, rifles and lots of grenades. In most cases their victims' weapons were still tied to their crossbars. The war diary of Kawamura's 9th Infantry Brigade puts the casualties of his Mukaide Detachment, who were the vanguard, at seventy dead and fifty-seven wounded, but this might not cover various attachments. Some Australian accounts claim ten times as many killed, but this is much too high. The entire action took twenty minutes and there was certainly no time for body counts.

What is indisputable is that unblooded Australian troops had the satisfaction of killing a lot of Japanese without suffering, at the ambush site, a single casualty themselves. For some weeks Bennett had been telling his commanders that this was the kind of thing they should and would be doing when they went into bat. Thanks to the length of the latest withdrawal, Heath's divisions had been able to disengage totally and the Japanese advance had not got its teeth into the rearguard with their usual piranha-like persistence.

This had allowed time for the kind of meticulous planning that is the hallmark of most successful murder. So that the enemy would not be suspicious of an intact bridge, for the last 30-mile stretch through the state of Negri Sembilan to the Johore border the Indian sappers had been ordered to spare all but the major structures. For the eager Mukaide Detachment the Gemencheh bridge, with its carefully hidden charges and fuse wires, was just another crossing closer to Singapore.

The battalion in charge of the ambush was Lieutenant-Colonel Frederick Galleghan's 2/30th. Galleghan was the most senior battalion commander in the entire 8th Division, a tall man, held in some awe by his men who called him 'Black Jack'. Most of the officers in charge of Australia's volunteer infantry battalions came from professional or land-owning backgrounds, 1940s Australia being nowhere near as classless as its accent. But Galleghan, who had some West Indian blood, was the shrewd and energetic son of a docker. In 1919 he had been a twenty-two-year-old sergeant when he returned from the trenches, where he had been twice badly wounded, to resume a successful career in the civil service. But, like Bennett, he had acquired a taste for soldiering and was soon commissioned into the militia, commanding his first battalion in 1932 and establishing a reputation as a disciplinarian and a man who liked to get his own way.

'The reputation not only of the AIF in Malaya, but of Australia, is in the hands of this unit,' Galleghan had warned his company commanders on the eve of the ambush. Black Jack himself, who had recently celebrated his forty-fifth birthday, was in exuberant mood. 'Colonel Ned Kelly of Australia,' he barked at an unfortunate Indian sergeant asking who he should say had removed the drum of field telephone cable just hijacked from his truck by Galleghan's grinning signallers. On the whole, the amount of Australian swagger endured by Heath's exhausted Indians as they passed through their lines was insufferable. This included trying to shoot out the headlights of drivers moving at night under anything more than slit-shaped blackout beams, the Indians having learned that the risks to life and limb from a crash far outweighed those of an air raid. The inevitable result was that, whenever possible, the Indians – either assuming Japanese snipers had infiltrated the route or sick of high-handed Australians – fired back.

Galleghan's 2/30th, a New South Wales formation, were the point battalion deployed as a buffer slightly west of the border town of Gemas astride the trunk road. Its orders were to hold the Japanese for at least twenty-four hours and then fall back behind the Gemas River, where the rest of Bennett's battalions were mixed in with some of the Indian formations Wavell had made available. B Company were the most forward of all the Australian infantry, 3 miles ahead of the rest of the battalion hiding in the fringes of the thick jungle around the Gemencheh bridge.

Duffy had been the winner of a draw Galleghan had organized to decide which of his four companies would get the ambush site and with it the honour of firing the first shots for the 8th Australian Division. B Company's 120 or so men had taken up their positions the day before, moving into their hides in small groups and eventually installing an open-line field telephone system linking all three platoons to Duffy's company HQ. Two other field telephone cables stretched back the 3 miles to the battalion – there was the usual mistrust of wireless and no attempt to use it. One line went to Galleghan's HQ and the other to a battery of Australian 25-pounders whose forward observation team were with Duffy. As soon as the bridge was blown it was intended that they would call down fire on Japanese cyclists and transport milling about on the far bank, thanking their lucky stars and wondering what they were going to do next.

This was the only part of the plan that went wrong. Both Duffy and Galleghan, who came up for a last-minute inspection the night before, had noticed that the telephone cables running alongside the road to battalion HQ and the artillery were easily seen. But orders to camouflage them had not been properly carried out and the first of the enemy infantry Duffy allowed through the trap before he blew the bridge cut them, probably out of sheer force of habit for by now they had been cutting British field telephone wire for almost the length of Malaya.

After the ambush most of these Japanese turned back to help their comrades at the bridge, forcing Duffy's outnumbered company to split into two main groups and find their way back to the battalion on compass bearings through the jungle rather than along the road. The Australians had expected to do this and fought their way through several sudden and bloody clashes *en route* where they seem to have given at least as good as they got. All but ten of their number, most of whom were believed to have been killed, made it back to the battalion within the next twenty-four hours. The last man to arrive, who had briefly been captured, was dressed as a Tamil.

By this time Galleghan was embroiled in a major fight. As usual, the Japanese powers of recovery were phenomenal. Six hours after the ambush they had repaired the Gemencheh bridge to the point where tanks could cross. The cut timber which enabled them to do this came from a local sawmill half a mile north of the river. Although its machinery had been destroyed by Australian engineers, they failed to set the planks on fire, perhaps because they feared that this might alert the Japanese to the idea that the enemy had plans for the bridge ahead.

Shortly after nine o'clock next morning, Japanese tanks supported by infantry were up to Galleghan's main position across the main road and the railway. Luckily, apart from 25-pounders and mortars, there were a couple of 2-pounder anti-tank guns waiting for them. This was no thanks to Black Jack, who appears to have had only a very shaky idea of what Shimada's tanks got up to at Slim River and had made it plain that he thought them redundant against an enemy hopelessly addicted to the bicycle. A third gun had actually been sent away.

The Australian gunners were not equipped with captured Italian Bredas but the 2-pounder anti-tank gun which, when the British Army first took delivery of it in 1938, was reckoned to be the best of its type in the world. Over the next three years the Germans produced armour it could not always penetrate but against T95s it was more than adequate – so much so that Lance-Sergeant Kenneth Harrison, who was commanding one of the 2-pounders Galleghan had accepted with such ill grace, began to suspect that at 250 yards his armour-piercing rounds were going straight through them and changed to high-explosive ammunition.

These burst on contact, and the flash enabled me to see where we were hitting, and to adjust the sights accordingly. With both guns pounding away at it, the second tank did not return our fire for long but, try as we might, we could not set it on fire. Eventually our infantry sent a message, 'Tank destroyed. Save ammunition.' It was difficult to tell how badly it was damaged because of the smoke and flame from the other one.

But it was far from over. Cleverly, the Japanese poured oil on one of their burning tanks to create a smoke-screen, nudged it out of the way and came on. They were emerging from a bend on a narrow stretch of the trunk road, essentially a cutting, knowing that on both sides of the road there was an anti-tank gun waiting for them: Harrison could not help but be impressed by their courage.

Two shells toppled a Japanese infantry carrier on its side. 'It lay there with men crawling out like wood bugs from a burning log.' Harrison gave orders to switch back to armour-piercing rounds and fire them through a burnt-out tank behind which an intact one lurked. Retribution was not long in coming. The guns were exposed, the camouflage nets over them an attempt to hide them from the air, not the ground, and the gunners' only protection was the armoured shield they crouched behind to serve the gun. Harrison's loader was hit in the head by shrapnel, then, far more seriously, as he slumped down his shoulder was smashed by the full force of the recoiling breech springing back to eject the empty shell case. Most of his war would be spent in Australia on a disability pension for the arm he would never use properly again. Within a few minutes, shrapnel from another near miss peppered the man who had replaced him down the entire left-hand side of his body, head to toe. No one could be spared to help him and he dragged himself away, mortally wounded.

Now his gun was down to two men. Harrison took over the loading while the gun layer, Gunner Joseph Bull, aimed and fired with a press of the trigger pedal. But by now the cutting was so full of smoke they were quite unable to make out a target. They fired blindly, dividing the road into four sections and aiming into each one in turn. The trouble with this was that it used up too much ammunition. They adopted a new fire plan. They would wait until a tank fired, then aim at its red muzzle flash; the near misses went over them with a chilling *whooosh*. A stray tank shell felled a rubber tree which came to rest immediately in front of their gun. They fired back through the tree, praying that a thick branch would not detonate a round so close to the gun. By the time they realized that the tanks had stopped firing, they had four shells left. The other gun was not much better off. As the ringing in their ears began to subside, they became aware of a new sound. It was the infantry to their right, cheering them while they waved their rifles in the air. 'We waved back rather lamely,' wrote Harrison who was twenty-three and not all that long ago had been working as a storeman in Melbourne. 'But that was without doubt the proudest moment either of us will ever know.'

At least four tanks were totally destroyed, one of them finished off by a fluke when an open turret pocketed a mortar bomb like a billiard ball. When the flames reached their ammunition the pyrotechnics were impressive. Some of the Australians were reminded of Empire Day fireworks back home. Several more were non-runners and were towed off while the infantry pinged .303 off their hides to speed them on their way.

Galleghan followed up this success with a company-sized local counter-attack. This worked well although the artillery support laid on for it was not as effective as it might have been because, as usual, the Japanese had moved in close and it went over most of them. But it did buy the Australians more time and one platoon came back tugging two of the small infantry guns Yamashita's troops dragged around with them. Eventually, they were halted by the machine-guns of Japanese light tanks operating from a lane between rubber trees and, covered by 25-pounder fire, withdrew with their wounded.

One of them was being carried by Corporal Frederick Abbotts, a former Grenadier Guardsman born in Birmingham who at forty was old for the infantry and had probably lied about his age to enlist. The tall English immigrant had himself been badly hit in the chest but nobody realized until he delivered his burden to the aid post. The corporal came from what was then the small country town of Taree on the Sydney–Brisbane rail line, where the air was no doubt considerably cleaner than his native Birmingham, and lived to see it again.

The Australians had organized their medical facilities well. The wounded were brought back from the field aid posts to a casualty clearing station at Segamat by ambulance and the Australians were impressed by the way the Japanese appeared to respect their red crosses and withheld their fire. Within twenty-four hours most of their cargoes were 75 miles south, at the former mental hospital the sultan had made available to Bennett in Johore Bahru where, apart from a few airmen, most of the patients were suffering from malaria and typhus or had hurt themselves in road accidents. For the first time, Vivian Bullwinkel, Mona Wilton and the other nurses found themselves cutting away old and grubby field dressings, and uniforms stiff with mud and blood, being careful to return the pockets that contained wallets, photographs, rosaries and lucky charms.

By mid-afternoon, some twenty-four hours after Duffy had blown the bridge over the Gemencheh River, Galleghan decided that his battalion had done enough and it was time to get out. This was not easy. The Japanese were pressing hard, all his companies tended to be heavily engaged and it was always a delicate business to break contact without it turning into a rout.

A troop of four 25-pounders bogged down in a rain-soaked rubber estate lane, where every round fired had hammered their traversing ring platforms★ deeper into the mud, was almost overrun by infantry. One gun and limber was eventually extracted and towed away. But there was no time to save the other three guns though breech blocks and sights were removed before they were abandoned. Lance-Sergeant Harrison's 2-pounder was also left behind after the agitated driver of a Bren gun carrier refused to give its crew time to attach it. The little gun, which had served them so well against the tanks, was left in the middle of the road. As they drove away, Harrison squirmed at this humiliating and undeserved end to their impressive debut, imagining 'the derisive laughter with which the Japanese would greet such an obvious sign of panic'.

But by and large the Australians had done well and they knew it. So did the Japanese, who had expected another Slim River. Tsuji declared that the Australians had 'fought with a bravery we had not previously seen'. In almost two days' fighting, they had inflicted far more casualties on the Japanese than they had sustained themselves. Galleghan's total losses were seventeen killed, fifty-five wounded and nine missing. One of the dead and four of the wounded were officers.

And while they were fighting, on 13 January, the long-awaited reinforcements had docked in Singapore unhindered – thanks to low cloud – by air strikes. Brigadier Cecil Duke's 53rd Brigade – two battalions of Norfolks and one of the Cambridgeshires – was in the

★ The gun was placed on a circular traversing ring platform so it could be turned 360 degrees and fired in any direction. When it was under tow the platform was placed on the limber.

process of disembarking. So were the fifty-one crated Hurricanes that were confidently expected to be the first step towards ending Japanese air superiority. It was thought that assembling and testing them should take no more than a week.

Most people had no idea about the arrival of the Hurricanes, which were dispersed to various places around the island where RAF technicians could assemble them in secret. None the less, suddenly there was a feeling in the air that the rot had stopped. Nor were there any doubts about who was responsible. On Singapore Radio one speaker described the Australians as 'our seawall against the vicious flood'.

It seemed that the mood was contagious. Even the air force, whose offensive actions were increasingly confined to night attacks against enemy-held airfields, surprised the Japanese, and possibly themselves, by sending thirty aircraft on a daylight raid to bomb transport and tanks on the trunk road north of Gemas. Six Singapore-based Dutch Glenn Martin bombers participated in the operation, along with six Blenheims and eighteen Buffaloes. The Glenn Martins bombed from a high altitude, then the Blenheims and Buffaloes went in low. How much damage they did is unclear. Flight Lieutenant Don Jackson, the RAF commander of the Blenheims, was annoyed to see that his aircraft aimed for the smoke and dust raised by his first strike instead of going down the length of the convoy. Even so, it robbed the Japanese of that comfortable feeling that they need not concern themselves with the sound of aircraft engines because they were always theirs. And some of their aircrews learned the hard way that it did not pay to be complacent. A Japanese fighter pilot surprised by Mowbray Garden in his Buffalo while 'larking on the tops of the clouds', crash-landed in Johore where he held an inquisitive crowd of Malays at bay with a pistol, then shot himself in the head.

In a press interview, a jubilant Bennett promised that his men would not only halt Yamashita but put him on the defensive. Then disturbing reports began to come in of Japanese landings at the mouth of the Muar River, which were pushing back the 45th Indian Brigade and threatening the Australians' left flank.

Lieutenant-Colonel John Williams, whose battalion of mainly teenaged Jats were part of the Muar River deployment, was leading his battalion on foot towards the village of Bakri when they came under rifle fire. The colonel went forward to investigate and peered cautiously over a muddy bank. There was a cry, perhaps two cries – one from the dying Williams who had just been decapitated, or very nearly so, by a samurai sword and the other from the Japanese officer who had so satisfactorily dispatched his enemy in preferred Bushido fashion.

Horatio Duncan's half-trained 45th Brigade, some of their vehicles still wearing the yellow desert camouflage intended for their advance training in Iraq, were up against Nishimura's Konoye Imperial Guards Division, Emperor Hirohito's personal troops. Its officers were desperate to prove that they were not chocolate-box soldiers but the best Japan had to offer, even if ceremonial duties at home had kept their swords sheathed since they had fought the Czar, almost forty years before. Recruits were selected from all over the country according to physique; they tended to be taller than average and less likely to use spectacles. They were equipped with the best their country possessed, had honed their battle skills to be as good as constant practice would allow, and were only too aware that the China veterans in the other divisions were longing for them to fail. To put Duncan's novices in the same ring with Nishimura's Guards, who already had the advantage of aerial superiority and tanks, was ludicrous. But there had been no public weigh-in. Nobody knew how steep the odds for this particular bout were and, in any case, for Percival there was very little choice.

Duncan's brigade had the normal complement of three infantry battalions: the 7/6th Rajputana Rifles, 4/9th Jats, 5/18th Royal Garhwal Rifles. (The 'Royal' was bestowed because of the number of Victoria Crosses the regiment's several battalions had won in the 1914–18 war.) It was supported by a battery of eight Australian 25-pounders under the command of a Major William Julius, a stocky regular soldier from Darwin known to his gunners, and not entirely without affection, as 'The Black Bastard'.

They were deployed so that the Rajputs held the wide river mouth where the ferry was, the south bank town of Muar itself and about 9 miles upstream; then came the Jats, thinly stretched along another 15 miles of winding river bank towards the hillier country to the east. Both battalions straddled the river because Bennett, inspired by the success of Galleghan's ambush with a company well forward of his main position, had insisted that each put two companies – half their strength – on the north bank. The Australian gunners also had an observation post there. The Garhwalis, in reserve and ready to go in either direction, were entirely on the south bank. They were camped inland, a couple of miles east of Muar harbour, at the crossroads village of Bakri, where Duncan had established his headquarters in an isolated white-painted building at a road junction at the edge of the village padang.

It took Nishimura no more than twenty-four hours to get the destruction of the Indian brigade well under way. First he feinted towards Muar, swallowing up the two isolated Rajput companies north of the river so effortlessly that Duncan's HQ never did learn the manner of their passing. The only man who made it back to the south bank was the driver from the Australian gunners' observation post who happened to be at the ferry point guarding a suspected civilian fifth columnist and swam the 400 yards across at nightfall.

Soon the Guards were coming across the river themselves. They used a variety of craft. The best were a kind of light assault boat that had come all the way down from the Thai beach-heads. These were augmented by a collection they had made locally of the small sampans the Malays used to get around their rice paddies. Ultimately, they also pirated the boats the British had gathered in places on the south bank both to deprive the Japanese of their use and bring back the forward companies when they judged the moment was right.

Some particularly insolent attempts at daylight crossings were repelled by artillery and machine-gun fire; the Australian gunners, cheerfully engaging them with direct fire, were delighted to be able to see what they were aiming at. But while this was going on another Guards regiment, about the equivalent of a brigade, crossed the river quite easily upstream where the Jats were thinly spread and attacked Muar from an easterly direction. The remaining two Rajput companies fled, and battalion commander Lieutenant-Colonel Lewis and most of his officers were picked off as they tried to rally their men. A few Rajputs, along with most of Major Julius's gunners, managed to fall back on brigade HQ at Bakri where Duncan was organizing the Garhwalis, his brigade reserve, to recapture the town. But before the attack could be mounted, their Lieutenant-Colonel James Woolridge was killed returning from a dawn reconnaissance patrol. The counter-attack failed and most of the Garhwalis' remaining British officers were killed or wounded, the adjutant and a lieutenant after they had each seized Bren guns from frightened sepoys and tried to hold a position in a rubber estate. In some disarray, the Garhwalis returned to Bakri, which was coming under increasing artillery and air attack. The Austra-lian gunners began to call them the 'Galloping Garhwalis'.

Not long after this, Williams was beheaded when leading his Jats back to Bakri. In their remoter upstream positions they had been easily by-passed by the Japanese though, unlike the Rajputs, they had at least managed to extract the two companies Bennett had obliged them to place north of the river. The death of Williams meant that, in the space of a little over twenty-four hours, Duncan had lost all three of his battalion commanders, each of them a dedicated, middle-aged pro-fessional killed leading his troops from the front and trying to set the best example. So much for the derided 'Curry Colonels', an easy laugh for any between-the-wars British music hall comedian capable of gripping a monocle and stressing the last syllable in Poonah.

By now Duncan had been reinforced by an Australian battalion. Bennett had sent him the 2/29th, a unit recruited mainly in Victoria and commanded by the genial Lieutenant-Colonel James Robertson, who lived in Geelong where he owned a garage and supplied fuel across the state. Robertson had just turned forty-seven and, like almost all of Bennett's battalion commanders, had returned in 1919 with wound scars, a Military Cross and a belief, which kept him in the militia, that survivors had a duty to pass on their experience.

Bennett was somehow under the impression that no more than 200 Japanese had got into Muar – it was already more like ten times that – and that the 2/29th would soon see them off and return to the Gemas area. Nor did he feel that the entire battalion was necessary for the task in hand and kept back a company and a platoon, perhaps 160 men in all. But he did think it might be a good idea to provide some anti-tank guns. It was decided that four would go under a Lieutenant Bill McCure, along with Harrison and some of the other sergeant gun commanders who had done so well at Gemas. There were plenty of volunteers to replace the men killed and wounded in the previous action.

To his amazement, McCure discovered that Robertson felt exactly the same way about his anti-tank guns as Galleghan had before they met the tanks at Gemas. He made it plain that he regarded them as an encumbrance imposed on him by Bennett. 'I don't want you to interfere with us in any way,' McCure was told. 'I don't expect the Japanese to use tanks, so for my part you can go home.'

Robertson was leading his battalion into action for the first time and perhaps it is not all that surprising that he was not his usual, amiable self. Also it was true that mingling artillery of any kind with the forward infantry could be a nuisance because riflemen, who might be better used elsewhere, were often required to protect them from attack while they worked their guns. Robertson was already more than a company under strength. No doubt the colonel was more welcoming to Hedley Metcalf, an Australian who was the official Malayan Ministry of Information photographer, and Frank Bagnall, a newsreel cameraman from an Australian Army Film and Photographic Unit. The prospect that their battle debut might be well reported back home was worth more than a regiment of anti-tank guns as far as morale was concerned.

Robertson's battalion arrived at Bakri during the afternoon of 17 January. Brigadier Duncan explained to him that he was waiting for Williams and his Jats to arrive, after which he intended to launch a counter-attack. Meanwhile, the Australian infantry took up a position about a mile and a half west of Bakri, towards Muar and the coast. Before he departed, Robertson took the opportunity to unburden himself of two of the four anti-tank guns, one of them Harrison's, which were left guarding brigade headquarters.

At about midnight Major Julius, the Australian battery commander, turned up at Robertson's HQ and confirmed all his prejudices about the artillery by asking for protection for his 25-pounders. It seemed that the Garhwalis, who were supposed to be screening them, had disappeared. Ninety of the 2/29th were told to go and babysit the battery while it provided harassing fire for the most forward of the Garhwali companies, which was trying to disengage and reorganize. Shortly afterwards came the first indication that the Japanese had located at least some of Julius's guns when counter-battery fire ignited an ammunition trailer and the position had to be abandoned. As the night wore on, the Japanese shelling intensified and with it the feeling that they were preparing to attack.

It came at 6.45 a.m., shortly after dawn. It was spearheaded by nine

T95 tanks commanded by Captain Shiegeo Gotanda, who came from Kagoshima, Japan's most southerly port, sometimes known as the 'Naples of the Orient' and one of the few parts of the country that ever came close to being as sticky as Malaya. Gotanda, inspired by, and no doubt envious of, Shimada's success at Slim River, had volunteered to charge into Bakri and do it without infantry support the way the dashing Watanabe had done it at the Slim road bridge.

Colonel Masakazu Ogaki, the Guards officer in charge of the Muar operation, had some reservations about this, particularly the lack of infantry protection from anti-tank guns and Molotovs. Also, there was always a chance that the British would use their field artillery in an anti-tank role as they had eventually done at Slim. In the end, it was decided that if the infantry did not travel with the tanks they would not be all that far behind. Some would also try to exploit Gotanda's attack by hooking around the Australians and establishing a road-block behind them.

To get to Bakri, Gotanda had to pass through a narrow, fairly high-banked cutting with thick vegetation on either side. Waiting for him there, around a bend and slightly off the road, was a 2-pounder under Lance-Sergeant Clarrie Thornton, a mature young man of twenty-four from a farm amidst the Snowy Mountain-sourced streams of the Riverina pasturelands. At the end of the cutting McCure had deployed another of his anti-tank guns.

Six tanks approached in single file. There was no artillery preparation; no cover other than the fast-melting early morning mist. Within a minute, Thornton's crew had hit the first, third and fourth machine, but they all trundled resolutely on. The only indication of anything amiss was wisps of what might have been white smoke rising delicately from some parts of them and the lack of accurate return fire – in some cases of any return fire at all. As Harrison and the others had discovered at Gemas, armour-piercing rounds could go in one side of a T95 and out the other, easily penetrating plate which was nowhere more than 12 millimetres thick. Their interiors might resemble a butcher's shop but, as long as the engine was intact and the throttle was open, the tank went on.

For some reason, the kind of high-explosive shells that had worked so well at Gemas were not lying beside their gun. By the time McCure and his batman had delivered some, the tanks had not only gone by but the vanguard of Ogaki's infantry had been glimpsed advancing either side of the road. The young farmer and his crew who, according to McCure, were all in high spirits pushed the gun into the middle of the road. With their backs to the advancing infantry, they began firing their newly delivered high explosive into the rear of the tanks. At the same time, the T95s were being hit from the gun the other end of the cutting, which was in a slight hollow and did not open fire until the nearest tank was 40 yards away. All six of these tanks were immobilized and eventually totally destroyed. So were three more that appear to have waited for the Japanese infantry, presumably because the fate of the tanks that had proceeded according to plan, without rifle support, was plain to see. By now a sniper had managed to get close enough to Thornton, who probably stood out as the man in charge, to give him a hip wound. But this had not stopped him and his crew from turning their gun around and starting to punch holes in the other tanks in the same deliberate way. Only when it was obvious that they were no longer any threat did Thornton consent to be carried off to a field dressing station. He was awarded an immediate Distinguished Conduct Medal.

The Gotanda tank company, which would receive a unit citation, had been wiped out. 'A glorious death,' declared Yamashita, though he may have had some sympathy with a Japanese history of the Imperial Guard, which concluded that brave men had been squandered. Some of the tank crews attempted to escape from their crippled machines only to be cut down by the waiting infantry. Others turned them into beleaguered fortresses, working their guns as long as they had ammunition to fire from them and the strength to squeeze a trigger – 'until one by one they were smashed, set on fire, rendered useless and uninhabitable,' recalled Lieutenant Ben Hackney, a grazier from Bathurst, who was among the nearby infantry.

Also watching the death throes of Gotanda's tanks were the cameramen Metcalf and Bagnall, who had spent the night at Duncan's brigade HQ at Bakri and appear to have turned up just as the action came to a close. They could hardly believe their luck. These were the images everybody had missed at Gemas, when Harrison and the others had been cheered by the infantry – 'some of the few really good pictures that were taken of the war in Malaya,' wrote Ian Morrison of *The Times* in his wartime book, *Malayan Postscript*. It was all there: smoking tanks with dead crewmen lying alongside them and the Australians only a few yards away, crouched behind their small, high-velocity guns. Since it was not long after first light, and the nightly battle against mosquitoes had only just ended, some of the gunners were still wearing their roll-up Bombay Bloomer shorts, let down almost to their ankles.

That the cameramen were far more excited by anti-tank gunners than his infantry was probably an irony not lost on Robertson, a fair-minded man, but he had no time to dwell on the error of his ways. He was off on the back of a dispatch rider's motorcycle to an urgent conference Duncan had called with the newly arrived commander of more Australian reinforcements, Lieutenant-Colonel Charles Anderson's 2/19th Battalion.

Anderson was a wealthy South African Scot born in Cape Town in 1897 and probably the only member of Percival's forces who had ever before fought in a jungle campaign. In 1917, serving as a lieutenant in the King's African Rifles, he had won a Military Cross chasing the elusive General von Lettow-Vorbeck around East Africa in what turned out to be World War I's most chivalrous sideshow. (At one point a captured British veterinary officer was exchanged for three bottles of whisky.) After the war he lived in Kenya and, despite the myopia that meant he never dared to venture out without three pairs of spectacles about his person, he established a reputation as a big game hunter. Then, in 1934, Anderson left Nairobi to settle with his Australian wife at Crowther in New South Wales, where he had bought several thousand acres of sheep and cattle grazing. Six months before the outbreak of the war in Europe, although by now he was the father of young children, he joined the militia and was given the rank of captain.

Anderson had commanded the 2/19th, which was very much a Riverina country battalion, for the last five months. He had taken over when the physician Dr Maxwell had been promoted to brigadier and given the 27th Brigade. The battalion was one of the first Australian units to land in Malaya, thoroughly acclimatized, well-trained, and longing to show what it could do. Percival must have hoped that this included performing miracles. For the 2/19th's arrival at Bakri was the result of his growing realization that what was happening on the Muar front was crucial. It threatened his continued tenure of that small part of the Malayan Peninsula that was still under British control, and thus the fate of Singapore itself.

At first Percival and Bennett had been inclined to believe that the Japanese incursion eastwards along the Muar River was a relatively minor ailment, though it obviously needed to be watched. The very worst prospect was that the Imperial Guard would eventually reach the trunk road, 30 miles east of Bakri at the Yong Peng intersection. If they succeeded in doing this, they would have cut the only line of communication to Bennett's Westforce 70 miles to the north.

None the less, so soon after the Australians' success at Gemas had given everybody's morale a boost, the generals were determined that they should not be panicked into unnecessary retreat – what Percival sometimes regarded as Heath's 'withdrawal complex'. Bennett had long been of the opinion that a lot of the British withdrawals in the north had been brought about by gigantic bluffs committed by relatively small Japanese forces. It was a feeling that permeated the entire bewildered army, regardless of rank. 'If a handful of Japanese were reported in our rear the whole British Army must perforce retire – infantry guns and armoured cars – often without firing a shot,' recalled Mortimer Hay, Malaya's Acting Chief Inspector of Mines, who was serving as a lance bombardier in the same light battery as Ross, the idealistic young civil servant who had been so horrified by the British Army joining in the looting around Kuala Lumpur.

More often than not, these feelings were the result of not being able to see the big picture and the very real chances of being cut off. But this time, bolstered by Bennett's confidence, it was decided to try and contain the Muar front, 'stabilize' was Percival's word, and Robertson's battalion and the anti-tank guns were sent to shore things up. Then suddenly it became plain that this would not do.

Percival was informed that the latest intelligence reports, which probably meant wireless intercepts, indicated that the Japanese presence in the Muar area was not small but consisted of almost the entire Imperial Guards Division. Even worse, some of it had been landed further down the coast and was now preparing to cut the Muar–Bakri line from the south. Percival knew that the chances of holding up this division for any length of time with the forces available 'were remote'. None the less, it was imperative that sufficient delay should be imposed to allow Bennett to bring south the two Australian and six depleted Indian battalions he had in the Gemas–Segamat area. To hold the door open for them, Percival's immediate response was to dispatch to Bakri Anderson's 2/19th, which was part of the other Australian brigade that had been left to defend Johore's eastern coastline around Mersing. Then he began to examine the other cards he had to play.

It was not an inspiring hand. Bennett's six infantry battalions were now equally divided and scattered north, west and east in groups of two. Alongside the two northern ones, the Australian commander had the six depleted battalions of Barstow's 9th Indian Division, among them Arthur Cumming's much-reduced 2nd Sikhs of Kuantan airfield fame. Between Muar and Bakri, corseting Duncan's sagging 45th Brigade, were the two western ones. On the east coast, the remaining two Australian battalions were on their own. In the southern part of Johore the shattered 11th Division was trying to refit and some parts of it were already in Singapore. Among the latter were the remnants of Stewart's Argylls, who were about to be merged into a composite battalion with 200 Royal Marine survivors off the *Prince of Wales* and the *Repulse*.

Then there were Brigadier Duke's East Anglian Territorials who had arrived in Singapore less than a week before. 'It had been thought that the move to the mainland was for the purposes of training in jungle warfare and to have a few days in which to settle down ashore after three months at sea,' begins a somewhat rueful account of this period in the Royal Norfolks' regimental history.

Contrary to popular legend, neither Duke's brigade nor either of the other two 18th Division brigades shortly to land at Singapore were untrained or trained exclusively to fight in the Middle East. Nor did they arrive wearing thick European-theatre battledress. Before they left England the previous October they had all been issued with the same shorts, shirts and pith helmets worn by all British soldiers east of Suez. (Jungle-green, pioneered by the Dutch in the Netherlands East Indies, was first issued in 1943 to British forces in Burma.) Like most Home Army battalions, at the height of the invasion scare they had spent much of their time on coastal defence duties. But since then they had done a lot of the kind of training – field firing, night operations, route marches – designed to turn them into tough and proficient infantrymen with the basic ability to fight anywhere.

Obviously, the more time they had to familiarize themselves with the terrain they were campaigning in, whether it be desert or jungle, the better they would perform. Although they had been brought up to strength with conscripts, the core of the East Anglian infantry battalions and the Northumberland Fusiliers remained Territorial Army and their morale was good. In most units there existed the same framework of closely knit regional backgrounds as among the Australian volunteers. And to guide them there was, among the senior officers and NCOs, the same small percentage of 1914–18 veterans. Otherwise, apart from the same air raids endured by British civilians, very few of them had seen any action. The Norfolks were quite entitled to imagine they would get time to settle in. Had they gone to the Middle East, as was originally intended, they could certainly have expected to have been acclimatized by training well behind the lines and then sent to a quiet area to be gradually introduced to combat.

But Percival had no time for such niceties. Nor, after all their brigade exercises, could he send them into action as a unit. First, Duke was relieved of his 2nd Cambridgeshires to strengthen coastal defences around Batu Pahat from where, only a short while ago, the Japanese had shipped the iron ore from the nearby mines they owned. A Guards battalion had already landed there and disappeared into the hinterland. Then one of his two battalions of Norfolks, the 5th, were sent to replace Anderson's Australians. 'This breaking up of an organized formation is, of course, contrary to all military teaching,' admitted Percival. 'But, with so many danger points and so few troops to guard them, it proved most difficult to avoid.'

Equally unavoidable was the necessity of landing Duke's brigade without its heavy equipment. The 18th Division was not what the British called 'tactically loaded'. Since there had been no intention of sending them into action immediately, they were not travelling with their transport and artillery support on the same ship. All this had to be scrounged, often from the Australians, who had been in Malaya long enough to build up a certain surplus. Feeling particularly sorry for themselves were the brigade's gunners, Philip Toosey's Hertfordshire Yeomanry, aka the 135th Field Regiment. Since they were separated from their guns and Quad tractors there was talk of employing them as infantry until these arrived. An indignant Toosey reacted by first pestering the Australians to part with some spare 25-pounders they were keeping in their Singapore depot and then, in the absence of Quads, rounding up anything civilian or military that was capable of towing them and painting them green. Called up for service north of the Causeway were some of Singapore's municipal dust carts.

This, then, was the brigade Percival was scattering around Johore in a bid to plug all the obvious gaps. 'They were a fine body of men but almost dazed by the position in which they found themselves,' reported one of the officers Anderson had left behind in a small rear party to help the 5th Norfolks settle in. The Poms were gratifyingly Pom, delighting Australian eyes by unloading into the monsoon mud strapped sea trunks, bulging valises and, if the 2/19th's battalion diarist is to be believed, even those collapsible canvas hip baths pioneered by Kitchener's officers in the Sudan. Most of these things had not been opened since they left Liverpool three months before and, without a regimental depot in Singapore where they could store them, they were obliged to carry it all with them. Besides, the Norfolks believed they would be in Johore for several weeks if not months. It was bound to be a while before they had finished training and reinforcements had been built up to the point where they could start pushing the Japs back. 'Your first job is to get the [officers'] mess going,' the Norfolks' CO was overheard telling his second-in-command, while the Australians tried to keep a straight face.

At Bakri there was precious little for the Australians to laugh about. A low-level air attack roaring in across the padang had scored a direct hit on the white bungalow that was brigade headquarters, just as Duncan was holding his 11 a.m. conference, an event well-advertised by the vehicles parked outside. Almost all of Duncan's staff, including his entire signals section, were killed or wounded. Only the brigadier and his brigade major escaped unscathed, though Duncan, who was covered in other people's blood, was in a state of shock.

Despite their aerial superiority, Japanese close support bombing was rarely as effective as this. Dismembered bodies were scattered over a wide area. Part of somebody's stomach was hanging from a nearby tree. Lieutenant Ben Hackney, who, since watching the destruction of the tanks, had had his left leg broken by a bullet below the knee, was one of several wounded lying in a truck parked in the padang when the bombs landed. By the time his war was over, Hackney would have far worse things to remember, but the images etched on his mind that day would never be erased. 'Just beside the road a naked waist with two twisted legs lay about two yards from a scarred bleeding head with a neck, half a chest and one arm.'

Major Julius, the commander of the Australian artillery battery, was among the seriously hurt, though it was thought he might survive if he could reach the casualty clearing station at the Yong Peng intersection in time. An attempt to evacuate him was foiled by a road-block and he was killed when the vehicle he was in and the armoured car escorting it were destroyed. One bloodied survivor came staggering back. 'The Black Bastard was dead,' wrote Gunner Russell Braddon. 'Our best soldier had not survived and . . . we were now surrounded.'

Road-blocks were becoming a feature of the fighting around Muar because the Imperial Guard were now attacking the road to Bakri from the south as well as the east. One of their first victims was Colonel Robertson, who ran into one as he tried to get to brigade HQ the day before the bombing on the back of the dispatch rider's motorbike. Fatally injured, not by the bullet which hit him in the leg but by falling off the bike at speed, he was picked up by a Bren gun carrier about 500 yards beyond his battalion's eastern perimeter. Before he died, the Geelong garage proprietor who could so easily have decided to sit this war out called in McCure, the anti-tank lieutenant, and admitted how wrong he had been. 'Bill, but for you and your guns none of my boys would be alive now,' he told him.

Since then, the block had been cleared by a company-sized attack with mortar support from Anderson's battalion, and an enormous cheer went up when a relief column came through with food, ammunition and the other two anti-tank guns. Some of the same vehicles evacuated all but twelve of their wounded and the cameramen Metcalf and Bagnall with their precious film. Hedley Metcalf's pictures of the gunners before the burning tanks would soon be receiving wide circulation and, for a few days at least, would lull Australian and British newspaper readers into believing that the tide might have turned in Malaya.

Duncan, who had already had more than his share of setbacks, was heavily concussed by the bombing which, by some bizarre caprice of high explosive, he had so miraculously survived. It was agreed that the South African Anderson, the CO of the newly arrived 2/19th, who had not been at the conference, would take over command of the brigade at least until such time as Duncan had fully recovered. In any case, operationally it had become more or less an Australian brigade with two of Bennett's battalions and an Australian gun battery. It could have been two batteries but Anderson sent away a UK British unit, reinforcement from Singapore garrison. Like Robertson he felt it was not artillery country and protecting them would be a drain on infantry resources. Before they left they handed over 500 spare rounds to the Australian gunners.

The only blot on Anderson's homogeneous command were 1,000 or so mainly teenaged Indian stragglers, a little over a battalion's worth. 'I felt extremely disturbed that it was necessary to have had to employ such immature and partly trained troops,' said Anderson, who professed 'the highest regard' for the Indians he had fought alongside during the campaign in German East Africa. 'Most of the troops were, I should say, about seventeen years old and had adolescent fluff on their cheeks; six months formed, and it takes them four months to teach them to wear boots!!!'

Anderson had a point. These deracinated peasants, who had lost almost all their British officers killed or wounded, not least their three dead battalion commanders, were surely the saddest and cruellest measure of British desperation. The largest number who had retained any cohesion at all, and then only because they had seen little of the enemy, were the late Colonel Williams' Jats. They were beginning to come into the positions around Bakri, hungry and thirsty and having lost a lot of their kit. Being strict Hindus and revolted by the idea of using the utensils of the unclean, the Jats irritated the Australians by declining canteens and mugs and wasting precious drinking water by trying to catch it in their cupped hands, elbowing each other out of the way as they did so. Sergeant Harrison, the anti-tank gunner, and his crew had to produce their pistols to keep order. 'Eventually they were given a fair share in bulk and left to work out their own distribution.'

As he recovered, Duncan began to try and restore some confidence and order among the Indians, but the Australians mostly regarded them as a rabble and treated them accordingly. Some of Braddon's battery noticed that the Indians' Lee-Enfield rifles were much newer than their own, which had probably been new at Gallipoli, and decided that exchange was no robbery.

Australian morale remained high. Unlike the Indians, they were well-trained and the teenagers in their ranks were the exception not the rule. Furthermore, Anderson's men had already enjoyed the kind of success Bennett expected of them with a counter-attack west of Bakri on the Japanese who had inserted themselves between the two Australian battalions. By applying one of the outflanking movements they had been practising for almost a year, they trapped over 200 of the enemy between two companies. 'The Japs literally ran around in circles,' reported Lieutenant Patrick Reynolds, a platoon commander and, like so many Australian infantry officers, a grazier in civilian life. 'It all went off as we'd been taught to expect. The boys were in great heart about it all.' Even so, Reynolds soon learned the hard way that this was an opponent who did not give in easily.

The section on my right was again pinned down by automatic fire. Lying amongst a heap of about fifteen apparently dead Japs, I was signalling to the other section when suddenly one of the corpses came to life, holding a grenade in his right hand and raising himself from the ground with his left. I shot at him, the grenade exploded simultaneously, and half his head was blown off. Two pieces of the grenade hit me, one under the right arm and the other on the side of my head . . . As I fell I called out to Sergeant Small to 'push home the attack' . . . We had practised this type of movement dozens of times in training . . .

Then, only a few yards away, Reynolds noticed another grievously wounded member of the Imperial Guard.

I saw him pushing his rifle laboriously towards me, so I picked up my pistol and, with my left hand, took careful aim and pulled the trigger for all my worth. It just wouldn't fire. I can remember feeling extremely annoyed about this. Luckily my batman saw the Jap up to his tricks and shot him . . .

For the Australians, all the rumours they had ever heard about Japanese bravery, or 'fanaticism' if you were at the wrong end of it, were coming true. But it seems that several of the Japanese, though prepared to die rather than be captured, were playing dead in the hope that the Australians would move on and leave them to fight another day.

Sergeant Desmond Mulcahy's particular Lazarus was a fallen sergeant of the Konoye Guards. He was about to search him for the letters and unit identification beloved by battalion intelligence officers, when the dead man sprang indignantly to his feet with a grenade in his right fist. Mulcahy grabbed his left hand to stop him pulling the pin. This was good thinking but it allowed his opponent to bludgeon him about the head with his grenade while he did his best to fend him off with left jabs. Mulcahy shouted for help and, while he was holding the man's arms, the Guards NCO, so far from the pomp and circumstance which had moulded his military career, was first bayoneted and then shot.

More puzzling was the case of the unarmed man who got to his feet and charged Private 'Bluey' Watkins, a Welshman born in Swansea. Watkins had sportingly thrown down his rifle and took on his assailant only to have the bout ended by a .303 fired at such close quarters it left him deaf for a while. There appears to be no good reason why this particular Japanese could not have been restrained and captured. But it seems that it rapidly became the norm, as it did almost everywhere the Imperial Japanese Army ever met western troops, to regard almost any attempt to take them alive as much too risky. 'From that first engagement we learnt not to trust their wounded,' remembered Charles Warden, a private in B Company during the fight outside Bakri and, five months short of his seventeenth birthday, one of the 2/19th's under-age infantrymen.

Both sides could be unpredictable. At Slim River the Argylls' Lieutenant Primrose had shot a Japanese officer in the stomach at close range and survived a beating to be taken prisoner. Yet the Japanese had casually murdered those wounded prisoners unable to walk rather than be inconvenienced by them.

By the time they had made sure of every Japanese they could see, and counted all the bodies, Anderson's battalion reckoned they had killed 140. Among them was an officer wearing a distinctive white shirt, who died leading an ill-advised charge. 'He was hit by Bren and Tommy and rifle fire and his shirt just flew into little pieces,' observed Warden. Australian losses had been ten killed and fifteen wounded. With this and the destruction of the tanks the Australians had started as well at Bakri as they had at Gemas, but it would turn out to be their high-water mark.

By dawn on 20 January, Anderson had been ordered to pull out of Bakri towards Yong Peng and save what he could of 45th Brigade, which Nishimura's Guards were now trying to slice up salami fashion with road-blocks so they could deal with it piece by piece. Particularly hard hit by this was the late Colonel Robertson's 2/29th. Only about 200, including seven officers, managed to fight their way through and join up with Anderson's men. About the same number, perhaps slightly more, could not get through. Most were in the rearguard where the major who had taken over command of the battalion was killed by machine-gun fire, along with several others, while trying to get across a stretch of open land. Another 150 or so, including some Jats, walked into a maze of jungle-covered swamp where they were both machine-gunned by the Japanese and shelled by their own artillery giving them covering fire from Bakri and never dreaming that anybody but the enemy would be off the road. Among the casualties was a young man with a friend called Jim. Lance-Sergeant Harrison and everybody else in the vicinity, which probably included the Japanese, knew this because he was in such agony he kept pleading for Jim to kill him. Eventually there was a single shot and then Harrison heard the boy ask, 'Oh, Jim, what did you do that for?'

Eventually they found a way out of this hellhole, carrying their wounded, though not always their rifles, as far as a friendly Chinese village where they were left. Next day, they broke up into small parties. One of these consisted of Lieutenant McCure, Harrison and ten of their anti-tank gunners. Like all British fugitives in Malaya they soon saw that progress in the jungle was so slow that it might take them weeks to overtake the Japanese advance. They decided that the quickest way back to friendly forces was to get to the coast, get hold of a boat and sail it to Singapore.

Certainly, this seemed a more sensible plan than trying to catch up with Anderson and the rest, who, they imagined, must by now be well on their way to the Yong Peng intersection on the trunk road.

But Anderson's column was nowhere near there. It had taken them two agonizing days and nights to fight their way along a mere 15 miles of road to a little humpbacked bridge of white reinforced concrete which spanned the unremarkable dung-coloured waters of the River Simpang Kiri at Parit Sulong. They were right up to the bridge but all their attempts to cross it had been thwarted by well-placed machine-guns.

Equally frustrated had been attempts by Brigadier Duke's 53rd Brigade to come the other way and relieve them: particularly a confused British night attack to regain full control of Bukit Belah, a hill which commanded a narrow pass along the road from Yong Peng to Parit Sulong – a defile in Indian Army speak – and regarded as the key to keeping it open. Moorhead, who had given up command of the amalgamated 6/15th Brigade to return to his beloved Punjabis, had been killed when once again he dashed forward to stop the newly landed and trigger-happy Norfolks from firing on his men who rarely spoke more than a few words of English. This time it was the Japanese he was ordering to ceasefire. Lieutenant-Colonel Moorhead was the fourth British commander of an Indian battalion to be killed in four days. 'My heart is broken,' said one of his havildars. 'There will never be a man more brave than he.'

By now, many of the Australians in the 2/19th were feeling much the same about the South African-born Charles Anderson. The first road-block to hold Anderson's column up as it moved east towards the Yong Peng intersection was not astride the road itself but on a low ridge of rubber trees which dominated it. The South African urged his men to charge it, singing 'Waltzing Matilda'. Once they had overcome the initial shyness with which Australians almost invariably greet an outsider's request for the sheep rustler's anthem, they had obliged with considerable enthusiasm. Among them was the sixteen-year-old Charles Warden.

I was about to go over the top of a rotting tree trunk when I saw a Jap on the other side with a light machine-gun who had just killed Tom Howard on my right, and in his haste to bring his gun to bear onto me it fell over on its legs [bipod] . . . I momentarily took cover . . . took a quick look over the top and saw a pair of legs and backside. So I shot him in the hips. He gave a yell and was certainly not dead but it slowed him down . . . I then saw the face of a Jap lying down beside a rubber tree about 12 feet away . . . I fired a quick shot at him and at the same time I was knocked backwards off balance and felt a terrific burning pain in my left shoulder and shoulder blade. I looked round again and saw Charlie Dutton throwing a grenade . . . and at the same time he was hit badly and his face hit the ground in front of me and he lay still.

Pinned down, the Australians threw their grenades by getting up on their knees and then ducking down again, Warden contributing with his good arm. Two more, including his platoon commander, were hit doing this. It was about then that Anderson came charging up at the head of another platoon. A corporal pointed out the whereabouts of two machine-guns that were holding them up. Anderson, accompanied by a Private Donnelly who acted as his batman cum bodyguard, announced that he would try and deal with them, after which everybody must get up and charge.

Sometimes crawling, sometimes moving from tree to tree, Anderson approached the Japanese with the kind of painstaking attention to detail he might have given a wounded lion in a Kenyan thicket. Behind him came the faithful Donnelly. Once he was close enough to be reasonably sure that his grenades would be on target he let fly. When one of the survivors unwisely put his head up, the bespectacled Anderson yelled out 'Mine, Donnelly!' and immediately killed him with his .455 revolver. In a wild charge, his men caught up with him and the position was taken. Clutching his bleeding shoulder wound, Warden watched the last moments of the action as Anderson continued to fine-tune, 'telling people to move here and fire there [which] helped a lot to relieve the strain'. As they moved on, the exploits of this big game hunter who was leading them reverberated down the column, a comic-book hero come to life.

The reality, of course, was somewhat grimmer. Bennett's Australians had hardly been in action for a week and here were two of his battalions – one-third of his available infantry – one of them already badly reduced and both surrounded and fighting for their lives. In all, with two companies of Jats and a mixed company of Rajputs and Garhwalis, the column was about 1,200 strong. Anderson had done his best to arrange them into a phalanx of which the core was the mile or so of road occupied by his transport with his infantry on foot all around them. Front and rear were a couple of UK British anti-tank guns that had been sent to Bakri at the last moment. There were also the tracked Bren gun carriers which, in the Australian battalions, carried belt-fed, water-cooled Vickers machine-guns which had a high rate of fire. In the centre were the four remaining 25-pounder guns with their beetle-like Quad tractor tows, the wireless wagon, trucks containing food, ammunition and, increasingly, the wounded for the couple of Indian Army ambulances with them had long since reached capacity. When-ever possible they had moved at night and spent the daylight hours under cover in the rubber, unless the ground was too soggy to move off the road for fear of getting bogged down. When this happened the transport, often three abreast and moving at a funereal pace in first gear, were an easy target for air or artillery strikes and several of the wounded were hit again. A machine-gun burst stitched a line of holes in the vehicle Lieutenant Hackney was lying in. 'I heard a peculiar grunt beside me, and looking around saw that the poor fellow sitting there, already badly wounded, had been killed. His body slumped forward, revealing a fresh blood patch where a bullet had entered his back.'

By the time they got to Parit Sulong Brigadier Duncan, who had recovered from his concussion and was commanding the rearguard, had been killed after rallying his dispirited Jats and personally leading a successful bayonet charge to retrieve lost vehicles. 'A very able and gallant officer,' declared Anderson, but for many of the young Indians the way the Japanese had been able to account for every one of their senior officers was deeply depressing. Who was going to lead them? This was not winning.

At the front of the column the Australians had been obliged to fight their way through the toughest road-block yet with a barricade composed of gutted Australian transport pushed there from a nearby rear echelon vehicle park which had been overrun. It had yielded only after a 25-pounder, manhandled to within 75 yards of its target, had blown the trucks into pieces small enough to be tossed aside and Bren gun carriers had got to within a few feet of machine-gun nests and used their Vickers on them until the water-coolers blistered the gun-ners' hands. Some of the Australian gunners who were acting as infantry – there was not enough artillery left for all of them – had removed from their trucks the axes they used to clear rubber trees for gun emplacements. Now they were using their axes on both people and barricades with a berserker lack of discrimination. 'Every man was fighting mad,' related the 2/19th Battalion's diarist, and certainly enough of them were to make a difference.

It had been thought that this was their last hurdle and the relief was tremendous. Identity discs were removed from their latest dead, who amounted to about twenty, and shallow graves hurriedly dug; space was found in their trucks for the freshly wounded, and they were on their way. As far as Anderson was concerned, Parit Sulong was not in Japanese hands and from there it would be plain sailing for the 20 miles to Yong Peng, where a casualty clearing station awaited his wounded and there would be sleep for all his troops, most of whom had known nothing more than catnaps for four days now.

But the bridge at Parit Sulong, which had been briefly held or at least patrolled by the Norfolks until the Japanese got into the high ground behind them, had been firmly in Japanese hands for the last two days. Lieutenant Walter Greenwood, an intelligence officer at 53rd Brigade HQ who had been in the country a week, had seen them arrive. Out on a one-man motorcycle reconnaissance, Greenwood had stopped with his feet still astride his machine on the western end of the bridge when he had noticed, off the road, about 50 yards away, a file of men approaching. 'They were wearing shorts and for a moment I wondered whether they were coolies of some sort. Then I saw the bandoliers of ammunition. They started shouting, "Hello Johnny" but I had started the bike up and was off. I knew they were Japanese.' Back at Brigadier Duke's HQ near Yong Peng, he was introduced to Percival and Heath who were visiting, but Greenwood thought they seemed unimpressed by his news.

Anderson's column reached Parit Sulong after a long night march at 2 a.m. on 21 January. The village straddled the river and its western edge was about half a mile from the bridge. By dawn the Australians had established beyond all doubt that the Japanese possessed all of Parit Sulong both sides of the bridge. The day was spent in some of the fiercest fighting they had yet seen. It was not until mid-afternoon that the Australians had won control of the western half of the village, where the Japanese had torn up the floors and dug themselves into the foundations of the wooden houses, prising apart planks to make loopholes. Once again it was the Bren gun carriers, low and little bigger than a beach buggy, which won the day, bringing their Vickers up to not quite point-blank range so that they could depress the barrels. When even the Guards' nerve broke and they started to make a run for it, the Australian riflemen were waiting for them with their Lee-Enfields and grenades.

But while the head of the column was gaining ground, and eventually reached the river and almost the bridge itself, the rearguard and the flanks were beginning to buckle. Tanks and artillery from Muar had caught up with the Guards and, not all that surprisingly, their support was beginning to make a difference. Stocks of 25-pounder shells and mortar bombs, which would have been used to try and blast a passage across the bridge, were running low as the Australians tried to keep the back door closed. Most of the walking wounded, among them Lieutenant Pat Reynolds with his right arm in a sling from the grenade shrapnel he had received from 'the corpse', were helping to guard the flanks. Those, like Ben Hackney, who could not walk but could use their hands and were not in too much pain, found therapy in filling ammunition belts with .303 for the Vickers guns.

But the plight of the badly wounded, many of them with four-day-old injuries that were beginning to stink of gangrene, was awful. Morphine was in desperately short supply, as was the South African brandy that also helped to relieve pain and restore morale. The two doctors serving in the Australian infantry battalions as medical officers persuaded Anderson to see if the Japanese would allow their thirty worst cases, men who would obviously die unless properly treated, to cross the bridge under a flag of truce and proceed to Yong Peng. Perhaps they were inspired by the chivalrous behaviour of the Japanese at Gemas, when they had declined to fire on the 2/30th's ambulances. It was a faint hope but there was no alternative.

Under a white flag two truck loads of wounded were driven up to the crest of the humpbacked bridge and a parley took place with an English-speaking officer. It was soon established that the Guards would be happy to treat the wounded themselves as soon as the entire column had surrendered. In the meantime the wounded would remain on the bridge as a road-block and the trucks would be machine-gunned if they attempted to go back. But the hostages had other plans. Once it was dark, a lieutenant, his upper body swathed in bandages after a bullet had entered his throat and exited through a shoulder blade, got a wounded driver to help him slip the handbrakes on both vehicles.

Despite their injuries, and their inability to see very much, they then managed to reverse noiselessly and without mishap off the hump-backed bridge towards the Australian lines, from which flashes and bangs were coming in all directions.

By now Anderson's column had been compressed into a triangle-shaped perimeter with its apex at the bridge and a baseline of about 1,000 yards no more than 1,500 yards away and often less. The two UK British anti-tank guns, which appear to have been Italian Bredas, and 25-pounders firing over open sights stopped several of the tanks and the crippled machines made an effective road-block. But the Bredas were overrun and their crews killed or wounded, and one of the 25-pounders was lost, though its dial sight and breech block were removed when it became bogged down and the infantry around it began to pull out.

As darkness fell, a tank-hunting team armed with Boys rifles, Molo-tovs and grenades crept among the Japanese armour, finishing off the cripples and trying to get at the tanks sheltering behind them. The intrepid sergeant who led them was killed when flames from his first victim silhouetted him for the machine-gunner in the next T95 he was approaching. One of the more surprising combatants was Anderson's chaplain, the Reverend Henry Wardale-Greenwood, an English Pres-byterian minister from Durham in his early thirties who had lived in Australia for some years before the war and was the muscular sort of Christian. When he was not ministering to the wounded, Wardale-Greenwood, who like all army padres held the rank of captain, was out lending more temporal assistance with a 2-inch mortar he and his batman had acquired.

Throughout the night the Japanese kept up the pressure with their own mortaring and hit-and-run attacks. Fatigue was now one of the greatest problems. Captain Joe Pickup, who commanded a platoon of ten Bren gun carriers, found himself going from carrier to carrier shaking his men awake. 'I made them clean guns at every halt and check and fill belts. I hit them, slapped them and almost drowned them with water but they kept going and munched the dog biscuits [issue hard tack biscuits] and the small ration of bully beef.'

Even for Australian country boys a Malayan night under the cover of a rubber plantation or on the jungle fringe was very black indeed. Warden found that, after a while, they did not mind the occasional Japanese mortar round because they rarely seemed to cause much injury, as they tended to explode in high trees; also, they kept them alert and less likely to be taken by surprise. So did Japanese jitter parties trying to establish exactly where the Australian positions were by coming into earshot and calling, 'Where are you, Joe?' in what they fondly imagined was Indian English. This happened all over Malaya. Sometimes, tired of no response, they might sign off with an unequivocal, 'Tommowoh yoh die!'

After their first night on the road, when there had been several Australian casualties because of mass firing at shadows, fire discipline was strictly imposed. Instead the Australians were supposed to wait until enemy scouts were close enough to use their 17-inch bayonets on them, and the most unlikely soldiers sometimes did. Gunner Braddon, recently a Sydney law student, was on watch when 'a vague figure flitted towards us' and his exhausted comrades refused to be shaken awake. When this apparition was three rubber trees away Braddon made his decision.

I moved alone to the tree in front of me and, as the Jap ran crouching towards it, stepped out from behind it and presented him with a firmly held rifle and bayonet. Upon this he promptly impaled himself. At the moment of impact, as I tucked my right elbow securely against my hip and moved my left foot slightly forward, I found myself thinking, 'Just like a stop volley at tennis.'

Next morning Braddon saw that his victim had very white teeth and wished he would shut his mouth. The willingness of Japanese soldiers to terrorize their enemy and stage these solitary attacks by throwing a grenade, sniping or rushing in with the bayonet, often more like crazed assassins than soldiers, was probably something very few western armies could match. Stewart's Argylls, with their three- or four-man 'Tiger patrols', had probably been the only infantry battalion in Percival's command who came even close. Along the Bakri–Parit Sulong road the Japanese appear to have started out as small patrols then fanned out to attack individually, sometimes as a diversion while a larger attack was made elsewhere.

Lance-Havildar John Benedict, an Anglo-Indian serving in a company of the Queen Victoria's Own Madras Sappers and Miners, shot a Japanese who had been lurking in an unoccupied slit trench and then jumped an Australian sergeant who was obviously getting the worst of it. Benedict had a special interest in the Parit Sulong bridge because it was one of several along the Muar–Yong Peng road he had prepared for demolition over the last week. The charges were already in place; all they needed was a detonator. Once they had captured the bridge and got the column across it they could blow it to kingdom come and prevent the Jap tanks from following them in a couple of minutes. Few of the Indian sappers doubted that these tough Australians would win the day, though after a sepoy was mistaken for an infiltrator and bayoneted they did their best to stay home at night.

The main indication of the whereabouts of Anderson's brigade HQ area was the signals truck parked among the carriers and other vehicles – with a faint glow emanating from its transmitter and the steady pips and peeps of outgoing morse clearly audible. Its antenna was attached to the nearest rubber tree. It was manned by two of the three signallers loaned to 45 Brigade from Bennett's divisional HQ for liaison when the brigade first came under his command. The third man had been killed and their original wireless badly damaged at Bakri and they had constructed a replacement from parts salvaged from several different transmitters. All that was missing was a working morse key, so they transmitted by tapping the loose ends of their terminals together.

All the code books had gone up in smoke and messages were being transmitted in clear, though sometimes lightly coded because it was assumed that the Japanese would be monitoring. 'Look up at sparrow fart,' Bennett's HQ advised after Anderson requested an air drop of morphine for the wounded – something of a novelty in early 1942. Come the dawn, Anderson hoped for bigger and better things than air drops, for signals had indicated that Duke's 53rd Brigade, despite the earlier setback in which Moorhead had been killed, was about to try to relieve them. In the course of the afternoon, hopes had been raised by the occasional rolling rumble of artillery fire from the east.

As promised, at first light next day two Tiger Moths of the Malayan Volunteer Air Force had turned up to drop, at a little over tree-top height, supplies of morphine and food. Their appearance seems to have surprised the Japanese infantry for, despite having a top speed of only 100 mph, they got away with it. So did three more biplanes a couple of hours later. Two of these were Albacores, which had covered cockpits and were the Royal Navy's latest torpedo launcher, intended to replace the ageing Swordfish on their carriers. The third was a Shark, an old aircraft whose normal employment was dangerous enough for it earned its keep towing targets on which anti-aircraft gunners could practise their skills. This was all Pulford could spare. A fighter escort of Buffaloes had failed to make the rendezvous.

As well as food and medicines the Singapore-based biplanes also carried machine-guns and four 250-pound bombs. Anderson had hoped they would bomb the machine-gun positions around the bridge which were holding them up. But for some reason they flew west towards Muar, then turned south and, appearing suddenly from low cloud, bombed and strafed the long columns of Japanese traffic crawling down the coast road towards Batu Pahat. Sergeant Pilot Peter Ballard, a tall New Zealander, was flying the Shark and was the last of the three to attack. 'Each aircraft let all bombs go at once – one attack only, and we all got the hell out of it as quickly as possible.' On their way back to Singapore they sighted enemy fighters but they were flying in rain and the Japanese did not see them.

At Parit Sulong, the Australians ran around picking up the air drop which, to the intense annoyance of hungry young men, turned out to contain canned beetroot when what they wanted was all the bully beef they could carry. The day got much worse. For once, the British artillery had been far from impressive. The gunfire from the east that Anderson's column had heard had been ranging shots from a battery firing at the limit of its range and unable to get on target. Apparently there had been problems with the air burst fuses brought on by humidity and Brigadier Duke was insisting there could be no attack without artillery support.

The gunners were supposed to be providing it for Lieutenant-Colonel Mordaunt Elrington's 2nd Loyals, a regular North Country battalion normally part of the Singapore garrison and now attached to Duke's 53rd Brigade and his somewhat demoralized 6th Norfolks. For some time Elrington had been pleading with Percival to send his battalion to the mainland, where the situation had obviously become much too serious for amateurs. Most of his regulars were of the same mind. 'They wanted to show the Japs where to get off,' recalled Lieutenant Tom Henling-Wade, his intelligence officer, who had been educated in England but came from an old Anglo-Chinese family in Shanghai where he had worked as a cub reporter on the *Shanghai Times*. He was a friend of Lieutenant Newland of the Leicesters, one of the heroes of Kampar.

For two days the Loyals had been poised to attack the high ground at Bukit Belah and fight their way through to the Australians at Parit Sulong, while, to Bennett's enormous fury once he realized what was happening, Duke saw mission impossible and found fresh reasons for delay. Elrington would have done it without artillery preparation, relying on an element of surprise. But when it had finally been cancelled all surprise had been lost. For too long the Loyals had been formed up and waiting for the word in an exposed position of *lallang* grass with little tree cover. The Japanese had spotted them and called in an air strike: nine men had been killed and thirty wounded. Before they could get over this, the Guards they were supposed to be attacking, accompanied by a few tanks which had travelled south from Muar and then turned north, came rushing down the hill and attacked them instead. The Loyals' two forward companies were scattered and many taken prisoner. Henling-Wade discovered Elrington, whom the young officer greatly admired, sitting with his head in his hands 'cursing the brigadier and his artillery' for the fiasco which had all but destroyed his battalion. Percival thought the attempt should never have been made in the first place: 'the chances of a single battalion advancing 7 miles through that type of country were, in my opinion, quite remote.' But the attack was Bennett's idea and presumably he felt he could not deprive him of this chance, however remote, to relieve his cut-off Australians.

Anderson, of course, knew nothing of all this. At dawn on 22 January, as reports came in from all points of his triangular perimeter that they were finding it harder to hold, he decided to make one last attempt to get across the Parit Sulong bridge by frontal assault. They had, after all, smashed their way through every other road-block since Bakri, and it was unlikely that the Japanese on the other side had been reinforced. On the contrary, their numbers may have even been reduced by the need to reinforce their people on Bukit Belah trying to hold back Duke's brigade for, in a way, they too were surrounded.

On the hump of the bridge the Japanese had thrown together three sets of barricades, one behind the other. They were made up of the usual sandbags, 40-gallon oil drums and timbers provided, in case of air-raid damage, by the local Public Works Department. These barricades seem to have been covered by heavy machine-guns on some high ground behind the bridge and by two light machine-guns no more than 100 yards away, where its walls ended on the south bank. Left and right of these, the Japanese had men dug in along the bank so that they could not be immediately outflanked by parties coming across in rafts or boats. (There was no chance of this. Anderson had neither the men to spare, nor the boats.)

The bridge was only 20 feet wide and no more than 30 Australians took part in the actual assault, though at least 100 men, including some of the wounded and about 20 Indians, were giving covering fire from the wrecked houses just before the bridge. Casualties among junior officers had been heavy and the attack was led by some of the sergeants and corporals who had been in the thick of things for the last four days. Corporal Arthur Robb had a bloody bandage around his head. Almost everybody was short of sleep. Some had queasy stomachs because the stagnant water in the 8-foot-wide storm drains either side of the road was all they had to drink and it was not always possible to boil it.

It began with one of the carriers charging the first barricade, but all this succeeded in doing was pushing it back onto the second. The corporal in command and his gunner then threw grenades over the jumble of sandbags and oil drums. Before long both men were wounded but the driver managed to reverse the carrier and get them back. While the intense supporting fire suppressed the machine-guns on the high ground behind the bridge, corporals Robb and Ivers now led a charge on foot and reached the sandbags, which at least afforded them some protection. There were about sixteen of them in all and they threw a shower of grenades towards the Nambu light machine-gun crews at the end of the bridge and then started to clamber over. The Japanese must have held their fire until they were all in view, or perhaps one of their own grenades fell from a nerveless hand, because all appear to have been killed. Yet there seems to have been a feeling that Japanese fire was diminishing, or the fate of the others was not clear, because another eight men under Sergeant Jim Clark dashed up to support them. Sporting metaphors are always sadly inadequate on these occasions; but one does almost get the impression of something akin to a rugby touchline ruck, with the forwards gathering around the ball in a loose scrum, convinced that one more shove will win the try. Sandbags began to give way, more grenades were thrown and, for the first time, the third barricade was reached. Clark and two of his men were on top of it when the Nambus waiting for them on the other side killed them. The five Australians left alive on the bridge somehow managed to remove themselves without further casualties.

Anderson ordered an end to this sacrifice of his bravest and best. It was obviously useless. The narrow bridge was too well defended to force a passage with anything less than a tank. He made the decision he had been dreading. They would have to abandon their badly wounded to the mercy of the Japanese, blow up their remaining field guns, break as many working parts as possible in their vehicles and walk to Yong Peng through jungle and swamp. At 9 a.m. an officers' conference was called; they were told they would move out by companies and given compass directions to take them on what would be a circuitous, north-easterly route to Yong Peng – 12 miles away as the crow flies and more like 20 the way they were going.

All the wounded capable of walking were to go with them. About 150 stretcher cases would be left behind, of whom just over 100 were Australian, including three lieutenants. One of these was Ben Hackney, the 14-stone, rugby-playing grazier, who in addition to his smashed left leg had, since leaving Bakri with Anderson's column, collected two splinter wounds in his right leg, one behind the knee and the other in his calf, and a third in his back. Throughout the column's ordeal the wounded had been particularly vulnerable to shelling or air strikes because it had often not been possible to move their transport off the road and hide it in the rubber. At one point, when their driver could not be found, Hackney had dragged himself into the cab and somehow moved their truck. No padres or medical officers were remaining with the wounded. Hackney and the other two lieutenants incapable of moving much – A. Tibbitts and B. Crawford, in civilian life a clerk and a school teacher respectively – were expected to oversee the formal handing over of the wounded to the Japanese. Tibbitts appears to have been the most mobile of the three.

Barry Quigley, a forty-year-old private who was Crawford's batman and quite capable of walking, having no more than a relatively minor injury to his right forearm, volunteered to stay. It appears this was mostly to look after the badly wounded Crawford with whom he seems to have had one of those close master–servant relationships that quite often developed between young officers and their batmen, though in Crawford's case he was only nine years younger than Quigley. Undoubtedly, once the batman had made his brave decision it seems to have been generally welcomed because it was realized that there should be at least one almost able-bodied man to guide the Japanese to the officers and be around to offer what comfort he could before they arrived.

Among the Indian wounded who remained behind was Lance-Havildar Benedict, the Sappers and Miners NCO who had saved the Australian sergeant from the infiltrator. Since then he had been shot in the leg. It seems to have been a flesh wound for Benedict had managed to get around on it for several hours before he reported for treatment. Some of the Australian wounded who could hobble along on this kind of less serious leg injury had been persuaded to 'give it a go' by officers and friends determined to help them escape, but the Indians had very few officers left to take an interest in their welfare and many of the Australians found them comic at best. There were at least three others from Benedict's sapper company with him, including their havildar-major, who did not appear to be badly wounded if they were wounded at all. Extracting those capable of walking from the trucks without panicking the men who were about to be deserted was a delicate business. Corporal Jack Collins, who had been badly hit in the upper right arm which had 'started to smell a bit and was giving me some curry', heard a sergeant explaining to a stretcher case that the only reason he was asking those who could stand to get out of the truck was 'to give the other chaps more room'. Collins himself, though feverish and in considerable pain, decided to make the effort and go. 'I thought the Japanese would not show much consideration for any wounded.'

Yet allowing injured men you were unable to evacuate to fall into the hands of the enemy was not an outrageous concept, at least not among western armies. During the ebb and flow of the North African campaign's desert battles, in which the Australians were playing such a big part, it had become quite a common occurrence. There were occasions when British, German and Italian medics found themselves working alongside each other in field aid stations that had changed hands several times in a single day. And though Japanese atrocities against their fellow Asians in China were well known, the recent fate of some of the Argyll and Indian wounded at Slim River was not. As it happened, the only indication of how the Japanese might treat wounded prisoners was a good one and that was the respect they had appeared to show for the Australian ambulances at Gemas. True, there was the business of the badly wounded men held hostage on the bridge itself, but they had not actually harmed them and it could have been that they watched the trucks escape and decided to do nothing about it.

By 11 a.m., some five hours after the last attempt to get over the

Parit Sulong bridge had failed, most of Anderson's column was on foot and heading east. The exceptions were the wounded, a small rearguard of about twenty men, a cut-off platoon on the perimeter who did not receive the withdrawal order but eventually escaped to the west coast, Padre Greenwood, Anderson himself, his adjutant, his intelligence officer and his signallers. Before the latter smashed the radio they had so lovingly put together, they received a final message from Bennett which, though entirely redundant, must have offered some comfort. 'You may at your discretion leave wounded with volunteers, destroy heavy equipment and escape. Sorry unable to help after your heroic efforts. Good luck.'

The Japanese were slow at first to close in on the Australian positions. They contented themselves with sniping, mortaring, bringing up their machine-guns and sending in patrols to probe the enemy defences, fearful that the wily Australians might be trying to lure them into one of their ambushes. For a short while, the wounded lieutenants Hackney and Tibbitts lay under a wrecked utility truck supporting the rearguard with a Bren gun until their ammunition ran out, when they stripped it down and threw the pieces in several directions.

By 2.30 p.m., the fire around the convoy, both incoming and out-going, had stopped and the wounded knew they were on their own. Hackney and Tibbitts talked of how soon they would be reacquainted with all the things they had never realized were so good before, such as 'a wash; being in other than bloodstained, torn, filthy clothes; a bed and sleep'. Then, mostly from the west, the first of the Imperial Guard arrived and so began the torture and gradual massacre of Anderson's wounded.

It started with them bayoneting and shooting all those entirely incapable of moving away from the vehicles and crossing a small bridge which spanned the deep drainage ditch on the right of the road. Even men doing their utmost to crawl there were not spared but clubbed about the head with rifle butts or pierced with bayonets. It soon became apparent to Hackney that many of their tormentors took a malicious delight in prodding or kicking obvious wounds and derived consider-able satisfaction from 'any visible sign of pain'. Incapable of standing on either leg, he at last got over the bridge with his arms around the shoulders of Tibbitts and another man who both continued to support him while all three were pummelled with rifle butts.

Once across, the prisoners were assembled before some low buildings, which turned out to be a Public Works Department bungalow and its adjoining sheds and garages. They sat in a circle in front of these buildings, naked apart from their boots as they had been made to remove all their clothing so they could be searched, presumably for weapons or any interesting maps or papers. All requests for medical attention and water were refused. More men died. Some of the Guards had a sense of humour. One of the older corpses, already stiff with *rigor mortis*, was made to 'stand' by propping a table top against a truck and leaning the body against it. This served as a kind of macabre billboard. Passing troops in trucks or on bicycles stopped to break their journey south for some fun with the arrogant and contemptible enemy who had allowed themselves to be taken alive. Hackney was among those nearest to the road and a frequent target. 'The wound in my back attracted the attention of many who, whenever possible, took a delight in kicking and belting the place.'

Nor was this hatred confined to the white men. An Indian with half his hand blown off and a copiously bleeding thigh wound was first beaten into insensibility. After a while he started to come round and sit up, but this was noticed. Hackney watched as the man was subjected to a frenzied bout of kicking until he lay there 'groaning and jabbering'. This incensed his particular tormentor who picked up a rifle 'then thrust the bayonet into him time and time again' before pushing him into a deep and brimming drainage ditch. Still the Indian clung to life but when his head surfaced and he gasped for air he was shot. At least one Japanese officer would have found this scene almost as distressing as Hackney. Not very far away at Muar, Major Fujiwara and his propaganda team were addressing Indian prisoners about the benefits of Japan's Asian Co-Prosperity Scheme, and in particular their opportunity to end British rule at home by joining something he called the Indian National Army.

By this time the wounded prisoners were in a very distressed condition. Their rags of uniform had been returned to them but, with the exception of six officers, the three Australian lieutenants and three from the Indian Army, they had all been locked up in conditions of desperate overcrowding. First they had been crammed − most of them still screaming for water − into a shed outside the main bungalow which, according to Hackney, was 'a stinking, scrambling hell hole, full of tortured, groaning, delirious, wounded soldiers'. Then both wounded and dead were shifted into two rooms in the main bungalow building.

This move caused more loss of life when those unable to manage the outside steps to the bungalow were bayoneted or shot. Others received more wounds but were able to drag themselves inside.

The six officers were made to sit on these steps, which must have been infinitely preferable to being inside among the tangled bodies of the living and dead, both smeared with blood and excrement. This is where they were sitting when two staff cars drew up and out of one of them, 'amidst much shouting, saluting and bowing', stepped Lieutenant-General Takuma Nishimura, the Guards' divisional commander, accompanied by his retinue of staff officers. As he passed them the officers were motioned to stand up and Hackney was helped to his feet by the others. He noticed Nishimura's sword 'hanging low with a great deal of brown cord at the hilt, knee-high boots and spurs all glistening'.

The general appears to have given the prisoners – by now degraded into an almost subhuman state – a cursory glance, then issued an order through his aide-de-camp, Captain Shoichi Nonaka, to 'dispose' of them. Some years later Nonaka would be very clear that he used this word, '*Shobun*' in Japanese, but insisted that he used it in the sense that they should be 'disposed of' by being sent to the rear. Two other staff officers present were just as adamant that Nishimura gave precise instructions that the prisoners should be executed by firing squad, which is exactly what happened not long after the general – ignoring pleas from the captive officers that their men needed water and medical treatment – had gone on his way.

But not before another act of almost surreal cruelty. Some of the prisoners were let out of the bungalow to find their captors waiting for them with water and cigarettes which they held just out of reach while a party of Japanese war correspondents took pictures of the captives, about to receive them. When the correspondents had gone, the water was poured away, the cigarettes pocketed, and the men bundled back inside.

There were several survivors of the messy and prolonged mass execution, which took place around dusk near the river bank, and ended with the screams of men who had plenty of life left in them being burned to death. While most of the Australians, the majority roped together like a chain gang, were first shot, some of the Japanese officers decided it was time the samurai swords they carried – often family heirlooms – tasted blood, and practised their skills on the Indians, perhaps because the average Asian collar size tends to be smaller than a Caucasian's. Lance-Havildar Benedict, who was not tied, was escorted to the bank by three Japanese, as was his company havildar-major beside him. As they approached the river, Benedict managed to knock the rifle out of the hands of one of his executioners, dived in and, in the gathering gloom, swam under water for some distance. While all the Japanese in the vicinity were shooting wildly into the river, the company havildar-major seized his chance and also escaped. For some time, Benedict hid among some trees that had dropped into the river, listening to the shots and the awful screaming that followed the flare of petrol-fed flames. Perhaps he moved in the water, because he became aware of someone on the other bank calling softly for help. He swam across and found Sapper Periasamy with a great gash in his neck from some latter-day samurai who might as well have been using a bow saw. He was being held up by another of his men who was clearly exhausted. He helped them cross to his hiding place among the fallen trees.

The only officer to escape was Hackney. All six officers had been cruelly tied together: first their arms were tied behind their backs and then another length of rope was looped around their bound wrists, which were tugged up towards the shoulder blades as the rope went around their throats, pulling their heads back, then returned to their wrist and on to the next man. As the line moved off, with Hackney at the end of it, his two broken legs refused to support him and he collapsed. His captors responded by stabbing him with their bayonets and kicking him so badly that his right eyebrow became bloodily detached and fell over his eye. When this failed to get him back on his feet they tried to get the other prisoners to drag his 14 stones along, but this meant that nobody was moving. Eventually, they cut him free of the chain, gave him another good kicking so that his back wound bled freely, and left him lying there watching as 'the line proceeded slowly, some still being dragged, of which a few occasionally raised themselves to their knees only to be again thrown off balance'.

As soon as they were out of sight the shooting started and there was no mistaking what was happening. Hackney realized that his only hope was to play dead, which was not very difficult. He was covered in blood from his matted hair to the freshly opened wounds on his legs where 'one bayonet had gone through the bandage and entered the calf above the exit hole of the bullet'.

I could see the flickers of fire which occasionally would burst out very brightly. The prisoners were being burnt, and many were screaming and yelling terribly . . . I was determined even more than before that, no matter what pain I was suffering, how my body ached . . . I would remain 'dead' until such time as the Japs departed . . . Many times one or more of them came across my body; some just passed by, others would satisfy themselves by previously used methods – kicking and hitting mostly on the head. Some unfortunately used their bayonets, most just pricking me in the back. On two occasions they were more than pricks; once the Jap jumped and grunted as he lunged forward but fortunately he was too far away and the bayonet entered my side between the ribs and apparently did no harm; the other when a bayonet point struck my right elbow making it useless for several days . . .

More painful than the bayonet wounds was the sudden tugging at his feet by a passing Guardsman, who had evidently taken a fancy to his brown, Australian-issue boots, whose removal stretched his broken legs into an agonized jangling of twisted nerve ends. Still the face-down Hackney managed to remain silent and conceal his shallow breathing. Eventually, when he was satisfied that the last Japanese had left the scene, he drank copiously from a nearby puddle of water, and with his hands still bound behind him, turned himself over and shuffled back to the PWD buildings on his bottom. He got his back to the brick corner of the foundations and sawed his bonds against its rough edge until they frayed and snapped. Shortly afterwards he met up with two other survivors: Sergeant Ron Croft, a salesman before he volunteered, and an Australian private. Both reeked of the petrol that had been poured over them, though, unlike the private, the sergeant was not badly burnt. Croft got the other man into the cover of some jungle and then came back for Hackney. Although he was much smaller than the lieutenant, the NCO managed to carry him in a fireman's lift to the same place and it is hard to understand why, if he was capable of doing this, he had not tried to walk away with the other wounded unless like Quigley, who died, he had volunteered to remain behind.

A little over 800 men got back to Yong Peng, of whom 499 were Australians from the two infantry battalions and the 25-pounder battery, all of which were reduced to a skeleton and would have to be completely rebuilt by reinforcements. The rest were the remnants of Duncan's ruined 45th Brigade which had precisely three British officers left on its ration strength. Anderson got in about twenty-four hours after he left Parit Sulong and impressed Bennett by reporting to him immediately 'before he washed or fed' and talking 'as if the whole battle was merely a training exercise'. When the full extent of his exploits became known – and there were plenty of eyewitnesses to the way he had stalked machine-gun nests and his inspired leadership – he was awarded a Victoria Cross.

At least 100 of the Australian walking wounded got through, though some of them were no longer walking but being carried on makeshift stretchers of groundsheets and timber. Among those still on their feet was Corporal Collins, whose gangrenous right arm was giving him even more 'curry' by the time he reached Singapore, where it was amputated from the shoulder. (Three days later, along with other seriously wounded from the Bakri–Parit Sulong fighting, he was on a ship bound for Java and back in Australia by the end of February.) A few died on the way to Yong Peng, one of the stretcher-borne within an hour of the road where an advance party had ensured the ambulances were waiting. Most were lost crossing rivers, despite the unravelled turbans and rifle slings used to help the non-swimmers. Surprisingly, there seem to have been almost as many Australians in this category as Indians.

One small party, among them the wounded anti-tank gunner Clarrie Thornton who had done so well at Bakri, became separated, got lost and were captured when they mistook a company of bivouacking Japanese encountered in a deserted compound for some of Brigadier Duke's Norfolks. At first, not realizing how many there were, Private Charles Edwards and the others had taken up firing positions and then both sides froze.

A Jap officer with a drawn sword appeared right under the spout of Jimmy Harrison's rifle. It looked funny, with sword in air and neither the Jap officer nor Jimmy moving, each having the other covered. More Japs followed all round us and those in the distance came closer. The game was up and we took heed of the two sergeants and rose and left our arms on the ground . . . The Japs gave us some food and water and I thought, not so bad after all.

These particular Imperial Guards, who were the only Japanese division in the Muar area, treated their prisoners quite decently and, although there was some beating up when they were handed over to another unit, their treatment never began to approach the terror that had been inflicted on the wounded at Parit Sulong. There are several theories as to why the massacre, with all its calculated sadism, happened. Later, much later, some Japanese officers would explain to Anderson and others that it was revenge for the heavy casualties the Australians had inflicted, including the killing of a brigadier and two colonels – one of them perhaps the officer in the white shirt whom Warden watched being shot to pieces.

Without question, among their seriously wounded was the colonel commanding the Third Regiment, the Guards' most prestigious unit. Yamashita, a former commander of the Third himself during his time in Tokyo, insisted that he would choose the colonel's replacement and this, not surprisingly, worsened the already poor relations between himself and Nishimura. It is not clear whether Yamashita had yet heard something of the murder of the Australian wounded, though later he would condemn it. While Yamashita's humanitarian tendencies should not be exaggerated, there is no doubt he wanted officers who understood that atrocities blackened their cause. He had displayed no mercy towards Japanese soldiers arrested for murder, rape and pillage in Penang and had ordered their immediate execution. Had it been Yamashita, and not Nishimura, who came across Anderson's wounded in the bungalow at Parit Sulong, his most likely reaction would surely have been some harsh words about their appalling condition and unambiguous orders that they be sent to the nearest field hospital.

Nor was this kind of behaviour entirely unknown. Four days after the massacre, another of Percival's brigades had been obliged – this time after fierce fighting around Batu Pahat – to abandon its transport and take to the jungle after Japanese road-blocks had stopped them going south down the coast road. Forty-five British stretcher cases, mostly 2nd Cambridgeshires borrowed from Duke's 53rd Brigade and now getting towards the end of their second week in Malaya, had to be left behind. With them remained two medical officers, several orderlies and the Reverend Noel Duckworth, their battalion padre, who had been the Cambridge cox in the exciting 1936 boat race, when they came from behind to beat Oxford by five lengths. The first Japanese officer they met shook Duckworth's hand and gave them canned food, water and cigarettes. Behind his back, a few of his men collected wrist watches and, more unfortunately, some of the British medical supplies, but there was no attempt to mistreat the wounded.

Percival regarded the Australians' dogged fight against the numerically superior Imperial Guard between Muar and Parit Sulong as one of the epic encounters of the Malayan campaign, and considered that the delay they imposed had saved a large part of his army from being cut off and annihilated at Yong Peng.

But that was all. The Muar battle also marked the end of any serious attempts to hold onto part of Johore. There would, after all, be no Lines of Torres Vedras across this particular peninsula. By the time Padre Duckworth was surrendering his wounded, British defences had unravelled to the point where Percival had decided there was nothing left to do but withdraw to Singapore.

Percival's last chance of making a stand in Johore had been to hold the southernmost lateral road across the peninsula; this ran from the port of Batu Pahat, which lies in an estuary about 7 miles inland, to Mersing on the east coast. But, in the space of a few days, Yamashita had dashed any lingering hopes that the tide could be turned with a three-pronged attack, striking on both coasts as well as down the trunk road and railway that were the spine and nervous system of the central front.

On the east coast, the Japanese at last took advantage of their naval and air superiority to make the major landing there that Percival had long feared, and for which the two of Bennett's six infantry battalions that had yet to see major action had been held in readiness. The port of Endau, from where iron ore from Japanese-owned mines had once been sent to Tokyo, had been abandoned by the British several days before, when everybody pulled back to the Mersing–Batu Pahat line. On 26 January a Hudson patrolling the coast spotted two Japanese transports escorted by at least two cruisers, four destroyers and several minesweepers and patrol craft heading in that direction.

The scene was now set for the last offensive action of Pulford's squadrons, an aerial charge of the not-so-light and extremely slow brigade, their crews fully aware that the odds were horribly stacked against them. In deference to their age and general lack of mobility, the lumbering Vildebeest biplane torpedo bombers had mostly been used to make night raids on the abandoned RAF strips in northern and central Malaya. Now they were ordered to make a mass daylight attack on shipping. This was slow getting off the mark. Either because of Japanese jamming or wireless malfunction, the Hudson's crew who had observed the approach of the Japanese task force towards Endau were unable to tell Singapore what they had seen until they had returned to base. By the time the RAF were over the ships many of the troops they were carrying were either ashore or had transferred to their landing-craft and were well on their way there.

Twenty-one Vildebeest, their entire available strength, and three of the more contemporary, though not much faster, Albacores, with their enclosed cockpits, attacked in two waves about three hours apart. Accompanying them were nine Hudsons and the entire bombing force was escorted by fifteen Buffaloes and eight of the newly arrived Hurricane fighters. These had been in action for almost a week now and performed marginally better than the Buffaloes but, against all expectations, quite failed to make the Japanese air force rue the day they ever chose to tangle with the RAF. They were simply not quite good enough and, even if they had been, there were not nearly enough of them.

The Hurricanes that came to Singapore were not, like the latest Spitfires, an air superiority fighter. They were of a type partly intended for a ground support role in the Middle East, which was why they came complete with sand air-intake filters and twelve machine-guns instead of the normal eight. Below 20,000 feet, the added weight of these conspired to make the plane a sight less manoeuvrable and some-what slower than the Zero. Some accounts also dwell on the lack of combat experience of most of the pilots, among them future Australian prime minister John Gorton who survived a crash which smashed his face against his gunsight and saw him left for dead. (In the initial batch of twenty-four pilots there were five Australians, four Canadians and a Texan.) But one of the Battle of Britain veterans leading them was lost on the Hurricanes' first day in action and it was an English novice, Pilot Officer Jimmy Parker, who killed the man responsible.

There were not many novices in the Vildebeest squadrons, which had been based in Singapore since long before the war and were predominantly regular RAF, though the commander of one of them was Cyp Markham, a popular local figure who had worked in the Education Department for the last ten years and was originally in the Malayan Volunteer Air Force. There was also quite a strong contingent of Australian and New Zealand air gunners. Several of the crews were not long back from a night raid.

Leading the first wave was Squadron Leader Tim Rowland, whose wife Veronica and baby son were staying with their friends the Glovers, because the journalist's home was considered safer than married quar-ters near the much-bombed Seletar airfield. After all their years of training, the Vildebeest squadrons had so far dropped a total of six torpedoes in action, during an abortive attack in rough seas off Kota Baharu on the first day. Now, once again it was decided that conditions were unsuitable for a torpedo attack – apparently the waters around

Endau were too shallow – so the Vildebeests were loaded with bombs: either six 250-pound bombs or two 500-pounders and two 250-pounders. This was half as much again as the faster Hudsons could carry.

Endau was only 90 miles away and even the Vildebeests got there in less than an hour. Emerging over their targets through broken cloud at about 2,000 feet, the stately old biplanes, staggering towards them with their huge bomb loads, must have been an anti-aircraft gunner's dream. Rowland's aircraft was one of the first to go, exploding in mid-air before he had even started his bomb run. Soon the Zeros from Kuantan had joined in and the sea was smouldering with little petrol fires. RAF Flight Lieutenant Tom Lamb dived towards the beaches which were 'seething with troops'.

It's a wonder the old crate didn't fall apart. Within seconds the sky was thick with aircraft . . . it was disconcerting to see rows of holes appearing all over the place in the fabric and hear the twang of parting wires. I could hear Sharp [his Australian gunner] blazing away and I heard him shout that he had got a Zero. At one time I could see five parachutes in the sky and two aircraft going down in flames . . . I dropped my bombs at little more than tree-top height . . . doing some vicious skids whenever attacked. Suddenly Gil Sharp gave a shout . . . A shell had got him right through the knee and the lower half of his leg was hanging off. Wills [sergeant observer] took over the gun. The Japs continued to attack for a considerable distance but finally they gave me up as a bad job.

While Sergeant Wills applied a tourniquet to Sharp's leg, Lamb nursed the shredded aircraft back to Seletar where they had a 'terrible job' removing the gunner from his cramped rear cockpit and getting him into the ambulance. In all, the RAF had lost ten Vildebeest (plus two written off on landing), two Albacores, two Hudsons and a Hurricane. Thirty-eight aircrew were missing, most of whom would turn out to have been killed, among them both Vildebeest squadron leaders. Initial reports that they were 'missing' would sustain the hopes of their wives for months if not years ahead.

Some shot-down aircrew did survive crash landings or parachute descents into the area the Japanese were beginning to move into, and, according to their luck or initiative, got back to British lines. At least one was summarily executed by the wreckage of his aircraft. Another wounded pilot was picked up by HMS *Thanet* only to find himself swimming for his life again a few hours later when the old British destroyer was sunk.

Despite the odds against them, which were about as bad as those faced by the Vildebeests, *Thanet* and Australia's *Vampire* staged a hit-and-run night torpedo attack against the tightly defended convoy. Few if any of their torpedoes hit anything. It was thought that some were fired too close to achieve their depth settings and passed under their targets. Both ships used their guns; then *Thanet*, caught in searchlights, was hit in the engine room and her crew began to abandon the ship, which was now a sitting target. It would have been suicide for *Vampire* to stop and attempt to pick them up but Commander Moran did his best to shield them by laying a smoke-screen around *Thanet* before making good his escape to Singapore.

This was the first time the navy had tried to engage enemy ships in these waters since the Australian destroyer had been part of Admiral Phillips' disastrous search for the original Japanese invasion fleet. This time there were unconfirmed reports that the troop transports had been damaged and that a destroyer, possibly holed by one of the few torpedoes that worked, had beached herself. But the RAF made similar claims and neither service seriously interfered with the landings. Over fifty of *Thanet*'s crew, including her captain Lieutenant-Commander Davies, struggled ashore. From there, most found boats and got back to Singapore, bringing with them the shot-down airmen they had previously rescued as well as others encountered on the way. Some of these sailors were survivors from the *Prince of Wales* and *Repulse* and this was the second time they had been sunk in two months.

Another thirty men, one of them a Sub-Lieutenant Danger who was *Thanet*'s torpedo officer, were plucked out of the sea by the Japanese destroyer *Shirayuki*, which landed all except Danger into army custody in Endau where they were murdered. The motive for this atrocity is unclear. Revenge for heavy casualties suffered elsewhere? Because they were considered an encumbrance to advancing troops? Ingrained xenophobia? Possibly a combination of all three. Danger, something of a prize because he was the first RN officer to be captured by the Imperial Japanese Navy, was taken to their base at Indo-China's Cam Ranh Bay to be interrogated about things a sub-lieutenant off a 1918 destroyer was unlikely to know very much about. He survived this and the rest of his long captivity.

Once ashore, the Japanese by-passed Mersing, which the Australians had, in any case, been ordered to leave as part of the phased withdrawal to Singapore. They then joined up with troops who had made an arduous trek down from Kuantan and began to move south along the jungle fringe of the main road which led to Johore Bahru. Abandoning Endau and Mersing without a proper fight – there had been not much more than a few patrol actions – had been galling for the Australians who had spent almost a year lovingly preparing its defences, including the laying of hundreds of mines. Then, in the pitch black of early morning at the Nithsdale rubber estate just north of Jemaluang, there was consolation of sorts when the 2/18th Battalion ambushed the Japanese vanguard.

All of Bennett's battalion commanders wanted to emulate, and preferably improve on, what Black Jack Galleghan's 30th had achieved at Gemas. The 2/18th was commanded by a wiry New South Wales grazier with piercing blue eyes named Albert Varley, whose son Jack, a lieutenant, had been with Anderson at Parit Sulong. They did not let him down. There was no bridge to blow up beneath enemy cyclists but, unlike at Gemas, no field telephone lines had been cut either. Once the leading battalion of the 55th Infantry Regiment had been allowed into the killing zone and pinned down with Brens and rifles, sixteen 25-pounders, plus Varley's own mortars, opened up on cue.

Come the dawn, the Japanese found themselves with two companies of Australians ahead of them and two behind and, as soon as they gave a position away, terrorized by British artillery. The Japanese, part of Yamashita's 18th Division and some of those unfortunates who had been wading through oozing swamps and widening jungle tracks for their light artillery pieces all the way from Kuantan, were not at their best. Being cornered by these comparatively fresh and cocky Australians developed, by their own admission, into 'an appalling hand-to-hand battle'.

But before he could finish it, Varley's artillery support was withdrawn and he received firm orders to disengage and pull back to Jemaluang. By 27 January, Percival, Heath and Bennett had fine-tuned their time-table for withdrawal to fortress Singapore to put everybody on the island with the Causeway blown up behind them by 1 February. Brigadier Harold Taylor, Varley's immediate superior, had been called back to supervise the deployment of the outer bridgehead around the Johore end of the Causeway. Lieutenant-Colonel Varley was to be in command of Eastforce. This was essentially the two battalions of Taylor's 22nd Australian Brigade less Anderson's battered 2/19th, which was being rebuilt in Singapore out of some suspiciously raw Australian reinforcements hastily dispatched from recruit camps.

Varley did as he was told, but he had no way of communicating with his two most forward companies, the ones that had popped up behind the Japanese and were now finding it difficult to extricate themselves. One was almost completely wiped out, with six officers and ninety-two men missing. Months later, the remains of some of these soldiers were discovered by Australian prisoners, surrounded by spent .303 cases where they had obviously fought to the last, confident perhaps that help would come at any moment. They had, after all, been winning. The battalion had undoubtedly inflicted far more casualties on the Japanese – enough to make them withdraw to Mersing to await reinforcements and allow Eastforce to withdraw to Johore unmolested.

Westforce was not so well placed. Batu Pahat was garrisoned by the 6/15th Brigade, its main elements being Esmond Morrison's British Battalion – since the decimation of the Argylls at Slim River probably the best UK infantry in the field – the 2nd Cambridgeshires and the 5th Norfolks, both hardly off the boat before they had been detached from Duke's brigade and flung in at the deep end.

The other Norfolk battalion in Malaya, the 6th, was also in the vicinity, still recovering after their chaotic night action alongside Moorhead's Punjabis, when they had tried to keep the defile open for Anderson's column. Most of their 100 or so dead were listed as missing* because there had never been time to find and bury them. They had been obliged to reduce their rifle companies from four to two, and among the other casualties had been their shattered CO, Lieutenant-Colonel Ian Lywood, who was sent back to Alexandra Hospital in Singapore suffering from what his friends said was malaria and his detractors 'nervous strain'.

The Australians blamed Lywood's battalion for losing Parit Sulong bridge. A platoon from this battalion patrolling the area (it had taken over from an Australian one commanded by Varley's son), having noticed the absence of traffic from the Bakri direction, and heard an awful lot in the week they had been in the country about how good

* In other theatres, particularly North Africa, 'missing' often turned out to mean taken prisoner, but most of Malaya's missing are still missing.

the Japs were at sneaking up behind you, had abandoned it. This may not have been in the spirit of Horatius but it is unlikely that a thirty-man platoon would have held the bridge against a determined Japanese assault. The problem was that there were simply not enough troops to garrison all the possible choke-points along the road.

Now Lywood's second-in-command had taken over and once again the battalion's task was to help the Punjabis keep a road open. This time it was the coastal highway which ran the 25 miles from Benut, near the tip of the peninsula and where what was left of the 11th Indian Division had its HQ, up to Batu Pahat. On its way there it passed through the fishing villages of Rengit and Senggarang. The 6th Norfolks had a company in both places and were already having to deal with infiltrators.

Because of their tin-mining interests in the area the Japanese knew it well. At the beginning of the Muar operation they had already inserted a battalion by boat, which had promptly disappeared into the jungle-covered slopes of the local hills to wage a local guerrilla war on British lines of communication. These were considerably reinforced when Nishimura's Imperial Guards, Yamashita's right flank, moved south from Muar. Travelling by bicycle along country tracks, they had penetrated deep into British territory, press-ganging the locals into porterage whenever they could. Once Batu Pahat had been by-passed they had turned west towards the coast road, searching for places to establish road-blocks and do to its garrison what they did to Anderson on his calvary between Bakri and Parit Sulong. Meanwhile, the Japanese had attacked the port frontally and established a foothold because at one stage the defenders, fearing they were about to be outflanked, had started to withdraw only to be ordered to return.

Commanding the 6/15th at Batu Pahat was Acting Brigadier Bernard Challen, who had taken over from Moorhead after the latter had chosen to return to his Punjabis and, given the high casualty rate among Indian Army battalion commanders, to face his almost inevitable death. Challen, also from a Punjabi regiment and grateful to get into the field from a grinding logistics job at Heath's Indian Corps HQ, had seen the threat to his rear coming for several days and been asking for permission to pull back to Senggarang some 10 miles down the coast. Billy Key, the latest commander of 11th Indian Division and his immediate superior (after the Slim River debacle Paris had gone back to commanding 16 Brigade) had been sympathetic and so had Heath.

But the final decision was Percival's. At the very least, he wanted to hold Batu Pahat's large airfield, which was only 60 miles away from Singapore, until the arrival of the other two brigades of the 18th East Anglian Division which were due any day. Eventually, he bowed once more to the inevitable and 'with a heavy heart' allowed Challen to leave.

As it was, Percival's approval came too late to save Challen and very nearly his brigade. Having withdrawn to Senggarang, and met up with the company from the 6th Norfolks there without incident, he had not gone much further south when he met his first road-block. It was cleverly sited, about 500 yards beyond the bridge over the next river, thus denying him the space to get across the enormous number of vehicles which encumbered all British brigades in Malaya and so often made them less mobile than the Japanese cyclists. Challen's 3,000 or so men required about 250 vehicles, which took up at least a mile of road even moving both sides of it. Understandably, he was anxious to get them all across the bridge, then blow it up behind him before the Japanese pursuit from Batu Pahat bottled them up. Enemy aircraft were already beginning to take an unhealthy interest in his column, though so far without much effect.

Logs and barbed wire had been placed across the road and covered by machine-guns and mortars dug in among the rubber on either side. Attempts to smash through it, some of them led in person by the Cambridgeshires' Lieutenant-Colonel Thorne, met with the usual implacable Japanese defence and quickly petered out when the junior officers or sergeants became casualties. 'Just another case of the troops being too tired for effective action,' noted Percival. And it was true that no amount of hard training in northern Europe could have prepared them for belonging to an army that had known nothing but retreat in an enervating climate. Even so, subalterns were going down with the kind of ninepin inevitability associated with the Somme. In the space of seventy-two hours the 6th Norfolks alone would have six second lieutenants and one captain killed.

To add to Challen's problems, his wireless communications with divisional HQ were down. 'Where are you? Where are you?' demanded Key's desperate signallers, persistent as a bird call. Eventually, the answer came in a handwritten note extracted from a message container dropped from the open cockpit of Flight Lieutenant Harry Dane's Malayan Volunteer Air Force Tiger Moth, all the RAF could

muster by way of a search party. Dane, in civilian life the manager of
the Perak Hydro-Electric Company, had avoided Zeros by flying at
tree-top height until he witnessed the bumper-to-tail congestion over
the Senggarang stretch of the highway. Since by now it was well
known that the Japanese had nothing as old-fashioned as a biplane in
Malaya, the occupants of these vehicles had waved rather than shot
at him.

Never one to sit on his hands, Key decided to help Challen out by
assembling from the few spare troops at his disposal a relief column to
distract the enemy road-blocks by nibbling away at them from the
opposite direction. It was commanded by Major Charles Banham, an
artillery officer from Toosey's Hertfordshire Yeomanry who were now
supporting 11th Indian Division and had managed to replace some of
their dustcart towing vehicles for Quads. It consisted of 112 infantry –
battle casualty replacements for the 6th Norfolks recently arrived from
Singapore – who were in trucks. In addition, there was a fleet of
ambulances to bring back Challen's wounded; two armoured cars from
the Straits Settlements Volunteer Force; four Bren gun carriers, of
which two were from the Norfolks and two manned by Moorhead's
Punjabis; and a brace of 25-pounder field guns towed by the newly
acquired Quad tractors. One of these carried Lieutenant Ben Bolt
whose twenty-first birthday it happened to be. Like Toosey he was
from Merseyside and his parents, who lived at Hoylake on the estuary
of the River Dee, knew his commanding officer.

Banham led his column in one of the Punjabi carriers, accompanied
by a gunner and a driver. They had not gone 5 miles when, just north
of Rengit and its little garrison of Norfolks and Punjabis, they hit a
road-block. Almost immediately they came under fire from all sides
and very quickly another road-block was established behind them.
One of the armoured cars was damaged and had to be abandoned. War
being no respecter of birthdays, Bolt was killed trying to get a gun into
action over open sights. It was only because of the bravery of a
Bombardier (artillery corporal) Thompson who, despite the narrowness
of the road, managed to execute a three-point turn in a Quad, that
several of the wounded were brought safely back down the road to
Benut before the trap was closed. Both guns and most of the vehicles
were abandoned. Some of the Norfolks under Company Sergeant-
Major Melville Rudling managed to get away and find temporary
sanctuary with the outpost at Rengit which was deployed around the

50-foot water-tower from which the village's supply was distributed at a uniform pressure. This position rapidly came under siege.

One carrier got through the ambush, its caterpillar tracks scaling the felled rubber trees across the road like some determined insect. It contained Banham and his Punjabi crew who, no doubt hoping others would follow, pressed on towards Challen's brigade some 3 miles up the road. In the process the Yeomanry officer had to hurdle at least three (five according to some accounts) similar barricades, a mechanized point-to-point. Whether these obstacles were all manned or not is unclear. Perhaps there was a reluctance to fire at a single carrier for fear of giving away their position. Whatever the reason, Challen was about to mount a full brigade group attack when Lance-Naik Naranjan Singh revved his shot-up carrier over the logs of the final barricade and tumbled Banham into the arms of the Cambridgeshires.

Challen might have taken the view that if a single Bren gun carrier could get through then a whole brigade should have no problem, but he chose not to. Once Banham had given him the details of his journey, he decided there was no way his tired battalions, with all their vehicles, would be able to fight their way through the road-blocks and he cancelled his attack. Also from Banham he learned that evacuation to Singapore appeared imminent, though the major, of course, had no notion of the exact date. But it was obvious that if his brigade became involved in a protracted battle to clear road-blocks it might be abandoned on the mainland. Challen now found himself – though on a slightly bigger scale – in the same position as Anderson's column at Parit Sulong and he made the same decision. His wounded, along with Padre Duckworth and the doctors, would be left to the mercy of the enemy who, in their capricious way, would display it in a manner which could hardly be faulted. The vehicles and guns would be destroyed and they would walk out.

Challen had in the region of 3,000 men under him, more if the detachments at Senggarang and Rengit *en route* were included. And once off the coast road and its bridges there were several rivers to cross. The first to reach Key's divisional HQ at Benut were about forty Punjabis from Moorhead's old 3/16th, who had fought their way out of the encirclement around the Rengit water-tower. Company Sergeant-Major Rudling, who had led his surviving Norfolks into the Rengit perimeter after Banham's column had been ambushed, had also escaped. But he lingered with another Norfolks company sergeant-major to

give covering fire with a Bren gun and never did catch up with his
main party, who were guided to safety by two Malays Rudling had
been ordered to shoot as suspected spies. He had been unable to bring
himself to do this, perhaps because he was recently arrived and had not
been over-exposed to the fifth column mania. (Or was it simply that
he had too much common sense and decency?)

Then, a day later, came 1,200 men, Cambridgeshires, Norfolks and
about 300 Indians who were designated 'Cavalry' because they rode
about in trucks and a few armoured cars, though now they had neither.
They had been guided to Benut by a colonial policeman named Wallace. These men, the first sizeable party to arrive, were the rearguard
and it soon became apparent that the rest of the column had fallen into
some confusion during a night crossing of a river, many of them losing
their weapons.

'When dawn broke the exhausted men of the Cambridgeshires and
6th Norfolks were in a poor state of discipline,' wrote Sir Compton
Mackenzie in a history he had been commissioned to write by the
British Indian Army of its World War II campaigns. The book was
published in 1951, four years after that army had passed into history.
In it, the novelist and former intelligence officer usually does his best
not to cause offence, apart from sometimes returning Gordon Bennett's
casual contempt for Indian soldiers with something similar for the
Australians. But the plummeting morale of some of these East Anglian
Territorials, who had not on the whole suffered heavy casualties, taxed
even Sir Compton's formidable powers of obfuscation. 'A burst of
machine-gun fire and a salvo of mortar bombs scattered the leading
company. The panic spread; many men were drowned in the swamp.'

Challen went forward and managed to calm some of the men and
then went off in search of Colonel Thorne, who was rarely very far
from the front himself. Shortly after this, the brigadier took a wrong
turn and became hopelessly lost. Accompanied by his Indian orderly,
he made his way towards the road to try and get his bearings and ran
into some Japanese who shot his orderly. Challen hid until dark then,
though sometimes fired at, walked along the edge of the road, climbed
a barricade – ignored by the Japanese sentries guarding it, who presumably thought he was one of their own – stole a bicycle and rode for a
while before returning to the jungle. At dawn on the 29th, more than
twenty-four hours after he had become separated from his command,
he was leaving a hut where he had spent the night when he gave a

small Imperial Guards patrol the kudos of taking the most senior British prisoner to date.

In his absence, Colonel Morrison of the British Battalion, whose hard core of regulars had not been infected by the panic that had gripped some of the others, had taken command and restored order. Morrison realized that the Japanese had cut them off and they would never get south in a formed body. He decided that the answer was to get his 1,500 men back to the coast, somehow send word to Singapore and get the navy to pick them up after dark. This, of course, was a very tall order. For a start, there was not all that much of the navy left. But over the next seventy-two hours this was exactly what was done.

Morrison set up a defensive perimeter in the trees around a coastal hamlet some 3 miles south of Rengit and less than a mile from the main coastal road, along which the first Japanese motor traffic had begun to appear on its remorseless journey south. Two officers in separate sampans, in case one was intercepted or met with some other mishap, sailed the 15 miles south to divisional HQ and the navy responded by sending their Yangtse River gun-boats *Scorpion* and *Dragonfly*. The gun-boats' shallow draft was ideal for the work at hand, though they still needed to tow lines of little boats, sampans and dinghies, to get in among the mangroves and take the troops off. There were the inevitable comparisons with Dunkirk and George Chippington, the Leicesters' lieutenant who had fought down the length of Malaya, was by no means certain he was going to make it.

He was hiding in the decaying wreck of a big wooden junk tossed up by a storm. Many of his platoon were non-swimmers. To get to this staging post, he had already suffered the longest night in his young life, waiting in the dark with them in the mangroves for the dawn to come up and the tide to go down, the Indian Ocean lapping their shoulders. Nor were they alone. 'We were sharing the water with innumerable other creatures having the time of their lives scooting about on the surface scattering phosphorescent showers of light almost level with our faces.' He began to think of poisonous snakes and large crocodiles: 'the tide turned not a moment too soon for the little chap alongside me . . . his chin tilted at an acute angle heavenward.'

They had their walking wounded with them in the junk – several had injuries from mortar splinters – who, owing to some oversight, and much to the fury of the Leicesters' doctor, had not been removed before the able-bodied during their first night's contact with the gun-boats. Chippington knew that if the navy failed to return, these men were doomed, for they had neither the food nor the medical supplies they would need for an arduous trek through Japanese lines.

As darkness fell we sat on the high deck at the stern gazing anxiously out to sea. Time passed but no long, low shadow appeared. Slowly our confidence began to ooze away. Perhaps something had gone wrong and they were not coming back for us. Perhaps we had been abandoned – written off . . . Then we heard a sound, a very faint but distinct sound . . . The clouds moved away, revealing those very welcome black bobs on the dark sea moving steadily towards us. The wounded went first, some in considerable pain as they were helped down into the boats, but no one complained.

Chippington and his men got to Singapore on 1 February. The island had been severed from the mainland the day before when, at 8.15 a.m., Indian sappers, using mainly naval depth charges, had blown a 70-foot-wide gap in the Causeway's reinforced concrete and stone. At the Johore Bahru end, the withdrawal had gone amazingly smoothly, and even with some panache. The Japanese had not pressed the rear-guard unduly. Instead, the British had departed the Malayan Peninsula on a reassuring, if slightly whimsical note of British pageantry, with the two surviving Argylls pipers playing across Varley's Australians and the 2nd Gordons, a Singapore garrison battalion who had relieved the Loyals. The Argylls, who had been steadily rebuilding since Slim and, with the latest staff and hospital releases, now 250 strong, had been brought out of the reserve to provide the final rearguard. Last to leave had been Colonel Ian Stewart himself, accompanied by his batman, Drummer Hardy.

Accounts vary as to exactly what the pipers played. Eric Linklater says it was 'A Hundred Pipers' and 'Hielan' Laddie', while his fellow Scot and novelist Compton Mackenzie suggests that the Gordons also had a piper present who played 'Jenny's Black E'en', while a third account insists it was 'Blue Bonnets O'er the Border'. Whatever it was, it was music to Japanese ears if not to Sultan Ibrahim, abandoned in his palace with his portraits of the House of Windsor, awaiting the arrival of the conquerors. At a final lunch with Bennett he had deplored the way the British heads of Johore government departments and even hospital staff had left without a word of farewell. His only consolation was that his youngest wife had changed her mind and decided not to leave for Singapore and perhaps elsewhere. Romania was, after all, allied to Germany and officially at war with both Britain and the United States.

Stewart, ever the enthusiast about anything his Argylls were involved in, gloried in the clockwork efficiency of an operation that 'ought to have cost dearly [but] had been carried out without the loss of a single casualty'. While this was true of the final musical interlude, it was an outrageous glossing over of the facts and Stewart must have known it. Challen's command had been very lucky but the price of getting back to Singapore had been several hundred missing, all their artillery and transport and about 80 per cent of their Bren guns. On the central front it was even worse: an entire Indian brigade had disappeared.

This was Brigadier George Painter's 22nd Indian Brigade, which had been much depleted in the Kuantan fighting and basically consisted of Parkin's 5th Sikhs and all that was left of the hospitalized Cumming's Frontier Force Regiment and the 2nd Royal Garhwal Rifles. Three days before the gap was blown in the Causeway, the weakened brigade, which still probably numbered the best part of 2,000 men, had been cut off and then vanished as they tried to escape through some of the thickest jungle in the peninsula.

It had happened because of sins of both commission and omission. The brigade was part of the genial Arthur Barstow's 9th Indian Division. Barstow and Bennett got on well together. 'One of the most efficient British leaders with whom the Australians were associated,' was the assessment of the AIF's commander. This happy state of affairs mainly existed because Barstow, who was fifty-three and had spent his entire career in the Indian Army where he was known as 'Whiz Bang Sikh', was determined to prove to Bennett that, properly led, his men were as good as the Australians any day. Who better than Barstow, then, to be astride the railway during the delicate business of the final withdrawal, on the right flank of Maxwell's Australian 27th Brigade, which was next to him on the roughly parallel trunk road. Barstow kept his two brigades – behind Painter's 22nd was Lay's 8th – well forward. Some might have said too far forward, for it was not always easy to replenish them with food and ammunition, but Barstow was not going to be accused of allowing the Australians to be outflanked. Then it all went wrong.

Lieutenant-Colonel Trott, an Australian-born Indian Army officer on Barstow's staff, would later describe Brigadier Lay as 'all washed up' and blame him for much of what followed. This is probably unfair, though it might be true to say that Lay had never quite recovered the verve he had displayed when he counter-attacked at Gurun, and a lot of people were never as good as that in the first place. A railway bridge between the two brigades was blown up prematurely, probably accidentally, and with it went the telephone line that ran alongside the rails, the only link between the brigades. Painter had already sent back most of his wheeled transport and Bren gun carriers, and with them had gone brigade HQ's wireless truck. Without the telephone line, Lay was unable to inform Painter that he had moved further back. Elements of the Japanese 5th Division, never slow to exploit a chance like this, soon spotted the gap and inserted themselves between the two units. Painter was cut off.

Then Barstow arrived on the scene with Colonel Trott and another Australian, a Major Moses who was a liaison officer from Bennett's staff. As soon as he realized what had happened, Whiz Bang Sikh lived up to his nickname in no uncertain fashion. First of all, and in Trott's presence, he exploded all over the wretched Lay. 'You've sold the show . . . Hell take you, man, get a battalion on that high ground.'

Without pausing for a reply, Whiz Bang strode off to the railway line, determined to get up to Painter and alert him to the danger. Accompanied by the two Australian officers and his Sikh batman, he boarded what sounds like the kind of push-pull, flat-bed maintenance trolly often featured in silent films. First stop was Prem Sahgal's 2/10th Baluch, Lay's forward battalion, whom he ordered to return to their old positions down the track. While the Baluch sorted themselves out, the four pressed on. At the demolished bridge the trolly was abandoned while they clambered across its broken girders and proceeded along the raised railway embankment on foot. Barstow was well in the lead, his face glistening under the distinctive red band around the crown of his major-general's service cap. When the Japanese opened fire he was seen to roll down the right of the embankment. The others went to the left. Several times they tried to cross it and get to the general but the fire was too fierce. Later the Japanese would recover his body. After Admiral Phillips, Whiz Bang Barstow was the second highest ranking officer on either side to be killed in the conflict.

The Baluch tried to regain contact with the 22nd but they were no more successful than their general. To make matters worse, Bennett, for all his admiration of Barstow, did not take the missing brigade's plight into consideration when he ordered the withdrawal of Maxwell's 27th Brigade on schedule. This meant that Painter's left flank was exposed and his men were in danger of being completely surrounded. The inevitable decision was made to walk around the Japanese in a long jungle detour.

This soon became another of those nightmare ordeals, increasingly familiar to Percival's scattered infantry. It was some time since any rations had got through to the brigade; the chapattis in one unguarded food dump had been looted by civilians. Even before they started, it was at least twenty-four hours since most of Painter's men had eaten very much. Some of the walking wounded scarcely qualified for that category, hobbling behind as best they could on sticks they had cut themselves. In addition, Parkin's Sikhs had twelve stretcher cases with them, who had been injured during a highly successful local counter-attack with Sikh and Muslim Punjabi companies competing to see who could get closest with the bayonet. Neither Parkin nor any of his officers, British or Indian, would consider abandoning their wounded, often their bravest and their best, and nor would any of the forty-eight Punjabis of both confessions (Sikhs are also from the Punjab) involved in carrying them. Captain Denis Russell-Roberts, Parkin's transport officer, supervised the stretcher-bearers' night crossing of a jungle swamp.

Shortly all four men were floundering in the bog. The man on the off fore position suddenly staggered, his knees were shaking wildly. He sank to one knee with a shout of terror in his hoarse voice and the stretcher lurched over on its side ... This was an awful moment and it happened over and over again in one form or another. I think it was the groans and at times the shrieks of the wounded which struck the deepest note of horror ... On the other side of the crossing the same difficulties were encountered. There the wounded man would almost inevitably find himself tilted backwards at the same steep angle with his head close to the level of the mud and his body uncomfortably positioned in a semi-vertical position. And through this hell passed twelve stretchers, twelve wounded men who were by now gangrenous, delirious and half-mad, forty-eight gallant men who carried the stretchers ... a slow-moving picture of unforgettable misery.

It could not last. Painter had only recently recovered from injuries received in an air crash and was not a fit man. His moods became mercurial. One day he would declare he was unable to take another step and beg Parkin to take over; the next he would set such a cracking pace that good men were left behind because somebody had failed to rouse them when they fell asleep immediately on resting, as everybody did (except at night when it sometimes became so cold that men who had been asleep on their feet all day awoke shivering). Contact was lost with an entire company, about 100 men, of Parkin's battalion like this.

In the end, they did leave the wounded, but only after they had encountered some Tamil rubber workers who directed them to a large dispensary on their estate where they could be looked after. They were carried there by a company of Sikhs under three British officers with orders to catch up with the rest of the brigade or make their own way south depending on how far it was. Some of the men wept to see them go. Russell-Roberts watched two of the walking wounded he had been keeping an eye on follow them, young Punjabi Muslims with filthy, mud-stained bandages, one hobbling along with the aid of his stick. 'I shall never forget those two young men as they followed behind the stretcher cases. They were both smiling and their eyes were bright. Dear God, what guts they had.'

A chance to ambush 300–400 Japanese carousing noisily in a kampong was declined. By now, almost everybody but Parkin and some of his men were too exhausted to take any kind of offensive action. The brigadier declared they would not be fit to fight again until they had got back to Singapore and rested. All they needed was sleep, a lot of sleep, food and a bath. He asked Parkin to look after the rearguard. Then they were ambushed and some of the Indians flung down their arms and surrendered, though not too many from the 2nd Sikhs. The diminutive Parkin in his well-tied turban, Thompson in hand, urged his men to fire at every Jap they could see, though Russell-Roberts doubted whether most of them had much more than ten bullets left. Later a viceroy commissioned officer explained that there had been confusion because some sepoys thought the brigadier wanted to surrender and were surprised when the order came to fight. Had they not observed, whenever the column rested, that a white flag appeared on a branch near where the brigadier was lying? It seemed that Painter's brigade major, who had decided 'Brigade HQ' should be properly designated if only with a soiled piece of white rag, had a lot to answer for.

Their numbers dwindled. Some simply announced they could not walk another step, sat down and refused to budge. Twenty of the men who had taken Parkin's wounded to the dispensary, including the three British officers, avoided Japanese patrols, reached the Straits of Johore and were picked up by a naval launch looking for stragglers. The brigadier failed to keep a rendezvous with Parkin, rushing off with a new Chinese guide before the others could catch up with them. This turned out to be their good fortune because, shortly afterwards, Painter and what was left of his command encountered a battalion of Japanese and surrendered. The others had no idea this had happened and expected to run into them all again at any moment.

The day after the Causeway was blown, Colonel Parkin, who had inspired everybody around him to keep going, arrived in Singapore with twenty-four of his men, three Indian and four British officers. In the closing stages of their journey they had hijacked a Chinese truck to get to a kampong on the northern side of the straits, from where they could see the naval base. Russell-Roberts and a couple of others had gone across in a sampan to get the navy to send a launch for the rest. He noticed that the water was covered with a thick black scum of oil from the navy's holed fuel-tanks. As they approached they were nervous that they would be fired at by their own side; but they came alongside the steps that led up to the pier of the base's yacht club without challenge to be greeted by four 'smiling Indian sepoys' who turned out to have been washing dishes in the club house.

Over the next couple of days, a few more stragglers from Painter's brigade reached the island. By 3 February the grand total had reached sixty-two officers and men. The last was a British signalman called Winterbottom who removed his boots and swam across. None of these appear to have brought news of Painter's capture and it was some time before Percival's HQ could bring themselves to accept that his brigade was lost. Dane and other daring Tiger Moth pilots went searching for them but brought back nothing more than fresh holes in their four wings for the fitters to patch and glue.

At night, the search was continued by a couple of officers from the newly arrived Sherwood Foresters, part of the 18th East Anglian Division, which was now almost all on the island and had been allotted positions on its northern shore. Captain 'Black Bill' Thirlby, a keen yachtsman, had discovered an abandoned RAF launch armed with twin Lewis guns. Along with Lieutenant John Goatley, the battalion's intelligence officer, he would go to the broken end of the Causeway, switch off the engines and then drift towards the enemy-occupied shore, calling into the darkness, 'Are there any British troops there?' But the only reply was the 'tok, tok, tok' of the nightjar, which sounded remarkably like a small engine coming towards them and made them reach for their machine-guns.

There were, of course, plenty of British imperial troops still at large on the other side of the water, but mostly well out of earshot. The loose ends of Percival's shaken command were distributed the length and breadth of the peninsula. In Kota Baharu bazaar some of the Dogra soldiers of Key's old brigade, who had given the Japanese such a bloody nose on the beaches there, were learning to pass themselves off as locals. On Penang Island, deep in its mountain forest, were seven Leicesters under a Sergeant Bennett. With the help of some courageous Chinese, they had been hiding out there ever since Jitra and the ambush of their battalion as Morrison led it singing into Alor Star. In central Malaya, often still not all that far from Slim River, there were scores of Argylls in various states of repair as malaria, blackwater fever and beri beri began to take their toll. Dr Ryrie, the Scottish doctor who had witnessed Kuala Lumpur's moment of anarchy, was looking after one party of his countrymen, who had taken refuge in the jungle near his leper colony at Sungei Buloh, keeping them alive on what food he could spare. The Japanese were suspicious of him but, terrified of leprosy, they seemed willing, for the time being at least, to let the doctor stay on. Lindsay Robertson, who had enjoyed such a brief moment as the battalion's commander, was leading a small party of determined men south and had made it plain that he did not intend to be captured. Others were heading for the west coast in the hope of getting a boat across the Malacca Straits to Dutch Sumatra. Among these was the Australian anti-tank gunner Harrison, who had wreaked such havoc at Gemas and had spent a few days with some Chinese guerrillas before heading west. Most of the evaders were helped by the more politically aware Chinese, often at a terrible price. A sick Argyll officer gradually recovering his health because of the bundles of food delivered daily to a certain tree by the teenaged daughter of a Chinese school teacher one day discovered with his lunch a note in English: 'They took my father and cut off his head. I will continue to feed you as long as I can.'

Near Parit Sulong, a strange Ben Gunn figure with filthy matted hair, long bushy beard and wild, staring eyes haunted the Malayan villages in the area. This was the Australian Lieutenant Ben Hackney of the 2/29th Battalion, survivor of the massacre of the Australian and Indian wounded at Parit Sulong who, unable to walk, had told Sergeant Croft to go on. He was being fed by nervous locals who were not as hostile as the more middle-class Malays, particularly the school teachers and doctors, who had organized the pro-Japanese Malayan Youth Union. They would not allow him into their homes but would put food out for him, the way people sometimes feed stray cats. Hackney was living from day to day, giving time for his legs to mend, determined not to be recaptured. Already this had been the fate of his fellow survivor, Lance-Havildar Benedict, who had been caught with his two comrades in the Sappers and Miners while they were trying to find a boat at Muar. This time they were reasonably treated. Nor did their new captors show much interest in the prominent half-healed gash in Sapper Periasamy's neck.

Not all the British on the northern side of the straits were evaders. The SOE stay-behind parties had gone into action. After a shaky start, when most of his explosives were stolen, Spencer Chapman had not only succeeded in recovering them, but was also beginning to refine his ambush techniques, supplementing War Office plastic explosive with some distinctly sweaty mining gelignite they had acquired.

I hit Sartin on the shoulder and we all pressed our bodies down into the soft soil. Harvey and I pulled the pins out of our grenades. As far as we could make out on reconstructing the scene later, the bomb must have exploded beneath the petrol tank and ignited that too . . . the flash was followed by a steady and brilliant blaze which lit up the whole scene like a stage setting. As I threw my grenades, I caught a glimpse of another large closed truck crashing into the burning wreckage and the third one turning broadside on with a scream of brakes. After the explosion there was a harsh stutter as Harvey emptied his Tommy gun in one burst up the road. I did the same then found myself racing down the path, floodlit by the funeral pyre of Jap lorries.

But these attacks on Yamashita's long lines of communication were pinpricks as even Spencer Chapman, who was not often burdened by false modesty, would have probably admitted. In many ways, he seems to have regarded it as a kind of apprenticeship in guerrilla warfare. There were not enough SOE teams to make any difference, just as there were not enough Hurricanes.

One British soldier who was only too aware of the power of the Imperial Japanese Army was Company Sergeant-Major Rudling, who had known mixed fortunes since he had broken out of Rengit. Although he had managed to get some wounded away in one of the small boats picking up members of Challen's brigade along the coast, he had not been able to escape himself. Instead he had become a member of one of the increasingly small mixed bands, all heading south along jungle tracks and trying to keep parallel with the road. Twice he had shot his way out of ambushes and on the second occasion lost his rifle when he had to swim a river.

Unarmed, lost and alone he was befriended by a Chinese charcoal burner who ordered his son to put him on the road to Johore Bahru. When they could hear that there were Japanese close by, the boy indicated to Rudling that he should remove his boots which the sergeant-major did rather reluctantly, tying them firmly by their leather laces and hanging them around his neck. Then, just when he thought it was all clear and he was thinking of putting them on again, they bumped into a solitary Japanese. 'He was so surprised at seeing us that I had a momentary advantage and I was able to swing my boots around his neck. I pulled them tight and was able to dispose of him quietly.'

The Chinese boy – he appears to have been a teenager – seems to have taken this surprising use of British army bootlaces in his stride, for he calmly assisted Rudling in concealing the garrotted man in the undergrowth. Shortly after this they found the road and the sergeant-major, his boots back on his feet, said goodbye to the boy. But by the time he arrived at the coast the last British troops had crossed the Causeway and Rudling, who had narrowly escaped being walked into a Japanese road-block by an insistent Malay, had been without food and water long enough to become careless and probably a bit disorientated. He blundered into a Japanese artillery position, tried to run away, tripped over an ammunition box in the long grass and was captured.

To his surprise, after an initial threat of execution, the Japanese treated him quite well; they gave him ointment and bandages for some jungle sores that had developed on his legs and fed and watered him. Rudling thought the enemy's field guns looked rather like the British 25-pounder except that they had old-fashioned-looking wooden wheels. He had plenty of time to study them because he was anchored to one of these wheels, tied up in the usual Japanese way with a long rope that went around his neck and then bound his wrists. He did not get much sleep. All night his captors and other batteries along the coast were shelling across the straits. Yamashita had begun the siege of Singapore.

# PART FIVE

# The Besiegement

On the island itself there was to be no talk of a siege, at least not as far as the newspapers were concerned. At the 4.30 p.m. press conference at Fort Canning the military spokesman and chief censor, an officer who had been given the job because he had broken his leg, forbade the use of the word in their news stories because 'it would have a depressing effect on local morale'. The assembled reporters, among them Ian Morrison of *The Times*, protested. The spokesman stuck to his guns. They might say the island was 'besieged' but were not to use the word 'siege'. Semantics of this kind always infuriate journalists. They begin to compete to be as offensive as possible. Morrison felt that the officer, whom he later admitted was 'a charming person and did his best', needed a lesson in English grammar. 'I pointed out that it was inconsistent to permit us the use of a certain English verb but to deny us the use of the noun which is cognate with that verb, for possible ill effects which that English noun might have on a population whose native tongue was not English.'

At length, a compromise was reached. They might use 'investment', which Morrison thought 'a horrid word'. But worse was to come. Next morning, when *The Times*' correspondent checked his cable to see if the censor had heaped any other indignities on his prose, he discovered that not even 'investment' had survived. Overnight it had mutated into 'besiegement'. Morrison was appalled. 'It is a word not even to be found in the English dictionary.'* Sub-editors in *The Times*' office must have thought that their Singapore correspondent was suffering from shell-shock when they received a message beginning, 'The besiegement of Singapore began . . .'

Winston Churchill did not need *The Times* to tell him what was happening. Almost two weeks before Morrison's story appeared the prime minister had sent Wavell a very clear message on how he saw the immediate future of Britain's richest colony:

---

* Times (and for that matter *The Times*) change. Within half a century 'besiegement' was in the *Shorter Oxford*: 'The action of besieging; the being besieged.'

I want to make it absolutely clear that I expect every inch of ground to be defended, every scrap of material or defences to be blown to pieces to prevent capture by the enemy and no question of surrender to be entertained until after protracted fighting in the ruins of Singapore city.

The words came in a reply to a cautious telegram Wavell had sent the prime minister on Singapore's chances of withstanding a siege after the setbacks in Johore:

Preparatory measures for the defence of the island being made with limited resources available. Success will depend on numbers and state of troops withdrawn from Johore, arrival of reinforcements and ability of air force to maintain fighters on island. If all goes well, hope prolonged defence possible.

Wavell passed on Churchill's *Götterdämmerung* exhortations to Percival, who pointed out that he could either inflict a scorched earth policy or hold the island for as long as possible but he could not do both. 'Singapore would become a complete inferno ... to put [an] extensive scorched earth policy into effect immediately would so undermine the morale both of troops and public as to prejudice seriously our ability to hold.'

Churchill conceded that Percival had a point and in a note to the chiefs of staff sought to tone down his rhetoric, though he stressed that the naval base should be rendered 'utterly useless for at least eighteen months', with all its docks and workshops destroyed, arguing, perhaps a little disingenuously, that this should not cause alarm because 'they are all in military areas, from which the public is rigorously excluded'. Otherwise, demolition preparations should not be permitted to weaken the island's defences 'which, as the general rightly says, must be prolonged to the last possible hour. Every day gained is vital.'

It was now quite clear that even Churchill was reconciled to something Brooke, his senior soldier, and probably Wavell had come to terms with ever since the Japanese had sunk the *Prince of Wales* and the *Repulse* and gained a foothold in northern Malaya. Barring a miracle, the fall of Singapore was almost inevitable. All that could be done was to hold out for as long as possible and buy time to reinforce the Dutch East Indies where Australian, perhaps even American, reinforcements were expected.

Ever since it had been accepted that the island's big guns meant that an overland attack down the Malayan Peninsula was much more likely than seaborne assault, it had always been assumed that the nearest front line Singapore could tolerate was northern Johore. Any closer and the enemy's artillery would be able to neutralize the naval base. Because of this there had never been any attempt to turn 'Fortress Singapore' into a real fortress, with all-round defence like Malta or Gibraltar or, for that matter, what the Germans were in the process of doing with unbelievable thoroughness to the occupied Channel Islands.

Even at this late stage Churchill was shocked to discover the true state of affairs:

I ought to have known. My advisers ought to have known and . . . I ought to have asked . . . the possibility of Singapore having no landward defences no more entered my mind than that of a battleship being launched without a bottom. I saw before me the awful spectacle of the almost naked island.

There had been some belated attempts to rectify this. Not quite three weeks into the campaign, Brigadier Ivan Simson, Malaya Command's Chief Engineer and the man Duff Cooper had made head of civil defence on the island, had pleaded with Percival over two hours of late-night Boxing Day drinks to allow him to begin building defences on Singapore's northern shore. At this point Percival was far from convinced, insisting that such defences would undermine both military and civilian morale by giving the impression that he was contemplating a total withdrawal to Singapore and withstanding a siege. In this he had the support of Major-General Frank Keith Simmons who was then in charge of the island's garrison and whose official title was Commander Singapore Fortress.

Not long afterwards Percival changed his mind. Within two weeks of his meeting with Brigadier Simson, the situation in mainland Malaya had deteriorated to the point where he was beginning to fear that the enemy might attempt to land on the island, particularly on the north-western coast which was closest to the mainland, before their conquest of the peninsula was completed. Even so, with the battle for Johore still undecided, Wavell was as convinced as Percival that, for the sake of morale, Singapore's defences should only be improved with the utmost discretion. On 19 January, only twelve days before the Argyll pipers played the last men across the fractured Causeway, the supreme commander sent a telegram reminding him:

Your preparations must of course be kept entirely secret . . . troops must not be allowed to look over shoulders. Under cover of selecting positions for garrison of island to prevent infiltration by small parties you can work out schemes for larger force and undertake some preparation such as obstacles and clearances . . .

In any case, there was no way Percival could embark on the kind of major defence works on the north shore that Simson contemplated: clearing fields of fire by tearing out mangrove swamps, laying mines and barbed wire, building pillboxes and digging bunkers and trenches, the latter always difficult in Singapore where the water-table was so near the surface. The manpower, mostly Chinese and Tamil, required to perform these miracles was simply not available. Although refugees from the peninsula had increased Singapore's labour pool, the risk of getting too close to the British military had also increased. A marked intensification of air raids against the naval base, the docks in Keppel harbour and the airfields, where the labourers' main task was filling in bomb craters from the last raid, made it hard to keep even the most desperate of them on the job for very long. Nor was the Royal Navy, whose larger ships traditionally carried a small complement of Chinese stewards and laundrymen, exempt. Captain Peter Cazalet, commander of the light cruiser *Durban*, which was escorting convoys in and out of Singapore, found himself faced with a mutiny from his Chinese civilians on board who were subject to military discipline. Eventually, after 'hours of oriental parley', it was settled through the mediation of the ship's Chinese canteen manager. Cazalet was by no means unsympathetic – though he could be pushed too far.

We have not treated the Chinese well in peace time . . . they have no real loyalty towards us and why should they have? All the same, like most people, they react to fair and considerate treatment – or most of them do. On Friday however, one little bastard refused duty. He refused to get food from the refrigerator. Said he was Assistant Wardroom Wine Steward and fetching food from a refrigerator would make him lose face. The trouble is if I send him to prison I am doing exactly what he wants (and he knows it!) So I've temporized and punished him lightly. Now I learn he says he wants to join the Japanese Army!

Percival sought to alleviate the labour shortage by drafting in troops. A few former dockers from the Argylls and the Loyals found themselves briefly back in their old occupation, sometimes working alongside disgruntled Gurkhas who deeply resented the notion that they had been transformed into coolies. But the turnaround of ships was never fast enough; several were hit and took casualties in the docks long after they should have sailed, though none were sunk. Priority went to the RAF and some reinforcements made their first contribution towards the island's defence by filling in bomb craters on an airfield, preferably at night.

According to Churchill's wishes, the destruction of the naval base had begun with the sinking of its German-built floating dock even before the withdrawal to Singapore was completed. Judging by General Bennett's reaction in a diary he was keeping, Percival's fears about the implementation of a scorched earth policy were well founded.

We were here to defend the naval base rather than the city of Singapore. This demolition of docks, even before we withdrew to the mainland, reflected the lack of confidence in our cause. The morale of the men is undoubtedly affected when they find demolitions going on behind them. It is an admission of defeat.

Nor was it easy to keep it a secret. The well-connected Morrison soon gained access with Rob Scott, his former boss at the Far Eastern Bureau of the Ministry of Information before he took up his job with *The Times*. They were accompanied by Henry Stokes, an Australian radio correspondent. The base was coming under occasional mortar attack from across the straits but it was a large area and only when they walked too close to the shore did they have one near miss. None of them were prepared for the scene that greeted them. Morrison would later describe it as 'my most tragic memory of the whole Malayan campaign'. Britain's most potent symbol of its resolve to defend its South-east Asian possessions had been reduced to a monument to abject, panic-stricken flight.

There were some Indian sentries at the gate but they did not bother to ask us what we wanted . . . the naval base police had been disbanded . . . one acre was knee-deep in their uniforms. Shirts, turbans, truncheons, gas masks, leather belts, wooden lockers, were lying about in a wild mess . . . It was so unlike the Navy to tolerate mess of any sort. We later salvaged fifty of the gas masks as we knew there were hospitals in Singapore that had none at all . . .

there were twenty huge cylindrical oil tanks. Four were on fire. A strong breeze was fanning the flames and scattering the smoke ... We walked through the various machine shops. Here were the great furnaces where huge blocks of iron and steel could be forged and rolled, enormous hydraulic presses ... Here were lathes of many types ... Here was the huge boiler shop, with great boilers still there. Here was the storeroom for wireless equipment, rows of shelves with every conceivable form of wireless device ... Towering over the storeroom and machine-shops was the great crane which could lift an entire gun turret out of a battleship. A mortar shell had scarred slightly one of its girders.

Some salvage was tried. The skeleton crew of the Australian destroyer *Vendetta*, in Singapore for a major refit after her adventurous two years with Cunningham in the Med, retrieved her innards from the base workshop, stowed them aboard and were towed all the way back to Australia by a couple of tugs. There was a less successful attempt to rescue the base's lathes and other machinery for Australian factories where they were worth their weight in gold. Unfortunately, weight was the main problem. Most of it was too heavy to shift.

Ships' crews were invited to the base, on a first-come-first-served basis, to avail themselves of extra ammunition and anything else that caught their eye. Cazalet, like most captains, was averse to stuffing his ship with unnecessary explosives, but took a few more rounds for *Durban*'s ready-use supply (the ammunition at the guns rather than in the ship's magazines) as well as finding room for extra depth charges. Stores were thrown open and sailors told to help themselves. There was no attempt to organize distribution. Men picked up anything they might be able to wear, barter or sell. Even the journalist Morrison acquired a new length of rope for which he had no use whatsoever. Cazalet, who always thought the base staff a venal bunch, was appalled. In the journal he had started to keep, he wrote, 'This is the first time I have felt utterly ashamed of my own service.'

I wondered whether we should do anything about it. Putting senior officers under arrest is a tricky business but it did pass through my mind ... Anyway, it's much too late now to retrieve the situation. The harm has been done ... one semi-bright spot, this casual abandoning of stores and complete lack of organization will not seem odd to the army and RAF who are used to it and so our name will not stink as much as it should. We have always said that the naval base at Singapore was rotten to the core. We've now reached the core. In any case, I hope there will be a Court of Enquiry which must be followed by a crowd of courts martial . . . I could understand if they had been heavily bombed and were getting a bit shocked. This was not the case. The yard and base generally has suffered very little. Compared to Portsmouth, Liverpool, etc. it has not suffered at all.

Cazalet was not to know that it was not the relatively small amount of bombing and shelling that had brought about this state of affairs but Churchill's order. Even so, his contention that a lot of valuable equipment might have been saved had it been done in a more sea-manlike manner is hard to fault. Instead, he discovered Rear-Admiral Jack Spooner, the most senior naval officer left on the island, still in his office 'charming as usual but blathering about what the general ought to have done three weeks ago etc. etc.' Now Spooner was about to hand over the base to the army who were going to use it as a strong point. What was left of the navy in Singapore, about 300 men, was moving to the waterfront at Keppel harbour. Spooner had set up a demolition programme but had since cancelled it. If the army had to abandon the base it would be up to them to destroy what remained.

Bennett was right about the effect on morale. Not surprisingly, the Royal Navy's departure from the brand new Asian bastion the British taxpayer had built for it at such enormous cost and with considerable fanfare, proved even more demoralizing than the loss of Phillips' battle-ships. Within a very short time rumours began to spread, among both troops and the civilian population, that there was no intention of defending Singapore and all the military would be evacuating to Sumatra. This theory was supported by the growing realization that most of the RAF, its airfields in the northern part of the island now under artillery fire, had already left. All that remained were a few Hurricanes at the old civil airport at Kallang. (In theory, this was not as bad as it sounded. Those Hudsons and Blenheims that were left would operate out of Dutch airfields which still placed them well within range of most targets in Malaya.)

Realizing that he had to stop the rot, Percival issued a statement announcing that, after nearly two months of struggle against an enemy with both air and naval superiority, the battle of Singapore had started. And he concluded with a rousing, if somewhat cynical rendition of Singapore's second favourite F-word.

Our task has been both to impose losses on the enemy and to gain time to enable the forces of the Allies to be concentrated for this struggle in the Far East. Today we stand beleaguered in our island *fortress*. Our task is to hold this *fortress* until help can come – as assuredly it will come. This we are determined to do.

But if it was not a fortress, and in later years Percival would be adamant that it was no such thing, then neither was it Churchill's 'Naked Island'. Lieutenant Abbott of the East Surreys, about to come off the staff and return to the British Battalion he had left at Kampar when he went down with malaria, noted that civilians fleeing the bombing on Singapore city itself were unlikely to find much peace. 'The island is by now crammed with troops, the roads are blocked with transport, and every available piece of land seems to be in use for some kind of defensive work.'

Many of these soldiers belonged to the remaining two brigades of Beckwith-Smith's 18th Division, which had arrived just too late to save Johore or, perhaps more likely, to be mauled in the attempt as the Norfolks and Cambridgeshires of Duke's 53rd Brigade had been. A few more divisional support troops, among them the machine-gunners of the Northumberland Fusiliers, were still a few days' sailing time away. None of these men were aware of how close they had been to being diverted at the last minute from Singapore to Burma, where a Japanese offensive had begun.

Churchill had returned from his last summit with Roosevelt aware of how important China – which absorbed so much of Japan's military energy – had become to the Americans. The US aid reaching Chiang Kai-shek's forces through the port of Rangoon and then along the 350-mile Burma Road to China was vital. Once he had adjusted to the idea that a 'prolonged defence of Singapore' might not be possible, the prime minister suggested abandoning the island to its fate and sending the remainder of the 18th to where they might do more good. 'An ugly decision,' admitted Churchill but while the chiefs of staff were considering it Sir Earle Page, Australia's special envoy in London, got wind of this blasphemy and informed Canberra. From there came the strongest telegram Churchill had yet received from prime minister John Curtin, with whom his relations were already acerbic enough, which described any such move as 'an inexcusable betrayal'. It was not the time to ruffle Australian feathers. Two of the three AIF divisions in the Middle East were coming back home to face the Japanese threat. If need be, it was hoped that, as a *quid pro quo* for the 18th Division, one of these could be diverted to Burma. So the big American liners continued on course, were comfortably missed by some high-altitude bombers as they passed through the Sunda Straits, then raced through the darkness of their last night at sea before Singapore. The rest of Beckwith-Smith's division, who had spent most of the last three months afloat, would take their chances alongside Bennett's men.

The first thing Reginald Burton, the captain in the 4th Norfolks, noticed when the *Manhattan*, now the USS *Wakefield*, docked at Keppel harbour were the lines of people waiting to board other ships to take them away from Singapore. Many were civilians but there were also airmen and sailors whom he discovered were mostly survivors from the *Prince of Wales* and *Repulse*. He found this disconcerting. Burton envisaged a long, bitter siege, something like England in 1940 but with much more prospect of land action. Surely every able-bodied man capable of squeezing a trigger was needed on the island?

They were taken, at breakneck speed, to a tented camp in a rubber estate that had been prepared for them. Their drivers were from the Australian transport company of mainly 1914–18 veterans that had made such a name for itself on the mainland. They prided themselves on driving fast and liked to give newcomers a thrill, taking bends 'like movie stuntsmen' according to Burton. His driver told him about the long retreat down the peninsula but thought things were about to change for the better. 'We'll come good on the island,' he said, obviously unaware that his unit was about to be sent to Java. Singapore was choked with transport. As they roared through the city Burton spotted some European women 'in summery dresses' trying to cross the road and waved. Smiling they waved back. He found their presence reassuring. Things could not be that bad.

But smiling European women in summery dresses were not as good a barometer as Burton thought. On the contrary, for Percival they had just become another problem. At the end of January Miss Phyllis Harrop, who worked in the Police Commissioner's Chinese Affairs Department in Hong Kong, managed to escape to the neutral Portuguese colony of Macao following the Christmas Day surrender of the colony. She brought with her harrowing tales of murder and rape by the victorious Japanese. One of the worst atrocities had occurred at a temporary hospital set up at St Stephen's Boys' School where fifty-six patients and staff had been killed, including a nurse who was bayoneted while she tried to shield a patient. British nurses were then repeatedly raped, having first been locked in a room from which they were removed one at a time to be the plaything of any passing Japanese soldier. (An unwilling witness to the nurses' violation was a wounded soldier from the Middlesex Regiment hiding in a broken wicker laundry basket.)

Up until now Percival had held fairly relaxed views concerning the evacuation of civilians. For while he agreed that there were genuine *bouches inutiles* (the military's preferred term for mouths so useless they did not earn their rations), he also saw that many women were making an important contribution to the war effort as nurses, drivers or in civil defence, while officers' wives were working as cypher clerks in various headquarters. After the messy departure of the Europeans from Penang, there was also the vexed question of race and Shenton Thomas's determination that it would never again be a factor. For once Percival was inclined to agree with the governor. 'If the European women were sent away why should not the Eurasian, Chinese and other Asiatic women who were working side by side with them?'

On 21 January, ten days before the final withdrawal to the island, Percival sent the War Office a message saying that a total of 5,200 European women and children had been evacuated and that all but 600 of the 4,800 that remained had applied for a passage out. (These figures are obviously rounded up, but they are the only ones that seem to be available.) About 5,000 Indians, including men, were returning to India and Shenton Thomas was hoping that Canberra would suspend its 'White Australia' policy and take 5,000 Asian refugees, mostly Chinese. In the end all he could get out of them was permission for fifty Chinese and the same number of Eurasians to land.

Then Miss Harrop turned up at Macao, was interviewed by MI6 and alarm bells began to ring. The Foreign Office, far from treating Miss Harrop's revelations as a propaganda *coup*, kept them under wraps for another month when they were eventually hinted at in a story that appeared in London's *Evening Standard*. But in Singapore, although few people outside the War Council knew the reason why, the evacuation of European women was suddenly accelerated. Even then it was considered that evacuating too many nurses would have a grievous effect on morale. Gordon Bennett was particularly opposed, and deaf to pleas from Colonel Arthur Dernham, his Director of Medical Services who appears to have known about the rapes in Hong Kong. In the end, Dernham decided to get at least some of the nurses off by shipping them out with Australian wounded on their way home. At about this time the British also sent a hospital ship to Ceylon with some of their worst wounded from Alexandra Hospital. Among those on board was the young fighter pilot Tim Vigors, still suffering from terrible burn wounds he had collected over Penang, and the Argylls officer Bal Hendry, the rugby forward who had emerged intact from his hand-to-hand encounter at the country railway station, only to be badly hit during an air strike at Telok Anson several days later.

By now there was an anchored, zeppelin-shaped Japanese observation balloon floating over Johore Bahru. Angus Rose, the Argylls major, saw it for the first time while playing a round of golf with Ian Stewart to celebrate the colonel's DSO, which the War Office had just announced along with other awards in the *Straits Times*. The Argylls had done particularly well. Rose thought the balloon looked like 'a sausage on a stick'. As they played, some Japanese bombers came over and dropped all their bombs at once in what by now just about everyone was calling a 'diarrhoea attack'. The bombs fell close enough for them to hear the whistle and put Rose off a tricky putt.

Despite the air raids and now shelling – some rounds had reached the grounds of Government House – Singapore, like some faded society beauty determined to put on a brave face, could still show you a good time. Accompanied by his wife Ruth, Russell-Roberts, one of the few survivors of Painter's lost 22nd Brigade, went off to Wassiamull's, the fashionable ladies' outfitters in the High Street, and bought enough material for two pairs of men's pyjamas which an Indian tailor he knew would run up for him. On their way to lunch at the Cricket Club they dropped into St Andrew's Cathedral and 'offered up a prayer of thankfulness for our reunion'. In the evening they went with some friends to the Tanglin Club to drink highballs and ended up at a house party. The hostess had just returned from her nursing duties at Alexandra Hospital. Her husband, an Indian Army officer, was with his regiment. Their living room was without a roof and their windows without glass but there was plenty to drink. The next night they investigated Raffles Hotel and discovered, behind the blackout, Dan Hopkins and his dance band still in full swing. During the day Russell-Roberts pulled every string he knew to get his wife, who was working for the RAF as a cypher clerk, out on the next boat. A week before, some ships had left with plenty of room on board. Now, even though most people were unaware of the rapes that had occurred in Hong Kong, with Japanese patrols plainly visible through binoculars from the northern shore the word had got round: get your women out.

It was expected that more evacuation ships would be available soon because some people were still trying to land on the island. This was the last of the 18th Division: the machine-gunners of the 9th Northumberland Fusiliers, easily one of Beckwith-Smith's most tightly knit Territorial units; a battalion of the Reconnaissance Regiment with their armoured cars and Bren gun carriers; and the 125th Anti-Tank Regiment, equipped with the 2-pounder guns that the Australians had used to such good effect, plus some transport units and divisional workshops.

The Northumberland Fusiliers had left Bombay on 23 January on a different ship from the one that had brought them to India in the convoy that included the American liners. This time they were on the motor vessel *Felix Roussel*, a Free French ship of the Messageries Maritimes line which was in Suez when France capitulated and had been seized by the British, whose appetite for merchant shipping was prodigious. The *Felix Roussel* was a small liner that had plied between Saigon and Marseilles. It had a lot of good woodwork on its upper decks, where a large carved elephant guarded the entrance to the first-class saloon. It had two rather smart square funnels, which gave it the appearance of a rakish steam yacht, but one of them was false and for cosmetic purposes only. A few members of its original crew remained aboard, having elected to fight for de Gaulle and sail for the Allies rather than be repatriated to Vichy-controlled Marseilles. These included one French officer and there were also some French petty officers and stewards. Otherwise, most of the crew were Vietnamese or North Africans.

Its new master was a Sunderland man, a British merchant marine officer called Snowling whose most recent employment had been as a Suez Canal pilot. At the beginning of Snowling's command the ship had been employed mainly to carry Indian Army units to the Middle East, then return to India with Italian prisoners. After their experience of the American ships, the Fusiliers considered the French vessel, which had been carrying numbers it had never been designed for, to be in a filthy condition and they spent a lot of their time cleaning her up. When some men began to get stomach trouble, a rumour went round that dead rats had been discovered in her fresh-water tanks. Despite its eighteen months of pressed military service, and recent striking examples of Japanese air power, the ship's air defences consisted of two twin 1918 vintage Lewis machine-guns and five Marlin light-automatics, virtually a sub-machine-gun.

In the same convoy were two freighters and another trooper, the coal-burning *Empress of Asia* carrying the Reconnaissance Corps Battalion, the anti-tank gunners, a field ambulance and the divisional workshops. The *Empress* was older and even dirtier than the *Felix Roussel*. A slow ship whose old steam turbines had a voracious appetite, she had first seen service as a trooper during the 1914–18 war. Her stokers were mainly Liverpool Irish and some carried documents showing they were citizens of the neutral Irish Free State – then hardly twenty years old. Stoking boilers in the bowels of a ship under air attack was a nerve-racking experience enough without the nagging feeling that it was not your war anyway. The master of the *Empress* had already experienced occasions when air-raid warnings had caused jumpy stokers to leave their posts and come on deck. When this happened, the *Empress* almost immediately lost steam, slowed down and became an easier target.

Their escort was the cruiser HMS *Exeter*, one of the warships that in 1939 had cornered the pocket battleship *Graf Spee* at the River Plate. The Royal Navy thought the convoy had a good chance of passing through the Bangka Straits undetected and would arrive in Singapore with the dawn on 5 February. But on the morning of Wednesday 4 February, with just less than twenty-four hours to go, they were spotted in the Bangka Straits by some high-flying Japanese bombers which were probably returning from a raid on Singapore. Some of them still had bombs on board and they dropped them without result while the *Exeter* returned fire just as uselessly.

None the less, there was little reason to celebrate. The convoy had been spotted, its destination was obvious and it had to be assumed that the Japanese would do everything in their power to stop it getting there. Lieutenant-Colonel Lechmere Thomas, a regular soldier of forty-five and popular with his Territorials, called his battalion together and told them that he had been given a choice. They could either turn back and put in at Batavia for a while, then try to time another run that would take them to Singapore mostly under cover of darkness. The freighters, one of which was carrying all the battalion's motor transport still in its desert colours, had already decided to do this. Or they could carry on regardless to Singapore where most of the division were already preparing to repel a Japanese landing and where the support of its machine-gun battalion would be very welcome.

It is unlikely that many of Thomas's men were surprised to learn that their colonel had chosen the last option. Nor would the battalion remain in its passive, passengers' role. Thomas explained that Captain Snowling had accepted his offer that the Fusiliers should bolster the ship's defences with their own weapons. Twenty-four of their Vickers medium machine-guns were to be brought up on deck from the hold and set up about the ship, their greatest concentration being on the stern. Before they were dismissed Thomas told them, 'I want men who want to fight and those that are yellow, may the Lord have mercy on their souls.' This went down very well, though it would have been hard to guess at the excitement most of them were feeling as they set about preparing the ship's defences in the phlegmatic and purposeful way of their region.

The Vickers, with the distinctive corrugated sleeves around their barrels, looked impressive enough. But the best anti-aircraft weapon at their disposal was in the hands of the battalion's anti-aircraft platoon, a stopgap, post-Dunkirk innovation intended to raise the morale of infantry battalions by giving them something to take on Stuka dive bombers. These platoons were armed with Brens mounted on tripods. More important, instead of being fitted with the familiar banana-shaped magazine which carried 28 rounds they were fed by 100-round drum magazines – very similar to the ones fitted to the old Lewis guns. Every third bullet in these magazines was yellow tracer so that the firer could see where his shots were going and adjust his aim accordingly. This platoon had received some training in deflection shooting – firing slightly ahead of a moving target – and the most vulnerable moments of a fighter bomber's attack. They had also been taught to develop a 'hosing technique' which kept an aircraft under constant fire. They were under the command of a Lieutenant Treacher, known as 'Treacle' by his fellow subalterns. Thomas ordered Treacle to establish his main position on a platform above the bridge. Another team were on the *Roussel*'s false funnel.

Each company headquarters also had a Bren for protection, and these were also set up on tripods. Jack Phillips, W Company's clerk, found himself manning one on the bow. Phillips was a twenty-one-year-old grammar school boy with a stutter who, like many of the battalion, had been brought off the Mole at Dunkirk by the Thames paddle steamer *Royal Daffodil*. He was one of eighteen men aboard the *Felix Roussel* from the moorland village of Rothbury, where his father, who had won a Distinguished Conduct Medal at Arras in 1916 for bringing in a wounded Fusilier under machine-gun fire, was the local newsagent.

The drivers and mechanics of the two Royal Army Service Corps supply companies on board also had three Brens which they set up. And, as a last resort, the firepower of *Felix Roussel* was bolstered by 100 Fusiliers armed with rifles who were positioned on each of the two hurricane decks that ran the length of the ship. Others became part of fire-fighting or ammunition parties, ready to form a chain and pass up ammunition for the Vickers and the Brens from the holds.

At dawn on 5 February, the thirteenth day of their voyage, they were, as planned, in sight of Singapore. It was hardly a welcoming prospect. The first thing the soldiers and sailors aboard the *Felix Roussel* saw was the thick pall of black smoke hanging over the island from the burning oil tanks at Singapore naval base.

Breakfast was served in shifts and afterwards those not on duty at the guns did some physical training designed to stop them becoming physically softened by all these cruises at His Majesty's expense. Look-outs were hoping to catch the first sight of the Hurricanes that were supposed to be escorting them into harbour. It was beginning to look as if the Northumberlands' machine-guns would not be needed after all. At 10.30 the pilot came aboard to guide them through the British sea mines and into Keppel harbour. It was almost exactly at that moment that the Japanese air force made its long-awaited appearance and the usual 27-strong formation in three 'Vs' of nine began to attack the two troop ships and HMS *Exeter* with bombs and machine-gun fire.

Colonel Thomas had set up his battalion headquarters just below the bridge on the deck of the first-class saloon, which was reached by a broad wooden staircase with an elephant's head carved into its top. He sat at a small table with his adjutant surrounded by several attentive subalterns who had been unable to find an active role in the defence of the ship and had to content themselves with being the colonel's eyes and ears, rushing off to any part of the vessel Thomas directed them to, to report on the situation there. Among them was

Second Lieutenant John Webb who commanded W Company's
13 platoon and had celebrated his twentieth birthday just before they
left England – one of the youngest subalterns on board. He was feeling
particularly peeved because he had done a course on using Bren guns
against aircraft but 'Treacle' Treacher was a full lieutenant and felt he
needed no assistance from a lowly one-pipper.

The Japanese bombed and strafed the *Roussel* lengthwards, starting from either the bow or the stern: sometimes two aircraft seemed
about to collide as they launched their attacks simultaneously from
opposite directions. The noise was greater than anything any of the
Fusiliers had ever experienced in France or even on the range at Traws-
fynydd in Wales where they had practised laying down parabolas of
indirect 'concentration fire' with their Vickers the way the artillery
lobs shells. The crescendos were supplied by the bombs and the scream
of Mitsubishi engines at maximum revs. The chorus was constant
and sustained machine-gun fire like the sound of a hail-storm on a tin
roof.

'When you went below decks,' recalled Webb, 'it was as if you
were locked inside a tin can which people were beating with sticks.'
Snowling jinxed his ship from side to side as much as he dared while
proceeding through a channel in mined waters. The Japanese could
not have chosen a better place to attack. The ships had so little room
to take evasive action that it was almost as if they were on rails. Quite
early on the Japanese managed to score a direct hit on the *Felix
Roussel*. Two small bombs fell close to the false funnel, killing Treacle's
two-man Bren crew there as well as three RASC men and wounding
another fourteen soldiers. A fierce fire started, then another bomb hit
a nearby water tank and the resulting deluge put the fire out.

Thomas rushed to the scene and told everybody that the damage
was superficial and they were doing a good job. As it happened, the
colonel was right. The damage was negligible and the curtain of fire
being stitched by Thomas's orchestra of Vickers, Brens, Lewis guns,
Marlins and rifles seemed to be taking effect. Some of the Fusiliers
were already claiming they had shot down one aircraft and possibly
damaged another. Webb thought the AA platoon with their drum-
magazined Brens inflicted most of the damage. In the bow, Phillips
was vaguely aware of the noise but entirely concentrated on 'getting
at the bastards'. They took it in turns to spot and fire. As the action
wore on, he noticed that the twin-engined planes grew bolder and

came lower. He tried to 'hose' them the way he had been taught. 'I remember watching fascinated as one of them dived down at us and released two bombs which seemed to be directed at me. They exploded in the sea about 50 yards off us.'

Well astern of the French ship, the *Empress of Asia* was not doing so well. Although army volunteers had replaced most of her mutinous stokers they could not keep her steam up. Bren gunners had added their firepower to the ship's anti-aircraft defences but it was slower, and not half as prickly as the *Felix Roussel*, and the Nells began to smell blood and gang up on the stricken ship. Soon several fires had started. The worst was amidships which effectively cut her in two, preventing people from getting from one end to the other. Eventually her master dropped anchor on a sandbank just outside the harbour and gave the order to abandon ship. A fleet of small boats and a destroyer dashed to the rescue and all but seven of the almost 2,000 men aboard were saved, though many were suffering from smoke inhalation and burns. All the anti-tank guns and vehicles aboard were lost, as was a large consignment of rifles intended to arm a newly raised formation of Singapore Chinese volunteers. A few days later an attempt was made to salvage some of this valuable equipment, but the *Empress* was still smouldering and her hull was so hot that the salvage party could not get within 10 feet of it. Despite Japan's overwhelming air superiority and their earlier successes against the battleships, this was the only ship the British lost from a Singapore supply convoy.

On the *Felix Roussel*, the Northumberland Fusiliers, having fought their way through almost unscathed, were going into Singapore with their tails up. Second Lieutenant Webb recalled the *Exeter* coming alongside and much flashing of Aldis lamps as signals were exchanged from the bridge. Then it was announced over the ship's public address system that the *Exeter* had congratulated them on shooting down at least two, possibly three aircraft. There was an exchange of cheering. 'Three cheers for the *Exeter*. Hip-pip-hooray!' 'Three cheers for the *Roussel*. Hip-pip-hooray!' (A year later a Commander Witzel, Director of the Fighting French Mercantile Marine, would see to it that a memorial plaque was placed on the main first-class staircase of the ship: 'In remembrance of the men of the 9th Royal Northumberland Fusiliers who gave their lives defending this ship.')

Not everybody was in such high spirits. The adjutant took Colonel Thomas to what had been the first-class bar – now the officers' wardroom

– and asked the lascar in charge for two whiskies only to be firmly told that the bar was '*fermé*'. '*Mais, voici le Colonel,*' protested the adjutant, motioning towards Thomas. '*Et moi. Je suis un général,*' said the barman, unimpressed. He was eventually persuaded to open up.

They buried their dead at sea before they put into Keppel harbour with the Northumberlands' padre officiating. Webb had always thought a burial at sea would be rather dreadful but he found it very dignified. The bodies were on stretchers and went over broadside on. There was no last post. The battalion's bugler, Fusilier George Errington, was on one of the stretchers.

In the bow of the ship, Phillips was staring at the way the black clouds of oil smoke hung over the island, blotting out the sun. He was not the only British Expeditionary Force veteran on board who was reminded of Dunkirk and the way a similar pall of smoke had always hung in the air. Singapore was burning.

42. In besieged Singapore Chinese civilians trim the spare rubber off locally made gas masks. This factory was turning out 1,000 a day

43. Soldiers and civil defence workers of all races try to deal with a line of blazing trucks hit after an air attack on Keppel harbour

44. Singapore burning. For the combatants on both sides, an abiding memory of the battle for the island was the oil smuts from the naval base's burning fuel tanks, which blackened skin and uniforms alike

45. (*Below*) Chinese women mourn a dead child by a bombed rickshaw rank, the wheel of one machine buckled by the blast. There were not enough air-raid shelters

46. Yamashita's industrious engineers soon repaired the gap blown in the Johore Causeway. British stragglers, cut off on the mainland, had already discovered they could scramble across it at low tide

47. The first tanks to land on Singapore Island were towed across the Straits of Johore on ingenious pontoons

48. The delicate moment of surrender. An Australian or British soldier being searched by his captors

49. A portrait of two young Australian nurses. Elizabeth Pyman (*right*) got safely back to Fremantle on a ship that left Singapore on 12 February. Next day her friend Ellen Keats was among those nurses who survived shipwreck and landed at a beach on Bangka Island only to be murdered there

50. Badly wounded Sergeant 'Pony' Moore of the 1st Cambridgeshires felt in his blood-soaked shirt pocket for a photograph of his wife and newborn son. But the bullet that had entered his chest had also robbed him of his wife's face. He burst into tears

51. The expensive car of a departed civilian evacuee is pushed unceremoniously off the dock at Keppel harbour. In the foreground are some opened and abandoned suitcases. A few of the earlier evacuees took their cars with them, but towards the end ships' captains were limiting their passengers to one suitcase per person

52. On the evening of the first day of the ceasefire Major Harry 'Flossie' Flower of the Northumberland Fusiliers towers over the victors as he negotiates the return to his lines of about 160 British soldiers the Japanese had rounded up contrary to the agreed terms

53. An unknown Japanese artist's impression, later produced as a lithographic print, of the formal signing of the agreement to surrender at the Ford factory. Percival is in the centre foreground, showing his left profile

55. The honeymoon period. Arm in arm in one case, jubilant Japanese pose for a picture with their captives soon after the surrender. At this stage very few British soldiers were aware of the atrocities that had occurred

54. Civilians watch from the balconies of Singapore's General Post Office with its imposing royal crest as the first Japanese troops march into the city centre

56. The honeymoon begins to wane and calculated humiliation begins. Australian POWs are made to sweep the streets in front of an Asian crowd

57. Major Tominaga, who once bragged about how he had beaten up a European woman doctor for giving medicine to another civilian internee, was a capricious camp commandant, suddenly capable of small kindnesses. His death sentence was reduced to ten years' imprisonment after some of his former prisoners spoke on his behalf

59. Near-naked (they are wearing Japanese underwear which covers the genitals) war crime suspects at Changi jail kowtow to a British military policeman, but one apparently not quite enough. Few POWs wanted revenge but many of their liberators wanted to take it for them

58. Lieutenant-General Shinpei Fukuyei was not so lucky. He was shot by firing squad in the same place on Changi beach where, on his orders, the botched execution of four Australian and British prisoners occurred for the 'crime' of attempting to escape

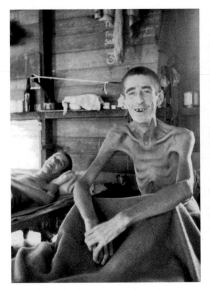

60. One of the most-photographed of the rescued prisoners was Jack 'Becky' Sharpe, a regular in the Leicesters. He was reduced to this skeletal state after three years of systematic starvation and torture in Outram Road jail for an escape attempt

61. Shortly after the liberation a soldier touches up the names on the wooden crosses of some of the 800 prisoners in the cemetery at Changi. Later they will be replaced by headstones. Some of the 12,000 Australian and British servicemen who died building the Thailand–Burma railway still lie in unmarked graves

62. Vivian Bullwinkel, the nurse who miraculously survived the Bangka Island massacre when twenty-one of her colleagues died, at a reception with her mother on her return to Australia in 1945

63. The Australian grazier Ben Hackney, who played dead then crawled away from the massacre of the wounded at Parit Sulong, back in the saddle in 1946 and healed in body if not in mind. His testimony would help see General Takuma Nishimura hanged

Singapore was burning because Yamashita feared that the British would, as a last resort, use the oil stored in their big tanks at the naval base to turn the Straits of Johore into a blazing lake which would consume his first wave of boats and men in a Viking funeral. To prevent this he decided the oil should be burned off and ordered his artillery to shell the tanks and the air force to bomb them. Oil can be much harder to ignite than most people think, but by the time the reporter Morrison visited the base, four tanks were alight and later more were set on fire. The billowing clouds of black smoke from the tanks settled over the entire island, mingling with the smoke from lesser fires such as rubber stocks smouldering in the godowns at the docks at Keppel harbour.

Soon the smell of this smog rarely seemed to be out of anyone's nostrils for long and when it rained the rising smuts of burned oil returned to earth as liquid soot. Combined with their constant sweating, it made front-line soldiers, who were always several hot showers short, feel even filthier than usual. It also added to the misery of the civilians, especially for the growing number of people whose water supply was running to waste somewhere because a pipe had been fractured by a bomb or a shell.

The seed for Yamashita's fears had been planted during his last visit to Berlin when he was informed that Churchill's scientists were claiming that, as one of their anti-invasion measures, they had perfected a way to create a 'burning sea'. The truth was that the British had been trying to set the sea on fire since shortly before the war started but had never quite been able to bring it off over a wide area in a consistent and dependable manner. Naturally they were quite happy to let the Germans think they had by planting stories to that effect in the neutral American press. For home consumption the story was allowed to grow, and there were even 'eyewitness accounts' of charred German corpses, presumed to have been from some kind of reconnaissance in force, being washed up on British beaches.

After conducting some experiments of their own, Yamashita's

engineers had concluded that, although it was easy enough to get fairly still water in a pond or sluggish river to burn, it would be much harder in a large tidal area such as the Johore Straits. Harder but not impossible, and Yamashita was not going to take any chances. Nor were his fears entirely unfounded. Although there never seems to have been any attempt to set the entire straits alight, Brigadier Simson's engineers did come up with incendiary booby traps (petrol mixed with some tar-like adhesive to make a primitive sort of napalm) intended to be placed in the mangrove creeks and detonated either electronically or with a tracer bullet.

Eventually, the besieged grew accustomed to the mantle of smog that had settled upon them. Few if any were aware that the Japanese had, to a small extent, scored an own goal. As the smog thickened, it became increasingly difficult to spot from aircraft or their captive balloon where their artillery shells were landing and correct accordingly. Instead they had to fire blindly onto map references and tended to waste ammunition which was in short supply.

This was particularly galling because, despite the Imperial Japanese Army's general neglect of its artillery arm and its custom of scattering it about in penny packets under infantry control, for the assault on Singapore Yamashita had managed to concentrate the biggest number of field guns his army had yet seen in Malaya. In all there were in the region of 200 guns and heavy mortars in range of Singapore, some recently arrived by road and rail from the 25th Army's Thai beach-heads or along the shorter route from the newly opened port of Endau. None of Warren's few hastily trained SOE 'stay-behind' parties, apprentice saboteurs who at first found it depressingly difficult to blow things up, had managed to cause more than a few hours' delay down either of these routes.

British artillery had dominated on the peninsula. Without this edge things would certainly have gone even worse for them though more than forty-eight guns (two regiments) are unlikely to have ever shelled the same target at the same time. On the island Percival still had a slight artillery advantage over Yamashita, with a total of 226 guns of all calibres. These included the twenty-nine big garrison artillery pieces which everybody associated with the image of Singapore as a fortress. Three of the five 15-inch naval guns could make a full 360-degree turn on their swivel mountings to face the enemy across the straits. But the magazines buried deep beneath their thick concrete bonnets still contained nothing but armour-piercing shot that would burrow deep into the ground before exploding just as they were designed not to go off before they had penetrated a warship's armoured hide.

The six 9.2-inch and eighteen 6-inch guns did have a few high-explosive shells at their disposal but, being essentially anti-shipping weapons, like the 15-inchers they all fired on a flat trajectory and could not lob shells to cover a wider area. What they could do was blow ships out of the water. They covered the sea approaches to the Straits of Malacca and the Johore Channel for 25 miles in any direction and so far the Imperial Japanese Navy had shown a marked reluctance to come anywhere near the island's southern coast. To defend the northern beaches Percival was relying mainly on his 25-pounders but he was concerned that, if they were to withstand a prolonged siege, he might not have enough ammunition for them and had restricted harassing fire to twenty rounds a gun a day.

Yamashita wanted every one of his guns to have 1,000 rounds each to fire before the softening up barrages started. The heaviest cannon he had were 105 mms, which fired a 68-pound shell. Most were Krupps 1890s pattern 75 mms of various types, which delivered a missile 11 pounds lighter than the British 25-pounders. As Melville Rudling, the captured Norfolks' sergeant-major, had discovered, many of them had wooden rather than pneumatic wheels and looked rather old-fashioned. But there was nothing antiquated about the shells they fired. And not once during the fifty-five days of fighting down the peninsula had either side laid on a barrage with anything like this number of guns.

But if he now had almost as many guns as Percival, as well as considerable air support, Yamashita still had far fewer men available for his assault on Singapore than Percival had to defend it: about 30,000 compared to something approaching 90,000. Percival says 'in the region of 85,000' and Wavell, in a message to Churchill, that it could have been as low as 60,000, though he thought this would suffice 'providing the troops can be made to act with sufficient vigour and determination'.

What is beyond question is that the three Japanese divisions preparing to cross the straits were all tried and tested combat troops who had tasted nothing but victory without, in the main, incurring heavy losses. Behind them, stretching back to the beaches on southern Thailand's Kra Isthmus and ultimately to those distant echelons still in Indo-China, was a logistical tail of some 50,000. Percival's equivalent were all crammed onto the island where, just to get them into the right frame of mind, they had been told that in future they would be responsible for guarding their own gun emplacements, offices and workshops. This was the cause of much foreboding among those old sweats who had long since come to regard the army as no more or less than a steady job with a pension at the end of it.

Major Basil Peacock, a Territorial Army officer with a Military Cross he had won as an infantry subaltern in 1918, was commanding a searchlight battery when the order came through. He was alarmed to discover that even his regular sergeant-major had not fired a rifle for ten years. How could this be, asked Peacock, a dentist by profession and a keen Territorial, when standing orders required every soldier, regardless of rank or corps, to qualify on the range once a year? 'He whispered that the ammunition was fired at targets by one or two enthusiasts from the unit who were reasonable shots.'

Quite apart from these unofficial non-combatants there were at least 6,000 recognized non-combatants to be found in the sixteen field ambulance units, three casualty clearance stations and seven military hospitals maintained by the Australians, British and Indians. Little wonder that Percival estimated his teeth arms as about 70,000 – 'the equivalent of four weak divisions'.

'He who defends everything defends nothing,' declared Frederick the Great, and it is unlikely that Percival was unaware of the clever Prussian's famous advice on these matters. But he had a difficult decision to make. Should he fight Yamashita on the beaches or, in the case of the island's north-west shore, among its mangroves? Or should he hold back, see where his thrust was coming and then try and crush it with overwhelming force? He decided on the first option.

The island of Singapore has 72 miles of coastline. It was obvious that the enemy's main thrust was bound to be on its northern shore and perhaps another general might have risked concentrating more of his infantry there to the detriment of the other coasts. The Manchesters, for instance, the regular machine-gun battalion that had arrived on the island from Palestine in 1938, were still in their pillboxes on the south coast and had yet to fire a shot in action. But Percival simply could not bring himself to do it. He had, after all, been outflanked all the way down Malaya. What if Yamashita combined an attack on the northern shore with a simultaneous seaborne landing on another, or

even an airborne assault with the fledgling, and as yet unused, parachute
brigade that was supposed to be lurking in Indo-China? What, indeed,
if he did all three? It would be a hollow victory repelling an attack in
the north if Keppel docks or Kallang airfield had just fallen. Much
better to have the entire coastline covered and then draw off formations
to face the most obvious threat. Meanwhile, his mobile reserve would
be Paris's weak 12th Indian Brigade, whose best unit was the Plymouth
Argylls – the amalgamation of Stewart's battalion with the Royal
Marines off Phillips' battleships. (After the obligatory brawl in the
Argylls' canteen at Tyersall barracks they worked quite well together
though, like the Hindus and Muslims in the Indian battalions, they
were kept in separate companies.)

What was unquestionable was that Yamashita's main attack would
come on the northern shore. The only question was which end? Wavell
plumped for the west of the Causeway where the waters now rushed
through the gap blown at the Japanese end. This was the obvious point
of entry because the straits were at their narrowest here, between 600
and 2,000 yards, the upper reaches of the Skudai River estuary was a
good place to hide small boats and the Japanese would have less time
on the water when they would be at their most vulnerable. He advised
that the 18th Division, easily the freshest and strongest formation, be
positioned there. But it was not up to supreme commanders to dictate
to their generals in the field exactly how to deploy their troops.
Percival, perhaps because he thought the western side of the Causeway
a little too obvious, decided the main landings were more likely to
come to the east of it and deployed the three East Anglian brigades
there alongside two Indian, one of them Selby's Gurkhas.

In overall charge on this flank was Sir Lewis Heath with all five
brigades under his 3rd Indian Corps, which retained the title though
not its character for three of its brigades were now UK British. Given
the lateness of the hour, to the non-military mind the well-used
metaphor of rearranging a stricken liner's leisure seating may well
spring to mind. But this was all to do with trying to create order out
of chaos, and a chain of command, in preparation for the battle ahead.
The reality was never so tidy. In those days the city occupied 9 of the
island's 350 square miles. A mass of men with field kitchens as well as
field guns, and communal latrines that were not for the faint-hearted,
were living in or on the edge of rubber estates and jungle or on the
coast. Some were in requisitioned housing, some under canvas or

sleeping under their camouflaged vehicles, and more than a few in waterlogged holes in the ground being bitten to death by mosquitoes without even the consolation of a moonlight view of the nearby Straits of Johore.

If they knew, few cared that, following Major-General Barstow's death on the railway and the disappearance of Painter's 22nd Indian Brigade (not to be confused with 22nd Australian), Lay's 8th Brigade, now all that was left of the old 9th Indian Division, had been absorbed by Billy Key's 11th Indian Division and Beckwith-Smith's 18th Division put alongside it so that once again Heath commanded a two-division Corps. To many of these men even company headquarters seemed a remote concept. As ever, their horizons, particularly the infantry's, were limited to their mates: the dozen or so men with whom they shared food, drink, tobacco, jokes and, very occasionally, their deepest fears.

West of the Causeway Percival placed Gordon Bennett's 8th Australian Division, which had been strengthened by the most recent Indian reinforcements to reach Singapore in the form of the three Punjabi battalions in Brigadier George Ballantine's 44th Indian Brigade. It was from the same division, and just as green, as the late Brigadier Duncan's 45th, which had disintegrated between Muar and Parit Sulong. Bennett let them remain on the south-western sector, which was regarded as one of the least likely landing spots. He put his Australian brigades either side of the Kranji River. Duncan Maxwell's 27th dug in to the east of the river up to the Causeway where they linked up with the Gurkhas. West of it were the three battalions of Harold Taylor's 22nd Brigade spread along 9 miles of creeks and mangroves.

As soon as they saw it, some of Taylor's officers started to complain that they were far too thin on the ground to hold the territory they had been given, which in any case was not a good position. Lieutenant Frank Gaven of the 2/10th was reminded of the mangroves on the Hawkesbury River back home and thought it was hopeless.

It was impenetrable with all the streams coming in along the foreshore . . . forward defence in this situation was an impossible task. There were no defences or fortifications and no field of view of an enemy approach. It was a situation that would not offer the troops a glimmer of hope.

On the face of it, Bennett's men and not the East Anglians were the best division Percival had. Not surprisingly, the Australians had fared much better than the first Cambridgeshires and Norfolks to arrive, who had been catapulted into action without any time to prepare, one day afloat on a converted liner and almost the next on a sea of confusion in the jungles of Johore. The 8th AIF were well acclimatized and had not been worn down by the agonizing seven weeks of withdrawal down the length of Malaya. Above all, they had recent successful battle experience. 'I thought that, of the troops which had had experience of fighting on the mainland, it was the freshest and the most likely to give a good account of itself,' Percival would recall.

But all was not well in Gordon Bennett's kingdom, where a persistent and apparently unshakeable malaise was being allowed to erode morale. In the three weeks since the Australians had first strode so confidently into battle, provided the world with pictures of smouldering Japanese tanks and briefly become the darlings of local press and radio, much had changed. Bennett had convinced his men they would stop the rot. Instead they had found themselves on the same whirligig of fight and flight as the rest of Percival's army. Two of their battalions had been all but destroyed and it had been discovered that the reinforcements sent to rebuild them were not trained soldiers but men who had only been in the army for a few weeks. During range practice at the Australian depot in Singapore, one was alleged to have been discovered reloading his rifle a round at a time, unaware of the workings of its magazine. Bennett estimated it would take months to get the 2/19th and 2/29th battalions, the core of Anderson's column, back to their old form.

The Old Digger from the transport company who had assured the Norfolks' officer Burton that it would 'come all right on the island' was an exception. The Australian infantry who had been ordered to leave the untested defence works they had so lovingly prepared on Johore's east coast, to come to rest behind a mangrove swamp with inadequate fields of fire and in unprepared positions were not amused. This lack of preparation on the island bewildered them as much as the smoke which rose unchecked from the empty naval base, where Indian sappers were rumoured to be preparing demolitions. Wasn't the naval base what they were here to protect? Where were the apron fences of barbed wire, the mine fields and machine-gun nests they had left behind at Mersing?

For many of these soldiers, Singapore had only ever been a drunken night out in Lavender Street. They were as ignorant of the true state of its fortifications as the British prime minister. It never seemed to occur to Percival, concentrated as he was on stopping the enemy no further south than Johore, that in a worst-case scenario it might be the very absence of defences on Singapore's northern shore that would undermine morale. Admittedly, some had become so bloody-minded that no amount of barbed wire and mines would have persuaded them that Singapore was anything other than a hopeless case. One of Peacock's searchlight crews, put down among an Australian unit with orders to probe the straits at night, were told that their light would be shot out if they attempted to use it because it was bound to draw fire.

Nor was it only the rank and file who were suffering from poor morale. One of the greatest pessimists among the Australians was Brigadier Duncan Maxwell, the tall, bullnecked physician in command of 27th Brigade, who were manning the sector between the Causeway and the Kranji River. Maxwell, who had celebrated his fiftieth birthday a few days before his brigade had fired 8th Division's opening shots with their devastating ambush at Gemas, had once been a favourite of Bennett's. When his predecessor had returned to Australia because of ill-health, Bennett had refused to look outside his own division for a replacement, although in the Middle East there were several eligible Australian lieutenant-colonels, all battle-tested battalion commanders. He had even insisted on giving Maxwell the job over the head of the brigade's senior battalion commander, the dour 'Black Jack' Galleghan who, as commander of the 2/30th Battalion, had overseen the Gemas affair.

Maxwell had the usual good 1914–18 record most of Bennett's battalion commanders had. He was one of two sons of a Tasmanian bank manager who had both been with the Light Horse at Gallipoli before transferring to the infantry and serving in France, where both were commissioned in the field and subsequently survived wounds and won Military Crosses. At 6 foot 3 inches, Maxwell was 2 inches shorter than his elder brother and was known as 'Little Maxwell'. After the war he graduated in medicine at Sydney University while his elder brother went to Malaya and became a rubber planter. (When the Australian army arrived he offered his services and was employed as a staff officer at 8th Division's headquarters with the rank of major.) 'Little' Maxwell had nothing more to do with the military until the last days of peace before Hitler invaded Poland. Then 'despite some misgivings arising from the contrast between the duty of a doctor and a combatant' he returned to the militia and was soon in charge of a battalion.

Once the fighting started in Malaya, Maxwell's 'misgivings' appear to have returned in a big way. Within two weeks of going into action he had begun to badger Bennett about how fatigued his men were getting in the enervating climate and to object to any more demands being made on them before they were properly rested. Before long an exasperated Bennett was reminding Maxwell how much longer Heath's divisions had been in the field and telling him to stop 'wet nursing' his soldiers. At this point some divisional commanders might have fired Maxwell, but it was not in Bennett's nature to admit he had made a mistake. Yet by the time they were taking up their positions on the island Maxwell had become almost openly defeatist. Colonel Thyer, the Australian commander's chief of staff, recalls him telling Percival in person that he thought lives should not be wasted in a hopeless fight for Singapore. Shortly afterwards he confided in Thyer that, as a doctor, he felt that it was his job to save lives. Percival makes no reference to this in his own gentlemanly account of the campaign, in which he seems to have adopted a policy of not mentioning a person at all if he could not find a single good thing to say about them. Dr Maxwell does not appear in his index.

The Australian brigadier was not alone. There were others in responsible positions who were preaching that the game was up. The 1st Cambridgeshires, the second and last of that regiment's battalions to come to Singapore, arrived at the end of January on the USS *West Point* after almost three months at sea. Waiting to greet them were 'a number of high-ranking officers' who were soon telling Lieutenant-Colonel Gerald Carpenter, their CO, that his battalion had arrived too late to make any difference. Carpenter's response was to tell Lieutenant 'Bunny' Gates, his intelligence officer who had been standing next to him, to keep this to himself and ask company commanders to get their men off the ship as quickly as possible.

Some of this gloom in high places filtered down, but it seems that most people, both military and civilian, were either blissfully unaware of it or tried to ignore it. Instead they girded themselves for the best prospect at hand: a long siege. 'In any case, it's doubtful if we could withdraw from Singapore even if we wished to,' Percival told a press conference with what the reporter Morrison would describe as 'a

slightly nervous laugh'. Government announcements assured the population that there was enough food on the island to last at least six
months: 125,000 pigs, plenty of rice and so much flour that the Food
Controller boasted he would be happy to ship some of it back to
Ceylon. True, the pipe which brought water over from the reservoirs
in Johore had been severed when the Causeway was blown up, but
the island's three reservoirs – the Seletar, Peirce and MacRitchie –
were brimming to their banks.

'Singapore must stand; it SHALL stand,' Sir Shenton Thomas had
declared in one of his broadcasts, and the *Straits Times*, in a rare show
of solidarity with the governor they had wished to replace with Duff
Cooper, started to print this rallying cry on its front page every day.
Morrison went to Government House to interview Thomas for *The
Times*. He was always glad to see the press, if only to scotch rumours
that he and Lady Thomas had fled the island for India. A couple of
days before he had been photographed in his shirt sleeves helping to
clear away the rubble from bombed houses in China town. That
morning there had been a new development. Some of Yamashita's
105 mms, using special ammunition that made their warheads rather
lighter than usual, had managed to land some rounds in his grounds,
though whether this was by accident or design was hard to say. The
army estimated that the nearest place the guns could be in Johore was
a good 10 miles away. Before they adjourned to his study the governor
took him to see the holes they had made and 'with a certain pride'
some rather larger ones from aerial bombing. In his study Thomas
admitted that he was puzzled by examples of defeatism and low civilian
morale. He spoke of Malta and Tobruk and said he was glad to be in
Singapore at a time when it had the chance to write another 'epic in
imperial history'.

Later in the year Morrison would write that Thomas was 'sanguine
to the verge of complacency' and it was true that, because the civil
defence programme had been so neglected, few people could shelter
behind walls as thick as those at Government House. In a radio talk, a
senior civil defence officer admitted that, unlike Malta, the only shelters
most people had were 'drains and ditches'.

As the air raids increased, the Stapledons had several small bombs
fall into their own and neighbours' gardens, often burying themselves
well into the ground before they exploded. Kathleen Stapledon noticed

that her 'fat and jovial' Chinese majordomo, the 'Boy' who often delighted her by procuring fish – difficult to get now that all the Japanese fishermen had been interned – rarely took cover.

He used to stay in the garden watching the planes. He often asked me where our planes were and I found it difficult to answer him. He said we would easily beat the Japanese because each one of our soldiers had a gun, whereas in China one rifle was shared between ten men and as one man was killed so another took up the rifle.

Then one day she came home to be told by her *ayah* that the 'Boy' had gone shopping, been knocked off his bicycle by a bomb or a shell and been taken to hospital. He had sent word that he wanted to see them. The *ayah* had no idea which hospital he had been taken to so they went to the nearest one. But there was a problem.

We didn't know his name. All the male Chinese servants in Singapore are known simply as 'boy'. They told us that the easiest way would be to look for ourselves. We went through several clean and tidy wards in which Chinese, Indian, Malay, Javanese and Tamil patients were mixed together and seemed to be quite happy. We found him after a while, wreathed in smiles at the sight of us. They had operated on him that morning and he assured us that he would be back to work in a few days.

Kathleen Stapledon was working in the teleprinter room of the RAF's communications centre at the much-bombed old civil airfield at Kallang which, being on the southern coast and theoretically out of artillery range, was where the last squadron of Hurricanes in Singapore was based. The pilots lounged around in easy chairs, Battle of Britain style, waiting for the next scramble. Morrison called on them just after one of their number had failed to return.

Never have I admired people more than I admired those boys. They were tired out. They had been flying infinitely longer hours than fighter pilots are supposed to fly. The strain was all too evident . . . They knew they would have to go up in another hour or so . . . The most phlegmatic was a Canadian pilot who sucked philosophically at his pipe. He had joined an RAF squadron at the beginning of the war.

The nearest most people got to a pilot was at the Alhambra, watching Ronald Reagan in *International Squadron – The Foreign Legion of the RAF*. The only cinemas that had closed down were a couple being used to store rice. The rest were still open and, though few of them had changed their films since Christmas, there were often queues of all races at their doors as people sought a couple of hours' escape from the awfulness outside.

Rumours abounded. One of the most persistent was that hundreds of Japanese paratroopers were landing. These invariably turned out to be the white puffs of smoke from the bursting anti-aircraft barrage. Percival was still not sure on which side of the Causeway Yamashita would launch his main attack. Curiously, apart from the SOE stay-behind teams, who were operating much further north, the only attempt to establish some kind of listening post in Johore before the final withdrawal to Singapore was made by the Secret Intelligence Service. Two days before the Causeway was blown, MI6 had inserted one of its intelligence officers, three Royal Signals operators under Sergeant John Cross, and a considerable amount of heavy wireless equipment, to set up a relay station to which Chinese agents equipped with suitcase radios could send their messages for passing on to Singapore or Wavell's HQ in Java. But this had nothing to do with anything as vulgar as military reconnaissance.

For this Percival had to rely on patrols being able to sneak across the straits in sampans, lie low and get back with their information. They were not equipped with (just about) portable suitcase radios: nobody in the army had ever seen them. East of the Causeway patrols from Burton's company of the Norfolk regiment found, as they may well have been intended to, items of Japanese equipment on Ubin Island. This, coupled with an increase of artillery fire on the East Anglian Division's area, seemed to suggest that Percival was right and the Japanese were coming that way. Then two Australian patrols both confirmed a heavy build-up of troops opposite their western sector.

Both the Australian patrols, five in one and three in the other, were volunteers from Taylor's 22nd Brigade. One was from 2/20th Battalion, the other from the reinforced 2/19th which had just lost Colonel Anderson, who had been hospitalized with the dysentery he had probably picked up from drinking bad water at Parit Sulong. These were the northern- and southern-most battalions on Taylor's thinly manned 9-mile north-west coastal front, and both patrols had investigated the areas immediately opposite them, slipping across the straits in sampans after dark on 6 February and returning the following night.

The wider area had been covered by the three-man patrol led by Lieutenant Dal Ottley, a replacement officer at the 2/19th whose habitual pipe gave him a gravitas beyond his twenty-six years. He and the sergeant and corporal who accompanied him, a Dempsey and a Donnelly, knew the territory they were exploring well from weeks spent training there. Wearing their rubber-soled brown canvas PT shoes, armed only with revolvers and each equipped with a compass, they went through the familiar rubber estates carefully marking on their maps the locations of gun batteries, mortars and headquarters. Unless they were occupied by the enemy, kampongs were deserted, most of their livestock was gone, and it was obvious their inhabitants had been cleared out of what had become a military area.

A little further north Lieutenant Roy Homer's five-man patrol from the 2/20th observed lines of field guns 50 yards apart and came close enough to a field kitchen to contemplate adding some grenades to the pot. Coming back they discovered the tide had gone out and had the nerve-racking task of pushing and pulling their boat noisily through the mud before they were into knee-deep water and the beginning of a twenty-minute paddle back to their own shore. Neither patrol had seen very much in the way of Japanese small craft which seemed to indicate that, even if the largest part of Yamashita's army was concentrated against the Australians, it was not ready to attempt a landing.

And yet people in Singapore with any knowledge of Japanese history, including the Australian government's representative Bowden, had

been predicting that Yamashita would try to take the island by
11 February. This was *Kigensetsu*, Shinto's most important holiday celebrating the birth of Emperor Jimmu Tenno, the brutal earthling descendant of the sun goddess Amaterasu and founder, some 2,000 years
before, of the divine imperial dynasty.* But it was already 7 February.
Surely the Japanese did not expect to complete their conquest of the
island in less than four days? Perhaps they would launch their attack
on *Kigensetsu*? But would they risk the possibility of failure tainting the
sacred day, the appalling loss of face? Or was it one of those cases, they
asked each other over their *stengahs*, whispering so as not to alarm
the Boy polishing the glasses behind the bar, where failure was not
contemplated?

Yamashita was convinced that Singapore was his for the taking and
well aware of how pleased his masters would be if he completed his
conquest by *Kigensetsu*. It had taken him a mere fifty-five days to
conquer British Malaya at a cost of 1,793 Japanese dead and 2,772
wounded. In that time, he informed Tokyo, he had advanced 700
miles, repaired 250 bridges, killed an estimated 5,000 enemy troops
and captured another 8,000, including two Indian Army brigadiers –
Painter and Challen. This last figure would turn out to be something
of an underestimate for, as the jungle fugitives were driven by hunger
and disease to surrender themselves or were flushed out by their patrols,
it swelled to over 11,000, most of them Indians. The majority were
incarcerated in the appallingly overcrowded Pudu jail, a large stone-
built late-Victorian building erected by the British in Kuala Lumpur.

And soon Singapore itself would be no more than one vast prison
camp, for it would only be a matter of days before the Japanese navy
and air force between them tightened their blockade and the British
could neither escape nor reinforce. Yet there was no possibility that
Yamashita's three divisions could settle down for a long siege. They
were needed elsewhere in South-east Asia: Sumatra, Java, New Guinea,
New Britain and all the smaller islands to the east beckoned. So, quite
apart from the satisfaction of completing his mission by the 11th, speed
was imperative for more pressing reasons – not least, to keep Percival
off balance. The longer Yamashita left it, the better prepared the enemy
would be and, although they would undoubtedly win in the end, the

---

* Perhaps the essential difference between Shintoism and Christianity is that when
Jimmu gave a last supper he had all his guests assassinated.

greater the Japanese casualties. On the other hand if he rushed it and got it wrong, this wounded British lion might come out fighting and turn the Straits of Johore into a moat clogged with the bloated corpses of his army.

When he arrived at the straits, Yamashita had promised Tokyo he would attack within a week. Zero hour was set for shortly after sunset on 7 February. Yet, when two of his divisional commanders asked for another twenty-four hours to prepare he agreed without any display of impatience. He knew they would not have asked for it unless they needed it.

But there was some action on the 7th. All day the fifty-two guns of various types that were supporting Nishimura's Imperial Guards Division on the Japanese left flank had been shelling the part of the coast held by the East Anglians and up to Changi, the easternmost point of the island, where some of the British 15-inch guns were positioned. Then, under cover of darkness, a battalion of Imperial Guards boarded their collapsible assault boats, which were powered by some disagreeably noisy outboard engines, and headed for Ubin Island at the eastern mouth of the Johore Straits. Its nearest landfall was about half a mile away. To the astonishment, and no doubt the delight, of the Guards, despite making noise enough to wake the dead, their landing was unopposed. Although the island was not without tactical importance – its highest point overlooked Changi a mile away – Percival had regretfully decided he did not have enough troops to defend it. Instead, it had been twice patrolled by the unblooded 4th Norfolks who had suffered their first fatality when they started shooting at each other in the dark.

The absence of a garrison gave Yamashita and his staff some cause for concern. Only the Guards' more senior officers were aware of it but the attack was a feint designed, as were all the other warlike noises east of the Causeway, to keep Percival's eye off the western sector where Yamashita intended to attack with almost the entire weight of his army. Did undefended Ubin indicate that the deception had failed? Were the bulk of Percival's forces waiting for him on the north-west coast?

At dawn Guards officers climbed Ubin's highest peak, some 300 feet above sea level, and anxiously examined the enemy coast ahead through their binoculars. But this did not tell them very much. The smoke from the burning oil tanks was thicker than ever. Their only consolation came

from the British artillery. It had evidently dispensed with its shell
rationing and was firing dozens of rounds over Ubin as it tried and
mostly failed to locate the Guards' guns on the mainland. Unlike the
concentrated batteries to the west of them, to make them appear more
numerous these guns were dispersed in ones and twos through the
rubber. Every time one of them fired the British would return it with
interest – hardly the action of people who had discovered they were
dealing with a decoy duck.

This indeed was the case. Both Percival and Bennett were delighted
with the work the Australian patrols had done. Harassing fire was
ordered on some of the troop concentrations they had located. Even
so, the information they had brought back was not conclusive. Where
were the boats? Bennett ordered another patrol to go over that evening.
Meanwhile, Japanese artillery fire on the western sector had been on
the increase for the last couple of days and was getting worse. So were
air strikes. Bennett's HQ, in a rubber estate north-west of Bukit Timah
village on the Jurong road, was first bombed and then received over
100 shells in a little over half an hour. Slit trenches had saved all but
one unlucky soldier and the administration branch's office truck was
wrecked, which allowed Bennett to make soldierly remarks about how
'a little less paper in this war will improve matters'.

The bombing and shelling followed Bennett to Brigadier Taylor's
headquarters in the large village of Ama Keng about 3 miles from the
nearest forward positions along the mangroved coast. 'The brigadier
appears somewhat shaken,' Bennett rather meanly noted in his journal.
He and Harold Taylor had never got on and it was too late now for a
whiff of cordite to forge more comradely feelings. Their latest row had
been over Taylor's suggestion that his brigade should have prepared
fall-back positions along the Kranji–Jurong switch line. Bennett would
not tolerate such 'looking over your shoulder' defeatism.

A 'switch line', as the name suggests, was a line a formation could
switch to, usually by pivoting on a flank. Percival had identified two
places to which his forces could pull back from parts of the coast and
yet still control the largest part of the island and its vital reservoirs.
Basically, these involved lopping off its western and eastern extremities
while retaining the central and longest sections of its northern and
southern shores. The Serangoon line cut off Singapore's eastern, oyster-
like nose, abandoning Changi and its guns to its fate. On the western
side the Kranji–Jurong switch line was the 5-mile gap between the

headwaters of the Jurong River, which emerged on the south coast, and the Kranji, whose broad north-coast estuary marked the boundary between the two Australian brigades. The rivers themselves were rarely more than a quarter of a mile across and would have to be well patrolled against enterprising and determined infantry but it would be difficult to get armour and artillery over them. These lines were very much last resorts, the water-tight doors that had to remain shut – otherwise Singapore was sunk.

Although Bennett thought it was not yet necessary to prepare positions along the Jurong line, he was fully aware, as was Percival who had inspected 22 Brigade's positions with him, that they were too thinly held. To try and thicken them Bennett had raided his rear echelons and added to his tactical reserve an extra formation he named the Special Reserve Battalion. Apart from a few infantrymen plucked from a reinforcement pool for the recently arrived 2/4th Machine-Gun Battalion, it was mostly composed of clerks and storemen from the ordnance corps, and surplus drivers and mechanics. Probably the most 'special' thing about it was the number of young men in its ranks wearing spectacles who, although they were all volunteers just like the infantry, thought things must be desperate indeed if their services were required as riflemen. But Bennett had no alternative, and at least it was a genuine attempt to turn every man in uniform into a fighting soldier, something the Japanese army would have had no problem with at all.

More obvious warriors were Dalforce, Chinese volunteers from all of Singapore's parties and factions, including some strangely tattooed members of its *demi-monde*, united for once by their common desire to trample the 'shrimp barbarians'. They were the brainchild of Lieutenant-Colonel John Dalley, a colonial policeman well versed in their ways. Even the sporting rifles and shotguns they had been issued in lieu of the promised captured Italian carbines, lost on the burned-out *Empress of Asia*, had failed to dampen their enthusiasm for the task at hand. Their main drawback was that, to most European eyes, they looked no different to the Japanese and most of them were wearing little by way of uniform. All that identified them as friendlies were white headbands.

A company of about 100 Dalforce were attached to Taylor's brigade. He put them alongside the 2/10th, his northernmost battalion, where they quickly learned the virtues of digging in. By 7 p.m. on Sunday 8 February, the Japanese barrage, which had started at ten o'clock that morning along the length of the north coast, was now firing almost entirely on the Australians on the west coast of the island and had reached a long and lingering 'drumfire' crescendo. One of Taylor's company commanders timed the incoming rounds and discovered that in the space of a single minute they had received more than one a second. Lieutenant-Colonel Varley, commander of the 2/18th Battalion, thought that for concentrated shell-fire it beat anything he had known in 1914–18. 'Pozières was the heaviest shelling I experienced in that war. In two and a half days I lost fifty out of fifty-six men.'

And yet this time Varley's casualties were remarkably light. The battalion commander noted: 'The German shells seemed much more effective.' This is not all that surprising. In 1916 the Kaiser's 5.9-inch rounds were heavier than anything the Japanese were throwing at them; but there were other factors that minimized casualties. On Singapore the Australians were dispersed in two- or even one-man slit trenches and fox holes and, even when the shells landed close, the explosion tended to be absorbed by soil even soggier than the Somme in places. Unless a man was caught in the open, it needed almost a direct hit to kill or maim him. Heavy mortars were more effective; fortunately for the Australians, the Japanese had a limited supply of ammunition for these.

But if it was not what their fathers and the Old Diggers in authority over them had suffered in France, it was still a terrifying ordeal. Neither side in the Malayan campaign had experienced a sustained barrage like this. And, as usual, it had rained heavily and many of their holes were waterlogged pits. Men began to crack up. Ashamed, some of them put their trembling down to a sudden onset of malarial shivers. Mercurial mood swings were commonplace. Sergeant Tom Fardy admits he went from scared to highly belligerent. 'Then you settle down and, when the men see you settled, it rubs off and everyone feels more settled.'

During the lulls, when the fire swung away from one battalion area and onto another, a few walking wounded and the occasional stretcher case would head towards the aid posts at battalion HQs. Some did their best to disguise their shock or fear and perhaps a certain relief that they were honourably departing from the field. 'Square this up for me with those yellow bastards,' yelled a private of the 2/20th to his mates as he was being carried away with a tourniquet on the leg which would soon be amputated. Something, probably a mortar bomb, had exploded in a tree directly above his trench. Most had less serious wounds, some from flying stones and clods of earth rather than shrapnel. At the 2/19th's aid post, a tented dug-out, the medical officer had persuaded brigade to send up four extra orderlies so that the lightly injured could be patched up and returned to their positions. Rum sometimes helped to console those who thought they had won a ticket back to sanity and a hospital bed for a couple of days. At least one man refused to be evacuated. Lieutenant Dal Ottley, who had led the most successful reconnaissance patrol across the straits, came in just about standing with multiple shrapnel wounds. After they were dressed he hung around battalion HQ, which was itself being shelled, trying to help out.

By this stage all the battalion commanders were beset by communication problems because, as usual, they were reliant on field telephones to keep in touch with their company commanders and the shells were cutting the cables to pieces. Radio links set up with Taylor's brigade HQ at Ama Keng worked only intermittently. Newly serviced radios had been returned to all the battalions that morning. Colonel Kappe, the regular soldier in charge of the Australian division's signals, thought it had a lot to do with unskilled operators who were not persistent enough. As the shelling went on and the breaks became harder to repair, most communications were carried out by runner or dispatch riders, often scrambling around country tracks on dimmed headlights. Mixed in with the infantry's most forward positions were the observation posts of the Australian artillery batteries, whose telephones were also useless and who had the usual reluctance to attempt to use radio. As a last resort, they did have Verey pistols and agreed signals to the batteries hidden in clearings in the rubber that would bring fire down on various parts of the coast.

The strength of the barrage had convinced the Australians that an attack must now be imminent. 'Soon the leaves will be falling,' warned Brigadier Taylor, whose HQ was constantly under fire. He had given orders that, if they appeared in danger of being overwhelmed, battalions should first coalesce around their headquarters and then fall back and form a line starting at his HQ at Ama Keng so they were protecting the northern approach to Tengah airfield. He had not told Bennett about this plan because he knew the latter would disapprove, just as he had turned down his suggestion to prepare defences along the Kranji–Jurong line. In any case, it was a contingency plan. It would obviously be much better to blow the Japs out of the water and never let them set foot on the island in the first place.

The moon was scudding about the clouds, casting weird shadows. It was in its last quarter and would not be fully risen until 1.30 next morning. Yet none of the searchlights were operating on 22nd Brigade's front. The brigade major had given orders that they should not be illuminated because they had boat patrols out. He had called Brigadier Ballantine, commander of the 44th Indian Brigade to the south of them, and asked him what he was doing about lights. Ballantine told him his beach lights would start making their sweeps as soon as it got dark. The major told him that the Australians found there was light enough to see without them. Perhaps he had in mind the intermittent flaring up of some slow-burning fuel tanks on the east bank of the Kranji estuary in the territory occupied by Maxwell's 27th Brigade. At about 8.30 p.m. the barrage began to subside and for the first time the men of the 2/20th Battalion's D Company began to make out the sound of the boat engines it had been masking. When there was no mistaking what the sound was, Private Col Nicol fired a long burst on his Bren gun. In the absence of a working field telephone it was the agreed signal that the landings had started.

The reason the Australian patrols had not seen many boats was because the Japanese engineers in charge of them had hidden them in the jungle and rubber estates that bordered the Skudai River just above its estuary. One of the causes of the twenty-four-hour delay was that it had proved such hard work hacking out tracks wide enough to carry them to the harbours that had been prepared for them. Apart from a few dozen sampans of various sizes, commandeered for scouting and various other tasks, there were three kinds of boat involved.

The largest were fifty or so of the smallest of the steel-hulled landing-craft used in the landing on the Thai beaches and at Kota Baharu, which had been brought down by rail and road. At a pinch they could hold about fifty men. Some of these carried heavy machine-guns. A few had been fitted with wooden platforms to enable mortars to be fired from them. But the mainstay of Yamashita's lilliputian fleet were the collapsible assault boats with the outboard motors the Imperial Guard had used for their diversionary attack on Ubin Island. Intended for river crossings, these were ingenious, lightweight affairs of plywood with moulded rubber joints which came in two sections and could, claimed their manufacturers, be put together by a trained man in two minutes. They normally had at least one sapper as coxswain and carried twelve average-sized Japanese infantry with their equipment, though the longer-legged Guards preferred to limit their capacity to eight. It was also possible to link two or three of them together, fit a deck and carry field guns and even light tanks on them.

By dusk on the 8th, the confused scenes at the Skudai as the infantry assembled and the engineers directed them to their boats, often having to yell above the firing of the batteries hidden nearby, did not augur well for the night ahead. The tide was well on the ebb. There were fears that fully laden craft, even the assault boats, which were almost flat-bottomed, would run aground. To avoid this the engineers had the infantry wading out to embarkation points that were almost midstream in some cases. Once a man had dropped his rifle aboard and started to pull himself over they were easily capsized. This happened a couple of times and the upturned craft went drifting downstream pursued by irate coxswains in the boats with the outboard motors attached.

Then, in the Japanese way, suddenly all was order and calm and off they sailed towards the Skudai's wide mouth, a regatta of some 150 boats, sometimes bumping into each other as they followed the ebb tide out along its narrowing channel. Yamashita's first wave did not need their own propaganda machine to tell them, as it had done with increasing frequency over the last eight weeks, that they were making history. Not a few thought of those who had died to get them this far and tapped a pocket to ensure that the tin – flat British tobacco ones were ideal – containing a little of a comrade's ashes and bone was safe. Since there was rarely any time for full cremations and Shinto rites they would cut off a finger, or sometimes an entire hand, and when they had a moment cremate it themselves; at times, over a slow fire, this was a dreadful business that had them retching. Some of these ashes would be put aside for the family and the rest would go in their own tin. Often friends had vowed that, one way or another, they would get to Singapore together, and now one of them was keeping that promise.

As they emerged from the river mouth, spread out, line abreast, into the straits and began to approach the enemy shore, they heard for the first time the whistle of their own shells arcing over them and then the comforting sound of their explosions not even a kilometre away. How far across the water would the British allow them to get before they began to fire back?

Col Nicol, the Bren gunner from the 2/20th's battalion, fired the first shots at about 300 yards. It was probably as well that he had little idea of what he was shooting at. The best part of two divisions, the 5th and the 18th, were heading Nicol's way – not all at once, Yamashita did not have enough boats for that, but in waves of 4,000 at a time. Facing them were the 3,000 or so Australian infantry who had spent most of the day under bombardment.

Yamashita had chosen the positions occupied by Taylor's 22nd Brigade as what the Germans called the *Schwerpunkt*: the point where he would concentrate his forces to punch a hole through one small part of Percival's thin perimeter then spread out behind it. Once it was certain that an attempt at a landing was under way two things were supposed to happen. Major Peacock's UK British and Malay searchlight crews should have begun to reveal the Japanese boats and, however much their coxswains twisted and turned, held them in their beams long enough for the Vickers and anti-tank guns to begin to take their toll. And, although almost all the field telephone lines were cut, the red and white Verey flares should have called in the kind of artillery fire on all the obvious landing places that the Japanese had learned to fear. Neither of these things occurred.

The failure of the searchlights to come on in the Australian sector was never properly explained. Despite his brigade major's talk of a total blackout while boat patrols were on the water and the moonlight being good enough to see by anyway (which patently it was not), Brigadier Taylor himself always insisted that he had given his three battalion commanders discretion to illuminate the beach lights as they saw fit. In any case Taylor, the Deputy Government Analyst for New South Wales and a scientist by training, had ignored Bennett's order to send another patrol across the straits because, by the time it was dark, the continuing barrage seemed to make a full-scale attack more imminent. The only Australian patrol to go out that evening was a lieutenant and two men from Maxwell's 27th Brigade on the eastern side of the island's Kranji estuary. Yamashita did not intend to attack this sector until the following night when the Imperial Guard, less the battalion still making the diversion on Ubin Island, would be launched against them. The patrol had ended in disaster when the lieutenant was lost after a Japanese-manned sampan rammed them, though not before he had tossed a grenade into it. The men with him swam back to Singapore's north shore trying to keep their heads above the oil sludge on the water, but the lieutenant was never seen again.

With the enemy so close, less than half a mile away across the straits in most cases even before they had boarded their boats, switching the lights on was a calculated risk for both the crews and anyone near them. Obviously the Japanese would do their best to extinguish them with anything that could be brought to bear from artillery and heavy machine-guns to small arms. Only a few days before the landings started, *The Times*' correspondent Morrison had visited a searchlight crew, positioned in scant cover on one of the northern beaches, who had cheerfully described themselves to him as 'a suicide squad'. One of the reasons Taylor was chary about using them was because he felt there had not been enough time to devise proper protection for them, either by digging in or by using sandbags, something that might have been done weeks before if the labour had been available to permit Simson to start work on the northern shore defences, and if Percival had been inclined to let him. When the lights failed to come on Taylor assumed it was because, like the field telephones, their generator lines had been cut by shell-fire; but of the four lights in his sector this only applied to one of them. At the other three, the crews waited for orders to switch on that never came.

More important than the lack of illumination was the absence of heavy and sustained artillery fire. As they watched the dark shapes come closer and gradually take form, the dug-in infantry held their breath and waited in vain for their own barrage to tear them apart. 'Yet the seconds crept by and still there was no response, all the time the enemy craft came closer,' noted one anguished eyewitness.

There was a simple reason for this. Once the field telephone lines had been cut, the Verey flares being fired by forward observation officers were hard to spot at batteries concealed on the fringes of jungle or rubber estate clearings a couple of miles away. Morse signal lamps, similar to the ones the navy used, pleading L C D F – 'Landings – coastal defensive fire' – were even harder to spot. At the three battalion headquarters in Taylor's brigade, divisional wireless operators supplied by Colonel Kappe, Bennett's senior signals officer, proved just as incapable of getting through to brigade HQ on their malfunctioning sets as the half-trained infantry signallers with their slow morse and clumsy tuning techniques.

Yet these gunners had been preparing for this moment for at least a week. All their arcane calculations, involving range, calibration, fuse times, charges and the air burst spread tables which enabled shrapnel to fall over a designated area, had been made, the ammunition prepared and neatly stacked into separate piles. It appears that the only thing that had been omitted was some stringent testing of the alternative signalling arrangements if field telephone lines went down. The Verey flares, serious fireworks fired from a large-bored single-shot pistol, arced across the sky then burst and, for a few tantalizing seconds, bathed the boats in brilliant light, better than any searchlight, as they drifted down onto the water. Not surprisingly, the forward observation officers, who now found themselves running out of flares, were tearing their hair out. 'We train and we practise for years and now we get nothing,' despaired the man in the 2/19th Battalion's sector whose latest flares had at least enabled a Vickers gun to mow down the occupants of one of the nearest landing-craft. 'Can't they hear anything going on up here in front?'

It was getting noisy. Although, for the most part, the Australian artillery still remained stubbornly silent, the infantry were firing their 3-inch mortars as fast as they could drop the bombs down their tubes. And, on the 2/20th's front, two Vickers guns had blown up a barge carrying some sort of explosives which – a blazing beacon – drifted obligingly across their front exposing several of its siblings to their fire. The Japanese responded with machine-gun and mortar fire from the bigger landing-craft, mooring one to the poles of a Malay fish trap about 100 yards offshore. They also set up mortars and machine-guns on the tiny unoccupied island of Sarimbun about 400 yards from the positions held by Varley's 2/18th. Where they could see a target, this failed to suppress the Australian fire in any significant way and there was no doubt that casualties were being inflicted on the attackers; but the majority pressed stubbornly ahead, seeking out those dark spots from which no fire appeared to be coming.

The first Japanese heroes of the landings on Singapore were the coxswains the engineering corps had supplied, steering their craft towards the enemy shore under fire as the infantry they carried crouched in a tangle of limbs and equipment at their feet. Not surprisingly, they had a high casualty rate. Among them was Leading Private Kiyoichi Yamamoto who was hit by shrapnel, probably from a mortar bomb, which badly wounded him in his stomach, chest and right hand as well as damaging the steering. In the dark it was impossible for his passengers to see how grievously hurt he was and, though he was gasping for breath, he insisted on staying at what was left of the wheel until they were all ashore. Only then did Yamamoto collapse and die though, according to his citation, not before he remembered to wish His Imperial Majesty a long life with a last '*Tenno heika banzai!*' When they picked him up it was discovered that his right lung was protruding through his shattered rib cage and almost his entire uniform was soaked with blood.

That some of Taylor's Australians inflicted considerable casualties on the first Japanese to land is beyond doubt. When, at about 1 a.m., Sergeant Arai Mitsuo of the 18th Division jumped from the bow of his boat with the second wave, 'a cold hand stroked his ankle'.

Nine corpses floated in the water, head upward, in a line next to each other. A chill ran down Arai's spine. Were they shot while crossing, and then washed up, or after they had landed? But reflections be hanged! Quick! Cut off a wrist or a finger of each dead man. Chop, chop, chop. Into a box, there's no time to bury them. Just a quick prayer. Rest in peace. Then forward! He must fire the green 'success' rocket: Regimental Command has landed – the sign for 18th Division General Mutaguchi Renya to embark on the third wave across the straits.

By the time Sergeant Arai was paying his gruesome respects to the dead the time was right to fire his green success rocket, for the Japanese had more than a mere toehold on the island. In the space of four hours Taylor's 22nd Brigade had been overrun and disintegrated. A combination of factors had led to this state of affairs. Although the artillery did eventually start to meet requests for defensive fire, only two troops – eight guns – fired heavily out of thirty available 25-pounders and 4.5s. Two other troops scarcely fired a shot. When at last some of the gunners became aware of the infantry's cries for help, usually from news brought by dispatch riders, the wording of their messages was often desperately vague. 'Bring down fire everywhere,' read one.

Whatever the reason, the absence of a proper artillery response, beach lights and decent fields of fire combined with a thinly manned and porous line that was easily infiltrated plus, at Yamashita's chosen *Schwerpunkt*, the vastly superior numbers of forces that fell on any position showing an inclination for prolonged resistance, all proved too much for the Australians. They would probably have proved too much for any troops – even, had the roles been reversed, the Japanese. Then, quite apart from these fearful odds, they were doomed by Taylor's humane and sadly unworkable orders that, if they felt they were at the brink of being overrun, platoons should fall back on company headquarters and, if necessary, companies to battalion HQs. Like Bennett, Percival had no knowledge of Taylor's instructions and, in his gentle memoir of the campaign, permits himself a rare hint of impatience with such dismally amateur tactics, 'at night in thick country and in the middle of a battle which in many places was being fought at close quarters'.

In such circumstances, the only way to fight the battle is for the advanced posts to hold on and for reserves to counter-attack up to them if the opportunity arises. The result in this case was much confusion and disorganization, groups of men becoming detached and lost in the close country. Those are the conditions which produce stragglers and that there were stragglers in this case cannot be denied.

But Taylor, who had an excellent 1914–18 record, was a scientist not a staff-college-trained professional soldier well versed in the theory as well as the practice of war. Inevitably, the stiffest resistance in his brigade was against those few Japanese who, despite the lack of searchlights, were unlucky enough to be spotted in the boats and at their most vulnerable. A small party who ventured as far south as the territory occupied by Ballantine's Punjabi teenagers were greeted by lights and artillery, and the survivors soon headed back north into the welcoming darkness of the Australian sector.

Taylor's orders were an open invitation to run away rather than stick to isolated positions as, for example, some of the British Battalion had at Kampar on the mainland. Once the enemy was ashore, it was almost inevitable that the most forward sections and platoons would begin to withdraw sooner rather than later. There were no prizes for being last man off the beach, only the risk of solitary annihilation. It did not take the enemy long to work out what was happening.

'For the defending Australians, it was kill or retreat,' said Ochi Harumi, a machine-gunner in the 5th Division whose unit came up against the 2/20th Battalion. 'For the Japanese it could only be kill or be killed.' Ochi recalled how a rearguard armed with Thompson guns tried to hold them up as, 'like rabid dogs', they chased them into the bush.

Among Ochi's quarry was Private Len Serong. In secondary jungle in the dark it was terrifyingly easy to lose your companions. Serong made the mistake of pausing to tie a loose bootlace and never caught up with his section again. Before he was captured he would spend a month in the same patch of jungle living off fruit, abandoned rations and what friendly locals gave him. For the landing on Singapore, almost all the Japanese junior leaders – lieutenants, sergeants and corporals – were equipped with cheap wrist compasses with luminous dials. Their orders were simple. No matter how dispersed they had become they were to head south or south-east, depending on where they had landed, and rendezvous at the much bombed and shelled Tengah airfield. (It had been abandoned by the RAF several days before, shortly after its station commander, a group captain who had done his utmost to raise the morale of his ground crews, had shot himself following an official reprimand for a delay in getting his Hurricanes into the air.)

Between the coast and Tengah were mangrove swamps, creeks, bogs, deep and fast-flowing rivers, some roads, then the village of Ama Keng with Taylor's brigade HQ just south of it, and finally the airfield. Both sides were now heading in the same direction, scrambling along rain-soaked muddy jungle tracks in the dark. Inevitably, some collided.

Corporal Clarence Spackman, a dairy hand from Western Australia, was one of about ten machine-gunners armed with rifles and fixed bayonets who were trying to find a way through a swamp to 2/18 Battalion's HQ when they bumped into a party of Japanese led by an officer brandishing a sword. It seems that at first both sides were too shocked to shoot. Spackman bayoneted the officer, seized his sword and then used it on a man who had rushed to the officer's help. In the *mêlée* that followed, most of Spackman's section were wounded, but they stuck together and all of them came out of it alive.

Spackman was part of the 2/4th Machine-Gun Battalion, mostly recruited in Western Australia, who were supporting Taylor's brigade along its 9-mile front. Spackman's section was part of Lieutenant Terence Meiklejohn's platoon, four Vickers guns in all. In order to give themselves a decent field of fire the two sections had dug in, about 400 yards apart, close to the water where they had been able to shoot through gaps in the mangrove swamp. Both had come under frequent grenade attacks but the Japanese had made no attempt to finish them off with a frontal assault. Instead, they had gone round them.

Meiklejohn's men had fought on until shortly after 1 a.m., their four guns firing about 20,000 rounds between them, and only pulled out when the infantry around them had announced they were withdrawing because they were 'surrounded'. Spackman's section had dismantled their Vickers' working parts and dumped them because, unlike Meiklejohn's platoon, their escape route lay through a swamp and there was no way they could carry their heavy weapons through it. (The Vickers' basic design was unaltered since they came off Sir Hiram Maxim's drawing board in 1883 and they weighed 40 pounds.) Meiklejohn's men were carrying their dismantled guns when they surprised some Japanese who were sprawled across a track and appeared to be resting. The lieutenant shot several with his revolver and at least one was rendered *hors de combat* by a blow from one of the tripod stands the Vickers were mounted on. Meiklejohn, who was twenty-one and a warehouseman according to his army records, then reloaded his pistol, told his men to run for it and was killed trying to give them covering fire as they got away.

The lieutenant had at least known the satisfaction of directing a lot of fire at the enemy before he died. Other Vickers platoons from his battalion had not seen any Japanese or fired a single shot before the infantry informed them that they were pulling out. Since these escape routes almost invariably lay through thick bush and over various waterways – several men were drowned trying to cross them – at least one of these platoons suffered the additional humiliation of being obliged to spike their unblooded Vickers by scattering the working parts. If these machine-gunners had not seen anything to shoot at, then neither had the men alongside them. But the riflemen had been encouraged to pull back if they felt they were in danger of being overrun, and it was dark and there were undoubtedly a lot of Japanese around.

This is not to say that all or even most of Taylor's brigade retired without firing a shot. Some did, some didn't. As was so often the case, it was the men Taylor could least afford to lose who most frequently appeared on the casualty lists. Both the lieutenants who led the reconnaissance patrols across the straits died. Ottley of the 2/19th was found, still clutching a Bren gun, outside the ambushed ambulance that had been taking him and others to a casualty clearing station. He should not, of course, have had a Bren gun in an ambulance, but then neither should an ambulance have been ambushed. Homer of the 2/20th would die of wounds in Alexandra Hospital. In the first twenty-four hours of fighting on Singapore this battalion lost seven officers killed, three wounded and one captured. Among them was their commanding officer Lieutenant-Colonel Charles Assheton, a civil engineer from Tamworth in New South Wales, who had been born in 1901, just too young for the 1914–18 conflict and too old, if he had chosen to be, for the next one. He died shortly after dawn, organizing a rearguard of three Bren gunners on a knoll, sparsely covered in rubber saplings, in order to cover the withdrawal of some wounded by road towards Tengah airfield.

The men who had gathered about him from his own and Varley's 2/18th Battalion were still, more or less, a disciplined body with a sting in their tail. Most suffered from the 'confusion and disorganization' Percival refers to. It might be argued that this is the norm in battle, common to triumph and defeat alike, and the best-laid plans rarely remain unchanged after first contact with the enemy. But it seems to be a trick of good generalship somehow to harness this chaos. Yamashita laid down one inland objective: Tengah airfield and get there any way you can. It is just possible that the Australians might have been able to hold onto at least some of their positions had they been ordered to stay put, been properly wired into them and if they had been supplied with enough ammunition, rations, cigarettes and perhaps a little rum. Meiklejohn's machine-gunners held for the best part of five hours and, with the Japanese showing no desire to press matters with them, might well have continued to do so if the neighbouring infantry had not abruptly announced their departure.

Dawn might have risen on a patchwork quilt of opposing forces. The Australians would still have been holding large pockets along the coast and making it difficult for Yamashita to reinforce in daylight. Behind them, cut off, exhausted and uncoordinated parties of Japanese, some of them beginning to run out of ammunition, might have been ripe for counter-attack as they congregated around Tengah airfield and the British artillery at last came into its own.

Instead, when the sun came up on 9 February 1942, the largest part of Taylor's brigade had been turned into a rabble. Most were filthy with a gooey combination of mud and the oil smuts that were in the humid air. Many were unarmed and incongruously clad in underpants, boots and helmets, having stripped off and abandoned their weapons and ammunition pouches in order to cross rivers and swamps in the dark. (Brens, which at 22 pounds were more than twice the weight of a rifle, were usually the first to go.) All were short of sleep and long on adrenalin.

At first Taylor tried to hold a line north of Tengah airfield and Bennett rushed reinforcements to him in the shape of the 2/29th Battalion, the drivers and clerks of the Special Reserve Battalion, and some machine-gunners who had not been committed to the coastal defences. The 2/29th, almost destroyed at Bakri, was mostly composed of reinforcements, and the sight of these 'veterans' heading south and obviously determined to put as much distance as possible between themselves and the Japanese was an unnerving one. 'Efforts were made to stop these men and weld them into new positions but only a few remained,' reported Colonel Kappe, Bennett's chief signals officer. 'It is unfortunate to relate that one party of fifty under an officer, after being steadied and persuaded to occupy a locality, soon afterwards vacated it without orders.'

An entire company of Varley's 2/18th did not stop running until they got as far south as the village of Bukit Timah on the outskirts of Singapore. Here they paused long enough to arrange some transport to convey them to the Australian general base depot in the city. Later they would claim that, throughout their journey, they had encountered no other Australian troops, though they would have had to pass through the 2/29th and the Special Reserve Battalion at Tengah airfield. 'This is not understood,' commented Colonel Kappe in his long and mostly unpublished narrative of the campaign, and his pain is only too obvious.

'Not all men are heroes though the readers of military histories who have no practical experience may get that impression,' wrote Percival, recalling that during the last great German offensive in the spring of 1918 he had discovered in a French village British stragglers from twenty-one different units. 'Even our military regulations admit that there will be battle stragglers in the instructions they contain for the organization of stragglers' posts.'

Brigadier Taylor had made no provision for this kind of safety net. As a result, what started as straggling, which might be defined as the temporary displacement from forward positions of soldiers willing to return to the fray, soon began to look more like mutiny and desertion. The division that had raised everybody's hopes when at last it 'went in to bat', as Bennett put it, with the ambush at Gemas less than a month before, would never be put back together again: a diagnosis that must have occurred to Brigadier Maxwell, the defeatist doctor, who had been watching these events with some apprehension from his position west of the Causeway where the two battalions under his command were about to be attacked by almost an entire division of Imperial Guards.

On the day Taylor's broken battalions were drifting away from the coast and even to Singapore city itself, Duncan Maxwell, who commanded Bennett's 27th Infantry Brigade, did an odd thing. He got rid of both his battalion commanders within the space of a few hours.

The first to go was Lieutenant-Colonel Albert Boyes, much to the surprise of all those who considered his 2/26th to have done well in the rearguard on Johore, where after two bayonet charges the admiring Japanese had accused them of 'suicidal resistance like wounded boars'. Maxwell declared Boyes to be 'unsatisfactory'. It is hard to work out what Maxwell had against him unless his view was founded on the two things that made Boyes unusual for a battalion commander in Bennett's division. He had not, though he was easily old enough to have done so, fought in World War I. And yet, after gaining his commission at the age of twenty-two in the closing months of that conflict, he had elected to stay on and become one of Australia's tiny cadre of regular soldiers.

Perhaps Maxwell, with all his doubts and his determination that young lives should not be wasted, was irritated by the presence of this unblooded professional who had seen very little of the awful difference between theory and practice. Boyes' successor was the same age but Lieutenant-Colonel Richard Oakes, another grazier member of Australia's landed gentry, had like Maxwell served in France with the 1st AIF, first as a machine-gunner then as a member of the Australian Flying Corps.* Oakes had been second-in-command to Anderson in the 2/19th Battalion but missed the retreat from Bakri and Parit Sulong bridge because he and a few others had been left behind at Jemaluang.

The other banished battalion commander, albeit in theory only on a temporary basis, was Black Jack Galleghan, the CO of the 2/30th who had fired the 8th Division's first shots when he supervised the ambush at Gemas. There was no love lost between him and his briga-

---

* The forerunner of the RAAF just as the Royal Flying Corps was the forerunner of the RAF.

dier. Galleghan, who had been senior to Maxwell before Bennett promoted him, had never bothered to hide his resentment. But he was highly regarded and there was no way Maxwell could fire him with any credibility. However, Black Jack had a problem. He had become partially deaf. Whether this was the result of a near miss by a bomb or shell or an infection of some kind is unclear. Whatever was causing it, his hearing loss seems to have made it difficult for Galleghan to follow what was going on at brigade conferences. Which is where Dr Maxwell stepped in. He ordered him to hand over his battalion to his second-in-command, a Major Ramsay, and report to hospital for treatment. To be fair, Galleghan might have been in excruciating pain and happy to follow doctor's orders. If so, for Maxwell it was a happy coincidence. The two men most likely to question his decisions had now left the scene.

It was Monday 9 February. Galleghan departed shortly after midday. By then Boyes had already left for the AIF's base depot, covering his embarrassment by explaining to his incredulous company commanders that he was needed for a special job elsewhere. Meanwhile, the 2 miles of shore line between the Causeway and the broad Kranji River estuary covered by Maxwell's two battalions was beginning to come under the kind of artillery and air attack that had been the prelude to the previous night's landings in Taylor's sector.

But, for the moment, the expanding Japanese bridgehead remained entirely west of the Kranji, where Taylor, having now pulled back from Tengah airfield, was doing his best to absorb the reinforcements he had been sent with what was left of his brigade and hold the Kranji–Jurong switch line. Fugitives from the coast were still trickling through, many of them deaf to pleas to stay and fight. 'Quite out of control and leaderless and stated they had had enough,' noted Lieutenant-Colonel Pond, the commander of the reconstituted 2/29th, with its large number of raw recruits. Pond feared their condition might be infectious and was glad to see the back of them.

As the Japanese strength across the Kranji grew Maxwell began to agitate to withdraw from the shore line and turn to his left to face them across the river. Bennett refused. Despite all the mitigating circumstances, he was already furiously embarrassed by the performance of 22nd Brigade and would shortly be telling Taylor that he and his men were 'a disgrace to Australia and the AIF'. The last thing he wanted was Australian troops looking wobbly elsewhere. Furthermore, it was by no means certain that the Japanese landings on the north-west coast were their main thrust. It would make sense for them to seize the Causeway area held by 27th Brigade with its direct road route to the city. All he could bring himself to do was give Maxwell permission to detach two companies to face west and guard his left flank against any attempt to cross the river or come down its main eastern tributary, the Pangsua. Otherwise he was to stay put.

In the 1914–18 years Maxwell had never commanded more than a company in action. He had always felt indebted to Bennett, his military mentor, flattered by the faith he had shown in him and by no means certain he deserved to command a brigade. But over the last month, from the beginning of the Australian involvement in the land campaign on the Malayan Peninsula, the Gallipoli veteran had made it plain that the debt he felt towards the young men under his command was stronger than anything he owed Bennett. If Maxwell had anything to do with it there would be no useless sacrifice, no Lone Pines for this generation.

Once the Japanese had landed on the west coast the brigadier was haunted by fear that their next move would be to cross both the straits and the river at the same time and cut off and annihilate his two remaining battalions now that Pond's 2/29th had been taken away from him and sent to Taylor. So he decided to disobey Bennett and give himself a new set of orders. In the event of a landing, he would resist long enough to allow the engineers to destroy the 2 million gallons of commercial motor fuel at the Woodlands fuel depot just west of the Causeway. They had already done a reconnaissance. Then he would withdraw from the Causeway area altogether and place not just two companies but his entire brigade facing the river. They would no longer be deployed on a west–east axis but a north–south one with one battalion behind the other just east of the main Bukit Timah road. Once there he could either deny the enemy the road or (more likely) use it to escape south into the city with his command intact. Naturally, Maxwell made no attempt to warn Selby's Gurkha brigade on his right flank that they might suddenly find themselves with new neighbours. How could he? Even Bennett would have been unable to leave him in command.

That afternoon he briefed his two battalion commanders on his contingency plan and put Colonel Oakes in charge of the actual withdrawal. He later admitted this was an error of judgement, saying in his disarming fashion: 'I suppose I did it because I'm a doctor in civil life and did not know enough of soldiering.'

But Oakes was a grazier and no more qualified to disengage two infantry battalions from a night action than a medical practitioner. Maxwell himself would remain at his brigade HQ which was at least 5 miles away from its forward positions, a habit he had got into in his desire to stay close enough to Bennett's divisional headquarters for easy consultation, which was the way to stay on the right side of him. Oakes talked to Ramsay about the contingency plan and neither of them was very happy about it. Ramsay felt he was only caretaking for Black Jack and knew his colonel would hate to see the 2/30th move out of its present position without a very good reason.

They had A Company supported by anti-tank guns spread out around the end of the Causeway in the area known as Woodlands. Then, above them, on some higher ground known as Hill 95, was C Company with a platoon of four Vickers guns from the 2/4th Machine-Gun Battalion with really good fields of fire across the straits to Johore Bahru itself. Captain Duffy's B Company, the ambushers at Gemas, were alongside the road about 600 yards from the petrol tanks that Lieutenant Arthur Watchorn of the Royal Australian Engineers was set to destroy. D Company was in reserve. It was deployed with battalion HQ about a mile due south of the Causeway on the now defunct water pipe-line from the Johore reservoirs, which ran overground in a more or less straight line to the city. On their left was the entrance of a little river called the Mandai, which served as the battalion boundary. The 2 miles of shore line between the Mandai and the estuary of the Kranji were occupied by the three forward companies of Oakes' 2/26th.

In their smaller sector, Maxwell's brigade were much thicker on the ground than Taylor's men, even without one of their battalions, and Nishimura suspected that his Imperial Guards might suffer heavy casualties. The British had been forewarned by the previous night's landings. And he knew the narrow sector between the Causeway and the Kranji was likely to be a tougher nut to crack than the longer and more thinly manned positions where the 5th and 18th divisions went ashore. Yet he could hardly object. Yamashita had originally intended to keep the Guards in reserve and send them in for the *coup de grâce* once he had established a secure bridgehead. This had infuriated Nishimura. For all he knew, the British might surrender within hours of landing. Was the

Guards' role in this historic battle to be limited to the diversionary raid
on Ubin Island? The humiliation was unthinkable. Nishimura had
sulked until Yamashita relented. An assault on the Causeway sector
would, after all, take some of the pressure off the other two divisions
and, if they could get astride the main road to Singapore, it would be
easier to insert the tanks he intended to ferry across the straits.

The Guards' objective was so narrow that Nishimura decided the
first wave would consist of no more than one battalion. At about
8.30 p.m. the Japanese barrage lifted and within the next half hour the
boats carrying men of the 4th Guards Regiment started to come ashore
on the 2/26th Battalion's front. Initially, their main landing point was
a smashed wooden pier where shell-fire had partly cleared barbed wire
and various other obstacles. Shortly afterwards, landing barges appeared
at the mouth of the small river, the Mandai Kechil, close to the petrol
tanks about 400 yards west of the Causeway in the 2/30th's area. For
the first twenty minutes there were the same delays in summoning
artillery and heavy machine-gun support that Taylor's men had experienced. Once again, shell-severed cables meant that the field telephones
and searchlights were down. And it turned out that some of the Verey
gun cartridges were not only unseen but unfired, having become
swollen by the humidity and impossible to load. But even before the
artillery joined in, the Australians were giving the Japanese a hard time.
On the 2/26th's front, some of those who did get ashore found their
opponents in no mood to withdraw. In a patrol encounter at Kranji
village a corporal felled a man with his empty Thompson and they
were seen wrestling furiously with each other on the ground until an
Australian bayonet intervened. In the 2/30th sector, shouts and screams
from where the mud flats met the sheen of the water indicated that
their mortars and supporting Vickers were hurting.

Ramsay was more reluctant than ever to leave the 2/30th's position
but Maxwell was not around to see how well they were doing and
communications with brigade headquarters kept going down. Oakes
had his orders and he was conscious that he was not aware of the big
picture. There was no doubt that, for the moment at least, they were
holding. What was equally undeniable was that Taylor's brigade had
had a bad time and they could no longer be certain of their left flank.
Were the Japs crossing the Kranji and coming behind them?

At about midnight, communications with brigade HQ were restored
long enough for Maxwell to confirm that he should begin to withdraw

as soon as the fuel tanks had been destroyed. But there was a delay. A lucky Japanese shell had burnt out Lieutenant Watchorn's parked truck containing all his explosives. The lieutenant and some of his party had gone off in search of some more. Before they left, just in case they failed to find any or in case the storage tanks had been overrun by the time they got back, the sappers opened the valves and started the slow process of draining some of the 2 million gallons of high octane fuel they contained into the nearest stream.

When Watchorn and his men returned it was almost 4 a.m. and the Japanese had indeed gained a little ground. As they laid their charges, they sometimes imagined they could hear the enemy shouting to each other. Half an hour later they set them off. Watchorn got a Military Cross for what happened next. First came a blinding yellow flash. Then lava trails of blazing spirit spurted along the adjacent creeks and found fresh sustenance in the petrol that the opened valves had already deposited in them. By now the flames were unstoppable. On they blazed, into the Mandai Kechil where they followed its flow down towards the mangroved edge of the straits, feeding with supreme indifference on plywood-hulled assault boats and men alike. The British had at last succeeded in setting the sea on fire.

Caught up in this inferno was Corporal Tsuchikane Tominosuke, the youngest son of a small businessman from Kawagoe, an industrial town with a fifteenth-century castle some 20 miles outside Tokyo. Not all that long ago, he had been a clarinettist in a youth band playing conscripts off to the China war at the local railway station and yearning to go with them. Singapore was an even better cause, the removal of the arrogant Anglo-Saxon from his Asian bastion. On his wrist Tsuchikane wore a silver bracelet given to him by an Indian family he had befriended in Alor Star. The Greater East Asia Co-Prosperity Sphere was not an empty slogan. It was something worth dying for.

When he had killed his first man, one of Anderson's Australians, in a bayonet duel around Bakri, he felt he had somehow grown up, passed a test. But the confusion and terror he experienced during his battalion's landing just off the Causeway came as something of a shock. Tsuchikane had managed to leave his boat intact and was taking cover in a mangrove swamp when the narrow beach-head was lit up by Watchorn's explosion and came under machine-gun and mortar fire. After a while, he persuaded himself to leave this flimsy cover and go and search for his men. At first all he found were some strangers trying to give a dying boy the will to live. Writing about it years later, he felt sufficiently removed from the bewildered young man on the beach – he was twenty-two at the time – to write about himself in the third person.

Tsuchikane had stumbled into another company's position. Quickly he began to move back in the direction he'd come from. Another shell exploded near the soldiers he had just left.

'Mother! Mother!'

'Don't die! Don't die – you must not!'

'*Tenno heika banzai* – Long live the Emperor!' Tsuchikane pulled himself together, moving cautiously to find his unit. Close to him, fire lashed out over the mangrove and set it on fire. It spread quickly, feeding on oil poured into the straits . . .

'Mother! Mother!' The moaning voice could still be heard. It was a picture of hell – *Abiyokan* – Buddhism's worst of all hells. Stumbling along the edge of the beach, Tsuchikane's gun felt slippery in his hands. Fire in all directions threatened to engulf him. Where to go? It seemed impossible to advance or retreat! Then he stumbled across Corporal Nemeto. 'We'll burn to death just standing here – let's attack!' Corporal Nemeto yelled to Tsuchikane. Shouting out their battalion and platoon names, they advanced . . . One then two comrades joined them. Soon they were five black figures looking all alike, with only the whites of their eyes glinting in the darkness. They were all covered with the heavy black oil . . . 'Advance!' Nemeto shouted.

The first Nishimura heard of the burning water was an account from an officer of the engineers who was one of the boat handlers. He assured the general that the casualties were heavy, among them the commander of the Kobayashi regiment who had last been seen 'swimming in a sea of fire'. This tended to be backed up by several Guardsmen who swam back to the Johore shore, including three from Corporal Tsuchikane's company. Nishimura, already convinced that both he and his division had been slighted, was furious. He made no secret that he blamed Yamashita and his staff. 'Reckless forcing of a passage without adequate preparation causes unnecessary casualties.'

The 5th and 18th divisions had encountered nothing like this. Why had the toughest beach been reserved for his Guards? It was typical of the prejudice they had to endure from the rest of the army. They loved to see them fail. Accompanied by a staff officer, Nishimura charged into Yamashita's forward HQ in the Sultan of Johore's palace only to discover that the army commander had already crossed the straits for the island several hours before.

As it turned out, this was as well for Nishimura, who would surely not have survived the climb-down he would shortly have had to make had he become involved in a face-to-face shouting match with Yamashita. Instead, Nishimura dispatched an aide-de-camp with a message to say that, if the casualties were as bad as he feared, he intended to call off his landings and put his division through the beach-head already secured by 5th Division. This unfortunate aide caught up with Yamashita, who was accompanied by Tsuji, at the forward HQ he had established on the northern boundary of Tengah airfield.

The army commander was breakfasting on dry bread, no doubt much to the approval of Tsuji who, with his feet planted firmly on the soil of Singapore, was in ebullient mood and not about to let some whinging popinjay of a Guards officer spoil it for him. According to his own account, Yamashita let Tsuji ask most of the questions. It was soon established that General Nishimura had not as yet made any independent assessment of the situation by sending a staff officer. He was acting on the reports of a few panic-stricken men who had fled the flames in the hours of darkness. Yamashita was disgusted and told Nishimura's aide that, as far as he was concerned, the Guards Division could 'do as it pleases in this battle'. For good measure, Tsuji added that the 5th and 18th divisions could take Singapore on their own. The chastened man then crept away to bear these tidings to his commanding officer. A few hours later, Yamashita received a report from Nishimura's HQ saying that their initial information had been mistaken. It turned out that their losses were not significant after all and they were advancing.

Maxwell had, of course, missed a golden opportunity to inflict something like the kind of casualties Nishimura believed he was taking. If he had been there to be inspired by the fight his two battalions were putting up, rescinded his illicit orders to withdraw and properly exploited the tremendous luck provided by the web of waterborne flame Watchorn had accidentally contrived, it might have been a different story. But Maxwell was not there and Oakes followed his orders and began to pull out. Nor was disengagement always done cleanly. How could it be otherwise as the dawn revealed just how close some of their positions were?

The Imperial Guard, having passed through the torments of *Abiyokan*, had their blood up and were looking for revenge. First Corporal Tsuchikane was involved in a grenade duel with the Australian rearguard. In his excitement the baseball-pitching skills he had acquired at senior high school almost undid him, because he threw his first one much too long and was nearly killed by the pineapple variety that came back and rolled within 2 metres of the rubber tree he had dived behind. The second one he got right. Then they all charged with fixed bayonets. Some of the Australians, now badly outnumbered, started running. Tsuchikane chased one down, pushed him to the ground and heard a 'deathly yell' as he impaled him with his bayonet and then withdrew the blade. The corporal noticed that others were neither running nor fighting.

Having lost their nerve, some soldiers were simply cowering in terror, squatting down and avoiding the hand-to-hand combat in a wait and see position. They, too, were bayoneted or shot without mercy.

At about the time the Imperial Guard were beginning to comprehend that they had won the day, Wavell began what would turn out to be his last visit to the island for some time. He arrived from his Java HQ in a Dutch Catalina flying boat. In order to minimize their chances of being intercepted by Japanese fighters, the pilot had hoped to land at or just before dawn. But the sun was well up by the time they touched down in a great shower of spray in Keppel harbour and chugged over to the old Imperial Airways mooring near the slipway which led to Kallang, the 'Empire's Greatest Airport', where the fresh strawberries from Australia used to be landed. Now, most of the glass had been blown out of its art deco buildings and there were sandbags at the entrances and scorch marks on the walls. Its 700 yards of bomb-acned runway was a nightmare for those who still had to use it.

Wavell was accompanied by three aides-de-camp, one of them a Dutch aristocrat. But for once his youngest ADC, the Western Desert veteran and fellow mono-optic Captain Sandy Reid Scott, was absent, being in New Delhi with Lady Wavell. This would have unforeseen consequences. As so often happened during the supreme commander's peregrinations around his vast territory – he had just been in Burma where the Japanese were beginning to threaten Rangoon – the signal announcing his visit had apparently not yet landed on the right desk so there was nobody to meet him. Kallang airfield was just coming to life and his aides went off in search of somebody who could provide transport.

Wavell's arrival had coincided with the final evacuation from Singapore of the RAF. Their remaining Hurricanes, easier to spot in the island's confined airspace than they were over Malaya, had thrilled troops too long accustomed to regarding all aircraft as hostile by diving through Japanese formations with their throttles wide open and chasing them low across the straits. This was the kind of Battle of Britain flying the Australians in particular, who had only ever seen it on cinema newsreels, were longing to watch. The day before, the fighters had been on operations from dawn to dusk. They had claimed at least eight enemy aircraft destroyed for the loss of three of their own, with casualties of one pilot killed and one plucked from the sea and hospitalized. The third had been unhurt after a forced landing.

But that was their last day. Singapore's Few were getting fewer and there were no replacements. Kallang was now being bombed so regularly it had become as untenable as the island's abandoned north coast airfields. It was increasingly difficult for the ground crews, few of them Hurricane trained, to maintain aircraft scattered about the field in any cover they could find. And the air-raid warnings which saw them dropping their spanners and competing for the nearest slit trench were shorter as well as more frequent. Ground security was also becoming a problem and there had been recent proof that the fifth column was not always a figment of the imagination. One coughing Hurricane, its pilot lucky to land in one piece, was discovered to have been trying to fly on a choking mix of aviation fuel and the latex rubber used to poison its tanks.

Shortly after the Catalina had moored and disembarked its passengers, eight Hurricanes departed for the two airfields near Palembang in southern Sumatra placed at Wavell's disposal by the Dutch. Three more Hurricanes would follow, together with an abandoned Buffalo considered, at least for the adventurously inclined, to be more or less airworthy.* The Blenheim, Hudson and what was left of the

---

* The Buffalo reached Sumatra, but two out of these eleven Hurricanes crashed because of mechanical failure: the engine of one overheated and its sergeant pilot baled out; the other had fuel-feeding problems and made a forced landing on a small Dutch island about 100 miles south of Singapore. Since it was unlikely to have been recovered – at least by the British – it was never established whether this machine had also received the latex rubber treatment.

Vildebeest squadrons were already operating from the Sumatra air strips from where they were continuing to try and curb Japanese air power with night raids against the same northern Malayan airfields on which the entire defence of the colony had once hinged. Together with forty or so more Hurricanes that had flown into Sumatra off the British carrier HMS *Indomitable* on 25 January, these squadrons were all part of the build-up of Wavell's next line of defence, for which every day that Singapore held out and tied up Yamashita's troops bought him extra time to prepare.

The supreme commander and his aides eventually stopped an army truck which happened to be passing and ordered the driver to take them to Percival's Sime Road HQ south of the Bukit Timah golf course. It was a humid, overcast day and bursts of anti-aircraft fire indicated that the Japanese air force was already in the air. As they moved off, the RAF was about to mount its last offensive operation from Kallang. It was probably as well that Wavell was unaware of this last sortie for, although the courage it required was undeniable, so was its desperation. Flight Lieutenant Harry Dane, the amateur pilot who had located Challen's missing brigade in Johore, and another weekend flier of the Malayan Volunteer Air Force were about to take off in their Tiger Moths and each drop eight 20-pound fragmentation bombs on the invaders from the racks fitted to the biplanes' lower wings, released by a lever in the cockpit. Perhaps the Japanese were too astonished to take effective action, for both pilots and machines survived to follow the rest of the RAF to Sumatra the following day.

One of Wavell's aides had called Percival from Kallang to warn him of their impending arrival at the Sime Road headquarters where Percival had spent the night on a camp bed in his office, snatching what sleep he could. They found him 'composed, very tired, and presenting a controlled stoicism'. But there can be no doubt that never in his worst nightmares had he expected Singapore's defences to unravel so quickly. All hopes that the Australians might display some of their famous resilience and bounce back were evaporating and he had told Sir Shenton Thomas as much the previous evening. 'Things look grim. Percival tells me the Australians are very half-hearted. Still, we hope for the best,' wrote the governor in a note dated 9 February to a colleague at the Colonial Office in London, to whom he was sending for safekeeping the Singapore War Council files as well as the latest pages of his personal diary.

If things sounded grim to the governor they must have looked even worse to Wavell as he took in the sights on his way up to Bennett's new headquarters which, since the debacle on the beaches, had moved south-east of Bukit Timah village and closer to the city. There was still a steady stream of Australians, often unarmed and blackened with oil soot, making their resolute way into Singapore. Some of them were shouting that the fighting was over. Percival thought many of them looked more like coal miners coming off shift than fighting soldiers. 'It is difficult to keep one's self-respect in these conditions, especially when things are not going too well.'

Their arrival at Bennett's headquarters was greeted by a Japanese air raid which almost killed all three generals, something Yamashita might have regarded as a mixed blessing. Percival's car was wrecked and in it his favourite field glasses. It turned out that the nearest bomb to the room they were in was a dud, but the rest were close enough to have them scrambling for cover under tables and chairs. Bennett took the bombing calmly enough but otherwise he did not radiate his normal confidence.

'He had always been very certain that his Australians would never let the Japanese through and the penetration of his defences had upset him,' Percival would write with cruel understatement. Perhaps, at this point, the General Officer Commanding British troops in Singapore might be forgiven a little *Schadenfreude*. For almost a year he had been accommodating this arrogant egomaniac with the hair-trigger temper who was commanding what should have been one of his best assets. Despite the growing dissatisfaction and whisperings among Bennett's Australian staff, not only had the press overrated him – even the normally perceptive Morrison sang his praises – but so had Wavell who, after the disaster at Slim River, had given him command of northern Johore.

Disillusionment had soon set in after Bennett's faulty dispositions at Muar when he had deployed 45 Indian Brigade on both sides of the river. The obvious disintegration of Taylor's battalions had completed the process and Bennett knew it. Now, in front of their impassive supreme commander, it fell to Percival to break the news to him that the latest reports from 11th Indian Division indicated that Maxwell had ignored his orders and had withdrawn. The Australian brigades had opened the floodgates. Only the day before, Bennett had assured Percival that the 27th would be staying put but, as usual, his head-quarters was too far back to monitor what was going on. The way was open for Yamashita to start his advance on Bukit Timah, which was full of stores and munitions, and after that the city itself.

It would have been out of character if at this point the full horror of his personal situation had not dawned on Bennett. Unless these holes were plugged it would not be Brooke-Popham who would be remembered for losing Malaya and Singapore because he lacked the nerve to make the pre-emptive strikes which would have secured the Thai beach-heads and sunk much of the invasion fleet from the air. Nor Admiral Phillips for the dent he left in morale by losing his much-hyped battleships, and with them any hope of approaching naval parity, without managing to sink a single Japanese ship. Nor would blame be pinned on the lack of preparation of Murray-Lyon's division at Jitra and Gurun, where his teenaged sepoys had broken, or the dismal performance, in the main, of the few UK British anti-tank guns at the Slim River disaster and the way the Australians had demonstrated what could have been done at Bakri. Nor on whoever was responsible for not sending enough aircraft to do the job and the absence of any British tanks whatsoever. Nor Heath for his demoralizing succession of premature withdrawals. Nor Percival for all his Pommy diffidence and inability to inspire as a leader and the way he had failed to build decent defences on the island's northern shore. No, it would be none of these. It would be Gordon Bennett, commander of the 8th Australian Division, whose men had run away on Singapore.

His visitors' next stop was General Heath and they left Bennett to get on with organizing the defence of the Kranji–Jurong switch line where the remnants of Taylor's brigade had fallen back. To reinforce Taylor and Ballantine's Punjabis, who with the collapse of the Australians would also have to pull back to the switch line from their unchallenged coastal positions or be cut off, Percival had already sent his only available reserves: Paris's weak 12th Indian Brigade, whose Plymouth Argylls and Hyderabads hardly amounted to 800 men between them (the equivalent of one full-strength battalion whereas most brigades have three), and the equally gaunt 6/15th Brigade, whose stars were the British Battalion supported by various Indian amalgamations. One of these, the Jat Battalion, was commanded by Lieutenant-Colonel Arthur Cumming VC, the hero of Kuantan airfield, who had talked his way out of hospital even though he was still in bandages.

Percival had also given Bennett a fall-back plan marked 'Secret and Personal' – copies had also gone to Heath and Keith Simmons who was in charge of the city's seaward defences – showing the last-ditch perimeter he intended to hold around Singapore city, which would include the reservoirs and Kallang airfield. But this was intended as a last resort and things had begun so badly for them since Yamashita landed on the island it seemed impossible that their luck would not change.

At noon Wavell and Percival reached the north coast headquarters of Billy Key's 11th Division where they discovered Gurkhas and Garhwalis trying to fill the gaping cavity to their west caused by Maxwell extracting his battalions. Eight 'wet and naked' Japanese were discovered hiding in a trench by a section of Gurkhas led by a British officer and all killed. They may have been survivors from one of the landing-craft caught up in Watchorn's fire who had eventually managed to struggle ashore. None of Key's staff could work out why the Australians had left. All they knew was that the Japanese had not been slow in exploiting it and there were fears they had already occupied the Hill 95 feature overlooking the straits from where the Australian machine-gunners had enjoyed such a good field of fire. A counter-attack was being organized with a preliminary bombardment from Toosey's Yeomanry gunners who had been borrowed from the 18th Division. Key told Toosey to forget about ammunition rationing. Watching the barrage from the naval base about 3½ miles away was Terence Hewitt, the former Darjeeling planter and liaison officer with Selby's 28th Gurkha Brigade who had established their headquarters there. 'All his [Toosey's] guns, twenty-six of them, fired 900 rounds for a period of ten minutes. We could see the hilltop about 3½ miles from us and it was covered in smoke.'

The hill was recaptured but two of Selby's junior British officers were killed. One was the captain who had discovered the naked Japanese in the trench, the other a lieutenant called Coombes, who died on his twenty-first birthday. Inevitably, there were bitter feelings about the absent Australians. Hewitt recalled that Ray Selby was 'angry and upset'. To make matters worse, it was decided that the little hill was now too vulnerable to Japanese mortar fire and the Gurkhas withdrew, though throughout the day Toosey kept up regular harassing fire to discourage its reoccupation. Meanwhile the Garhwalis, the Gurkhas' Himalayan neighbours and old enemies, were trying to ferret the Japanese out of some nearby rubber estates. As usual, the Japanese snipers concentrated on their British officers and they lost even more than the Gurkhas. Among the six to be killed was their commanding officer, Lieutenant-Colonel Smith. Sometimes there were no UK British to pick off. Subadar Gul Din Khan was nearby, commanding a company of Pathans of the 1st Frontier Force Rifles, otherwise known as the Cookies because they were once Coke's Rifles. With four others, Khan charged a machine-gun nest and was the last to die, falling almost on top of it. By this time the rest of his men had worked their way behind the Japanese and were ready to pounce.

Wavell congratulated the gunners on their performance and they felt rather pleased with themselves. Even so, at Toosey's HQ, Lieutenant Alexander, the doctor's son who had noticed how 'scrawny and pallid' his gunners were on the ship out, thought they might have been less critical of the Australians had they been in closer contact with the enemy. This was not a view likely to be shared by the supreme commander and Percival. Having stopped *en route* to inspect the heavy guns at Changi, where they were mortared by the Imperial Guard on Ubin Island, they had returned by mid-afternoon to Bennett's HQ where more bad news awaited them. While they were away the Kranji–Jurong line had been lost.

It had started with an almost parade-ground obsession with line straightening. A modest Japanese advance eastwards along the Jurong and Tengah roads had caused one formation after another to notice that their neighbours had moved a little behind them and, sometimes without a shot being fired, they had responded by dressing back so that their flanks were not exposed. The Argylls' Colonel Stewart thought the green Australian 2/29th were behaving 'with great coolness'* under a wounded Pond, who refused to leave the field though he did, for a while, allow Stewart to take both battalions under his wing. They went back a quarter of a mile so that they could enjoy the fire support of the Argylls' armoured cars. But Stewart generally knew what he was doing. Other battalions were not so well handled and repeatedly shuffled a little too far back and then the whole process had to be repeated. It seems that this had a lot to do with Bennett foolishly disclosing to Taylor Percival's secret contingency plan for a last-ditch perimeter around the city which, in his exhausted state, had the brigadier looking over his

---

* 'If the 93rd had to choose a unit with whom they would like to go into battle, they would not look beyond the 2/29th Australians,' wrote Stewart in his account of the Argylls' part in the campaign.

shoulder at these fresh deployments instead of concentrating on holding the switch line. There was only one instance of utter panic when Ballantine's three battalions of Punjabi boy soldiers ended up 4 miles from where they should have been and might have gone further had most of them not found themselves standing on a beach. Only then were their officers able to calm them down and lead them back.

Percival, with Wavell standing alongside him, asked Bennett when he intended to counter-attack and was told within a few hours. Units would move into position during the hours of darkness and then attack along a broad front at first light, pushing the Japs westwards back towards Tengah airfield and the coast. Taylor's brigade, though still a shadow of its former self, had been slightly strengthened by a unit Bennett referred to as X Battalion. This was not a battalion at all but turned out to be about 200 strong and was made up mostly of stragglers from the 2/19th and 2/20th battalions whose headquarters had more or less dissolved leaving no battalion structure to return men to. It was commanded by Colonel Boyes, sacked from his last battalion command by Maxwell only the day before, and included some highly respected officers from both battalions. Another makeshift unit under Taylor's command was Merrett Force, named after Major Robert Merrett of the 2/20th, a millinery manufacturer in his late thirties who, in all the terror and confusion that followed Yamashita's initial landings, had discovered he could persuade men to stay with him and fight. (Whether he enjoyed the same success as a hatter is unrecorded.)

Shortly after Wavell had left Bennett, the supreme commander had yet another glimpse of the other side of Australian morale when he visited General Simmons at his HQ near Keppel harbour. While he was there Simmons received a call from a naval officer wishing to sink some Australians, evidently deserters, who had just hijacked a launch. Permission was reluctantly refused.

Prior to his early morning return flight to Java, Wavell joined Percival for dinner at Flagstaff House, the quarters he shared with Air Vice-Marshal Pulford. Before the meal began a telegram arrived from Winston Churchill. The words were meant to provoke and inspire. But they were founded on a nagging suspicion, which had started for Churchill in the spring of 1940 during the Norwegian campaign, had been reinforced a year later by the fall of Crete and was now confirmed by what was happening in Singapore. 'Our soldiers are not as good fighters as their fathers were,' he would shortly be telling his old friend

Violet Bonham Carter. 'We have so many men in Singapore, so many men – they should have done better.'

The prime minister was resigned to the temporary loss of the island. It was the manner of its passing that worried him. He wanted his famous siege. What he dreaded was the kind of operatic, premature and shameful surrender that Wavell had imposed on the 130,000 Italians captured in Libya almost exactly a year ago. Fear of loss of face is not an entirely Asian phenomenon. 'I feel sure these words express your own feelings,' Churchill added in an obvious attempt to sweeten the pill; but without doubt this was the harshest message he ever sent to any of his generals.

There must at this stage be no thought of saving the troops or sparing the population. The battle must be fought to the bitter end at all costs. The 18th Division has its chance to make its name in history. Commanders and senior officers should die with their troops. The honour of the British Empire and of the British Army is at stake. I rely on you to show no weakness or mercy in any form. With the Russians fighting as they are and the Americans so stubborn at Luzon the whole reputation of our country and our race is involved.

There were few precedents for what Churchill was demanding. The last senior British officer to die with his troops was General Gordon, killed in 1885 by the Mahdi's mediaeval army at Khartoum after a ten-month siege. Hong Kong, the most recently lost colony, held out for eighteen days and hardly fought to the last man. Like Percival, Lord Cornwallis's forces had outnumbered those of his besiegers but, in October 1781, he surrendered to Washington at Yorktown, thus ending the American War of Independence though not his career, which flourished for another quarter of a century. Even Singapore had its Cornwallis Road. Over the last hundred years, British soldiers campaigning in Afghanistan, Zululand and the Sudan had all, from time to time, fought to the death, but this was usually because their opponents did not take prisoners under any circumstances. In South Africa they had frequently surrendered to the Boers, among them the war correspondent and half-pay Hussars lieutenant Winston Churchill.

It is unlikely that Percival thought for one moment that Churchill expected him to go down throwing his emptied revolver at a roaring banzai charge. But both Wavell and he seem to have seized on his message as their cue to admonish the fainthearts. For distribution to all divisional and brigade commanders Wavell, rather proud of his own literary ability, gave the prime minister's words a light rewrite and for good measure inserted:

The Chinese, with an almost complete lack of modern equipment, have held the greater part of their country against the full strength of the Japanese . . . It will be disgraceful if we yield our boasted Fortress of Singapore to inferior enemy forces . . . I look to you and to your men to fight to the end and to prove that the fighting spirit that won our Empire still exists to enable us to defend it.

Percival, not to be outdone, then added a covering note of his own complaining that the behaviour of some troops – he did not specify their nationality – had not been what it should have been.

It will be a lasting disgrace if we are defeated by an army of clever gangsters many times inferior in numbers . . . The spirit of aggression and determination to stick it out must be inculcated in all ranks. There must be no further withdrawals without orders. There are too many fighting men in the back areas. Every available man who is not doing essential work must be used to stop the invader.

But it was much too late for exhortations of this kind. Yamashita and his 'clever gangsters' were determined to keep up the momentum of their attack and they had the wherewithal to do it. By about 9 p.m. all the formations taking part in Bennett's dawn counter-attack the following day had settled for the night into what were supposed to be their start lines. At his HQ in a Public Works Department compound near the quarries worked by the village of Bukit Panjang, Brigadier Archie Paris was sitting down to dinner, no doubt with a bottle of something interesting on the table, for Paris prided himself on living well in the field. The commander of 12th Brigade was not very confident about the prospects of tomorrow's attack because, like his good friend Stewart of the Argylls, he thought it very likely that the Japs would attack first. Even so, he was by no means prepared for what happened next.

He had not finished his meal when one of the two-man tracked reconnaissance vehicles the Japanese called tankettes rolled up at his gates. Nobody had expected the enemy to get armour onto the island quite so quickly. There was even a school of thought that the Japanese did not have tank landing-craft in the straits and would need to repair the Causeway first. Paris's sentries had at first mistaken it for a Bren gun carrier. Then the crew of a parked Argylls' armoured car, who happened to be in their vehicle, recognized it for what it was and opened fire. Soon, led by the brigadier with his revolver, everybody else was shooting at it. Whether lost or simply curious, the tankette's crew soon got the message and disappeared into the night. The brigadier had little doubt that they would be back.

Yamashita had towed his armour across the straits on rafts made up of three pontoons joined together and capable of supporting up to 16 tons' worth of heavy vehicles or armour, perhaps slightly more. Most of them had been landed in the area abandoned by Maxwell's brigade east of the Kranji, from where they could easily get onto the main road south. Behind the tankette were at least thirty T95 medium tanks. Three miles down the road, in the Bukit Timah area, there were supposed to be some Australian anti-tank guns. Paris dispatched his brigade major, Angus MacDonald, an Argyll from a wealthy Highland family, to try and locate them and set up a block. As MacDonald headed south in the baby Fiat he had recently acquired from the growing stock of vehicles dumped by civilian evacuees, Paris rushed over to the Argylls' HQ to break the news to Stewart that it looked as if his rebuilt battalion was about to face the kind of 'night filleting attack' with tanks that had ruined them at Slim River. They must buy time for MacDonald to set up something to stop them.

There was no time to start sawing down trees or preparing anything like proper defences. The battalion had been facing west. The north was supposed to be friendly territory. All that was available for road-blocks were a few abandoned vehicles and the battalion's own motor transport, which was parked across the road. Two blocks were set up, one after the other, each covered by an anti-tank rifle which would penetrate the sides but not the fronts of the T95 medium tanks. No Molotov cocktails were available, but they did have twelve anti-tank mines. In charge of them was Captain David Wilson, who had to oversee the delicate business of unpacking, assembling and arming them in the dark: six to each block and mostly placed on the verges where it was hoped they might blow an outside track. The mines had only just been put down and an Argylls' armoured car, which had been mounting watch ahead, was being guided back through them, when the dim outline of a T95 became visible as it approached the first block and the shooting started.

It took the Japanese twenty minutes at most to smash through the Argylls' obstacles, after which the latter retired about 100 yards into the rubber to the east of the road, but not in the kind of disorder that had occurred at Slim River, certainly not 'filleted'. At least one tank exploded one of Wilson's mines. The armoured car the battalion called 'Stirling Castle', which like all their Lanchesters carried an anti-tank rifle as well as machine-guns, held them up for a while until it was wrecked. By some miracle its crew survived and limped off into the night. The lieutenant in charge of the first block was killed as the tanks pushed their way through. On the second, the Boys anti-tank rifle was manned by two officers – Captain Mike Blackwood and Jim Davis, one of the Royal Marine lieutenants. They lay on their bellies where the road rose slightly to accommodate the circular entrance of a flood culvert, so they were shooting slightly upwards and were difficult to see. 'The night was as black as the Earl of Hell's waistcoat,' recalled Angus Rose, who was nearby. The pair were not much more than 20 yards away from the lead T95, which was trying to open the block by nudging one of the heavier trucks aside. The Boys, with its bruising recoil, appears to have pierced this tank. Some of its three-man crew may well have been hurt. They seemed reluctant to advance and tried to keep their unseen tormentors at bay by spraying machine-gun tracer in all directions. This would sometimes be mingled with an occasional round of high explosive from their small cannon. Then Blackwood and his companion, who knew it would not be long before the Japanese infantry sought them out, crawled away and the tanks nosed cautiously around the last block and moved on.

It was too late. The Argylls had won. They had bought enough time for MacDonald to get the 3 miles down the road and, somewhere on the southern outskirts of Bukit Timah village, not far from the Ford factory, find not only some unflappable Australian anti-tank gunners but also a British howitzer battery, which prepared to fire over open sights. The first tanks appeared as MacDonald was donating his baby Fiat to the road-block. There was an exchange of fire and the defenders claimed to have knocked out the first two tanks. Behind them the rest of the Japanese armour halted, line ahead on the road, and remained there with the reasonable expectation that, whatever else the dawn

would bring, it would not be RAF air strikes. It was 10 February and
the eve of *Kigensetsu*, the anniversary of the foundation of the Japanese
Empire 2,602 years ago, and they were a little over 6 miles from Raffles
Place. But this was not to be the night that Yamashita entered the city
of Singapore.

On the morning of the Sacred Day, shortly before nine, Japanese aircraft flying below the island's sooty cloud layer began to drop over British lines something the latter had not seen before. These were twenty-one blunt-ended tubes about 18 inches long with festive strips of coloured ribbons rather than tail fins at one end. Some must have disappeared into various densities of greenery where their remains may linger yet. Others hit more accessible places and it was noted that they failed to explode but lay apparently dormant, their gay ribbons inviting investigation. Once curiosity had overcome fear, and the braver or more foolhardy had picked them up, they were discovered to be hollow, made of wood and with an end that was easily removed to reveal the paper furled inside.

The twenty-one copies of Yamashita's *Kigensetsu* invitation to Percival, in English, to surrender were not addressed to him by name but to the 'British High Command'. The message was sweetened with the kind of flattery the British had themselves used to persuade numerically superior Italian forces to give up in Africa and its style would have been familiar to General Heath. Above all, it stressed the futility of continuing a resistance among thousands of non-combatants which 'would not add anything to the honour of your army'.

Your Excellency, I, the High Command of the Nippon Army based on the spirit of Japanese chivalry, have the honour of presenting this note to Your Excellency advising you to surrender the whole force in Malaya. My sincere respect is due to your army which, true to the traditional spirit of Great Britain, is bravely defending Singapore which now stands isolated and unaided. Many fierce fights have been fought by your gallant men and officers to the honour of British warriorship. But the development of the general war situation has already sealed the fate of Singapore ... I expect that Your Excellency accepting my advice will give up this meaningless and desperate resistance and promptly order the entire front to cease hostilities and will dispatch at the same time your Parliamentaire according to the procedure shown at the end of this note. If on the contrary Your Excellency should neglect my advice and the present resistance be continued, I shall be obliged, though reluctantly from humanitarian considerations, to order my army to make annihilating attacks on Singapore. In closing this note of advice, I pay again my sincere respects to Your Excellency. (signed) Tomoyuki Yamashita

1. The Parliamentaire should proceed to the Bukit Timah road.
2. The Parliamentaire should bear a large white flag and the Union Jack.


Yamashita was not yet in a position to make 'annihilating attacks' on Singapore but he was getting close to it. The tank attack north-to-south down the Bukit Timah road, which had been brought to a halt almost at the final approaches to the city, had more or less coincided with a Japanese push from the west. Starting in the early hours of the morning, most of the forces Bennett had mustered for the counter-attack intended to recapture the Kranji–Jurong line had been rolled up.

The only exception was Cumming VC and his newly formed battalion of Jats. During the fighting in the early hours of the morning, Cumming had lost touch with the best part of two of his companies, which had been overrun along with the battalions either side of them. Come the dawn, unaware that his flanks had caved in and faithful to his orders, Cumming had led his remaining 250 men, including 10 British officers, as far west as the hill covered in thick bracken and patches of rubber that was their second objective and occupied it against scant opposition. He had been able to do this because, quite by chance, the Jats had passed between the two main thrusts of Yamashita's advance eastwards astride the lateral Choa Chu Kang and Jurong roads. Hidden on their hillside, the Jats listened to the disturbing sounds of heavy firing behind them. Cumming sent out patrols which soon confirmed his worst fears. They were cut off and the units which should have been either side of them were in some disarray.

Among the worst hit had been Boyes' hotchpotch X Battalion which had literally been caught napping, its exhausted collection of stragglers asleep at its forming-up point for their attack on a small hill a little south of the Jurong road. Sentries, either surprised or asleep, had not given the alarm, and some of the Australians had been bayoneted on the ground in their blankets. Boyes and most of his senior officers had been killed trying to rally their outnumbered men in a confused close-quarters encounter fought partly in the dancing light of a petrol dump ignited by Japanese grenades. The two other forward Australian formations, Merrett Force and the Special Reserve Battalion with its mixture of machine-gun battalion reinforcements and drivers and clerks, were also badly mauled. First they were hit on their start lines and, as the dawn broke, the Japanese kept up the pressure, rarely allowing them to disengage. On one occasion, some of the Australians and a company of Leicesters and the Surreys from 6/15th Brigade's British Battalion joined together to buy time with a counter-attack that developed into a bayonet charge in places. But, by about the time Yamashita's peace proposals were dropping to earth, the withdrawal of the Australians, the British Battalion and some of Ballantine's Punjabis was turning into the next best thing to a rout.

As they made their way across a saucer-shaped depression *en route* for the city's Reformatory Road, where Brigadier Taylor had already set up his HQ in premature compliance with Percival's worst-case scenario, they were ambushed from a huddle of huts that straddled their line of retreat. About 400 of the British Battalion, with their backbone of regular NCOs, stuck together and reached Reformatory Road. Some of the young Indian soldiers, the same recruits who had bolted the day before, would not be led. A subadar who charged a machine-gun team died alone.

Yet for a few the fighting was once again a savage, close-quarters affair in which both sides made full use of their long bayonets. With the enemy all around him, Lieutenant Victor Mentiplay of the Special Reserve Battalion had managed to find cover in some bushes when he heard screams and saw one of the Australian wounded being bayoneted. According to Major Saggers, his battalion commander, Mentiplay then went berserk.

He charged the Jap with his bayonet. The Jap, who was on slightly higher ground, met the attack, and Vic's rush carried him onto the point of the Jap's bayonet, which entered his throat under the chin and came out the back of his neck. The bayonet missed his jugular vein by a fraction of an inch . . . he threw himself backwards off the bayonet and fell on the flat of his back. Pulling his revolver from his waistband he shot the Jap and then, seeing red, rushed at the other Japs in the vicinity . . .

Mentiplay emptied his revolver then threw it at a machine-gun crew who must have assumed it was a grenade and stayed down long enough for him to get away. Bleeding profusely from his neck wound, he staggered into a village duck pond and, half-submerged, hid under the foliage of an overhanging branch until the Japanese had moved on. In a nearby hut he discovered a grievously wounded British officer and a companion, less seriously hurt, who might have been his batman. The officer wanted Mentiplay to shoot him but he refused and eventually made his way back to the Reformatory Road line from where he was removed to hospital. Major Saggers' description of Mentiplay's action sounds very much like a citation for a medal, though there is no record of the lieutenant getting any kind of reward other than medical attention and clean sheets to lie between.

But for every Australian to enter Singapore in the back of an ambulance there were scores more wandering its streets, looking for somewhere safe to sleep where they would not be discovered and immediately sent back to the front line. Next on their wish list were food, alcohol and then (occasionally) sex, though not necessarily in that order. A small but increasing number had decided to desert and were either trying to board the ships leaving Keppel harbour with the last of the civilian evacuees or, failing that, to find a small craft in which they could get to the Dutch territories of Sumatra or Java. A few were almost certainly the recently arrived reinforcements who, in some cases, had only been in the army a matter of weeks and expected Fortress Singapore to be a training camp not a battlefield. (Bennett probably had a legitimate grievance when he complained that the Australian reinforcement depots in Mandate Palestine were bursting with trained men who should have come to him.)

Some of these young recruits had decided that volunteering for the AIF was a big mistake and were trying to go home within hours of the first reports of the Japanese landings. The journalist Ian Morrison, who followed his wife to Java on a Dutch ship which left Keppel harbour at dusk on the 11th, noted that 'three Australian soldiers who had come aboard the previous night' went ashore in the launch that took the pilot off. This appeared in a wartime book published in London nine months later, when any mention of deserters would have been censored. Morrison's own point of departure came when he discovered that Bennett had told the official Australian war correspondent to get out.

An AIF stragglers' post was established at the Botanical Gardens leading to the inevitable Pommy gibes that this was the nearest most Australians ever got to jungle warfare. Criticism also came from a surprising quarter. 'I don't think the men want to fight,' General

Bennett informed an exhausted Captain Frank Gaven of the 2/20th, who had been one of the stalwarts of Merrett Force, when they met at the Gardens.

Gaven did not mince words. 'The men are very tired,' he told Bennett. 'Their rations have been irregular and inadequate, they have been constantly in contact with the enemy and they feel they have been badly let down. I feel that too.'

'Well, you go and have a good rest and rejoin your brigade,' said Bennett when he had heard him out. Gaven was not telling him anything new. Crowds of fed-up Australians were all over town. Not long after dawn Major Moses Ashkanasy, a lawyer who was Bennett's deputy assistant adjutant-general, had almost got himself shot when he pulled up alongside a group sipping mugs of hot cocoa at a Salvation Army mobile canteen and accused them of being deserters. It turned out that they were some of the survivors from X Battalion, most of them lightly wounded, and in no mood to take any lip from red-faced majors back at base. Safety catches were slipped and it was only the intervention of the captain who had led them to safety – a grazier called Richardson from the 2/20th who had been one of Boyes' company commanders – that cooled things down. 'We're all wounded,' Richardson shouted. 'Get back to headquarters and tell them that X Battalion has been wiped out.' Captains do not usually tell majors what to do but Ashkanasy beat a hasty retreat to his car, promising to arrange transport for them.

By this time it was common knowledge among senior officers on Singapore that the Australians had broken, though for decades after it was rarely mentioned in print and some contemporary reports were not released by the Public Record Office in London until the 1990s. Even the imperturbable Wavell had allowed his mask to slip when he called to say goodbye to Shenton and Daisy Thomas. 'He sat in our sitting room, thumping his knees with his fists and saying, "It shouldn't have happened" over and over again,' recalled the governor who had decided to send out with the supreme commander all but one of his code books. Lady Thomas had turned down the chance to leave with the cyphers, preferring to remain with her husband. In any case, she was starting to feel unwell and it would turn out that not even the governor's wife was immune to the dysentery that was beginning to break out in Singapore.

Perhaps Wavell's agitation contributed, a couple of hours later, to him stepping out of his car parked at the edge of the Catalina landing stage on his blind left side – something unlikely to have happened if his young ADC Reid Scott, also missing his left eye, had been with him. The supreme commander plummeted 6 feet onto the rocks and barbed wire below, broke two small bones in his back and lay there calling for help. In considerable pain, he spent some time bobbing about in a launch while the Catalina's Dutch crew struggled to dismantle a machine-gun mounting across the door before he could be carried on board, where a large neat whisky and aspirin put him to sleep.

From his hospital bed in Java, Wavell dictated a signal to Churchill which made it plain to anyone familiar with the deployment of the Singapore garrison that all was not well with the Australians: 'Japanese with usual infiltration tactics getting on much more rapidly than they should in west of island . . . Morale of some troops is not good and with none is it as high as I should like to see . . . Everything possible is being done to produce more offensive spirit and optimistic outlook.'

But obviously not enough. 'Singapore will probably be captured by tonight or tomorrow,' Rear-Admiral Jack Spooner, the commander of the naval base, was writing in his admiral's green ink within forty-eight hours of the first landings. 'The present state of affairs was started by the AIF who just turned tail, became a rabble and let the Japs walk in unopposed.'

The admiral's comments came in a note to the same Captain Cazalet who had been equally disapproving about Spooner's handling of the closing down of the naval base. Cazalet was heading back to Singapore with his cruiser *Durban* so that he could provide an escort for the ships taking out RAF technicians, Australian and British nurses, and most of the remaining civilian evacuees who still wanted to leave. Spooner's note accompanied the delivery to *Durban* of three metal trunks and a suitcase, with instructions to get them to his wife Megan, who had left for Batavia a couple of days before. 'You must go by midnight. All good luck and tell my wife I will follow soon.'

Spooner was wrong. Surrender was by no means hours away. It was true that Yamashita had pierced the thin crust of Percival's west coast defences and was now occupying a wedge-shaped slice with its apex at Bukit Timah village, 6 miles from the city centre. Determined to give the Emperor something for *Kigensetsu* he had even issued a communiqué claiming to have entered the north-western part of the city, thus anticipating its expansion by about half a century. Not only the city but about three-quarters of the island remained in Percival's hands and, although smoke was rising from its many wounds, Singapore still had plenty of troops willing to fight for it if only they were pointed in the right direction and properly led.

Three days after the Japanese had landed, Second Lieutenant John Webb of the Northumberland Fusiliers, the machine-gun battalion of the fresh 18th Division, was on Hill 95 admiring the view of the straits, the broken Causeway and the Japanese maritime traffic below. Like most of his battalion, Webb's men had not fired a shot in action since they had fought their way into Keppel harbour against Japanese air attack aboard the *Felix Roussel* six days before. That morning, the lieutenant had imagined that all this was going to change when he received orders to take two of the platoon's four Vickers guns to support the 5/14th Punjabis in an attack on the hill where the Gurkhas had lost two of their British officers. The day before there had been an inexplicable withdrawal by a company of the normally reliable 1st Frontier Force Rifles.

But the reoccupation of this high ground, first abandoned by Maxwell's Australians, was unopposed. It appeared that the Japanese, now well established in the north-west corner of the island, were more concerned with their push on the city than exploiting any gaps east of the Causeway. The Punjabis discovered a British field telephone set in working order and made a call to their brigade headquarters. It occurred to Webb that if only they had an artillery spotter with them, they could make it very uncomfortable for the Japanese boats flitting across the waters below them with impunity.

Then somebody came on the field telephone and said we had to get off the hill because we were surrounded. Of course, we weren't surrounded but off we went, back down the hill in single file, down a deep ravine, carrying the Vickers guns, the tripods, the ammunition. Down we all came, all very thirsty.

Because his intelligence was poor and he thought Yamashita was much stronger than he was, Percival was slow in concluding that the landings on the west coast probably constituted the main Japanese thrust. No attempt was made to risk withdrawals from other places to expel them with overwhelming force before they had time to build up their strength. Which was why, almost two and a half days after the Japanese had first landed, people like Webb and his platoon found themselves being marched uselessly up and down hills overlooking the straits.

With Wavell's encouragement, Percival's first move toward re-arranging his defences had been to ask Heath to form a scratch brigade and send them to the race course east of Bukit Timah village, where there were big food, fuel and ammunition dumps. It was inevitable that Heath would send some of the UK British battalions which now made up the majority of his 3rd 'Indian' Corps. He chose the 4th Norfolks from 54th Brigade, and the 1/5th Sherwood Foresters from the 55th. The third battalion was 18th Reconnaissance Corps who, having lost all their vehicles, had in most cases been plucked from the blazing *Empress of Asia* in little more than their underwear and hastily equipped with whatever could be found. There was also a battery of 2-pounders from the Royal Artillery's 85th Anti-Tank Regiment.

They were to be known as Tomforce, for they were all to come under Webb's commanding officer, Lionel Thomas of the North-umberland Fusiliers. Thomas was the obvious choice for the job. At forty-five, he was a senior lieutenant-colonel and the most readily available for a stint as acting brigadier because machine-gun battalions rarely worked as a whole but tended to be deployed in platoon-sized packets wherever their support was most needed. This apart, Thomas had arrived in Singapore with a reputation as something of a firebrand for the way he had organized the air defences on the *Felix Roussel*. Within twenty-four hours, to plug another gap, Heath would stitch together another makeshift brigade. Massyforce, under Brigadier Tom Massy-Beresford, included the 1st Cambridgeshires from his own 55th Brigade (he had already lost the Sherwood Foresters to Tomforce) plus the 4th Suffolks from 54th Brigade, and the much depleted 5/11th Sikhs from the late 'Whiz Bang Sikh' Barstow's 9th Indian Division. Detaching individual battalions like this was intended to leave intact, with all its brigade and divisional headquarters, the administrative and tactical trunk of 18th East Anglian Division. But it must have been agonizing for Beckwith-Smith, who had secured the division its place overseas by winning the 1941 'Exercise War of the Roses', to watch his creation being fed piecemeal into the battle.

Tomforce was ordered to recapture Bukit Timah village and, more importantly perhaps, the hill the village is named after which is about a mile away and east of the railroad. Elements of Yamashita's 5th and 18th divisions had seized the hill that morning. Operating in

Bennett's western sector they came under his overall command and although, unlike a growing number of Australian troops, they were at least going in the right direction, he was soon less than satisfied with their performance. A staff officer was dispatched with a note for Thomas urging him to 'press his attack with more vigour'. But he was killed when his vehicle was strafed and eventually the message was delivered by Bennett's aide-de-camp, Lieutenant-Colonel Gordon Walker. If Thomas made a written reply it does not appear to have survived. Possibly he ignored it. It is not hard to imagine how Bennett might have responded in similar circumstances. Tomforce was, after all, three green battalions, one of them shipwrecked not quite a week before.

They advanced along the Bukit Timah dual carriageway, the best road on the island. Behind them the road was crammed with a misery of refugees, Chinese, Indian and Malays from the Japanese-occupied north-west, either walking or packed into an assortment of trucks, buses, bullock carts and even grossly over-laden trishaws pedalled by sinewy opium addicts. Straddling the road was 18th Reconnaissance, which had scrounged a few Bren gun carriers to replace those lost on the *Empress of Asia*. To their right were the Norfolks and to their left the Sherwood Foresters. Their frontage was about 2,000 yards across.

Captain Reginald Burton was leading the 4th Norfolks' D Company because its commander had gone down with a bad dose of the virulent tinea they called 'Singapore Foot' and was shuffling about in gym shoes with the aid of a thumb stick. They had spent the night in fox holes a little south of the race course, where Burton had dreamed of those Saturday afternoons at his prep school in Torquay when his mother would sometimes call to take him on the beach to build sand castles. When he awoke he saw that they had dug themselves into a gentle and thinly vegetated slope with good fields of fire. In the circumstances, it had seemed to Burton a much better idea to sit tight and let the Japanese tide try and breach their fortifications.

They advanced in extended order, A Company ahead of them, and then closed up to go down the straight of the well-kept race course. The first of the various dumps was here and Burton saw that looters had already been busy with some crates of tinned food. Once they had left the race course they found the overground pipe-line that, until a few days ago, had run across the Causeway with the island's additional water from the mainland's Gunong Pulai waterworks. They followed it up towards the summit of the hill. Burton led his men towards a clump of trees on the skyline from where he heard 'sporadic bursts of firing'.

I realized that at last we'd come to grips with the enemy . . . We started to climb the hill and very quickly we ran into the wounded from A Company making their way painfully back . . . Some men were limping, others being helped along by less severely wounded comrades . . . For a moment our own men wavered. They had friends, even relations, among the wounded, and their immediate reaction was to lend a hand. This was their first real experience of action . . . However, we quickly managed to get them on the move and as we neared the crest the momentum of our advance increased.

Tomforce may not have impressed Bennett but it won the admiration of at least one Japanese officer watching the dogged British infantry below him. ' "This is gallantry, is it not?" I said to myself, and involuntarily I was lost in admiration,' wrote Tsuji, who was running about the battlefield in his usual manic way. Earlier that day he had very nearly been killed by the most potent symbol of Fortress Singapore.

From Changi on the island's east coast the three 15-inch guns of the Johore battery, so called because of Sultan Ibrahim's generous donation towards their upkeep, had first joined in the battle three days before the landings by firing a few shots on troop concentrations around the railways in southern Johore. But by the 11th they had joined in the battle in earnest by traversing to fire at targets on the island itself, particularly in the Bukit Timah area, which was well within their 21-mile range. Fortunately for Tsuji, even at this late stage it had not proved possible to find and deliver the rarer high-explosive 15-inch shells with the large spread of shrapnel intended for land warfare. All but one of the 250 rounds in the Johore battery's underground magazine were of the armour-piercing variety, designed to pierce then disembowel battleships. They weighed almost 2,000 pounds, about as much as a small car, and could make holes in the ground as big as suburban swimming pools though considerably deeper. They had to be winched up from the magazine on an ammunition hoist on which there was a sign, a legacy of peace-time skylarking, forbidding men to ride on it. The gunners of the Royal Artillery's 9th Coastal Regiment were as blind as those on the *Prince of Wales* or *Repulse* and, once a target area had been decided, relied on observation posts which could monitor their 'fall of shot' in any direction. These posts fed the battery's Fire Direction Table the bearings and ranges they had worked out with their Barr and Stroud range-finders and the wonderful brass stereoscopic telescopes, all British-made optics, which provided three-dimensional images. Years of practice had reduced the hoisting and loading time for the huge shells to the point where each of the three guns had a rate of fire of two rounds a minute.

Tsuji and his batman had abandoned their car because the road was too cratered, which should have served as a warning. They were going in an easterly direction towards the important crossroads village of Bukit Panjang, about 2 miles north of Bukit Timah, when the first round blew them off their feet:

. . . the blast jarred our spines. The flash seared my eyes, and I was thrown into the roadside ditch. In my agitation I thrust myself into an earthenware drainage pipe . . . one discharge – two discharges . . . I had no experience of such heavy projectiles, which tore holes in the ground 15 or 16 metres in diameter and 4 or 5 metres deep . . . Crouching like a crab inside the earthen pipe I imagined what would happen if a shell fell on me . . . I had landed on the island with the intention of dying but unconsciously I drew myself further into the pipe.

By the time Tsuji and his orderly, having survived the expenditure of several thousand pounds' worth of ammunition, had reached the top of Bukit Timah, the 15-inch guns had switched their attention to the village below, which had already come under a considerable amount of 25-pounder fire. From his vantage point, Tsuji watched the shells burst and thought it was being annihilated. But the British attack, which was becoming increasingly subject to air strikes, was petering out. The Reconnaissance Corps' battalion had met with strong resistance at the Bukit Timah railway station while to the left of them the Sherwood Foresters had enjoyed mixed fortunes. John Goatley, the Foresters' intelligence officer, who had gone out at night looking for stragglers in Thirlby's boat after the Causeway was blown, remembers the distance from their start line to the objective as being about five miles. 'The country in between was a disagreeable mixture of secondary jungle, plantations, gardens, houses, and roads.'

Throughout their advance he was at the side of the popular Lieutenant-Colonel Harold Lilly, a long-serving Territorial Army officer who, like most of the Midlanders he commanded, was a Derbyshire man. Although he was not a regular soldier, the dapper Lilly was wedded to his Foresters the way Stewart was to his Argylls. He had first been given the command of the battalion in 1934. The following year, his civilian occupation – he was a director of the Derby-based commercial printers Bemrose – took him to Greece for four years and he was obliged to relinquish it. Then, on his return to England just before the outbreak of war, he managed to get the 1/5th returned to him.

Lilly had been commissioned into the regiment in 1915 and captured the following year at Gommecourt when, after a successful attack, he and his platoon became cut off and he was obliged to surrender to the prisoners he had taken. This was Lilly's first time in action since then. (He had been away in England on a course when the battalion were caught up in the 1940 blitzkrieg in France, where they had fought a spirited action against Rommel's Panzer grenadiers, only to have the best part of a company taken prisoner because of a map-reading error.) Goatley recalled that Lilly was trying to coordinate the Foresters' advance by keeping in touch with his company commanders by radio, and experiencing the same technical difficulties that had beset almost every other battalion commander throughout the campaign. He was concerned that the Japanese were actually further forward than suspected. There had already been some patrol clashes and Goatley, like most of the officers, was carrying a rifle as well as his holstered revolver to make his rank less obvious to snipers. Then he heard the crack of a near miss – 'I knew someone was after me':

. . . about 50 yards away was a large clump in the fork of a tree. He fired at me twice more, all close and I became convinced he was in this clump, this growth in the tree. I was lying on the ground by this time and I fired three shots into the growth. There was no more firing. I couldn't see a body but he didn't fire back.

Somewhere ahead of Goatley, also clutching a rifle and 'feeling very light-hearted', was Captain Norman Thorpe, the second-in-command of C Company and another Derbyshire Territorial whose family were half of Lancaster & Thorpe, the county's biggest opticians, where he worked. During their first two weeks on the island, Thorpe had thought his men 'depressingly slack and careless'. But after the Japanese landed he found that the 'completely indifferent' attitude adopted by his Midlanders matched his own phlegm. 'I myself only feel mildly excited and hardly feel it concerns me,' he noted in his diary.

As they advanced, they passed through Australians, Indians and some of the regulars from the amalgamated East Surreys and Leicesters in Morrison's British Battalion. These were the remnants of the formations dispersed the previous day, before they had been able to make their counter-attack and recover the Kranji–Jurong line. Some were utterly demoralized, and told the Foresters in their new-looking tropical kit not to be such damn fools. But a few, mostly East Surreys, joined Thorpe, including two men with a Lewis gun, the 1914–18 light machine-gun much heavier than the Bren, an indication that they were probably old sweats who knew how to use it.

Thorpe led his men into a thickly overgrown Chinese cemetery where they were bombed and strafed by half a dozen aircraft which had been circling the area for some time. Although Japanese close air support lacked any ground-to-air radio direction and was nowhere near as professional as the Luftwaffe's (or as good as the Allies would become before very long), this was no consolation to troops who had none at all. These aircraft, as was often the case with the smaller fighter bomber types, did not inflict any casualties, but they had no sooner gone than the Japanese infantry opened fire with a heavy machine-gun and once more everybody dived for cover. Thorpe wriggled forward between the bushes and the gravestones but not many followed. It was always difficult to maintain control in what the army called 'close country'. Most of his Foresters were content to lie where they found themselves, among the old dead, until all the disagreeable noises had ceased. By the time Thorpe had crossed the railway and entered the outskirts of Bukit Timah, there were no more than a dozen men with him – including a lieutenant – when it should have been more like sixty. Then, as he was passing a hut, Thorpe came under machine-gun fire again.

Two men including a man from the Surreys who had joined me were hit, and so I left a Bren with Lieutenant Sherlock and worked round the left with grenades and a few men to try and winkle the post out. I got close enough to throw a grenade or two, which worried them, but had to abandon my intention owing to sniping from several points which cost me another man with a bullet through his arm. I was now convinced that the battalion had not gone through here and therefore must be over to the left.

As so often in this campaign, Bukit Timah was not a tidy battlefield. Ahead of Tomforce, and behind the hilltop position Tsuji was on, about 200 of Stewart's cut-off Argylls had fragmented into a dozen or so small parties. After they had delayed the Japanese armour long enough for Major MacDonald to set up the anti-tank guns, Stewart had retired about 100 yards into the rubber to the east of the road. He had intended to lie low there, silent and not giving away their positions by firing at shadows, until first light, when they would ambush the infantry reinforcements which would surely follow up the T95s. But by 4 a.m. the Japanese, whose English-speaking mimics with their 'Is anyone there?' had largely failed to lure the Argylls out of cover, were already beginning to send large patrols into the rubber. One of these came within 10 yards of Stewart's battalion HQ and killed four men, including his mortar officer, Lieutenant Albert Gispert, an accountant from Kuala Lumpur and a transfer to the Argylls from the Federated Malay States Volunteer Force. Gispert, who had Spanish antecedents, was popular and athletic and left a lasting legacy. Sixty years after his death the Hash House Harriers cross-country running club he founded in Malaya has branches all over the world.

Stewart decided that he could not afford to start a dogfight in the dark when the enemy had the tactical advantage of controlling the road and they would have to withdraw to their emergency rendezvous point – an experimental dairy farm on the northern side of Bukit Timah hill. This was not too much of a problem for the Plymouth element of the reconstituted Argylls, the two companies of Royal Marines off the battleships, who were closer to the farm. They got away with their wounded, including a stretcher party carrying Lieutenant Douglas Weir, a young colonial policeman who had been shot in the stomach. Like Gispert, Weir was one of thirteen local transfers from the volunteer forces, police and civil service granted temporary commissions in the Argylls the previous month. These volunteers were mostly, but by no means all, of Scottish extraction and delighted to get into the best-known infantry regiment in Percival's command. Hubert Strathairn, a friend of Weir's, had held a Territorial Army commission in the Black Watch before he came out to Malaya as a police cadet in January 1940, when the European war was still only three months old. But there had been little chance for these newcomers to bond with the regiment. Strathairn was probably not the only one who thought that the three weeks' cramming they did on map reading and fieldcraft might have been better spent getting to know their men.

Around midnight, Weir had been leading three Argylls, one of them awarded the Military Medal for his bravery in northern Malaya, on a patrol near the road when, before he had a chance to use his Thompson, he was hit at close range by a single rifle bullet. 'I was knocked off my feet, like being hit hard at rugby.' A tank came up and for the next twenty minutes or so sprayed the rubber trees around them with intermittent bursts of tracer. Weir crawled off unaided to an *attap* rubber tappers' hut he had noticed. Once inside, he fumbled in the dark for his issue field dressing then struggled to snap apart the tight stitching which sealed its canvas cover.

Later I learned the bullet had passed through my stomach from left to right, just missing my liver and bowel. At the time all I knew was that where it had gone in felt as if I'd been hit by a hammer. But when I put my hand there it came away dry. I thought I must be bleeding internally and began spitting in my palm to see whether I was bringing up any blood. I'd heard that if you got to a hospital within six hours of receiving a stomach wound you'd a good chance of surviving. This was providing you didn't develop a temperature.

For four hours Weir lay in the hut, holding his dressing in place, looking at his watch, occasionally spitting in his palm and hoping the Argylls he had been leading would find him. But if they were looking for him they were not trying very hard. Then he heard the Royal Marines passing by and called out to them. They carried him for miles until they found an abandoned ambulance and drove him to hospital.

Stewart and his HQ company were also able to escape but the two forward companies – A and D, who comprised the rump of the Argylls – were cut off. Regimental Sergeant-Major Sandy Munnoch, the Hogmanay bongo drummer, somehow weaved his wiry frame around the Japanese to reach them with the dismal tidings that, once again, it was every man for himself. But there was one crucial difference between Bukit Timah and Slim: the city was so close they could almost smell it and there seemed a good chance that a counter-attack would push the Japanese back.

The sergeant-major himself took command of one party and led it south-eastwards around the MacRitchie reservoir to reach British lines without mishap. Others were not so fortunate. Lieutenant Donald

Napier, who had slowed the Japanese pursuit with his neat ambush on the railway at Slim, died pistol in hand during a sudden collision with the enemy. They were following the water pipe-line, which was by far the easiest and most obvious cross-country route into the city. In the same scrimmage Lieutenant John Love, one of the temporary commissioned officers and not long escaped from his civil servant's desk, came close to being throttled with the lanyard cord of his own revolver, worn around the neck to prevent the weapon being snatched. In this case an Argyll did come to the new officer's rescue and the strangler was left bellowing on the ground from a bullet in the bottom.

The survivors from this party escaped, leaving Napier in the monsoon ditch where he had fallen. But twelve others, who appear to have bumped into the Japanese confronting Lilly's Foresters around Bukit Timah village, were taken prisoner. First they were tied up with barbed wire, then bayoneted, then shot. One man survived. Private Hugh Anderson, who had six bayonet wounds, was left for dead and rescued by local Chinese who, at considerable risk to themselves, hid him in their home and nursed him back to health. Also taken prisoner in a separate incident a little earlier was Lieutenant Hubert Strathairn whose treatment was so different to Anderson's it is hard to believe they were captured by the same army.

Strathairn was on a lone scouting mission around the dairy farm buildings, trying to establish whether the rendezvous was still in British hands, when he was wrestled to the ground by three or four Japanese who immediately relieved him of his watch as well as his pistol. For the first twenty-four hours he was guarded by a soldier who obviously relished making frequent apologies for his imminent execution. But when Strathairn was led away it was to a major with fluent English and a gentle sense of humour. Having ascertained that his prisoner could drive a car and a motorcycle, he was required to push a bicycle to which most of the major's kit appeared to be attached. In return the major allowed Strathairn to sleep in his tent and generally looked after his welfare. When some wounded prisoners from the East Anglian Division appeared, the young policeman easily persuaded his chivalrous captor to get a doctor for them.

Strathairn had been in a party led by Captain Michael Bardwell, an Assam tea planter from an old Highland family – heir apparent to Argyllshire's Connel Castle – and a cousin of Angus Rose. Bardwell, who was twenty-three, was one of the luckier Slim River fugitives, having reached the sanctuary of Sumatra after a 150-mile voyage in an open boat. Eschewing rest and recuperation, he inveigled a Tiger Moth pilot into returning him to Singapore where he delayed reporting to the Argylls long enough to marry his fiancée, a nurse who was the daughter of the colony's leading architect, then see his bride safely aboard a ship bound for Australia.

Bardwell had led his party to the outskirts of the dairy farm, the rendezvous point Stewart had laid down, just before dawn. Shortly afterwards, Hubert Strathairn volunteered to go off on his lone reconnaissance. It was hoped he would find some farm workers who would tell them where the Japanese were. Like all policemen, he had been required to learn Malay and was the obvious choice. The farm was just behind the hilltop Japanese positions from where Tsuji would shortly be admiring the *élan* of the advancing Norfolks. By the time the lieutenant was sneaking around its outbuildings it had probably been occupied by the Japanese for several hours. Drawing the correct conclusions from Strathairn's failure to return, Bardwell and his men tiptoed away on a more circuitous route to the city, taking a compass bearing from the smoke rising from the burning godowns at Keppel harbour.

At the beginning of the day, Percival had left these fires behind him to drive up an almost deserted Bukit Timah road to see how Tomforce was doing. He felt 'terribly naked' as Japanese aircraft, apparently indifferent to anti-aircraft fire, circled overhead looking for targets. 'Why, I asked myself, does Britain, our improvident Britain with all her great resources, allow her sons to fight without any air support?' It is not clear when exactly Percival was made aware of Yamashita's invitation to surrender. Sometime in the late afternoon or early evening of 11 February, after his return from Bukit Timah, is the best guess, for he was not in direct radio contact with his HQ, though he may have been reached by a dispatch rider. It was not until nine o'clock that evening that he telegraphed a copy to the injured Wavell in Java. It was accompanied by a comment showing that the 'nakedness' he felt during his morning trip up the Bukit Timah road was still very much in his mind. 'Have no means of dropping message so do not propose to make a reply which would of course in any case be negative.'

It is hard to imagine that Wavell would have expected anything else. But for Percival much had changed between setting out from his HQ near the golf club that morning and returning to it at the Fort Canning bunker in the evening, where he had ordered it to be transferred because the Japanese were now too close. The enemy had made substantial gains on the south-western outskirts of Singapore and were no more than 4 miles away from Keppel harbour. By late afternoon, Japanese infantry 'swarmed' (Percival's word) around the two 15-inch guns of the south coast's unblooded Buona Vista battery as British engineers blew them up. The enemy were now beyond the battery and pressing forward towards the Alexandra Hospital and barracks complex. A little further north, what was left of Taylor's 22nd Australian Brigade, which seemed to be composed of a hard core of men who wanted to fight, had delighted Percival by holding its ground 'most gallantly'. But they were hard pressed and, although Bennett was loath to admit it to Percival, he knew that a growing number of his disillusioned, belligerent and often drunken infantry were now roaming the streets of Singapore with only one thing in mind and that was a boat home. Bennett, having long decided that he deserved a better war than becoming a prisoner of the Japanese, was thinking along much the same lines.

The Tomforce counter-attack had finally ground to a halt. There were probably never enough of them to dislodge the Japanese from Bukit Timah and, after three months at sea, none of the East Anglian Division's battalions had had the chance to work up to the level where there was any reasonable hope of success. 'What we lacked was blooding,' said Brigadier Massy-Beresford, who would shortly be told to take over Tomforce from Colonel Thomas and merge it with his own Massyforce.

You have got to begin gently. If we had gone to Africa we would have been put into strict training, then into a reserve position and then into a non-quiet position. It would have all been worked up. But to plunge them into that place was hopeless. One couldn't have expected anything better.

Even so, as far as the Japanese were concerned, the introduction of these fresh British troops was to be taken very seriously. Medium bombers, Nells and Bettys, were switched away from targets in Keppel harbour and the city to deal with them. When they hit the British infantry they were flying in their standard 27-aircraft formations but much lower than usual. Pressed against the ground, Burton felt the earth shake 'like an enormous jelly' and was reminded of the wobbling cake-walk platforms he used to try and walk at fun fairs. Among the casualties were two wounded Norfolks who went through his position on a delivery bicycle, the worst hit crouched in the box in front and the other pedalling. 'How they kept their balance was as mysterious as how they'd acquired their transport.'

By nightfall Colonel Thomas, realizing that his *ad hoc* brigade was getting nowhere, had ordered them back to their original start line or close to it. Once again the Norfolks passed through the race course where a bombed fuel dump was ablaze. But, to Burton's great regret, they did not return to their original position with the good fields of fire. Instead they went to a rubber-planted hillock that lay between it and the oval track.

The Japanese wasted no time following them down from Bukit Timah hill. They teased them with probing attacks accompanied by strings of mortar-thrown crackerjack rifle simulators, which left a distinct whiff of fireworks in the air different to gunsmoke. Pale moonlight cast sly shadows among the silver trees where the Norfolks crouched, firing at anything that moved and much that did not. 'But if I wait too long, sir, I'll be killed,' one told Burton as he tried to restore some fire discipline before they all ran out of ammunition. Not everybody was shooting shadows. After twelve hours in the field, Burton and his batman at last had their first good look at the enemy when an upward crawl through thorny undergrowth to the crest of a slight rise revealed in the half light, 'little men in breeches and puttees . . . They were collecting their dead.'

Next morning, the Norfolks were again ordered to withdraw. It was not an easy business. The Japanese pursued them with mortar fire and had the range nicely judged. By the time they had disengaged Burton discovered he was the only officer in his company still on his feet. The other four officers had all been wounded. The company commander, slowed by his foot complaint, was hit in the back by a mortar splinter. Two platoon commanders had been shot in the leg and another had had his knee cap sliced off by a mortar bomb. The battalion had also lost the lieutenant commanding its Bren gun carriers. These officers were often selected for the role because they were suspected of having a bit of cavalry dash about them. Ordered to rescue some isolated Norfolks, he had charged to the scene with his half a dozen open-topped carriers spitting fire only to be decapitated by another dashing young officer who, Samurai sword in hand, dropped into his vehicle from a tree. Eventually the carriers escaped by driving straight down the Bukit Timah highway, surprising in the process some Japanese tanks which they briefly engaged with Boys rifles, before escaping intact to rejoin the battalion amidst the tropical tudor splendour of Singapore's Adam Road.

This teak-panelled bastion of the European *Tuan Besars*, with rattan furniture still awaiting sundowners on the verandas of immaculate bungalows, lawns not long cut now desecrated by slit trenches, the nets on the tennis courts only just beginning to sag, and the extravagant shrubberies of scarcely restrained tropicana already in want of the garden boys' attention, had become part of Percival's final defence perimeter around the city. There would be no more retreats. There was nowhere to go.

Given the failure to recapture Bukit Timah, the growing mutiny of much of Bennett's division and the uncertainty over where Yamashita would strike next, Percival's decision to gather his forces around the city was inevitable. It was one of those rare occasions when both he and Heath thought the time had come to withdraw: 'We agreed it was no good leaving troops guarding the northern and eastern shores of the island when there was such imminent danger of losing Singapore town itself.'

It was decided to concentrate the garrison in a 28-mile perimeter, with Keppel harbour at one end of its remaining coastline and Kallang airfield at the other, an area of some 30 square miles. Into this would be crammed around a million civilians and perhaps 100,000 military, including some Australian and Indian units in a considerable state of confusion. If there was to be any hope at all of the prolonged last stand Churchill had demanded – and it was not yet seventy-two hours since the Japanese had first landed – water would obviously become as important as ammunition.

Originally, Percival had intended that his perimeter would encompass two of the island's three reservoirs, the Peirce and the MacRitchie. But the loss of Bukit Timah made this no longer feasible as it would create a long finger of a salient, vulnerable to amputation at the knuckle. So it was decided to give up the Peirce and the north bank of the MacRitchie. A water supply was ensured by dominating MacRitchie's south-eastern shore, from where underground pipes ran down the eastward slope of the Braddell Road to gravity-feed the vital Woodleigh pumping station. The station itself was accommodated by a discreet bulge in the British front line.

The trek back to the city redoubt had started by early evening on the 11th, when it was realized that the counter-attack on Bukit Timah had failed. The shell of the naval base, with all its fuel tanks pumping black smoke since the engineers had finished off what the Japanese had started, was finally vacated by Selby's Gurkhas, John Webb's Northumberland Fusiliers machine-gunners and Philip Toosey's

Yeomanry artillery by the following morning. For some of them, conceding this – the most fortress-like stretch of the northern coast – without being allowed to fire a shot in its defence, was the first indication of how much trouble they were in. Yeomanry gunner Lieutenant Stephen Alexander was probably one of many who found it difficult coming to terms with no longer being 'a tight little Jap-proof island like, say, Malta':

My own resolve in facing the enemy . . . was badly shaken . . . there was no longer any doubt that henceforth there would be equivocation, civil disturbance and second thoughts about death or glory.

Some naval officers lingered, reluctant to abandon ship. To Webb's amazement, an RN captain, who he thought was the Chief Signals Officer, emerged from a neat married quarters bungalow near the wireless station and assured him that he was free to borrow any of his books. Next day, exactly a week after they had arrived off Keppel harbour all guns blazing aboard the *Felix Roussel*, Webb and his score or so of men with their four Vickers guns were in action for the first time. Their task was to support the 2/10th Baluch, who were fighting a rearguard action against the Imperial Guard at the village of Nee Soon. The village is in the middle of the island, at the important junction of the Madai Road from the west and the Thomson Road, which ran south from the naval base to the city, skirting the eastern banks of the reservoirs.

Once again a gaping hole had appeared in the left flank of 11th Indian Division, because Duncan Maxwell's 27th Australian Brigade had moved south. This time it was not entirely Maxwell's fault. His two battalions had fallen apart after an uncoordinated attempt to make them the northern half of a pincer movement – designed to coincide with Tomforce's attack on Bukit Timah – attacking the Japanese rear. Some of his Australians had attempted, like the cut-off Argylls, to move down the water pipe-line route south, only to be ambushed from behind its brick buttresses.

The Australians' disarray appears to have been caused mainly by an unprecedented failure in communication and chain of command, seasoned by the confusion and hesitation Maxwell now brought to almost any military endeavour. As his battalions moved about on the overcrowded roads of the visibly shrinking entity that was British

Singapore, traffic jams, poor navigation and air attack all combined to fragment them into their constituent companies or even platoons. Nor did it help that the breakdown in radio and field telephone links meant that the only sure way of delivering a message was by word of mouth. In the end, the two battalions were scattered, exhausted, dispirited and, as they came closer to the city, constantly meeting other Australians telling them the game was up. All the King's horses could not have put 27th Australian Brigade back together again.

At Nee Soon, the British commander of 2/10th Baluch's A Company, who had fought the Japanese down the length of the peninsula, was giving Webb, who was young even for a second lieutenant, the benefit of his experience. 'First they attack your front, get all your attention, then they go for a flank, then we pull out before we're surrounded.'

But when it happened it was not quite like that. This time, the Baluch were supported by the kind of firepower that was uncommon on the peninsula: two anti-tank guns with Geordie gunners from the Royal Artillery's 85th Regiment and the four belt-fed Vickers which, like the 2-pounders, were divided between the two forward companies, A and C. Admittedly Webb thought the fields of fire for his Vickers were poor, but that could not be helped. They were in secondary jungle at the edge of a rubber estate. It reminded him of the kind of undergrowth to be found in an English wood.

Since he had arrived in Singapore, Webb had heard a lot of stories about how unreliable some of the Indian troops had become. Only that morning, three companies of the reconstituted and mainly adolescent 1/8th Punjabis, who had been on the 2/10th's right flank, had fled after a heavy mortar attack and had to be hurriedly replaced by the Garhwalis. But he was impressed by the Baluch who, though often very young as well, seemed an efficient bunch.

There were various bangs Webb did not quite understand and the A Company commander allowed him to share his shallow trench. It turned out they were being mortared. There was some small arms fire, and it seemed that the Japanese infantry were closing in. The first of his Vickers to open up was the left-hand section supporting C Company, which was commanded by Prem Sahgal, by now the battalion's most senior Indian officer: first one gun, then the other gun, then both together. Webb found the noise of his platoon firing their first shots in the defence of Singapore 'wonderfully reassuring'.

Then he heard some Bren gun carriers moving up, making the laboured rumbling sound peculiar to all tracked vehicles, whatever their size. His companion informed him that if they were carriers, they were nothing to do with his battalion, because they had long since lost all theirs. 'As he was speaking there was a terrific crack. We both thought it was another mortar bomb and flattened ourselves.'

When he raised his head, Webb could smell burning, and there was a lot of smoke in the air. There were two more high-velocity cracks, then the Vickers section he had deployed just behind the 2-pounder opened fire. He ran over to them. It turned out that the gunners had knocked out, one after the other, three tanks coming down an estate road. At least one was burning. At a range of less than 200 yards, his Vickers had then riddled the crews, and perhaps a few infantry piggybacking on the armour, as they huddled for cover in a storm drain.

This little victory at Nee Soon blunted the Imperial Guard's advance and allowed Key's 11th Indian Division to disengage. Not everybody was so lucky. Norman Thorpe's Foresters had a good start to the day when they got a Bren gun onto some Japanese moving in the open. But the Japanese responded by bringing up their light armour, and the Foresters were caught without any anti-tank weapons, having left their 36-pound Boys rifle with their transport. Thorpe was one of the first to hear the 'rumbling down the road' and knew exactly what it was.

Under fire they could not return, some of the men broke and began to run, but Major Robinson managed to get them back to the trenches. However, as we were experiencing considerable losses without any hope of reply, [Paul Robinson] decided to pull the men out. Unfortunately, we found it impossible to steady the men once they were moved, so we found ourselves with only a few . . . mostly injured.

Among the wounded was Lieutenant Goatley, on an errand for Colonel Lilly, who had given up on the radio: 'John, go and tell Tigger [Major Price, D Company] to change his front and swing right.' Before Goatley could deliver the message, one of the tanks had started hosing down the rubber with its machine-gun and a bullet found his right leg. Goatley could feel the blood squelching in his boot as, using his rifle for support, he hopped back towards Lilly to explain that it was not Tigger's fault that he was not swinging right. 'Better do something about that,' said Lilly, glancing at his leg, and Goatley staggered off in search of somebody who would change the field-aid dressing he had tied around the wound.

Later, the Foresters resented accusations from some of their officers that the tanks had unnerved them and they had failed 'to steady'. When the tanks opened fire, Private Ron Morrell, a twenty-year-old miner's son from Nottingham, was lying near the edge of the road behind a big log, watching his cover growing smaller by the second as an invisible axe chipped great chunks of wood off it. 'We pulled back into the rubber. We didn't run away. We just parted to let them go through. What else could we do? We had nothing to stop them.'

If Yamashita's armour was really unlucky – and the odds were very much in its favour – as it moved down the main road to Bukit Timah, it came under indirect fire from the distant 15-inch coastal battery, whose projectiles were capable of turning it into a smudge on the road. But not for much longer because most of the eastern part of the coast was being given up and with it one of the showpieces of Fortress Singapore. At 1 p.m. Changi Fire Command was ordered to have the three guns readied for demolition by 6.30 that evening. 'Battery will fire away all ammunition possible.'

The gunners spent part of the afternoon putting down harassing fire on the north-western part of the naval base they had been installed to defend. Why this particular target was chosen for their swan song is unclear. Enemy forces could hardly have been observed in the vicinity because the British no longer possessed either the aircraft or the high ground to spot them. Most likely it was because of a sneaking suspicion that not enough had been done to transform the base into the kind of wasteland Churchill demanded. After a short reprieve, the final order to go ahead with the destruction of the guns came at 6.45 p.m. Two hours later, the battery, and all the precision tools that enabled it to kill from afar, was a tangled wreck. It had fired a total of 194 rounds in Singapore's defence, almost 80 per cent of its magazine capacity. To boost the engineers' demolition charges, fifty-six shells were left. One breech block landed a quarter of a mile away.

Smaller guns fared better. Several regiments of field artillery, mostly 25-pounders, struggled to get back to the new perimeter from the north-eastern sector through traffic jams dominated by horn-crazy Indian drivers. The Japanese air force failed to exploit this as brutally as it should have. The 118th Field Regiment became enmeshed in the chaos at a junction of five roads, where the old-fashioned-looking fighters that had preceded the Zero – the ones with their fixed spatted landing gear that the Allies had codenamed 'Claudes' and 'Nates' – strafed and dropped small bombs. Gunner Fergus Anckorn, the conjuror Wizardus at the 18th Division's concert parties, who was behind the wheel of a Quad towing tractor, recalled one such low-level attack:

I could see the pilot's face so plainly, he couldn't have been more than 100 feet up. I saw [the plane] dip and he had a bomb between the wheels, and I saw the bomb drop down. We were out of our lorries and threw ourselves on the ground. But when I got up my friend was dead and there wasn't a mark on him anywhere. My tin hat had been blown off me. I didn't know where that had gone to, but I hadn't felt a thing.

Lieutenant Alexander of Toosey's 135th thought the Japanese bombing had become 'devil may care', and was astonished to witness Sikh Bofors crews 'actually bring down planes'. When he reached Singapore, he found his colonel with the brigadier who commanded all the Royal Artillery's guns on the island, 'consoling himself with whisky and talking wildly about the hopeless infantry, the criminal Australian Imperial Forces, the brilliant 135th Field Regiment, and his own vow never to surrender, never to be captured alive, and never to leave by boat'.

Yet this last was exactly what some of the most distinguished of Percival's front-line soldiers were about to do. Given that the intention was still to resist Yamashita for as long as possible, an unusual addition had been made to the airmen and sailors permitted to leave. It had been decided to salvage from the infantry a cadre who had learned how to fight the Japanese, and who would bring their experience to training the fresh battalions that would have to be raised. The orders were quite explicit: 'The people selected are to have outstanding ability in the field and no consideration is to be given to consequent loss of efficiency of the battalion.' This was not the survival of the fittest then, but rather an attempt to preserve some of the bravest and the best, often the category least likely to survive when left to their own devices.

First to go were four Argylls: Stewart and his buccaneering second-in-command Angus Rose, assassin of the Japanese brigadier, and David Wilson, the man who blew up a bridge with some string, a delicately tied grenade and a machine-gun. The fourth was Arthur Bing, the self-effacing sergeant-major who had blistered his hands on the emptied Thompson he used as a club during the *mêlée* at the country railway station.

The Laird of Achnacone only agreed to go when Brigadier Paris promised that the Plymouth Argylls would not be committed to any further offensive action but restricted to defending their barracks area in the Tyersall Park cantonment. This was not a difficult pledge to keep. Since the tank attack down the Bukit Timah road, Stewart's command was once again greatly reduced. The Argyll element was down to about sixty, although a hundred or so stragglers were yet to come in. As for his Royal Marines, many had been reclaimed by the navy: for an escort to take captured Japanese aircrew to Sumatra; for a bodyguard for Admiral Spooner, who intended to move in the same direction soon; and for a guard platoon at Keppel harbour, where deserters desperate for a passage out were becoming harder to control.

Once the Argyll evacuation party received their departure orders, a Royal Marines captain with an Argyll officer as his number two took command of the remnants of the Plymouth Argylls. Wilson felt like a condemned man who had just heard he had been reprieved, but Rose recalls only feelings of shame: 'We were no better than rats deserting a sinking ship.'

Most of their last hours on the island were spent underground: first in Malaya Command's 'Battlebox' – the bunker at Fort Canning, with its warren of passageways, humming generators and rooms too overcrowded by sweating staff officers for the air conditioning to be effective; then in another, slightly smaller, lucifugous establishment, occupied by 'Singapore Fortress Command', whose fief had shrunk to the harbour. Finally, perhaps because their departure was considered sensitive and the less visible they were to those who had to stay behind the better, they were taken to a Chinese house in the Thomson Road that served as the headquarters of Dalforce.

John Dalley, the Special Branch officer who recruited among the Chinese Communists he had formerly hunted down, seems to have settled for providing guides and scouts for regular forces. Given the lack of proper small arms for his half-trained volunteers, this was probably the most useful employment for them. Few doubted their courage and commitment, but it was unlikely that their sawn-off shotguns made much difference during the initial night landings in the mangrove swamps. Almost inevitably there had been mistaken clashes with the Australian infantry, who shot dead one of their leaders following repeated challenges in English.

Other military evacuees were brought to Dalley's HQ. Among them were RAF officers and some Japanese-speakers from Percival's staff who, besides being valuable assets, were felt to be at some risk. Almost all of them had learned the language during the late pre-war years, when their civilian occupations had taken them to Japan – at this time, all westerners were routinely regarded as spies. One of General Heath's interpreters, who would not leave for another two days, had already served a six-month jail sentence in Japan for alleged espionage. Knowledge of the MAGIC decrypting machine that the Americans had given the British to break the Japanese diplomatic code was probably another ticket out. The machine itself was presumably long gone, or lying in deep water.

Not long after midnight, they all left for the harbour, driving on the blinkered headlight beams required by blackout regulations, the drivers straining their eyes looking for rubble and craters in the road. A veiled moon struggled to rise above the oil smoke. Every few minutes, the city was lit up by spears of flame from the latest conflagrations, or sudden flashes of gunfire on the horizon.

They were leaving on Peter Cazalet's light cruiser HMS *Durban*, which would be the flagship of an escort for a convoy bound for Batavia, Java's main port,* that was forming up in the roads. The other warships were the destroyers *Jupiter* and *Stronghold*, and the converted straits steamer *Kedah*, now transformed by the addition of a brace of 4.5s on her stern into HMS *Kedah* and rather grandly referred to as a sloop, although, of all the escorts, she would be carrying the most passengers. The last time many of the civilians among the 700 people crammed onto her decks had been aboard, they had been travelling in rather more style, as they cruised up to Penang for the races. Among them was Maurice Glover, the managing editor of the *Malayan Tribune* group. Only five days before, he had sent his wife Julienne to India in the battle-scarred *Felix Roussel*, the ship that had delivered the Northumberland Fusiliers. He had then settled down with Tim and Tom, his wife's adored labradors, for what he had expected to be a long siege. One of the last things he had done before leaving had been to put the dogs in his car and join the line of expatriates who had taken

* Now Djakarta.

their pets to the veterinary clinic to have them killed. It would be years before Glover could forgive himself for this.

Waiting on the quay for the *Durban*, which would not come in until 2 a.m., Colonel Stewart and his party listened to the battle-thunder from the west. It was obvious that Yamashita was still concentrating his thrust from that direction and making no real attempt to invest the city. To the east there was little action: lazy blobs of red tracer floated across the night sky, a descending flare snagged and died on a canopy of rubber. From behind them shells whizzed overhead from the British 9.2- and 6-inch batteries on the island of Blakang Mati opposite the harbour. The guns had been turned away from the sea approaches they normally covered to seek out these targets on land and, unlike the destroyed 15-inch monsters, there were a few high-explosive as well as armour-piercing shells available for both calibres.

Every time the gun on Blakang Mati fired, Kathleen Stapledon noticed how the blast flapped her trousers against her legs. She was standing on the deck of the SS *Gorgon*, a small Blue Funnel liner anchored in the roads, not far from where the coastal gunners were firing inland. Next to her was her friend Billy, an Australian woman who had worked with her at the RAF communications centre until they both boarded the *Gorgon* the previous day. The ship had come in from Australia a couple of days before, laden with tinned food. When the crew discovered that most of the dockers had fled, because of the air raids, they unloaded the ship themselves.

Like many of the wives who had stayed on, Kathleen had left under protest, and only when her husband insisted. There had been very little notice and the two permitted suitcases were not full. At the last moment, she had scooped up some table silver and cutlery, wrapped them in a silk petticoat and stuffed them among her clothes. Partings of this kind were a wretched business. There could be no certainty that couples would meet again, and many did not. Nor was it always those who remained who died. Few realized it, but soon Japanese naval and air supremacy would make it more dangerous to go than to stay. Women registered on evacuation lists would often be telephoned at home or their place of work and told they had an hour to pack and get down to the docks. 'The men said goodbye to us cheerfully, waving and saying they would come down next morning, but none of them came. They realized too well how painful it would be for all of us.'

Twenty-four hours later, the SS *Gorgon* had got no further than an anchorage in the roads, and during that time the ship had been boarded by two gangs of deserters. The first consisted of sixteen British soldiers on a motor launch. They had followed a similar vessel, which brought out wealthy nationalist Chinese like those who had been executed in Penang. Kathleen Stapledon watched the deserters come aboard.

There was no one to stop them. They were armed and looked very determined. They went straight to the captain and demanded to be taken with us. Their story was that they had been told to get out as best they could . . . They commanded the deck with their rifles and we thought that if the captain refused to take them, some of us would surely get shot. As soon as they heard they could come along, they collected their rifles and gave them up. It was clear that they had seen heavy fighting and appeared dazed and strung up . . .

To avoid a repetition of this, the *Gorgon*'s master took his ship a little further out to sea but, an hour later, thirty-two Australian soldiers under a sergeant came out to the vessel in sampans. Kathleen was amazed at the way they managed to paddle through the swell. There was a brief struggle with some of the *Gorgon*'s crew, who were in a launch at the bottom of the gangway.

It was a ghastly sight. They shouted, 'Take us! Oh, take us – don't leave us behind.' We then hoped they would get aboard safely . . . Directly they appeared on deck our feelings changed . . . all of us were feeling bitter and distraught at the thought of our husbands left behind, most of them unarmed . . . who knows what mental and physical strain had led them to take this cowardly step? . . . I approached the sergeant and asked him why they had come. He said that Singapore was falling and they thought they might as well leave. They could do nothing . . . I told him they should have stayed and done their best. After all, they were armed, and many civilians, including our husbands, had stayed, though they had no means of defending themselves. He then told me that they got lost and didn't know to whom they ought to report . . . the women ignored them though some of the men made much of them and bought them drinks.

Whether this hospitality was extended by the two US Army liaison officers among the official military evacuees aboard the *Gorgon* is not recorded. They can hardly have been impressed by the conduct of their allies, though these incidents might have made them even prouder of the stand MacArthur was making in the Bataan Peninsula.* But the situation worsened. Another 140 or so Australians fought their way onto the *Empire Star*, the largest ship in the convoy, which was still berthed in Keppel harbour and was therefore the most accessible.

The Belfast-registered, 12,500-ton *Empire Star* was a Blue Star line freighter, which before the war had plied between Fremantle and Singapore carrying frozen meat. Her present master was Captain Selwyn Capon, a Norfolk man who had been awarded an OBE for services rendered in the 1914–18 conflict and who, in his fiftieth year, had helped to evacuate the British Army from Dunkirk. His ship had arrived in Singapore from Australia two days before, with enough ammunition aboard to blow Keppel harbour into Bukit Timah. Once they discovered the nature of his cargo, dockers had become even more unavailable than usual, and the ship had been hastily unloaded by his crew, with pauses for air raids. When they had finished, Capon had been told to stand by to take on service personnel and civilian evacuees. Nobody seemed to know exactly how many. In peace time, the *Empire Star* had accommodation for only sixteen fare-paying passengers, but her holds were big and reasonably clean.

Most of the servicemen – Capon estimated there were just over 1,500 of them – turned out to be RAF ground crew and technicians trying to catch up with squadrons that had already departed for Java. Some heavy machine-guns came on board with them, which Capon thought would be a useful addition to his anti-aircraft armament of four Lewis guns and a 3-inch high-angle cannon made with zeppelins in mind (a 6-inch piece on the bow was for surface action). One of the first things he did with this extra firepower was allow the crew of a Hotchkiss gun to set up shop on the starboard wing of his navigating bridge, one of the best lookouts on the ship.

In one of the holds, which had its hatch off so that passengers would be reasonably cool once they were under way, there were about 100 Australian and British military nurses who had accompanied 80 stretcher cases aboard. The rest of the Australian nurses were due to

* Their reports on this incident, and the general state of Bennett's infantry in Singapore, probably contributed to the well-documented and ill-judged contempt for the fighting qualities of Australian troops demonstrated by Lieutenant-General Douglas MacArthur when, a couple of months later, he fled the Philippines and set up his HQ in Brisbane. This would change when he saw how well some of the Australians were performing in New Guinea.

leave the next day on the *Vyner Brooke*, the White Rajah of Sarawak's stylish loan to the war effort, aboard which Sister Vivian Bullwinkel had once been wined and dined. Bullwinkel would be among them, along with Mona Wilton, the country girl who had gone to the Sultan's ball. Like Bullwinkel, she was a non-swimmer.

Then there were the civilians. Long after dark, backlit by burning buildings and cowering at stray shots from homesick and muddle-headed Australians, passengers continued to come aboard the *Empire Star*. Some had stepped out of Bentleys and Chevrolets still gleaming from their *syces*' last polish, then seen their cars pushed into the water by police and soldiers who were keeping the quay clear for essential traffic. At the foot of the gang-plank, some hard-pressed military policemen clubbed back angry and often drunken Australian deserters who were trying to hack their way through the crush with rifle butts and boots. A small party of Argylls under Captain Eric Moss, the battalion's splendidly moustached pipe major, had been roped in to reinforce the beleaguered redcaps after escorting some nurses to the ship. At one stage, Moss was convinced that he had ejected all the stowaways at pistol point, but it was a big ship and they were persistent. Nor did all of them use the gangway. At least one party silently came alongside in a small boat and found a way up.

The civilians particularly incensed the deserters. They did not see them for what they were, mainly wives, some accompanied by their children, who had lingered because they hated to be parted from their husbands. (Colonel Stewart's wife Ursula and their baby daughter Cherry Linnhe were on the *Kedah*.) They were just a useless bunch of pampered Poms, some with bulging suitcases, who should have been prised away from their lotus existence weeks before. Some Australians – by no means all of them deserters – were convinced that more of their wounded would have been evacuated if it had not been necessary to find places for these civilians.

Later, Capon tried to find out how many were aboard his ship, and his crew counted 2,161, but he thought the true figure was 'appreciably in excess' of this figure. To save space, it was decided to reduce the civilians' already small luggage allowance. After a while, gangs of Australians started to overwhelm the opposition and get aboard. One was led by an officer, a captain in the Australian Army Service Corps. Pressed against the rail of the upper deck, RAF Corporal John Dodd was watching a tearful young woman clutching a small boy argue with the purser's checkers, who were demanding she left most of her luggage behind. Suddenly, about twenty Australians knocked them aside and surged up the gangway.

Captain Capon had had enough. He knew that more deserters lurked in the shadow of the blazing godowns, waiting for the right moment to rush his ship. He ordered the gangway pulled up, lines cast off and engines started. On the quay the young woman with the small boy was left staring incredulously at the widening gap between herself and the ship. Not far away from her stood the Argylls' Captain Moss, whose sense of duty had not allowed him to accept an invitation from Capon for him and his men to remain on board ('You are surely not going back?'). Now he noticed that, even at this late stage, one Australian had not given up. A sergeant, his chevrons clearly visible, was pulling himself up the remaining hawser that held the drifting *Empire Star* – her engines not yet properly started – to Singapore. 'I called to him to come down but he took no notice, so I drew my revolver and fired. I don't know whether he was hit but he fell off.'

Cazalet's convoy assembled in the dark for their 500-mile trip south to Batavia. When they were about 10 miles out, Glover looked back at Singapore and thought it looked 'as if the whole place was burning'. There had been some consternation aboard *Kedah* when, evidently uncertain whether they were friend or foe, searchlights on Blakang Mati sought them out, illuminating on the decks a multitude of anxious, blinded faces. As it happened, British fears that Yamashita might yet try and outflank them by landing troops on the south coast, or even raid the harbour itself, were groundless.

The Japanese High Command was confident that Singapore could not hold out much longer, and the Imperial Navy was leapfrogging across its waters towards the next item on the imperial shopping list: Sumatra and its southern oil fields around Palambang. Vice-Admiral Jizaburo Ozawa was sailing south and was about to cross the equator with his three cruisers, half-dozen destroyers and single aircraft carrier. They were escorting transports laden with two infantry brigades recently transferred from Hong Kong, which was already well into its second month in the Greater East Asia Co-Prosperity Sphere. Their destination was the Bangka Strait, between Bangka Island and the estuary of Sumatra's Moesi River, about 50 miles downstream from the oil fields of Palambang and two of Wavell's recently established airfields.

This was exactly where Cazalet was heading with his packed ships.

The straits marked the half-way stage on the most direct route to Batavia. To go around Bangka Island would add at least another 50 miles to their journey, and the less time they spent on the water and vulnerable to air attack the better.

The convoy did not leave Singapore as quickly as they would have liked; the thick smoke made it difficult to find a buoy that marked their passage through a minefield, and they had to drop anchor until dawn. For about three hours they steamed steadily south. Then, shortly after 9 a.m., as Cazalet passed through the Durian Islands about 50 miles south-west of Singapore, the first aircraft of the day were spotted. Six twin-engined bombers, Nells or Bettys, chose the *Empire Star* and came in low. Corporal Dodd, who was optimistically engaging one of them with a Thompson gun, dived for cover when he realized that they were close enough for him to make out the markings on the bombs they were about to drop. There were three direct hits on her overcrowded decks, killing fourteen military and crew and seriously wounding forty or so more, who were tended by the nurses. Among the dead were some of the deserters. As the second attack came in, two of the Australian nurses on deck were seen to throw themselves over the wounded they were treating. When it was over, fire parties were tackling several different blazes, a lifeboat had been damaged, there were holes in the deck and hatch covers, and the engineering officers' cabins had been wrecked.

But the Japanese had not emerged unscathed. The RAF gunners on the navigating bridge, more effectively equipped than Corporal Dodd, had sent at least one of them into the sea with a burst from their Hotchkiss; another had staggered off belching black smoke. Perhaps they were put off by these losses or, since the fires on the *Empire Star* were soon extinguished, they did not realize how effective their first strike had been. Whatever the reason, the Japanese aircrews changed their tactics. For the next four hours, relays of bombers, mostly operating in squadrons of nine, untroubled by fighters or any plausible anti-aircraft fire, tried to sink the *Empire Star* and the *Durban*, the biggest targets available, with the kind of formation bombing that had given the crippled *Prince of Wales* her *coup de grâce*.

Over such a prolonged period, the chance that at least one of these ships would be sunk was high. At one point, Capon's lookouts counted almost sixty aircraft. Thanks to the magnificent conning skills demonstrated by both captains, the *Empire Star* and the *Durban* survived – but only just. In his report to the Blue Star line, Capon said that bombs he had dodged with sudden turns to port or starboard had landed only 10 or 20 feet away. Yet the only discernible damage – for he had no way of knowing if plates had been sprung in the hull – was that the already wrecked lifeboat had been blown off its davits. Some of the near misses made his ship seem to jump out of the water. Below decks, the nurses made sure everyone had their lifejackets on and organized sing-songs for the children.

The *Durban* had two gun turrets put out of action, and the triple torpedo tubes were blown overboard. The Argylls contingent did not take to war at sea with their customary *élan*. Ian Stewart and Angus Rose took cover under the wardroom table, where Rose found that a copy of Erskine Childers' *The Riddle of the Sands* he had picked up quite failed to transport him to the North Sea.

The book wasn't really making any sense at all. I had to read the last two pages again – then suddenly, there was God's own crash and a blinding flash. For a moment I thought the wardroom had taken a direct hit and I couldn't quite understand why I was still alive. I sat up and put my hand on a red hot splinter. The wardroom was still there but the ship's side was one mass of ugly gashes and the pungent fumes of cordite permeated the whole room . . . If a fairy godmother had appeared and asked me whether I would like to take a free passage back to Singapore on a magic broomstick, I think I would have accepted the offer.

Among the serious casualties was an RAF officer hit in the chest. He had been acting as a stretcher-bearer with David Wilson, the Argylls' only casualty with a flesh wound from a ricochet that had caught him in the back of the head. 'The ship's doctor slapped a bandage round my head, injected me with some sort of pain killer and sent me back to my job.' On the bridge, Cazalet himself was slightly wounded by a splinter in the hand.

Still unaware that Ozawa was heading towards the Bangka Straits, the convoy seems to have more or less split up. The *Kedah*, the smallest vessel, positively dawdled. Her skipper picked his way around the broken jigsaw of the Riau Archipelago, where a gentle surf was break-ing on beaches of startling beauty, until he found what he was looking for: a well-wooded little bump rising some 300 feet above sea level, where they could drop anchor and hide until nightfall from all but the most intrepid wave-hoppers. *Kedah*'s luck held, as did the luck of every other ship in Cazalet's convoy. Battered and bleeding in two cases, they all passed through the straits only hours before the arrival of the Japanese warships and had reached Batavia by the following evening. By then Cazalet had been on his bridge ever since he had left the same port some seventy-five hours before, cat-napping in an armchair put there for that purpose. 'Curiously enough, I was not as tired as I expected except that I was beginning to get bad attacks of cramp in the legs from standing up so long.'

But before they could rest, while the *Durban* was patched up as best she could be and her wounded taken ashore, Cazalet had one more duty to perform. The *Gorgon* had by-passed Batavia, sailing directly for Fremantle with its hundreds of evacuees, among them Kathleen Stapledon, who was still refusing to talk to the forty-eight deserters aboard. She would arrive there on 19 February, exactly a week after leaving Singapore. What happened to the deserters is unclear. The British were probably sent to India as soon as passage could be arranged and then transferred to units serving on the Burma front. (It is, of course, always possible that one or two of them may have melted into Australia.) Once the *Empire Star* had unloaded her RAF contingent and their equipment, all part of the second line Wavell was trying to build in the Dutch East Indies while Percival bought him time, she was to follow *Gorgon* to Fremantle. But first Capon wanted the Australian deserters removed. Six had been killed in the first bombing strike. This left just over 130 of them aboard – the exact figures vary. Some of them were still armed and trouble was expected.

Tired though he may have been, Cazalet had obviously given the matter some thought. He decided to avoided confrontation by dispatching to the *Empire Star* his first lieutenant and the most motley crew they could devise: thirty seaman volunteers dressed in scarecrow scraps of uniform. The deserters, as Cazalet had hoped, seem to have found them a reassuring sight, imagining perhaps that kindred spirits were merely transferring them to another Australian-bound ship. Somehow, those who still had guns were persuaded it was the most natural thing in the world to ground arms on the deck of the *Empire Star*. Then they allowed themselves to be formed up and marched, after a fashion, off the ship, across the dock and around a corner where the *Durban*'s forty Royal Marines were waiting with fixed bayonets and transport to deliver them to a Dutch jail.

Australia's Labour prime minister John Curtin had already been informed by Vivian Bowden – Canberra's man in Singapore, who was about to take a boat himself – of the deserters on the *Empire Star*. Suspecting that the British were in no mood for half measures, Curtin had promptly sent a cable to Wavell (it arrived in Java a few hours before the *Empire Star*), advising him that the death penalty must not be imposed on Australian soldiers without the approval of his government. Wavell knew what was expected: 'In absence of confirmed evidence from Singapore impossible to sustain charges of desertion,' he replied. In any case, there was so much else to think about.

Cazalet's was the last organized convoy to get through to Batavia; but they were by no means the last ships to try. For some days, Radio Tokyo had been promising 'There will be no Dunkirk for Singapore', and they meant it. There was, of course, little comparison with the 1940 evacuation of Lord Gort's men across the Channel where Britannia indubitably ruled the waves; then, the RAF was at least able to challenge the Luftwaffe's superiority, all the evacuees were servicemen and ultimate safety lay only 40 miles away.

In the wake of the *Empire Star* and HMS *Durban*, there started in the 2,000 square miles of islands south-east of Singapore a maritime massacre of horrific scale which reached its zenith on St Valentine's Day 1942. Total casualties far exceeded the number of those lost on the *Prince of Wales* and the *Repulse*. Among them were Admiral Spooner and Air Vice-Marshal Pulford, who were marooned on a beautiful but pestilential island where their sinking motor-torpedo-boat ran aground. They were among those who succumbed, after several weeks, to a particularly vicious strain of malaria. Another fatality was the popular and energetic Captain Kenneth Atkinson, the 'Captain of Dockyard' at the naval base, who had so yearned for his wife to join him. After leaving the base he became in effect Admiral Spooner's chief of staff and left Singapore at the same time as him, on a slow-moving tug called the *Ying Ping*. They were sunk by a cruiser in the Bangka Straits. Out of the seventy-eight on board, there were thirty-two survivors. One of them, who was with Atkinson on the bridge, remembered his last words as they watched the cruiser: 'This may be our last moment.' And immediately after, 'They've fired.'

It has been estimated that of 5,000 people travelling in some forty-four vessels, of which over forty were sunk, only about 1,250 eventually reached India or Australia. Even more would have died if it had not been for Warren, the Royal Marines colonel seconded to SOE, and his assistant Major Ivan Lyon, the wiry yachtsman from the Gordon Highlanders with the tiger tattooed on his chest. In the weeks before Singapore fell, they had set up a chain of food and water dumps on the islands, usually in the hands of trusted locals, that would enable escapees in small boats to reach the mouth of Sumatra's Indragiri River. From there, they would travel across the island to its Indian Ocean port of Padang where, with any luck, a ship would be waiting.

Inevitably, many of the victims were civilians who were almost invariably mixed in with troops as they had been in Cazalet's convoy. Some were sunk, rescued, then sunk again as they hopped between islands. The Insect-class gun-boat *Grasshopper* spent two hours trying to beat off a very determined air attack, watched with a professional eye by the six captured Japanese aircrew the Royal Marines had escorted on board. When the *Grasshopper* was eventually beached, the behaviour of these prisoners was said to be magnificent: 'All pretence at guarding them was dropped and they went about calmly and efficiently helping the wounded.' The fate of these Japanese is uncertain. At least one account has them being flown from Sumatra to Ceylon by Catalina.

The ships and boats of this fugitive fleet that were not destroyed from the air were shot to pieces in the Bangka Straits, with a couple of honourable exceptions when the Japanese navy accepted surrender and thereby saved the lives of hundreds of women and children. From about noon on the 13th, Ozawa's cruisers and destroyers were, in the memorable words of Lieutenant Geoffrey Brooke, the officer from the *Prince of Wales* who would survive this too, holding its narrowest part 'like a gang of thugs across an alleyway'.

Most of the craft about to get mugged in or around these waters had been, like the more fortunate *Kedah*, 'taken up from trade', as the navy put it, for use as minesweepers and patrol boats. Not a few went down spitting defiance, notably the flat-bottomed, three-decker, coal-burning Yangtse river boat *Li Wo* and its captain Tom Wilkinson, who like his vessel had been requisitioned from the Indo-China Steam Navigation Company and given a commission. Wilkinson announced to the ship's company, apparently to cheers, that rather than try to run from a Japanese convoy he was going to attack and 'take some of the bastards with us'. When he had run out of the little ammunition he had for his 4-inch gun, with an RAF air gunner clearing the enemy's bridge with a Lewis gun, he rammed and set on fire a troop transport before *Li Wo* was sunk by the transport's escorts. Wilkinson went down with his ship.

A few old guns and lots of grey paint had turned these ships into legitimate targets. Survivors bobbing around on rafts and bits of wreckage, such as those from the *Li Wo*, who were machine-gunned in the water, were not. 'All around the rafts and swimmers were dismembered limbs, dead fish and wreckage, drifting with the currents,' wrote Oswald Gilmour, an engineer in the Public Works Department, who was one of the swimmers.

By far the worst atrocity was committed by the Japanese army. For almost two days the *Vyner Brooke* did very well, lying up among the islands during the day and steaming at night. At the entrance of the Bangka Straits her master, Richard Borton, managed to avoid the search-lights of the naval picket there by switching off his engines and drifting through them. Others had not been so lucky, or perhaps not so skilful. The 300 passengers he had managed to get on board, 65 of them the remaining Australian nurses, could not have been in better hands.

Next day, Borton's luck ran out. There was no cover in the straits and he was trying to reach the mouth of Sumatra's Moesi River, which is not very far from their northern end, when the Japanese air force found them. His ship survived the first attack with minor damage and no casualties. A couple of hours later, the Japanese returned and one of the first bombs went straight down the funnel. Another exploded between decks, where many of the passengers had taken cover. The nurses did what they could to comfort the wounded. An old gentleman dying from a hideous stomach wound sang 'Rule Britannia' while a nurse from Queensland patted his hand. Then they abandoned ship.

Mona Wilton went over the side with her friend Wilma Oram who could swim. They were both wearing lifejackets, but this was the last Oram saw of her friend. Wilton was among the twelve nurses of the sixty-five on board who are assumed to have drowned or been killed when Japanese fighters strafed the slowly sinking *Vyner Brooke* along with any survivors bobbing about in their line of fire (cork life-preservers prevented even the strongest swimmers from getting under water). Fifty-three nurses, some baling madly in a shrapnel-riddled lifeboat but the majority on rafts or clinging to an upturned boat and bits of wreckage, were left to be washed by an easterly current onto various Bangka Island beaches.

Bangka had just been occupied by some of the infantry Admiral

Ozawa had escorted south. They had begun to collect the growing number of shipwrecked enemy personnel from the duckshoot their navy and air force were having in the coolie lines that had once accommodated Chinese labourers at Muntok, the island's capital. Within twenty-four hours, thirty-one of the nurses from *Vyner Brooke* found themselves in this temporary internment camp. The remaining 22 were on a remote beach near a village named Radji, along with about 100 civilians and servicemen, not only from the *Vyner Brooke* but from several other sinkings. Among them was the non-swimmer Vivian Bullwinkel. She had been among those clinging to the capsized boat, which had taken seven hours to come ashore.

Many of them, including two of the nurses, were wounded. It was decided that their only option was to give themselves up to the Japanese, and Bill Sedgeman, the *Vyner Brooke*'s first officer, led a party to Muntok to make contact in the hope that they would organize either a boat or stretcher-bearers to take the injured to a hospital. Some women and children capable of walking followed him, reasoning that it would be quicker than waiting for the Japanese to send transport (in the event, a wise decision, for they were all interned). Matron Irene Drummond told the nurses it was their duty to remain where they were, with the wounded.

About 10 a.m. next day, Sedgeman reappeared with a patrol of about thirty Japanese, China veterans from the 229th regiment of the 38th Infantry Division under Captain Masaru Orita. Some of the nurses noticed they were not carrying any stretchers. The men who could walk were separated from the women and taken to a small bay out of sight of the beach, where they were lined up facing the sea. Among them was Ernest Lloyd, a stoker, who had no doubt what was going to happen next when one of them was asked to rip up his shirt to make blindfolds. Lloyd and two others dived into the sea and started swimming. Only the stoker survived the firing squad behind them. One bullet had gone through his left leg and shoulder, another had creased his scalp. Half-submerged, he floated around some rocks and was washed up on a spit of sand where he passed out.

On the beach, Orita stood with his legs apart, his thumbs hooked in his belt. Bullwinkel thought the young officer looked detached, even bored, as if he wanted to be somewhere else. The sound of the shooting was almost muffled by the surf. Then the firing party returned, wiping their fixed bayonets with bits of rag, bunched together and chatting among themselves. Prodded by bayonets, it was now the nurses' turn to be forced into line. Some of them were supporting their two wounded colleagues, Wight and Halligan. An elderly English woman who had refused to be parted from her seriously hurt husband was also made to join them. The Japanese motioned them to start walking towards the sea. No blindfolds were offered. 'Chin up, girls. I'm proud of you and I love you all,' said Matron Drummond in a low voice.

The line was not even. When the shootings started, Drummond, the wounded Wight and Casson, who was supporting her, were hit before they had reached the water. By this time most of the others had waded quite far out. Even Bullwinkel, captain of games at Broken Hill High School in 1932, who was easily the tallest, was almost up to her waist. Nobody tried to dive into the water and swim away, which in her case was out of the question anyway. She was thinking that very soon now she would be seeing her father again.

I was just at the end of the line and the bullet that hit me struck at the waist line and just went straight through ... They all knew what was going to happen to them but no one panicked: they just marched ahead with their chins up.

When it was over, the Japanese bayoneted the dozen or so stretcher cases the nurses had been looking after on the beach and, according to stoker Lloyd, who emerged from hiding to limp by them next morning, appear to have used them on some of the nurses, presumably to finish them off. The stoker also mentions that the women's bodies were in 'various stages of undress', but this may have been caused by bullets, which sometimes do odd things to clothing, or by bayonets or the action of the sea. There was never any suggestion of rape from Bullwinkel, the only nurse to survive – thanks to the tendency of the small Arisaka round to pass straight through people without, if they were lucky, damaging vital organs. It seems that the massacre occurred because Orita did not want to be burdened by the wounded, and the tidiest way to dispose of them was to put them and the witnesses back into the sea. This was the kind of solution the Japanese army would not have thought twice about using in China.

Bullwinkel lived, floating as Lloyd had done, not quite face down, her cheek on the surface, periodically vomiting the salt water she had swallowed and afraid to lift her head far to do this in case the Japanese were still on the beach. The wound in her back was burning but she dared not touch it. The non-swimmer allowed the shallow water to carry her where it would until a slack tide abandoned her on the sand. When she summoned the courage to look up, the enemy had gone. Somehow, she made her way across the beach to the thick undergrowth at its edge and collapsed.

Next morning Bullwinkel awoke with a raging thirst and remembered a nearby stream they had found during their time on the beach. She was kneeling at its bank, hands cupped, when a male voice demanded, 'Where have you been, nurse?' Later, in a moment of exasperation, she would rebuke him for his habit of calling her nurse and instantly regret it: 'I am a sister in the Australian Army Nursing Service, address me as Sister.'

The voice was that of Private Kinsley, who probably belonged to the 18th Division, for he talked of not having been on Singapore very long. Shrapnel had sliced his left upper arm to the bone, which was visible through the flesh. Lying among the wounded on the beach he had somehow survived two bayonet thrusts to the upper and lower midriff – one of which had punctured a lung – and had crawled into the jungle after the Japanese had departed.

The two of them hid in the jungle behind Radji beach for two weeks, fed by women from a nearby kampong, who brought them fish, rice and pineapple wrapped in banana leaves, and ignored their headman's urging that the whites should 'give up to Japan man, get food'. Bullwinkel never seems to have learned Kinsley's first name, but he did tell her he was from Yorkshire where he had a wife called Elsie. Kinsley was curious about her German surname and she told him of her great-grandfather, who came to London from Hanover in the 1840s and ran a pub in Whitechapel. A grandson, her father, had emigrated to Australia.

Bullwinkel's wound healed fast. There was no infection and afterwards she would say that the salt water probably did more to heal it than any amount of being prodded around in hospital. All Kinsley's injuries were infected. Bullwinkel did her best to keep them clean, bathed them and dressed them with coconut fibre. She was touched by the will to live displayed by this soldier so far from home, but she knew too much about the nature of wounds to hold out much hope for him outside a hospital.

It was after hearing from a local man that women with uniforms like her own had been seen in a camp in Muntok that they decided to risk giving themselves up. After a long barefoot trek – the exhausted nurse supporting Kinsley, who could just about walk with the aid of a staff – they reached a metalled road. A Japanese naval officer, lounging in the back of an old open-topped tourer, ordered his driver to stop, picked them up, gave them each a banana and drove them to Muntok. Before long, Kinsley was in a hospital, albeit of the primitive prisoner-of-war kind, and Bullwinkel was breaking the news to the nurses, overjoyed to see her, that twenty-one of the sisters would not be joining them. This became the best-kept secret in the camp, since it was assumed that the Japanese would never allow the only witness of such a despicable deed to live. Sister Bullwinkel last saw Private Kinsley in hospital; he had sent a message that he wished to see her. The drugs that might have saved him were unavailable and he was dying. They whispered their thanks to each other and she held his hand until the end.

In the next bed lay the stoker Ernest Lloyd, also sworn to secrecy over the murder of the nurses. Like Bullwinkel and Kinsley, he had given himself up in the knowledge that he was unlikely to meet the same troops again, and in the hope that what he had seen and experienced was an aberration.

The massacre on Radji beach was carried out in cold blood. The men who committed it had not recently been in action or taken casualties. Neither the Dutch nor the British had any organized ground forces on Bangka to oppose the Japanese landings there. This was not the situation at the Alexandra Hospital in Singapore city on Saturday 14 February, the day the *Vyner Brook* was sunk, when the building suddenly found itself in no man's land and embroiled in the battle.

One of the patients there was Gunner Anckorn. The day before, Wizardus had finally run out of whatever it was that had enabled him to walk away – at least twice – from situations where people feet away from him had been killed. Towing a replacement 25-pounder back from an ordnance yard to his gun position, he was caught up in an air raid, with bombs falling all around him.

I knew I'd been hit but when you've been hit properly you don't know where you've been hit you just know you've been jolly well hit . . . The

Quad was on fire. I went to open the door and found that my right hand was hanging off just by the skin . . . I lay on the seat and I kicked the door open and then I jumped and when I was in mid air I was hit again through the back of the knee into the knee cap and that brought me down.

He was dragged into an anti-aircraft gun position where somebody applied a tourniquet to his wrist. Shortly afterwards he found himself in the Fullerton Building, where one of the city's mushrooming emergency casualty clearing stations had been set up in the ground floor normally occupied by the General Post Office. Army surgeons were operating on its famous 300-foot-long counter. Anckorn remembers one of them leaning over him and saying, 'I'm sorry, son, I can't save your hand. It's got to come off.' 'And I said to him, "Well, OK take it off. Save me." You get your priorities.'

He told the orderly to put me out and the orderly put this gauze pad over my nose and poured ether on it and, as he was doing it, the orderly looked at me and said, 'Aren't you the conjuror we saw in Liverpool?' And I said, 'Yes I am.' And he said, 'You can't take his hand off, sir. This man is a conjuror.' And the last words I heard as I went under was the surgeon saying, 'I'll see what I can do.'

When he woke up he was in a bed which he later discovered was in an overcrowded ward of Alexandra Hospital. He had probably been given quite a lot of morphine because he kept drifting in and out of consciousness, and even when he felt awake he suspected he was dreaming. Shells were apparently landing close by. Sometimes he thought he could feel their blasts. It was night and the orderlies were putting blackout boards on the windows, but as fast as they put them up they were blown out again. In one of his waking moments he asked the man to the right of him, who was not on a bed but on a stretcher on the floor, if he still had a right hand. The man picked up his arm and, for the first time, Anckorn saw there was a stump or lump at the end of it, bandaged up like a boxing glove. Then his neighbour put his hand inside the boxing glove and counted, finger by finger, 'This little piggy went to market', until the last little piggy had gone all the way home and Wizardus knew he had not made his last stage appearance after all. He drifted back to sleep. When he woke again he was obviously dreaming because there were Japanese in the ward, but he noticed that his neighbour seemed to be staring in the same direction.

I said, aren't they Japanese soldiers and he said yes they are. I said what are they doing? He said they're taking people on the front lawn and killing them. I said, 'Oh I see.' Then I went off again. The next time I woke up the Japanese were back in the ward, going from bed to bed with fixed bayonets. As they came up my line of beds, I thought to myself I'm going to be dead in thirty seconds. Now there's not the slightest fear here at all because when there's no hope then you have no fear. It's only when you think you could dive out the window and run you're frightened. You accept it. I said out loud to myself two things: 'I'll never be twenty-four'. The other one was, 'Poor Mum'. They got close to my bed for my turn of bayoneting. I was lying there, I couldn't move anything and I didn't mind being killed as long as there was no pain, but I didn't want to see it happen. So I put my head under the pillow and when I came up for air they'd gone and there were four people left alive in the ward. I have two theories about this: one is that in their hurry and not seeing a head on the pillow they might have thought the bed was empty. The other thing was that I was lying there with my hand on my chest and there was a big hole in the back of it and blood was pouring down on the floor and I think they might have thought that I had already been bayoneted.

It was the worst atrocity of the campaign. Some 320 men and one woman, the Eurasian wife of a Royal Army Medical Corps man, were murdered at the Alexandra Hospital. In all, about 90 RAMC people died, many of them trying to protect some of the 800 patients in the hospital at the time. An orthopaedic surgeon who tried to push aside bayonets miraculously survived with wounds in a hand and a leg after what should have been a fatal thrust was deflected by his cigarette case.

Among the dead was a corporal in the Loyals, impaled on the operating table; a Hurricane pilot; a padre; the 6th Norfolks' commanding officer, recovering from his malaria; and a Japanese prisoner, possibly mistaken for a Gurkha. One recent admission killed was Lieutenant John Brownrigg of Lilly's Sherwood Foresters, who had been considered one of the bravest of the brave by the men of a battalion which, like all the green 18th Division infantry, was desperately trying to find its feet. He was the firstborn by an earlier marriage of Lady Phillips, the widow of Admiral Phillips, who thus lost both a husband and a son in the campaign.

The initial assault on the hospital, which had red crosses on its roof, lawns and hanging out of windows, appears to have been provoked by some Indian troops who briefly used their Brens on the Japanese as they fell back through the hospital grounds where the fountains used to play. A British officer is said to have led some of them to the roof from where they gave covering fire to the troops retreating below them. But if the first wave of General Mutagachi's 18th Infantry Division to enter the Alexandra had blood in their eyes because they had taken casualties from behind the red cross, the next wanted loot.

Lieutenant Walter Salmon, a Leicester from the British Battalion, was trying to read a biography of Clive of India when a lone Japanese entered his ward armed with nothing more than a long-bladed knife 'hanging from a string round his neck'. Salmon watched him pick up an empty boot and hit an officer over the head with it until he surrendered his watch. 'He then walked around the room taking watches, cigarette cases and anything else that took his fancy . . . he came and sat on my bed, staring at me, swinging this knife to and fro. I kept looking at the book. It seemed an eternity before he saw the silver identity disc round my neck, snatched it off and went away.'

Alexandra Hospital had been overrun by Yamashita's latest thrust against Percival's final perimeter. It had come down the south-west coast against the flank held by the 1st Malay Brigade, north-west of Blakang Mati Island. This brigade consisted of two mainly British-officered Malay battalions, the rump of the 2nd Loyals and various other detachments including George Chippington's platoon from the British Battalion. The Malays were all regulars but they were something of an unknown quantity. They had never fought and did not have the same quarrel with the Japanese as the Chinese, so belatedly invited to the fray thanks to Colonel Dalley. And, unlike the Chinese, few of the Malays came from the island itself; most were from villages in the now Japanese-occupied mainland.

For unblooded troops, some of the Malays did surprisingly well. With the support of the 6-inch and 9.2 coastal batteries on Blakang Mati Island firing over their heads, they made the 18th Division's progress over the Kasr Panjang ridge a painful business in places. One company so stubbornly defended a low hill over the Kasr Panjang Road that when they were finally overrun exultant members of the

56th Infantry Regiment found the body of its commander, Lieutenant Abnan bin Saidi, and hung it upside down from a tree.

And, on the eve of the outrages at the Alexandra Hospital, more of the heavy casualties that might have provoked it were inflicted by some of the 1st Malay's D Company and Chippington's platoon. Shortly before dusk, they watched incredulously as 'more Japanese than we had encountered at any one time' advanced, bunched together down a straight road towards their well dug-in position, which the enemy had evidently persuaded themselves was abandoned. Waiting for them on a hill with good fields of fire were seven Brens, a 3-inch mortar, a 2-pounder anti-tank gun and about thirty rifles.

The defenders were probably outnumbered by at least ten to one, but concertina barbed wire both sides of the road made it impossible for the Japanese to take cover. Chippington, who would one day follow his father into holy orders, had agreed with the other officers that they would not fire until the enemy were within 150 yards. Once it was dark and the shooting had stopped, an officer crawled down a storm drain alongside the road to watch the enemy carry away their dead and wounded, and tried to work out how many there might be. According to an English-speaking Japanese lieutenant in conversation with a prisoner sometime later, 500 were killed; but it is not only the enemy's losses that soldiers tend to exaggerate. About 100 dead and 300 wounded sounds more plausible. What is without doubt is that there were no British or Malay casualties, and a lot of Japanese were killed.

A direct result of the sanguinary lessons being administered by the 1st Malay Brigade was one of the most concentrated Japanese barrages of the island battle since the initial landings, despite Yamashita's growing concern about his shortage of artillery ammunition. Their target was the heavy gun support being given the 1st Malay from Blakang Mati. Dozens of shells landed on the north-west tip of the island and succeeded in knocking out both the 6-inch guns, leaving the enemy to concentrate on the 9.2 battery, which had fired so much their barrels were becoming dangerously worn.

Lack of artillery support could easily have been remedied by the Australians to the north of the Malay Brigade and on their right flank, but Bennett was determined to conserve his 25-pounder ammunition and had instructed both his gunners and machine-gunners to give fire support only to those units still under his command. However tempting the target, the plight of their neighbours was to be ignored.

This was one of the first indications of how near Bennett was getting to a unilateral declaration of independence. He had already rallied all the Australian troops still prepared to obey orders into his own all-round defensive position, so that they were dug in not only on their sector of the line but behind and on both flanks as well. Within this inner Australian keep of Percival's crumbling castle, technicians who had never expected to be called on to fire a shot in anger were learning, with varying degrees of enthusiasm, to be infantry. 'Three chaps at least were terrified of the idea of becoming front-line troops,' discovered Staff Sergeant Alec Hodgson, an English immigrant in the Australian engineers who was trying to recall enough of his British Army training circa 1917–18 (he had not seen much action) to transform his workshops section into riflemen.

Meanwhile, hundreds of trained infantrymen were loitering around the docks. At a conservative estimate, the total number of Australians in the process of drifting away from the battle now numbered in the region of 7,000. Of the 22nd Infantry Brigade alone, at least 2,400 – about half – were unaccounted for.

Trying, Canute-like, to turn this tide was Captain A. G. Menz of the Australian Provost Company, whose daily reports to Bennett's HQ told the whole sorry tale.

Soldiers are becoming very sullen and they are so numerous . . . Some AIF very reluctant to return to the line, saying 'There is no organization there' . . . Arms and equipment being discarded all over Singapore. Wharves crowded with soldiers viewing chances of getting off in boats . . . morale shocking. A lot of men hid themselves . . .

Bennett had already sent Army HQ Melbourne a signal indicating that his own surrender might not be far off. 'If enemy enter city behind us will take suitable action to avoid unnecessary sacrifices,' he had cabled. There was not the slightest indication that 8 Australian Division might somehow have contributed to this possibility, and that the number of his men prepared to make any kind of sacrifice was greatly reduced; nor that he had decided that, whatever happened, he would do his utmost to reach Australia ahead of reports of his division's performance in Singapore.

To the north of the Australians, Major-General Beckwith-Smith had at last gathered most of his 18th Division infantry together, the exceptions being the 5th Bedfordshires and Hertfordshires, who were near the west coast attached to the 1st Malay Brigade. But the Cambridgeshires, Norfolks and Suffolks, and Foresters (less a company that had become detached and was somehow fighting in the Australian sector) were learning fast and, as they were mostly unaware of what was going on elsewhere, morale was generally good. 'I think we felt that our division was all that was needed to put things right,' recalled machine-gunner John Webb of the Northumberland Fusiliers. The lieutenant's own platoon found themselves in a position to do a lot of damage. 'To our delight we discovered that we had a real field of fire at last – up to 1,000 yards over a golf course.'

House fighting amidst the tropical tudor splendour of Adam Road, Colonel Carpenter's 1st Cambridgeshires had discovered that the Boys anti-tank rifles worked wonders. Not only did their huge .55 rounds tend to ricochet around buildings like enraged hornets, they also made jagged holes in outer walls through which Thompsons and Brens could be poked and emptied. There was a lot of door-kicking, close-quarters fighting here: small rooms and garden corners cleared with Thompsons and grenades, the little 2-inch mortars fired almost horizontally through windows. Japanese snipers took their toll. One crawled up a storm drain and picked off a captain in the Northumberland Fusiliers. Carpenter encouraged counter-snipers, who laid out their bag like exotic birds so that everyone could admire the enemy's clever camouflage – though in these cases, not quite clever enough.

Like all these Territorial Army battalions, the Cambridgeshires benefited from a cadre of regular sergeant-majors and sergeants. Some of them were very tough customers indeed. Sergeant Stanley 'Pony' Moore, one of the 2-inch mortar artists, crawled back from a night patrol, still clutching his Thompson, with three bullets and grenade shrapnel in his chest that had made a hole which measured 4 by 9 inches. He was given tea laced with brandy and enough morphine to allow him to die in peace. Then, as he was about to be planted in a suburban garden, Moore suddenly exhibited enough signs of life to find himself in Alexandra Hospital in time for the massacre. Delirious, he had no idea how he survived it. His only clear memory is of reaching into a torn shirt pocket to extract a photograph and finding that his wife's face had been obliterated by one of the bullets in his chest. He burst into tears but, against all odds, he lived to see her again.

The 1st Cambridgeshires, who would turn out to be Beckwith-Smith's star turn, had undoubtedly benefited from the confidence built by some small successes as they fell back on the Adam Road position. The most notable of these came after a tip-off from some of Colonel Dalley's Chinese scouts. A large party of Japanese had been observed encamped on the north-western shore of the Peirce reservoir where they were lighting campfires, starting the day with a swim and callisthenics, and generally exhibiting an unhealthy contempt for the opposition. The Cambridgeshires brought up a dozen or so Brens and some 2-inch mortars. As soon as the happy campers were up and splashing about, they began their slaughter with impunity from the opposite bank at a range of about 400 yards. One of the ambushers, Private Jesse Adams, reported 'much confusion' as those in the water tried to get out and those out in.

But by no means all their victims were Japanese. There appears to have been a large number of Indians among them. The most likely explanation is that these were some of the teenaged Punjabis who had bolted under the mortar fire at nearby Nee Soon, who should never have been anywhere near a front line in the first place. They were now being treated according to the special dispensation encouraged by Major Fujiwara Iwaichi and his acolyte Captain Mohan Singh, late of the 1/14th Punjabis, who had gone over to the Indian Independence League at Jitra. It must have come as a terrible shock to discover that the Japanese side of the line could be just as dangerous.

Now, Fujiwara was about to bring off his greatest *coup* of the campaign. In Heath's eastern sector of the perimeter, his agents succeeded in suborning almost an entire battalion. The 2/10th Baluch, the unit John Webb had admired at Nee Soon, was one of the few to have survived the peninsular fighting sufficiently intact not to require amalgamating with another battalion. In the process they had lost many of their best men and, as usual, these had been replaced by the rawest of recruits. Then came a self-inflicted wound. Their popular commanding officer, Lieutenant-Colonel James Frith, was included in the official Indian Army evacuation list of men being sent back to raise fresh battalions. Although Frith was still awaiting a place on a ship out (he would never get one), his replacement, an officer of considerable experience but from another regiment, had already taken over.

Fujiwara had several teams of Indians who had gone over to Mohan Singh's Indian National Army in Malaya operating for him on the island. According to the Japanese intelligence officer, the man chiefly responsible for the defection of the 2/10th was one Captain Allah Ditta, who got close enough to them to start shouting invitations. 'They stopped shooting and listened to his speech in silence . . . and replied with a cheer. At that moment the resistance of the Indian regiment crumbled and its soldiers discarded their arms and joined the INA.'

Subsequent events put this kind of Damascene conversion in some doubt. Two of the battalion's Indian company commanders would eventually desert to the INA. One had only recently joined them and had already been reprimanded by the new CO for allowing a Bren gun position to be overrun when it should have done 'great execution'. The other was Prem Sahgal who, despite his nationalism and the wounding slights he and other Indian officers had endured from Malaya's European clubland, had fought throughout the campaign with enough distinction to be nominated by Colonel Frith for inclusion with him in the official evacuation party.

The catalyst for Sahgal's conversion to the INA was Lakshmi Swaminadhan, the radical young doctor who would become the commander of the INA's Rani of Jhansi women's regiment (named after the Indian heroine of the 1857 uprising) and eventually his wife. But at the time of the 2/10th's defection, although she was living not far away from the battalion's last position at Paya Lebar, about half a mile north-east of Woodleigh pumping station, they had not yet met, nor had Lakshmi yet heard of anything as exciting as the Indian National Army.

It seems that the recruits of the 2/10th, frightened and aware of the growing disintegration of Percival's command, were ripe for desertion. Many years later, when membership of the INA had received some belated recognition in India and it would have done Sahgal no harm to have claimed to have plotted the whole thing, he gave his own account of the end of the 2/10th and his capture:

Nothing was happening . . . an orderly came up and said, 'Leigh sahib sends you his salaam.' Now Bertie Leigh was commanding the company in front of me. I thought he wanted something. So I picked up my equipment, didn't even put it on properly, and walked along the ditch to where his company was. Suddenly I saw half a dozen Japanese. The battalion was half young recruits, you know, and before they knew what was happening the Japanese had crept in. Leigh had tried to warn me but I had got the message wrong. Here I was, about to be evacuated, and I had walked into this!

Shortly afterwards the Japanese had tied up and decapitated with a samurai sword the Australian-born lieutenant who was Sahgal's second-in-command, so it was with some relief that he realized the Japanese took a more generous view of Indian officers, especially admirers of Gandhi. He was taken to see a colonel who was seated behind a small table eating an omelette with a bottle of cognac on the table. The colonel invited him to take a drink. 'I picked up a glass and poured one that big, and drank it. And then, for the first time, it struck me what had happened. Until that moment I had been paralysed.'

The alcohol level in the shrinking, stinking, dangerous and increasingly foul enclave that was British Singapore was falling, although the city was far from dry. Orders had gone out on Friday the 13th to destroy all existing stocks as it was widely believed that the availability of hard liquor had been a significant contribution to the Rape of Nanking. This was not easy. Singapore was the main distribution centre for spirits and wines for the entire Far East, including Japan. Police Inspector Harvey Ryves, formerly based in Perak, started his bottle-breaking duties at Café Cyrano in the Orchard Road and then went on to a bonded warehouse in Hare Street.

The task was hopeless because the godown contained thousands of bottles . . . the fumes alone produced light-headedness. One inspector put his drunkenness down to them but privately I thought he was stretching poetic licence . . . a Tamil was so hopelessly intoxicated that he lay flat on his back on the road outside the warehouse . . . one merely had to lie with one's head in the drain and drink . . . Guy [a police colleague] rolled up in the afternoon and the connoisseur was so scandalized that he rescued two high-grade bottles of champagne . . . I was satisfied with a humble, but none the less excellent, case of sparkling lager.

Water was in short supply, not because the pumping station at Woodleigh had failed but because the shells and bombs falling throughout the city had severed too many pipes which, in a country without frost, were all near the surface. Thousands of gallons were going to waste, often under the rubble of wrecked buildings. At the General Hospital a 10-foot-deep pit had been dug in its main lawn, about 150 feet long and 15 feet across. It was to be left to fill with rain water as an emergency supply but, as casualties increased, it had been decided to use it as a mass grave. Among the volunteers helping to fill it was William Churchill, Deputy Commissioner for Civil Defence, who felt that his job had 'petered out' into meaningless paper work. He discovered that, even in death, certain distinctions were maintained:

European bodies, mostly soldiers, were laid at one end and Asiatics at the other. After endless carrying of heavy stretchers, it was necessary to get down inside this pit and stack the dead standing on end and, for health reasons, carefully cover each corpse with earth. Shells bursting nearby in no way heartened one for this task: the idea of being blown up among those packed corpses.

Although all the military nurses had been evacuated, often under protest, there were plenty of civilian nurses at the General Hospital. Many of them were the wives of colonial civil servants and policemen who had refused to evacuate because their husbands had been ordered to stay on. Some of the 'deserters' in this category would argue that they had gone because they were determined to get their wives out and this was the only way they could do it.

On Sunday 15 February, the *Straits Times*, now reduced to a single sheet, had as its splash: 'STRONG JAP PRESSURE – Defence Stubbornly Maintained'. Next to it was the announcement that Colonel Anderson of the Australian Imperial Forces, the hero of Parit Sulong, had been awarded the Victoria Cross. There was also a brief paragraph urging people to conserve water.

The newspaper still carried under its title the slogan: 'Singapore Must Stand; It SHALL Stand – H. E. Governor'. But Sir Shenton Thomas and his sick wife had been obliged to make one small compromise and move into the Singapore Club in the Fullerton Building after shells had hit his Government House, killing twelve staff and Gurkha guards who were sheltering under the back veranda. Thomas himself had crawled under the wreckage to see if he could do anything to help, only to discover they had all been killed by the blast.

That Sunday the governor did not go to St Andrew's. For several days now the Australians had been using the cathedral as a hospital for military and civilians alike, and all its pews had been removed to the Padang to make room for stretchers. A brief service had been held there that morning by the Reverend Jack Bennitt, the young missionary priest who had felt so guilty about leaving wartime Britain for the easy life in Singapore. Bennitt had got his wife and daughter out, but refused to be evacuated himself.

Percival, up at 6.30, had attended a Communion Service conducted by an army padre in the Fort Canning bunker. He had already read his telegrams. The most important one came from Wavell and it gave him permission to surrender. 'Time gained and damage to the enemy are of vital importance . . . When you are fully satisfied that this is no longer possible I give you discretion to cease resistance . . . Inform me of your intentions. Whatever happens I thank you and all your troops for your gallant efforts of last few days.'

A commanders' conference was called for 9.30 a.m. The only one who could not make it was Beckwith-Smith, who reported heavy enemy infiltration of his 17,000-yard front the night before. The 4th Suffolks and the Foresters had been pushed back by a tank attack. Carpenter's Cambridgeshires had clung on to their positions but were left in a thumb-shaped salient. The Commander Royal Artillery announced that the Bofors guns, which had been enjoying some success against low-flying aircraft, would run out of ammunition that afternoon, as would supplies of 25-pounder artillery shells. Chief Engineer Brigadier Simson revealed that there was a good chance that most of Singapore city would run out of water by the next day. Bennett and Heath, who still had his pregnant wife with him, had both been urging surrender for several days and apparently saw no reason to change their minds.

The decision to comply with the surrender terms Yamashita had offered four days before was taken unanimously, but when some of the finer points were being discussed Bennett suddenly suggested, 'How about a combined attack to recapture Bukit Timah?' Major Cyril Wild, a former executive on the Rising Sun Petroleum Company (a subsidiary of Shell), who was on Heath's staff and was one of the few British Japanese-speakers left on the island, noted that this was greeted with silence. 'I formed the impression at the time that it was made not as a serious contribution but as something to quote afterwards.'

At 11.30 a.m., Wild was acting as interpreter when he accompanied Brigadier Terence Newbigging, Percival's senior administrative officer, and Hugh Fraser, the Straits Settlements Colonial Secretary, as they crossed the lines carrying white and Union flags. Both ways, their most dangerous moments occurred on the British side. Going, an angry captain in the 5th Suffolks who, like many of the 18th Division, thought they had a lot more fight left in them, shoved a revolver in Newbigging's chest and demanded to see his identity card. Coming back, Wild reported 'an inaccurate burst of pistol fire, delivered at somewhat unsporting range, from a Provost Corporal'.

A Japanese flag flown for ten minutes from the Cathay Building indicated that Percival had agreed to the terms and would meet Yamashita at the Ford factory. They met there at 4.30 p.m. and the negotiations were predictably one-sided. Percival wanted a ceasefire at 10 p.m. but settled for 8.30. However, Yamashita did agree that for the next twenty-four hours, 1,000 British troops could retain their arms to keep law and order, and he allowed only a small number of his men to enter Singapore the next day.

Among those who used this interlude to escape by small boat to Sumatra, and thence to India or Australia, was Gordon Bennett who, shedding various travelling companions with all the facility of a multi-stage rocket, reached Australia in twelve days. He was the only senior commander to leave his men at the moment of surrender and, although an official inquiry cleared him of any wrongdoing, he never held a field command again. He retired from the army in 1944.

Yamashita took Malaya and Singapore for 3,506 killed and 6,150 wounded. Percival's casualties are estimated at 7,500 killed and 10,000 wounded. About 120,000 prisoners were taken. In his week-long campaign on Singapore Island itself, Yamashita lost almost as many men as he did on the peninsula: 1,713 killed and 2,772 wounded. This works out at 640 casualties a day, which by the end of the twentieth century any western power, let alone Japan which hardly has an army at all, would consider exorbitant.

Afterwards, Yamashita liked to boast that his victory was based on a bluff because he was outnumbered and running out of artillery shells. On paper he did have half the men, but his three first-class homogene-ous divisions backed by total air and naval superiority cannot be compared to Percival's heterogeneous, ramshackle command. In the end, there was not much more than the 18th Division and a few attachments left. If the British had continued to resist, the worst that could have happened to Yamashita was that there would have been a humiliating wait for reinforcements. There was no way Percival was ever going to push him back off the island.

Understandably, the Japanese were very pleased with themselves. The day after the surrender, Major-General Imai, chief of staff of Nishimura's Imperial Guards Division, met the Indian Army's Major-General Billy Key, who had played some very bad hands with great skill. Imai unrolled a large map of South-east Asia and they spoke in French. Also present was Colonel Harrison, Key's chief of staff who later made some notes.

'We Japanese have captured Malaya and Singapore,' declared Imai pointing at the map. 'Soon we will have Sumatra, Java and the Philippines. We do not want Australia. I think it is time for your British Empire to compromise. What else can you British do?'

'What else can we do?' demanded Key, and Harrison watched with some foreboding as his general cupped his big hands around all the places Imai had mentioned. 'We can drive you back. We will eventually occupy your country. This is what we can do.'

General Imai, as well he might, looked dubious.

# Epilogue

On 5 September 1945 HMS *Kedah*, the old faithful borrowed from the Straits Steamship company, was allowed – in one of those sentimental gestures rather dear to the Royal Navy – to lead the Fleet back into Singapore after an absence of three and a half years.★ A week later, Admiral Lord Louis Mountbatten, Britain's Far East supremo, took the formal surrender of Japan's South East Asia Command at Singapore's City Hall to which the Japanese generals – lean after months of Allied blockade – were marched, swordless and forlorn.

General Key's defiant prophecy had come to pass, though hardly in the way he might have expected during his conversation with General Imai, who was now on his way to a Siberian prison camp from which he would not return. On 6 August the first atomic bomb had been dropped on Hiroshima, recruiting ground for Yamashita's 5th Division; three days later the second fell on the ship-building town of Nagasaki, where much of the 18th Division had been enlisted. It took another six days for all the factions of the army to accept Emperor Hirohito's decision to surrender. Even then, the announcement came only after diehards had failed in their attempt to find and destroy the recording the Living God had made for his radio debut which, at noon on 15 August, was transmitted to an incredulous nation.

It was through radio, passed on by word of mouth from the few who risked their lives to run clandestine sets, that the remnants of Percival's defeated army first heard the news of their deliverance from an outrageous captivity which, far more than battle, had decimated their ranks. Worked and starved into emaciated wrecks, 12,000 alone had died while building 260 miles of railway from Thailand to Burma through jungle-covered mountains with river views that would

★ The long war had devoured the two stars of Cazalet's convoy. Seven months after the fall of Singapore the *Empire Star* was lost in the North Atlantic, torpedoed by a U-boat. Most of her crew were saved but the indomitable Capon, who had been awarded a CBE for his handling of the ship under Japanese bombing, got into the one boat that was never seen again. HMS *Durban* ended her days as one of the floating foundations for the artificial Mulberry harbour off the Normandy beach-heads.

become a later generation's picture postcards. The area had one of the unhealthiest climates in the world and was the kind of white man's grave that had killed off most of Raffles' children. Cholera, malaria, beriberi, blackwater fever, diphtheria, and tropical ulcers that rotted flesh to the bone were never far away. Among the dead was Kathleen Stapledon's 'Steepy' who was one of many so weakened by disease and malnutrition that they died in the first days of liberation.

And yet, in the main, it had all started gently enough. While hundreds of Chinese were massacred with captured Bren guns on the island's beaches, it looked as if the Japanese were disposed to be magnanimous in victory as far as the British were concerned. During the first forty-eight hours after the surrender, British and Japanese troops, often equally exhausted, stood each other looted drinks and cigarettes, and even posed arm in arm for photographs. It seems unlikely that this would have happened had their circumstances been reversed. 'Little men from Mars, a week's stubble on their faces, sunburned and dirty, creatures from Hell with their funny boots with two separate toe pieces,' thought the machine-gunner Lieutenant Webb, who had certainly not posed for a photograph.

Then, for a while, these Martians became almost invisible. The Australian and British prisoners were ordered to concentrate at the Changi cantonment on the east coast: 6 square miles of airy three-storey barracks buildings and married quarters bungalows near the new jail, with sea on three sides. The main drawback was that it was intended for, at most, 5,000 men and there were somewhere in the region of 50,000.★

It was some 16 miles from the city centre. Some of the Argylls went at least part of the way by truck, with a piper playing. Most of the captives walked with what they could carry, sometimes singing 'Tipperary' and other 1914–18 marching songs, or this war's more plaintive, 'There'll always be an England'. Some Indian and Malay civilians jeered at them. The Chinese watched, stony faced. Among the latter was Lee Kuan Yew, an eighteen-year-old student at Raffles College. 'I saw them tramping along the road in front of my house for three solid days,' said Singapore's president in a speech he gave in Australia in the 1970s, 'an endless stream of bewildered men who did not know what had happened, why it had happened or what they were doing here in Singapore in any case.'

---

★ There has been argument over the precise figures ever since. There were at least 15,000 Australians.

At Changi, the Japanese gave them some barbed wire and allowed them to immure themselves with double-apron barbed-wire fences between the lines allotted to each division. Their immediate guards were not Japanese but Sikhs armed with Lee-Enfields, who appear to have been the forerunner of the Indian National Army, although it was unclear at this stage how many were Indian Army turncoats and how many had been locally recruited, sometimes from the police.

For a short while these guards, who, until the Japanese put a stop to it, sometimes beat up prisoners with their rifle butts if they failed to salute them, were the only blot on what would come to be considered Changi POW camp's golden age. Some of the prisoners started calling it Changi University. It was decided that the best answer to boredom was education. For those who simply wanted to catch up, there were classes in English, arithmetic and geography. More advanced students could learn most European languages plus Malay. There were lectures in engineering, law and medicine – though the latter tended to be confined to people whose studies had been interrupted by the war.

Some sports equipment was discovered intact and the high point in the first few weeks was a series of three 'test matches' between England and Australia. The Australians were captained by the Test wicket-keeper Ben Barnett, but the series was won by England, mainly thanks to three centuries scored by the county player Geoff Edrich, who was a sergeant in the Norfolks. When a Sikh guard refused to return one of Edrich's sixes outraged spectators rendered him unconscious.

The Japanese do not appear to have taken much interest in the Changi Ashes. In any case, baseball not cricket was their game and they played it with POWs held at Pudu jail in Kuala Lumpur, among them the Australian gunner Russell Braddon, who was cut off at Bakri. As well as this fraternization, there occurred the execution of recaptured escapees and the kind of brutal beatings where eyes as well as teeth were removed. About 1,200 Australian and British prisoners, along with a few Dutch and New Zealand airmen, would shortly be transferred to overcrowded Changi from various holding centres on the mainland. The 10,000 or so Indian prisoners taken in the north were kept separately, as they were in Singapore, the easier to be pressed by INA recruiters.

As food ran short and energy levels began to dip, sport was phased out. So was foot drill, part of initial attempts to maintain military discipline in a community where, over the next three and a half years, by far the most powerful force was a camaraderie which knitted a kind of enduring philanthropic safety net. It was not impenetrable: King Rats did exist and no doubt some men died because others stole – but, on the whole, this net was always there. As the Japanese shunted their human booty around their prisoner-of-war gulag, from the copper mines of Formosa to the shipyards of Nagasaki, men went out of their way to look after each other. The Aussies called it mateship.

The only recorded case of murder in Percival's army is a Conradian tale of cannibalism and screams in the night in a grossly overcrowded lifeboat as men maddened by drinking sea water began cutting throats, drinking blood and throwing each other overboard. On board the Dutch ship *Rooseboom* when she was torpedoed two days' sailing time from Colombo were 500 British escapees, civilian and military, who had somehow travelled down the fugitive trail set up by Warren and Lyon to the Sumatran port of Padang. Among them were the dapper Brigadier Archie Paris and two of the Argylls chiefly responsible for stopping the tank attack down the Bukit Timah road: Paris's brigade major, Angus MacDonald, and Captain Mike Blackwood who had held up the tank column with a Boys rifle.

After the torpedo struck, 135 people found themselves either in or clinging to the lifeboat, which was intended for 30. By the time it came ashore on an island off Sumatra, twenty-eight days and 1,000 miles later, four were left: two Javanese seamen, Doris Lim, a young English-speaking Chinese woman from Shanghai who had been working as an assistant to a newsreel cameraman, and Sergeant Walter Gibson of the Argylls, a tough little regular, who was not quite 5 foot 5. The first hints of the story emerged in 1949 when Gibson gave evidence in an Edinburgh court that Major Angus MacDonald was dead, so that his estate could be settled. In 1952 Gibson published a short account of his ordeal, *The Boat*, and the way the dozen or so who had remained more or less sane rid themselves of the five soldiers – led by a Liverpudlian – he called the 'murder gang'.

Then we were at their throats. We struggled and stumbled and rolled wrestling at the bottom of the boat. We did not seem to put them overboard one by one so much as to rush them overboard in a body. Three, as they came to the surface, got their hands to the gunwale and tried to drag themselves back. It was a confusion of pleadings and curses and choking half-smothered obscenities. Relentlessly, we battered at their fingers with rowlocks. We were down to the elemental now. It was, we told ourselves a dozen times that night, either them or us.

Two weeks after the surrender, the British and Australians in Changi POW camp had run out of supplies of canned food. Japanese rations mainly consisted of rice, which that generation of army cooks took some time to learn to cook, and fish that Japanese quartermasters had rejected as unfit for their troops. 'To gaze on a sack of rotting shrimps moving slowly under the impulse of a million maggots was a poor prelude to meals,' observed an Australian sergeant. Changi outdoors soon became one great kitchen garden. Almost every open space was under cultivation, often supervised by students from the university's agricultural department. Poultry were kept, and a lot of the eggs went to the hospital.

For all its overcrowding and the outbreaks of dysentery that were beginning to worry the medical officers, for one man this honeymoon period was almost literally that. While all the other civilian internees, who numbered about 2,500 – of whom 400 were women and children – were being held in Changi jail, General Sir Lewis Heath had managed to smuggle his pregnant wife into his bungalow quarters. She remained there undetected until June, when she had a miscarriage and, after hospital treatment, was sent to the women's section of the civilian internment camp set up in the jail. Here she found Lady Thomas, recovered from the dysentery which had beset her during her last days at Government House but separated from her husband, who was held with all the other men in a separate wing.

The governor had felt that it was his duty to stay, and that by not running away he would help redeem British prestige. In this he was right. Sixty years later, in the heart of Singapore's thriving financial centre, there is a Shenton Way. But it availed him and Heath nothing to keep their wives on the island. For the Heaths it was particularly tragic because, after Lady Heath's miscarriage, British army doctors found she had aplastic anaemia and required repeated blood transfusions. 'We would ask that, if it is at all possible, endeavour should be made to move her to a temperate climate.'

There would be no early repatriation for Lady Heath. In the initial stages of the Far East war the exchange of some civilians, mainly diplomats, had occurred. As a result Canberra's external affairs department had assured Vivian Bowden, their representative in Singapore, that the Japanese would respect his diplomatic status and release him.

Instead, this led to his death. Having been persuaded to remain on the island long after it was prudent to do so, Bowden was captured aboard one of the few vessels of the fugitives' flotilla that the Japanese had the grace not to sink on sight. It was escorted to Muntok, the capital of Bangka Island, where the Australian nurses were massacred. The white-haired Bowden had first met the Japanese army in the late 1930s when he was Australia's trade commissioner in Shanghai and thought he knew how to handle them. Taken ashore with the other passengers, he lost no time trying to convince a pair of low-ranking guards of his identity. They responded by attempting to steal his watch. A scuffle ensued and Bowden was dragged off and shot.

Unlike his wife, Heath – like Percival and Shenton Thomas – ended up in a place that at least had some temperate moments. In August 1942, all senior officers of the rank of full colonel or above were shipped out of Singapore, 400 of them packed in what Percival would describe as 'the hold of a very small and dirty cargo ship'. This rust-bucket took them to Formosa, where they remained for two years. But they did not finish their war there. After a journey which took them through Japan and Korea, in October 1944 they arrived in the sub-zero temperatures and deep snows of Manchuria. It was here, in balmier weather, on 18 August 1945, that they were liberated by the Russians who, ten days before, had at long last entered the war against Japan.

Percival and Heath never had the easiest of relationships. Adversity seems to have brought the two closer together. Three and a half years with jailers as capricious as the Imperial Japanese Army must have bonded them just as it did their men. While they remained in Singapore, the Japanese – who liked to point out that they had never ratified the Geneva Convention requiring POWs to divulge no more than their name, rank and number – had tried to strong-arm both generals into revealing secrets. Percival spent two weeks in solitary in a cell in Changi jail before his captors relented. Heath wrote his interrogators a polite but dignified letter explaining why he was willing to talk about things that were in the public domain but not about others, such as India's fixed defences, that were not. It ended: 'If I have to pay the extreme penalty for my refusal to divulge official secrets, I shall have the satisfaction of terminating with honour my participation in a campaign which has been so disastrous to our arms.' The samurai were unimpressed and, despite or because of his withered arm, beat Heath up. This was probably mild by Japanese standards, but it was hardly the 'trade union of generals' to which a furious British Labour minister would refer when, after Alamein, Montgomery gave General Ritter von Thoma dinner and sent him on a guided tour of the pyramids.

Then, out of the blue, about two months after this unpleasantness, there arrived at Percival's quarters some sweating Japanese orderlies bearing 150 bottles of beer, and thirty tins each of butter and cheese, accompanied by a note from Yamashita: 'As a small token of my personal interest in your welfare and a practical contribution to your own comfort . . .'

Yamashita had been lionized by the Japanese press, who called him the 'Tiger of Malaya'. This made Tojo even more determined to deny him the imperial audience he craved. Instead, the prime minister found a diversionary role for the Tiger that was both useful and almost guaranteed to deny him the chance of expanding his reputation. He was ordered, as a matter of urgency and without stopping over in Tokyo, to proceed directly to Manchuria and take command of the army that had been given such a drubbing by Zhukov in 1939. Germany and Italy were constantly urging their Axis partner to declare war on the Soviet Union and draw off some of the troops between them and Moscow. This was the next best thing. The sudden arrival of Japan's star general on their borders was bound to worry Moscow. But for the foreseeable future Tojo had no intention of going to war with Stalin. In a world at war, Manchuria was a military backwater and the man he considered his arch-rival would not prosper there. However, Percival did meet Yamashita again.

In September 1944, following Tojo's political demise, the Tiger was sent to the Philippines. An American offensive appeared imminent and the incumbent commander was suspected of being too fond of girls and golf to prepare for it. Shortly afterwards, MacArthur, as promised, returned in overwhelming force. In the process they repatriated Captain James Gilbert and five of his gunners from Yorkshire's 122 Field Regiment; they had been rescued by Filipino guerrillas after US dive bombers sunk a crammed ship, drowning most of several hundred Singapore prisoners being taken to Japan. Manila was almost destroyed as its kamikaze naval garrison threw a wild and terrible wake for themselves in an orgy of rape and murder, while the American artillery reduced their cover brick by brick. One thousand Americans died; about 16,000 Japanese. Quite separately from all this, Yamashita and his starving, fever-ridden soldiers had fought a brave and skilful rearguard action until they were cornered in the pine-covered highlands of northern Luzon, where they showed the white flag on 2 September 1945.

The next day, there was a surrender ceremony at Baguio, the hill station and summer capital, attended by Percival and the US General Jonathan Wainwright, who had been captured in the Philippines in 1942. MacArthur had invited them to fly in with him from Japan where, the previous day, they had all been aboard the USS *Missouri* to witness his formal acceptance of Japan's capitulation. 'As Yamashita entered the room I saw one eyebrow lifted and a look of surprise cross his face – but only for a moment . . . he showed no further interest. He was much thinner and worn-looking and his clothes bore testimony to the rough conditions in which he had been living.'

Five months later, the Tiger of Malaya was wearing GI fatigues when he stepped onto the gallows at a small local prison outside Manila to be hanged as a war criminal. On MacArthur's orders he had been stripped of his tired uniform with its shabby rows of medal ribbons for being 'a blot upon the military profession and a stain upon civilization'.

As senior commander in the Philippines, Yamashita had been condemned for the sailors' sack of Manila, although they had not been directly under his command and he had ordered a withdrawal from the capital. From the start, the general's three American lawyers, all civilians in uniform, had been convinced of his innocence and, however much MacArthur wanted a kangaroo court, Yamashita's defence was far from token. His appeal went to the US Supreme Court in Washington where one of the two dissenting judges, a former Governor-General of the Philippines, called the process a 'judicial lynching', but a final plea for clemency was swiftly rejected by President Truman. A few hours before his execution, Yamashita ate some bread and asparagus washed down with beer and then went to sleep, snoring loudly until the hangman and a weeping Shinto priest arrived. A last poem was found:

> The world I knew is now a shameful place
> There will never come a better time
> For me to die.

It has been alleged that Yamashita's ignominious end was victor's justice, brought on by MacArthur's rage at being led on such a dance by Yamashita's inferior forces. But even if the appeals had been successful, Yamashita would almost certainly have had to answer to the British for the killing of 'anti-Japanese elements' among Singapore's Chinese. The victims were mostly but not exclusively male and members of the volunteer forces, including the civil defence, the Communist Party or organizations which collected funds for the struggle in mainland China. No one is certain how many died in the two weeks of killings, which started three days after the surrender. Cyril Wild, the tall Japanese-speaking officer who had interpreted for Percival at the surrender negotiations at the Ford factory, and who would shortly become the senior British war crimes investigator with the rank of full colonel, thought it was 'considerably in excess of 5,000'. In the 1980s, building workers in Singapore were still unearthing their bones. Some Singaporean Chinese insist that the true death toll in what became known as the *sook ching* pogrom was more like 50,000.

Whatever the numbers, there were plenty of reliable witnesses to the horror of it all. Some marooned British coastal gunners the Japanese had yet to round up from an islet off Blakang Mati had a grandstand view of a machine-gunner on a Keppel harbour tug firing long bursts at the bobbing heads of bound targets who had just been pushed overboard. At Changi, British prisoners burying Chinese killed on the main beach near their camp managed to rescue a few wounded who had played dead, and to hide them in their hospital until they were strong enough to be smuggled out.

Yamashita persuaded Wild, who interrogated him while he was awaiting trial in the Philippines, that he had no knowledge of these massacres. But here he appears to have been on shakier ground than in his denial of the Manila atrocities. There was no doubt that, immediately after the surrender, Yamashita had been concerned to nip any incipient anarchy in the bud. Looting had begun to subside after severed heads on long bamboo poles began to make their appearance. Four, two of them rumoured to be Japanese, had been placed on Raffles bridge. ('A most effective measure,' noted the Indian nationalist Dr Lakshmi Swaminadhan who, after years of British oppression, was beginning to warm to the new order.)

But, for the Japanese, much more worrying than the looting were their fears that an urban resistance movement could rise from the ashes of a Singapore rich with discarded small arms. Yamashita gave the job of dealing with all those unlikely to appreciate the benefits of Japanese rule to his zealous – not to say fanatical – chief planning officer, Colonel Masanobu Tsuji, who worked with a will. Meanwhile, the Tiger mulled over his plans to have a memorial built by prisoners for the fallen from both sides near Bukit Timah.

By September 1945 Tsuji had vanished. The last sighting the British had of him was the morning after Emperor Hirohito's iconoclastic broadcast, when he had been spotted leaving army headquarters in Bangkok dressed in the saffron robes of a Buddhist monk. He found sanctuary in Nanking, scene of the greatest war crime Japanese troops had ever committed, but Chiang Kai-shek's Chinese Nationalists were pragmatists and they knew they needed a lot of help if they were ever going to beat Mao Tse-tung. Four years later, Tsuji was back in Japan. The Korean war had started and by 1950 the Americans were sufficiently impressed by Tsuji's anti-communist credentials to drop all war crimes charges against him, including a gruesome beheading in Burma of a captured US pilot followed by a symbolic act of canni- balism. Not long afterwards, the British did the same. Yet by then they not only had the *sook ching* massacres against him, he was also suspected of inciting the Alexandra Hospital atrocity – not, as was originally thought, because Indian troops had fired at the Japanese from its grounds, but because of casualties incurred from British artillery.

At home, Tsuji became a celebrity, an outspoken link with the past. He wrote a series of highly successful memoirs, including his account of the Malayan campaign which was first published in English in Australia in 1960 with an introduction by Gordon Bennett. 'Like many soldiers in all countries he seems subject to strong religious influences,' wrote Bennett of the man who liked to boast that he ate the roasted livers of his enemies to give him strength.

Tsuji was elected to the Diet, first as an independent and then as a founder member of the new right-wing Democratic Party, later the Liberal-Democrats. As his political career took off he began to move away from his American benefactors. Tsuji's main platform was that Japan must restore its military and adopt a policy of armed neutrality, which should involve the recognition of Communist China. In 1957 he caused a tremendous stir in Japan by making a surprise visit to Peking where, despite the lack of diplomatic relations between the two countries, he was received by premier Chou En-lai, who appears to have been no more troubled by Tsuji's war record than Chiang Kai-shek.

But the accusations of war crimes would not go away and his party would not trust him with a ministerial role. On the contrary, a new generation of Japanese began to regard Tsuji as a throwback, more banzai than brains, and his popularity waned. In 1961, Tsuji decided to demonstrate the kudos a neutral Japan could obtain. He went on a one-man peace-keeping mission to Laos, which like the rest of Indo-China was drifting into civil war, and met with the communist Pathet Lao. After he returned to government-held Vientiane his movements were restricted. Once he was spotted wearing the kind of monk's saffron he had first put on to slip out of Bangkok in 1945; then he was seen in shirt and trousers, apparently about to board a Russian airliner for Hanoi. This was the last positive sighting. It seems that, somewhere in Indo-China, his past caught up with him. In 1968 a Japanese court declared that Masanobu Tsuji must be presumed dead.

By then he would have been sixty-six and would have lived over twenty years longer than Lieutenant-General Saburo Kawamura who had led his 9th Brigade down the length of the Malayan Peninsula to Singapore. Immediately after the surrender, Kawamura had been made commander of the city's garrison and in June 1946 he was hanged in Changi jail together with a Kempetei (secret police) colonel for his part in the killing of the Chinese. Five other Japanese officers were sentenced to life imprisonment, including Lieutenant-General Takuma Nishimura, the former commander of the Imperial Guards Division which had provided some of the death squads.

Nishimura had escaped the gallows by one dissenting vote on the panel of five officers who were required to make a unanimous decision on death sentences – but not for long. Four years later, the general was seized by the Australians who wanted him for the murder of Anderson's wounded at Parit Sulong. With other convicted war criminals, Nishimura had been *en route* for home, where in theory they would complete their sentences, when he was plucked off a ship in Hong Kong. In June 1951, convicted on the testimony of Lieutenant Ben Hackney, he was hanged at the Australian base in the Admiralty Islands, north of New Guinea, where he had been tried by a military court.

Once they re-took Malaya and Singapore and the Dutch East Indies, and saw the condition of the men and women the Japanese had held prisoner, there can be no doubt that the British and Australians were looking for revenge. By the time they were found in a remote camp in Sumatra, eight of the Australian nurses in Bullwinkel's group had died of malnutrition. When he saw their emaciated state and heard Bullwinkel's own story one Australian doctor, a practising Christian well known for his gentle nature, recommended that their guards be 'forthwith slowly and painfully butchered'. Major Masaru Orita, who had been a captain when Bullwinkel noticed how bored he looked while overseeing the murder of her friends on Radji beach, was discovered to be in Russian hands. He was handed over to the Australian military mission in Tokyo but killed himself before he could be interrogated.

There were cases of instant retribution. Before Hiroshima, in anticipation of British landings on Malaya's west coast in early September, commandos from Special Operations Executive were preparing Thai guerrillas for a general uprising. South of the border Spencer Chapman, who had survived over three years in the jungle, was doing the same thing with a team of liaison officers attached to the Chinese Communists of the Malayan Peoples' Anti-Japanese Liberation Army. In Thailand, an Australian prisoner reported that, immediately after the Japanese capitulation, a British major from Special Operations Executive attached to Thai guerrillas 'went on the rampage killing many Japs'. But he did not approve of the commando's actions: 'He impressed me as a man who had seen too much of war and and was jumpy and nervous.'*

This was an almost universal attitude among the prisoners themselves. Enraged outsiders were sometimes made to feel as if they were intruding in a family quarrel. Liberation swept aside cherished dreams of revenge. There is an account of a Welsh gunner working in one of the Formosa mines beating a particularly brutal guard to death with his own club and stuffing his body down a latrine, for they were yet to be formally liberated – but such incidents were rare. Some of those who had been on the railway even felt they might have more in common with the Japanese, whose living conditions had often been not much better than their own, than they did with their liberators.

Who were these strange creatures in their unfamiliar jungle-green, long-trousered uniforms? Whatever happened to khaki and Bombay Bloomer shorts? And then there were their equally unfamiliar Sten guns and jeeps and all sorts of other good things the prisoners had had to do without, such as radios that worked and the mepacrine tablets that turned skins as yellow as the Japs were supposed to be but apparently kept the malaria away.

---

* He was right. Most of the Thai SOE mission had started their active service against the Germans and Italians. One, Peter Kemp, had even started a little earlier on the same side as the Germans in the Spanish Civil War.

One of the exceptions among the ex-prisoners was the Japanese-speaking Colonel Wild who investigated, interrogated and wrote reports on suspected and convicted war criminals with considerable relish. Asked what could be said in favour of Lieutenant-General Shinpei Fukuye after he had appealed against his death sentence, Wild had answered, 'Practically nothing.' On 27 April 1946, Fukuye, who in August 1942 had become the officer commanding all prisoners in Malaya, was hooded, led out to Changi beach and shot in the place where he had ended the honeymoon period between Percival's defeated army and their captors by executing four escapees. As an added humiliation, Fukuye had arranged that the firing squad should be made up of four Sikhs from the Indian National Army. To the disgust of the Australian and British officers whom the Japanese forced to witness the event, one of the Sikhs was identified as a certain Captain Rana, a product of Dehra Dun, who held the King's commission.

The condemned men, two of them still in their hospital pyjamas – for they had been picked up half-starved after a 200-mile trip in a small boat – behaved with great dignity, declining blindfolds and returning the salute their officers gave them. Perhaps not surprisingly given the small number of rifles involved in the execution, it had been as botched an affair as the shooting of the sepoy mutineers in 1915. One of the escapees sat up after the first volley and announced, 'You have shot me through the arm. Please shoot me through the heart.' When Rana fired again, he was hit in the leg and shouted, 'For God's sake, shoot through the heart.' In the end each of the escapees received over ten shots, the Indians having to reload their magazines to do it.

By November 1945, Wild was able to report that Captain Rana was under arrest in Delhi. What happened to him after that is unclear. Presumably he was one of several thousand INA soldiers who either deserted to the British once they reached Burma – where, to their disgust, they found that the Japanese had used one of their best battalions as road workers – or had surrendered there. Among the latter category was Colonel Prem Sahgal, lately Captain Sahgal of the 2/10th Baluch and the betrothed of Dr Lakshmi Swaminadhan, who was shortly to be captured in eastern Burma by some Karen guerrillas commanded by a British officer. At the end of April 1945, Sahgal had given himself up to a Gurkha battalion and spent the first hour or so of his new captivity helping the British officer who was 'looking after him' do the *Times of India* crossword. British intelligence officers put

INA men in three categories: white for those who had only ever joined in order to desert and get back home; grey for those deemed to have become confused without the direction of their officers; black for rabid nationalists. Prem Sahgal was black.

Eight months later, convicted with two other INA officers of treason by a court martial assembled at the Red Fort in Delhi, he had been sentenced to be cashiered from the service, forfeit all pay and allowances, and be transported for life. Transportation usually meant being sent to the penal colony in the Andaman Islands, only recently vacated by the Japanese, but this part of the sentence was commuted by Auchinleck, the Indian Army's commander-in-chief. Some of that army, and by no means just its British officers, were outraged by such leniency when, among the thousands of Indian soldiers who had died in the war, were those who had been murdered by the Japanese for refusing to join Bose's battalions. But Britain's new Labour government was determined to quit India – its freedom (and partition) was less than two years away – and was in no mood to create martyrs. After independence, the armies of both India and Pakistan imposed their own sentence on officers who had joined the INA and never allowed any of them to rejoin.

India was the jewel in the crown and, without its jewel, the crown lost its lustre. In the years after the war, it became fashionable to say that the fall of Singapore marked the beginning of the end of the British Empire, but this was no more true than that other enduring myth – that the island fell because its coastal guns were 'pointing the wrong way'. The empire could never have survived the loss of India, and India was going long before Singapore fell. Yet, as things worked out, British Singapore proved rather more resilient.

After the war, the Tuans and the Mems were, by and large, welcomed back. The statue of Raffles, which had been hidden away in a museum, was returned to its plinth in front of the Victoria Theatre and, for good measure, a replica was erected at the mouth of the Singapore River, where the founder had landed. Long after the French and Dutch had rather bloodily departed from their more homogeneous South-east Asian possessions, the British stayed on – mostly because there were always enough people who believed they were better than the alternative.

On the Malayan Peninsula, the Chinese communist guerrillas whom Spencer Chapman had helped to arm and train turned against the

British, as both sides had always suspected they would. But the Malays and a good many of the Chinese were not with them. After a twelve-year campaign characterized by deep jungle penetration, weeks of boredom, good intelligence and savage ambushes, the British eventually won. They called it the Malayan Emergency, rather as the Japanese used to refer to significant pre-war clashes in China as 'Incidents'. And the guerrillas were no longer guerrillas but 'CTs', which stood for 'Communist Terrorists'. The Emergency was not another Vietnam, though later the British sometimes liked to pretend to the Americans that it was; but they were the only western power to mount a successful counter-insurgency operation in South-east Asia after World War II. This was at least partly because Singapore provided a secure base for the British and Commonwealth troops deployed in Malaya: Canberra bombers used the lengthened runways from which the Vildebeest biplanes had once taken off on their mad, brave sortie against the Japanese ships at Endau; the secure moorings from where Phillips had set out looking for trouble now served the frigates and fast patrol boats that policed the long coasts of the peninsula for gun-runners.

Nor was this by any means the swan song of the British military on Raffles' treasure island. In 1963 Malaya, fully independent since 1957, and Singapore, self-governing since 1959, were encouraged by London to join with the old British territories of Brunei, Sarawak and Sabah in northern Borneo and form Malaysia. The Indonesian dictator Sukarno objected. Most of Borneo was Indonesian just as it had once been mostly Dutch. If the British were leaving, surely the territories should revert to him?

When UN-sponsored plebiscites confirmed that Sarawak and Sabah wished to join Malaysia, Sukarno decided to throw enough bricks through Malaysia's front windows to make Malaysia and its British backers wish they had left the UN out of it. He called it 'Confrontation'. Indonesian infantry, sometimes in small parties and sometimes 200 or 300 strong, began to raid logging camps, villages and police stations in Sabah and Sarawak. Hit-and-run attacks began on Singapore and Malaya. The island's offshore bunkering stations that had burned so brightly in 1942 were shot up, Singaporean fishing vessels were pirated, bombs were set off in the growing city itself. Across the straits in Johore, an Indonesian platoon took over an old Japanese bunker opposite Changi and defended it with a stubbornness that would have won the approval of its original occupants, until they were dislodged by the Malay Regiment and air strikes. Indonesia's own aircraft regularly teased the RAF by coming close enough for fighters to be scrambled and then turning back.

Britain's response to the pinpricks of Confrontation, which eventually ended when Sukarno was overthrown in 1966, was immediate and massive. Its latest aircraft carrier, HMS _Eagle_, arrived, easily the biggest ship in those waters since the _Prince of Wales_. So did Javelin fighters, Vulcan bombers, Bloodhound surface-to-air missiles. Royal Marine Commandos, Gurkhas, the Parachute Regiment, the Rifle Brigade and the Special Air Service all skirmished regularly and with increasing success against Sukarno's infiltrators in Borneo. Australia and New Zealand sent small contingents. There were 60,000 British troops in the area. Singapore's service economy boomed.

In retirement in his native Hertfordshire, Arthur Percival must have marvelled at, and no doubt envied, the response his country could make when it was not also fighting a major European war. After thirty-two years' service he had retired from the army in 1946 with the honorary rank of lieutenant-general, but not with the knighthood that normally went with it and on the lower pension of a major-general. For five years he served as honorary colonel of his old regiment, the Cheshires, and he became deputy lieutenant for Hertfordshire and director of the county's Red Cross Society, but none of the honours and middle-ranking Commonwealth governorships that might have been expected ever came his way – not even those quaint sinecures that exist in the Channel Islands.

There can be no doubt that he was being punished for what the headlines which greeted the publication of the official history in 1957 called 'The Shame of Singapore'. It was not so much that he was blamed for losing the island. Singapore could only have been saved if Air Chief Marshal Brooke-Popham and Admiral Phillips had considered the mere presence of Japanese ships off the Malayan coast reason enough to sink them. He was being punished for losing it too quickly and with too little glory, for being the gangling man in the silly shorts surrendering to the little men in the high boots.

He bore all this with fortitude. His account of the campaign, _The War in Malaya_, published in 1949, is remarkably restrained. To read between its lines the reader has to know the story very well indeed. Never once did he say – not in public at least – 'Look, in the end most of the Australians fell apart, some of the Indians were not much better and I had this green British division which was beginning to settle down but needed a lot more time.'

But there was one body of men who did honour Percival. These were the British veterans of the Far East Prisoners of War Association who elected him their Life President and whose reunions he attended until his death in 1966. When troops lose a battle they tend to blame their commanders and these men had not just lost but suffered a captivity from which many of them would never recover. The Sherwood Foresters had about 50 killed in Singapore, and 292 died in captivity. 'With hindsight and given the opportunity they might well have decided to fight on,' notes Clifford Housley, the battalion's historian.

One of those who did have the opportunity and took it was Temporary Lieutenant Thomas Wilkinson of the Royal Naval Reserve who had gone down with his three-decker river boat HMS *Li Wo* after ramming the Japanese transport in the Bangka Strait. When the few who survived the sinking of the *Li Wo* and their captivity had returned and told their story, Wilkinson was awarded a posthumous Victoria Cross. Various other awards were made to the survivors, especially the gun crews.

But one man whose conduct aboard the *Li Wo* cried out for recognition was the RAF air gunner who stuck to his Lewis gun and finished the Japanese transport's machine-gunners as well as clearing the ship's bridge with his devastating fire. The problem was, nobody knew his name or could ever recall seeing him again after the ship sank. All they could remember about him was that he was a sergeant and possibly UK British, although given the composition of the RAF at the time he could easily have been from anywhere in the Commonwealth, or even an American.

It might be possible for some industrious researcher at least to discover which unit he was likely to have come from. But perhaps we should allow this sergeant to remain Singapore's unknown soldier, caught up in his hopeless battle, forever engaging the enemy more closely.

# Acknowledgements and Sources

It took me over three years to research and write this book and the debts of gratitude incurred stretch from Northumbria to Canberra. During that time the veterans of the campaign in Malaya and Singapore got even thinner on the ground. Yet, despite the vile treatment most of them endured as prisoners, an amazing number of these who were 20 to 25 years old at the time – the privates and lieutenants – were still around and willing to tell me about the fighting they did before they were ordered to surrender.

I have to thank Robert Chesshyre, a writer for the *Telegraph* magazine and old friend from our days on the *Observer*, for his introduction to an entire tribe of Northumberland Fusilier Territorial Army machine-gunners living, as the majority always have done, in the border country with Scotland around Berwick-on-Tweed. Most of the men Captain Henry McCreath took away to war with him from Liverpool docks in October 1941 came from villages or urban terraces within a few miles of his own home in Berwick, where the McCreaths brewed a profitable fertilizer out of local herring oil and imported phosphates. Over sixty years later, Henry McCreath had no difficulty in putting me in touch with many of the survivors, for ever since they returned he had kept an eye on their welfare and helped to organize their regular reunions. It was from him, and men like Jack Phillips and John Webb (a 'southerner' from York), that I learned how the Fusiliers had sailed into their nightmare captivity with all guns blazing only ten days before the garrison surrendered.

During the closing stages of the battle, the command of the machine-gunners passed into the hands of Major (later Colonel) Henry 'Flossie' Flower, who went into captivity with them; his insistence on the chores of basic hygiene is credited with saving many lives. Sibylla Jane Flower, his daughter, has become Britain's greatest authority on Japan's Allied prisoners-of-war and her forthcoming book on the subject is the product of fourteen years' research. Ms Flower, whom I was fortunate enough to meet in February 2002 at Singapore University's 'Sixty Years On' conference, very generously helped steer some of my own inquiries in the right direction.

Among those I might not have found without her help was Wizardus, also known as Gunner Fergus Anckorn, the magician of his divisional concert party. In his flat at Westerham in Kent one showery April afternoon, he described at length the greatest trick of his career: escaping a Japanese bayonet while lying wounded and helpless in his bed during the Alexandra Hospital massacre.

Few of the survivors of the campaign are perhaps quite so clustered as the Northumberland Fusiliers. In the village of Swinton in Berwickshire James McLean recalled how he was wounded with the Argylls in northern Malaya, and in Hertford Douglas Weir how, some weeks later, he was shot through the stomach in Singapore while serving with the same battalion. In Nottingham, Ron Morrell of the Foresters explained what it was like to come under a Japanese tank attack, while in Haslemere in Surrey I found John Goatley, a Foresters' lieutenant wounded in the same action.

In Australia I was fortunate to interview three of the surviving RAAF air-crew who, in the opening hours of the Far East war, tried to sink the Japanese invasion fleet off Kota Baharu. In Canberra I met Clarence 'Spud' Spurgeon, and in Melbourne Alan Morton and Russell Rayson, who were all on Hudsons. I am particularly grateful for the hospitality and assistance I received from the former air gunner Alan Morton, who is the Secretary of the Sembawang Association and editor of its informative newsletter. At New South Wales' Colliray Beach Services Club, Don Wall of the AIF's 2/20th gave me a copy of his meticulously researched and revealing battalion history, *Singapore and Beyond*. Near Newcastle, along the same coast, I met Victor Levi, then 92, a signaller with Taylor's 27th Brigade, whose father, having reduced his age from 60 to 45 to enlist, also survived a captivity that men less than half his age did not. In Melbourne, Basil Atkinson allowed me to look at the letters of Major Charles Atkinson, a beloved elder brother who was 27 when he succumbed to encephalitis and became the first Australian to be buried at Changi POW camp.

Rear Admiral Guy Griffiths, who was one of the Australian midshipmen aboard HMS *Repulse*, kindly agreed to meet me for lunch and, in the shadow of the Sydney opera house, told me about the last voyage of the battle cruiser. He also put me in touch with his shipmate, Hubert Bowen, the teenaged Welsh chorister, who settled in Sydney after his last RN posting had taken him there. On the same subject, David Stevens, Director of Historical Studies at the Royal Australian Navy's Sea Power Centre in Canberra, was very generous with his time and his files as were his colleagues, naval archivist Joe Struezele and assistant naval historical officer David Griffin. I am greatly obliged to Dr John Reeve, senior lecturer in naval history at the Australian Defence Academy, who invited me to his home for a stunning tutorial on the sinking of the battleships. (He also put me in touch with his Uncle William, who was asleep on the deck of HMAS *Vendetta* when the first Japanese bombs on Singapore interrupted his dreams.)

'The men who did the fighting are now all busy writing,' runs a line in some anonymous Noël Cowardish verse that circulated in Changi POW camp. Dr Peter Stanley, principal historian at the Australian War Memorial (AWM), made an enormous contribution by drawing my attention to the first full-length history of the campaign, compiled in captivity by Lieutenant-Colonel Charles Kappe, Bennett's chief signals officer, who had the advantage of being locked up with most of the available sources. Typed on the backs of procurement forms and naval signal pads, with hand-written inserts, it is an invaluable document, though at times one needs to bear in mind that, when things go wrong, people tend to blame somebody else.

Steven Bullard, Dr Stanley's colleague at the AWM and in charge of their Japan Research Project, introduced me to the Japanese documents contained in the Allied Translator and Interpreter Section – a mixture of propaganda and operational orders. 'The most formidable fighting insect in history,' Field-Marshal Sir William Slim, the victor of the Burma campaign, once described the Japanese soldier. The Swiss historian Henry Frei, who lived and worked in Japan, died shortly after he had attended the sixtieth anniversary conference on the fall of Singapore, where he gave a taste of the book he had almost completed, *Guns of February – Ordinary Japanese Soldiers' Views of the Malayan Campaign and the Fall of Singapore*. It certainly makes them less insect-like and I have quoted from it. And yet, though atrocities beget atrocities and all armies commit them from time to time, it fails to answer why, in their case, undisputed valour was so often besmirched by some despicable cruelty. Perhaps nobody, including the Japanese, knows the answer.

In Britain the National Archives (Public Record Office), the National Army Museum, Oxford's Bodleian Library (Rhodes House) and King's College War Studies Centre all yielded some treasures, but most of my research there was done in the Borough of Lambeth, directly under the cupola of the Imperial War Museum, where the reading room is located. Here the staff of Roderick Suddaby, chief keeper at the Imperial War Museum's Department of Documents, not only produced every file I asked for, but also made some extremely helpful suggestions of their own. In addition to the papers held there I was also most grateful for additional material on the Reverend Jack Bennitt and his wife Nora furnished by their son Martin, until recently the Agence France Presse Bureau Chief in Nicosia, and some details on Admiral Sir Peter Cazalet's earlier World War II career given to me by his son, Adrian. So that I could better understand what the Japanese had to contend with at Kota Baharu, Colonel James Anderson of the Royal Engineers, then defence attaché at the British High Commission in Cyprus, unravelled the arcane business of barbed-wire defences for me. In Singapore David and Gloria Dudley-Owen spent hours mining the 1941–2 archives of the *Straits Times* on my behalf.

There is an enormous historiography on the Malayan campaign, much of it out of print and quite a lot privately published and in limited circulation.

In Nicosia, where I live, Ruth Keshishian and her team at the Moufflon book shop eventually located every volume I ever mentioned to them, including books that had not been in print for more than half a century. In this department, I am also indebted to Ron Morrell of the Sherwood Foresters who not only gave me his hand-written account of the campaign but generously handed over his entire library on the subject. A bibliography of most of the books I consulted is listed, and they are identified in the source notes below. Minor changes to grammar and spelling have been made to some of the quotations.

## Abbreviations

AWM – Australian War Memorial
IWM – Imperial War Museum
NAM – National Army Museum

## The Treasure Island

p. 6 'Veiled autocracy', Imray, *Cricket in the Backblocks*, p. 7.

p. 9 'shot civilians like schoolboys catapulting birds', Richard Winstedt, *Start from Alif: Count from One*, Kuala Lumpur Press, 1969, p. 165. Quoted by Nicholas Tarling in the December 1982 issue of the *Journal of the Royal Asiatic Society*. Most of the account of Singapore's mutiny is based on Tarling's long and informative essay on these events.

p. 10 'Their self-imposed efficiency', ibid.

p. 10 'The expression on his face was one of such terrible agony', Shennan, *Out in the Midday Sun*, p. 100.

p. 11 'It is sufficiently far from Japan', Admiralty papers, PRO 1/8571/295.

p. 11 'That extraordinary fellow', Jenkins, *Churchill*, p. 396.

p. 12 'Suppose the Japanese', ibid., p. 395.

## Part One: Dancing in the Dark

### Chapter 1

p. 17 *Some planters, veterans*, Shennan, *Midday Sun*, p. 170.

p. 18 *Furtive visits to the bordellos*, ibid., p. 172.

p. 18 *colour bar*, Morrison, *Malayan Postscript*, p. 38.

p. 18 'Eurasians, Indians, Ceylonese, a Sikh bowler', Shennan, *Midday Sun*, p. 124.

p. 18 *redundant Tuans*, Imray, *Cricket*, p. 58.

p. 19 *Arab revolt in Palestine*, King-Clark, *Free for a Blast*, p. 254.

p. 21 *'Its main feature was the large, airy anteroom'*, ibid., p. 249.

p. 22 *had donated an additional half a million pounds*, Murfett et al., *Between Two Oceans*, p. 164.

p. 22 *'more guns on Singapore Island'*, Sydney Morning Herald, 10 March 1938.

p. 23 *students at London's Imperial Defence College*, Kirby, *The Chain of Disaster*, p. 33.

p. 25 *'where everybody quickly gets to know'*, Percival, *The War in Malaya*, pp. 13–14.

p. 25 *'There were clashes of interests'*, ibid., p. 18.

p. 26 *'I think he wanted to be liked'*, Elphick, *The Pregnable Fortress*, p. 215.

p. 26 *'People as a whole were not interested'*, Percival, *War in Malaya*, p. 14.

p. 27 *'shrimp barbarians'*, Snow, *The Fall of Hong Kong*, p. 31.

p. 27 *put the figure at 227,400*, Chang, *The Rape of Nanking*, p. 25.

p. 30 *lost twelve killed and sixteen wounded*, Wilson, *The Sum of Things*, p. 27.

p. 30 *Wilson was impressed by his first glimpse*, ibid., p. 52.

p. 32 *Unable to endure the shame*, Hoyt, *Japan's War*, p. 101.


## Chapter 2

p. 34 *'firangi rascals'*, Sahgal, *A Revolutionary Life*, p. 4.

p. 34 *'Being self-willed and obstinate'*, ibid., p. 8.

p. 35 *'Give me blood and I promise you freedom'*, Toye, *The Springing Tiger*, p. 41.

p. 35 *'would have done credit to any crack infantry unit'*, Sahgal, *Revolutionary Life*, p. 49.

p. 35 *beginning to call him 'Netaji'*, ibid., p. 44.

p. 37 *'fat and jovial'*, Stapledon papers, IWM 85/31/1.

p. 38 *'brilliantly lit up'*, private papers of Reverend Albert John 'Jack' Bennitt made available to the author by his son, Martin Bennitt.

p. 41 *'far too dangerous'*, Vichy and British officials, Singapore meeting, 26.12.40, PRO FO 371/15773504.

p. 42 *'perfect picture'*, Sir Frederick Weld, quoted in *Singapore's 100 Historic Places*, p. 32.

p. 42 *'seize this pretext'*, ibid., PRO FO 371/15773504.

p. 43 *sat Professor Mayer May*, Cruikshank, *SOE in the Far East*, p. 74.

p. 43 *'specimen copies of the leaflets'*, PRO FO 371/15773504.

p. 44 *known as the 'flying barrel'*, Saville-Sneath, *Aircraft Recognition*, p. 78.

p. 46 *had left his spinning bed*, Bishop, *Fighter Boys*, pp. 226–7.

p. 47 *'It is on a par with our Buffalo'*, Shores, Cull and Izawa, *Bloody Shambles*, p. 43.

p. 47 *while the RAF was bad*, Ferris, paper delivered at sixtieth anniversary conference at Singapore University, in *Sixty Years On: The Fall of Singapore*, edited by Brian Farrell and Sandy Hunter, p. 116.

p. 47 *than was visited on the Kaiser's High Seas Fleet*, Winston, *Cunningham*, p. 113.

## Chapter 3

p. 49 *'quoted to future generations as an example'*, Brooke-Popham papers, Liddell Hart Centre, King's College, London.

p. 53 *'not be lost upon Japan'*, Churchill, *The Second World War*, vol. 3, p. 14.

p. 55 *'had never cooked an egg'*, Wigmore, *The Japanese Thrust*, p. 72.

p. 55 *'the hope of seeing a British newsreel'*, Stapledon papers, IWM 85/31/1.

p. 56 *'Japan's peaceful cooperation'*, *Asahi* newspaper, 30.7.42, quoted in telegram from British embassy in Tokyo, PRO FO 371/27882.

p. 58 *'Welcome to the AIF'*, Braddon, *Naked Island*, p. 29.

p. 58 *'Once again one cannot help thinking'*, PRO FO 371/27882.

p. 58 *'How courteous is the Japanese'*, Nash, *The Face is Familiar*, pp. 233–4.

## Chapter 4

p. 59 *steel girders*, Brendon, *The Dark Valley*, p. 542.

p. 59 *from Shakespeare and Goethe*, Steiner, *Behind the Japanese Mask*, p. 72.

p. 60 *Some western missionaries*, ibid., p. 34.

p. 60 *10 per cent of its farmland*, *Encyclopaedia Britannica*, vol. 29.

p. 60 *'slashed it to shreds'*, Steiner, *Japanese Mask*, p. 38.

p. 61 *kiken shiso*, ibid. p. 107.

p. 61 *In any case, Japan did not have anything like*, *Oxford Companion to the Second World War*, p. 613.

p. 61 *It was decided that baseball*, Steiner, *Japanese Mask*, p. 96.

p. 62 *'There is nothing more dreadful than crazy persons'*, ibid., pp. 36–7.

p. 63 *'War is the father of creation'*, Steiner, *Japanese Mask*, p. 47.

p. 64 *'the natural objective still remains'*, Wigmore, *Japanese Thrust*, p. 87.

p. 64 *'We are both Asiatics'*, Hoyt, *Japan's War*, p. 199.

p. 66 *'all conceivable data'*, Tsuji, *Singapore 1941–42*, p. 4.

p. 66 *'From an old sea captain'*, ibid., p. 6.

p. 67 *'Although our country'*, ibid., p. 302.

p. 67 *'In the Japan of recent years'*, ibid., p. 308.

p. 69 *'All the seas'*, ibid., p. 213.

## Chapter 5

p. 70 *'to get a go at a Hun before this war ends'*, AWM PR 1514.

p. 70 *'a hatred of Malaya'*, 2/19th Battalion Association, *The Grim Glory*, p. 48.

p. 70 *an . . . article on Bennett's command*, *Australian Women's Weekly*, 12.4.41.

p. 71 *'have a gay time'*, quoted by Wigmore, *Japanese Thrust*, p. 71.

p. 71 *'Hello darlings'*, papers of Sister Mona Wilton, 2/13th AGH, AWM PR 98/92.

p. 72 *Large and dewlapped and almost seventy*, Payne, *Eyewitness*, p. 166.

p. 72 *'What a night we had'*, Wilton papers, *op. cit.*

p. 72 *'I am sending you Mona's last'*, ibid.

p. 73 *'wouldn't move from her house during the Blitz'*, Manners, *Bullwinkel*, p. 25.

p. 73 *'He was very active'*, Bennett, *Why Singapore Fell*, p. 21.

p. 74 *'there was the double danger'*, Percival, *War in Malaya*, p. 27.

p. 74 *'I could not have said it'*, Kinvig, *Scapegoat*, p. 122, letter from Betty Percival, 14.9.39.

p. 75 *'The news of my impending departure'*, Percival, *War in Malaya*, p. 26.

p. 76 *'A man of my own way of thinking'*, ibid., p. 31.

p. 78 *'Crosby is too often influenced by the existing mood'*, PRO WO 193/917.

p. 78 *at the same country inns*, ibid., p. 172.

p. 80 *rowed for fourteen hours across*, Skidmore, *Marines Don't Hold Their Horses*, pp. 28–30.

p. 80 *thought rifles were of more use*, Cross, *Red Jungle*, p. 57.

p. 81 *'might as well expect a chief of police'*, Cruickshank, *SOE in the Far East*, p. 72.

p. 81 *John Becker*, Elphick, *Pregnable Fortress*, pp. 173–212.

pp. 84–5 *'The safety, honour and welfare'*, Mason, *A Matter of Honour*, p. 465.

p. 85 *fifty-six Indian Commissioned Officers a year*, ibid., p. 464.

p. 86 *'I stayed in a Japanese home'*, Somerville, *Our War*, p. 28.

p. 86 *'only way to run the country was with the lathi and the boot'*, ibid., p. 12.

p. 86 *'When an English girl went in'*, Fay, *The Forgotten Army*, p. 56.

p. 87 *'How can we when we don't take senior Malays?'*, ibid., p. 54.

p. 87 *'I hope you're not trying to rush things, Prem'*, Fay, *Forgotten Army*, p. 56.

p. 88 *'give a lead to the other British women'*, Percival papers, IWM P21 F39.

## Chapter 6

p. 89 *'Why has everyone got their wife here'*, Atkinson papers, IWM 85/36/1.

p. 90 *'How I wish you were here'*, ibid.

p. 92 *perils of becoming 'swollen-headed'*, Middlebrook and Mahoney, *Battleship*, p. 77.

p. 93 *ordered to change into lightweight white ducks*, author's interview in

Melbourne with Chief Petty Officer (retd) Hubert Bowen, who made sure it never happened to himself.

p. 94 *administered two canings during his tenure*, Brooke, *Alarm Starboard*, p. 47.

p. 94 *'If they do, they'll find they've bitten off more than they can chew'*, ibid., p. 85.

p. 94 *'the sense of complete security'*, Duff Cooper, *Old Men Forget*, p. 300.

p. 95 *'Disfigured the smiling landscape'*, ibid., p. 244.

p. 95 *'the Japanese were, as a people, addicted to suicide'*, ibid., p. 291.

p. 96 *'Prince of Wales, Repulse, Jupiter, Electra, Express'*, Cazalet papers, IWM P432.

p. 97 *'told that the essence of naval warfare'*, Percival, *War in Malaya*, p. 95.

p. 97 *'would rapidly result in our losing the war'*, Hough, *The Hunting of Force Z*, p. 110.

p. 97 *'ought to serve as a deterrent on Japan'*, PRO CAB 65/24.

p. 98 *a total of 676 aircraft and 446 tanks*, Wigmore, *Japanese Thrust*, p. 103.

p. 98 *they had 145 aircraft*, Shores, Cull and Izawa, *Bloody Shambles*, p. 58.

p. 98 *Percival recalled faulty 'interrupter gear'*, Percival, *War in Malaya*, p. 104.

p. 99 *to replace the Brownings*, Hough, *Force Z*, p. 82.

p. 99 *'a feeling of relief'*, Percival, *War in Malaya*, p. 64.

p. 100 *ankle bones were visible*, author interview, Melbourne, 2.8.02.

p. 103 *'cold-blooded proposals'*, Potter, *A Soldier Must Hang*, p. 12.

p. 104 *demobilizing four divisions*, Akashi Yoshi, emeritus professor, Nanzan University, at 'Sixty Years On', international conference, Singapore University, February 2002.

p. 105 *'Before Vienna I knew little'*, Potter, *A Soldier Must Hang*, p. 14.

p. 105 *'in the afternoon Kitty came to see me'*, ibid., p. 31.

p. 107 *'more like a bank clerk'*, Akashi Yoshi, op. cit.

p. 108 *badly trained and wondered if they were up to the job*, Tsuji, *Singapore 1941–42*, p. 32.

p. 109 *'AIF to maintain health and morale at government expense'*, Wigmore, *Japanese Thrust*, p. 96.

p. 109 *'very senior'*, ibid., p. 97.

p. 110 *Congratulating Brooke-Popham*, Chung, *Operation Matador*, p. 226.

p. 110 *'damned near gaga'*, ibid., citing MRGN 1/6 Margesson Papers, Churchill College Archives. Duff Cooper to David Margesson (Lord), Secretary of State for War, 1.10.41.

p. 110 *'We can get on alright with Buffaloes out here'*, Brooke-Popham papers, Liddell Hart Centre, King's College, London.

p. 111 *From Saigon, Edward Meiklereid*, PRO FO 371/15773504.

## Part Two: The Bloody Beaches of Kota Baharu

### Chapter 7

p. 115 *On 3 December*, PRO WO 208/871.

p. 118 *67 crashes resulting in 48 deaths*, Shores, Cull and Izawa, *Bloody Shambles*, pp. 36–42.

p. 119 *'Corporal Fujimoto and Corporal Yoshida attacked from the rear'*, Allied Translator and Interpreter Section South West Pacific Area, AWM 55 5/24.

p. 120 *'only a demonstration against Thailand'*, Percival, *War in Malaya*, p. 109.

p. 120 *'improper to print such alarmist news'*, Glover, *In Seventy Days*, p. 72.

p. 121 *'We were all ready waiting for the flag to fall'*, Percival, *War in Malaya*, p. 109.

p. 122 *'like some frightful oath'*, Morrison, *Malayan Postscript*, p. 74.

p. 123 *'I said to myself'*, author interview, Melbourne, July 2000.

p. 123 *Orion was having her bow repaired, ibid.*

p. 124 *a convenient beacon*, Glover, *Seventy Days*, p. 77.

p. 125 *Also on the list*, Montgomery, *Shenton of Singapore*, p. 1.

p. 126 *'One lot went for the base area'*, Shenton Thomas diary, Rhodes House, Oxford.

p. 127 *The sight of coolies from the Public Works Department*, Bennitt, private papers.

p. 127 *'all caught on the hop'*, Shenton Thomas diary.

p. 127 *'a bold enterprise'*, Percival, *War in Malaya*, p. 113.

p. 127 *would see them in Sydney for Christmas*, Middlebrook and Mahoney, *Battleship*, p. 89.

p. 127 *Prince of Wales was being fussed over in dry dock*, Brooke, *Alarm Starboard*, p. 93.

p. 127 *only Lieutenant Yoshimi Shirai*, Shores, Cull and Izawa, *Bloody Shambles*, p. 86.

p. 128 *When Vigors threatened to take off, ibid.*, p. 87.

p. 129 *'An enormous number would be drowned'*, Wrigglesworth, *The Japanese Invasion of Kelantan in 1941*, p. 59.

p. 130 *'Get up, you silly bastard'*, Gibbes in *Apakhabar*, RAAF Newsletter.

p. 130 *military operator tried and failed to ration these calls*, Hall, *Glory in Chaos*, p. 83.

p. 132 *a fifth of its original strength*, Wrigglesworth, *Invasion of Kelantan*, p. 40.

p. 132 *'could not relax for a moment'*, Allied Translator and Interpreter Section, AWM 55 5/24, Yokoyama Ryuichi, *The Malayan Campaign 1941–42*, Imperial Japanese Army.

p. 133 *first stirrings of sea-sickness*, Tsuji, *Singapore 1941–42*, p. 93.

p. 133 *'skip bombing'*, *Oxford Companion to the Second World War*, p. 1010.

## Chapter 8

p. 138 *'digging the ground frantically'*, Allied Translator and Interpreter Section, AWM 55 5/24.

p. 138 *'a kind of tear gas'*, Elphick, *Pregnable Fortress*, p. 296.

p. 138 *almost 12,000 mustard gas shells*, PRO WO193/711.

p. 140 *'The next thing I knew'*, Shores, Cull and Izawa, *Bloody Shambles*, p. 89.

p. 141 *obliging Lieutenant Tadatsuen Tokaji to break off*, ibid.

p. 141 *'in the pouring rain to watch the bombing'*, Condon, *Frontier Force Regiment*, p. 349.

p. 142 *they'll never take off in this*, Bulcock, *Of Death but Once*, p. 36.

p. 142 *'long wisps of smoky cloud'*, Morton, communication to the author, August 2002.

p. 143 *noticed that his hands were sweating*, ibid.

p. 143 *'I flung the thing down'*, author interview with Spurgeon, Canberra, July 2002.

p. 144 *drilled a 2-inch hole*, communication to the author from Morton, August 2002.

p. 144 *'turned their craft towards us'*, author's interview with Rayson, Melbourne, 2.7.02.

p. 144 *'Right ho, Dusty, there's your chance'*, Hall, *Glory in Chaos*, p. 90.

p. 145 *'the first round does not necessarily decide the contest'*, Rose, *Who Dies Fighting*, p. 33.

p. 146 *talked of 320 killed*, Tsuji, *Singapore 1941–42*, p. 93.

p. 146 *'One section of non-commissioned officers'*, ibid., p. 165.

p. 147 *a lone figure in a tiny Malayan prahu*, Hall, *Glory in Chaos*, p. 103.

p. 148 *shattered his lower jaw and passed through his mouth*, ibid., p. 401.

p. 148 *Records of the 59th Sentai*, Shore, Cull and Izawa, *Bloody Shambles*, p. 92.

p. 149 *discovered that, in both cases, they were unloaded*, ibid., p. 248.

p. 149 *Fowle decided they could no longer operate from Sungei Patani*, ibid., p. 249.

p. 150 *not greeted with much enthusiasm*, ibid., p. 106.

p. 150 *ground crews, who were clambering aboard trucks*, Elphick, *Pregnable Fortress*, p. 328.

p. 151 *almost certainly the ground crew's 'sniping'*, Warren, *Singapore 1942*, p. 63 (among others).

## Chapter 9

p. 153 *'Thus began the long series of evacuations'*, Percival, *War in Malaya*, p. 118.

p. 153 *'For the first and last time in my life'*, Bulcock, *Of Death*, p. 43.

p. 154 *an RAAF sergeant drew his revolver*, Hall, *Glory in Chaos*, p. 107.

p. 155 *too congested*, ibid., p. 102.

p. 155 *'strongly suggested'*, ibid., p. 108.

p. 155 *'not in the scheme of things'*, Shores, Cull and Izawa, *Bloody Shambles*, p. 101.

p. 156 *'If you don't shut up you won't hear the Japs'*, Bulcock, *Of Death*, p. 41.

p. 156 *'told that the Japs were landing'*, author interview with Rayson, Melbourne, 7.7.02.

p. 156 *'The little flame of panic'*, Bulcock, *Of Death*, p. 41.

p. 157 *'blew the door-lock off a private car with his pistol'*, ibid., p. 43.

p. 157 *'How is this possible? They are all sahibs'*, Elphick, *Pregnable Fortress*, p. 337.

p. 157 *three of the airmen were found guilty*, Sibylla Jane Flower, from her paper 'Allied Prisoners of War: the Malayan Campaign 1941–42', delivered at 'Sixty Years On' conference, Singapore University, February 2002.

p. 158 *Two of the Blenheims were totally destroyed*, Shores, Cull and Izawa, *Bloody Shambles*, p. 106.

p. 158 *seeing no sign of the promised fighter escort*, ibid.

p. 158 *honed by over eight years of RAF*, Laffin, *British VCs of World War 2*, pp. 200–201, 232.

p. 159 *By this time Scarf's left arm was shattered*, Shores, Cull and Izawa, *Bloody Shambles*, p. 106.

p. 159 *Between them they steered the Blenheim*, Elphick, *Pregnable Fortress*, p. 588.

p. 159 *in a coffin obtained from a local jail*, Briggs diary, IWM 82/24/1.

p. 159 *His crew were also decorated*, Shores, Cull and Izawa, *Bloody Shambles*, p. 106.

p. 160 *'many innocent men being shot'*, papers of Harvey Ryves CBE, IWM 84/30/1.

p. 162 *'full of underlined sentences and an obvious code'*, Elphick and Smith, *Odd Man Out*, p. 90.

p. 163 *Tall and athletic*, ibid., pp. 84, 96, 104, 176.

p. 164 *'bodies of men of both sides were moving across'*, Condon, *Frontier Force*, p. 352.

p. 165 *'like little spiders routed by mosquitoes'*, AWM 55 5/24.

p. 166 *slip through the Japanese in ones and twos*, Condon, *Frontier Force*, p. 355.

## Part Three: The 300-year-old Tradition

The definitive account of the sinking of the *Prince of Wales* and *Repulse* will surely always be *Battleship* by Martin Middlebrook and Patrick Mahoney.

For these chapters I also consulted Geoffrey Brooke's autobiographical *Alarm Starboard*, a frank and exciting tale by a young officer on the *Prince of Wales*; the war correspondent O'Dowd Gallagher's rather overlooked *Retreat in the East*, which has some nice reportage about his experiences on the

*Repulse*; Shores, Cull and Izawa's *Bloody Shambles*, which gives a good idea of what was happening on the Japanese side; Richard Hough's *The Hunting of Force Z* for some details on the ships' construction and a description of Phillips; Henry Leake's *Endure No Makeshifts*, for its moving description of a young midshipman's last days with his doomed father; and Bon Hall's *Glory in Chaos* for the view from the RAAF Hudson with the ringside seat. As well as meeting with naval historians in Canberra (see my acknowledgements) and examining various Admiralty records at the PRO, I also interviewed three survivors and an Australian seaman from one of the escort destroyers which picked them up.

## Chapter 10

p. 171 *'We are off to look for trouble'*, Gallagher, *Retreat in the East*, p. 14.

p. 171 *'Japs would be a bit of a pushover'*, author's interview, Hubert Bowen, Sydney, 26.7.02.

p. 172 *'keen to get into action'*, author's interview, Admiral Guy Griffiths, Sydney, 24.7.02.

p. 172 *his hobby was repairing watches*, Hough, *Force Z*, p. 107.

p. 173 *no fan of the younger man*, Winton, *Cunningham*, p. 1.

p. 173 *'One day, Tom'*, Ismay, *Memoirs*, p. 240.

p. 174 *'It will take three years to build a new Fleet'*, Winton, *Cunningham*, p. 211.

p. 174 *near fatal obsession to qualify for a private pilot's licence*, Jenkins, *Churchill*, pp. 349–50.

p. 175 *battleships had accounted for at least five of their tormentors*, Brooke, *Alarm Starboard*, pp. 87–8.

p. 175 *To complete the joy of the Prince of Wales' crew*, ibid., p. 89.

p. 175 *large number of stoppages*, PRO ADM 1/12181.

p. 175 *'Even if the British attacked'*, *Japanese Official History*, p. 247.

p. 176 *'The fiercest serpent may be overcome by a swarm of ants'*, Carver, *The Warlords*, p. 396.

p. 177 *'I've always been a very poor swimmer'*, Sir Henry Leach, telephone interview, 14.2.04.

p. 178 *'Oh let 'em come, let's have a crack at them'*, ibid.

p. 178 *lost sight of them in a squall*, Middlebrook and Mahoney, *Battleship*, p. 127.

p. 179 *he had developed a bad toothache*, ibid., p. 119.

p. 179 *the captain had muttered 'Difficult man'*, Leach, telephone interview, 14.2.04.

p. 180 *'fat transports lie off the coast'*, PRO ADM 199/1149.

p. 180 *'a cold, uninteresting, help-yourself supper'*, Middlebrook and Mahoney, *Battleship*, p. 136.

p. 181 *his grandfather's caul*, ibid., p. 262.

p. 183 *'I have most regretfully cancelled the operation'*, PRO ADM 199/1149.

p. 184 *'I may have spoken out of turn'*, Gallagher, *Retreat in the East*, p. 24.

p. 185 *orchids in a glass water jug*, ibid., p. 16.

p. 187 *the can of petrol being used to ensure full cremation*, Bulcock, *Of Death*, p. 47.

p. 188 *'We all "saw" things'*, ibid., p. 47.

p. 189 *'so peaceful standing on a long mile of deserted sand'*, Lomax, *The Railway Man*, p. 64.

### Chapter 11

p. 190 *'The enemy is making a landing'*, Gallagher, *Retreat in the East*, p. 26.

p. 191 *The shot had come from the Prince of Wales*, ibid., p. 27.

p. 191 *'well and truly locked in'*, Middlebrook and Mahoney, *Battleship*, p. 169.

p. 191 *the bugler's call caught Ordinary Seaman Taffy Bowen*, author's interview, Sydney, July 2002.

p. 194 *large flakes of paint*, Gallagher, *Retreat in the East*, p. 29.

p. 195 *left them firing 36 rounds*, Middlebrook and Mahoney, *Battleship*, p. 176.

p. 196 *a little puzzled by their absence*, ibid., p. 119.

p. 196 *In a ringside seat*, Hall, *Glory in Chaos*, p. 138.

p. 196 *'no torpedo bombers about'*, Middlebrook and Mahoney, *Battleship*, p. 181.

p. 198 *'The heavy jarring of the 5.25s'*, Brooke, *Alarm Starboard*, p. 97.

p. 198 *Katsujiro Kawa, and all his crew*, Shores, Cull and Izawa, *Bloody Shambles*, p. 118.

p. 198 *'a lurid column of water'*, Hall, *Glory in Chaos*, p. 139.

p. 199 *swirling up the steps*, Middlebrook and Mahoney, p. 201 (quoting Lieutenant Dick Wildish).

p. 200 *'not up to much'*, Gallagher, *Retreat in the East*, p. 16.

p. 202 *'I pushed the throttles forward'*, Shores, Cull and Izawa, *Bloody Shambles*, p. 120.

p. 203 *'as though we were a destroyer'*, Middlebrook and Mahoney, *Battleship*, p. 193.

p. 203 *'God, did we move!'*, ibid., p. 192, quoting Able Seaman S. C. Baxter.

p. 203 *six rounds of .38 revolver ammunition'*, Hough, *Force Z*, p. 142.

p. 203 *spit it out when they tasted warm salt water*, Gallagher, *Retreat in the East*, pp. 30–31.

p. 204 *'TO ANY BRITISH MAN OF WAR'*, National Archives, PRO ADM 199/1149.

p. 204 *'Thanks to providence have so far dodged'*, Hough, *Force Z*, p. 145.

p. 207 *taken on about 18,000 tons of water*, Middlebrook and Mahoney, *Battleship*, p. 220.

p. 207 *'an important ship that was being bombed'*, Shores, Cull and Izawa, *Bloody Shambles*, p. 122.

## Chapter 12

p. 209 *'hardly shuddered and ploughed steadily on'*, Middlebrook and Mahoney, *Battleship*, p. 222.

p. 211 *This honour was reserved for Fukumatsu Yamamoto*, Shores, Cull and Izawa, *Bloody Shambles*, p. 121.

p. 211 *constantly volunteering to serve on motor torpedo boats*, Brooke, *Alarm Starboard*, p. 92.

p. 211 *flopped into the sea on its belly*, Shores, Cull and Izawa, *Bloody Shambles*, p. 121.

p. 212 *'it was clear the men inside had only seconds to live'*, Brooke, *Alarm Starboard*, p. 105.

p. 212 *'Being a kid like, I turned to help him'*, author's interview, Sydney, July 2002.

p. 214 *he swam the fastest crawl*, author's interview with Hubert Bowen, Sydney, July 2002.

p. 214 *'You can stop swimming now, Taffy'*, ibid.

p. 214 *'I told them they looked like a couple of Al Jolsons'*, Gallagher, *Retreat in the East*, p. 36.

p. 215 *her crew gave her a last cheer*, Hubert Bowen to author, Sydney, July 2002.

p. 215 *bandsman they knew hanging in the chains of the paravane*, ibid.

p. 215 *'You've put up a good show'*, Hough, *Force Z*, p. 147.

p. 215 *considered a bit on the quiet side*, Admiral Guy Griffiths to author, 24.2.04.

p. 216 *'Here you are, sir'*, Hough, *Force Z*, p. 148.

p. 217 *'What have you come alongside for?'*, Middlebrook and Mahoney, *Battleship*, p. 232.

p. 217 *'Come back, you yellow bastard!'*, ibid., p. 246.

p. 217 *'It was surprisingly tiring work'*, Brooke, *Alarm Starboard*, p. 108.

p. 218 *'All the ropes swung down, heavy with men'*, ibid., p. 108.

p. 219 *'Guns before men'*, Middlebrook and Mahoney, *Battleship*, p. 251.

p. 220 *'obvious that the three destroyers'*, Vigors in the *Daily Express*, 27.2.48.

p. 221 *'very large, unconscious Royal Marine, wounded and clogged with oil'*, Hayes, *Face the Music*, p. 202.

p. 221 *amazing himself by placing them neatly together*, Gallagher, *Retreat in the East*, p. 42.

p. 221 *place his camera and plates in a lifebelt locker*, ibid.

p. 222 *'a bloke here called Captain Tennant'*, Vince Cesari to author, Singapore, 15.2.02.

p. 222 *'They urged them to leave'*, Leach, *Endure No Makeshifts*, p. 10.

p. 224 *'made one hell of a mess of even fifty or sixty'*, Shores, Cull and Izawa, *Bloody Shambles*, p. 125.

p. 224 *'going down with his ship'*, telephone interview with Sir Henry Leach, 14.2.04.

p. 225 *'derrick boom wedged firmly over my thighs'*, Middlebrook and Mahoney, *Battleship*, p. 252.


## Part Four: Retreat and Reinforcements

### Chapter 13

p. 229 *'The worst single piece of news'*, Cooper, *Old Men Forget*, p. 301.

p. 229 *'We were not safe then'*, Morrison, *Malayan Postscript*, p. 60.

p. 229 *'His reception was poor'*, Stapledon papers, IWM 85/31/1.

p. 230 *'Blown clean away at one fell swoop'*, Morrison, *Malayan Postscript*, p. 60.

p. 230 *'Are you sure it's true?'*, Churchill, *The Second World War*, vol. 3, p. 551.

p. 231 *'They came in mass'*, Fay, *The Forgotten Army*, p. 59.

p. 233 *'It caused great hindrance'*, Kawamura Saburo, Summary of the Malayan Operation of the Fifth Division, IWM AL 5181.

p. 235 *'A few score men'*, Percival, *War in Malaya*, p. 117.

p. 236 *When Heath wanted labour to improve them*, Kappe papers, AWM MSS 1393.

p. 237 *stretched some 35 miles*, Underhill, *The Royal Leicestershire Regiment*, p. 90.

p. 238 *'Suddenly I saw some of my trucks'*, Greer, quoted in Holmes and Kemp, *The Bitter End*, p. 99.

p. 239 *'scattered like chaff'*, Kappe papers, AWM MSS 1393.

p. 241 *'that Private Watkins was improperly dressed?'*, Abbott papers, IWM 89/15/11.

p. 241 *Second Lieutenant Oto*, Tsuji, *Singapore 1941–42*, p. 12.

p. 243 *'It was mediaeval'*, interview with Jack Sharpe, Singapore, February 2002.

p. 243 *He dropped to one knee*, ibid.

p. 243 *'Unconsciously breaking into a run'*, Tsuji, *Singapore 1941–42*, p. 122.

p. 245 *confusion and exhaustion*, Percival, *War in Malaya*, p. 134.

p. 245 *'scenes of indescribable confusion'*, Underhill, *Royal Leicestershire Regiment*, p. 93.

p. 247 *'The fellows are done in by now'*, Abbott papers, IWM 89/15/11.

p. 248 *'My God! That's a Jap!'*, Percival, *War in Malaya*, p. 140.

p. 248 *an anti-tank gun also entered into the spirit*, Kappe papers, AWM MSS 1393.

p. 248 *the whistle jammed to a constant scream*, ibid.

p. 248 *which shivered visibly*, ibid.

p. 249 *was killed when a mine went off*, Warren, *Singapore 1942*, p. 100.

## Chapter 14

p. 250 *drew his pistol*, Murray-Lyon, Indian Office, London, L/WS/1/952.

p. 252 *'There's nothing we can do but leave them'*, Abbott papers, IWM 89/15/11.

p. 252 *'one of the strongest natural positions'*, Percival, *War in Malaya*, p. 132.

p. 253 *'Well, he may be mad'*, Abbott papers, IWM 89/15/11.

p. 254 *'Get round the bastards'*, ibid.

p. 254 *'We arrive back on the road and start to crawl'*, ibid.

p. 254 *'stabbed in the buttocks with burning chopsticks'*, Tsuji, *Singapore 1941–42*, p. 134.

p. 255 *'an elderly officer, a stranger'*, Chippington, *Singapore – The Inexcusable Betrayal*, pp. 78–9.

p. 257 *'If the 11th Division was defeated at Jitra'*, Kappe papers, AWM MSS 1393.

p. 258 *'Each man was near breaking point'*, Abbott, *And All My War is Done*, p. 22.

p. 258 *'seem like slaves'*, Tsuji, *Singapore 1941–42*, p. 135.

p. 258 *'RAF – Rare as Fairies'*, interview with Ernest Agass, London, February 2002.

p. 259 *'The usual mêlée ensued'*, Shores, Cull and Izawa, *Bloody Shambles*, p. 132.

p. 260 *'which we had only ever seen in Dorothy Lamour films'*, Lieutenant J. E. Whitaker, IWM 97/6/1.

p. 261 *'every single man we could lay hands on'*, Percival, *War in Malaya*, p. 143.

p. 261 *'Hello, Singapore, this is Penang calling'*, Morrison, *Malayan Postscript*, p. 70.

p. 262 *'They accompanied me to the hospital'*, Shores, Cull and Izawa, *Bloody Shambles*, p. 135.

p. 262 *he had waited six hours*, Glover, *Seventy Days*, pp. 112–13.

p. 263 *'a very discreditable affair'*, Shenton Thomas diaries, Rhodes House, Oxford.

p. 263 *'evacuate the troops first and leave the women'*, Charmley, *Duff Cooper*, p. 161.

p. 263 *British citizens who had insisted on staying*, Shenton Thomas diaries, Rhodes House, Oxford.

## Chapter 15

p. 265 *'much hope of saving Singapore'*, A. Brooke, *War Diaries*, p. 212.

p. 265 *'our new enemy, the yellow Huns of the East'*, Bennett, *Why Singapore Fell*, p. 69.

p. 266 *'I got so angry'*, Henry McCreath to author, Berwick-on-Tweed, January 2002.

p. 267 *'towards us over the horizon'*, Fergus Anckorn to author, Westerham, Kent, 30.4.02.

p. 267 'We didn't have companionways', ibid.

p. 268 'Lots of milk, bread', Fusilier J. F. Taylor's diary, regimental museum, Alnwick Castle, Northumberland.

p. 270 called him 'Busty', James McLean to author, Swinton, Berwickshire, 30.1.02.

p. 271 With two kilted pipers, a drummer and a little dog, Moffatt and McCormick, Moon over Malaya, p. 33.

p. 271 'British standards', Stewart, History of the Argyll and Sutherland Highlanders 2nd Battalion 1941–42 (henceforth 2nd Argylls), p. 4.

p. 272 'Once a force has been launched into the jungle', ibid., pp. 35–6.

p. 273 'The force of the bullets', Moffatt and McCormick, Moon over Malaya, p. 70.

p. 273 'the perfect answer to a machine-gunner's prayer', Stewart, 2nd Argylls, p. 23.

p. 274 'There is rarely a drawn battle in the jungle', ibid., p. 42.

p. 274 'Hearing Jap voices I cut some lotus leaves', ibid., pp. 124–7 (Appendix II, 'An Escape from the Japs', by Major R. W. Kennard, MC).

p. 274 'There was a lot of moaning and groaning', ibid., p. 125.

p. 276 'Captain Hendry thereupon picked up the least dead-looking Jap', Stewart, 2nd Argylls, p. 57.

p. 277 'Tired and worn after several days', Morrison, Malayan Postscript, pp. 101–2.

p. 277 During one leapfrog, Deakin, Kappe papers, AWM MSS 1393.

p. 279 'It was impossible to make even the remotest guess', Tsuji, Singapore 1941– 42, p. 139.

p. 281 'Destroyers against battleships', Stewart, 2nd Argylls, p. 58.

p. 281 saw an eye lying near a boot, Moffatt and McCormick, Moon over Malaya, p. 94.

p. 282 'refused to let itself be stampeded off the road', Stewart, 2nd Argylls, p. 59.

p. 283 'All seemed to have a Scottish dislike', ibid., p. 62.

p. 283 'It was well into the night', Moffatt and McCormick, Moon over Malaya, p. 97.

## Chapter 16

p. 284 'we were preparing for the usual New Year', Straits Times, 1.1.42.

p. 284 'all in the dark as there was an alert', Atkinson papers, IWM 85/36/1.

p. 285 'What a funny place', Shores, Cull and Izawa, Bloody Shambles, p. 278.

p. 286 'meek and acquiescent', Shenton Thomas diary, Rhodes House, Oxford.

p. 286 '. . . there are no air-raid shelters, no trenches', PRO/National Archives, PREM 3/499/2.

p. 286 '. . . a nice, good man', ibid.

p. 287 '. . . a fine dashing attractive fellow', ibid.

p. 287 'I found the country far more beautiful', Duff Cooper, Old Men Forget, p. 299.

p. 287 *'better than a better man'*, PRO/National Archives PREM 3/499/2.

p. 287 *born in Australia and already thirty*, Moremon and Reid, *A Bitter Fate*, pp. 133–4.

p. 288 *'Unless the unforeseen happens'*, PRO/National Archives PREM 3/499/2.

p. 288 *'He has a heavy task'*, Bennett, *Why Singapore Fell*, p. 85.

p. 289 *'The whole scheme wild and half-baked'*, A. Brooke, *War Diaries*, p. 215.

p. 289 *'A pretty tall order'*, Connell and Roberts, *Wavell*, p. 71.

p. 289 *'It was almost certain'*, Churchill, *The Second World War*, vol. 3, p. 600.

p. 290 *'immense capacity for taking hard knocks'*, Pownall, *Chief of Staff*, p. 95.

p. 290 *'All materials of war, including the general'*, Wavell, *Soldiers and Soldiering*, pp. 14–16.

p. 290 *'I breathe the air of the South'*, Potter, *A Soldier Must Hang*, pp. 64–5.

## Chapter 17

p. 294 *recently been a clerk*, Wigmore, *Japanese Thrust*, p. 185.

p. 294 *'A bird came and perched on a bough near my stand'*, Rose, *Who Dies Fighting*, p. 71.

p. 294 *'I had gone about 30 yards or so'*, ibid.

p. 295 *'There was a good deal of shouting going on'*, ibid.

p. 296 *Once police, acting on one of his plots*, Elphick, *Pregnable Fortress*, p. 141.

p. 298 *'I felt so like a Crusader'*, Spencer Chapman, *The Jungle is Neutral*, p. 19.

p. 299 *'For God's sake stop calling me sir'*, Barker, *One Man's Jungle*, p. 198.

p. 299 *'as it can move very fast'*, Spencer Chapman, *The Jungle is Neutral*, p. 93.

p. 299 *iodine and potassium permanganate for blacking up*, Barker, *One Man's Jungle*, p. 200.

p. 300 *'We have already organized for many years to fight'*, Rose, *Who Dies Fighting*, p. 55.

p. 300 *'Some wore green, others grey, khaki or even dirty white'*, Spencer Chapman, *The Jungle is Neutral*, pp. 26–7.

p. 301 *Naval Arsenal's factory in Nagoya*, Mayer, *The Rise and Fall of Imperial Japan*, p. 46.

p. 301 *estimated 4 million Stens*, Archer, *Jane's Pistols and Sub-machine Guns*, p. 182.

p. 302 *'Frequently one or two men armed with a tommy-gun'*, Bennett, *Why Singapore Fell*, p. 75.

## Chapter 18

p. 303 *'My soldiers began to get tired'*, Kawamura papers, IWM AL 5181.

p. 304 *'I remembered a thought'*, McEwan, *Out of the Depths of Hell*, p. 32.

p. 304 *The Lanarkshire Yeomanry's monocled commander*, ibid., pp. 19–20.

p. 305 *'polo-playing playboy'*, Sharpe interview, February 2002.

p. 306 *'a continuous stream'*, Tsuji, *Singapore 1941–42*, p. 160.

p. 307 *Bren guns further up the hill*, Chippington, *Inexcusable Betrayal*, p. 121.

p. 307 *found himself face to face*, ibid., p. 118.

p. 307 *'immediately awarded'*, 88th Field Regiment, RA, in Malaya, PRO WO 172/43.

p. 309 *talk in old Indian Army circles*, Russell-Roberts, *Spotlight on Singapore*, p. 285.

p. 311 *a steamer with ten landing-craft in tow*, Kappe papers, AWM MSS 1393.

p. 311 *casualties were one killed and one wounded*, Papers of Mortimer Cecil Hay, Lance-Bombardier, Light Battery, Volunteer Forces, Rhodes House, Oxford.

p. 311 *begged to be allowed to go there immediately*, ibid.

p. 311 *'Unfortunately neither the navy nor the air force'*, Percival, *War in Malaya*, p. 197.

p. 313 *the 'pluck' demonstrated*, ibid., p. 149.

p. 313 *'often failed to take the most elementary precautions'*, ibid., p. 200.

p. 314 *A fighting patrol of Deakin's 5/2 Punjabis*, Stewart, *2nd Argylls*, p. 69.

p. 314 *allowed the Japanese to get so close*, author's conversations with General Shahid Hamid of the Pakistani Army, once Colonel Hamid, Indian Army Service Corps, who served in Malaya. He died in Rawalpindi in 1993.

p. 314 *ninety killed and wounded*, Stewart, *2nd Argylls*, p. 71.

p. 315 *emerged from the last chest-deep swamp*, Tsuji, *Singapore 1941–42*, pp. 160–61.

p. 315 *'The "getaway" was uneventful'*, 88th Field Regiment, RA, PRO WO 172/43.

p. 315 *disappointed to find themselves heading south again*, McEwan, *Depths of Hell*, p. 32.

## Chapter 19

p. 316 *Takumi would never have got it, alleged his critics*, Tsuji, *Singapore 1941–42*, p. 165.

p. 318 *'obstinately defended'*, Tsuji, *Singapore 1941–42*, p. 166.

p. 318 *A jemadar was observed*, Condon, *Frontier Force*, p. 362.

p. 319 *there was a lingering affection for the .455*, author's conversations with Shahid Hamid; also in 1995 with Colonel Tony Simonds, who became a friend of Cumming after they had both retired to Cyprus. Cumming died in 1971.

p. 319 *seven Japanese with bayonets fixed*, Condon, *Frontier Force* (citing Captain Ian Grimwood as main source for its chapter on Malaya), p. 368.

p. 322 '*the brigade commander's responsibility*', Russell-Roberts, *Spotlight on Singapore*, pp. 42–3.

## Chapter 20

p. 324 *Wilson-Stephens became aware of something in the glass*, Kappe papers, AWM MSS 1393.

p. 326 '*the usual one of gaining time*', Stewart, *2nd Argylls*, p. 76.

p. 327 *Two of these cuttings, which were about a mile apart*, Kappe papers, AWM MSS 1393.

p. 327 *shortage of Boys anti-tank rifles*, Hewitt papers, IWM 85/35/1.

p. 327 *like a lollipop stick*, Moffatt and McCormick, *Moon over Malaya*, p. 110.

p. 327 *A Tamil labourer who had wandered through the front lines*, Kappe papers, AWM MSS 1393.

p. 328 '*Sixty dead Japanese had been counted*', ibid.

p. 329 '*Like all regiments the Argylls had their rubbish*', Stewart, *2nd Argylls*, p. 94.

p. 332 *Shimada's leading T95 went over one of the anti-tank mines*, Kappe papers, AWM MSS 1393.

p. 332 *They began to drop Molotov cocktails on them*, ibid.

p. 332 *making a lot of noise*, ibid.

p. 333 '*hang on at all costs*', ibid.

p. 334 '*Turbaned soldiers ducked around him*', Moffatt and McCormick, *Moon over Malaya*, p. 105.

p. 334 '*I heard his engine revving up*', ibid., p. 109.

p. 336 *The experiences of this party*, Stewart, *2nd Argylls*, p. 81.

p. 338 *never expected this sort of thing to happen to them*, Flower, 'Sixty Years On' conference, p. 209. Ms Flower, the greatest authority on the fate of the campaign's POWs, mentioned this as a widely held belief in the paper she delivered at the 2002 conference in Singapore.

p. 338 *Before long he realized the man was dead*, Stewart, *2nd Argylls*, p. 84.

p. 340 *Mooney drew his. 455*, Hewitt quoting Mooney's orderly, who saw it; IWM 85/35/1.

p. 341 *he had shot himself*, Warren, *Singapore 1942*, p. 139.

p. 343 *Arthur Harrison, the division's chief of staff*, PRO CAB 106/55.

## Chapter 21

p. 346 *almost killed on the day*, Connell and Roberts, *Wavell*, p. 66.

p. 346 '*I have never seen two men look so tired*', ibid., p. 84.

p. 346 '*somewhat critical*', ibid., p. 85.

p. 347 'We could not afford to leave the east coast weakly defended', Percival, *War in Malaya*, p. 208.

p. 347 'going into bat', Bennett, *Why Singapore Fell*, p. 100.

p. 347 'We must take certain risks', Connell and Roberts, *Wavell*, p. 88.

p. 348 'My God, I thought, he's gone and murdered', Fay, *Forgotten Army*, p. 62.

p. 349 'Pillars of smoke and flame', Percival, *War in Malaya*, p. 210.

p. 349 Wilson's solution was to tie down, Wilson, *Sum of Things*, p. 66.

p. 350 'a disgrace which the native peoples', Kappe papers, AWM MSS 1393.

p. 350 'An Indian emerges from the crowd', Ryrie papers, Rhodes House, Oxford.

p. 351 somewhat unfair dissatisfaction with Percival, Pownall, *Chief of Staff*, p. 76.

p. 351 'He is such a one for pleasure', Charmley, *Duff Cooper*, p. 158.

p. 351 Diana fortified by a large gin, Cooper, *Old Men Forget*, p. 305.

p. 351 'I shall see him out with a sigh of relief', Montgomery, *Shenton of Singapore*, p. 109.

p. 352 'he was a civilian', Smyth, *Percival and the Tragedy of Singapore*, p. 256.

## Chapter 22

p. 353 'Japanese bodies, bicycles', Kappe papers, AWM MSS 1393.

p. 355 trying to shoot out the headlights, Harrison, *The Brave Japanese*, p. 43.

p. 356 'These burst on contact', ibid., p. 27.

p. 357 'It lay there with men crawling out', ibid., pp. 29–32.

p. 358 'We waved back rather lamely', ibid., p. 33.

p. 358 twenty-three and not all that long ago, Horner, *The Gunners*, pp. 294–8.

p. 358 Empire Day fireworks back home, Kappe papers, AWM MSS 1393.

p. 358 been badly hit in the chest, Wigmore, *Japanese Thrust*, p. 219.

p. 358 respect their red crosses, ibid., p. 220.

p. 359 'the derisive laughter', Harrison, *Brave Japanese*, p. 37.

p. 360 A Japanese fighter pilot, Shores, Cull and Izawa, *Bloody Shambles*, pp. 295–6.

## Chapter 23

p. 361 'The Black Bastard', Braddon, *Naked Island*, p. 57.

p. 364 'I don't want you to interfere with us', Finkmeyer, *It Happened to Us*, p. 10.

p. 366 'A glorious death', Allied Translator and Interpreter Section, AWM 55 5/24.

p. 366 brave men had been squandered, History of Japanese Imperial Guard, p. 15, NAM.

p. 366 'until one by one they were smashed', Wigmore, *Japanese Thrust*, p. 227.

p. 369 'thought that the move to the mainland', Kemp, *The Royal Norfolk Regiment*, p. 108.

p. 370 *municipal dust carts*, Toosey interview, IWM 12749/52, Sound Archive.

p. 370 *'They were a fine body of men'*, Wigmore, *Japanese Thrust*, p. 226.

p. 371 *'Your first job'*, ibid., p. 226.

p. 371 *'Just beside the road a naked waist'*, ibid., p. 233.

p. 372 *'The Black Bastard was dead'*, Braddon, *Naked Island*, p. 63.

p. 372 *500 yards beyond his battalion's*, Kappe, papers, AWM MSS 1393.

p. 372 *'but for you and your guns'*, Harrison, *Brave Japanese*, p. 47.

p. 373 *'Most of the troops were'*, NAM 7709–62.

p. 373 *'Eventually they were given'*, Harrison, *Brave Japanese*, pp. 51–2.

p. 373 *the Indians' Lee-Enfield rifles were much newer*, Braddon, *Naked Island*, p. 60.

p. 374 *'my right was again pinned down'*, 2/19th Battalion Association, *The Grim Glory*, p. 201.

p. 374 *Sergeant Desmond Mulcahy's particular Lazarus*, ibid., p. 200.

p. 374 *sportingly thrown down his rifle*, ibid.

p. 375 *'we learnt not to trust their wounded'*, ibid., p. 233.

p. 375 *had killed 140*, Wigmore, *Japanese Thrust*, p. 232.

p. 375 *'He was hit by Bren and Tommy and rifle fire'*, ibid.

p. 376 *'Oh, Jim, what did you do that for?'*, Harrison, *Brave Japanese*, pp. 57–8.


## Chapter 24

p. 377 *'I was about to go over the top'*, 2/19th Battalion Association, *Grim Glory*, p. 234; also Ward, *Snaring the Other Tiger*, pp. 209–10.

p. 378 *'Mine, Donnelly!'*, 2/19th Battalion Association, *Grim Glory*, p. 212.

p. 379 *'I heard a peculiar grunt beside me'*, ibid., p. 215.

p. 379 *'A very able and gallant officer'*, Wigmore, *Japanese Thrust*, p. 239.

p. 380 *'They were wearing shorts'*, interview with Walter Greenwood, February 2002 at IWM.

p. 381 *a bullet had entered his throat and exited*, Bennett, *Why Singapore Fell*, p. 141.

p. 382 *'I made them clean guns'*, 2/19th Battalion Association, *Grim Glory*, p. 215.

p. 383 *'Tommowoh yoh die!'*, author interview with Don White, 2/20th, Australia 2002.

p. 383 *'like a stop volley at tennis'*, Braddon, *Naked Island*, pp. 75–6.

p. 384 *their original wireless*, Bennett, *Why Singapore Fell*, p. 143.

p. 385 *'Each aircraft let all bombs go at once'*, Shores, Cull and Izawa, *Bloody Shambles*, p. 338.

p. 386 *'the chances of a single battalion'*, Percival, *War in Malaya*, p. 232.

p. 386 *thrown together three sets of barricades*, 2/19th Battalion Association, *Grim Glory*, pp. 222–3.

p. 389 *'started to smell a bit'*, ibid., p. 240.

p. 389 *'I thought the Japanese would not show much consideration'*, ibid., p. 240.

p. 390 *'You may at your discretion'*, Bennett, *Naked Island*, p. 142.

p. 390 *'a wash; being in other than bloodstained'*, Wigmore, *Japanese Thrust*, p. 246; from 'Dark Evening', Hackney's unpublished memoir.

p. 391 *'then thrust the bayonet into him'*, Hackney's sworn testimony for Nishimura's trial, taken before Mr Justice Mansfield, Sydney, 12.11.45.

p. 393 *'one bayonet had gone through the bandage'*, ibid.

p. 394 *'I could see the flickers of fire'*, ibid.

p. 395 *'A Jap officer with a drawn sword'*, 2/19th Battalion Association, *Grim Glory*, p. 249.

p. 396 *killing of a brigadier and two colonels*, Flower, 'Allied POWs', paper at 'Sixty Years On' conference, Singapore University, February 2002, p. 214.

## Chapter 25

p. 399 *sand air-intake filters and twelve machine-guns*, Probert, *Forgotten Air Force*, p. 56.

p. 399 *it was an English novice*, Shores, Cull and Izawa, *Bloody Shambles*, p. 325.

p. 399 *Rowland, whose wife Veronica and baby son*, Glover, *In Seventy Days*, p. 81.

p. 400 *either six 250-pound bombs*, Hall, *Glory in Chaos*, p. 351.

p. 400 *exploding in mid-air*, ibid., p. 353.

p. 400 *'It's a wonder the old crate didn't fall apart'*, AWM 3DR1/6066.

p. 400 *the RAF had lost ten Vildebeest*, Probert, *Forgotten Air Force*, p. 58.

p. 401 *where they were murdered*, Francis Richard, article in *Naval Historical Review* – Journal of the Naval Historical Society of Australia, vol. 23, 2002.

p. 402 *'an appalling hand-to-hand battle'*, Allied Translator and Interpreter Section, Wigmore, *Japanese Thrust*, p. 269.

p. 403 *six officers and ninety-two men missing*, ibid., p. 268.

p. 403 *'nervous strain'*, a veteran of the campaign who wishes to remain anonymous.

p. 406 *Both guns and most of the vehicles*, Toosey interview, IWM 12749/52, Sound Archive.

p. 408 *'in a poor state of discipline'*, Mackenzie, *Eastern Epic*, p. 371.

p. 409 *'We were sharing the water'*, Chippington, *Inexcusable Betrayal*, p. 162.

p. 410 *'As darkness fell'*, ibid., pp. 165–6.

p. 411 *'Whiz Bang Sikh'*, Elphick, *Pregnable Fortress*, p. 593.

p. 412 *'You've sold the show'*, from transcript of Major-General Kirby's interview with Trott in Australia when he was preparing his official history, PRO CAB 106/151.

p. 413 *'Shortly all four men were floundering'*, Russell-Roberts, *Spotlight on Singapore*, p. 99.

p. 414 *'I shall never forget'*, ibid., p. 103.

p. 414 *a white flag appeared*, ibid., p. 109.

p. 416 *'Are there any British troops there?'*, interview with John Goatley, Haslemere, 10.3.02.

p. 416 *Dr Ryrie, the Scottish doctor*, journal, Mss. Ind. Ocean. s. 250, Rhodes House, Oxford.

p. 416 *'They took my father and cut off his head'*, Russell-Roberts, *Spotlight on Singapore*, p. 283.

p. 417 *'I hit Sartin on the shoulder'*, Spencer Chapman, *The Jungle is Neutral*, p. 80.

p. 418 *'He was so surprised at seeing us'*, Rudling papers, IWM P478.

## Part Five: The Besiegement

### Chapter 26

p. 423 *'It is a word not even to be found'*, Morrison, *Malayan Postscript*, pp. 145–6.

p. 424 *'I want to make it absolutely clear'*, Churchill, *Second World War*, vol. 4, p. 47.

p. 424 *'measures for the defence of the island'*, Connell and Roberts, *Wavell*, p. 113.

p. 424 *'Singapore would become a complete inferno'*, ibid., p. 142.

p. 425 *'I ought to have known'*, Churchill, *Second World War*, vol. 4, p. 49.

p. 426 *'preparations must of course be kept entirely secret'*, Connell and Roberts, *Wavell*, p. 111.

p. 426 *'We have not treated the Chinese well'*, Cazalet papers, IWM P432.

p. 427 *'We were here to defend the naval base'*, Bennett, *Why Singapore Fell*, p. 165.

p. 427 *'There were some Indian sentries at the gate'*, Morrison, *Malayan Postscript*, pp. 149–50.

p. 428 *'utterly ashamed of my own service'*, Cazalet papers, IWM P432.

p. 429 *'charming as usual but blathering about'*, ibid.

p. 430 *'Our task has been both to impose losses'*, Percival, *War in Malaya*, p. 259.

p. 430 *'The island is by now crammed'*, Abbott papers, IWM 89/15/11.

p. 431 *every able-bodied man*, Reginald Burton to author at Newton Abbott, 3.5.02.

p. 431 *'We'll come good on the island'*, Burton, *Railway of Hell*, p. 8.

p. 431 *harrowing tales of murder and rape*, Phyllis Harrop, quoted in message from Macao's British Consulate received by Foreign Office on 2.2.42, PRO CO 980/82.

p. 432 *'If the European women'*, Percival, *War in Malaya*, p. 179.

p. 432 *Percival sent the War Office a message*, from paper delivered by Kent

Fedorowich, Senior Lecturer in British Imperial History at University of the West of England, Bristol, at 'Sixty Years On' conference, Singapore University, 2002.

p. 432 *Thomas was hoping that Canberra would suspend*, ibid.

p. 432 *Miss Harrop turned up*, PRO 980/52.

p. 432 *a story that appeared, Evening Standard*, London, 5.3.42.

p. 433 *Dernham decided to get at least*, Manners, *Bullwinkel*, p. 42.

p. 433 *'a sausage on a stick'*, Rose, *Who Dies Fighting*, p. 121.

p. 433 *went off to Wassiamull's*, Russell-Roberts, *Spotlight on Singapore*, p. 126.

p. 433 *Dan Hopkins and his dance band*, ibid., p. 129.

p. 434 *Felix Roussel was a small liner*, details of ship from documents supplied to author by Northumberland Fusiliers Henry McCreath, John Webb and Jack Phillips.

p. 436 *'I want men who want to fight'*, from the diary of Fusilier J. F. Taylor, Royal Northumberland Fusiliers regimental museum, Alnwick Castle.

p. 436 *best anti-aircraft weapon at their disposal*, details of Brens used in anti-aircraft role from Fusilier veterans John Webb and Jack Phillips.

p. 436 *known as 'Treacle' by his fellow subalterns*, author's interview with John Webb, January 2002, and subsequent correspondence.

p. 437 *brought off the Mole at Dunkirk*, author's interview with Jack Phillips, Singapore, February 2002, and subsequent correspondence.

p. 437 *Colonel Thomas had set up his battalion headquarters*, author's interview and correspondence with John Webb, January 2002.

p. 438 *'locked inside a tin can which people were beating with sticks'*, ibid.

p. 438 *'getting at the bastards'*, author's interview with Jack Phillips.

p. 440 *'Mais, voici le Colonel'*, author's interview with John Webb.

p. 440 *Singapore was burning*, author's interview with Jack Phillips.


## Chapter 27

p. 441 *'burning sea'*, Dear and Foot, *Oxford Companion to the Second World War*, p. 377.

p. 442 *fire blindly onto map references*, Tsuji, *Singapore 1941–42*, p. 236.

p. 443 *twenty rounds a gun*, Murfett et al., *Between Two Oceans*, p. 339.

p. 443 *'in the region of 85,000'*, Percival, *War in Malaya*, p. 261.

p. 443 *could have been as low as 60,000*, Connell and Roberts, *Wavell*, p. 162.

p. 443 *'troops can be made to act with sufficient vigour and determination'*, ibid.

p. 446 *'It was impenetrable with all the streams'*, Wall, *Singapore and Beyond*, p. 52.

p. 447 *'Of the troops which had had experience of fighting'*, Percival, *War in Malaya*, p. 262.

p. 447 *reloading his rifle a round at a time*, Wall, *Singapore and Beyond*, p. 91.

p. 448 *their light would be shot out*, Peacock, *Tinker's Mufti*, p. 162.

pp. 448–9 *'despite some misgivings arising from the contrast'*, Wigmore, *Japanese Thrust*, pp. 29–30.

p. 449 *'wet nursing' his soldiers*, Murfett et al., *Between Two Oceans*, p. 357.

p. 449 *he thought lives should not be wasted in a hopeless fight*, ibid.

p. 449 *'a number of high-ranking officers'*, Moore, *Battalion at War*, p. 11.

p. 451 *'stay in the garden watching the planes'*, Stapledon papers, IWM 85/31/1.

p. 451 *'We didn't know his name'*, ibid.

p. 451 *'Never have I admired people more than I admired those boys'*, Morrison, *Malayam Postscript*, p. 178.

p. 452 *'Two days before the Causeway was blown'*, Cross, *Red Jungle*, p. 15 (Cross did not identify his employers as MI6 but later accounts did).

## Chapter 28

p. 453 *rubber-soled brown canvas PT shoes, armed only with revolvers*, 2/19th Battalion Association, *Grim Glory*.

p. 453 *came close enough to a field kitchen to contemplate adding*, Wall, *Singapore and Beyond*, p. 56.

p. 453 *including the Australian government's representative*, Wigmore, *Japanese Thrust*, p. 353.

p. 456 *dispersed in ones and twos through the rubber*, Tsuji, *Singapore 1941–42*, p. 235.

p. 456 *'a little less paper in this war will improve matters'*, Bennett, *Why Singapore Fell*, p. 173.

p. 456 *'The brigadier appears somewhat shaken'*, ibid.

p. 458 *sudden onset of malarial shivers*, Don Wall to author, Australia, July 2002.

p. 458 *'Then you settle down'*, Wall, *Singapore and Beyond*, p. 64.

p. 460 *lightweight affairs of plywood with moulded rubber joints*, Wigmore, *Japanese Thrust*, p. 334.

p. 461 *longer legged Guards preferred to limit their capacity*, Tsuji, *Singapore 1941–42*, p. 225.

p. 461 *150 boats, sometimes bumping*, Frei, *Guns of February*, p. 86.

p. 461 *containing a little of a comrade's ashes and bone*, ibid. Also Allied Translation and Interpreter Section South West Pacific Area, AWM 55/RR 68/12/46.

## Chapter 29

p. 462 *discretion to illuminate*, Kappe papers, AWM MSS 1393.

p. 463 *'a suicide squad'*, Morrison, *Malayan Postscript*, p. 145.

p. 463 *generator lines had been cut by shell-fire*, Kappe papers, AWM MSS 1393.

p. 463 *'Landings – coastal defensive fire'*, 2/19th Battalion Association, *Grim Glory*, p. 308.

p. 464 *'We train and we practise for years'*, ibid., pp 308–9.

p. 465 *remembered to wish His Imperial Majesty a long life*, Allied Translations, AWM 55/RR 68/12/46.

p. 465 *'a cold hand stroked his ankle'*, A. Mitsuo Shingaporu Senki (*Singapore War Diary*, Tokyo, 1984) translated by Professor Henry Frei and read by him in the paper he delivered at 'Sixty Years On' conference, Singapore University, February 2002.

p. 465 *'Bring down fire everywhere'*, Wigmore, *Japanese Thrust*, p. 310.

p. 466 *'at night in thick country and in the middle of a battle'*, Percival, *War in Malaya*, p. 270.

p. 467 *For the defending Australians, it was kill or retreat*, Frei, paper at 'Sixty Years On' conference, Singapore University, February 2002.

p. 467 *'like rabid dogs'*, ibid.

p. 467 *made the mistake of pausing to tie a loose bootlace*, Wall, *Singapore and Beyond*, p. 66.

p. 467 *had shot himself following an official reprimand*, Probert, *Forgotten Air Force*, p. 58.

p. 467 *Spackman bayoneted the officer, seized his sword*, Kappe papers, AWM MSS 1393.

p. 468 *Meiklejohn's men had fought on until shortly after 1 a.m.*, ibid.

p. 468 *at least one was rendered hors de combat*, ibid.

p. 470 *'Not all men are heroes'*, Percival, *War in Malaya*, pp. 270–71.

## Chapter 30

p. 472 *'suicidal resistance like wounded boars'*, Wigmore, *Japanese Thrust* p. 279, citing Allied Translation and Interpreter Section, AWM 55/RR 68/12/46.

p. 472 *Maxwell declared Boyes to be 'unsatisfactory'*, Warren, *Singapore 1942*, p. 233.

p. 473 *'Quite out of control and leaderless'*, AWM 8/3/29.

p. 473 *'a disgrace to Australia and the AIF'*, War Diary 22nd Brigade AIF, AWM 52/8/22.

p. 475 *'because I'm a doctor'*, Warren, *Singapore 1942*, p. 235, citing AWM 73/7, Maxwell 26.1.53.

p. 478 *'Tsuchikane had stumbled into another company's'*, Frei, *Guns of February*, p. 89.

p. 480 *'Having lost their nerve'*, ibid., p. 97.

p. 481 *latex rubber used to poison its tanks*, Shores, Cull and Izawa, *Bloody Shambles*, p. 366.

p. 482 *about to take off in their Tiger Moths*, ibid., p. 378.

p. 482 *'composed, very tired, and presenting a controlled stoicism'*, Connell and Roberts, *Wavell*, p. 156.

p. 482 *'Australians are very half-hearted'*, Shenton Thomas's shorter diary, Rhodes House, Oxford.

p. 483 *'It is difficult to keep one's self-respect'*, Percival, *War in Malaya*, p. 276.

p. 485 *Eight 'wet and naked' Japanese*, Mackenzie, *Eastern Epic*, p. 387.

p. 485 *'All his [Toosey's] guns'*, IWM Sound Archive 12749/52.

p. 485 *'angry and upset'*, ibid.

p. 486 *Among the six to be killed*, Warren, *Singapore 1942*, p. 238.

p. 486 *With four others Khan charged a machine-gun nest*, Mackenzie, *Eastern Epic*, p. 389.

p. 486 *less critical of the Australians*, Alexander, *Sweet Kwai Run Softly*, p. 57.

p. 487 *a call from a naval officer wishing to sink some Australians*, Kinvig, *Scapegoat*, p. 209.

p. 487 *'Our soldiers are not as good fighters'*, Jenkins, *Churchill*, p. 681, citing conversation with Violet Bonham Carter quoted in Harold Nicolson's *Diaries and Letters*.

p. 488 *'must at this stage be no thought of saving the troops'*, Churchill, *Second World War*, vol. 4, p. 87.

p. 489 *'It will be a lasting disgrace'*, Wigmore, *Japanese Thrust*, p. 341.

p. 490 *rafts made up of three pontoons joined together*, ibid., p. 334.

p. 490 *Argyll from a wealthy Highland family*, Moffatt and McCornick, *Moon over Malaya*, p. 180.

p. 490 *the delicate business of unpacking, assembling and arming them*, Wilson, *Sum of Things*.

p. 491 *British howitzer battery, which prepared to fire over open sights*, Wigmore, *Japanese Thrust*, p. 346.

## Chapter 31

p. 493 *'Your Excellency, I, the High Command of the Nippon Army'*, Wigmore, *Japanese Thrust*, p. 353.

p. 494 *Cumming had led his remaining 250 men*, PRO CAB 106/106 and 106/14. After the surrender Cumming and ten of his British and Indian officers continued to evade the enemy, caught a boat to Sumatra and got on the escape line to India.

p. 495 *'He charged the Jap with his bayonet'*, Wigmore, *Japanese Thrust*, p. 349.

p. 496 *The officer wanted Mentiplay to shoot him*, ibid.

p. 496 *'I don't think the men want to fight'*, Wall, *Singapore and Beyond*, p. 102.

p. 497 *'The men are very tired'*, ibid.

p. 497 *'Well, you go and have a good rest and rejoin your brigade'*, ibid.

p. 497 *'We're all wounded'*, ibid., p. 97.

p. 497 *'He sat in our sitting room, thumping his knees'*, Montgomery, *Shenton of Singapore*, p. 131.

p. 498 *plummeted 6 feet onto the rocks and barbed wire*, Connell and Roberts, *Wavell*, p. 160.

p. 498 *'Morale of some troops is not good'*, ibid., p. 162.

p. 498 *'Singapore will probably be captured by tonight or tomorrow'*, ibid.

p. 498 *'The present state of affairs was started by the AIF'*, Cazalet papers, IWM P432.

p. 499 *'Then somebody came on the field telephone'*, John Webb to author, York, 30.1.02.

p. 501 *'press his attack with more vigour'*, Bennett, *Why Singapore Fell*, p. 182.

p. 502 *'I realized that at last we'd come to grips with the enemy'*, Burton, *Railway of Hell*, p. 22.

p. 503 *'the blast jarred our spines'*, Tsuji, *Singapore 1941–42*, pp. 253–5.

p. 504 *'I knew someone was after me'*, Goatley to author, Haslemere, March 2002.

p. 504 *'feeling very light-hearted'*, Housley, *First In, Last Out: History of 1/5th Sherwood Foresters 1939–46*, p. 33, quoting Lieutenant Norman Thorpe's diary.

p. 505 *'I myself only feel mildly excited'*, ibid.

p. 505 *not to be such damn fools*, ibid.

p. 505 *'Two men including a man from the Surreys'*, ibid.

p. 506 *He had intended to lie low there*, Stewart, *2nd Argylls*, p. 111.

p. 506 *'Is anyone there?'*, ibid.

p. 507 *'I was knocked off my feet'*, author's interview with Douglas Weir, London, March 2002.

p. 507 *Weir crawled off unaided*, ibid.

p. 507 *'Later I learned the bullet had passed'*, ibid.

p. 508 *bellowing on the ground from a bullet*, Rose, *Who Dies Fighting*, p. 140, from Sergeant Charles Wallace.

p. 508 *relished making frequent apologies*, telephone interview with Hubert Strathairn, 2004.

p. 509 *'Why, I asked myself'*, Percival, *War in Malaya*, p. 279.

p. 510 *'What we lacked was blooding'*, Holmes and Kemp, *The Bitter End*, p. 170, quoting from their interview with the late Brigadier T. Massy-Beresford.

p. 510 *'like an enormous jelly'*, Burton, *Railway of Hell*, p. 22.

p. 511 *'How they kept their balance'*, ibid.

p. 511 *'But if I wait too long, sir, I'll be killed'*, Reginald Burton to author, May 2002.

p. 511 *'little men in breeches and puttees'*, ibid.

p. 511 *another had had his knee cap sliced off*, ibid.

p. 511 *decapitated by another dashing young officer*, ibid.

## Chapter 32

p. 513 *'We agreed it was no good leaving troops'*, Percival, *War in Malaya*, p. 281.

p. 514 *'My own resolve'*, Alexander, *Sweet Kwai*, p. 5.

p. 514 *To Webb's amazement, an RN captain*, John Webb to author, York, 2002.

p. 515 *'First they attack your front'*, ibid.

p. 515 *'wonderfully reassuring'*, ibid.

p. 516 *smell burning, and there was a lot of smoke*, John Webb to author, York, 2002.

p. 516 *'rumbling down the road'*, Housley, *First In, Last Out*, p. 36.

p. 516 *'John, go and tell Tigger'*, author interview with John Goatley.

p. 517 *'We pulled back into the rubber'*, Ron Morrell to author, Nottingham, January 2002.

p. 517 *'Battery will fire away'*, Royal Artillery Museum and Singapore National Archives.

p. 517 *One breech block landed*, ibid., quoting Sapper Roy Blackler, Royal Engineers.

p. 518 *'I could see the pilot's face so plainly'*, Anckorn to author, January 2002.

p. 518 *'consoling himself with whisky and talking wildly'*, Alexander, *Sweet Kwai*, pp. 58–9.

p. 519 *'We were no better than rats'*, Rose, *Who Dies Fighting*, p. 145.

p. 520 *shot dead one of their leaders following repeated challenges*, Wall, *Singapore and Beyond*, p. 71.

p. 520 *served a six-month jail sentence*, Bradley, *The Tall Man Who Never Slept*, p. 28.

p. 520 *One of the last things he had done*, Glover, *Seventy Days*, p. 203.

p. 522 *'There was no one to stop them'*, Stapledon papers, IWM 85/31/1.

p. 522 *'It was a ghastly sight'*, ibid.

p. 523 *allow the crew of a Hotchkiss gun*, Elphick, *Pregnable Fortress*, p. 560, quoting Selwyn Capon's report to his bosses at the Blue Funnel line.

p. 524 *more of their wounded would have been evacuated*, Wall, *Singapore and Beyond*, p. 108.

p. 524 *RAF Corporal John Dodd was watching*, Norman, *Road from Singapore*, pp. 34–5.

p. 525 *'You are surely not going back?'*, Moffatt and McCormick, *Moon over Malaya*, p. 167.

p. 525 *'so I drew my revolver and fired'*, ibid.

p. 525 *'as if the whole place was burning'*, Glover, *Seventy Days*, p. 211.

p. 526 *close enough for him to make out the markings*, Norman, *Road from Singapore*, p. 37.

p. 527 *'The book wasn't really making any sense at all'*, Rose, *Who Dies Fighting*, pp. 148–9.

p. 528 *'Curiously enough, I was not as tired as I expected'*, Cazalet papers, IWM P432.

p. 529 *death penalty must not be imposed on Australian soldiers*, Warren, *Singapore 1942*, p. 335.

p. 530 *'like a gang of thugs across an alleyway'*, Brooke, *Singapore's Dunkirk*, p. 21.

p. 533 *'Chin up, girls. I'm proud of you'*, Manners, *Bullwinkel*, p. 81.

p. 533 *soon now she would be seeing her father again*, ibid., p. 80.

p. 533 *'various stages of undress'*, Brooke, *Singapore's Dunkirk*, p. 146.

p. 534 *'address me as Sister'*, Manners, *Bullwinkel*, p. 90.

p. 535 *'I knew I'd been hit'*, author's interview with Fergus Anckorn, 2002.

p. 536 *'I'm sorry, son, I can't save your hand'*, ibid.

p. 536 *'This little piggy went to market'*, ibid.

p. 537 *'aren't they Japanese soldiers'*, author interview 30.4.02 and IWM Sound Archives 22926.

p. 537 *Some 320 men and one woman*, 'Narrative report on Alexandra Hospital Massacre' by P. Burton, IWM 168/2588.

p. 537 *one of the bravest of the brave*, author's interview with Ron Morrell, 2002.

p. 538 *'hanging from a string round his neck'*, ibid.

p. 539 *'more Japanese than we had encountered'*, Chippington, *Inexcusable Betrayal*, p. 216.

p. 539 *'500 were killed'*, ibid., p. 222.

p. 539 *100 dead and 300 wounded*, Webber papers, IWM 88/33/1.

p. 540 *'Three chaps at least were terrified'*, AWM PR91/141.

p. 540 *Of the 22nd Infantry Brigade alone*, Murfett et al., *Between Two Oceans*, p. 361 (Notes to Appendix Three), citing War Diary 22nd Brigade (AWM 52/8/2/22), PRO CAB 106/162, Kirby, *The Loss of Singapore*, pp. 384–91, Wigmore, *Japanese Thrust*, pp. 335–45.

p. 540 *'Soldiers are becoming very sullen'*, Diary, 8th Aus. Div. Provost Co., AWM 52/18/2/21.

p. 541 *'we had a real field of fire'*, author interview with John Webb, York, 2002.

p. 542 *A large party of Japanese had been observed*, Moore, *Battalion at War*, p. 29.

p. 542 *'much confusion'*, ibid.

p. 543 *'stopped shooting and listened'*, Fujiwara, *F-Kikan – Japanese Army Intelligence Operations in Southeast Asia 1941–45*, p. 145.

p. 543 *'Nothing was happening'*, Fay, *Forgotten Army*, pp. 68–9.

p. 544 *'I picked up a glass'*, ibid., p. 70.

p. 544 *'The task was hopeless'*, Ryves papers, IWM 84/30/1.

p. 545 *'European bodies, mostly soldiers'*, W. F. N. Churchill papers, IWM 85/36/1.

p. 546 *'Time gained and damage'*, Percival, *War in Malaya*, p. 292.

p. 546 *'I formed the impression'*, Bradley, *The Tall Man Who Never Slept*, p. 29.

p. 547 *'an inaccurate burst'*, ibid., p. 31.

## Epilogue

p. 550 *'Little men from Mars, a week's stubble'*, Webb to author, February 2002.

p. 550 *'I saw them tramping'*, Josey, *Lee Kuan Yew*, p. 255.

p. 551 *the county player Geoff Edrich*, Obituary, *Daily Telegraph*, 10.1.04.

p. 553 *'To gaze on a sack of rotting shrimps'*, Wigmore, *Japanese Thrust*, p. 513.

p. 553 *'We would ask that'*, Heath papers, IWM P442 Sub-folder LMH 11.

p. 554 *'If I have to pay the extreme penalty'*, ibid.

p. 555 *'As a small token'*, Kinvig, *Scapegoat*, p. 230.

p. 556 *'As Yamashita entered the room'*, Percival, *War in Malaya*, p. 326.

p. 556 *'The world I knew'*, Potter, *A Soldier Must Hang*, p. 206.

p. 557 *Some marooned British coastal gunners*, Ward, *The Killer They Called a God*, p. 20.

p. 558 *dressed in the saffron robes of a Buddhist monk*, ibid., pp. 262–3.

p. 558 *of inciting the Alexandra Hospital atrocity*, ibid., p. 320 (quoting Major-General Akashi).

p. 559 *'slowly and painfully butchered'*, McKernan, *This War Never Ends*, p. 73.

p. 560 *'He impressed me as a man'*, Wall, *Singapore and Beyond*, p. 205.

p. 560 *There is an account of a Welsh gunner*, McEwan, *Out of the Depths of Hell*, pp. 121–2.

p. 560 *creatures in their unfamiliar jungle-green*, Alexander, *Sweet Kwai*, p. 232 (among others).

p. 561 *'You have shot me through the arm'*, AWM 144/14/65.

p. 561 *Wild was able to report that Captain Rana was under arrest*, Bradley, *The Tall Man Who Never Slept*, p. 102.

p. 561 *do the Times of India crossword*, Fay, *Forgotten Army*, p. 360.

p. 564 *60,000 British troops in the area*, Murfett et al., *Between Two Oceans*, p. 315.

p. 565 *RAF air gunner who stuck to his Lewis gun*, monograph on *Li Wo*, compiled from survivors' accounts by Commander R. W. Palastre MBE, IWM 67/111/1, and *Times* obituary of Chief Petty Officer Charles Rogers, 6.3.97.

# Bibliography

Alexander, Stephen, *Sweet Kwai Run Softly*, Merriotts Press, Bristol, 1995.

Barber, Noel, *Sinister Twilight*, Cassell, London, 2002.

Barker, Ralph, *One Man's Jungle*, Chatto & Windus, London, 1975.

Bayley, Christopher and Harper, Tim, *Forgotten Armies*, Allen Lane, London, 2004.

Bennett, Gordon, *Why Singapore Fell*, Angus & Robertson Ltd, Sydney and London, 1944.

Bloodworth, Dennis, *The Tiger and the Trojan Horse*, Times Books, Singapore, 1986.

Bond, Brian (ed.), *Diaries of Sir Henry Pownall* (vol. 2), Leo Cooper, London, 1974.

Braddon, Russell, *The Naked Island*, Werner Laurie, London, 1956.

Bradley, James, *Cyril Wild – The Tall Man Who Never Slept*, Woodfield, Fontwell, 1991.

Brendon, Piers, *The Dark Valley*, Jonathan Cape, London, 2000.

Brooke, Alan, *War Diaries* (eds. Dancher and Todman), Weidenfeld & Nicolson, London, 2001.

Brooke, Geoffrey, *Alarm Starboard*, Patrick Stephens, Cambridge, 1982.

Brooke, Geoffrey, *Singapore's Dunkirk*, Leo Cooper, Barnsley, 2003.

Bulcock, Roy, *Of Death But Once*, Cheshire, Melbourne and London, 1947.

Burton, Reginald, *Railway of Hell*, Leo Cooper, Barnsley, 2002.

Buruma, Ian, *Inventing Japan*, Weidenfeld & Nicolson, London, 2003.

Callahan, Raymond, *The Worst Disaster*, Cultured Lotus, Singapore, 2001.

Chang, Iris, *The Rape of Nanking*, Penguin, London, 1998.

Charmley, John, *Duff Cooper*, Macmillan (PaperMac), London, 1987.

Chippington, George, *Singapore – The Inexcusable Betrayal*, The Self Publishing Association, Hanley Swan, 1992.

Chung, Chit Ong, *Operation Matador*, Times Academic Press, Singapore, 2001.

Churchill, Winston, *The Second World War* (vols 1–6), Penguin, London, 1985.

Connell, John and Roberts, Michael, *Wavell*, Collins, London, 1969.

Cooper, Duff, *Old Men Forget*, Rupert Hart Davis, London, 1953.

Cross, John, *Red Jungle*, Robert Hale, London, 1957.

Cruickshank, Charles, *SOE in the Far East*, Oxford University Press, Oxford, 1986.

Day, David, *The Great Betrayal*, Oxford University Press, Melbourne, 1992.

Edwards, Jack, *Banzai, You Bastards!*, Corporate Communications, Hong Kong, 1997.

Elphick, Peter, *The Pregnable Fortress*, Coronet Books, London, 1995.

Elphick, Peter and Smith, Michael, *Odd Man Out*, Hodder & Stoughton, London, 1993.

Falk, Stanley, *Seventy Days to Singapore*, Robert Hale, London, 1975.

Farrell, Brian and Sand, Hunter (eds), *Sixty Years On*, Eastern Universities Press, Singapore, 2002.

Fay, Peter, *The Forgotten Army*, Michigan University Press, Michigan, 1995.

Frei, Henry, *Japan's Southward Advance and Australia*, Hawaii Press, Honolulu, 1991.

Frei, Henry, *Guns of February*, Singapore University Press, 2004.

Gallagher, O'Dowd, *Retreat in the East*, Viking Press, London, 1945.

Gibson, Walter, *The Boat*, W. H. Allen, London, 1952.

Glover, E. M., *In Seventy Days*, Frederick Muller, London, 1946.

Hall, E. R. (Bon), *Glory in Chaos*, Sembawang Association, West Coburg, Aus., 1989.

Hamond, Robert, *The Flame of Freedom*, Leo Cooper, London, 1988.

Harrison, Kenneth, *The Brave Japanese*, Rigby, Sydney and Melbourne, 1966.

Holmes, Richard and Kemp, Anthony, *The Bitter End*, Antony Bird, Chichester, 1982.

Hough, Richard, *The Hunting of Force Z*, Fontana, London, 1964.

Housley, Clifford, *First In, Last Out*, 1/5th TA Battalion, Sherwood Foresters, Derby, 1995.

Hoyt, Edwin, *Japan's War*, Cooper Square Press, New York, 2001.

Imray, Colin, *Cricket in the Backblocks*, Book Guild, Crowborough, 1998.

Josey, Alex, *Lee Kuan Yew*, Times Books, Singapore, 1968.

Kennedy, John, *The Business of War*, Hutchinson, London, 1957.

King-Clark, R., *Free for a Blast*, Grenville, London, 1998.

Kinvig, Clifford, *Scapegoat*, Brassey's, London, 1996.

Kirby, S. Woodburn, *Singapore – The Chain of Disaster*, Macmillan, New York, 1971.

Laffin, John, *British VCs of World War II*, Sutton Publishing, Stroud (UK), 1997.

Lane, Arthur, *One God, Too Many Devils*, Chrysanthemum, Stockport, 1989.

Leach, Henry, *Endure No Makeshifts*, Pen and Sword, Barnsley, 2003.

Lomax, Eric, *The Railway Man*, Vintage, London, 1996.

Mackenzie, Compton, *Eastern Epic*, Chatto & Windus, London, 1951.

Manners, Norman, *Bullwinkel*, Hesperian Press, Carlisle, Western Australia, 1999.

Mayer, S. L. (ed.), *The Rise and Fall of Imperial Japan*, Bison Books, London, 1984.

McEwan, John, *Out of the Depths of Hell*, Leo Cooper, Barnsley, 1999.

McKernan, Michael, *This War Never Ends*, Queensland University Press, St Lucia, 2001.

Middlebrook, Martin and Mahoney, Patrick, *Battleship*, Allen Lane, London, 1977.

Moffatt, Jonathan and McCormick, Audrey, *Moon over Malaya*, Tempus, Stroud (UK) and Charleston (US), 2002.

Montgomery, Brian, *Shenton of Singapore*, Leo Cooper, London, 1984.

Moore, Michael, *Battalion at War*, Gliddon Books, Norfolk, 1988.

Moremon, John and Reid, Richard, *A Bitter Fate: Australians in Malaya and Singapore*, Department of Veterans' Affairs, Canberra, 2002.

Morrison, Ian, *Malayan Postscript*, Faber, London, 1942.

Morrison, Ian, *This War against Japan*, Faber, London, 1943.

Murfett, Malcolm, Miksic, John, Farrell, Brian and Shun, Chiang, *Between Two Oceans*, Oxford University Press, Melbourne and Singapore, 1999.

Norman, Diana, *Road from Singapore*, Hodder & Stoughton, London, 1979.

Owen, Frank, *The Fall of Singapore*, Classic Penguin, London, 2001.

Payne, Robert, *Eyewitness*, Doubleday, New York, 1972.

Peacock, Basil, *Tinker's Mufti*, Seeley, London, 1974.

Percival A. R., *The War in Malaya*, Eyre & Spottiswoode, London, 1949.

Potter, John Deane, *A Soldier Must Hang*, Frederick Muller, London, 1963.

Pownall, Henry, *Chief of Staff – The Diaries of Lt-General Sir Henry Pownall* (ed. Brian Bond), Leo Cooper, London, 1974.

Probert, Henry, *The Forgotten Air Force*, Brassey's, London, 1996.

Rose, Angus, *Who Dies Fighting*, Right Book Club, London, 1945.

Russell-Roberts, Denis, *Spotlight on Singapore*, Anthony Gibbs, London, 1965.

Sahgal, Lakshmi, *A Revolutionary Life*, Kali, New Delhi, 1997.

Saville-Sneath, R. A., *Aircraft Recognition*, Penguin, London, 1941.

Shennan, Margaret, *Out in the Midday Sun*, John Murray, London, 2000.

Shinozaki, Mamoru, *Syonan – My Story*, Times Books, Singapore, 1984.

Shores, Christopher and Cull, Brian, with Izawa, Yasuho, *Bloody Shambles*, Grub Street, London, 1998.

Slim, William, *Defeat into Victory*, Cassell, London, 1956.

Smyth, John, *Percival and the Tragedy of Singapore*, Macdonald, London, 1971.

Snow, Philip, *The Fall of Hong Kong*, Yale University Press, Newhaven, CT and London, 2003.

Spencer Chapman, Frederick, *The Jungle is Neutral*, Chatto & Windus, London, 1949.

Steiner, Jesse, *Behind the Japanese Mask*, Macmillan, New York, 1943.

Stewart, Ian, *History of the Argyll and Sutherland Highlanders 2nd Battalion 1941–42*, D. P. & G. Military Publishers, Doncaster, 2002 (first published 1947).

Tett, David, *A Postal History of the Prisoners of War and Civilian Internees in East Asia During the Second World War*, Stuart Rossiter Trust, Bristol, 2002.

Thompson, Peter and Macklin, Robert, *Kill the Tiger*, Hodder Headline, Sydney, 2002.

Trenowden, Ian, *Operations Most Secret*, William Kimber, London, 1978.

Tsuji, Masanobu, *Singapore 1941–42*, Oxford University Press, Oxford, 1988.

Wall, Don, *Singapore and Beyond*, 2/20th Battalion Association, Cowra, 1985.

Ward, Ian, *The Killer They Called a God*, Media Masters, Singapore, 1992.

Ward, Ian, *Snaring the Other Tiger*, Media Masters, Singapore, 1996.

Warren, Alan, *Singapore 1942*, Talisman, London and Singapore, 2002.

Wigmore, Lionel, *The Japanese Thrust*, Australian War Memorial, Canberra, 1957.

Wilson, David, *The Sum of Things*, Spellmount, Staplehurst, 2001.

Wrigglesworth, H. L., *The Japanese Invasion of Kelantan in 1941*, Jalan Hospital, Kota Baharu, 1991.

# Index

# COLIN SMITH & JOHN BIERMAN

## ALAMEIN: WAR WITHOUT HATE

'Excellent ... a remarkable achievement and ought to be recognized as one of the most successful histories of the Western Desert and North African fighting yet to have appeared' John Keegan, *Daily Telegraph*

A turning point in the Second World War, the battle of El Alamein was the culmination of a military campaign like no other. Fought across desolate arid terrain, the brutal fighting was matched by a camaraderie and respect between enemies as witnessed in no other theatre of war. Combining gritty personal testimonies with thorough journalistic investigation, John Bierman and Colin Smith present a compelling journey to the final confrontation between Rommel and Montgomery.

'A big pacey read which, as well as being an account of the battle itself, is a panorama of the desert fighting leading up to the sacking of General Auckinlech and the arrival of Montgomery' Allan Mallinson, *The Times*

'Here is a first-class account of the arduous hunt to run Rommel to ground' John Crossland, *Sunday Times*, Best Military History Books of 2002

'A new definitive account of the desert battle' *Daily Mail*